C0-AZS-028

SALES MANAGEMENT
Decisions, Strategies, and Cases

Fifth Edition

RICHARD R. STILL
Florida International University

EDWARD W. CUNDIFF
University of Texas at Austin

NORMAN A.P. GOVONI
Babson College

PRENTICE HALL, Englewood Cliffs, NJ 07632

Library of Congress Cataloging-in-Publication Data

Still, Richard Ralph (date)
Sales management.

Includes index.
1. Sales management. I. Cundiff, Edward W.
II.Govoni, Norman A. P. III. Title.
HF5438.4.S84 1988 658.8'1 87-25725
ISBN 0-13-786542-2

Editorial/production supervision and
interior design: Maureen Wilson
Cover design: Ben Santora
Manufacturing buyer: Barbara Kittle

Printed in the United States of America

10 9 8 7 6 5 4 3 2 1

ISBN 0-13-786542-2 01

Prentice-Hall International (UK) Limited, *London*
Prentice-Hall of Australia Pty. Limited, *Sydney*
Prentice-Hall Canada Inc., *Toronto*
Prentice-Hall Hispanoamericana, S.A., *Mexico*
Prentice-Hall of India Private Limited, *New Delhi*
Prentice-Hall of Japan, Inc., *Tokyo*
Prentice-Hall of Southeast Asia Pte. Ltd., *Singapore*
Editora Prentice-Hall do Brasil, Ltda. *Rio de Janeiro*

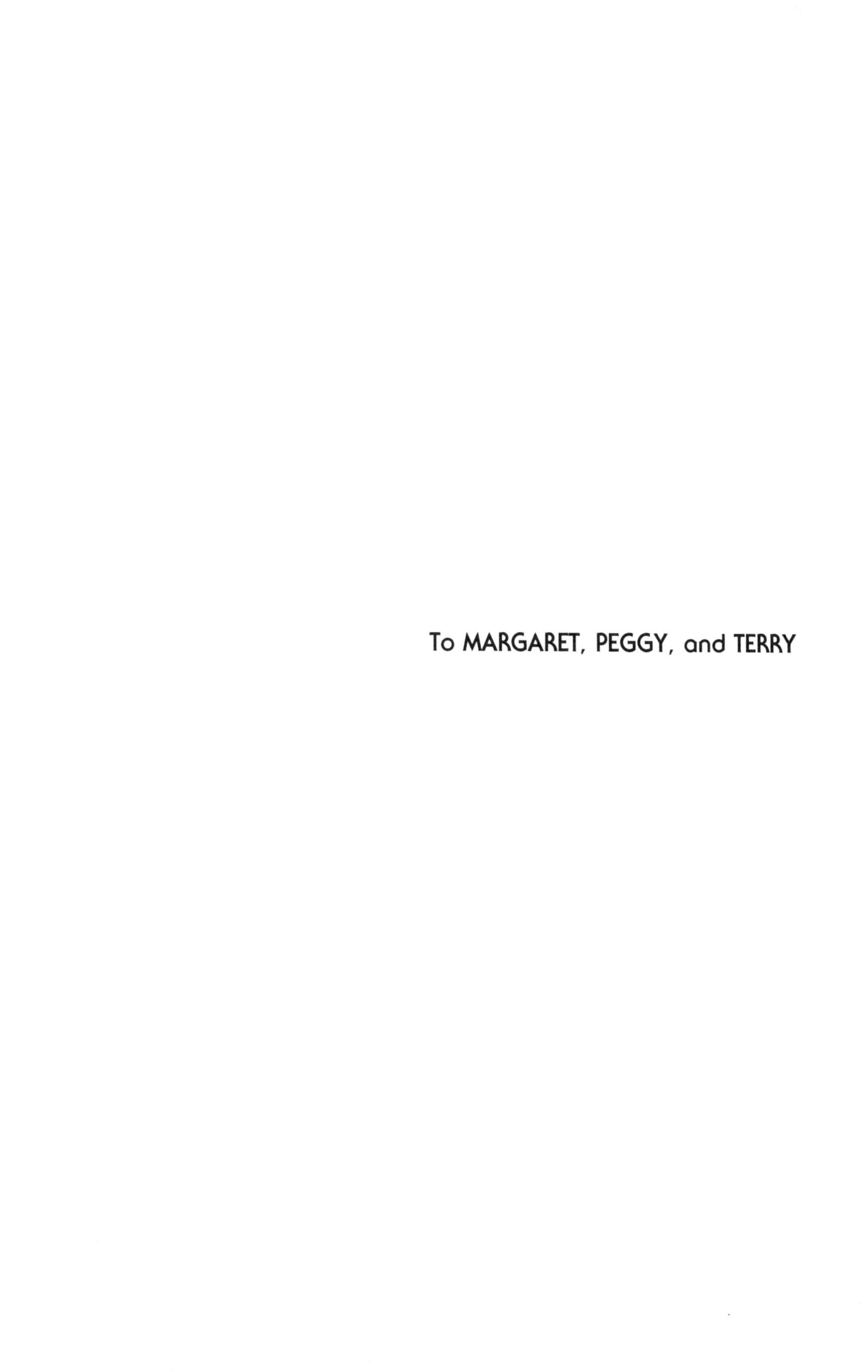

To MARGARET, PEGGY, and TERRY

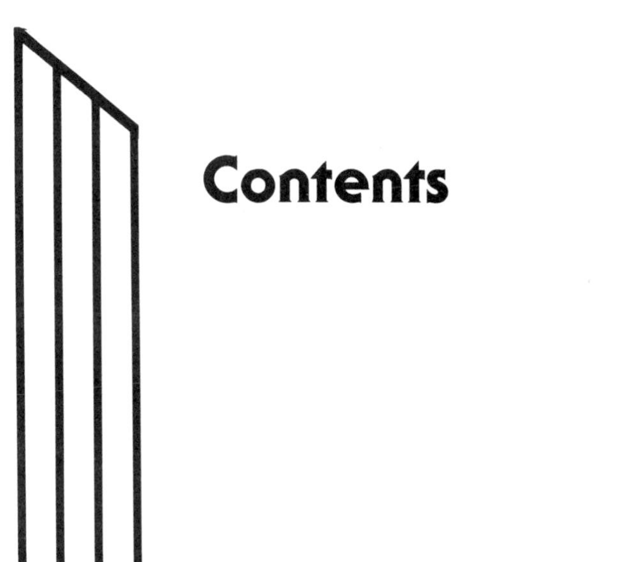

Contents

Preface

This book is aimed toward accomplishing three objectives: (1) to delineate the areas in which sales executives make decisions; (2) to analyze decision alternatives and criteria in these areas; and (3) to provide cases as real-world illustrations of decision situations. These objectives will have been accomplished if readers gain an understanding of the sales executive's functions in diverse circumstances.

The emphasis, as in previous editions, is on sales management, not on marketing. The main perspective is that of the sales executive as a participant in the marketing management team. Sales executives participate in, and sometimes are primarily or jointly responsible for, formulating strategies on the product line, on pricing, on physical distribution, on marketing channels, and on promotion. But their focus and primary responsibility consists of either the management of sales personnel or the maintenance of relationships with distributive organizations or both. Thus sales executives play roles both as planners of sales operations and as key figures in implementing not only sales programs but also important aspects of marketing strategies. In marked contrast to other marketing executives, the time orientation of the sales executive stresses the present—in getting things done, in making plans come true, in turning dreams into reality.

The management approach is applied to an analysis of the sales executive's job, the duties and responsibilities involved, and the planning and implementation of sales and marketing programs. Part I discusses the interrelationships of personal selling and marketing strategy, including the art of salesmanship, personal selling objectives, sales-related marketing policies, and the formulation of personal selling strategy. Part II shifts to the organizing of the sales effort both within the enterprise and relative to the distribution network. Part III is an in-depth analysis of the sales executive's primary responsibilities to the sales force. Part IV concentrates on techniques of controlling the sales effort, including sales budgets, quotas, territories, and sales and cost analysis. And because business organizations have more and more come to look on the entire planet as potential markets and sales executives have become ever increasingly involved in international business, Part V considers the emerging field of international sales management, emphasizing sales force operations across national boundaries.

For successful completion of this edition, we owe a great deal to a great many people. Our present and former colleagues at the Florida International University, the University of Georgia, Emory University, Babson College, and the University of Texas at Austin have given generously of their time and have shared the benefits of their teaching and business experience. A large number of executives provided materials for case histories, and our graduate students competently assisted in collecting the cases. Daniel Darrow of Ferris State College, Robert Collins of Oregon State University, and Kenneth C. Lundahl of Jamestown Community College read the entire manuscript for this edition and made sound and helpful suggestions. Whitney Blake and Maureen Wilson were among the many at Prentice Hall who gave us help and advice. Hilda Aguiar, Christina Suarez, and Sylvia Suarez typed the manuscript efficiently and cheerfully under the watchful eye of Irene Young. Our wives were our sources both of helpful criticism and of encouragement. For all this assistance, we express our sincere thanks.

Richard R. Still
Edward W. Cundiff
Norman A. P. Govoni

Sales Management and the Business Enterprise

1

Today's sales executives are professionals. They plan, build, and maintain effective organizations and design and utilize efficient control procedures. The professional approach requires thorough analysis, market-efficient qualitative and quantitative personal-selling objectives, appropriate sales policies, and personal-selling strategy. It calls for skillful application of organizational principles to the conduct of sales operations. In addition, the professional approach demands the ability to install, operate, and use control procedures appropriate to the firm's situation and its objectives. Executives capable of applying the professional approach to sales management are in high demand today.

Sales executives have responsibilities to their organizations, the customers, and society. Top management holds them responsible for (1) obtaining sales volume, (2) providing profit contributions, and (3) continuing business growth. The customers (most often, wholesalers, retailers, or industrial users) expect them to supply easily resalable products and services, backed up by supporting activities (e.g., training dealers' sales personnel, help in preparing local advertising, and the provision of credit) and assurance that the products and services are wise investments in the competitive marketplace. Society looks to them to assure the delivery of goods and services that final buyers want at prices that final buyers are willing to pay and—of increasing importance—to develop and market products whose potentials for damaging the environment are minimal. If the goods and services made and sold are needed and accepted by the buying public, and if these products are "socially responsible," then it is likely that management's objectives will have been achieved. Ultimately, a business's earnings depend upon how well, or how poorly, the interests of the firm, the final buyers, and society are blended. To the extent that these interests are in harmony, the firm experiences sales volume, net profits, and business growth.

EVOLUTION OF THE SALES DEPARTMENT

Prior to the Industrial Revolution, small-scale enterprises dominated the economic scene, and selling was no problem. The chief problem was to produce enough goods for nearby customers. Orders were obtained with minimum effort, and they were on hand before goods were produced. In most firms a single individual supervised all phases of the business, including both manufacturing and selling. Manufacturing problems received the most attention. Selling and other marketing problems were handled on a part-time basis.

With the Industrial Revolution, which began about 1760 in England and shortly after the American Revolution in the United States, it became increasingly necessary to find and sell new markets. Newly built factories were turning out huge quantities of goods of every description. Their continued operation demanded great expansions in the area of sales coverage, as adjacent markets could not absorb the increased quantities being manufactured. But even under these circumstances other business problems took precedence over selling. These were problems associated with hiring large numbers of workers, and acquiring land, buildings, and machinery. To solve them, large amounts of capital had to be raised. The result was that more and more businesses adopted the corporate form of organization—the day of large-scale manufacturing enterprises had arrived. Firsthand administration of all phases of the operation being beyond the capabilities of most individuals, authority was increasingly delegated to others. Separate functional departments were established, but sales departments were set up only after the activation of manufacturing and financial departments.

The advent of specialized sales departments helped to solve the organizational problems of market expansion, but another problem remained—communicating with customers. Little by little, manufacturers shifted portions of the marketing function to middlemen. At the start, goods were sold to retailers, who resold them directly to consumers. Eventually, some larger retailers began to purchase for resale to other retailers, and, as time passed, many of these evolved into wholesale institutions. Other wholesalers developed out of the import-export business. The manufacturer's sales department was becoming more remote from consumers, and it was increasingly difficult to maintain contact with final buyers and users of the product and to control the conditions under which wholesalers and retailers made their sales. Thus, in some respects, the addition of middlemen to the channel of distribution complicated the problem of market expansion.

Meanwhile, marketing activities conducted by the manufacturer's sales department grew in importance. Many tasks, such as advertising and sales promotion, became increasingly complex. One solution was to split the marketing function, a trend that is still continuing. New departments were and are being organized for the performance of specialized marketing tasks. Marketing activities today are carried on not only by the sales department, but by such departments as advertising, marketing research, export, sales promotion, merchandising, traffic and shipping, and credits and collections. In spite of this growing fragmentation of marketing operations, the sales department still occupies a strategically important position. The underlying responsibility for the making of sales has not shifted elsewhere. Businesses continue to rely upon their sales departments for the inward flow of income. It has been aptly said that the sales department is the income-producing division of business.

SALES MANAGEMENT

"Sales management" originally referred exclusively to the direction of sales force personnel. Later, the term took on broader significance—in addition to the management of personal selling, "sales management" meant management of all marketing activities, including advertising, sales promotion, marketing research, physical distribution, pricing, and product merchandising. In time, business, adopting academic practice, came to use the term "marketing management" rather than "sales management" to describe the broader concept. Then, the Definitions Committee of the American Marketing Association agreed that sales management meant "the planning, direction, and control of personal selling, including recruiting, selecting, equipping, assigning, routing, supervising, paying, and motivating as these tasks apply to the personal salesforce."[1]

The American Marketing Association's definition made sales management synonymous with management of the sales force, but modern sales managers have considerably broader responsibilities. Sales managers are in charge of personal-selling activity, and their primary assignment is management of the personal sales force. However, personnel-related tasks do not comprise their total responsibility, so we call their personnel-related responsibilities "sales force management."

Sales managers are responsible for organizing the sales effort, both within and outside their companies. Within the company, the sales manager builds formal and informal organizational structures that ensure effective communication not only inside the sales department but in its relations with other organizational units. Outside the company, the sales manager serves as a key contact with customers and other external publics and is responsible for building and maintaining an effective distribution network.

Sales managers have still other responsibilities. They are responsible for

[1]American Marketing Association, Committee on Definitions, *Marketing Definitions* (Chicago: American Marketing Association, 1960), p. 20.

participating in the preparation of information critical to the making of key marketing decisions, such as those on budgeting, quotas, and territories. They participate—to an extent that varies with the company—in decisions on products, marketing channels and distribution policies, advertising and other promotion, and pricing. Thus, the sales manager is both an administrator in charge of personal-selling activity and a member of the executive group that makes marketing decisions of all types.

Sales management is a key function in many kinds of enterprises. Manufacturing and wholesaling enterprises encounter a wide range of problems in sales management. Retail institutions, small and large, have sales management problems, even though the differences (when compared to the problems of manufacturers and wholesalers) are so great that retailing problems (at least in the academic world) are ordinarily considered separately. But some retailers have sales management problems more akin to those of manufacturers and wholesalers than to those of other retailers—the automobile dealer, the real-estate broker, and the direct-to-consumer marketer all are in this category. Firms selling intangibles, such as the insurance company, the stockbroker, the mutual fund, and the airline, have problems in sales management. Sales management problems exist even in companies not employing sales personnel as, for example, in the company that uses manufacturers' agents (rather than its own sales personnel) to reach its markets; indeed, the problems of managing a sales force of "independent outsiders" often are more complex than when sales personnel are on the company payroll.

OBJECTIVES OF SALES MANAGEMENT

From the company viewpoint, there are three general objectives of sales management: sales volume, contribution to profits, and continuing growth. Sales executives, of course, do not carry the full burden in the effort to reach these objectives, but they make major contributions. Top management has the final responsibility, because it is accountable for the success or failure of the entire enterprise. Ultimately, too, top management is accountable for supplying an ever-increasing volume of "socially responsible" products that final buyers want at satisfactory prices.

Top management delegates to marketing management, which then delegates to sales management, sufficient authority to achieve the three general objectives. In the process, objectives are translated into more specific goals—they are broken down and restated as definite goals that the company has a reasonable chance of reaching. During the planning that precedes goal setting, sales executives provide estimates on market and sales potentials, the capabilities of the sales force and the middlemen, and the like. Once these goals are finalized, it is up to sales executives to guide and lead the sales personnel and middlemen who play critical roles in implementing the selling plans.

Sales management, then, is influential in charting the course of future operations. It provides higher management with informed estimates and facts for making marketing decisions and for setting sales and profit goals. Largely on sales management's appraisal of market opportunities, targets are set for sales volume, gross margin, and net profit in units of product and in dollars, with benchmarks of growth projected for sales and profits at specific future dates. Whether or not these targets are reached depends upon the performance of sales and other marketing personnel.

SALES MANAGEMENT AND FINANCIAL RESULTS

Sales management and financial results are closely related. Financial results are stated in terms from two basic accounting formulas:

$$\begin{aligned} \text{sales} - \text{cost of sales} &= \text{gross margin} \\ \text{gross margin} - \text{expenses} &= \text{net profit} \end{aligned}$$

Sales management influences the "numbers cranked into these formulas." Sales, gross margin, and expenses are affected by the caliber and performance of sales management, and these are the major determinants of net profit. The cost-of-sales factor cannot be affected directly by sales management, but it can be affected indirectly since sales volume must be large enough to permit maintenance of targeted unit costs of production and distribution. Periodically, these formulas become the company operating statement and are used by the board of directors, and by stockholders, in appraising top management's performance. Moreover, top management uses these formulas in judging the effectiveness of sales management.

Sometimes, sales executives stress sales volume while neglecting gross margin and expenses. In these instances, even though sales volume increases, gross margin declines, expenses increase proportionately, and net profits are reduced. If these conditions prevail for long, profits disappear and losses appear. Often the best treatment for this situation is to shrink sales volume and expenses. Even with a lower sales volume, skilled sales management can reduce expenses and raise gross margin sufficiently to convert a loss into a profit.

It is also possible to err in the opposite direction, to overemphasize high gross margins and low expenses—because of a preoccupation with percentage relationships. Percentages of gross margin and expense are important, but sales management should be more concerned with dollar relationships. The important net profit is dollar net profit, not the percentage of net profit. It is small consolation to have satisfactory gross margin and expense percentages if total sales volume and net profits are inadequate. Sales management should worry more about sales and profit dollars than about percentage relationships.

The company maximizes its net profits if it obtains an optimum relationship among the four factors. Sales management, both in its planning and operating roles, aims for an optimum relationship among the *three* factors it can directly affect: sales, gross margin, and expenses. Sales management works with others (such as those in charge of production and advertising) to assure that sales volume is sufficient to attain targeted *cost of sales*, the fourth factor.

SALES EXECUTIVE AS COORDINATOR

Optimum marketing performance in terms of sales volume, net profits, and long-term growth requires coordination, and sales executives play significant roles in coordinating. Sales executives have responsibilities for coordination involving (1) the organization, (2) the planning, and (3) other elements in the marketing strategy. Higher-ranking sales executives are those most concerned with obtaining effective coordination, but sales executives at all organizational levels have some responsibility for coordinating.

Organization and Coordination

Coordination of the different order-getting methods (personal selling, advertising, and so forth) is achieved through a single responsible, top-ranking executive. Generally, this is the marketing vice-president, director of marketing, or marketing manager. This executive is responsible for minimizing the possibility that the different order-getting departments will work at cross-purposes or work toward sales goals independently (with little knowledge of what others are doing).

Inside the sales department, from the department head on down, all sales executives are responsible for coordinating the organizational units under their control. In sales departments that function smoothly, generally democratic administration is the rule. All subordinates affected by a decision are consulted in advance and are allowed to participate in making it—thus reducing the tendency to resist directives issued by superiors. Not only are there minimum opportunities for misunderstandings to occur, but subordinates as well as superiors are able to visualize the circumstances giving rise to decisions.

Planning and Coordination

The sales executive, having specialized knowledge of the market and of the capabilities of the sales force, is involved in achieving coordination in marketing objectives and drafts plans that achieve desired results at optimum cost, Sales executives determine the elements (personal selling, advertising, and so forth) that make up the marketing program, apportioning the relative amounts of each so as—at least theoretically—to equate its marginal effectiveness with that of other elements. Coordination among the marketing planners is essential if they are to lay out specific programs for achieving predetermined sales, profit, and growth objectives. The sales executive, as a member of the planning group, seeks to secure a marketing program that is both appropriate for market conditions and reflects the probable contribution of the sales force.

Coordination with Other Elements in the Marketing Program

Many responsibilities of sales executives relate to coordinating personal selling with other order-getting methods. Personal-selling efforts must be coordinated with advertising, display, and other promotional efforts if the total marketing effort is to achieve the desired results. Just as they must "build coordination into" the marketing plan, sales executives must achieve coordination during the plan's implementation.

Synchronizing personal selling with advertising is particularly important. Advertising may prove uneconomic unless the sales force capitalizes upon the interest aroused. Personal-selling effort is wasted in explaining details that might be explained by advertising, but when sales personnel and the advertising use the same appeals—if both tell the same story—promotional impact is magnified. The timing and sequence with which different phases of the personal-selling and advertising efforts are executed affect the firm's chances for marketing success. An advertising effort should be implemented within the context of the larger marketing effort, and the same is true of personal-selling effort.

Sales executives are involved in coordinating other promotional efforts with the personal-selling effort. Point-of-purchase displays, for example, are set up in retail stores where customers will see them at the precise time that tie-in advertisements appear in national and local media. It is the job of the sales force to achieve this timing and coordination. In a similar manner, the sales personnel alerts dealers to special couponing or sampling efforts so that they can benefit from heightened customer interest.

Coordination with the Distributive Network

Sales executives coordinate personal selling with the marketing efforts of the middlemen. Among the most important aspects are gaining product distribution, obtaining dealer identification, reconciling business goals, and sharing promotional risks.

Gaining product distribution. When a new product is introduced, sales executives are responsible for obtaining distribution. Unless the product is sold directly to final users, the sales department must persuade middlemen to associate themselves with the new product's distribution. Gaining distribution is not easy. Middlemen refuse to stock a new product unless the manufacturer's sales staff presents convincing arguments of its salability. Some manufacturers succeed in "pulling" their products through the distribution channel by means of heavy advertising to final buyers, but such instances of "forced distribution" are rare.

Regardless of the distribution channels used, the manufacturer of a new product, as often as not, faces distributor lethargy and dealer indifference and must use missionary selling. But, as frequently happens in marketing a new consumer product, even missionary selling may be handicapped because corporate chains and other integrated retailers commonly do not permit decentralized calls on their individual outlets. Thus, the manufacturer of a new product may have to build a demand for it in as many outlets as are initially willing to handle it and then prove the existence of an established market demand to the remaining "desired outlets" before adequate distribution is secured. Consequently, the sales executive must ensure that the manufacturer's initial promotional efforts are tied in with those of the middlemen who first stock the product. As distribution in more outlets is secured, the sales executive sees to it that progressively larger shares of the promotional burden are shifted to the middlemen. Thus, coordinating the promotional efforts of the manufacturer and its middlemen grows increasingly important as the product is made available in more outlets, and sales executives must adjust their coordinating efforts accordingly.

Obtaining dealer identification. In furthering the chances that the personal-selling effort will succeed, the sales executive must ensure that final buyers know which local outlets stock the product. Even if advertising succeeds in preselling the product, no sales will result if final buyers cannot find the outlets that stock it. Inadequate dealer identification results in clogged distribution channels—all the way from the dealer's stockroom to the factory. In some instances, dealers take the initiative in publicizing the availability of the product. But, in most cases, sales personnel promote dealer identification through providing store signs, furnishing preprints and reprints of advertisements, supplying advertising mats for local insertions, and assisting in building merchandise displays. In other cases, sales executives arrange for the placing of local advertising over the dealers' names.

The sales force plays a related role in marketing many consumer products, particularly those distributed through self-service retailers. It is important that consumers, once in the right retail stores, can locate the product with minimum difficulty. Display at the point of purchase bridges the gap between advertising impact and the retail sale. Whenever merchandising aids, such as interior display pieces or shelf markers, are used, sales executives must teach salespeople how to obtain the retailers' permission to use them. Timing is important in securing permissions—at the start of a special promotional campaign, for example, retailers are more willing to allow the erection of displays (particularly if they have ample supplies of the product on hand) than they are during slow selling seasons.

Reconciling business goals. Skillful coordinating by sales executives and the sales force minimizes the natural friction that develops because of conflicts, imaginary or real, between the business goals of the manufacturer and the middlemen. The less the manufacturer and the middlemen work at cross-purposes, the greater the return to both parties.

One approach is for the manufacturer to share business information with the middlemen. Certain information is imparted through trade advertising, but salespeople personalize much data for middlemen. When the results of marketing research studies, for example, have significance for individual middlemen, sales executives have special reports prepared for personal presentation and explanation by the sales force.

The manufacturer needs information on the operating situation and problems of the middlemen. Sales personnel, through regular and special reports, serve as the vehicles of communication. Sales executives recognize that only if timely information is available on the needs and attitudes of middlemen is it possible to provide them with effective promotional and other assistance. The sales executive makes periodic appraisals of existing marketing policies in the light of information provided by salespeople in the field, thus ensuring that those policies already in effect, as well as those newly formulated, are appropriate for the total marketing situation.

Sales executives ensure that sales personnel are fair and impartial in their dealings with middlemen. No outlet should be favored at the expense of another; all should receive equitable treatment. Salespeople need continual training to keep them abreast of current operating policies, practices and procedures; they require effective supervision to apply them fairly as well as properly. Providing this training and supervision is the responsibility of sales executives.

Sharing promotional risks. The marketing program often calls for the manufacturer and the middlemen to share promotional risks (such as through cooperative advertising). In these cases, sales executives ensure that the sales personnel make effective presentations designed to convince dealers to participate. Manufacturers utilizing selective or exclusive agency distribution stand to gain the most from sharing promotional risk with middlemen; in these situations, sales executives and the sales force play roles in both the initial selection of middlemen as well as in obtaining their consent to share promotional risks. Manufacturers using mass distribution do not find it feasible to delegate much promotional authority to their middlemen. However, regardless of the company's distribution policy, any steps that the sales executive takes to make the job of the middleman more interesting, more profitable, and more challenging facilitate the task of coordination.

Coordination and Implementation of Overall Marketing Strategy

When the overall marketing strategy is being put into effect, problems in coordination occur in timing and securing the best sequence of execution of the various phases. For example, if a new product is to be introduced at a trade show or exhibition, the sales executive coordinates with advertising executives to ensure that the proper interval elapses before advertisements appear or salespeople make calls on dealers in the product's behalf. Similar coordinating action ensures proper spacing of the advertising in relation to the call schedules of

FIGURE 1.1 Coordination and Timing by the Sales Department in the Introduction of a New Product

	First Month	*Second Month*	*Third Month*	*Fourth Month*	*Fifth Month*	*Sixth Month* 1st Week	*Sixth Month* 2nd Week	*Sixth Month* 3rd Week	*Sixth Month* 4th Week
General Sales Management	Supervision of Sales and Advertising Plans				Coordinating Final Sales Activities				Concentrated
Sales Branch Inventory Control			Setting Up Standard Stocks for Branches		Notifying Branches of Stock				Sales
Sales Branch Sales	Study of Problems by Branch Management	Recommendations to Management	Revising Territories and Personnel	Training New Sales Personnel re New Product		Preliminary Sales Approach to Key Accounts		Active Selling to Everyone	Effort
Sales Training		Prepare Training Bulletins		Distribute Bulletins and Other Sales Information to Sales Personnel		Distribute information for Jobber Sales Meetings			by Entire Sales
Sales Operation		Prepare Price Sheets and Other Price Information			Distribute Price Information				Organization
Coordination with Outside Departments									
Publicity	Inform Them of New Product		Prepare Publicity Material	Distribute "Stories" to Media		Break Publicity in Business Media	Break Publicity in Consumer Media		Continue Publicity
Sales Promotion	Work on Preliminary Planning	Approve Plans for Catalogs, Brochures, Sales Kits	Preliminary Layout and Copy	Final Proofs	Promotional Material Approved for Distribution	First Mailing to Users		Second Mailing to Users	Continuing Promotion
Advertising		Consult Ad Agency on Plans	Preliminary Layouts and Copy	Final Proofs	Reprints of Ads Sent to Sales Personnel		First Ads	Balance of First Month Ads	Continuing Ads

salespeople. Furthermore, sales executives see that field sales personnel integrate every phase and segment of the promotional programs of distributors and dealers.

Successful market introduction of a new brand is a severe test of the mettle and the level of competence possessed by all members of the marketing management team, including sales executives. Introduction of a new brand requires policies, strategies, and detailed plans, all of them appropriate to the company's marketing situation. Proper timing of the stages in the introduction plan is important because launching a brand at the wrong time, or faulty timing at any stage, kills or reduces the chances for success. All the promotional efforts in behalf of the new brand require coordination: advertising with personal selling and the manufacturer's total promotion with middlemen activities.

It is not enough for sales executives to know the techniques and problems of new-brand introduction. They must be capable of putting the plans into action, to implement them effectively. They must skillfully execute the program of market introduction. Figure 1.1 illustrates one sales department's planned coordinating action and emphasizes the importance of timing of coordination effort in the introduction of a new product. Notice, for instance, that publicity releases break at about the time that the product becomes available. Notice, too, that salespeople are alerted ahead of time, but not too far in advance for them to lose their enthusiasm.

SALES MANAGEMENT AND CONTROL

Sales executives control the personal-selling effort of the organizational units they head. The purpose is to ensure that sales department objectives are reached. Control is part of management, as are planning, organizing, and coordinating. The several phases of control are presented in the following discussion in the normal sequence, but in the "real world," several phases can occur simultaneously or overlap in time.

Sizing up the situation. Sales executives start by reviewing the personal-selling objectives of the firm. They analyze these objectives with respect to the present, the past, and the future, in an attempt to answer four questions:

1. Where are we now?
2. How did we get here?
3. Where are we going?
4. How do we get there?

After satisfying themselves that the company's personal-selling objectives, long range and short range, are reconcilable, sales executives appraise them relative to the plans, policies, and procedures that have been used, are being used, or are intended for use in the effort to reach personal-selling objectives. In the course of sizing up the situation, sales executives find and correct weaknesses or imperfections in the sales plans and the policies and procedures used in their implementation.

Setting quantitative performance standards. After ironing out planning weaknesses, sales executives set quantitative standards against which to measure performance. Standard setting requires continual experimentation, and most standards are far from precise. The ultimate test of a particular standard's appropriateness is whether it contributes more to personal-selling efficiency than it costs.

Intelligent standard setting requires identification of the individuals who are responsible for the activity or group of activities being put under control. No two salespersons or executives perform exactly alike, even though they may operate in circumstances identical in every other respect. Thus, standards are often expressed as ranges of acceptable performance. Although it is convenient to think of a standard as a fixed value, there should be an upper and lower limit within which human variation may take place. When the performance of an organizational unit passes either of these control limits, the danger flag is up, signaling that the situation is out of control.

Gathering and processing data on actual performance. The type and amount of information needed for controlling sales depend upon the standards selected. But, regardless of the nature of this information, it should not be in excess of sales management's real needs, nor should its cost of collection and processing be more than its worth. Consequently, sales management determines—at regular intervals—whether the information being reported is sufficiently important and being used often enough to justify its costs. Sales executives also keep in mind that changes in executives, basic policies, or other matters may alter the usefulness of information. Occasionally, too, they look for cases where the same or similar information is being obtained from more than one source, representing opportunities for savings through eliminating duplications in reporting. Sometimes, also, saving are realized through reducing or lengthening the intervals at which information is gathered and processed.

For standards to be of maximum value, sales executives must have information on actual performances soon enough to permit timely corrective action. An efficient system of sales control not only furnishes information necessary to managerial evaluation of performance but also promptly relays it, together with suggestions for actions, to the appropriate organizational unit. But information on actual sales performance is often slow in arriving on the sales executive's desk, considerably delaying performance evaluations. For example, many companies, perhaps even most, require sales personnel to make weekly sales reports; in such cases, a week or more may pass before the sales executive acts on the report. But progress is being made in improving the timeliness of sales control information. Utilization of electronic data-processing systems for handling sales control data has sped up information evaluation and feedback.

Evaluating performance. Evaluation of performance means comparing actual results with standards. Because of differences in territorial and other conditions, it is difficult to compare individual performances. However, it is possible to explain each individual salesperson's variations from standard. Departures from standard are classified into uncontrollable and controllable variations. Variations outside the control of the person being appraised include those caused by rapid and unexpected changes in economic conditions; changes in governmental activities; and wars, strikes, floods, droughts, and other natural disasters. Variations over which the person held responsible has responsibility include obtaining proper sales coverage, following up leads, selling a balanced line, securing adequate credit information, and the like. The principle is that subordinates should not be held responsible for conditions outside their control. In appraising performance, it is important to exclude uncontrollable variations.

Action to correct controllable variation. Management corrects the variation explained by factors within the control of the person being evaluated. Management, in other words, takes steps to move the individual's performance in the direction of the standards. The specific actions taken differ with the nature of the variation. But management's actions assume one or more of three forms: (1) direction, or pointing out more effective ways to perform certain tasks; (2) guidance, or providing additional instructions or training; and (3) restraint, or the installation of procedures and practices aimed at keeping results within desired bounds.

Adjusting for uncontrollable variation. The amount of uncontrollable variation in the comparison indicates the relative need for adjusting sales plans and policies. If uncontrollable variation suggests that present sales objectives are unrealistic or not in line with current expectations, basic revisions in the objectives are made. Thus, if a comparison of results with standards reveals substantial uncontrollable variation, adjustment of standards to attainable levels is in order.

SALES CONTROL—INFORMAL AND FORMAL

Informal control. Circumstances exist in which awareness of the changing situation, and the ability to analyze it, are adequate control devices. Effective sales executives have their "fingers on the pulse of the business"—they have an uncanny ability to detect situations that require attention. But the larger a company is, and the higher up in the administrative hierarchy the sales executive is, the harder it becomes to use "fingertip" control. As the business grows and the structure of the sales organization becomes more complex, the more pressing the need is for formal control. For effective management, a growing business needs dependable machinery to provide the facts for making workable decisions and for formulating appropriate policies.

Formal control and written sales policies. Early evidence of the introduction of formal sales controls is the appearance of sales policies in writing. No enterprise, however small, can survive for long without policies, but smaller firms often operate satisfactorily, even though they do not put their policies in writing. As the sales organization grows, the limits within which action is to take place in given situations is spelled out in detail. A large organization not only has more complex problems than a small organization but there is less chance that everyone will know what to do in every circumstance. The large organization needs written sales and marketing policies to ensure substantial uniformity of action. Uniformity is essential both among different persons handling similar problems and among the same persons handling similar problems at different times. Written policies also conserve executive time. Because policies are written, more time can be used for planning and making decisions on problems not covered by existing policies. Sales executives reserve time for handling "policy exceptions," and if they encounter enough exceptions of similar nature, a new policy is formulated and is put in writing.

Policy formulation and review. The process of policy formulation and review illustrates the dynamics of executive control. A good policy evolves from thorough study and evaluation of tangible information. However, many sales policies deal with subjects on which quantitative data are lacking, especially when management is experimenting with new ideas. When objectives are not set clearly (because of lack of information), results vary from the standard because of factors ("uncontrollable variations") beyond the control of the individual being evaluated. Thus, coincident to the scaling down of objectives, sales management reviews the original plans. Eventually, through successive revisions, policies initially based on inadequate data often become appropriate and "good."

Formal control over sales volume. One formal control, introduced early in the history of a firm, is that over sales volume. Estimating how much of a product can be sold in a specified future period is a prerequisite both for planning and control. Sales volume performance is best appraised by comparing it with potential sales volume. The "sales or market forecast," therefore, serves as a standard for evaluating sales performance. However, the periodic forecast of sales is not enough for effective control over sales volume. During the intervals between forecasts, sales management monitors such factors as industry sales trends, activities of competitors, and share-of-the-market percentages. Significant changes in these factors may call for changes in sales objectives, plans, policies, and procedures.

Budgetary control. Ultimately, formal control requires installation of sales budgetary controls and setting up of sales territories. Budgetary control represents an extension of control over sales volume to control over margins and expenses and, hence, over profits. When control reaches this stage, sales management can project individual profit-and-loss statements for such units as sales territories, products, marketing channels, and classes of customers. Through using such estimating devices as standard costs of distribution, sales management sets standards for controlling individual expense items and the gross margin. Through marketing costs analysis, sales management appraises sales performance against predetermined standards. In this way, the soft points, the areas where sales performance is below par, are brought to management's attention. The net result is to reduce the time between drops in performance and corrective action.

SALES CONTROL AND ORGANIZATION

Paradoxically, the points in the organizational structure at which effective control is exercised depend upon the degree to which management adheres to the philosophy of "decentralization." In the decentralized sales organization, greater control is exercised by executives lower in the hierarchy than is true in the centralized organization. The higher up executives are in the organization, the more they deal with "policy" or "control" exceptions than with the control mechanism itself. At all organizational levels except the top, situations falling outside the control limits are handed up to that executive who has authority to deal with them. For speed in the initiation of corrective action, the power to make decisions is delegated as far down in the organizational structure as is consistent with the caliber and experience of executives.

CONCLUSION

Sales management is a challenging profession. Top management hold sales executives responsible for obtaining sales volume, handling the selling operation so as to make contributions to profits, and seeing to it that the business continues to grow. Society looks to them to assure the delivery of products that final buyers want and can pay for and to use their influence to see to it that products are "socially responsible."

Sales managers have broad responsibilities. They recruit, select, and train sales personnel; provide them with reasonable assignments and goals; and motivate them to optimum effort. They coordinate the personal-selling operation with other order-getting methods (such as advertising), with marketing activities of the distributive network, and with the implementation of the overall marketing strategy. They control the personal-selling effort of the organizational units they lead, assuring that sales department objectives are reached. Modern sales executives are professionals—they recognize that their main assignment is to build and maintain an effective sales organization, but they must be skilled in planning, coordinating, and controlling to ensure that personal-selling activities make their optimum contribution to the marketing effort.

2 Sales Management, Personal Selling, and Salesmanship

Sales management, personal selling, and salesmanship are all related. Sales management directs the personal-selling effort, which, in turn, is implemented largely through salesmanship. In managing personal selling, the sales executive must understand the many activities comprising the salesperson's job (including salesmanship), know the problems sales personnel meet (including many in salesmanship), and suggest solutions (including ways to handle problems in salesmanship).

Personal selling is a broader concept than salesmanship. Personal selling, along with other marketing elements such as pricing, advertising, product development and research, marketing channels, and physical distribution, is a means for implementing marketing programs. Salesmanship is one aspect of personal selling—it is never all of it. Salesmanship is one of the skills used in personal selling: *it is the art of successfully persuading prospects or customers to buy products or services from which they can derive suitable benefits, thereby increasing their total satisfactions.*[1] At one time, the emphasis in salesmanship was almost wholly on persuasion; today while recognizing the significance of persuasion, the emphasis is on the benefits attractive to prospects and customers. One variation of benefit-oriented salesmanship is "consultative selling"—creating long-term, mutually *beneficial* sales relationships with customers by helping them to improve their profits through products and services.

Salesmanship, then, is seller-initiated effort that provides prospective buy-

[1]Irving J. Shapiro, *Marketing Terms: Definitions, Explanations, and/or Aspects* (New York: S-M-C Publishing Co., 1973), p. 147.

ers with information and other benefits, motivating or persuading them to decide in favor of the seller's product or service. Sales personnel interact in diverse ways with the different customers' personnel. In addition to knowing the product and its applications thoroughly, sales personnel have to be psychologists with some individuals, human computers with others, counselors or advisors with still others, and personal friends with others. Effective sales personnel adjust their personalities on every call, making sure that what they say and do is compatible with each prospect's personality.[2]

Both personal selling and advertising make use of salesmanship techniques. Both are means for motivating or persuading prospective buyers to buy. Advertising, often described as "salesmanship in print," utilizes nonpersonal presentations, which generally are less flexible than the personal presentations made by sales personnel. A unique attribute of personal selling is that sales personnel identify differences among buyers and pattern presentations according to individual peculiarities.

The sales executive needs to know a great deal about personal selling and salesmanship. Successful sales executives know the theoretical aspects and have learned, usually through field experience, how the theories relate to and work out in practice. While many sales executives, some of them outstanding, have had little or no selling experience, the normal progression in sales management is by that route. Sales executives must be in close enough touch with actual selling situations—and the continual changes in them—to understand the problems that sales personnel face daily.

BUYER-SELLER DYADS

Fundamental to understanding salesmanship is recognition that it involves buyer-seller interactions. Sociologists use the term "dyad" to describe a situation in which two people interact. The salesperson and the prospect, interacting with each other, constitute one example of a "buyer-seller dyad." Another is the interaction of a seller using advertising with a particular prospect in the reading, listening, or viewing audience. In both advertising and personal selling, the seller seeks to motivate the prospective buyer to behave favorably toward the seller. Whether or not the buyer reacts as the seller desires depends upon the nature of the interaction. The opportunity for interaction is less in the advertising case than in personal selling. However, advertising and personal selling often supplement or support each other, and the buyer reacts to their combined impact.

Franklin Evans researched buyer-seller dyads in the life insurance business. Prospects who bought insurance knew more about salespersons and their companies, and felt more positively toward them, than did prospects who did not buy. Furthermore, the more alike salespersons and their prospects were, the greater was the likelihood that a sale would result. This was true for physical

[2]P. J. Micali, *The Lacy Techniques of Salesmanship* (Homewood, Ill.: Dow Jones-Irwin, 1972), p. xii.

characteristics (age, height), other objective factors (income, religion, education), and variables that relate to personality factors (politics, smoking).[3]

Evans's findings have significance for sales management. Whenever possible, sales personnel should be assigned to prospects whose characteristics are similar to their own, thus improving the chance of successful dyadic relationships. Pairing salespersons with customers of similar backgrounds is more easily accomplished in industrial selling, where there are fewer prospects about whom information is needed, than in consumer-goods selling, where the number of prospects and customers per salesperson is much larger.

Henry Tosi studied dyads of wholesale drug salespeople and retail pharmacists who made buying decisions. When the buyer perceived the salesperson's performance to be similar to his or her concept of "ideal" performance, the number of sources from which purchases were made was low. Although this did not necessarily result in a larger percentage of purchases from the salesperson, customer satisfaction with the salesperson's behavior did at least allow the salesperson to get into the store. Tosi concluded that, in addition to the physical characteristics and personality and objective factors cited by Evans, the customer's perception of what that behavior should be is a necessary condition for the continuation of dyadic interaction.[4]

Another factor influencing buyer-seller dyadic interactions is the buyer's initial conditioning with respect to selling. Salespeople have been maligned, and the butt of nasty stories for generations. People are taught from childhood to beware of the tricky salesperson.

There are indications that salespeople, not as stereotyped, but as they actually perform, leave much to be desired in the impact they make on customers. Studies of the attitudes of buyers and purchasing agents reveal that many are critical of the salesperson's lack of product knowledge, failure to follow up, general unreliability, slavish adherence to "canned" presentations, blatant use of flattery, bad manners, commercial dishonesty, and so forth.[5]

Figure 2.1 is a conceptual model of "salesperson-buyer" dyadic relationships. This model, developed after an extensive literature search, views the sales process as being influenced by both salesperson and buyer, each a focal person influenced by personal characteristics and role requirements. Personal characteristics include personality, values, attitudes, past experiences, and the like. Role set requirements (for example, formal authority and organizational autonomy) interact with personal characteristics to shape needs and expectations. Fo-

[3]Franklin B. Evans, "Selling as a Dyadic Relationship—A New Approach," *American Behavioral Scientist* (April 1963), p. 78.

[4]Henry L. Tosi, "The Effects of Expectation Levels and Role Consensus on the Buyer-Seller Dyad," *Journal of Business* (October 1966), pp. 516-29. For additional support of the hypothesis that sales success is a function of the degree to which the prospect perceives the salesperson as fulfilling his or her attitudinal and behavioral expectations, see Edward A. Riordan, Richard L. Oliver, and James H. Donnelly, Jr., "The Unsold Prospect: Dyadic and Attitudinal Determinants," *Journal of Marketing Research*, 14 (November 1977), pp. 530–37.

[5]D. L. Thompson, "Stereotypes of the Salesman," *Harvard Business Review*, 50, no. 1 (January-February 1972), p. 160.

FIGURE 2.1 Conceptual Model of "Salesperson-Buyer" Dyadic Relationships

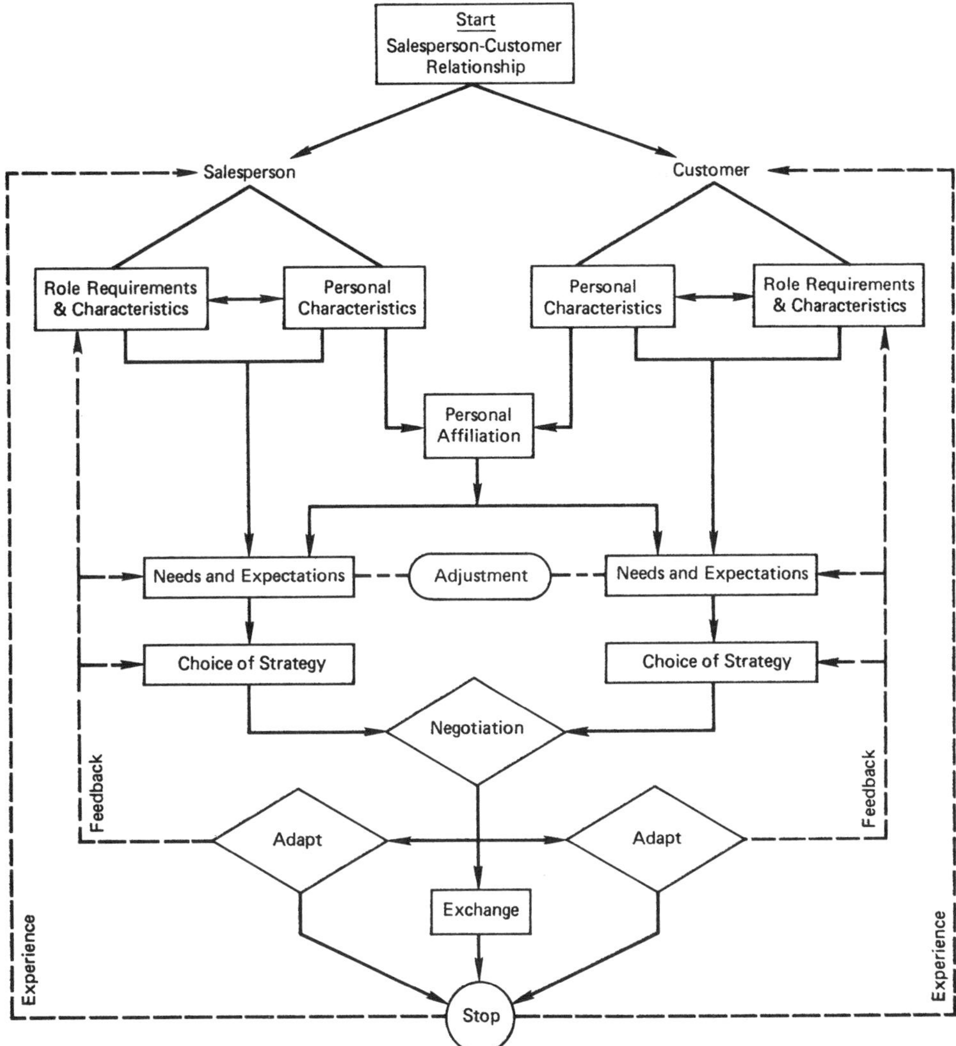

SOURCE: Reprinted by permission of the publisher from "The Personal Selling Process: A Critical Review and Model," by Rosann L. Spiro, William D. Perrault, Jr., and Fred D. Reynolds, *Industrial Marketing Management*, Vol. 5, p. 353. Copyright 1977 by Elsevier Science Publishing Co., Inc.

cal persons' perceptions of each other's needs may lead to adjustments of their own (see the "feedback" mechanism represented by the broken lines in Figure 2.1).[6]

Based on individual needs and expectations, each focal person develops a

[6]Rosann L. Spiro, William D. Perreault, Jr., and Fred D. Reynolds, "The Personal Selling Process: A Critical Review and Model," *Industrial Marketing Management*, 5 (1977), p. 352.

strategy aimed to negotiate a favorable exchange. That strategy may embrace persuasion, ingratiation, communication of facts or offers, friendship, and other elements. If the strategies are compatible, an exchange takes place. Otherwise, the salesperson and the buyer may stop interacting, or based on feedback from the unsuccessful negotiation, either or both may adapt by altering strategy, attempting to adjust needs and expectations, or modifying role requirements. Role requirements, as well as needs and expectations, often are determined by forces beyond the focal person's control, so one or both may find it impossible to adapt. For instance, to meet a buyer's expectations, a salesperson may need to set prices, yet this may be against company policy and beyond the salesperson's control. When the particular round of negotiations is terminated regardless of its outcome, the experience becomes input into future interactions of the salesperson and customer.

DIVERSITY OF PERSONAL-SELLING SITUATIONS

Considerable diversity exists among personal-selling situations, and it is helpful to distinguish between service and developmental selling. Service selling aims to obtain sales from existing customers whose habits and patterns of thought are already conducive to such sales. Developmental selling aims to convert prospects into customers. Developmental selling, in other words, seeks to create customers out of people who do not currently view the salesperson's company favorably, and who likely are resistant to changing present sources of supply.

Different sales positions require different amounts and kinds of service and developmental selling. McMurry and Arnold classify positions on a spectrum ranging from the very simple to the highly complex. They categorize sales positions into three mutually exclusive groups each containing subgroups, a total of nine subgroups in all:

Group A (service selling)

1. *Inside Order Taker*—"waits on" customers; for example, the sales clerk behind the neckwear counter in a men's store.
2. *Delivery Salesperson*—mainly engages in delivering the product; for example, persons delivering milk, bread, or fuel oil.
3. *Route or Merchandising Salesperson*—operates as an order taker but works in the field—the soap or spice salesperson calling on retailers is typical.
4. *Missionary*—aims only to build goodwill or to educate the actual or potential user, and is not expected to take an order; for example, the distiller's "missionary" and the pharmaceutical company's "detail" person.
5. *Technical Salesperson*—emphasizes technical knowledge; for example, the engineering salesperson, who is primarily a consultant to "client" companies.

Group B (developmental selling)

6. *Creative Salesperson of Tangibles*—for example, salespersons selling vacuum cleaners, automobiles, siding, and encyclopedias.
7. *Creative Salesperson of Intangibles*—for example, salespersons selling insurance, advertising services, and educational programs.

Group C (basically developmental selling, but requiring unusual creativity)

8. *"Political," "Indirect," or "Back-Door" Salesperson*—sells big-ticket items, particularly commodities or items with no truly competitive features. Sales are consummated through rendering highly personalized services (which have little or no connection with the product) to key decision makers in customers' organizations; for example, the salesperson who lands large orders for flour from baking companies by catering to key buyers' interests in fishing, golfing, blondes, or the like.
9. *Salesperson Engaged in Multiple Sales*—involves sales of big-ticket items where the salesperson must make presentations to several individuals in the customer's organization, usually a committee, only one of which can say "yes," but all of whom can say "no"; for example, the account executive of an advertising agency who makes presentations to the "agency selection committees" of advertisers—even after the account is obtained, the salesperson has to work to retain it.[7]

The more developmental selling required in a particular sales job and the more complex it is, the harder it is to make sales. The amount and kind of developmental selling depends upon the natures of prospects and customers, on the one hand, and the nature of products, on the other hand. The easiest sales are self-service sales: customers know their needs, know the products capable of satisfying these needs, sell themselves, and go through the checkout line. The most difficult sales require developmental selling *and* creativity—where sometimes the sales must be made on something other than the product's merit, or "multiple" sales are necessary to get the order, and where continual effort is required to keep the account.

THEORIES OF SELLING[8]

Is selling a science with easily taught basic concepts or an art learned through experience? In a survey of 173 marketing executives, 46 percent perceived selling as an art, 8 percent as a science, and 46 percent as an art evolving into a

[7]Robert N. McMurry and James S. Arnold, *How to Build a Dynamic Sales Organization* (New York: McGraw-Hill, 1968), pp. 11–16.

[8]Selling, in this section, is used synonymously with salesmanship. This is in line with the customary usage found in the literature of selling and salesmanship.

science.[9] The fact that selling is considered an art by some and a science by others has produced two contrasting approaches to the theory of selling.

The first approach distilled the experiences of successful salespeople and, to a lesser extent, advertising professionals. Many such persons, of course, succeeded because of their grasp of practical, or learned-through-experience psychology and their ability to apply it in sales situations. It is not too surprising that these selling theories emphasize the "what to do" and "how to do" rather than the "why." These theories, based on experiential knowledge accumulated from years of "living in the market" rather than on a systematic, fundamental body of knowledge, are subject to Howard's dictum, "Experiential knowledge can be unreliable."[10]

The second approach borrowed findings from the behavioral sciences. The late E.K. Strong, Jr., professor of psychology at the Stanford Graduate School of Business, was a pioneer in this effort, and his "buying formula" theory is presented later in this section. John A. Howard of the Columbia Graduate School of Business was in the forefront of those who adapted the findings of behavioral science to analysis of buying behavior; his "behavioral equation," discussed later in this section, attempts to develop a unified theory of buying and selling.

In this section we examine four theories. The first two, the "AIDAS" theory and the "right set of circumstances" theory, are seller oriented. The third, the "buying-formula" theory of selling, is buyer oriented. The fourth, the behavioral equation, emphasizes the buyer's decision process but also takes the salesperson's influence process into account.

AIDAS Theory of Selling

This theory—popularly known as the AIDAS theory, after the initials of the five words used to express it (attention, interest, desire, action, and satisfaction)—is the basis for many sales and advertising texts and is the skeleton around which many sales training programs are organized. Some support for this theory is found in the psychological writings of William James,[11] but there is little doubt that the construct is based upon experiential knowledge and, in fact, was in existence as early as 1898.[12] During the successful selling interview, according to this theory, the prospect's mind passes through five successive mental states: attention, interest, desire, action, and satisfaction. Implicit in this theory is the notion that the prospect goes through these five stages consciously, so the sales presentation must lead the prospect through them in the right sequence if a sale is to result.

[9]J. L. Goldstucker, B. A. Greenberg, and D. N. Bellenger, "How Scientific Is Marketing? What Do Marketing Executives Think?" *MSU Business Topics*, 22, no. 2 (Spring 1974), p. 41.

[10]John A. Howard, *Marketing Theory* (Boston: Allyn & Bacon, 1965), p. 71.

[11]See W. James, *Psychology* (New York: Henry Holt, 1908).

[12]E. K. Strong, Jr., *Psychological Aspects of Business* (New York: McGraw-Hill, 1938), p. 24.

Securing attention. The goal is to put the prospect into a receptive state of mind. The first few minutes of the interview are crucial. The salesperson has to have a reason, or an excuse, for conducting the interview. If the salesperson previously has made an appointment, this phase presents no problem, but experienced sales personnel say that even with an appointment, a salesperson must possess considerable mental alertness, and be a skilled conversationalist, to survive the start of the interview. The prospect's guard is naturally up, since he or she realizes that the caller is bent on selling something. The salesperson must establish good rapport at once. The salesperson needs an ample supply of "conversation openers." Favorable first impressions are assured by, among other things, proper attire, neatness, friendliness, and a genuine smile. Skilled sales personnel often decide upon conversation openers just before the interview so that those chosen are as timely as possible. Generally it is advantageous if the opening remarks are about the prospect (people like to talk and hear about themselves) or if they are favorable comments about the prospect's business. A good conversation opener causes the prospect to relax and sets the stage for the total presentation. Conversation openers that cannot be readily tied in with the remainder of the presentation should be avoided, for once the conversation starts to wander, great skill is required to return to the main theme.

Gaining interest. The second goal is to intensify the prospect's attention so that it evolves into strong interest. Many techniques are used to gain interest. Some salespeople develop a contagious enthusiasm for the product or a sample. When the product is bulky or technical, sales portfolios, flipcharts, or other visual aids serve the same purpose.

Throughout the interest phase, the hope is to search out the selling appeal that is most likely to be effective. Sometimes, the prospect drops hints, which the salesperson then uses in selecting the best approach. To encourage hints by the prospect, some salespeople devise stratagems to elicit revealing questions. Others ask the prospect questions designed to clarify attitudes and feelings toward the product. The more experienced the salesperson, the more he or she has learned from interviews with similar prospects. But even experienced sales personnel do considerable probing, usually of the question-and-answer variety, before identifying the strongest appeal. In addition, prospects' interests are affected by basic motivations, closeness of the interview subject to current problems, its timeliness, and their mood—receptive, skeptical, or hostile—and the salesperson must take all these into account in selecting the appeal to emphasize.

Kindling desire. The third goal is to kindle the prospect's desire to the ready-to-buy point. The salesperson must keep the conversation running along the main line toward the sale. The development of sales obstacles, the prospect's objections, external interruptions, and digressive remarks can sidetrack the presentation during this phase. Obstacles must be faced and ways found to get around them. Objections need answering to the prospect's satisfaction. Time is saved, and the chance of making a sale improved if objections are anticipated and answered before the prospect raises them. External interruptions cause breaks in the presentation, and when conversation resumes, good salespeople summarize what has been said earlier before continuing. Digressive remarks generally should be disposed of tactfully, with finesse, but sometimes distracting digression is best handled bluntly, for example, "Well, that's all very interesting, but to get back to the subject. . . . "

Inducing actions. If the presentation has been perfect, the prospect is ready to act—that is, to buy. However, buying is not automatic and, as a rule, must be induced. Experienced sales personnel rarely try for a close until they are positive that the prospect is fully convinced of the merits of the proposition. Thus, it is up to the salesperson to sense when the time is right. The trial close, the close on a minor point, and the trick close are used to test the prospect's reactions. Some sales personnel never ask for a definite "yes" or "no" for fear of getting a "no," from which they think there is no retreat. But it is better to ask for the order straightforwardly. Most prospects find it is easier to slide away from hints than from frank requests for an order.

Building satisfaction. After the customer has given the order, the salesperson should reassure the customer that the decision was correct. The customer should be left with the impression that the salesperson merely helped in deciding. Building satisfaction means thanking the customer for the order, and attending to such matters as making certain that the order is filled as written, and following up on promises made. The order is the climax of the selling situation, so the possibility of an anticlimax should be avoided—customers sometimes unsell themselves and the salesperson should not linger too long.

"Right Set of Circumstances" Theory of Selling

"Everything was right for that sale" sums up the second theory. This theory, sometimes called the "situation-response" theory, had its psychological origin in experiments with animals and holds that the particular circumstances prevailing in a given selling situation cause the prospect to respond in a predictable way. If the salesperson succeeds in securing the attention and gaining the interest of the prospect, and if the salesperson presents the proper stimuli or appeals, the desired response (that is, the sale) will result.

Furthermore, the more skilled the salesperson is in handling the set of circumstances, the more predictable is the response.

The set of circumstances, includes factors external and internal to the prospect. To use a simplified example, suppose that the salesperson says to the prospect, "Let's go out for a cup of coffee." The salesperson and the remark are external factors. But at least four factors internal to the prospect affect the response. These are the presence or absence of desires: (1) to have a cup of coffee, (2) to have it now, (3) to go out, and (4) to go out with the salesperson.

Proponents of this theory tend to stress external factors and at the expense of internal factors. They seek selling appeals that evoke desired responses. Sales personnel who try to apply the theory experience difficulties traceable to internal factors in many selling situations, but the internal factors are not readily manipulated. This is a seller-oriented theory: it stresses the importance of the salesperson controlling the situation, does not handle the problem of influencing factors internal to the prospect, and fails to assign appropriate weight to the response side of the situation-response interaction.

"Buying Formula" Theory of Selling

In contrast to the two previous theories, the third emphasizes the buyer's side of the buyer-seller dyad. The buyer's needs or problems receive major attention, and the salesperson's role is to help the buyer find solutions. This theory purports to answer the question: What thinking process goes on in the prospect's mind that causes the decision to buy or not to buy?

The buying formula is a schematic representation of a group of responses, arranged in psychological sequence. The buying formula theory emphasizes the prospect's responses (which, of course, are strongly influenced by internal factors) and deemphasizes the external factors, on the assumption that the salesperson, being naturally conscious of the external factors, will not overlook them. Since the salesperson's normal inclination is to neglect the internal factors, the formula is a convenient way to help the salesperson remember.

The origin of this theory is obscure, but recognizable versions appear in a number of early books on advertising and selling by authors who had experiential knowledge of salesmanship.[13] Several psychologists also advanced explanations similar to the buying formula.[14] The name "buying formula" was given to this theory by the late E.K. Strong, Jr., and the following step-by-step explanation is adapted from his teaching and writings.[15]

Reduced to their simplest elements, the mental processes involved in a purchase are

need (or problem) → solution → purchase

Because the outcome of a purchase affects the chance that a continuing relationship will develop between the buyer and the seller, and because nearly all sales organizations are interested in continuing relationships, it is necessary to add a fourth element. The four elements then, are

[13]See, for example, H. Tipper and others, *Advertising, Its Principles and Practices* (New York: Ronald Press, 1915), and W.W. Charters, *How to Sell at Retail* (Boston: Houghton Mifflin, 1922).

[14]See, for example, A. T. Poffenberger, *Psychology in Advertising*, rev. ed. (New York: McGraw-Hill, 1938), pp. 16–39.

[15]Dr. Strong's explanation is in his *Psychological Aspects of Business*, pp. 16–39. The explanation here is patterned after Dr. Strong's, but some terminology has been changed in line with modern usage.

need (or problem) → solution → purchase → satisfaction

Whenever a need is felt, or a problem recognized, the individual is conscious of a deficiency of satisfaction. In the world of selling and buying, the solution will always be a product or service or both, and they will belong to a potential seller.

In purchasing, then, the element "solution" involves two parts: (1) product (and/or service) and (2) trade name (name of manufacturer, company, or salesperson).

In buying anything, the purchaser proceeds mentally from need or problem to product or service, to trade name, to purchase, and, upon using the product or service, he or she experiences satisfaction or dissatisfaction. Thus, when a definite buying habit has been established, the buying formula is:

need or problem → product service and/or trade name → purchase → satisfaction/ dissatisfaction

To ensure purchase, the product or service and the trade name (that is, the source of supply) must be considered adequate, and the buyer must experience a (pleasant) feeling of anticipated satisfaction when thinking of the product and/or service and the trade name. In many cases, an item viewed as adequate is also liked, and vice versa, but this is not always so. Some products and services that are quite adequate are not liked, and some things are liked and bought that are admittedly not as good as competing items. Similar reasoning applies to trade names. Some sources of supply are both adequate and liked, others are adequate but not liked, still others are liked but patronized even though they are inadequate compared to competing sources.

With adequacy and pleasant feelings included, the buying formula becomes

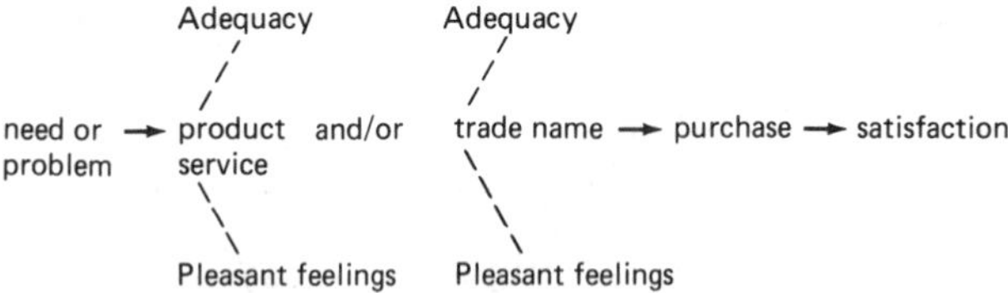

When a buying habit is being established, the buyer must know why the product or service is an adequate solution to the need or problem, and why the trade name is the best one to buy. The buyers also must have a pleasant feeling toward the product or service and the trade name.

Then, whenever the buyer's buying habit is challenged by a friend's remark, a competing salesperson's presentation, or a competitor's advertisement, the buyer needs reasons to defend the purchase, and, in addition, he or she needs a pleasant feeling toward both the product or service and the trade name. All this is represented by the dashed lines in the formula.

The primary elements in a well-established buying habit are those connected by solid lines, on the central line of the formula. Most purchases are made with scarcely a thought as to why, and with a minimum of feeling. And it should be the constant aim of the salesperson and advertiser to form such direct associations. Reasons (adequacy of solution) and pleasant feelings constitute the elements of defense in the buying habit. As long as they are present, repeat buying occurs.

The answer to each selling problem is implied in the buying formula, and differences among answers are differences in emphasis upon the elements in the formula.

Where the emphasis should be placed depends upon a variety of circumstances. Without going into detail, it may be said that

1. If the prospect does not feel a need or recognize a problem that can be satisfied by the product or service, the need or problem should be emphasized.
2. If the prospect does not think of the product or service when he or she feels the need or recognizes the problem, the association between need or problem and product or service should be emphasized.
3. If the prospect does not think of the trade name when he or she thinks of the product or service, the association between product or service and trade name should be emphasized.
4. If need or problem, product or service, and trade name are well associated, emphasis should be put upon facilitating purchase and use.
5. If competition is felt, emphasis should be put upon establishing in the prospects' minds the adequacy of the trade-named product or service, and pleasant feelings toward it.
6. If sales to new prospects are desired, every element in the formula should be presented.
7. If more sales to old customers are desired, the latter should be reminded. (Developing new uses is comparable to selling to new customers.)

"Behavioral Equation" Theory

Using a stimulus-response model (a sophisticated version of the "right set of circumstances" theory), and incorporating findings from behavioral research, J.A. Howard explains buying behavior in terms of the purchasing decision process, viewed as phases of the learning process.

Four essential elements of the learning process included in the stimulus-response model are drive, cue, response, and reinforcement, described as follows:

1. *Drives* are strong internal stimuli that impel the buyer's response. There are two kinds:

a. Innate drives stem from the physiological needs, such as hunger, thirst, pain, cold, and sex.
b. Learned drives, such as striving for status or social approval, are acquired when paired with the satisfying of innate drives. They are elaborations of the innate drives, serving as a façade behind which the functioning of the innate drives is hidden. Insofar as marketing is concerned, the learned drives are dominant in economically advanced societies.

2. *Cues* are weak stimuli that determine *when* the buyer will respond.
   a. Triggering cues activate the decision process for any given purchase.
   b. Nontriggering cues influence the decision process but do not activate it, and may operate at any time even though the buyer is not contemplating a purchase. There are two kinds:
      (1) Product cues are external stimuli received from the product directly, for example, color of the package, weight, or price.
      (2) Informational cues are external stimuli that provide information of a symbolic nature about the product. Such stimuli may come from advertising, conversations with other people (including sales personnel), and so on.
   c. Specific product and information cues may also function as triggering cues. This may happen when price triggers the buyer's decision.
3. *Response* is what the buyer does.
4. A *reinforcement* is any event that strengthens the buyer's tendency to make a particular response.[16]

Howard incorporates these four elements into an equation:

$$B = P \times D \times K \times V$$

where

B = response or the internal response tendency, that is, the act of purchasing a brand or patronizing a supplier
P = predisposition or the inward response tendency, that is, force of habit
D = present drive level (amount of motivation)
K = "incentive potential," that is, the value of the product or its potential satisfaction to the buyer
V = intensity of all cues: triggering, product, or informational

[16]This is a condensed version of the explanation contained in J. A. Howard's *Marketing Management, Analysis and Planning*, rev. ed. (Homewood, Ill.: Richard D. Irwin, 1963). We are indebted to the author for permission to include this condensation.

This model was later refined further by Professor Howard, working in collaboration with Jagdish N. Sheth. See their "A Theory of Buyer Behavior," in Reed Moyer (ed.), *Changing Marketing Systems: Proceedings of the 1967 Winter Conference of the American Marketing Association*, 1967, published by the American Marketing Association.

The relation among the variables is multiplicative. Thus, if any independent variable has a zero value, B will also be zero and there is no response. No matter how much P there may be, for example, if the individual is unmotivated ($D = 0$), there is no response.

Each time there is a response—a purchase—in which satisfaction (K) is sufficient to yield a reward, predisposition (P) increases in value. In other words, when the satisfaction yields a reward, reinforcement occurs, and, technically, what is reinforced is the tendency to make a response in the future to the cue that immediately preceded the rewarded response. After reinforcement, the probability increases that the buyer will buy the product (or patronize the supplier) the next time the cue appears—in other words, the buyer has learned.[17]

Buyer-seller dyad and reinforcement. In the interactions of a salesperson and a buyer, each can display a type of behavior that is rewarding, that is reinforcing, to the other. The salesperson provides the buyer with a product (and the necessary information about it and its uses) that the buyer needs; this satisfaction of the need is rewarding to the buyer, who, in turn, can reward the salesperson by buying the product. Each can also reward the other by another type of behavior, that of providing social approval. The salesperson gives social approval to a buyer by displaying high regard with friendly greetings, warm conversation, praise, and the like.

In understanding the salesperson-client relation, it is helpful to separate economic aspects from social features. The salesperson wishes to sell a product, and the buyer wishes to buy it—these are the economic features. Each participant also places a value and cost upon the social features. Behavior concerning these features of the relationship consist of sentiments, or expressions of different degrees of liking or social approval. Salespersons attempt to receive rewards (reinforcements) either in sentiment or economic by changing their own behavior or getting buyers to change theirs.

Salesperson's influence process. The process by which the salesperson influences the buyer is explainable in terms of the equation $B = P \times D \times K \times V$. The salesperson influences P (predisposition) directly, for example, through interacting with the buyer in ways rewarding to the buyer. The greatest effect on P, however, comes from using the product. The salesperson exerts influence through D (amount of motivation), this influence being strong when the buyer seeks information in terms of informational cues. If the ends to be served are not clearly defined, by helping to clarify these, the buyer's goals, the salesperson again exerts influence through D. When the buyer has stopped learning—when the buyer's buying behavior becomes automatic—the salesperson influences D by providing triggering cues. When the buyer has narrowed down the choices to a few sellers, the salesperson, by communicating the merits of the company brand,

[17]Howard states, however, that "additional reinforced purchases . . . increase P at a negatively accelerated rate [as] illustrated in the shape of the learning curve . . . ," ibid., p. 45.

can cause it to appear relatively better, and thus affect K (its potential satisfaction for the buyer). Finally, the salesperson can vary the intensity of his or her effort, so making the difference in V (the intensity of all cues).[18]

Salesperson's role in reducing buyer dissonance. According to Festinger's theory of cognitive dissonance, when individuals choose between two or more alternatives, anxiety or dissonance will almost always occur because the decision has unattractive as well as attractive features. After decisions, people expose themselves to information that they perceive as likely to support their choices, and to avoid information likely to favor rejected alternatives.[19]

Although Festinger evidently meant his theory to apply only to postdecision anxiety, it seems reasonable that it should hold for predecision anxiety. Hauk, for instance, writes that a buyer may panic on reaching the point of decision and rush into the purchase as an escape from the problem or put it off because of the difficulty of deciding.[20] It seems, then, that a buyer can experience either predecision or postdecision dissonance, or both.

Reducing pre- and postdecision anxiety or dissonance is an important function of the salesperson. Recognizing that the buyer's dissonance varies both according to whether the product is an established or a new one, and whether the salesperson-client relationship is ongoing or new, these are four types of cases involving the salesperson's role.

1. *An established product—an ongoing salesperson-client relationship.* Unless the market is unstable, the buyer tends toward automatic response behavior, in which no learning is involved and thus experiences little, if any, dissonance; but insofar as it does occur, the salesperson is effective because the salesperson is trusted by the buyer.
2. *An established product—a new salesperson-client relationship.* The salesperson, being new, is less effective in reducing dissonance.
3. *A new product—an ongoing salesperson-client relationship.* Unless the buyer generalizes from personal experience with an established similar product, the buyer experiences dissonance, especially if it is an important product. Because of the established relationship with the buyer, the salesperson can reduce dissonance.
4. *A new product—a new salesperson-client relationship.* The buyer needs dissonance reduction, and the salesperson is less capable of providing it.[21]

How can a salesperson facilitate the buyer's dissonance reduction? Two ways are (1) to emphasize the advantages of the product purchased, while stressing the disadvantages of the forgone alternatives, and (2) to show that

[18]Ibid., pp. 429–30.

[19]L. Festinger, *A Theory of Cognitive Dissonance* (New York: Harper & Row, 1957).

[20]J. G. Hauk, "Research in Personal Selling," in G. W. Schwartz (ed.), *Science in Marketing* (New York: John Wiley, 1965), p. 261.

[21]Howard, *Marketing Management*, p. 430.

many characteristics of the chosen item are similar to products the buyer has forgone, but which are approved by the reference groups.[22] In other words, the buyer experiencing cognitive dissonance needs reassuring that the decision is or was a wise one; the salesperson provides information that permits the buyer to rationalize the decision.

PROSPECTING

Efficient organization of time and thorough planning of work are earmarks of above-average salespersons. They look for ways to "stretch" productive selling time. They arrange travel and call schedules to economize on time spent en route and distance traveled. They make appointments to avoid prolonged waiting for callbacks. They do not waste time trying to sell to people who cannot buy or are not likely to do so. The planning work, which is essential in eliminating calls on nonbuyers, is called "prospecting."

Improvement in prospecting is one way to stretch productive selling time. Many sales personnel devote too little time to prospecting and, as a consequence, too much to calling on nonprospects. Salespersons who are proficient in prospecting apply their selling efforts productively; they do not call on nonprospects and can devote their full attention to those likely to buy.

Some companies use specialized personnel for prospecting, but most regard it as one of the salesperson's responsibilities. Even though salespersons may not do "all" the prospecting, they often have access to information on likely prospects that is not available to central office personnel.

Steps in Prospecting

The steps in prospecting are (1) formulating prospect definitions, (2) searching out potential accounts, (3) qualifying prospects and determining probable requirements, and (4) relating company products to each prospect's requirements.[23]

Formulating prospect definitions. Prospective customers must have the willingness, the financial capacity, and the authority to buy, and they must be available to the salesperson. Salespersons waste time when they attempt to sell individuals who have neither need for the product or money to pay for it. Salespersons waste time if they try to sell to the wrong persons; so it is important to ascertain which persons in each firm have the authority to buy. Although indi-

[22]G. Zaltman, *Marketing: Contributions from the Behavioral Sciences* (New York: Harcourt Brace Jovanovich, 1965), p. 63.

[23]For an interesting discussion on the importance of knowing as much as possible about the account in advance of making the sales call, see B. P. Shapiro, "Manage the Customer, Not Just the Sales Force," *Harvard Business Review*, 52, no. 5 (September-October 1974), pp. 130–31.

viduals may qualify as prospects in other respects, they may be inaccessible to the salesperson. The president of a large corporation, for example, may need insurance and be willing and able to pay for it, but a particular salesperson may have no way to make the contact.

In addition to meeting the stated requirements, there are other requirements unique to each company's customers. Starting with data on the profitability of present accounts, any characteristics typical of profitable accounts but not shared by unprofitable accounts should be detected. These identifying characteristics ideally should be ones recognizable from information appearing in directories or lists. Prospects in many businesses and professions, for instance, are readily identified from classified listings in telephone and city directories. Key characteristics that identify profitable accounts are assembled into descriptions of the various classes of customers, and these are the prospect definitions.

Searching out potential accounts. Using the prospect definitions, the salesperson combs different sources for the names of probable prospects, or "suspects," as they are called. Sources of prospect information include directories of all kinds, news and notes in trade papers and business magazines, credit reports, membership lists of chambers of commerce and trade and manufacturers' associations, lists purchased from list brokers, and records of service requests. Other sources are responses to company advertising, sales personnel of noncompeting firms calling on the same general classes of trade, conventions and meetings, bankers and other "centers of influence," and the salesperson's own observations. Salespeople selling services, insurance, for example, uncover prospects among their acquaintances; members of their professional, religious, and social organizations; and the referrals of friends. Another source of prospects is the "endless chain"—satisfied customers suggest, voluntarily or on request, other leads to the salesperson who served them.

Qualifying prospects and determining probable requirements. As information is assembled on each tentative prospect (i.e., "suspect"), it is easier to estimate the probable requirements of each for the types of products sold by the company. Prospects with requirements too small to represent profitable business are removed from further consideration, unless their growth possibilities show promise. Even after tapping all readily available information sources, additional information often is required to qualify certain prospects, and personal visits by salespersons may be the only way to obtain it. These visits may not bring in sales, but they save time, as prospects are separated from nonprospects.

Relating company products to each prospect's requirements. The final step is to plan the strategy for approaching each prospect. From the information assembled, it is usually possible to determine each prospect's probable needs. From what the salesperson knows about the company's products, their uses, and applications, he or she selects those that seem most appropriate for a particular prospect.

The salesperson's presentation is now easy to construct, and it is tailored to fit the prospect. The salesperson should have clear ideas about specific objections the prospect may raise and other obstacles to the sale that may be encountered. The salesperson is ready to contact the prospect, the only tasks remaining are making an appointment, deciding how to open the presentation, and determining how to persuade the prospect to become a customer.

SALES RESISTANCE

Prospects show sales resistance by pointing out real or imagined obstacles, and by voicing objections, sincere or insincere. In analyzing sales resistance, the salesperson needs skill in the accurate and rapid appraisal of people and their motivations. A prospect's expressed sales resistance is either an obstacle or an objection. An obstacle is real or unreal; an objection is sincere or insincere.

Obstacles to sales. Obstacles are real or apparent reasons that the prospect has for not buying. If the obstacle is real, it precludes the consummation of the sale. But if it is apparent, there are ways to circumvent it. A prospect says a temporary shortage of cash prevents buying—an obstacle, not an objection—and the salesperson helps the prospect to circumvent it by explaining a method for financing the purchase. Some obstacles can be circumvented, others cannot. When an obstacle arises, the salesperson determines whether or not there is a way to get around it. If the salesperson recognizes the specific obstacle and knows a way to circumvent it, the next move is to present the solution to the prospect.

Sales objections. Objections are never good reasons for failing to complete the sale, but they nearly always divert the salesperson's presentation from its main course. At best, an objection requires a satisfactory answer; at worst, it blocks the sale. Adroitness in handling objections is a difference between effective and ineffective salespeople.

Sincere objections trace to incompleteness, inaccuracy, or vagueness in the sales presentation. Prospects may not recognize the nature of their needs, or they may have doubts about the appropriateness of the product to fulfill those needs. Prospects may be confused in some respect, or may react unfavorably to the salesperson's personality. Except when personality conflict cannot be resolved (a real obstacle, not an objection), sincere objections are overcome by patient and thorough explanations.

Prospects raise insincere objections to discourage salespersons, to get rid of them, to test their competence, and as false excuses for not buying. When salespersons sense that an objection is insincere, they seek to regain the offensive as soon as possible. They do not permit an insincere objection to provoke an argument—one of the surest ways to lose a sale.

Some sales executives say that every objection, no matter how insincere, should be treated with the utmost courtesy. Others say that insincere objections should be ignored. The best defensive strategy often is the strong counterattack, and the salesperson should seek to regain the initiative as soon as he or she can gracefully do so.

CLOSING SALES

The selling tactics followed affect the ease of closing the sale. Low-pressure sales are closed more easily than are high-pressure ones. In low-pressure sales, prospects feel that they are reaching the buying decisions themselves, and primarily through rational processes of thought, so there is no need for extra push just before the sales are consummated. In high-pressure sales, the main thrust is to the prospects' emotions, so salespersons attempt to propel prospects into buying decisions. Often, the prospect regains normal perspective as the sale nears its climax, and, if this happens, the salesperson needs unusually effective persuasion to close the sale.

Every salesperson approaches certain closings with apprehension. At closing time, either the salesperson sells the prospect an order or the prospect sells the salesperson on a "no sale." Closing time provides an opportunity to register tangible proof of selling skill. Occasionally even the best salesperson must rely upon closing skill to make the sale.

Prospecting, if well done, puts the salesperson in the proper frame of mind for the close. The salesperson feels that a real service is being performed for the prospect, not that "a bill of goods is being sold." There is no doubt that the product is the best solution to the prospect's problems.

When the sales presentation is complete and clear, no difficulty is met in closing the sale. All obstacles to the sale and all objections have been removed, to the prospect's entire satisfaction. Basic agreement has been reached, and the prospect is ready to accept the proposal.

But even after an excellent presentation, and in spite of thorough prospecting, some prospects refrain from positive commitments. The natural tendency of many people is to let inertia guide their reactions—many are happy to leave things as they are, and salespersons leave empty-handed unless they jolt these prospects into buying. The skilled closer gives the extra push that triggers a buying response. But failures to get an order result as much from poor prospecting and inept presentations as from ineffective closing.

When an attempted close fails, the salesperson should normally try another. The refusal does not necessarily imply an unwillingness to buy; it may indicate the prospect's need for additional information or for clarification of some point. Some executives recommend that sales personnel attempt as many as five closes before giving up. Early closing attempts should be so expressed that a refusal will not cut off the presentation. A salesperson judges the sincerity of a prospect's refusal, surrendering gracefully when it is clear that no sale will be made.

The salesperson first uses an indirect close, that is, attempts to get the order without actually asking for it. The salesperson may ask the prospect to state a preference from among a limited number of choice (as to models, delivery dates, order size, or the like), so phrasing the question that all possible responses are in the salesperson's favor except for one: "None at all." Or the salesperson may summarize, emphasizing features that visibly impress the prospect, showing how the reasons for the purchase outweigh those opposed to it. Then the salesperson pauses for the prospect's response, which is expected to be, "Go ahead and write the order." Sometimes, the extra push may be a concession that makes the purchase sufficiently more attractive to make the sale. Or the salesperson may assume that the sale is made, write out the order, and hand it to the prospect for approval—if the prospect balks, the issue is clearer. Perhaps one last objection is voiced, but after it is answered, the sale is made. Many indirect closes are in common use, and books on selling contain numerous examples.

When one or more attempts at an indirect close fail, the salesperson uses the direct approach. Few prospects respond negatively to a frank request for the order. In fact, many people, especially those who are themselves engaged in selling, do not buy unless the order is asked for outright.

CONCLUSION

Sales executives must understand the jobs of those reporting to them. Of the tasks assigned to sales personnel, among the most important are those requiring application of selling techniques. When sales executives understand the tasks assigned to sales personnel, and have insight into how these tasks affect the thought processes and behavior patterns of sales personnel, they are ready to manage sales personnel. They have the necessary background to train sales personnel, to direct the sales force's efforts, and to evaluate individual salesperson's achievements.

Setting Personal-Selling Objectives

3

Marketing management in consultation with sales management determines personal selling's exact role in the promotional program. Figure 3.1 shows how personal selling fits into the promotional program. The marketing planning group sets personal-selling objectives, determines sales-related marketing policies, formulates personal-selling strategies, and finalizes the sales budget. The combined impact of these decisions constitutes the framework within which the sales force is managed. Generally, this means that the company fields its own sales force, but, occasionally, as in the insurance industry, personal-selling activities are largely shifted to middlemen.

TYPES OF PERSONAL-SELLING OBJECTIVES

The qualitative personal-selling objectives are long term and concern the contributions management expects personal selling to make in achieving long-term company objectives. These objectives generally are carried over from one period's promotional program to the next. Depending upon company objectives and the promotional mix, personal selling may be assigned such qualitative objectives as

1. To do the entire selling job (as when there are no other elements in the promotional mix).
2. To "service" existing accounts (that is, to maintain contacts with present customers, take orders, and so forth).
3. To search out and obtain new customers.

FIGURE 3.1 Personal Selling as Part of the Promotional Program

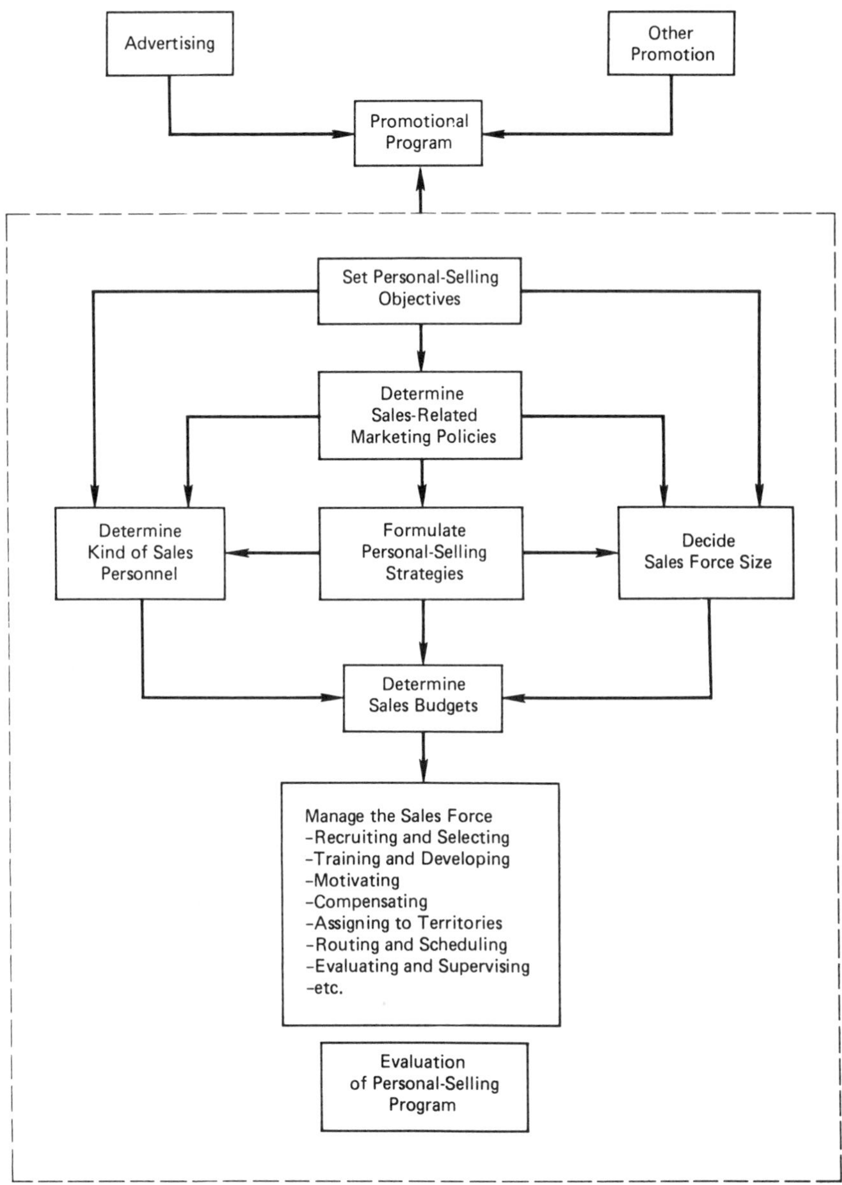

4. To secure and maintain customers' cooperation in stocking and promoting the product line.
5. To keep customers informed on changes in the product line and other aspects of marketing strategy.
6. To assist customers in selling the product line (as through "missionary selling").

7. To provide technical advice and assistance to customers (as with complicated products and where products are especially designed to fit buyers' specifications).
8. To assist with (or handle) the training of middlemen's sales personnel.
9. To provide advice and assistance to middlemen on management problems.
10. To collect and report market information of interest and use to company management.

The basic considerations in setting qualitative personal-selling objectives are decisions on sales policies and personal-selling strategies and their role in the total promotional program. After this role is defined, qualitative long-term personal-selling objectives are set. In turn, the qualitative personal-selling objectives become the major determinants of the quantitative personal-selling objectives.

The quantitative objectives assigned to personal selling are short term and are adjusted from one promotional period to another. The sales volume objective—the dollar or unit sales volume management sets as the target for the promotional period—is the key quantitative objective. All other quantitative personal-selling objectives derive from or are related to the sales volume objective. Thus, discussion here focuses upon the setting of sales volume objectives. Setting the sales volume objective influences the setting of other quantitative personal-selling objectives, among them the following:

1. To capture and retain a certain market share.
2. To obtain sales volume in ways that contribute to profitability (for example, by selling the "optimum" mix of company products).
3. To obtain some number of new accounts of given types.
4. To keep personal-selling expenses within set limits.
5. To secure targeted percentages of certain accounts' business.

SOME IMPORTANT TERMS

Before examining the planning and analytical work involved in setting sales volume objectives, it is important to define three terms: market potential, sales potential, and sales forecast. Some executives use these terms synonymously, but, as the following discussion indicates, there are good reasons for distinguishing among them.

Market Potential

A market potential is an estimate of the maximum possible sales opportunities present in a particular market segment and open to all sellers of a good or service during a stated future period. Thus, an estimate of the maximum number of low-priced pocket cameras that might be sold in San Mateo County, California, during the calendar year 1987 by all sellers competing for this market would represent the 1987 San Mateo County market potential for low-priced pocket cameras. A market potential indicates how much of a particular product can be sold to a particular market segment over some future period, assuming the application of appropriate marketing methods.

Sales Potential

A sales potential is an estimate of the maximum possible sales opportunities present in a particular market segment open to a specified company selling a good or service during a stated future period. To illustrate, an estimate of the number of low-priced pocket cameras that might be sold in San Mateo County, California, during the calendar year 1987 by the Eastman Kodak Company would be the 1987 San Mateo County sales potential for Eastman Kodak low-price pocket cameras. A sales potential represents sales opportunities available to a particular manufacturer, such as to Eastman Kodak Company, while a market potential indicates sales opportunities available to an entire industry.

Sales Forecast

A sales forecast is an estimate of sales, in dollars or physical units, in a future period under a particular marketing program and an assumed set of economic and other factors outside the unit for which the forecast is made. A sales forecast may be for a single product or for an entire product line. It may be for a manufacturer's entire marketing area, or for any subdivision of it. Such forecasts are short-term, or operating, sales forecasts rather than long-range sales forecasts, which are used for planning production capacity and for long-run financial planning. Long-range sales forecasts, although of interest, are so tentative that sales planners give them only passing attention. It is the short-term, or operating, sales forecast that is important to the sales executive. Keep in mind, then, that an operating sales forecast is a prediction of how much of a company's particular product (or product line) can be sold during a future period under a given marketing program and an assumed set of outside factors.

ANALYZING MARKET POTENTIAL

Market Identification

The first step in analyzing a product's market potential is to identify its market. Market identification requires finding out

1. Who buys the product?

2. Who uses it?
3. Who are the prospective buyers and/or users?

Some companies find answers to these questions in their internal records, but most companies, especially those that use long marketing channels, must use field research to obtain meaningful answers. In consumer-goods marketing, buyers, users, and prospects are identified and classified according to such characteristics as age, sex, education, income, and social class. In industrial-goods marketing, buyers, users, and prospects are identified and classified by size of firm, geographical location, type of industry, and the like.

Market identification studies reveal the characteristics that differentiate the market segments making up the product's market potential. Frequently they uncover unexploited market segments whose patronage might be obtained through redirecting personal-selling effort or changing promotional strategy. Sometimes, market identification studies provide, as a side result, customer data on such factors as purchase frequency, searching time expended, unit of purchase, and seasonal buying habits. When assembled and analyzed, these data help in estimating market potential.

Market Motivation

The second step in analyzing market potential is to detect the reasons why customers buy the product and the reasons why potential customers might buy it. Market motivation studies answer twin questions: Why do people buy? Why don't people buy? The answers help not only in estimating market potential but assist the sales executive seeking to increase the effectiveness of promotional programs.

Motivation research techniques vary, but the most widely used are the projective techniques, in which respondents project themselves, their attitudes, interests, and opinions into interpretations of special materials presented by the researcher. Analysis of results by trained specialists lays bare what goes on in buyers' minds, including, importantly, the real reasons for buying or not buying the product. Most motivation studies are directed toward explaining the buying behavior of ultimate consumers rather than industrial users. Information from motivation studies helps not only in estimating a product's market potential but assists in deciding

1. How best to present the product in sales talks.
2. The relative effectiveness of different selling appeals.
3. The relative appropriateness of various promotional methods.

Analysis of Market Potential

Having identified the potential buyers and their buying behavior, the third step is to analyze the market potential. Generally, market potential cannot be analyzed directly, so analysis makes use of market factors (a market factor is a market feature or characteristic related to the product's demand). For instance, the number of males reaching shaving age each year is one market factor influencing the demand for men's electric shavers. But not every male reaching shaving age is a prospective buyer of an electric shaver—some will be late in starting to shave, others will adopt other shaving methods, some will not have the money to buy a shaver or will prefer to use that money for something else, and still others will use borrowed shavers or, perhaps, will grow beards. Thus, using market factors for analyzing market potential is a two-step process:

1. Select the market factor(s) associated with the product's demand.
2. Eliminate those market segments that do not contain prospective buyers of the product.

MARKET INDEXES

A market index is a numerical expression indicating the degree to which one or more market factors associated with a given product's demand is present in a given market segment—usually a given geographical market segment. Market indexes are expressed in relative terms, such as in percentages, rather than in absolute numbers. In analyzing the market for furniture, for example, a market index might contain three factors: population, effective buying income, and number of marriages. In the United States, the most widely used single-factor market indexes are population as a percentage of U.S. total and effective buying income as a percentage of U.S. total. Many companies refine these indexes further by breaking them down into greater detail; for example, the population index is divided into subindexes covering different age groups and the income index into subindexes for different income groups.

Sales and Marketing Management, a trade publication for sales executives, publishes annually an issue giving Buying Power Index (BPI) data by state, county, city, metropolitan area, and even by the suburban components of metropolitan areas. The BPI combines effective buying income, retail sales, and population into a single index using weighting of factors of 5 for income, 3 for retail sales, and 2 for population. This particular combination and weighting of market factors serves as a satisfactory measure of market potential for many consumer-products marketers.

Other marketers construct their own market indexes, including different market factors and using different weighting systems. One producer of lighting fixtures includes data on new housing starts, and a maker of auto seat covers includes motor vehicle registrations. Other market factors frequently used in constructing consumer-goods market indexes are registrations of new automobiles, home ownership, marriage licenses issued, births, and deaths. Marketers of industrial products construct market indexes using such market factors as value added by manufacture, number of employees engaged in certain kinds of manufacturing, number of manufacturing establishments, person-hours worked, total value of shipments of particular items, and capital expenditures for new plant and equipment.

SALES POTENTIAL AND SALES FORECASTING

Sales potentials, as defined earlier, are quantitative estimates of the *maximum* possible sales opportunities present in particular market segments open to a specified company selling a good or service during a stated future period. They are derived from market potentials after analyses of historical market share relationships and adjustments for changes in companies' and competitors' selling strategies and practices.

A firm's sales potential and its sales forecast are not usually identical—in most instances, the sales potential is larger than the sales forecast. There are several reasons for this: some companies do not have sufficient production capacity to capitalize on the full sales potential; other firms have not yet developed distributive networks capable of reaching every potential customer; others do not attempt to realize their total sales potentials because of limited financial resources; and still others, being more profit oriented than sales oriented, seek to maximize profitable sales and not possible sales. The estimate for sales potential indicates how much a company could sell *if* it had all the necessary resources and desired to use them. The sales forecast is a related but different estimate—it indicates how much a company with a given amount of resources can sell if it implements a particular marketing program.

SALES FORECASTING METHODS

A sales forecasting method is a procedure for estimating how much of a given product (or product line) can be sold if a given marketing program is implemented. No sales forecasting method is foolproof—each is subject to some error. Some methods are unsophisticated, such as the jury of executive opinion or the poll of sales force opinion. Others involve the application of sophisticated statistical techniques, such as regression analysis or econometric model building and simulation. Two sales forecasting methods may be either sophisticated or unsophisticated, depending upon how they are used—the projection of past sales and the survey of customers' buying plans.

Well-managed companies do not rely upon a single sales forecasting method but use several. If different methods produce roughly the same sales forecasts, then more confidence is placed in the results. But if different methods produce greatly different sales forecasts, then the sales situation merits further study.

Jury of Executive Opinion

There are two steps in this method: (1) high-ranking executives estimate probable sales, and (2) an average estimate is calculated. The assumption is that the executives are well informed about the industry outlook and the company's market position, capabilities, and marketing program. All should support their estimates with factual material and explain their rationales.

Companies using the jury of executive opinion method do so for one or more of four reasons:

1. This is a quick and easy way to turn out a forecast.
2. This is a way to pool the experience and judgment of well-informed people.
3. This may be the only feasible approach if the company is so young that it has not yet accumulated the experience to use other forecasting methods.
4. This method may be used when adequate sales and market statistics are missing, or when these figures have not yet been put into the form required for more sophisticated forecasting methods.

The jury of executive opinion method has weaknesses. Its findings are based primarily on opinion, and factual evidence to support the forecast is often sketchy. This approach adds to the work load of key executives, requiring them to spend time that they would otherwise devote to their areas of main responsibility. And a forecast made by this method is difficult to break down into estimates of probable sales by products, by time intervals, by markets, by customers, and so on.

The Delphi technique. Several years ago researchers at the Rand Corporation developed a technique for predicting the future that is called the Delphi technique. This is a version of the jury of executive opinion method in which those giving opinions are selected for their "expertise." The panel of experts responds to a sequence of questionnaires in which the responses to one questionnaire are used to produce the next questionnaire. Thus, information available to some and not to other experts is disseminated to all, enabling all to base their final forecasts on "all available" information. Some contend that "this technique eliminates the bandwagon effect of majority opinion."[1]

Poll of Sales Force Opinion

In the poll of sales force opinion method, often tagged "the grass-roots approach," individual sales personnel forecast sales for their territories; then individual forecasts are combined and modified, as management thinks necessary, to

[1]J. C. Chambers, S.K. Mullick, and D. D. Smith, "How to Choose the Right Forecasting Technique," *Harvard Business Review*, 49 (July–August 1971), pp. 55–64.

form the company sales forecast. This approach appeals to practical sales managers because forecasting responsibility is assigned to those who produce the results. Furthermore, there is merit in utilizing the specialized knowledge of those in closest touch with market conditions. Because the salespeople help to develop the forecast, they should have greater confidence in quotas based upon it. Another attractive feature is that forecasts developed by this method are easy to break down according to products, territories, customers, middlemen, and sales force.

But the poll of sales force opinion approach has weaknesses. Not generally trained to do forecasting, and influenced by current business conditions in their territories, salespersons tend to be overly optimistic or overly pessimistic about sales prospects. They are too near the trees to see the forest—they often are unaware of broad changes taking place in the economy and of trends in business conditions outside their own territories. Furthermore, if the "forecasts" of the sales staff are used in setting quotas, some sales personnel deliberately underestimate so that quotas are reached more easily.

To some extent, the weaknesses of this method can be overcome through training the sales force in forecasting techniques, by orienting them to factors influencing company sales, and by adjusting for consistent biases in individual salespersons' forecasts. For most companies, however, implementing corrective actions is an endless task, because sales personnel turnover is constantly going on, and new staff members (whose biases are unknown at the start) submit their forecasts along with those of veteran sales personnel with known biases. In short, this method is based to such a large extent on judgment that it is not appropriate for most companies to use it as the only forecasting method. The poll of sales force opinion serves best as a method of getting an alternative estimate for use as a check on a sales forecast obtained through some other approach.

Projection of Past Sales

The projection of past sales method of sales forecasting takes a variety of forms. The simplest is to set the sales forecast for the coming year at the same figure as the current year's actual sales, or the forecast may be made by adding a set percentage to last year's sales, or to a moving average of the sales figures for several past years. For instance, if it is assumed that there will be the same percentage sales increase next year as this year, the forecaster might utilize a naive model projection such as

$$\text{next year's sales} = \text{this year's sales} \times \frac{\text{this year's sales}}{\text{last year's sales}}$$

This year's sales are inevitably related to last year's. Similarly, next year's sales are related to this year's and to those of all preceding years. Projecting present sales levels is a simple and inexpensive forecasting method and may be appropriate for companies in more or less stable or "mature" industries—it is rare in such industries for a company's sales to vary more than 15 percent plus or minus from the preceding year.

Time-series analysis. Not greatly different in principle from the simple projection of past sales is time-series analysis, a statistical procedure for studying historical sales data. This procedure involves isolating and measuring four chief types of sales variations: long-term trends, cyclical changes, seasonal variations, and irregular fluctuations. Then a mathematical model describing the past behavior of the series is selected, assumed values for each type of sales variation are inserted, and the sales forecast is "cranked out."[2]

For most companies, time-series analysis finds practical application mainly in making long-range forecasts. Predictions on a year-to-year basis, such as are necessary for an operating sales forecast, generally are little more than approximations. Only where sales patterns are clearly defined and relatively stable from year to year is time-series analysis appropriately used for short-term operating sales forecasts.

One drawback of time-series analysis is that it is difficult to "call the turns." Trend and cycle analysis helps in explaining why a trend, once under way, continues, but predicting the turns often is more important. When turns for the better are called correctly, management can capitalize upon sales opportunities; when turns for the worst are called correctly, management can cut losses.

Exponential smoothing. One statistical technique for short-range sales forecasting, exponential smoothing, is a type of moving average that represents a weighted sum of all past numbers in a time series, with the heaviest weight placed on the most recent data.[3] To illustrate, consider this simple but widely used form of exponential smoothing—a weighted average of this year's sales is combined with the forecast of this year's sales to arrive at the forecast for next year's sales. The forecasting equation, in other words, is

$$\text{next year's sales} = a\,(\text{this year's sales}) + (1 - a)(\text{this year's forecast})$$

The a in the equation is called the "smoothing constant" and is set between 0.0 and 1.0. If, for example, actual sales for this year came to 320 units of product, the sales forecast for this year was 350 units, and the smoothing constant was 0.3, the forecast for next year's sales is

$$(0.30)(320) + (0.7)(350) = 341 \text{ units of products}$$

Determining the value of a is the main problem. If the series of sales data

[2]For a good discussion of this technique, see R. B. Miller and D. W Wichern, *Intermediate Business Statistics* (New York: Holt, Rinehart and Winston, 1977).

[3]P. E. Green and D. S. Tull, *Research for Marketing Decisions*, 4th ed. (Englewood Cliffs, N.J.: Prentice-Hall, 1978), pp. 508–10.

changes slowly, a should be small to retain the effect of earlier observations. If the series changes rapidly, a should be large so that the forecasts respond to these changes. In practice, a is estimated by trying several values and making retrospective tests of the associated forecast error. The a value leading to the smallest forecast error is then chosen for future smoothing.[4]

Evaluation of past sales projection methods. The key limitation of all past sales projection methods lies in the assumption that past sales history is the sole factor influencing future sales. No allowance is made for significant changes made by the company in its marketing program or by its competitors in theirs. Nor is allowance made for sharp and rapid upswings or downturns in business activity, nor is it usual to correct for poor sales performance extending over previous periods.

The accuracy of the forecast arrived at through projecting past sales depends largely upon how close the company is to the market saturation point. If the market is nearly 100 percent saturated, some argue that it is defensible to predict sales by applying a certain percentage figure to "cumulative past sales of the product still in the hands of users" to determine annual replacement demand. However, most often the company whose product has achieved nearly 100 percent market saturation finds, since most companies of this sort market durables or semidurables, that its prospective customers can postpone or accelerate their purchases to a considerable degree.

Past sales projection methods are most appropriately used for obtaining "check" forecasts against which forecasts secured through other means are compared. Most companies make some use of past sales projections in their sales forecasting procedures. The availability of numerous computer programs for time-series analysis and exponential smoothing has accelerated this practice.

Survey of Customers' Buying Plans

What more sensible way to forecast than to ask customers about their future buying plans? Industrial marketers use this approach more than consumer-goods marketers, because it is easiest to use where the potential market consists of small numbers of customers and prospects, substantial sales are made to individual accounts, the manufacturer sells direct to users, and customers are concentrated in a few geographical areas (all more typical of industrial than consumer marketing). In such instances, it is relatively inexpensive to survey a sample of customers and prospects to obtain their estimated requirements for the product, and to project the results to obtain a sales forecast. Survey results, however, need tempering by management's specialized knowledge and by contemplated changes in marketing programs. Few companies base forecasts exclusively on a survey of customers' buying plans. The main reason lies in the inher-

[4]Ibid., pp. 509–10.

ent assumptions that customers know what they are going to do and that buyers' plans, once made, will not change.

Even though the survey of customers' buying plans is generally an unsophisticated forecasting method, it can be rather sophisticated—that is, if it is a true survey (in the marketing research sense) and if the selection of respondents is by probability sampling. However, since it gathers opinions rather than measures actions, substantial nonsampling error is present. Respondents do not always have well-formulated buying plans, and, even if they do, they are not always willing to relate them. In practice, most companies using this approach appear to pay little attention to the composition of the sample and devote minimum effort to measuring sampling and nonsampling errors.

Regression Analysis

Regression analysis is a statistical process and, as used in sales forecasting, determines and measures the association between company sales and other variables. It involves fitting an equation to explain sales fluctuations in terms of related and presumably causal variables, substituting for these variables values considered likely during the period to be forecasted, and solving for sales. In other words, there are three major steps in forecasting sales through regression analysis:

1. Identify variables causally related to company sales.
2. Determine or estimate the values of these variables related to sales.
3. Derive the sales forecast from these estimates.

Computers make it easy to use regression analysis for sales forecasting. One tire manufacturer, for instance, used simple regression analysis to determine the association between economic variables and its own sales. This company discovered that a positive correlation existed between gross national product and its own sales, but the correlation coefficient was too low to use in forecasting company sales. The same was true of personal disposable income and retail sales; their correlation coefficients with company sales were too low to use in forecasting company sales. The tire manufacturer measured the relationship between its own dollar sales and unit sales of automobiles and found a much higher degree of correlation (see Figure 3.2). The dots on this scatter diagram cluster closely around the straight line that is the result of the mathematical computation between the two series of data. If the correlation had been perfect, all the dots would have fallen on the line.

Where sales are influenced by two or more independent variables acting together, multiple regression analysis techniques are applied. To illustrate, consider this situation. An appliance manufacturer is considering adding an automatic dishwasher to its line and decides to develop a forecasting equation for industry sales of dishwashers. From published sources, such as the *Statistical Abstract of the United States*, data are collected on manufacturers' sales of dishwash-

FIGURE 3.2 Relation Between Company Sales of Tires and U.S. Automobile Sales

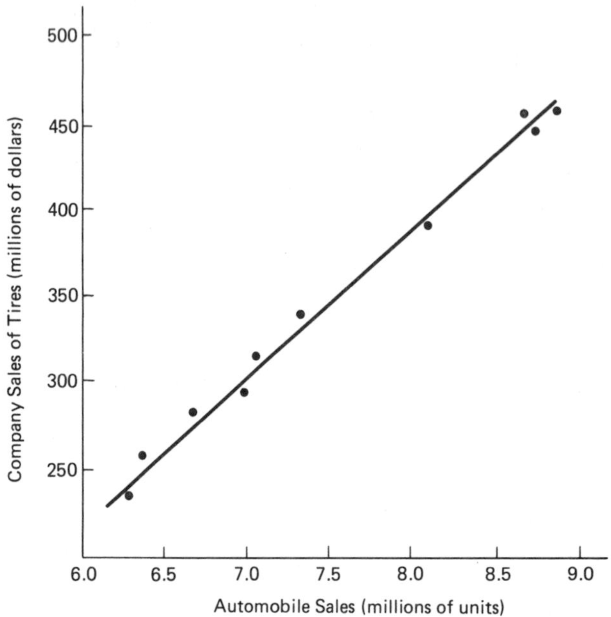

ers for a period of twenty years (the dependent variable). Also collected are data on four possible independent variables:

1. The Consumer Price Index for durables
2. Disposable personal income deflated by the Consumer Price Index
3. The change in the total number of households
4. New nonfarm housing starts

Then, the analysts use stepwise multiple linear regression to estimate the relationship among the variables. Figure 3.3 shows the computer printout used in developing the forecasting equation. Here is a step-by-step explanation of the program output:

Step 1. Means and standard deviation for all variables:
X(1) is Consumer Price Index for durables (CPI).
X(2) is disposable personal income deflated by the Consumer Price Index (DPI/CPI).
X(3) is the change in the total number of households (DNH).
X(4) is new nonfarm housing starts (NFHS).
X(5) is sales (the dependent variable).

Step 2. Simple pairwise correlation coefficients (note that sales volume is highly correlated with DPI/CPI and CPI).

FIGURE 3.3 Computer Printout Used in Developing an Equation for Forecasting Industry Sales of Automatic Dishwashers

```
                MULTIPLE REGRESSION ANALYSIS FOR: GRIMES
                PROJECT TITLE: SALES F(CPI, DPI/CPI, DNH, NFHS)
                                    Mean          Standard Deviation
Step 1     X(1)                 103.0000                6.5012
           X(2)                 373.2286               89.4190
           X(3)                   1.0299                0.3833
           X(4)                1428.8571              188.1014
           X(5)                 938.9524              739.3600
Step 2     CORRELATION COEFFICIENTS
           r(1,2)    0.836915
           r(1,3)    0.415448
           r(1,4)    0.486596
           r(1,5)    0.897006
           r(2,3)    0.443997
           r(2,4)    0.229535
           r(2,5)    0.980989
           r(3,4)    0.240009
           r(3,5)    0.469477
           r(4,5)    0.316022
Step 3.1   THE STANDARD ERROR OF Y WILL NOW BE 739.35996
                                Coefficient    Standard Error of Coefficient
           b(0)                 938.95238
              Coefficient of Determination is 0.00000
Step 3.2   THE VARIABLE X(2) IS NOW BEING ENTERED INTO THE MODEL
           WITH AN F = 485.51400
           THE STANDARD ERROR OF Y WILL NOW BE 147.20898
                                Coefficient    Standard Error of Coefficient
           b(2)                   8.11130              0.36812
           b(0)               -2088.41491
              Coefficient of Determination is 0.96234
Step 3.3   THE VARIABLE X(1) IS NOW BEING ENTERED INTO THE MODEL
           WITH AN F = 18.88398
           THE STANDARD ERROR OF Y WILL NOW BE 105.65553
                                Coefficient    Standard Error of Coefficient
           b(1)                  28.85239              6.63949
           b(2)                   6.35570              0.48272
           b(3)               -4404.97376
              Coefficient of Determination is 0.98162
Step 3.4   THE VARIABLE X(3) IS NOW BEING ENTERED INTO THE MODEL
           WITH AN F = 0.62558
           THE STANDARD ERROR OF Y WILL NOW BE 106.77186
                                Coefficient    Standard Error of Coefficient
           b(1)                  28.37586              6.73664
           b(2)                   6.27963              0.49721
           b(3)                  55.19663             69.78644
           b(0)               -4354.34552
              Coefficient of Determination is 0.98227
Step 3.5   THE VARIABLE X(4) IS NOW BEING ENTERED INTO THE MODEL
           WITH AN F = 0.25544
           THE STANDARD ERROR OF Y WILL NOW BE 109.18975
                                Coefficient    Standard Error of Coefficient
           b(1)                  26.09639              8.23421
           b(2)                   6.38803              0.55185
           b(3)                  50.42226             71.98926
           b(4)                   0.08159              0.16143
           b(0)               -4301.67933
              Coefficient of Determination is 0.98255
```

Step 3. Program enters independent variables in order of highest explained variation of the dependent variable:

3.1 Program states distribution of dependent variable (sales) before the first independent variable is added.

3.2 Variable X(2): DPI/CPI enters the model first. The standard error of Y is reduced to 147.209. The coefficient of determination is 0.96234; that is, X(2) explains approximately 96 percent of the variation in Y.

3.3 Variable X(1): CPI enters the model next. (This means that X(1) explains the greatest portion of the variation in Y left over after the entry of X(2) in the model.) The standard error of Y is now reduced to 105.65553. The coefficient of multiple determination is increased to 0.98162.

3.4 After the addition of variables X(2) and X(1), less than 2 percent of the variation in Y is left to be explained.

3.5 The results of the additions of X(3) DNH and of X(4) NFHS indicate that these variables are not statistically significant; this is shown by the low F values as well as by the t values:

$$t = \frac{\text{coefficient}}{\text{standard error of coefficient}}$$

Therefore, the effect of adding these two variables to the model is not to reduce the standard error of Y but, in fact, in this case it is increased slightly.

These results indicate, then, that

$$\text{manufacturers' sales of dishwashers (in thousands)} = -4{,}404.97 + (28.85 \times \text{CPI}) + (6.36 \times \text{DPI/CPI})$$

So if the manufacturer has estimates for the coming year that CPI will be 125 and DPI/CPI 550, its forecast of industry sales of dishwashers (in thousands) is

$$\begin{aligned} \text{sales} &= -4.404.97 + (28.85)(125) + (6.36)(550) \\ &= 2{,}699.28 \text{ (or approximately 2,700,000 dishwashers)} \end{aligned}$$

Evaluation of regression analysis for sales forecasting. If high coefficients of correlation exist between company sales and independent variables, the forecasting problem is simplified, especially if the variables "lead" company sales. The probable course of sales may then be charted, and the forecaster can concentrate on factors that might cause deviations. But it is necessary to examine other circumstances that might upset past relationships. A forecast made through regression analysis assumes that past relations will continue. A "lead-lag" association in which deviations regularly occur in related independent variable(s) prior to a change in company sales is a near-ideal situation, but it rarely holds except over short periods. Lead-lag relationships are common, but associations between the lead variables and sales in which the intervening time intervals remain stable are uncommon. Periods not only contract or expand erratically; they vary greatly during different phases of the business cycle.

If close associations exist between company sales and a reliable barometer, estimates are improved by experts' predictions of probable changes in the barometer. However, one danger in using regression analysis is that forecasters may put too much faith in the statistical output. They may abandon independent appraisals of future events because of a statistically developed forecast. It is wrong to place blind faith in any forecasting method. It is wise to check results with those of other forecasts.

Econometric Model Building and Simulation

Econometric model building and simulation is attractive as a sales forecasting method for companies marketing durable goods. This approach uses an equation or system of equations to represent a set of relationships among sales and different demand-determining independent variables. Then, by "plugging in" values (or estimates) for each independent variable (that is, by "simulating" the total situation), sales are forecast. An econometric model (unlike a regression model) is based upon an *underlying theory* about relationships among a set of variables, and parameters are estimated by statistical analysis of past data. An econometric sales forecasting model is an abstraction of a real-world situation, expressed in equation form and used to predict sales. For example, the sales equation for a durable good can be written

$$S = R + N$$

where

S = total sales
R = replacement demand (purchases made to replace product units going out of use, as measured by the scrappage of old units)
N = new-owner demand (purchases made not to replace existing product units, but to add to the total stock of the product in users' possession)

Total sales of a durable good, in other words, consist of purchases made to replace units that have been scrapped and purchases by new owners. Thus, a family that has a five-year-old machine trades it in to a dealer as part payment for a new machine and becomes part of the replacement demand (although only effectively so when the five-year-old machine, perhaps passing through several families' hands in the process, finally comes to be owned by a family that goes ahead and consigns its even-older machine to the scrap heap).

Replacement demand is measured by the scrappage of old units of products, that is, by the percentage of the total stock of the product in users' hands that is taken out of service through consignment to the trash pile, by sale to a junk dealer, or merely by being stowed away and never used again. Replacement demand in any one year does not include demand originating from the family that had a five-year-old machine that it traded to a dealer for a new machine, with the dealer reselling the old machine to another family who buys it second-hand. Only when a particular machine goes completely out of service is it regarded as scrapped, and, at that time (through a chain of purchases and trade-ins), some family becomes a part of replacement demand. Econometricians estimate replacement demand by using life expectancy of survival tables, which are similar to the life (or mortality) tables used by life insurance actuaries. An example is shown in Figure 3.4.

If some durable good has a maximum service life of eleven years and 10,000 units of the good enter service in some year, the table indicates that five years later, 8,621 will probably still be in service, and ten years later, 54. For this batch of 10,000 product units, scrappage is 1,035 in the fifth year (that is, 1,379 − 344, the difference between the accumulated total scrappage at the close of the fifth and fourth years, respectively). In the fifth year, then, 1,035 replacement sales trace back to the batch of 10,000 product units that entered service five years before.

New-owner demand is the net addition to users' stocks of the product that occurs during a given period. For instance, if 2,000,000 units of some appliance were in service at the start of a period and 2,500,000 at the end, new-owner demand was 500,000 during the period. Forecasting the number of sales to new owners involves treating the stock of the product in the hands of users as a "population" exhibiting "birth" and "death" characteristics, that is, thinking of it as being analogous to a human population.

Constructing this sort of econometric model requires going through three

FIGURE 3.4 Durable-Goods Survival Coefficients (Maximum Service Life: 11 Years; Average Service Life: 6.5 years)

Year	Survival/Coefficient
1	1.0000
2	0.9995
3	0.9946
4	0.9656
5	0.8621
6	0.6406
7	0.3594
8	0.1379
9	0.0344
10	0.0054
11	0.0000

steps. First, study independent variables affecting each demand category (replacement and new owner) and choose for correlation analysis those that bear some logical relationship to sales (the dependent variable). Second, detect that combination of independent variables that correlates best with sales. Third, choose a suitable mathematical expression to show the quantitative relationships among the independent variable[5] and sales, the dependent variables. This expression becomes the econometric model.

The procedure for building econometric models is simple, but finished models can take on formidable appearances. Consider, for example, this econometric model for forecasting sales of washing machines.[6]

$$S_{tc} = Y_t - y_t + Y_t \left\{ H_t \left[(0.03 - 0.0157) \left(\frac{(I_t + 3C_t)/P_t}{10^{0.01818t - 33.1143}} \right) \right] - 0.0000283 Y_t \right\}$$

where

S_{tc} = calculated value for forecasted sales of washing machines during some time period

Y_t = level of consumers' stock of washing machines in any period (as of January 1)

y_t = level of consumers' stock that would occur in the following period (as of January 1) if no washing machines were sold and scrappage rates remained the same

H_t = number of wired (i.e., electrified) dwelling units, in millions

I_t = disposable personal income

C_t = net credit extended (excluding credit extended for automobiles)

P_t = price index for house furnishings

$10^{0.01818t - 33.1143}$ = trend of real purchasing power over time

$I_t + 3C_t/P_t$ = real purchasing power

Thus, new-owner demand in this model is represented by $Y_t - y_t$, determined by applying appropriate survival coefficients to previous years' sales of washing machines and estimating consumers' total stocks of washing machines in each year. Replacement demand is represented by the other *symbols* in the equation and takes into account the number of wired dwelling units (washing machines are not sold to people who live in homes with no electricity), real purchasing power (disposable personal income plus credit availability divided by a price

[5]M. H. Spencer and T. Mattheis, "Forecasting Sales of Consumers' Durable Goods," *California Management Review*, 4, no. 3 (Spring 1962), p. 79.

[6]Ibid., p. 98.

index), and real purchasing power adjusted for the historical trend. Regression analysis was used to derive the numerical values in this model.

Econometric model building seems a nearly ideal way to forecast sales. Not only does it consider the interaction of independent variables that bear logical and measurable relationships to sales, it uses regression analysis techniques to quantify these relationships. Econometric models, however, are best used to forecast industry sales, not the sales of individual companies. This is because the independent variables affecting an individual company's sales are more numerous and more difficult to measure than are those determining the sales of an entire industry. Many companies use an econometric model to forecast industry sales, and then apply an estimate of the company's share-of-the-market percentage to the industry forecast to arrive at a first approximation for the company's forecasted sales.

CONVERTING INDUSTRY FORECAST TO COMPANY SALES FORECAST

Many companies forecast both their own sales and sales of the industry. Of those using multimethod forecasting procedures, nearly all—at one or more stages—provide for the making of an industry sales forecast. In fact, of the six sales forecasting methods discussed in this chapter, only in two—the poll of sales force opinion and unsophisticated forms of projecting past sales—is it normal to skip the industry sales forecast and forecast company sales directly. The general practice is to forecast industry sales early in the procedure and from it derive a company sales forecast for use as a check against forecasts arrived at through other methods.

Deriving a company sales forecast from an industry sales forecast requires an appraisal of company strengths and weaknesses (as well as marketing programs) against those of competitors. The result is an estimate of expected market share that (when applied to the industry sales forecast) results in a forecast of company sales. The poll of sales force opinion method leaves this appraisal up to the sales personnel—they focus on estimating how much the company can sell, not on how much the industry can sell. Unsophisticated forms of the past sales projection method implicitly assume that no changes will occur in the company's strengths and weaknesses nor in its marketing programs vis-à-vis those of its competitors. In the other four forecasting methods considered in this chapter, management makes this appraisal when it determines the company's probable market share percentage. Moreover, although some companies check such appraisals with sales personnel, in most the main appraisal of competitive position is made by executives better informed on the overall sales outlook than any salesperson can be.

Forecasting a company's market share varies in complexity from one industry to another. In the steel industry, the number of competitors is small and market share is stable, so determining a given company's market share is a simple task—a matter of projecting past trends and adjusting for anticipated changes in the company's relative strengths and weaknesses. But in the women's clothing industry, the number of competitors is large and market shares fluctuate widely, so determination of market share is difficult. The ability to evaluate a clothing style's salability is a key element in forecasting, and this requires both thorough knowledge of market trends and keen judgment. Most companies operate in industries that lie somewhere between these two extremes, with market shares neither as stable as in steel nor as volatile as in women's apparel. Forecasters in most companies need information on competitors' plans to launch new and improved products, advertising and selling plans, pricing strategies, and so on. When forecasters evaluate this information in relation to their own company's proposed marketing and selling plans, they are in a position to exercise informed judgment in predicting the company's probable market share. If, for example, a forecaster knows that a major competitor plans a substantial price cut on a product that many buyers buy mainly on the basis of price, it will be necessary to lower the estimate of the company's market share unless management is willing to match the price cut. Forecasting a company's market share is a matter both of examining past trends and of appraising impending changes in competitive relationships.

DERIVATION OF A SALES VOLUME OBJECTIVE

A sales volume objective for the coming operating period is the hoped-for outcome of a company's short-range sales forecasting procedure. A sales forecast (1) contains an estimate of sales tied to a proposed marketing plan or program and (2) assumes a particular set of economic and other forces outside the unit for which the forecast is made. The sales forecast estimate does not necessarily become the company's sales volume objective, but it provides an orientation point for management's thinking. Further adjustments in the sales forecast estimate are necessary whenever management decides to alter its marketing plan or program or changes occur in competitor's marketing strategies.

The sales volume objective should be consistent with management's profit aspirations and the company's marketing capabilities. It must be attainable at costs low enough to permit the company to reach its net profit objective, and the company's marketing forces (that is, its sales force, the advertising program, the dealer organization, and so on) must be capable of reaching the objective set. All three items—the sales volume objective, management's profit objective, and the company's marketing capabilities—are interrelated. Using the sales estimate in the sales forecast as a point of departure, management juggles these three items until it satisfies itself that the relationship between them is the best obtainable. Only then does the sales forecast result in the setting of a sales volume objective. At that time, the chief sales executive accepts responsibility for making the forecast "come true." Sales policies and selling strategies, formulated by the chief sales executive and his or her subordinates, must be put into effect in the grand effort to reach the sales volume, profit, and other objectives.

EVALUATION OF FORECASTS

Before submitting forecasts to higher management, sales executives evaluate them carefully, regardless of the extent of their personal involvement in the preparation. Every forecast contains elements of uncertainty. All are based on assumptions. So a first step in evaluating a sales forecast is to examine the assumptions (including any hidden ones) on which it is based. Sales executives should view each assumption critically and note particularly any that seem unwarranted, testing each by asking: If this assumption were removed, or changed, what would be the effect on the forecast? They should evaluate the forecasting methods objectively, asking such questions as: Are there any variations here from what past experience would seem to indicate? Has sufficient account been taken of trends in the competitive situation and of changes in competitor's marketing and selling strategies? Has account been taken of any new competitive products that might affect the industry's and company sales? Have inventory movements at all distribution levels (including those at wholesale and retail levels) been considered?

Sales executives should evaluate the accuracy and economic value of the forecast as the forecast period advances. Forecasts should be checked against actual results, differences explained, and indicated adjustments made for the remainder of the period. When the period's sales results are all recorded, all variations should be explained and stored for future use in improving forecasting accuracy.

CONCLUSION

Considerable planning and analysis precedes the setting of the company's sales-volume objective, that is, the dollar or unit sales volume that management seeks to obtain during a particular future period. Determining the market potential—the maximum possible sales opportunities present in a market and open to all industry members—requires identification of the market and determination of buying reasons. Sales potentials, representing the maximum possible sales opportunities present in given markets and open to a particular company, are derived from market potentials after analyses of past market share relationships and through making adjustments for recent or anticipated changes in company and competitors' marketing and selling programs. Estimates of sales potentials, however, differ from estimates contained in sales forecasts. An estimate for sales potential indicates how much a company could sell *if* it had all the necessary resources and desired to use them for this purpose, whereas a sales forecast estimate indicates how much a company with a given amount of resources can sell if it implements a particular marketing program.

The basic purpose of an operating sales forecast is to predict how much a company can sell during a specified future period under a given marketing plan. There are many different methods of sales forecasting, and we have considered six methods here. Most methods look forward and backward, each has merits and limitations, and all call for judgment on someone's part. The guiding rule is to select methods that stand the best chance of achieving the desired degree of accuracy at the most reasonable costs in terms of time and money. Converting an industry sales forecast into a company sales forecast requires assessment of company strengths and weaknesses vis-à-vis those of competitors and quantitative estimates of market shares.

The sales forecast estimate does not automatically become the company's sales volume objective. Adjustments are made for changes in marketing plans or in competition. The sales volume objective must be attainable at costs low enough to permit reaching the net profit objective, and it must be in line with the company's marketing capabilities.

4 Sales-Related Marketing Policies

Sales-related marketing policies impact upon the functions and operation of the sales department. These marketing policies delineate the guidelines within which the effort to reach personal-selling objectives is made. There are three major types: (1) product policies (what to sell), (2) distribution policies (to whom to sell), and (3) pricing policies.

Sales executives' roles in determining sales-related marketing policies vary from company to company. At one extreme, the sales executive's role is not to determine, but to administer, policies laid down by higher management. At the other extreme, the sales executive bears sole responsibility for determining sales-related marketing policies—subject, of course, to top management's approval. The most usual role is for the sales executive to participate as a member of an executive group charged with responsibility for determining all marketing policies.

Sales-related marketing policies directly influence the jobs of sales executives. These policies provide direction as sales executives plan how the company will reach personal-selling objectives, as they organize the sales effort, as they manage the sales force, and as they control the sales effort. Clearly, these policies constitute the company-imposed marketing framework within which sales executives and the departments they lead must operate.

PRODUCT POLICIES—WHAT TO SELL

The products a company sells determine its basic nature. As its organizers visualize opportunities to make and/or market certain products, the company comes into existence. As it grows, management makes key decisions on products—whether to drop old ones, whether to add new ones, whether to expand the product line or add new lines—and on product design and product quality as well as on product-related matters such as guarantees and service.

Relation to Product Objectives

Product policies serve as guides for making product decisions. They derive from product objectives. If a product objective, for example, states that "this company desires to make and market products requiring only a minimum of service after their purchase by consumers," then product policies spell out how this objective is to be attained. Or, if a product objective states that "this company desires to make and market only products superior to those of competitors in ways of great importance to users," then product policies define the nature of superiority from the standpoint of product users. Often product policies take the form of a series of short definitions or of questions arranged as a checklist.

Product Line Policy

Policies on the width of a product line are classified as either short line or full line. The company following a short-line policy handles only part of a line, while the company with a full-line policy handles all or most of the items making up a line. For example, a manufacturer concentrating exclusively on a cornflakes product has a short-line policy, whereas a company offering a complete, or almost complete, line of breakfast cereals has a full-line policy. Companies use short-line policies for some product groupings and full-line policies for others. Management decides for each product grouping whether the basis of competition should be specialization (short line) or wide selection (full line).

The extent to which a short-line policy should be pursued is governed by the amount of risk that management is willing to assume—the narrower the line, the greater the risk. If a firm concentrates on a single product, the rewards can be great. Product specialization enables the manufacturing division to achieve low unit costs. In turn, this may make the company almost invulnerable to price competition, even though the product is of the highest quality. But the penalty for failure is also great. If the product is displaced by substitutes introduced by competitors, the company finds itself "locked out" of the market.

The extent to which a full-line policy should be followed is determined by such factors as the number of items the sales force can sell effectively, the need for after-sale service, the desires of middlemen and product users, the expenses of promotion, and the effect on production costs. The wider the product line, the more the risk is spread. Thus, in sharp contrast to the short-line policy, risk is diversified over many products. But, while there is less penalty attached to failure of any one item, there also is less reward for the success of any item.

Changes in product offerings. All items in a product line should be reappraised at regular intervals. Reappraisals serve two purposes: (1) to determine whether individual items are still in tune with market demand and (2) to identify those that should be dropped from, or added to, the line. Unless the product line is reappraised regularly, market demand may shift, and more alert competitors may capture larger market shares.

Regardless of which executive or group formulates product policies, sales executives should participate in product line appraisals. Compared with other executives, they have the most intimate contact with markets. They should see that effective procedures are in place for receiving communications on product acceptance from the sales force, and should make this information available to those participating in product line reappraisals.

Reappraising the product line and line simplification. Each item in the line is compared with similar and competing items in other manufacturers' lines. The focus is upon identifying strengths and weaknesses, especially as to which features of each item consumers consider desirable or undesirable. Special attention is paid to significant trends in usage: How much is used? What is it used for? When is it used? Where is it used? The answers also have supplemental benefits; they provide insights useful in constructing sales presentations and in motivating the sales force and dealer organization.

The most critical factor in reappraising is profitability. Generally, an item in the line should not be retained unless it meets standards for profitability or shows promise of meeting them. Nevertheless, before an item is dropped because of inadequate profitability, other factors need to be considered. Will modifications in price policy or promotion cause the item to improve in profitability?

Even if the item would continue with a poor profit showing regardless of changes in price or promotion, do other factors indicate its retention? Some companies cater to customers and dealers who, logically or not, expect a full-line offering. If distribution is through exclusive agencies, for instance, dealers insist on a complete line. Repair and replacement parts are unprofitable for many manufacturers, but, because of needed service on major products, most manufacturers must retain them. Since markets are made up of segments with unique tastes and preferences, many companies find that some unprofitable products must be retained to help sell profitable products. This happens, for instance, when customers combine individual products into "product systems," as in the case of sprayer fixtures used with insecticides. Subject to exceptions such as these, unprofitable products should be eliminated from the line.

Under certain conditions, it is appropriate to drop a profitable product. This should happen if the resources required for marketing it could be used to better advantage on behalf of a product with a brighter future or in which the company has a greater investment. An item should be dropped if it causes sales personnel to divert their efforts from more profitable items. Products with slow turnover rates should be discontinued if dealers place more emphasis on the better selling products in the line. Finally, any item not fitting logically into the line is a candidate for elimination.

Reappraising the product line and line diversification. Management makes reappraisals of the line relative to growth objectives. These objectives are restricted as an established product line approaches market saturation. They are restricted, too, when the industry is dying, or when competitors succeed in making permanent inroads in a company's "natural" market. If action is long delayed in these situations, the survival of the firm itself is at stake. Often the indicated action is to add new products or even entirely new product lines.

Some firms diversify to survive, but most diversify to expand sales or to reduce costs. For example, a decision to shorten marketing channels causes parallel consideration on widening the line. If sales personnel are to write orders large enough to justify the higher costs of direct selling, new products are required. On occasion, too, top management assigns the sales organization a substantially larger task than previously. When sales volume must be expanded greatly, one solution is to add new products. Sometimes, also, new products are added to stimulate the sales force or dealer organization. An addition to the line not only has news value, it may help salespeople to earn larger commissions and assist dealers in increasing sales and profits.

The sales department is the division that pushes hardest for line diversification. Its intimate contact with the market enables it to keep close watch on the market acceptance of new products of other manufacturers. With the objective of holding or improving market share, sales executives press for new products. Consequently, any shift in customers' buying patterns may signal the need for line diversification.

Circumstances elsewhere in the company can result in new products. The production department initiates the search for new products if there are unused plant facilities or if seasonal sales fluctuations cause manufacturing irregularities. The treasurer advocates diversification if idle funds cause financial criticism or if there is an opportunity for profitable acquisition of a firm with related products. The purchasing department suggests new products, particularly when difficulty is experienced in procuring materials for the fabrication of existing products. Pressure for line diversification originates in the scientific research division, when it discovers or perfects a new product, and in the marketing research department, when it uncovers natural additions as the result of other studies. Occasionally, too, either through research or by chance, uses for industrial waste materials result in additions to the line.

Ideas for new products. Companies tap both internal and external sources of new-product ideas. Product ideas coming from within the company generally are related to regular operations. The sales department identifies unsatisfied needs in its day-to-day contacts with customers and prospects. The production department develops improvements in existing products. The research and development department turns up ideas for new products as a routine part of its activities.

Because they represent thinking undulled by close association with the established product line, ideas from outside the company are often unique. Here are a few examples:

A pottery company got its idea for a new display case from a museum exhibit. One plastics manufacturer secured an idea for a film-viewing device from an unsolicited outside suggestion; another plastics manufacturer got an idea for a similar device from a list of needed inventions published by a bank. A chemical company picked up an idea for an insecticide from a list of government-owned patents available for licensing.

Appraisal of proposed new products. What criteria should be used for appraising candidates for addition? As in the reappraisal of established offerings, the key question is: Will this item (line) add to profitability? Other factors include the nature and size of likely markets, competition, price policy, sales programs, and legal implications.

The marketing and production characteristics of a proposed product should be compared with those of the existing line. Ideally, an addition should be in alignment on both the marketing and production sides.

These natural additions round out the line and make marketing and production efforts more efficient and more profitable. The same sales force can sell the product and reap the benefits of goodwill built up for other items in the line; the new product's seasonal sales dovetail with present sales patterns; and the product broadens the market base (diversifies the company's business by adding new classes of customers).

Product Design Policy

The two main policy decisions on product design are (1) the frequency of design change and (2) the extent to which designs should be protected from copying.

Frequent introduction and promotion of design changes and improvements is an important marketing factor in many industries, as in clothing, automobiles, home appliances, and office machines. Through design changes that make the product more attractive, users are persuaded to replace old models, which in many instances are still usable, with new models. In addition to weakening buyers' sales resistance, changes in design reduce the emphasis on price, assist in the stimulation of salespeople and dealers, and provide new inspiration for the advertising department. However, a policy of changing designs frequently is not appropriate for all companies or for all types of products, since the successful promotion of a design change (especially if it is only in the product's external appearance) requires exceptional skill in the planning and execution of promotional programs.

Policy on design protection is related to policy on frequency of design change. In certain industries, such as in women's apparel, it is impractical to protect a new design. The rapid rate of fashion change makes legal protection impractical. Success in high-fashion fields depends upon the extent to which designs are adopted by competing firms so that the style becomes fashionable. Where design changes occur less frequently, design protection is practical and desirable, as in the home appliance, furniture, and jewelry industries. Legal protection is effected through design patents granted by the United States Patent Office for terms of up to fourteen years. While they are in force, these patents protect a company against use of the design by others.

Product Quality and Service Policy

For consumer durables, and most industrial goods, product quality and service are related. High-quality products require less service and low-quality products, more service. Buyers expect product performance to vary with the quality, so manufacturers with high-quality products have liberal service policies. Often product quality is a matter of characteristics built into a product that the buyer is unable to judge until after the purchase. Technical features are apt to be deeply hidden, and a liberal service policy helps to reduce the customers' reluctance to buy. The maintenance and improvement of product quality are important matters for the sales department—if quality deteriorates, for example, the sales department bears the brunt of customer and middleman dissatisfaction.

Manufacturers' service policies take different forms. The simplest merely provides for education of the buyer in the use and care of the product. Other service policies—particularly for industrial products and such consumer lines as air-conditioning and heating equipment—provide for product installation, inspection, and repair.

When a company adopts a formal service policy, sales management should make it part of the promotional program. An appropriate service policy facilitates the making of initial sales and helps in keeping products sold, stimulating repeat sales, and building customer goodwill. There is no legitimate place for a service policy that fails to accomplish these aims.

Many manufacturers, at least for a specified period after sale of the product, do not charge for service. "Free" service may be provided either under the terms of a written guarantee of as a matter of policy. When the buyer requests service a considerable time after the purchase, most manufacturers charge for it. Firms with centralized service facilities, or operating their own service stations, generally make the charge nominal. A nominal charge pays part of the costs and eliminates many unreasonable demands.

Companies that depend upon dealers or distributors to provide service have less control over the charge. It may be nominal, with the manufacturer absorbing part and the user the remainder, or it may be larger, and borne entirely by the user. Unless the manufacturer pays some of the cost, middlemen hesitate to assume responsibility for service.

Guarantee policy. Guarantees, or warranties as they are sometimes called, serve as sales promotional devices and as guards against abuses of the service policy. If the product does not perform as represented, the guarantor may promise to replace it, to refund the purchase price or a multiple of that price, to furnish the purchaser with a competitive product at no expense, or to remedy defects free of charge or for a small fee. When a guarantee is used for promotional purposes, its terms are liberal. When used for protection, its terms are hedged with conditions and restrictions.

It is unusual for a guarantee to serve both promotional and protective purposes well. It is weakened as a tool for sales promotion because it includes clauses to protect the manufacturer, and the absence of such clauses makes it less effective as a protective device. This does not mean that a promotional guarantee should lack protective provisions, or that a protective guarantee should be useless for promotional purposes. But the guarantee must emphasize one purpose, not both.

DISTRIBUTION POLICIES—WHO TO SELL

Distribution policies are important determinants of the functions of the sales department. The choice of a particular marketing channel, or channels, sets the pattern for sales force operations, both geographically and as to the customers from whom sales personnel solicit orders. The decision on the number of outlets at each distribution level affects the size and nature of the sales organization and the scope of its activities. Related decisions concerning cooperation extended to and expected from the middlemen influence sales operations and salespersons' jobs.

Policies on Marketing Channels

One of the most basic of all marketing decisions is that on marketing channel(s). Figure 4.1 shows the principal choices available. Manufacturers selling to the consumer market have a choice of five main channels, and those selling to the industrial market have four main options. Few manufacturers use only one marketing channel; most use two or more. Firms that sell to both the consumer and industrial market are in this classification, as are the many who sell through both chain and independent outlets. Recognize, of course, that the actual situation is

FIGURE 4.1 Marketing Channels Commonly Used in Industrial and Consumer Markets

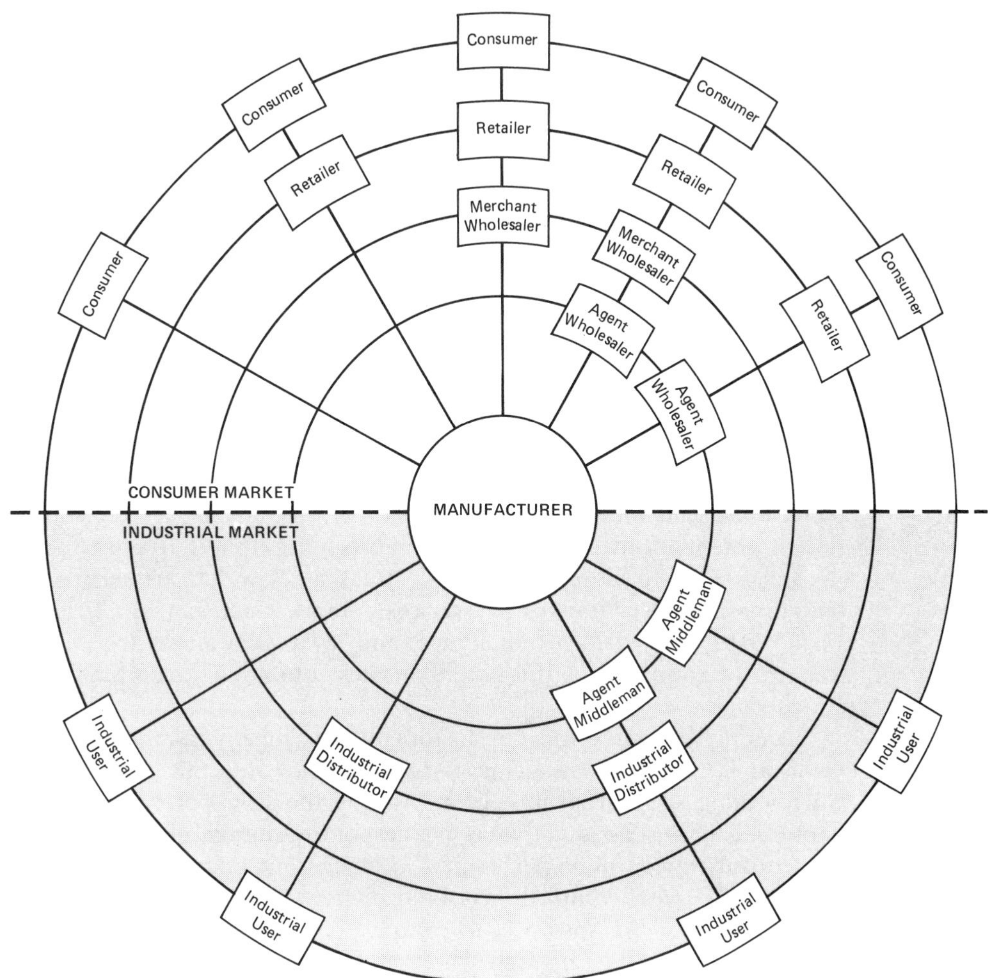

more complex than that depicted in the diagram. The toothpaste manufacturer, for instance, sells through both chain and independent outlets in the drug, grocery, variety, and department store fields.

Decisions on marketing channels are required more often than is commonly supposed. The obvious occasions are those following the initial organization of the enterprise, and when making additions to the product line. At these times, the desirability and appropriateness of different channel options are evaluated.

At other times—even though the product line is unchanged—reappraisals are advisable. Shifts occur in the nature and importance of the factors that governed the original selection. New institutions appear, marketing innovations develop, characteristics of markets change, and so on. Marketing is dynamic, and the effectiveness of different marketing channels is always changing. The sales executive keeps higher management apprised of changes in the factors affecting marketing channels (both those used and those available) and points out attention to the need for policy decisions.

The initial selection, or reevaluation, of marketing channels is a matter of determining which channel, or channels, affords the opportunity for the greatest profit. Channels, in other words, should be so chosen as to obtain the optimum combination of profit factors. This is no simple task. Neither maximum sales volume, nor minimum cost, should be considered alone; the most profitable combination of both must be sought. Furthermore, the time dimensions must be considered—management must look to the long-run effect as well as to the short-term impact upon net profits. The policymakers keep in mind all three profit factors—sales volume, costs, and resultant net profits—and they consider the effect of different channel options and combinations on each factor over both short and long periods.

Sales volume potential. For each channel option, the key question is: Can enough potential buyers be reached to absorb the desired quantity of product? The answers are found through market analysis. Raw data are secured from the company's own records, external sources of market statistics, and field investigations. When these data are analyzed, and after allowances are made for the strengths of competitors, the potential sales volume of each channel option is estimated.

Among the most important factors influencing any channel's sales potential are the ability of sales management, the excellence of its planning, and its skill in implementing sales programs. In appraising the sales potentials of alternative channels, one must assume that, regardless of the channel chosen, the sales management functions will be performed with the same degree of managerial competence. Otherwise, comparisons of alternative channels have little meaning. It makes little sense for instance, to compare a well-designed and skillfully executed plan for selling through wholesalers with a poorly designed and awkwardly executed plan for selling direct to retailers.

Comparative distribution costs. Distribution cost studies show that the costliest channels are the shortest ones. When a manufacturer decides to sell directly to the consumer, it assumes responsibility for the additional performance of marketing functions. It incurs higher costs as it steps up performance of selling, transportation, storage, financing, and risk bearing. If the manufacturer chooses to use the door-to-door direct-selling method, it faces problems on the selection, training, supervision, and general management of this class of sales personnel. If the manufacturer decides to open its own retail outlets, it has problems in selecting store locations and buildings, negotiating leases, designing store fronts, obtaining equipment, arranging store layouts, managing retail personnel, conducting retail advertising, and procuring retail-minded executives. The manufacturer using short channels has a higher gross margin to compensate for additional selling costs, but its net profits are often lower, because it may perform these functions less efficiently than the middleman. (Most middlemen carry a broader line of merchandise, and their fixed costs are spread over more products.) However, direct distribution has important nonfinancial advantages—more intimate contacts with consumers and closer control over the conditions of product sale. The manufacturer selecting direct-to-consumer selling must recognize that it will face a broad range of problems and incur additional distribution expenses. Furthermore, the shorter the channel, the more the manufacturer's selling costs tend to be fixed rather than variable in nature. This is important, especially with fluctuating sales volumes, because the break-even point is almost always higher when short marketing channels are used.

Direct sale is more common in the industrial than in the consumer field. But the costs of selling directly, even to large buyers, are still high. In the industrial market, it is common for direct-to-user sales personnel to need considerable technical education, their training is long and expensive, and necessarily their compensation is high when compared with that of less qualified persons. Nevertheless, selling directly to industrial users enables the manufacturer to provide special attention to each customer's needs. In many cases, this more than offsets the additional expenses.

Longer marketing channels result in lower selling costs for the manufacturer. When middlemen are used, they perform some functions that the manufacturer would otherwise perform. It is necessary to compensate middlemen for performing these functions. Consequently, when a manufacturer switches from short to longer channels, its own gross margins are reduced. However, there usually is a reduction in selling expense more than offsetting the loss in gross margin. Thus, the result of using indirect distribution is often higher profit per unit of product sold. In addition, the manufacturer shifts a wide range of problems to the middlemen and, in most situations, operates with a lower break-even point. The disadvantages of indirect distribution are (1) greater remoteness from final consumers and (2) less control over the conditions of product sale.

Net profit possibilities. Sales volume potentials are meaningful only when considered in relation to distribution costs. A channel with high sales potential may involve high distribution costs, causing low net profit. A second channel might not produce a worthwhile sales volume, even though it involves low distribution costs.

Those formulating policy on marketing channels must keep in mind the relationships among gross margin, expenses, and net profit. High gross margins, such as those obtained through using short channels, do not always mean higher net profits. Expenses of distribution are incurred for performing marketing activities. Choosing marketing channels is a matter of determining the extent to which the manufacturer should perform these activities and the extent to which their performance should be delegated to middlemen. The rule should be: determine which agency—the manufacturer or the middleman—can perform this particular activity most efficiently. If this rule is followed, the manufacturer's total costs of moving the product to final buyers should be lower, and its net profits should be higher.

Policies on Distribution Intensity

Choice of marketing channels is intertwined with policy on distribution intensity. At each level of distribution, decisions are made on the desired number of outlets. It is advisable to decide first upon the policy to be followed at the distribution level nearest the final buyer, because generally the same decisions must be applied at other distribution levels. Once the policy on distribution intensity is set, the sales executive's responsibility is to interpret and implement it. The sales executive, his or her subordinates, and often even the field sales personnel must decide to use or not to use particular distributive outlets.

Mass distribution. The company following a policy of mass distribution aims for maximum sales exposure by securing distribution through all those outlets from which final buyers might expect to purchase the product. This policy is used in distributing many consumer convenience items. Cigarettes, candy, and chewing gum, for instance, can be bought by consumers in food stores, drugstores, cigar stores, candy shops, variety stores, restaurants, theater and hotel lobbies; at newstands; and from vending machines. Often, the manufacturer using this policy needs not one but several marketing channels. But even though the manufacturer may maintain a sizable sales organization, its sales personnel cannot possibly sell directly to all retail outlets. Consequently, the manufacturer must determine how large each account must be before it is sold directly. In areas where retail outlets are concentrated, the manufacturer may find that it can sell directly to all accounts, large and small; in other markets, manufacturers secure distribution through wholesalers.

Selective distribution. Selective distribution means selecting only those outlets that can best serve the manufacturer's interests. Criteria are set up to provide guidance in the selection of accounts. These criteria relate to sizes of orders, volume of purchases, profitability, type of operation, and geographical location. In practice, selective distribution represents, directly or indirectly, an attempt to make every account a contributor to net profit.

The basic procedure is to set up criteria for the selection of accounts. An account analysis helps to identify the characteristics that differentiate profitable from unprofitable accounts. It may reveal that a small percentage of the customers contributes a large proportion of the total net sales and profits. It is not unusual for 20 percent of the accounts to produce 80 percent of the net sales, and even more of the net profits.

But there are exceptions to the general rule that only profitable accounts should be retained or solicited. Some losing accounts may be retained because of long-standing relationships, others because of their future promise. Furthermore, unprofitable accounts, if they contribute to the payment of overhead expenses, may add enough to sales volume to enable the firm to realize certain economies in manufacturing.

Usually, however, savings result from the elimination of unprofitable accounts. One manufacturer of industrial tools, for example, found that it was losing money on one-third of its dealers. By discontinuing sales to these dealers, it cut the number of salespeople by half. Through more effective use of the remaining sales staff and the surviving dealers, this manufacturer cut selling costs from 32 percent of sales to 18 percent.

Exclusive agency distribution. Exclusive agency distribution is an extreme form of selective distribution. The manufacturer makes an agreement, either written or oral, with a middleman in each market area stipulating that the distribution of the manufacturer's product or products within that area is to be confined solely to that middleman. Exclusive agencies are common in marketing automobiles, musical instruments, household appliances, machine tools, high-quality men's and women's shoes, and branded men's clothing and furnishings. In return, the middleman is expected to provide more aggressive selling (and sometimes product service, as in the case of appliances) than under milder forms of selective distribution or under mass distribution.

For many years, most such agreements were mutually exclusive; that is, they required the exclusive dealer to refrain from selling competitive lines. Section 3 of the Clayton Antitrust Act prohibits exclusive dealing when the effect is "to substantially lessen competition or tend to create a monopoly in any line of commerce."[1] For many years, court interpretation was that exclusive dealing was not illegal unless the actual or probable monopolistic consequences of the agreements could be shown in court. However, in the *Standard Oil Company of California* case, the court made it clear that the exclusive dealing contracts employed by the larger firms in an industry could result in a "substantial lessening of competition" and would likely constitute a violation of the antitrust laws.[2] This weakened the power of exclusive distribution, particularly of mutually exclusive contracts.

Implementing a policy of exclusive agency distribution presents a number of problems. In some markets, the most desirable dealers may be under agreement with another supplier, and the company may have to select a second- or third-rate dealer or open up its own outlet. Some middlemen want no part of an exclusive agency contract, perhaps because of the history of exclusive agencies in the food field.[3] If exclusive distribution is used at the wholesale level, the whole-

[1]38 Stat. 731, 15 U.S.C., Sec. 14.

[2]*Standard Oil Company of California and Standard Stations, Inc.* v. *United States*, U.S. 793, 69 S. Ct. 1051 (1949), p. 1062.

[3]It was formerly the practice of most manufacturers in the food field to grant exclusive agencies to grocery wholesalers. With the rise of corporate chains, most of the agreements were revoked, and manufacturers either opened their own sales branches or made their lines available to all wholesalers in each market area.

saler may not reach certain desirable outlets on the dealer level. It is sometimes difficult to sever relations with a middleman whose performance is unsatisfactory, and some middlemen accept an exclusive agency merely to deprive a competitor of it.

Using exclusive agency distributors does, however, have a number of attractive features. It is easy to develop distributor enthusiasm for the product and stimulate the distributor to sell it aggressively. The manufacturer should be able to persuade exclusive outlets to stock a complete line and to service the product or handle repair and replacement parts. Relations between sales personnel and the middlemen are likely to be of long duration, and, after the agreements have been reached, salespeople can focus more on "servicing" and less on "selling." The sales force should, therefore, be able to spend more time assisting dealers in planning local promotions of the product. Not to be overlooked either is the fact that the sales force can be smaller and subject to more effective supervision and control.

PRICING POLICIES

The sales executive's role in formulating pricing policies is advisory, but all sales executives are responsible for implementing pricing policies. Field sales personnel are the company employees whose jobs consist most directly of persuading buyers to accept the products at the prices asked. Field sales personnel do the actual implementing of pricing policies, but responsibility for implementation is the sales executive's alone. Because of their impacts upon the ease of making sales, then, pricing policies are of direct interest to sales executives and sales personnel.

Policy on Pricing Relative to the Competition

Every company has a policy regarding the level at which its products are priced relative to the competition. If competition is price-based, a company sells its products at the same price as its competitors. If there is nonprice competition, the choice is one of three alternative policies.

Meeting the competition. Meeting the competition is the most common choice. Companies competing on a nonprice basis meet competitors' prices, hoping to minimize the use of price as a competitive weapon. A meeting-the-competition price policy does not mean meeting every competitor's prices, only the prices of important competitors—"important" in the sense that what such competitors do in their pricing may lure customers away.

Pricing above the competition. Pricing above the competition is less common but is appropriate in certain situations. Sometimes higher-than-average prices convey an impression of above-average product quality or prestige. Many buyers relate a product's quality to its price, when it is difficult to judge quality before buying. A policy of pricing above the competition needs the support of strong promotion by both the manufacturer and the middlemen.

One tactic aimed toward obtaining the promotional support of dealers is to set high list (resale) prices. These prices, the prices that the manufacturer suggests the dealers use in reselling the products, include above-average markups. Middlemen pass the higher markups on to final buyers in the form of higher prices, but increased support by the dealers of the manufacturer's product more than offsets the sales-depressing tendency of the higher prices and may even increase total unit sales. For a product to compete at a price above the competition, it must either be so differentiated that buyers believe it superior to competitors' offerings or middlemen must enthusiastically promote it. The manufacturer's sales personnel play key roles, of course, in securing this kind of promotion from the middlemen.

Pricing under the competition. Not many manufacturers, at least those with sales forces, willingly price under the competition. However, some, such as in the clothing industry, price under their competitors and appear to have demonstrated, at least to their own satisfaction, that aggressive pricing increases market demand and keeps new competitors from entering the field. Sales executives, quite generally, dislike this alternative and contend that it causes sales personnel to sell price more than the product.

Policy on Pricing Relative to Costs

Every company has a policy regarding the relationships between its products' prices and the underlying costs. Long-run sales revenues must cover all long-run costs, but short-run sales revenues do not have to cover short-run costs. Sales revenue, of course, equals unit volume sold times price. Most companies follow a full-cost pricing policy under most circumstances, but most also spell out the circumstances under which departures are permissible.

Full-cost pricing. Under full-cost pricing, no sale is made at a price lower than that covering total costs, including variable costs and allocated fixed costs. The reasoning is that if short-run sales revenues cover short-run costs, they also cover long-run costs. Nevertheless, it must be recognized that the price buyers are willing to pay bears little relationship to the seller's cost—no one knows this better than the field sales personnel and the sales executive who leads them. Moreover, as cost accountants admit, it is next to impossible to determine "real" costs (especially with respect to allocating a share of fixed costs to a particular unit of product). Then, too, even if it were possible to determine real costs, there are times when prices on products already on hand must be cut below full cost to sell at all. There is a need, therefore, for a policy detailing the conditions under which prices that do not cover full cost may be used.

Promotion pricing. Particularly in industries producing consumer nondurables, pricing is a promotional tool. Thus, for instance, a company launching a new packaged convenience food may offer it at a "special low introductory price." A second example of the use of a low introductory price occurs when a company invades a geographical market in which a competitor is already well entrenched—Folger's coffee used this strategy when it brought its brand into markets east of the Mississippi in which Maxwell House was the long-established market leader. Other circumstances in which pricing is used as a promotional tool include ones in which management wishes to counter the effects of competitors' increases in promotional activity (e.g., heavier or more effective advertising, the use of instore demonstrators, or more frequent calls on customers by competitors' sales personnel) and to counter them quickly.

Contribution pricing. Using a contribution-pricing policy means pricing at any level above the relevant incremental costs.[4] Suppose that a seller is offered a special contract to supply a large buyer, who will not pay the going price. The buyer argues that the lower price is justified because of savings to the seller in selling time, credit costs, handling expenses, and the like. Still, the demanded price concession exceeds the likely savings, so that total sales dollars from the proposed transaction are not sufficient to cover total costs. Should the seller accept this proposition? The seller should accept the order *if* the resulting total sales dollars are sufficient not only to cover all incremental costs but to make a contribution to fixed costs and/or profits. After all, current sales at the going price may already cover the fixed costs, and the sale at a special price will not raise fixed costs (assuming the incremental costs are all variable), so this sale need not bear an allocated share of fixed costs to yield net profit. So long as the proposed price (times the number of units ordered) more than covers the out-of-pocket costs of the transaction, the excess is profit.

Three important conditions, however, should all be present for such offers to be accepted: (1) the company already has the necessary production capacity, (2) this capacity cannot be put to a more profitable use, and (3) the portion of the output sold below full cost is destined for a different market segment. All three conditions are important, but the third is critical to the continuance of going prices at full cost or above for the bulk of the output. As every salesperson knows, word that one account has been favored with a lower price travels at the speed of light to all other accounts in the market area.

Policy on Uniformity of Prices to Different Buyers

In pricing to different buyers, companies choose between (1) a one-price policy, under which all similar buyers are quoted the same price and (2) a variable-price policy, under which the price to each buyer is determined by individual bargaining. In the United States, most marketers of consumer goods adhere to a

[4]Incremental costs are those incurred in changing the level or nature of an activity, for example, making and/or selling a larger quantity of a product. Incremental costs may be either variable or a combination of variable and fixed costs.

one-price policy, even though many vary prices among different classes of customers and from one geographic region to the next.

The variable-price policy is common wherever individual sales involve large sums, as in many industrial marketing situations. The bargaining power of individual buyers varies with the size of the transaction. Moreover, as in the industrial market, a large buyer represents a greater potential for future business than does a small buyer, so a seller may make price concessions to gain or retain the large buyer's patronage.

There are two reasons sales executives consider the one-price policy attractive: (1) since prices are not negotiated with individual customers, sales personnel spend only minimum time discussing price and devote maximum time to "creative selling," and (2) there is no risk of alienating customers because of preferential prices given others. Furthermore, laws prohibiting price discrimination, such as the Robinson-Patman Act, make it safer legally for a marketer to apply a one-price policy than a variable-price policy.

Policy on List Pricing

A marketer distributing through middlemen either (1) does not suggest standardized resale (list) prices or (2) seeks to control middlemen's resale prices through list pricing. List pricing takes a variety of forms, the two most common being that of printing the price on the package or requiring sales personnel to suggest the resale price to buyers. List pricing is easiest to implement when the marketer utilizes selective or exclusive distribution, inasmuch as the difficulties of enforcement of suggested list prices multiply with increases in the number of middlemen. Effective enforcement of list pricing means assigning the additional role of "resale price reporter" to sales force personnel.

Policy on Discounts

Trade discounts. A manufacturer selling to both wholesalers and retailers may quote different prices, that is, offer different "trade discounts," to each class of customer. Under U.S. federal laws prohibiting price discrimination, discounts, to be legal, must be made available on proportionately equal terms to all similar customers. Wholesalers and retailers are not similar customers; each group performs a different distributive function. The law permits a manufacturer to charge a higher price to retailers than to wholesalers, even though some buyers in each class may buy in the same quantities. Policy on trade discounts depends on the importance (to the manufacturer) of each class of buyer and on the relative bargaining power of each class of buyer.

Quantity discounts. Quantity discounts are price reductions granted for purchases in a stated quantity or quantities and are normally aimed to increase the quantities customers buy. Through price reductions, sellers increase sales by passing on to buyers part of the savings that result from large purchases. These savings can be considerable, for it may take little, if any, more of a salesperson's time to sell a large order than to sell a small one. The same holds for order processing, order filling, billing, and transportation costs.

The firm using a quantity discount policy in the U.S. market must keep two legal restrictions in mind: (1) the discounts must reflect actual savings—the price reduction can be no greater than the actual savings resulting from the larger quantity ordered—and (2) the discounts must be available on proportionately equal terms to all similar purchasers.

Geographical Pricing Policies

One pricing policy of particular interest is that of who should pay the freight for delivering the product to buyers. The answer to this question is important to the sales executive, because it affects price quotations to buyers in different geographical areas. The farther away the customer is from the factory, the greater are the freight charges for a given size order. No matter what policy the company adopts, freight differentials are reflected one way or another in price quotations. Regardless of the policy on payment of shipping charges, its administration is the sales executive's responsibility. There are three alternatives: (1) F.O.B., or "free on board" pricing, under which the customer pays the freight; (2) delivered pricing, under which the seller pays the freight; and (3) freight absorption, a compromise between F.O.B. and delivered pricing.

F.O.B. pricing. The marketer using this policy quotes selling prices at the factory (or other point from which it makes sales), and buyers pay the freight charges. Each buyer adds freight to the factory price and determines total delivered cost. F.O.B. pricing results in variations in the resale price that middlemen put on the product in different areas. In consumer-goods marketing, F.O.B. pricing is used for items that are heavy or bulky relative to their value, for example, canned goods and fresh vegetables. In industrial marketing of raw materials and heavy machinery, F.O.B. pricing is also in widespread use.

Delivered pricing. The marketer using delivered pricing pays freight charges and includes them in its price quotations. The price is really an "F.O.B. destination" price, and the net return to the seller varies with the buyer's location. Delivered pricing is appropriate when freight charges account for only a small part of the product's price. It is a necessary policy when a marketer uses list prices. Standardized resale prices are likely to be obtained if middlemen pay a uniform nationwide delivered price—sometimes called a "postage stamp" price. Makers of chewing gum, candy bars, and many drug items, particularly patent medicines, use postage stamp pricing. Because middlemen all pay the same price, the resale price is roughly the same throughout the entire market.

A variation is zone pricing, under which the market is divided into zones and different prices are quoted to buyers in each zone. The manufacturer builds the freight charges into its quoted price (as in any delivered pricing policy), but it quotes different prices to buyers situated in different zones.

Policy on Price Leadership

All marketers should decide whether they will initiate or follow price changes. In some industries there are well-established patterns of price leadership. In selling basic industrial materials, such as lumber and cement, one company is the price leader and is usually the first to raise or cut prices; other industry members simply follow or, sometimes, fail to follow, as occasionally happens in the case of a price increase, thus causing the leader to reconsider and perhaps to cancel the announced increase. Similar patterns exist in marketing such consumer products as gasoline and bakery goods, where, usually market by market, one company serves as the price leader and others follow. Generally, price leaders have large market shares and price followers, small market shares.

Even when final buyers (for example, ultimate consumers) are not price conscious, producers know that the middlemen handling their products are sensitive to price changes. In response to even minuscule price changes, up or down, they will consider switching suppliers. Even the marketer of a consumer product competing on a nonprice basis must be alert to impending price changes; the important policy issue is whether to initiate or to follow price changes. The decision depends upon the marketer's relative market position and the image of leadership that it desires to build and maintain.

Product Line Pricing Policy

Pricing the individual members of a product line calls for policy decisions. The different items in a product line "compete" with each other; that is, a buyer buying one member of the line does so to the exclusion of others. One decision relates to the "price space" between the prices of individual members of the line. Having the right amount of price space is critical; too little may confuse buyers, and too much leaves "gaps" into which competitors can move and make sales. Sales executives contribute major inputs to this decision through their knowledge of the market, of buyers' motivations, and of competitors' offerings and prices.

Other important decisions concern the pricing of the "top" (highest-priced item) and the "bottom" (lowest-priced item) in the line. Companies price the "in-between" members of the line so that they account for the greatest sales volume, using the bottom of the line as a traffic builder and the top of the line as a prestige builder. As the traffic builder, the lower-priced item affects total sales far more than does the price of any other item. Price changes on it affect the sales of other line members. A price increase on the traffic builder causes higher sales on other line members. The same is true for the prestige builder; a change in the price of the top of the line influences sales of other line members.

Competitive Bidding Policy

In purchasing certain products, industrial and governmental buyers solicit competitive bids from potential suppliers and award the business to the bidder offering the best proposal. A proposal may be selected as best for a number of reasons (for example, price, delivery dates, reputation for quality), depending on which is most important to the buyer. In some industries, competitive bidding is the general rule, and individual manufacturers have no choice but to participate. In other industries, only a part of the volume is sold on this basis, and each manufacturer decides whether to participate. For example, a typewriter manufacturer who sells to industry on a uniform price basis must participate in competitive bidding if it wants orders from governmental agencies (since government purchasing agents at all levels of government are ordinarily required to request competitive bids on most purchases). Many manufacturers believe that competitive bidding reduces competition to a price basis; consequently, they avoid bid business unless the share of the total market involved is too large to ignore.

In competitive bidding the sales executive and the sales personnel play important roles. Their close contact with the market puts them in a good position to estimate how low a particular price must be to obtain the order. Furthermore, the long-term relationships developed between salespersons and their customers are important in giving the company a chance to make a "second bid" in those cases where industrial buyers give favored suppliers the chance to meet lower bids submitted by competitors. This chance does not exist in competitive bidding for government business, where closed bids are specified (that is, all bids are opened at the same time and there is no chance for high bidders to adjust their quotes downward). But an effective salesperson can often remove competition from closed government bids by persuading the purchasing agent of the value of a differentiating characteristic of the product so that the purchasing agent includes this characteristic in the written specification supplied to potential bidders.

CONCLUSION

Sales-related marketing policies influence the sales executive's job and effectiveness. They provide guidance in drafting plans for achieving the organization's personal-selling objectives, in organizing the sales effort, in managing the sales force, and in controlling the sales effort. Sales executives play different roles in deciding sales policies, but in all companies, they bear the main responsibility for implementing these policies. Product policies and distribution policies shape the basic nature of a company and set the pattern for its sales force operations. Pricing policies are important because the sales staff must persuade target buyers not only to accept the company's products but at the prices asked. Sales executives play a critical role in implementing sales-related marketing policies, making them work in ways that facilitate achievement of personal-selling objectives.

Formulating Personal-Selling Strategy

5

Sales management achieves personal-selling objectives through personal-selling strategy. Sales-related marketing policies provide the guidelines for making key decisions in personal-selling strategy on the kind(s) and size(s) of sales force required.[1] The decision on kind of salesperson defines the role(s) that sales personnel play in their contacts with customers and prospects. The decision on sales force size dictates not only the deployment of sales personnel but the frequencies and intensities of their contacts with customers and prospects. The effectiveness with which these roles are played by the sales force determines the extent to which overall personal-selling objectives are achieved.

A company's competitive posture is shaped by (1) the competitive setting, (2) overall marketing strategy, and (3) the effectiveness of strategy implementation. The kind of competitive setting is—for all practical purposes—beyond the control of management. But management influences the company's competitive posture as it makes key decisions on products, distribution, pricing, and promotion. Unifying these key decisions into an overall marketing strategy results in a plan for the kind of posture the company desires.

Making the planned competitive posture come true requires effective implementation of marketing strategy, that is, the successful conversion of marketing plans into realities. Implementing marketing strategy, of course, has both

[1]While most companies field a single sales force made up of one kind of salesperson, multiproduct companies may utilize different kinds and sizes of sales forces to sell individual product lines. Other companies sell the same or similar products to different market segments through separate kinds and sizes of sales force. For more on this topic, see Chapter 7.

short- and long-run aspects. Marketing management, with its planning orientation, concentrates largely on the long-run aspects. The implementation interests of marketing and sales management are intertwined, inasmuch as short-run accomplishments add up to long-run achievement. Marketing management depends upon sales management to lead the personal sales force in its effort to achieve personal-selling objectives and to produce "bottom-line" results in terms of sales volume, profits, and growth.

COMPETITIVE SETTINGS AND PERSONAL-SELLING STRATEGY

Individual companies operate in different competitive settings. Industries differ as to maturity and the number of competitors. These differences result in different competitive settings. Economists identify four basic kinds: (1) pure competition, (2) monopolistic competition, (3) oligopolistic competition, and (4) no direct competition. Assuming different levels of importance in each competitive setting are the various components of overall marketing strategy. How the importance of the personal-selling component varies is significant for sales management.

PURE COMPETITION

Pure competition, as defined by economists, is a market setting with large numbers of buyers and sellers, none powerful enough to control or to influence the prevailing market price. Economists assume, among other things, that (1) no single buyer or seller is so large relative to the market that it can appreciably affect the product's total demand or supply; (2) all sellers' products are identical, so buyers are indifferent as to which sellers they buy from; (3) no artificial restraints on prices exist (i.e., no governmental price fixing or administering of prices by individual companies, trade associations, labor unions, or others); and (4) all buyers are always informed about all sellers' prices.

If these assumptions represented the "real world" in an industry, no company would concern itself with marketing strategies of any sort. Each seller would be too small to gain business at the expense of its competitors through price cutting, and if it did cut the price, they would immediately match the cut. No seller could compete by offering a "better" product, because product differentiation is ruled out. No seller would push a product through personal selling or stimulate its sale through advertising, as this would be futile since all potential buyers buy only on a price basis and are already fully informed. In addition, the economist assumes implicitly that sellers and buyers are in direct contact, making it unnecessary to worry about marketing channels or physical distribution. The real world contains no known instances of industries operating under pure competition; consequently, we need not concern ourselves with this competitive setting.

MONOPOLISTIC COMPETITION

Most modern marketers operate in competitive settings that approximate monopolistic competition, which means that some or all of the assumptions of pure competition do not hold. More precisely, monopolistic competition exists when there is a large number of sellers of a generic kind of product but each seller's brand is in some way differentiated from every other brand. Furthermore, under monopolistic competition, it is easy for additional competitors to enter the market; for instance, retailers entering as private-label competitors. This competitive setting describes that of many products during late phases of their market growth and much of their market-maturity life-cycle stages.

Nearly every seller's brand of product, whether it be nailpolish remover or pet food, can be differentiated (at least in final buyers' minds) from competing brands. Most ultimate consumers appear convinced that different brands of even such "identical" products as aspirin, table salt, and flour are not exactly alike, providing individual marketers with opportunities to build brand preferences among buyers and hence to control a share of the market. Furthermore, most ultimate consumers (and even many industrial users) are not fully informed—frequently not even adequately informed—about the offerings of competing sellers. Sellers differentiate their "market offerings" through individualizing one or several components of overall marketing strategy. Unique packaging may differentiate the product (for example, table or picnic-sized shakers of salt); an unusual distribution method, such as house-to-house selling of cosmetics, may differentiate the product's distribution; or pricing gimmicks, such as "cents-off" pricing and list pricing, may differentiate the product's pricing.

However, the main way sellers of products in the market-growth and market-maturity stages differentiate them is through promotional strategy. Advertising differentiates the brand in the minds of final buyers and stimulates selective demand. Personal selling sees that the desired distribution intensity is secured and maintained and that middlemen provide the needed "push."

Competitive settings characterized by monopolistic competition provide marketing opportunities and clearly require skill in planning and implementing overall marketing strategy. Whereas the key element in the overall marketing strategy for these products is the ability to differentiate the product, even if ever so slightly, in some way(s), appropriate promotion (usually some blend of advertising and personal selling) is the *critical element in implementing* such an overall marketing strategy. Advertising's role is most often that of relating market messages to final buyers. Personal selling's role is that of servicing the distribution network and stimulating promotional efforts by the middlemen.

OLIGOPOLISTIC COMPETITION

Increasing numbers of marketers operate under oligopolistic competition, a competitive setting where the number of competitors is small enough that they are individually identified and known to each other and it is difficult for new competitors to enter the market. Each competitor is a large enough organization and has a large enough market share that changes in its overall marketing strategy have direct repercussions on the others. Each must weigh the possible reactions of each of its competitors in formulating and implementing its own overall marketing strategy. Oligopolistic competition develops in marketing many products either during a late phase of their market growth or an early phase of their market maturity.

In the United States and other developed countries, oligopolies exist in such industries as automobiles, appliances, personal computers, soaps and detergents, and shoes in the consumer-goods field and in data-processing equipment, steel, aluminum, textile machinery, and machine tools in the industrial-goods field. The successful firms keep on growing, and the less successful fail or disappear (through merger). The soap and auto industries provide dramatic examples, both having been reduced from numerous competitors to a small group.

Oligopoly produces the most aggressive competition. When a few large companies dominate an industry, the competitive moves of any one affects the entire market. When, for instance, one competitor introduces a new variation of a basic product (such as a new scent in hand soap), the other competitors risk a rapid loss in market share if they do not respond appropriately and almost instantaneously. For this reason, competitors' actions are watched closely, and marketing changes by one firm are matched or otherwise countered. Changes in one competitor's product, in its distribution, in its promotion—if they hold some promise of increasing its market share—are imitated, improved upon, or otherwise countered by competitors as rapidly as they can launch counteroffensives. Price changes by individual industry members can be and often are matched by others almost immediately. Industrywide price adjustments are often made so quickly that they appear to result from collusion, when, in fact, there has been none whatever.

Personal selling strategy under oligopolistic competition plays important roles in building and maintaining dealer cooperation, in servicing the distribution network, and in gathering information on competitors' activities. As under monopolistic competition, promotional strategy generally features both advertising and personal selling, with both playing highly critical roles, particularly in the successful implementation of overall marketing strategy.

No Direct Competition

Neither the monopolist nor the company marketing a radically new and different product in its market-pioneering life-cycle stage has direct competitors. But both have indirect competitors; both vie with sellers in other industries for the same prospects' interest and buying decisions, the monopolist on a long-term basis and the innovating marketer for the limited period it is free from direct competition. Both must initiate and stimulate primary demand—that is, demand for the product category—through promotional (personal selling and advertising) strategies aimed to influence final buyers and middlemen. Both need distribution strategies providing for marketing channels, middlemen's cooperation and the product's physical distribution, and the putting into effect of these distribution strategies requires the effective implementation of personal-selling strategy in terms of both kind and number of sales personnel. Both require a pricing strategy: the monopolist (at least in theory) being free to maximize profits through "charging what the traffic will bear," the innovating marketer choosing between either a price-skimming or a penetration-pricing strategy, depending mainly upon how soon it expect direct competitors to enter the market. Here, too, putting into effect the chosen pricing strategy calls for the effective implementation of personal-selling strategy. Further, both the monopolist and the innovating marketer seek to integrate their individual product, distribution, promotion (including personal selling and advertising), and pricing strategies into overall marketing strategies (that is, competitive postures) consistent with their long-term goals. This consistency is obtained when all elements of overall strategy are "in balance."

PERSONAL-SELLING OBJECTIVES AND PERSONAL-SELLING STRATEGY

The qualitative personal-selling objectives vary with the kind of competitive setting. These objectives concern the nature of the contribution management expects personal selling to make in achieving long-term company objectives. These objectives influence both the nature of the sales job (that is, the kind of sales personnel needed) and the size of the sales force. For instance, a company that expects its salespeople to do the entire selling job (as when it does not plan to use advertising or other forms of promotion) needs a different kind of sales staff, and a larger one, than does a company that expects its salespeople only to "service" existing accounts and backs them up with heavy advertising and other promotion. Qualitative objectives are long term and are carried over from one operating period to another. But when qualitative objectives change, there are changes in the nature of the sales job and in the size of the sales force.

The quantitative personal-selling objectives also vary with the kind of competitive setting. These objectives are short term and are adjusted from operating period to operating period. In all competitive settings, companies regard the sales volume objective—the dollar or unit sales volume that is to be obtained during the period—as the most critical. In all competitive settings, too, most companies benefit from assigning other types of quantitative personal-selling objectives as, for instance, one directing that sales volume be obtained in ways that contribute to profit objectives (for example, by selling the "proper" mix of products). In monopolistic and oligopolistic competitive settings, companies assign still other quantitative objectives, including ones specifying the securing and/or retaining of a certain market share.

Quantitative personal-selling objectives, like the qualitative personal-selling objectives, influence both the nature of the sales job and sales force size. A company, for instance, that increases its sales volume objective significantly either expects its sales force to perform differently (that is, changes the nature of the selling job), or increases the size of the sales force, or, perhaps, does both. Being short term and changing from one period to the next, the quantitative personal-selling objectives, however, impact more upon the size of the sales force than upon the nature of the sales job. That is to say that, in all competitive settings and in nearly all companies, changing the nature of the sales job is a rarer event than changing the size of the sales force. Changes in the nature of the sales job, in addition, usually flow from changes in key *qualitative* personal-selling objectives.

SALES-RELATED MARKETING POLICIES AND PERSONAL-SELLING STRATEGY

Sales-related marketing policies are the guidelines within which the company seeks to reach both qualitative and quantitative personal-selling objectives. They provide guidance on what to sell (product policies) and to whom to sell (distribution policies). Decisions on what to sell and to whom to sell shape the fundamental nature of a company and are important determinants of the kind of sales personnel and their total number (the two components of personal-selling strategy). Pricing policies, too, have an important impact, especially on the kind of sales staff; salespeople have to persuade target buyers not only to accept the company's products but at the prices asked. Sales-related marketing policies, like personal-selling objectives, vary with the competitive setting. It is important that they be attuned to a company's particular situation under conditions of monopolistic or oligopolistic competition, much more so than when there is no direct competition.

DETERMINING THE KIND OF SALES PERSONNEL

One key decision on personal-selling strategy is that on the kind of sales personnel. Making this decision requires consideration of qualitative personal-selling objectives—what contributions toward the company's long-term overall objectives should be expected from those performing selling jobs? What should be the duties and responsibilities of these individuals? How should their job performance be measured? Management must face up to these questions when it decides the kind of sales personnel it requires.

Each company has individualized requirements as to the kind of sales personnel best fitted to serve its needs. The reason goes beyond the fact that the qualitative personal-selling objectives of each company have some degree of distinctiveness. Each company deals with a unique set of marketing factors, such as the strengths and weaknesses of its products (what it sells), the motivations and buying practices of its customers and prospects (whom it sells to), its pricing strategy, and the competitive setting—the relative strengths and weaknesses of competitors. Furthermore, different selling jobs require different levels of selling and nonselling abilities, training, and technical and other knowledge. The bottler's driver-salesperson doing route selling has a considerably different job from that of the salesperson who sells complex industrial installations such as lathes and presses.

In determining the kind of sales personnel, then, we must understand what is expected of them: the job objectives, the duties and responsibilities, and the performance measures. Knowing the salesperson's job means knowing the particular job for the particular salesperson—it is common for different salespersons in the same company to have quite different jobs. Knowing the particular job helps management to avoid "putting square pegs into round holes." It helps in fitting the job to the person and the person to the job.

Product Market Analysis

No person is capable of selling all kinds of products to all kinds of customers. At one extreme, a salesperson sells a single product to many kinds of customers. At the other extreme, a salesperson sells a wide line of products to a single kind of customer. Most salespeople, however, have job assignments requiring them to sell *some* products to *some* kinds of customers. One way of categorizing selling jobs, then, is into three classifications: (1) product specialists, (2) market specialists, and (3) combinations of product and market specialization.

A critical step in sales job analysis is to define the nature of product-market interactions. It is advisable to construct a product-market grid (see Figure 5.1). Companies using product-market grids, of course, construct them showing much finer details of product-market interactions than that illustrated; this demands thorough analysis and classification of markets and products. The "boxes" indicate the different customers who might be sold the different products. As management decides which customers should be sold which products, some boxes are blacked in, others left empty. This helps to answer the question: Should our sales personnel be product specialists, market specialists, or a combination? Product specialization is indicated when the product is highly technical, requiring salespeople to advise on uses and applications. Market specialization is called for when the product is nontechnical but different kinds of customers have unique buying problems, require special sales approaches, or need special service. In many cases, analysis reveals that sales personnel need not only considerable knowledge of more than a single company product line and their applications but skills in dealing with more than one kind of customer.

FIGURE 5.1 Product-Market Grid for a Book Publishing Company

Type of Product	Type of Market: Campus Bookstores	Book Wholesalers	Business Buyers	Government Buyers
General Textbooks				
Technical and Reference Books				
Hardbound Fiction				
Paperbacks				

Determining the type and amount of specialization requires consideration of both the interdependence dimension and the expertise dimension. The four possible combination of these two dimensions (see Figure 5.2) results in four different kinds of selling roles.

If the dominant interdependence is between customers (rather than between products), sales personnel should be specialists. They should be product specialists when the needed dominant expertise is in product technologies. They should be customer specialists when the needed dominant expertise is in customers' applications. Customer specialists need the support of market managers who provide the needed prospect expertise through their specialization in applications in particular industries.

If the dominant interdependence is between products (rather than between customers), the selling organization needs staffing by full-line salespersons. If product technologies require the most expertise, salespersons sell the full line to all kinds of prospects and are supported by product managers who provide the needed product expertise. If customers' applications require the most expertise, salespersons sell the full line to particular kinds of prospects.

In addition to product-market interactions, other marketing elements affect the caliber of salesperson required. If most customers are large, for instance, salespeople need different talents than if most customers are small. The geographical location of a territory has a bearing on the best type of salesperson, particularly where local prejudice favors "natives" as opposed to "outsiders." If these or similar elements are important, appropriate grids assist in the analysis.

FIGURE 5.2 Types and Amounts of Specialization in Selling Organizations

DOMINANT INTERDEPENDENCE / DOMINANT EXPERTISE	BETWEEN CUSTOMERS	BETWEEN PRODUCTS
PRODUCT TECHNOLOGIES	Product Specialists	Full-Line Salespersons (Supported by Product Managers)
CUSTOMERS' APPLICATIONS	Customer Specialists (Supported by Market Managers)	Full-Line Salespersons Specialized by Kind of Customer

SOURCE: Adapted with permission from R. C. Rao and R. E. Turner, *Sales Force Specialization and Selling Effectiveness*, a working paper published by Queen's University, Kingston, Ontario, January 1978. Also see this same paper in Subhash C. Jain (ed.), *Research Frontiers in Marketing: Dialogues and Directions*, 1978, Educational Proceedings, American Marketing Association, Chicago. Also published in "Sales Management: New Developments from Behavioral and Decision Model Research," proceedings of Workshop Cosponsored by the American Marketing Association and Marketing Science Institute, April 6-8, 1978, Marketing Science Institute, Cambridge, MA. 02138.

Analysis of Salesperson's Role in Securing Orders

The role(s) that a company expects its sales personnel to play in securing orders influences the kind of sales staff required. All salespeople in some situations seek orders aggressively, but in others they need only take orders coming their way, the relative emphasis on order taking and order getting varying in different selling environments. The driver-salesperson for a soft drink bottling company is primarily an order taker, because the product has been strongly presold to consumers and retailers reorder automatically. The encyclopedia salesperson calling on householders most often functions as an order getter, since getting the order is the main goal.

Depending on whether promotional strategy places major reliance on personal selling or advertising, salespeople may be either active or passive forces in securing orders. If the promotional strategy of a manufacturer is to rely heavily upon advertising to attract business and build demand, marketing channels include several layers of middlemen, and the role of the manufacturer's salesperson is that of order taker primarily and order getter only incidentally. The opposite situation obtains when advertising is used mainly to back up personal selling—marketing channels contain a minimum number of layers of middlemen, and the salesperson's role is chiefly order getting.

There are cases both in consumer-goods and industrial-goods marketing in which the salesperson plays only a minor and indirect role in securing orders, the salesperson's major role being concerned with other matters. In consumer-goods marketing, the missionary salesperson's major role is to assist middlemen in making sales to their customers. Orders from customers, then, result indirectly, rather than directly, from the missionary salesperson's efforts. In industrial-goods marketing, the "sales engineer" plays two major roles: (1) advisor to middlemen and customers on technical product features and applications and (2) design consultant to middlemen and industrial users on installations or processes incorporating the manufacturer's products. Sales engineers, then, also secure orders indirectly, rather than directly, and as the result of playing their major roles as advisors and design consultants.

Choice of Basic Selling Style

Differences in marketing factors cause each company to have individualized requirements as to the kind of salesperson it employs. These differences cause each company to expect its own sales staff to play somewhat unique roles (in some respects) even relative to companies employing "similar" kinds of sales personnel. Nevertheless, sales job roles can be grouped into four basic styles that cut, to a large degree, across industry and company boundaries: trade selling, missionary selling, technical selling, and new-business selling.[2]

Trade selling. The trade salesperson develops and maintains long-term relations with a stable group of customers. For the most part, this is low-key selling, with little or no pressure, and the job is dull and routine. This selling style, which predominates in marketing food and apparel and in wholesaling, applies primarily to products that have well-established markets. Advertising and other forms of promotion are more vital to overall marketing strategy than is personal selling. One important responsibility of the trade salesperson is to help customers build up their volume through providing promotional assistance. For example, the salesperson for a line of breakfast cereals devotes much time to promotional work with retailers and wholesalers—taking inventory, refilling shelves, suggesting reorders, setting up displays, and the like.

Missionary selling. The missionary salesperson's main job objective is to increase the company's sales volume by assisting customers with their selling efforts. The missionary salesperson is concerned only incidentally with securing orders, since orders result from the missionary's primary public relations and promotional efforts with customers of the customers (indirect customers). The missionary salesperson's job is to persuade indirect customers to buy from the company's direct customers. For example, the salesperson for a pharmaceutical manufacturer calls on the retail druggist to acquaint him or her with a new product and to urge the druggist to stock it. Thus, the missionary seeks to persuade

[2]D. A. Newton, "Get the Most Out of Your Sales Force," *Harvard Business Review*, 47, no. 5 (September–October 1969), pp. 131–41.

pharmacists to buy from drug wholesalers, who are the direct customers. In some situations, missionary sales staff members call on individuals and institutions who do not buy the product themselves but who influence its purchase. The medical "detailer" who calls on doctors and hospitals to acquaint them with new drugs is an example. Missionary selling, like trade selling, is low key and does not require high-level technical training or ability.

Technical selling. The technical salesperson deals primarily with the company's established accounts, and the main job objective is to increase their volume of purchase by providing technical advice and assistance. The technical salesperson performs advisory functions similar to those of the missionary salesperson but, in addition, sells direct to industrial users and other buyers. The technical salesperson devotes considerable time to acquainting industrial users with technical product characteristics and applications and to helping them design installations or processes that incorporate the company's products. In this selling style, the ability to identify, analyze, and solve customers' problems is important.

Technical salespeople often specialize, either by products or markets. In selling large made-to-order installations, such as steam turbines and electric generators, different technical salespersons work with different items in the product line. Other technical salespeople specialize in servicing either industrial accounts or government procurement agencies.

New-business selling. The new-business salesperson's main job is to find and obtain new customers, that is, to convert prospects into customers. The salesperson specializing in new-business selling should be unusually creative and ingenious and possess a high degree of resourcefulness. Few companies, however, have sales personnel who do nothing but new-business selling; most firms expect their regular sales staff, who primarily do trade selling, to do new-business selling also. However, since it is rare for the same individual to possess both needed sets of talents and because there is a tendency for salespeople to neglect new-business selling in favor of servicing established accounts, some experts advocate the specialization of sales personnel into two separate groups, one to concentrate on retaining existing accounts and the other to focus on converting prospects into customers.[3]

DETERMINING THE SIZE OF THE SALES FORCE

Management makes its second key decision on personal-selling strategy when it decides the size of the sales force. Having determined the kind of salesperson that best fits the company's needs, management now determines how many are required to meet the sales volume and profit objectives. If the company has too few salespersons, opportunities for sales and profits go unexploited, and if it has

[3]G. N. Kahn and A. Shuchman, "Specialize Your Salesmen!" *Harvard Business Review*, 39, no. 1 (January–February 1961), pp. 94–95.

too many, excessive expenditures for personal-selling (even though they may bring in additional sales dollars) reduce net profits. It is difficult, perhaps impossible, to determine the exact number of salespersons that a particular company should have. Three basic approaches are used in approximating this number: (1) the work-load method, (2) the sales potential method, and (3) the incremental method. Each provides needed insights on the "right size" of sales force, although none produces a definitive answer.

Work Load Method

In the work load method the basic assumption is that all sales personnel should shoulder equal work loads. Management first estimates the total work load involved in covering the company's entire market and then divides by the work load that an individual salesperson should be able to handle, thus determining the total number of salespeople required. Companies applying this approach generally assume that the interactions of three major factors—customer size, sales volume potential, and travel load—determine the total work load involved in covering the entire market.[4]

The six steps in applying the work load approach are shown in the following example:

1. *Classify customers, both present and prospective, into sales volume potential categories.* (Classification criteria, other than sales volume or sales volume potential, can be used as long as it is possible to distinguish the differences in selling effort required for each class.) Assume that there are 880 present and prospective customers, classified by sales volume potential as

Class A, large	150 accounts
Class B, medium	220
Class C, small	510

2. *Decide on the length of time per sales call and desired call frequencies on each class.* (Several inputs are used in making these two decisions, for example, personal judgment, the opinions of sales personnel, and actual time studies). Assume that both present and prospective customers require the same amounts of time per sales call and the same call frequencies per year as follows:

Class A: 60 minutes/call × 52 calls/year = 52 hours/year
Class B: 30 minutes/call × 24 calls/year = 12 hours/year
Class C: 15 minutes/call × 12 calls/year = 3 hours/year

[4]See W. J. Talley, Jr., "How to Design Sales Territories," *Journal of Marketing*, 25, no. 3 (January 1961), p. 7.

3. *Calculate the total work load involved in covering the entire market.* In our example, this calculation is

Class A: 150 accounts × 52 hours/year	=	7,800 hours
Class B: 220 accounts × 12 hours/year	=	2,640 hours
Class C: 510 accounts × 3 hours/year	=	1,530 hours
	Total	11,970 hours

4. *Determine the total work time available per salesperson.* Suppose that management decides that salespeople should work 40 hours per week, 48 weeks per year (allowing 4 weeks for vacations, holidays, sickness, etc.), then each salesperson has available

   40 hours/week × 48 weeks = 1,920 hours/year

5. *Divide the total work time available per salesperson by task.* Assume that management specifies that sales personnel should apportion their time as follows:

Selling tasks	45%	864 hours
Nonselling tasks	30%	576 hours
Traveling	25%	480 hours
	100%	1,920 hours

6. *Calculate the total number of salespeople needed.* This is a matter of dividing the total market work load by the total selling time available per salesperson:

$$\frac{11{,}970 \text{ hours}}{864 \text{ hours}} = 14 \text{ salespeople needed}$$

The work load approach is attractive to practicing sales executives. It is easy to understand and easy to apply. Such large firms as Celanese, IBM, and AT&T have used this approach.

A basic flaw in the work load approach is that, as usually applied, it disregards profit as an explicit consideration. However, of course, management can take profit criteria into consideration in determining lengths and frequencies of sales calls. But the optimum length and frequency of any particular sales call depends upon many factors other than account size (in terms of sales volume or sales volume potential). Such factors as the gross margin on the product mix purchased by an account, the expenses incurred in servicing an account, and an account's likely responses to changed levels of selling effort all influence profitability.

Still another shortcoming traces to the inherent assumption that not only should all sales personnel have the same work load but that they all can and will utilize their time with equal efficiency. Although a relation exists between the amount of time spent on calling on an account and the size of the order received, some salespeople accomplish more in a shorter time than others can. The "quality of time invested in a sales call" is at least as important as the "quantity of time spent on a sales call."

Sales Potential Method

The sales potential method is based on the assumption that performance of the set of activities contained in the job description represents one sales personnel unit. A particular salesperson may represent either more or less than one sales personnel unit. If the individual's performance is excellent, that individual may do the job of more than one unit; if the individual's performance is below par, he or she may do less. If management expects all company sales personnel to perform as specified in the job description, then the number of salespersons required equals the number of units of sales personnel required. Generally, it must be noted, sales job descriptions are constructed on management's assumption that they describe what the average salesperson with average performance will accomplish. With that assumption, then, one can estimate the number of dollars of sales volume that each salesperson (that is, each sales personnel unit) should produce. Dividing this amount into forecasted sales volume—the company's sales volume objective—and allowing for sales force turnover results in an estimate of the number of salespeople needed. These relationships are summarized in the equation

$$N = \frac{S}{P} + T\left(\frac{S}{P}\right)$$

This reduces to

$$N = \frac{S}{P}(1 + T)$$

where

N = number of sales personnel units

S = forecasted sales volume

P = estimated sales productivity of one sales personnel unit

T = allowance for rate of sales force turnover

Consider a firm with forecasted sales of $1 million, estimated sales productivity per sales personnel unit of $100,000, and an estimated annual rate of sales force turnover of 10 percent. Inserting these figures in the equation, we have

$$N = \frac{\$1{,}000{,}000}{\$100{,}000} \times 1.10$$

N = 11 sales personnel units.

This is a simplified model for determining the size of a sales force. It does not, for instance, include the lead times required for seeking out, hiring, and training salespeople to the desired level of sales productivity. Actual planning models have built-in lead and lag relations to allow for such requirements. If two months of full-time training are required to bring a new salesperson up to the desired productivity, recruiting must lead actual need for the new salesperson by two months. Another assumption implicit in this simple model is that sales potentials are identical in all territories, which is similar to the assumption that the number of sales personnel units required is the same as the number of salespersons needed; where this assumption does not hold, the model should be adjusted accordingly.

Difficulties in making estimates for this model vary with the factor being estimated (*N*, *S*, *P*, or *T*) and the company. The crucial estimate of the sales productivity of one unit of sales strength relies heavily on the accuracy and completeness of the sales job description; it depends also on management's appraisal of what reasonably may be expected of those who fill the position. Estimating the sales force turnover rate is a matter of reviewing previous experience and anticipating such changes as retirements and promotions. In addition, both the estimates for unit sales productivity and the sales force turnover rate require management to have some means of evaluating the efficiency of individual salespersons and of determining the probabilities that individuals will remain with or leave the sales force during the planning period.

The estimate for forecasted sales volume deserves special comment. In many situations, the magnitude of the sales forecast is itself influenced by the planned size of the sales force. Indeed, since it takes time to add significant numbers to the sales force, a realistic sales forecast must take into account the number of salespersons (or sales personnel units) expected to be at management's disposal during the planning period.

In a new and rapidly growing company, potential sales volume often depends chiefly on the number and ability of its sales staff. Management, actually, may derive the sales forecast by multiplying the estimated sales productivity of its average salesperson by the number it has, can expect to keep, and can recruit and train during the planning period. As a company expands distribution geographically and its growth rate slows down, the procedure reverses itself. Under these circumstances, the number of sales personnel units required is determined by making the sales forecast first, and dividing it by the expected sales productivity of an individual salesperson, making adjustments for anticipated sales force turnover, lead times for recruiting and training, and other relevant factors.

Incremental Method

Conceptually, the incremental method is the best approach to determining sales force size. It is based on one proposition: net profits will increase when additional sales personnel are added *if* the incremental sales revenues exceed the incremental costs incurred. Thus, to apply this method, one needs two important items of information: incremental revenue and incremental costs.

To illustrate, assume the following situation. A certain company has found that its total sales volume varies directly and significantly with the number of salespeople it has in the field. Its cost of goods sold does not vary significantly with increases in sales, but holds steady at 65 percent of sales. All company sales personnel receive a straight salary ($20,000 annually per person) and in addition are paid commissions of 5 percent on the sales volume they generate. In addition, each salesperson receives a travel and expense allowance of $12,000 per year, that is, $1,000 per month. The company now has fifteen people on its sales force and wants to determine whether it should add additional staff. Its sales executives estimate the following increases in sales volume, cost of goods sold, and gross margin that would result from the addition of the sixteenth, seventeenth, eighteenth, and nineteenth salespersons.

With the Addition of Salesperson No.	There Will Be Additional Sales Volume of	−	Cost of Goods Sold of	=	Gross Margin of
16	$250,000	−	$162,500	=	$87,500
17	200,000	−	130,000	=	70,000
18	150,000	−	97,500	=	52,500
19	100,000	−	65,000	=	35,000

With the Addition of Salesperson No.	Gross Margin of	−	(Sales Salaries of	+	Commissions of	+	Travel and Expense Allowances of)	=	Net Profit Contribution of
16	$87,500	−	($20,000	+	$12,500	+	12,000)	=	$43,000
17	70,000	−	(20,000	+	10,000	+	12,000)	=	28,000
18	52,500	−	(20,000	+	7,500	+	12,000)	=	13,000
19	35,000	−	(20,000	+	5,000	+	12,000)	=	(2,000)

Next, they calculate the *net profit contribution* resulting from the addition of each salesperson. Adding the eighteenth salesperson brings in an additional net profit contribution of $13,000, but adding the nineteenth salesperson produces a negative net profit contribution of $2,000. Thus, the optimal size of sales force here is eighteen people.

Although this method is the most conceptually correct, it is also the most difficult to apply. It requires, first, that the company develop a sales response function to use in approximating (in terms of sales volume) the market's behavior in relation to alternative levels of personal-selling effort. (A sales response function is a quantitative expression that describes the relationship between the amount of personal-selling effort and the resulting sales volume.) For the response function to be useful in setting the size of the sales force, sales volume must be sensitive to changes in the number of sales personnel.[5] Not many companies have the research sophistication required for development of sales response functions, but some apply the basic concept.[6] It is doubtful that the incremental method is appropriate where personal-selling is not the primary means of making sales, that is, in cases where other forms of promotion, such as advertising, have stronger influences on sales volume than does personal-selling effort. Two additional problems in applying this approach are noted by T. R. Wotruba: "It fails to account for possible competitive reactions as well as for the long-term 'investment' effect of personal-selling effort."[7]

INDIVIDUALIZING SELLING STRATEGIES TO CUSTOMERS

The acid test of the appropriateness of personal-selling strategy comes when particular salespeople interact with particular customers. From the composite of all such interactions evolves the company's achievement of its personal-selling objectives. Management makes its first key decision on personal-selling strategy when it determines the kind of salesperson needed. It makes its second key decision when it determines the size of the company sales force. But after these decisions are implemented—after the desired number of the desired kind of sales personnel have been recruited, trained, and assigned to the field—each salesperson must individualize his or her own dealings with each customer. The job, when boiled down to its essentials, is to influence customer behavior in ways that both benefit the customer and contribute to the achievement of the company's personal-selling objectives.

Regardless of whether the salesperson's major role is that of order getter or order taker and regardless of the "basic selling style," the extent of the salesperson's success depends on the outcome of interactions with the customers. Each time the salesperson comes into contact with a customer, the salesperson says certain things, does certain things, and behaves and reacts in certain ways to what the customer says and does. What the salesperson says and does and how the salesperson behaves and reacts to the customers' behavior should, and generally does, vary from one sales call to the next.

The nature of the variation in the salesperson's approach to each customer, of course, is a matter of selling skill. This skill is a function of both how good the

[5]On this point and for an interesting report on a research study utilizing this approach, see Z. V. Lambert, *Setting the Size for the Sales Force* (University Park: Pennsylvania State University Press, 1968), especially pp. 4–7.

[6]See, for example, C. D. Fogg and J. W. Rokos, "A Quantitative Method for Structuring a Profitable Sales Force," *Journal of Marketing*, 37, no. 3 (July 1973), pp. 8–17.

[7]T. R. Wotruba, *Sales Management* (New York: Holt, Rinehart and Winston, 1971), p. 171.

salesperson's preplanning of each sales call has been and performance on the call itself. In doing the preplanning, the skilled salesperson analyzes a great deal of information about the customer and the nature of its business. What are its key objectives and problems? Who in the customer's organization makes and influences buying decisions, and what are their aspirations, needs, motives, fears, anxieties, drives, and the like? What rival sales personnel from what companies compete for the account's orders, and what are they like?

After analyzing these and similar items of information, the skilled salesperson sets definite goals to accomplish on each call. Next, the skilled salesperson plots the selling strategy to use on each successive call in an effort to achieve these definite goals, that is, what the salesperson plans to do and when. Then the salesperson makes the scheduled sales calls. If all goes according to plan, the salesperson achieves the goals set for each call, and thus the salesperson contributes to the achievement of the company's overall personal-selling objectives.

While the individual members of the sales force ultimately determine the success or failure of the company's overall personal-selling strategy, sales management has the important responsibility for helping them develop and improve their selling skills. How effectively salespeople perform their assigned tasks, in other words, is closely related to sales management's effectiveness in providing them with instruction on sales techniques.

CONCLUSION

Personal-selling strategy involves the implementation of sales policies to achieve personal-selling objectives. Formulating personal-selling strategy requires analysis of competitive posture to determine the kind of salesperson needed and the size of the sales force. Personal-selling strategy ultimately must be individualized for each customer and prospect; each salesperson, in the final analysis, determines how and when to do what in the contact with each assigned customer. Management makes the key decisions on personal-selling strategy, but each salesperson determines (through the quality of job performance) the effectiveness of that strategy in achieving the company's overall personal-selling objectives.

Cases for Part I

CASE 1-1

Scripto, Inc.

The Role of Sales and Marketing in Promoting a New Product

Scripto's new Electra lighter had been highly successful in the early introductory stages in 1985, and management hoped to make it the leader in the disposable lighter market. The new owners of Scripto, Tokai Seiki Co. Ltd. of Yokohama, Japan, acquired the company in the fall of 1984 and set out to achieve market dominance in its areas of writing instruments and lighters in the American market.

Scripto had a history of cycles of success and failure in its markets. Current management wanted to determine the extent to which these ups and downs were characteristic of the market or the results of managerial inconsistency.

COMPANY BACKGROUND

Scripto was initially incorporated as the Atlantic Manufacturing Company in 1923 and adopted the Scripto name in 1946. The company originally produced only mechanical pencils but gradually expanded its product line to include, besides mechanical pencils, ballpoint pens, fiber-tip pens, ink, components for its pens (one of the few writing-instrument manufacturers to offer this), lighters, and even wide-angle camera lenses. In 1969, Scripto acquired the Butane Match Corporation of America. Notwithstanding foreign subsidiaries in Mexico, Canada, England, and Ireland, Scripto's Atlanta Division was its largest, most important operation, as well as being the company's headquarters. Scripto was the world's largest combined manufacturer of pens and lighters.

Until the late 1950s, Scripto was successful and profitable in the writing-instrument industry. However, owing to managerial shortcomings and ill-advised decisions on capital expenditures and new products at a time when heavy competition made such decisions crucial, the company began to slide downward. By 1964, Scripto's share of the writing-instrument market had declined to 10 percent from a high of 16 percent a few years earlier. At the same time, Scripto dropped from second to fifth place in sales volume.

After 1964, under new management, Scripto spent heavily to improve production facilities, diversified its investments, reorganized management person-

EXHIBIT 1 Net Sales and Net Income, 1962–1972

Year	Net Sales	Net Income
1972	$28,378,819	$ 239,467
1971	30,979,108	20,012
1970	31,928,975	(1,074,558)
1969	31,229,204	(1,183,335)
1968	30,914,857	(173,145)
1967	30,462,424	715,777
1966	33,494,076	1,149,324
1965	28,714,981	1,546,138
1964	25,237,265	801,748
1963	26,344,306	1,536,181
1962	25,750,279	1,705,889

SOURCE: *Moody's Industrials,* 1973.

nel and positions, and gave new emphasis to the marketing program. The result was a reversal of Scripto's slide, with sales increasing by 40 percent in two years, 1964 to 1966. However, the revival was short-lived, because, from 1968 through 1970, the company operated at an average annual loss of more that $800,000, with the losses of each of the last two years at well over $1 million. In 1971, Scripto again was profitable, earning just over $20,000 net income. Indication that the company's financial crisis was over came in 1972, when Scripto had a net income of $239,467 on net sales of $28,378,819. Exhibit 1 shows the net sales and net income figures for Scripto, Inc., for the eleven-year period 1962–1972.

WRITING-INSTRUMENT INDUSTRY

Although writing instruments were used in early Egyptian times, the most rapid developments took place in the twentieth century. During the first half of the century, the fountain pen was extremely popular. It was with the invention of the ballpoint pen in 1945, however, that the writing-instrument industry began its rise to the multimillion-dollar level ($281 million in 1971), with ballpoint pen sales alone totaling $160 million (1.3 billion units) in 1971. In late 1963, when the Japanese entered the American writing market with the 49-cent Pentel fiber-tip pen, American firms set out quickly to produce an equivalent product before the Japanese could secure a major share of the market. Despite a shorter writing life than the ballpoint pen, porous-tip pens rapidly achieved consumer acceptance. From 1965 to 1971, porous-tip pen sales soared from $15 million to $60.7 million and were expected to increase 20 percent per year for several years thereafter. Exhibit 2 shows dollar sales of the various types of writing instruments from 1951 to 1971, and Exhibit 3 shows the average price by product for the same period.

EXHIBIT 2 Manufacturers' Sales of Writing Instruments by Product, 1951–1971

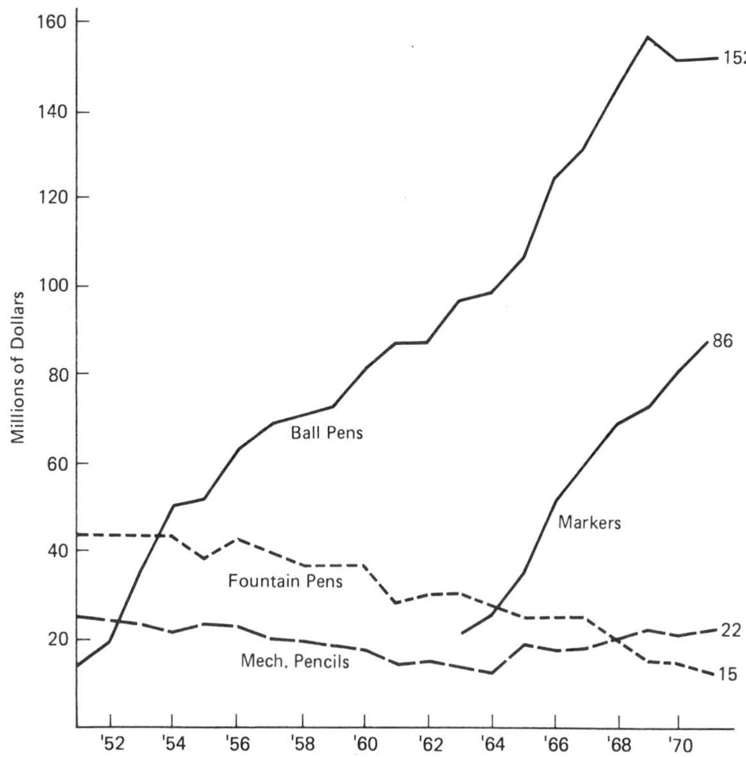

SOURCE: Writing Instruments Manufacturers Association

SOFT-TIP PEN MARKET

The number of soft-tip pen manufacturers had increased each year after 1963 until, by 1972, there were nearly forty such manufacturers. Gillette's Papermate Division dominated the market with its Flair pen through 1971, achieving 49 percent of the market sales. In early 1972, Scripto introduced its "19¢er" fiber-tip pen; in July, BIC introduced its Banana, and also in July, Papermate followed with its Write Brothers pen. Thus began the largest marketing and advertising war the porous-tip pen industry had yet experienced. Whereas the entire industry had spent only $2.7 million for advertising in 1971 (Flair accounted for $2 million of that total), Scripto spent nearly $750,000, BIC $3 million, and Papermate more than $1 million for Write Brothers during the first ten months of 1972 to promote the entry of low-priced porous-tip pens into the market.

All soft-tip pens were of similar appearance. The shaft and the cap of the pen were plastic and of the same color as the ink inside the pen (except for the

EXHIBIT 3 Average Price of Writing-Instrument Products, 1951–1971

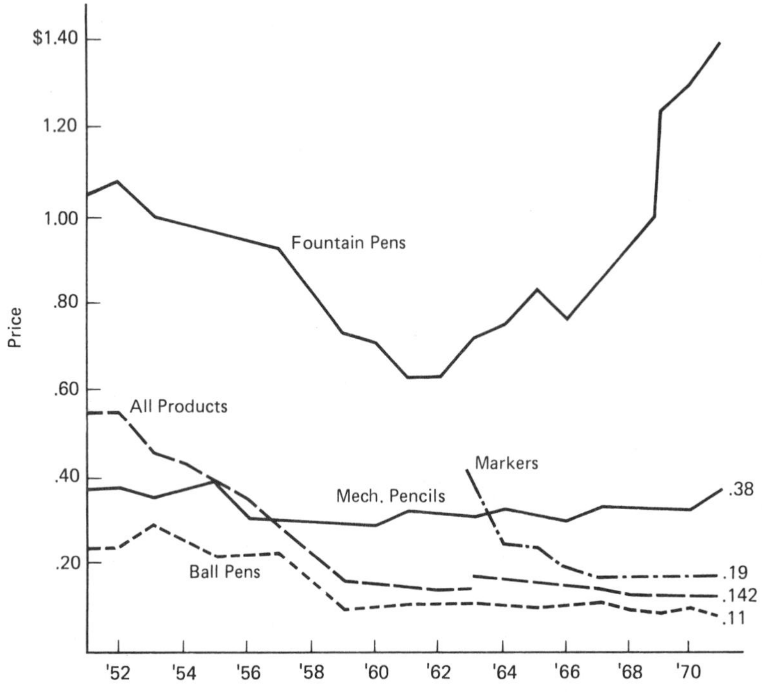

*All product lines adjusted in 1963 to include calculation for markers.
SOURCE: Writing Instruments Manufacturers Association.

BIC Banana, which had a yellow shaft). Scripto and Flair had twelve colors, while BIC and Write Brothers offered ten. Scripto's 19¢er was 30 cents cheaper than Flair's 49-cent retail price and 10 cents less than the BIC Banana and the Write Brothers markers.

The fiber-tip pen market consisted of two principal segments: students and various business usages. Advertising, which mainly appeared on network and spot television and also in newspapers and magazines, focused on these groups by emphasizing themes of individuality, distinction, and a pleasant experience from writing with porous-tip pens. Approximately 22 percent of annual writing-instrument sales occurred between mid-August and the end of September or during the back-to-school rush.

Scripto's Fiber-Tip Pens and Sales Strategy

Scripto first entered the fiber-tip market with the 49-cent Graffiti pen, which essentially was a "me-too" product. Other than the connotation of the name itself, the Graffiti had no single distinguishing feature. The trade was somewhat reluctant to accept it, because it meant carrying a product that lacked the selling power of the heavily advertised Flair. Graffiti's annual advertising budget was approximately $250,000. Scripto then began to search its resources for a porous-tip pen that would have greater appeal to the ultimate consumer, bolster the company's sagging writing-instrument business, and be profitable.

Consequently, in early 1971, Scripto started development of a fine-line marker that would equal Flair in quality, yet retail for considerably less. Within one year Scripto determined that it could produce large quantities of the new marker, sell it for 19 cents at retail, and still allow the standard margins for middlemen (10 percent for the wholesalers and 50 percent for the retailers), money to promote the product, and profit for the company. Scripto decided to adopt the same price and distribution strategy in marketing its new fiber-tip pen as Marcel L. Bich had so successfully applied when he introduced the BIC 19-cent stickpen in the late 1950s. Bich's successful application of this strategy had revolutionized the writing instrument industry and transformed the ballpoint pen from a luxury item (the average retail price in the late 1940s and early 1950s exceeded $1.00) to a utility item. His success was indisputable; in 1971, sales of BIC pens accounted for 65 percent of all retail pen sales and amounted to $39.5 million.

Scripto's philosophy behind the pricing strategy was to sell a quality pen for considerably less than the competition. It was believed that the low price would entice consumers to buy the pen if only to try it, and then the high quality of the pen would serve to secure repeat purchases from initial buyers. The rationale was that, after trying the 19¢er and realizing that it was a marker of quality equal to the higher-priced fiber-tips, yet at a much lower price, consumers would readily switch to the Scripto product. Therefore, by switching from a more expensive to a less costly pen, the consumer would lose nothing and save the difference between the purchase prices. Although the lower retail price meant less revenue per sale for the merchant and the manufacturer, the key to maintaining or increasing profits was to increase sales volume commensurately.

Distribution strategy was to introduce the product regionally rather than nationally, ensuring that orders, deliveries, advertising, and sales were well timed and coordinated and functioning smoothly in one region before moving to the next. By selling to general-line wholesalers who dealt with numerous retailers, the company could achieve extensive distribution throughout the region. As the product became established in the target regions and sales increased, the company could expand its advertising budget to foster greater product awareness among consumers and improve its production facilities to attain greater economies of scale. Management believed that, ultimately, these investments would stimulate sales even more.

As a result of successful test marketing in the Dallas–Fort Worth area, Scripto introduced the 19¢er in thirty-two major markets throughout the United States. Although the product never achieved market dominance, it helped to pull the company out of its financial crisis.

Relationship Between Sales and Marketing

In the past, Scripto had placed greatest emphasis on sales. This often resulted in the overall marketing plan being formed around the sales plan, with marketing relegated to a position of less significance than sales. For example, although budgetary restraints also were an important consideration, the company eliminated marketing research. From 1968 through 1970, the advertising program was greatly curtailed. In addition, there was no system of monthly sales forecasts to assist marketing planning and production scheduling efforts. To the extent that marketing plans were formulated, they were verbal, short range, and largely intuitive.

Since there was something of a preoccupation with sales at the expense of marketing, there was no marketing orientation, or systems concept, thinking uniting the various elements of the marketing mix into a coordinated program. Scripto management was determined to implement a conceptually sounder marketing program for the 19¢er and therefore was deeply concerned about the most effective relationship between sales and marketing.

After Scripto was acquired by Tokai Seiki, the management orientation shifted from sales to marketing. The parent company with sales of $170 million in 1984 was (with BIC) a major competitor in writing instruments and lighter markets. Scripto had been late in entering the disposable lighter market. In 1980 it had only 8 percent of that market, but by 1985 it sold 24 percent of the 500 million lighters sold nationally.

The new Electra lighter was introduced in 1985 with an advertising budget of $5 million, more than had been spent on lighter advertising during the previous six years. Stronger trade support was also planned with an expanded, better trained national sales organization and more promotional programs. This heavy promotional emphasis was felt to be justified by management because of the unique advantages of the new lighter, namely, a new electronic ignition system and a highly popular new design.

Does the announced new marketing orientation represent any real change from the company's historical sales orientation?

To what extent has the historical boom and bust performance of Scripto in its markets been the result of managerial mistakes or is it characteristic of the industries involved?

CASE 1-2

Sales and Marketing Executives of Greater Boston, Inc.

Sales and Marketing Management Association—Proposed Salesman-for-a-Day Program

The Executive Committee of Sales and Marketing Executives of Greater Boston, Inc., was considering a proposal under which students from several area colleges would each spend a day with SME-member company sales personnel to gain better insight into the world of selling. SME–Boston was a local chapter of SME–International, a worldwide association with about 30,000 members. SME–Boston had over 200 members, representing 190 companies.

Stuart Freeman, president of the Boston chapter, received the proposal for a "Salesman-for-a-Day" program from Tom Alden, a member of the marketing faculty at a local college. Several months previously Freeman and Alden had discussed together some of the problems in getting more college students interested in selling careers.

Alden mentioned that the majority of his students had no appreciation or feeling for selling simply because they had never done any. Also, it was his opinion that, among many college students, selling was considered a low-prestige job. As a result, he reasoned, many qualified graduates never even consider a career in selling. Alden then set about to develop a program through which college students could at least become familiar with the life of a personal salesman and gain some understanding of what selling is about. The result was his proposal, entitled "Salesman-for-a-Day," which he submitted to Freeman in the hope that the Boston SME chapter would consider it.

Under Alden's plan, sales executives of the various Boston SME-member companies would be contacted by mail, using SME-letterhead stationery, and asked to participate by identifying one or more salespeople who would agree to have a college student accompany them on their calls for a day. The salespeople then would be mailed a form on which they were to indicate the date, time, and place of meeting with the student. A student would be selected and his or her name forwarded to the participating salesman (which also served as confirmation that the plan was still on). Every effort would be made to assign a student to a salesman who sold a product or service of interest to the student. Finally, the student would meet the salesman and accompany him for the entire day. It was envisioned that the whole procedure, from contacting the sales executive to notifying the salesman of the name of the student and confirming the date, time, and place of meeting, would take no more than two weeks. If done at the beginning of the semester, ample time was guaranteed to arrange a time convenient to both the salespeople and the students.

While the initial program was to be strictly voluntary, Alden felt that each student should complete a questionnaire indicating the value of the salesman-for-a-day program to determine whether the program should be continued. Alden also foresaw the day when the salesman-for-a-day program would be made into a requirement for the selling and sales management courses that he taught. Further, he also had the idea that he could run a parallel sales executive-for-a-day program, if the proposed program met with success.

Alden was enthusiastic as to the possibilities of his salesman-for-a-day plan. Freeman shared that enthusiasm, especially since he had been searching for innovative programs to be pursued by the Education Committee. He believed this was a "natural" for that committee, and he agreed to present the proposal, with one amendment, to the Executive Committee for possible adoption. The amendment was that three of the participating people, a sales manager, a salesperson, and a student, would be invited to one of the regular monthly SME dinner meetings to discuss the results of the salesman-for-a-day program with the membership.

Should the Boston SME chapter have adopted the proposal? Why or why not?

CASE 1-3

Phillips Company

Manufacturer of Steam Power Plants— The Role of the Sales Force in the Company Image

Sam McDonald, vice-president of sales of the Phillips Company, was concerned with the potential role of his sales force in correcting his company's image in the electric utility industry. The Phillips Company, one of the leading manufacturers of steam power plants in the United States, was located in Philadelphia. The company was started by Aaron Phillips, who began manufacturing small steam engines in Philadelphia in 1846. Currently the company had annual sales in excess of $200 million and sold power plants to industrial users throughout the world. McDonald was concerned because public utilities, important users of steam power equipment, only accounted for 12 to 15 percent of Phillips' sales. Some utilities were good customers, but many other major utilities never bought from the company at all. Concerned with whether this low acceptance was a result of a poor image of steam power plants as a power alternative or a poor image of the Phillips Company as a source of steam power plants, McDonald suggested to top management that they explore the buying attitudes and motivation of electric utility companies as completely as possible. To remove the risk of personal bias, an outside research agency was called in to conduct the survey.

The research agency set out to find out what customers and potential customers really thought of the Phillips Company. Depth interviews were carried out with influential buying personnel in a selected sample of all electric utilities. The results that were presented to the executive committee in September were not too pleasant to hear. In general, Phillips' engineering skills were rated highly; product quality and workmanship were considered good. However, a number of respondents thought of Phillips as a completely static company. They were completely unaware of Phillips' excellent research operations and many new product developments.

The research organization pointed out other useful information about the Phillips Company and its market. Sales were normally personnel related; that is, personal relationships and personalities were important in the buying decision. The buying responsibility was widely dispersed for products sold by Phillips. As many as forty people, ranging from the president down, might be involved in a purchase. Many Phillips salespeople were not too well informed about the details of new product developments and would probably need additional training to be able to answer technical questions.

It was obvious to McDonald that Phillips' communications methods had failed completely to keep potential utility customers aware of changes taking place in the company and its products. Some method had to be devised to break down the communications barrier and sell Phillips products. At this point a disagreement developed between the advertising and sales departments as to how to go about changing the image. Representatives of the advertising department came up with two possible approaches that could be used separately or jointly. First, they might advertise in mass media to get across the Phillips story. Second, they could launch an intensive publicity campaign, blanketing all news media and particularly utilities trade media with information and press releases. McDonald's suggested approach started with a complete upgrading of information to the sales force about new-product developments and current research. Then, the sales staff could make presentations directly to prospects in the field. Flipcharts and visual aids could be used where appropriate. Alternatively, the company could try to schedule educational meetings for key electric utility personnel. This would require a traveling symposium, staffed by top personnel and equipped with audiovisual aids, that could spend several hours with groups of employees in selected utilities across the country.

What action should the Phillips Company have taken to change the company image in the public utility field?

CASE 1-4

Plastics Industries, Inc.

Manufacturer of Plastic Pipe—The Role of Personal Selling in Creating a Market

Management of Plastics Industries, Inc., was faced with the problem of promoting a new product to the market. The company had been organized in Beaumont, Texas, to manufacture pipe. It was founded by a group of wealthy individuals from the community, and total capitalization had been set with the expectation of four years of operation at a loss. By the second half of the third year of operation, the company had made a profit, and the room for future growth looked very promising. Nevertheless, management believed that sales were not increasing as rapidly as might be expected in light of the clear strengths of the product.

Plastics Industries manufactured plastic pipe by the extrusion process. Its manufacturing plant was located on the outskirts of Beaumont. The major capital investment consisted of an extruder, designed and specially built for the company in Germany at a cost of $250,000. The extruder was almost completely automated, so that only minimal training was needed to operate it. A staff of two engineers was maintained to service the machine. Polypropylene, available from major chemical companies, was used as the raw material, and it was available in a pellet form ready for manufacture. The finished pipe was called Plylene pipe.

The number of manufacturers of plastic pipe in the United States was small but growing. Several major companies, such as Dupont, Shell, and Hercules, were manufacturing or had manufactured plastic pipe. Dupont, a major supplier of the raw materials, had produced a plastic pipe under the Delrin brand name but recently had ceased manufacture of pipe and was buying Plylene pipe from Plastics Industries. The use of plastic pipe as a replacement for other types of pipe was a relatively new development. A first major product was polyethylene pipe, which was first introduced on the market as a nonpressure pipe suitable for mine-drainage operations. The chemical resistance of polyethylene made it a natural for this application; lack of resistance to acid mine waters had caused major corrosion problems with the steel pipe formerly used. Since that successful first, the polyethylene and, subsequently, polypropylene pipe industry had grown at a rapid rate. Some of the major oil companies began manufacturing plastic pipe for use in their fields. However, Plastics Industries quickly became a major supplier in this industry and soon was supplying twelve major oil companies.

Mr. Galloway, president of Plastics Industries, Inc., believed that the greatest single problem for the company, as well as for other makers of plastic pipe, was the setting of standards of quality. A number of laboratories were available for product performance testing. Galloway had made use of the services of the Battelle Memorial Institute in Columbus, Ohio, a leading researcher in the field of thermal polymers, to test samples of its product. But, until specific performance standards were established, no industry enforcement of quality levels was possible. Certain grades of Plastics Industries' pipe had been tested and accepted by the Food and Drug Administration and the Department of Commerce.

Plastics Industries maintained a sales force of three sales engineers, plus one factory representative to sell to major industrial users. These personnel were located in Odessa, Texas; Houston, Texas; and Tulsa, Oklahoma—all major oil-producing centers; they had concentrated their efforts almost exclusively on the oil industry. All orders were shipped directly from the factory, but the very high shipping costs indicated the need for distribution and warehousing points in the near future.

In the opinion of Galloway, the really big market for plastic pipe was in the home construction industry. He believed that this market was potentially at least five times as large as the present market, but so far neither the users nor middlemen were interested in the product. The image of plastic pipe was of a product that would easily break and, therefore, would not last as long as conventional pipe. The lack of quality standards in the industry had done nothing to improve the image. In addition, the building codes in most cities would have to be completely rewritten to permit the use of plastic pipe as a substitute for metal or other materials. Furthermore, middlemen and users required instruction in installation of plastic pipe. It was not a difficult process—sections were welded together with heat but the methods of cutting and welding needed to be explained to prospective users and distributors.

Galloway felt that a possible solution to the problem of selling the home construction market lay in advertising to the general public and to builders. He realized that Plastics Industries was too small to advertise in many major media, but to some extent they could benefit from the advertising of their major suppliers of raw material in trade magazines. He planned to reach the general public and builders through cooperative advertising on a shared-cost basis by suppliers. He was unsure as to the role of the sales force in pursuing this new market.

What should be the role of personal selling for a product such as this?

What kind or kinds of promotions would probably have been most productive for Plastics Industries?

Should the company go after the home construction market?

Would the job of the salesperson be changed if entry is made into the home construction market?

CASE 1-5

Benson's, Inc., Old Home Kitchens Division

Manufacturer of Fruit Cakes—Need for Marketing Research

The Five-Year Plan for changing the marketing program of Old Home Kitchens Division of Benson's, Inc., was completing its fourth year of implementation. The plan was introduced in an attempt to counteract recent declining profit margins on sales of Old Home Kitchens products, the largest volume of which was accounted for by the Old Home Fruit Cake. Basic to this marketing plan was a reevaluation of the company's distribution policy and redefining of the actual "business" that Old Home Kitchens was in. Management had decided that distribution would be effected exclusively through clubs and nonprofit organizations; in turn, this decision led to redefining the business, not as the fruit cake business, but as the fund-raising business. Together, these two reevaluations called for a third, an accurate description of the market. This task proved to be quite extensive in implications and formidable in approach.

COMPANY BACKGROUND

About fifty years ago, W. Howard Benson and his father opened the first Benson's Bakery in Athens, Georgia, with a product line consisting of bread, rolls, and cakes. The enterprise grew and expanded to include several regional bakeries in towns approximately the same size as Athens. From the very beginning, the Benson name was associated with high quality and personal attention of the owners. Never was Benson's far from the people it served. During the rationing days of World War II, Howard Benson gave away thousands of loaves of bread to hungry people. This generosity had always been evident in many aspects of the company, as recently exemplified by the student program at Old Home Kitchens, where students were allowed college credit for working as telephone salespeople.

Practically everything else about Benson's had changed, however. No longer a small regional bakery, the company had diversified into three main divisions: the Holsum Bakery, which baked and distributed Holsum bread and related products; Motel Enterprises, which owned and operated a Holiday Inn in Athens; and the Old Home Kitchens. The entire business was owned by the Benson family, with H. E. Benson, the son of Howard Benson, as the president.

OLD HOME FRUIT CAKE

Twenty years ago, Benson's introduced its Old Home Fruit Cake to civic clubs. The cake was loaf shaped, had the added distinction of being "presliced," and carried the *Good Housekeeping* Seal of Approval. The fruit cake was also sold through supermarkets, but fund-raising proved more profitable. The product line currently included three sizes of Old Home Fruit Cake, each consisting of 75 percent choice fruits and nuts and 25 percent pound cake batter, and a new Pecan Buttercake. It also included other taste tempters, such as candies, cookies, pound cake, and pecans. Still the Old Home Fruit Cake had continually been the overwhelming bestseller.

OLD HOME KITCHENS ORGANIZATION

J. B. Smith, executive vice-president of Benson's, Inc., was also general manager of the Old Home Kitchens Division. B. J. Stoll was marketing manager, and there were two sales managers. Old Home Kitchens was further divided into four areas: production (facilities located in Bogart, Georgia), distribution, commercial, and fund-raising. The commercial division packaged fruit cake under private brands for such independent distributors as Stuckey's, Pet Milk, and Charles Chips. The philosophy regarding private brands was that if Old Home Fruit Cake was to continue selling as well as it had, the image of "fruit cake" must be kept high. However, fund-raising accounted for 90 percent of the previous year's sales of somewhat over $5 million.

The Club Plan

Any nonprofit organization with a need to raise money could order the desired number of case lots (no individual cakes were sold). The cakes were then shipped prepaid and final payment was not due until December 31 of that year. (Benson's busiest season was just prior to Thanksgiving.) The Company sold direct to the organization and charged a flat rate so that when the products were sold at the suggested retail price, the organization could make a specified profit. An attractive brochure was available fully explaining the club plan to organizations making inquiries.

Competition

Fund-raising competition, like the fund-raising market, was difficult to pinpoint. The other large fruit cake producer was Claxton Fruit Cake Company of Claxton, Georgia, which sold its fruit cake exclusively through the Civitan Clubs. Benson felt that it had certain distinct advantages over Claxton: a better product, the added convenience of "pre-slicing," and a more aggressive sales strategy. Three years ago, Benson's surpassed Claxton in sales and became the number one producer of fruit cake. Other competition came from such projects as the sale of candy, cookies, light bulbs, and brooms. Stoll estimated that Benson's had 10,000 customers, 5,000 "dropouts" (those who had previously bought from Benson but for some reason had not continued to do so), and 40,000 inquiries (those writing for information about the club plan).

Advertising and Promotion

Tucker-Wayne Advertising Agency of New York had recently contracted with Benson's to promote the Old Home products. Previously, the account had been handled by the Lowe-Stevens Agency for several years and Stoll felt that it was time for a change. Coupon ads appeared in the September editions of a number of major publications, such as *U.S. News & World Report, TV Guide*, and *Better Homes and Gardens*, and most club magazines, such as the *Lion* and *Kiwanian*. Experience had shown that television was ineffective as an advertising medium, and no use was made of that medium. However, direct mail was an important part of the promotion campaign—over 750,000 pieces of mail were sent out in August to elicit inquiries from organizations (*not* individuals). Other promotions included printed materials, brochures, display posters, sales kits, advertising mats, and sample slices. Sample slices were mailed to each inquirer (over 40,000) and were included with orders. Also included with orders of more than sixteen cases of fruit cake were "Bonus Cakes," free Mainsellers that the club could sell to help pay freight charges. The yearly budget for advertising and promotion was $100,000.

REEVALUATION OF MARKETING STRATEGY

Until five years ago, Benson's marketed Old Home products through a sales force of about sixty college students employed during summer vacations. After a week's training, the students were assigned territories with coverage in the forty-eight contiguous states. Each student had the use of a company car and had an allowance for expenses. They contacted old accounts and new prospects, took orders, and made weekly call reports. Contacts were followed up by direct mail. Sales personnel were paid a salary and year-end bonuses.

Stoll, who came to Benson's as sales manager for Old Home Kitchens, had some previous experience in telephone selling and considerable experience in direct sales and the use of a part-time sales force. He implemented a research program that led to the adoption of an innovative plan called Phone Power. This plan consisted primarily of the installation of six WATS lines at the headquarters to be used for two months each. To gain complete coverage of the continental

United States, the lines were chosen as follows: one Georgia line, two for Area Three, two for Area Four, and one for Area Six. Browning Adair, sales manager in charge of Phone Power, installed by special legal permit a "monitor" by which he could listen in on the interviews, the purpose of which was to protect the customer as well as the interviewer and Benson's, and also to regulate and improve the content of the interview. A special line was run from Athens to Bogart so that touch-tone phones could be used, as it was known that they were 25 percent more efficient than regular dialing.

Phone Power required twelve part-time sales employees who worked in two shifts so that customers could be contacted at their own convenience and according to their respective time zones. These part-time salespeople were given a three-day sales training program and assigned territories. They were rated on a standard of performance, with interview completions averaging three per hour.

Obvious advantages of Phone Power over former sales methods were better regulated interviews and less time wasted in traveling and making second calls. Some orders were smaller than those generated by sales representatives, and certain types of calls were more difficult to conduct (such as "cold calls"), but the phones made it easier to contact customers to "feel out" inquiries, and interviewers were not forced to make immediate decisions concerning company policy about which they were not totally familiar. A special arrangement was worked out with the University of Georgia whereby students could receive five hours of college credit for telephone selling.

Along with Phone Power, the independent-agent program was introduced. The number of sales managers was reduced from five to two, one of whom was sent out on a Five-Year Plan to recruit agents, both full-time and part-time, to represent Old Home products in selected metropolitan areas. In its fourth year this plan was right on target, with forty-five agents throughout the United States. Phone Power supplemented the areas where there were no assigned agents. The agent program was motivated by the philosophy that local people were more successful in such an emotional selling atmosphere as club selling. They knew personally the people and organizations with whom they were dealing (Benson's actually leaned toward retired and semiretired personnel, to take full advantage of this acquaintance), and thus would be more likely to sway opinion toward a given project. Concentration of agents was according to population; for example, there were three agents in Los Angeles and its surrounding area but only one for the state of Virginia. The agents worked on a given percentage commission up to their quotas, then 10 percent on the next 10 percent of the basic quota amount, and 20 percent above that. They were also given their samples and selling tools. Grading was according to a standard of performance—that is, they made a certain number of contacts and reports to the company—but otherwise they were independent of Benson's Inc.

Both these projects had proved profitable in recent years, profits had increased along with sales, and the unfavorable growth trends had been corrected.

PROBLEM OF IDENTIFYING THE TARGET MARKET

The management at Old Home Kitchens was interested in knowing whether these trends were as promising as they seemed. So far, their clientele had conveniently been classified on the basis of "nonprofit" organizations. Surveys showed that 80 percent of families in the United States purchased fruit cake sometime during the year and that 75 percent of these did so before Thanksgiving. However, management did not have access to reliable data concerning the fund-raising market. There were many differences among the nonprofit organizations: degree of organization, whether structured or loosely bound: reasons for wanting to raise money; whether a one-time project or a continuous need; duration or stability of membership; life and purpose of the organization. Stoll wanted, among other things, some sort of demographic profile of the type of person who would most likely be a member of such a group so that he could predict future sales, determine the division's share of the market, and measure its competition. In other words, was the division's present level of 10,000 customers a high market penetration, or was the division at a low penetration with a potential of considerably more customers?

Tucker-Wayne Agency had talked at some length with Stoll about providing a research program to gather the needed information. Benson's had the alternative, of course, of trying its own hand at the effort. Previous company research, conducted primarily from a product-oriented viewpoint, had been of the survey type, with mail questionnaires. Stoll had tried various types and found that mail was just as effective for his purposes and much cheaper; therefore, Old Home Kitchens used it exclusively. There were also many national research centers that maintained indexes of consumer behavior and that were highly reputable in the field of market research. However, Stoll felt that the nature of the needed information warranted extensive personal attention. He believed that the advertising agency would serve best in this respect. The scope of the needed research was so great that the agency would have to contract out certain aspects. Actual plans had not been formulated, but the initial efforts would probably be carried out by means of a seminar-type question-and-answer program with participants consisting of a random sampling of the population—both club members and nonclub members. Stoll knew that the future of the division's business depended upon the information that he would receive from this research, and therefore he was willing to spend a considerable sum for it. He intended to implement the program within the next year.

Should the Old Home Kitchens Division of Benson's, Inc., have undertaken a marketing research program? If so, who should have done the research? What role should the sales personnel have played in the research?

Develop an outline for the marketing research. If you feel that there is no need for marketing research, state your reasons.

CASE 1-6

Scientific-Atlanta, Inc.

Manufacturer of Electronic Equipment—Decision on Adding a New Product by Acquisition

Top management of Scientific-Atlanta, Inc., was faced with a decision concerning whether or not to purchase from Spencer Kennedy Laboratories the design of a new two-way amplifier used in the Community Antenna Television (CATV) industry. Spencer Kennedy wanted to sell its amplifiers because of a lack of business caused by a Federal Communications Commission (FCC) freeze on new cable system construction. Scientific-Atlanta, Inc.'s management felt that purchasing the amplifiers would promise an expanded role in the CATV industry as well as help to make up for lost business resulting from a decrease in the military market, upon which the company was heavily dependent.

Scientific-Atlanta, Inc., was started in the 1950s by a group of engineers from Georgia Tech's research facility. Through diversification and innovative research and development, the firm grew to be a world leader in its branch of electronics, enjoying an outstanding reputation for its products and services. The company began by developing and producing high frequency antennas for military applications, such as rapid-scanning radar antennas. Eventually, Scientific-Atlanta developed products such as an electronic instrument capable of automatically measuring and recording signal patterns transmitted from high-frequency antennas, earth terminals, surveillance receivers, and manual and "slaved" satellite and missile-tracking systems.

For the CATV industry, Scientific-Atlanta, Inc., manufactured a microwave relay system and a full line of "head-end" equipment, which consisted of high-technology items such as a log-periodic antenna, a VHF preamplifier, a superheterodyne signal processor, and a solid-state demodulator. Head-end equipment was critical to the entire cable network, since it was here that the signal quality was either improved or degraded by preamplifiers, amplifiers, and other electronic devices filtering and preparing signals for the cable network. The head-end equipment cleaned up the signal by processing it, translated the frequency of the signal, and amplified the signal to a predetermined level going out of the head end. Scientific-Atlanta had about 30 percent of the head-end market.

The FCC freeze on new cable system construction prohibited further expansion in the top 100 television markets. Cable television systems were initiated in local areas where television reception was either poor or nonexistent. As long as CATV was limited to areas that could not otherwise get a good television signal, the broadcasters and the FCC were happy. However, with the proliferation of cable systems came greater pressure to expand into the cities, where 87 percent of the television sets were located. To enlist subscribers in areas where television reception was good, cable operators had to provide something new to differentiate the service. For example, differentiating features took the form of news and weather reports, the stock market tickertape, and time and temperature reports. Another extra provided was a channel from a distant metropolitan area: but when this feature was offered, the broadcasters and the FCC expressed concern. Ultimately, the FCC decided that the CATV industry required regulation, and the agency adopted rules that essentially prohibited any further expansion in the top one hundred television markets, but that left the remote areas open for continued development.

During the freeze, considerable thought and study went into the future potential of cable communications. For example, the Stanford Research Institute studied the economics of cable systems and developed projections on return on investment. The Sloan Commission investigated the impact of cable systems on American life. It was generally felt by industry experts that if the FCC permitted cable into the cities, the cable system would have to have capability for two-way communications, which required new technology. For example, the line amplifiers had to amplify in both directions, which meant additional electronics in the home. These technical problems were being solved. Scientific-Atlanta was in the process of developing a digital control center for a two-way system and planned to have it ready for the next National Cable Television Association trade show. The new amplifier offered for sale by Spencer Kennedy Labs was a two-way design. During the freeze, many of the applications for future systems were based on the capability for two-way communications, such as that required for pay television, polling, interactive educational programs, and burglar and fire alarms.

All in all, the horizons for CATV seemed promising. Scientific-Atlanta's management believed that to have a greater role in the CATV industry it was necessary to become a full-line supplier, which would be possible with the purchase of the Spencer Kennedy design. Although there were already over 5 million subscribers to cable television in more than 4,000 communities served by about 2,800 cable operators, it was estimated that there was considerable untapped potential. Becoming a full-line equipment supplier would throw Scientific-Atlanta, Inc., into direct competition with full-line suppliers such as Jerrold (which had 50 percent of the market), Theta-Com (20 percent), Anaconda, Sylvania, AEL, C-Cor, and Tocom.

The management of Scientific-Atlanta reasoned that a decision to purchase the new design would affect the company in three major ways: (1) the company would become a full-line supplier; (2) it would mean competing with companies that were formerly customers; and (3) being a full-line supplier would mean orders in the millions instead of orders in the thousands, thus tending to restrict the potential customers to cable system operators.

Management further believed that the financial aspects of the purchase would not be overly burdensome. In order to determine an appropriate price for the Spencer Kennedy design, a study was made to determine the cost of developing an amplifier from scratch. It was felt that the purchase of the new design would buy about one year's development time.

Should Scientific-Atlanta, Inc., have purchased the new two-way amplifier from Spencer Kennedy Laboratories? Justify your position.

What are the dangers of being overly dependent on one customer, such as the federal government? Are there any advantages?

CASE 1-7

Rebel Mills

Textiles Manufacturer—Reevaluation of the Product Line

The management of Bulldog Mills was concerned about a three-year sales decline of one of the products of one of its divisions. Bulldog Mills was a medium-sized manufacturer of textiles, with annual sales of over $98 million and with headquarters in Vicksburg, Mississippi. A Bulldog division, Rebel Mills, showed kitchen towel sales of $6 million for the previous year; however, it was the third consecutive year that Rebel's sales had declined. In addition, costs had increased to a level of $5.8 million, leaving a profit margin of $200,000, the company's lowest in twelve years.

Rebel Mills, located in Yazoo City, Mississippi, manufactured a limited line of textile products for household uses. For the household textiles market, Rebel Mills produced only kitchen textiles, with other divisions of Bulldog Mills producing bathroom and bedroom textiles. And, within the kitchen-textiles product line, which consisted of kitchen towels, dishcloths, and tablecloths, Rebel Mills made only kitchen towels. Also, no other division made the other two products in the kitchen-textiles line.

Rebel Mills' kitchen towels were distributed nationwide by a sales organization of nineteen sales representatives through a network of wholesalers and retailers. There were eight company salespeople, seven of whom operated out of New York City and who had responsibility for the Northeastern United States, as well as all major department store chain accounts regardless of the location of the chain's home office. The other company salesperson specialized in selling to grocery chains, in addition to monitoring the performance of four food brokers who also sold the Rebel Mills line. All company sales personnel received a salary plus a commission based upon a quota.

The four food brokers representing Rebel Mills sold to regional grocery chains located in different geographical areas of the United States. They received a 3 percent commission of all sales.

Besides the company sales staff and food brokers, Rebel Mills used seven manufacturers' agents who handled noncompeting lines of textile products. They received a 3 percent commission on all sales of Rebel Mills products.

For the past five years, Rebel Mills had manufactured private-label kitchen towels for four large department store chains, including the Harmony House brand for Sears, Roebuck and Co. Each of the private labels was manufactured to the buyer's specifications. The result was that five different weaves, including its own Rebel Mills brand, required varying amounts of yarn and machine time, thereby making it very difficult for efficient scheduling of machinery. Rebel Mills' cost of producing private labels was greater than had been anticipated and, coupled with heavy price competition for the business, was partly responsible for the steadily declining profit margin. At the same time, management was reluctant to abandon the private-label business, since it accounted for nearly 40 percent of Rebel's total kitchen towel sales. Sixty percent of Rebel Mills' business was done through company-directed channels.

Rebel Mills did a modest amount of advertising for its own brand. The company typically spent less than 2 percent of sales on advertising, with the previous year's expenditure amounting to $60,000. The entire amount was allocated to *Good Housekeeping* magazine for the sole reason of obtaining that publication's Seal of Approval. It was believed that displaying the Seal of Approval with Rebel Mills kitchen towels provided good point-of-purchase promotion.

Recent developments concerning its own brand of kitchen towels caused great alarm for Rebel Mills' management. During the past two years, a large number of accounts had been lost, and it was becoming increasingly difficult to obtain new accounts. Furthermore, there was growing customer dissatisfaction with Rebel Mills products. The sales staff strongly believed that these difficulties stemmed from the fact that Rebel Mills sold only kitchen towels and most customers, especially the volume buyers, preferred to purchase at least a complete line of kitchen textiles and, even more desirably, a complete line of household textiles, from a single manufacturer.

As a result, the sales force recommended that Rebel Mills begin as soon as possible to manufacture a complete line of kitchen textiles, to include kitchen towels, dishcloths, and tablecloths. The sales force further recommended that when it became financially feasible, Rebel Mills should also produce a complete line of bathroom and bedroom textiles to round out its household textiles offering.

Added to these difficulties, three other interrelated factors contributed to Rebel Mills' competitive disadvantage: (1) of the three main groups of household textiles, kitchen textiles provided the lowest profit margin, with kitchen towels allowing the smallest margin in its category; (2) the greater sales volume of the larger manufacturers enabled them to realize economies of scale; and (3) the combination of the first two factors led the larger manufacturers to lower the price of the kitchen-textiles product line to induce volume buyers to purchase the higher-margin bathroom and bedroom textiles. Cannon Mills, the industry leader, for example, followed this strategy.

It was in this setting that the management of Rebel Mills decided to evaluate fully the prospects of its kitchen-towel product line. It was generally agreed that some action had to be taken soon.

What alternatives were available to Rebel Mills' management with respect to its kitchen-towel product line? Evaluate each alternative, suggesting and defending that which you believe represented the best course of action for Rebel Mills.

CASE 1-8

United Airflow, Inc.

Manufacturer of Household Appliances—Salesperson's Job

United Airflow, Inc., was a manufacturer of air conditioners, dehumidifiers, humidifiers, vaporizers, and a variety of other small household appliances. The United sales force consisted of 200 people, accounting for about $125 million net sales volume annually. Thomas Rogers had been a salesperson for United Airflow for eight years, calling on department stores, discount houses, appliance stores, and hardware stores. His territory consisted of the western half of Ohio and southern Michigan. Rogers had been one of the leading salespeople for United Airflow over the past three years, ranking tenth among the entire sales force in sales volume. However, despite favorable business conditions in his territory, Rogers' performance had fallen off, with a current ranking of thirtieth in the sales force.

The branch sales manager in Toledo, the office from which Rogers worked, had a conference with Rogers to try to uncover the reasons for the sales decline. The sales manager believed that a first step should be to compare Rogers's daily call reports with the job description of a United Airflow salesperson.

Following is the "Specific Duties and Responsibilities" section of the job description for a United Airflow salesperson:

A. Present and potential customers
   1. Achieve sales volume goals as determined in cooperation with sales manager.
   2. Improve dealers' merchandising methods.
   3. Call on dealers regularly.
   4. Introduce new products by discussing with dealers the new products' selling features, new policies, and new campaigns as they apply to the new products.
   5. Explain United's advertising and promotion plans and assist dealers in carrying out local advertising programs, and make sure that all dealers are aware of current United Airflow advertising.
   6. Provide assistance in inventory control.
   7. Assist dealers in training salespeople, setting up point-of-purchase displays, solving retail management problems, and provide any other assistance deemed essential for the maintenance of a long-term relationship with customers.
   8. Provide feedback of information relating to market trends, demand preferences, dealer suggestions, competitive strategies, and all other information thought to be valuable for the preservation of the United sales operation.
   9. Handle complaints with an absolute minimum of delay and make sure there is a fair settlement.
   10. Secure new dealers by making a market analysis as suggested on the Potential New Dealer form, including selection of towns in which there is no dealer for United products, observation of competition, selection of most desirable dealer prospect, and presentation of the United Airflow sales program.

B. Contact architects, appliance dealers and installers, contractors, and subcontractors and sell them United products, or sell them on specifying United equipment for installation in new buildings and new homes. Keep these persons informed of new developments in the United Airflow line.

C. Keep abreast of competitive practices and dealers handling competing products by checking resale practices, sales plans, advertising, and new products.

D. Prepare all reports and correspondence promptly so as to maintain their timeliness.

E. Make effective utilization of time, being sure to take advantage of every opportunity which will help to sharpen sales skills and develop better all-around selling ability.

Following are Rogers' daily call reports for a typical week during the past several months:

Monday

Call 1. Nicholson Department Store. United customer. Took order for five Model 78 G9 small vaporizers.

Call 2. Drummond's Discount Variety. First call on prospective dealer. Interested in carrying toasters and radios. Call back later.

Call 3. Patton and Swain, Architects. Second call. Tried to interest them in United products. Not interested.

Call 4. Hicks Hardware. First call. Tried to interest in our complete line. Possible interest in smallest air-conditioning unit. Call back later.

Call 5. Klein and Sons. Department store. Buyer unavailable.

Call 6. Poindexter Construction Co. Home builder. Completely unapproachable the moment I mentioned United Airflow. Could not get reason.

Call 7. Tufts Hardware. First call. Happy with present line of small appliances and does not want to take on an additional line.

Call 8. Ames and Wade. Discount store. Sales poor in United dehumidifiers and humidifiers, but okay in air conditioning. Thinking of dropping the poor sellers and concentrating on better selling competitors. Will let me know next trip.

Tuesday

Call 1. Sawyer Construction Co. Developers. Tried to interest in air conditioners for apartment building complex. Appeared interested, but said to contact the architect.

Call 2. Hennessy Appliance Outlet. Regular customer. Needed help with a new point-of-purchase display. Couldn't oblige because of delay in getting the materials from the Promotion Department. Upset, but placed normal monthly order.

Call 3. Feinberg's, Inc., department store. Regular customer. Business slow, but expect it to get better.

Call 4. Herb's Hardware. Regular customer. Sales call interrupted when a long-lost pal of Herb's appeared on the scene.

Call 5. Skinner's Discount. Regular customer. Overstocked at present.

Call 6. Glick and Sons, department store. Regular customer. Took big order. Sales good. Complained about lack of advertising support by United.

Call 7. Cambridge Appliances. First call. Buyer too busy. Call back later.

Call 8. Franklin Hardware. First call. Has nothing in this product line, but is expanding store and seems interested in carrying these products. Has been contacted by two competitors. Will call back.

Call 9. Horwitz, Inc. Regular customer. Buyer out all week.

Call 10. Drucker and Hayes. Regular customer. Small order for vaporizers.

Wednesday

Call 1. Bosco and Baron. Large department store. Regular customer. Carries most complete offering of anyone in territory. Reviewed advantages of United Airflow products.

Call 2. Page's Bargainland. First call. Is in process of eliminating slow movers and not interested in taking on any new brands.

Call 3. Alberts and Machen. Architects for Sawyer Construction Co. Already placed order with competitor for 300 air-conditioning units for Sawyer's new apartments. Expressed little interest for future orders.

Call 4. Callahan's. First call. New discount store in Northeast Mall. Will consider. Call back later.

Call 5. Kirshner Associates. Shopping center developer. Has plans for new center. Call back later.

Call 6. Frost Brothers Appliances. Store closed. Reason unknown.

Call 7. Gridiron State University. First call. Done business with competitor for years and happy.

Thursday

Call 1. Thompson's Hardware. Regular customer. Not opened yet.

Call 2. Glenn and Driscoll. Regular customer. Buyer out.

Call 3. Frank's Greasy Spoon. First call. Will consider an air conditioner. Business slow. Call back later.

Call 4. Callahan Excavating. Building five homes now. Would like to install United air-conditioning units but complained about price.

Call 5. Snell, Bascom, and Birch. Real-estate developers. Used to be good customers but switched purchases to competitor for unstated reason. Happy with present supplier.

Call 6. Davis Stores, department store. Regular customer. Worked with three salespeople on selling techniques.

Call 7. Hardiman's Discount store. Occasional customer. Business booming. No order as don't want to change anything while business is good.

Call 8. Hoffman's House of Appliances. Regular customer. Complained about lack of good salespeople. No order.

Friday

Spent morning in weekly sales meeting at branch sales office. Made first call at 2:00 P.M.

Call 1. Upham's Appliance Store. Regular customer. Took small order.

Call 2. Gaudette's Appliances. Regular customer. Complained about competitive dealers' pricing tactics. Wondered if he could get United air conditioners, dehumidifiers, humidifiers, and vaporizers at lower prices.

Call 3. Roper and Sons. Appliance store. Regular customer. Buyer out.

Call 4. Kostick's. Department store. First call. Buyer out.

Call 5. Jeter and Jones. Hardware store. Regular customer. No order.

Call 6. Hoffman's House of Appliances. Regular customer. Owner-buyer out.

Compare the daily call reports of Thomas Rogers with the job description of a United Airflow salesperson. What strengths and weaknesses are apparent from the comparison?

CASE 1-9

Graham Manufacturing Company

Distributor of Highway Construction Equipment— Sale of a Truck-Mounted Power Shovel

In January, Shattuck Construction Company was awarded a $60 million contract for building a section of interstate highway crossing New York State. The contract called for clearing, paving, bridge building, blasting, and landscaping 50 miles of roadway, two lanes in each direction, in the vicinity of Syracuse.

Over a period of six months prior to the award of the contract, Fred Rennert, salesman for the Graham Manufacturing Company, had been calling upon the Shattuck Company for the purpose of selling a truck-mounted power shovel. Although the prospect concern had used all types of bulldozers, carryalls, trucks, and large shovels, it had never had experience with this particular type of power shovel. In January, Rennert finally persuaded John Shattuck, president of the Shattuck Company, to witness a demonstration of the product. Because Shattuck's time was limited, the demonstration's sole purpose was to acquaint him with the general operating procedures of the shovel.

Previous to the time of the sales interview recorded here, Rennert had talked with state engineers and other officials engaged in planning the new road. He had studied the technical aspects of the project and the major problems that would have to be faced in completing the prospect's contract. In addition, he had familiarized himself thoroughly with the various pieces of equipment used by the prospect on similar contracts in the past.

The following interview occurred on the day after the product demonstration. Rennert had learned on the same morning that the contract in question had been awarded to the Shattuck Company.

RENNERT: Good morning, Mr. Shattuck.

SHATTUCK: Good morning, Mr. Rennert.

RENNERT: I understand you have received the contract for the 50 miles of road construction east of here.

SHATTUCK: That's right, Mr. Rennert, and we have quite a job ahead of us.

RENNERT: This'll be the biggest job you've had since the war, won't it, Mr. Shattuck?

SHATTUCK: Yes. However, we did have one big job five years age, a big stretch of parkway near New York City. That was a dandy, at least from an engineering standpoint. We had our troubles on that job, and we missed our bid estimate by almost $400,000 because of the landscaping that was a part of the project.

RENNERT: Doesn't the state pay for any errors or mistakes they make in their survey estimate of the proposed project?

SHATTUCK: Yes, they do pay for their mistakes. However, that mistake was ours and we didn't get paid for it! You know, Mr. Rennert, what they say in this business—one mistake and you're backed up against the wall.

RENNERT: That's exactly why I'm here this morning, Mr. Shattuck, and that is why I gave you the demonstration yesterday. I am here to show you how to make more money by saving on construction costs right down the line. We realize that you have been in business a good many years and have the know-how, or you wouldn't be operating today. But I have studied your problems and I believe we have a machine that will reduce your operating costs by at least 10 percent.

SHATTUCK: Well, at the present I have two regular power shovels and a fleet of trucks, and I can't see how your machine will benefit me at all. I liked your demonstration yesterday but, of course, that is only one operation and I already have the equipment to do that.

RENNERT: That's true, Mr. Shattuck, but remember that your 1- and 2-yard shovels are not truck-mounted and therefore don't have the versatility that our shovel has. Isn't it true that most of the time on a rock cut or hill excavation those shovels are in the same spot for months at a time?

SHATTUCK: Yes, they are.

RENNERT: Well, our shovel is a mobile shovel. "Quick-Way" Model E has a 4/10 cubic-yard capacity bucket. It can be moved from place to place with the least amount of lost time or delay. It is ready for use as soon as it reaches its destination. There is no loading or unloading to consume time and run up costs. In many cases, you have small jobs, such as laying pipe, putting in culverts and ditch digging, all of which have to be done at almost the same time. With a "Quick-Way" shovel you'll be able to go from one job to another with a minimum of delay. You'll be able to use this shovel from the beginning of the operation right down to the end.

SHATTUCK: I don't see how I could use your shovel throughout the whole operation.

RENNERT: In the early stages you can use the clam shell or trench hoe for digging ditches and sluiceways. These can also be used for building up shoulders. The crane, which is 25 feet long, can be used for laying forms, putting out reinforcements of steel, and many other jobs of loading and unloading that must be done. When the concrete is ready to be poured, you can use the shovel boom and bucket for feeding the batch bins and loading the trucks with gravel.

SHATTUCK: That does sound practical, but I didn't know you could use a trench hoe or a crane with your shovel.

RENNERT: Oh, I'm sorry! I should have made that clear. The clam shell and trench hoe can be mounted on the shovel the same as a shovel boom and bucket can. There is also a 25-foot crane boom that can be mounted the same way, as you can see by these photos.

SHATTUCK: How long does it take to make a changeover to any one of these attachments?

RENNERT: It takes approximately two hours. However, the job is usually done at night when the machine is not in use.

SHATTUCK: That sounds good, Mr. Rennert. Now, I have a lot of bridge building in my work. Will your machine be of any use on these projects?

RENNERT: Absolutely! You can use the clam shell or the trench hoe for the digging, and the crane boom for laying the steel girders. Does that answer your question, Mr. Shattuck?

SHATTUCK: Yes, it does. I have heard that your type of shovel has a lot of competition from other road-building equipment. Is that true?

RENNERT: Yes, there are a lot of specific machines that we compete with. However, ours can compete with almost all of them. It is all four machines in one—the clam shell, trench hoe, crane boom, and shovel boom and bucket. You can see that this is a great saving in capital investment. You have one machine that does four different jobs.

SHATTUCK: Well, that certainly sounds economical.

RENNERT: It is economical, Mr. Shattuck. The "Quick-Way" shovel is operated generally by one man who can also drive the truck from job to job. The shovel has positive hydraulic controls and a wide-vision cab that gives the operator clear vision at all times. It has a 55-horsepower International engine that operates at low speeds. Therefore, your maintenance costs drop. It is full-revolving, making 7½ turns per minute. The shovel boom and bucket can dig to 3½ feet below ground level and can lift to a height of 11 feet above the ground for dumping. The trench hoe can dig to a maximum depth of 15 feet below ground level. The total height of the machine is 10 to 12 feet, depending, of course, upon the type of truck on which it is mounted. This passes all the requirements for highway bridges and trestles. It is also classed as a power shovel and, therefore, does not require license plates in New York State. One of the outstanding features of our shovel is that it has no dead weight to counterbalance the loads. By this, I mean that it is balanced right. Its weight is distributed proportionately throughout. This, of course, as you know, saves on repair costs and increases the utility of the machine.

SHATTUCK: We've had a lot of trouble with our large shovels because of this factor of counterbalancing. I have looked over your specification sheet and have noticed that there is a bronze bushing on the main spur gear. I would say that a roller bearing would be better because of the high speed at which your shovel operates.

RENNERT: Yes, you're right. The roller bearing would be faster, but this is the very reason for using a bronze bearing. When a ball bearing or roller bearing breaks down, there is likely to be damage to the shaft and the racer. On the other hand, when a bronze bearing wears, there's no damage to the shaft, and the machine doesn't have to be stopped immediately. This, I think, is a definite advantage in that the shovel can be kept in operation until time is available to get a new bearing and to get it installed. I would also like to point out to you that all our hydraulic clutches are interchangeable. If any one of them breaks down, it may quickly be substituted for by the clutch on the main boom lift, which has a mechanical stop and can temporarily be used in this way. You can see that this also saves on the number of parts that must be kept on hand to service the shovel.

SHATTUCK: Do you have any figures on the actual operating costs of your shovels over a period of years?

RENNERT: We have. We figured average cost per machine-year on twenty-five machines, a total of 130 machine-years. It was $2,325 repair and maintenance costs. Mr. Oldine, of the Oldine Contracting Company, bought a "Quick-Way" shovel two years ago and has had excellent results on this score. His total service costs have been $1,400 a year.

SHATTUCK: From what I have seen and from what you have explained, I'm interested in your shovel. Do you have the cost figures with you?

RENNERT: I have them right here. The basic machine plus the shovel boom and bucket comes to $28,241. The clam shell is $21,393. The trench hoe, $21,350. And the crane boom, $6,569. The prices are F.O.B. your place of business.

SHATTUCK: Your cost figures seem rather high since they don't include the price of the truck needed to mount the shovel.

RENNERT: No, Mr. Shattuck, experience has shown that it is possible to amortize the cost of our shovel over a two-year period. This also brings up another point. Our shovel can be mounted on any type of 5-ton truck. This is a distinct advantage over other truck-mounted shovels—they all require a specific type of truck on which to mount the shovel equipment. I have noticed that you have a Mack truck out in the lot which would be suited for our shovel. I have already looked at it and measured it. It's just the one for mounting our shovel on. That is, of course, if you can spare it.

SHATTUCK: Why, yes, I do have a few extra trucks, and that one you are speaking about is one of them.

RENNERT: I believe you'll agree that this is an added saving for you, and the price I have quoted, including attachments with outriggers, is reasonable.

SHATTUCK: Yes, it does make it sound better, but let me look over those specifications again. . . . Yes, I see. Just what is the capacity of this shovel? You know I have a lot of heavy work.

RENNERT: Well, with outriggers, the capacity over end or over side is 13,000 pounds at 10 feet and drops to 8,000 pounds at 15 feet. There is a 15 percent safety factor built in which increases its capacity correspondingly. I believe these capacity ratings will handle any work that you will encounter.

SHATTUCK: That would seem plenty. What attachments do you suggest I use?

RENNERT: I made a complete study of the attachments you will be using for this job. I would suggest the shovel boom and bucket, the crane, and the trench hoe or clam shell. The trench hoe would probably be more practical, but the final decision is up to you.

SHATTUCK: I think I agree with you. The trench hoe will handle my work. If I need it, you can always get me a clam shell, can't you?

RENNERT: Yes, I can have one for you within a few days' time. Now Mr. Shattuck, here's the contract. The basic machine, shovel boom and bucket, crane, and trench hoe total up to $56,160. This includes installation and mounting on your truck.

SHATTUCK: This seems to be in order. Where do I sign?

RENNERT: Thank you, Mr. Shattuck. I'll send a man over for your truck tomorrow. We'll be able to go right ahead with the work and have the shovel and truck back to you within two weeks. That will be in plenty of time for your work, won't it?

SHATTUCK: That will be fine. We plan to start operations in about two weeks, and I'll be able to use the shovel by that time.

RENNERT: Thanks again. I know you'll be satisfied with our "Quick-Way" shovel. I'll be here when you take delivery. I want to see that everything is as it should be. Goodbye, Mr. Shattuck.

SHATTUCK: Goodbye, Mr. Rennert.

Judging from the approach used, what facts had Rennert learned about the prospect?

How important was timing in this interview?

In opening the interview, did Rennert have a good plan of attack?

At what points in the interview did the prospect voice objections? Which objections, if any, were real, and which were excuses?

What methods were used by Rennert in answering the objections voiced by the prospect?

On the basis of this case, prepare a short outline of a job description for this sales position.

At what point in the interview was it apparent that Rennert was going to make the sale?

Analyze the closing technique used in this case.

Was Rennert wise to leave Shattuck almost immediately after getting the order? Why or why not?

CASE 1-10

Colonial Heritage Furniture Company

Manufacturer of Traditional American Furniture— Opening a New Account

The salesperson in this case, Jack Leonard, was employed by the Colonial Heritage Furniture Company, an old and well-known manufacturer of traditional American furniture. The prospect, Frank O'Keefe, was the owner and manager of O'Keefe Home Furnishings, a medium-sized, high quality retail furniture store in Waco, Texas. The sales interview recorded here took place late on a Wednesday afternoon.

LEONARD: Mr. O'Keefe? Good afternoon. I'm Jack Leonard from the Colonial Heritage Furniture Division of North Carolina Wood Product Industries. (Hands prospect a business card.)

O'KEEFE: Hmfh! I've heard of your line. Caswell Interiors are your exclusive franchised dealers in Waco, aren't they?

LEONARD: Well . . . that's what I'm here to see you about, Mr. O'Keefe. We are interested in opening a new account in Waco, and we would like very much to have our line represented in your store. You see, Mr. O'Keefe, we feel that Caswell is not doing a good enough job to warrant an exclusive franchise. Waco now has a population of over 150,000 and we think more Colonial Heritage Furniture should be sold here.

O'KEEFE: About three years ago, when I was interested in handling your line, I wrote to your firm. The answer I got was that Caswell was your exclusive dealer here and that I could refer my customers there if I so desired.

LEONARD: Three years ago, we had just opened their account. It would not have been fair to sell you any merchandise at that time. They gave us a large opening order with the understanding that they would be our only agency in the city. But they have done very little with our furniture, and conditions do not seem to be improving. We have been extremely patient and understanding with them. We missed a lot of business because we were loyal to Caswell. After three years' time, we feel justified in opening another account.

O'KEEFE: If they couldn't do anything with your furniture, why should I want it? I thought it was a good line to handle, but if Caswell has done as little with it as you say, evidently it isn't.

LEONARD: It's true Caswell was unsuccessful with Colonial Heritage, but I am certain you would do very well with it. (Looks around store.) I see you feature all the other well-known brands of traditional furniture Caswell didn't. It was the only traditional furniture they carried. They specialize primarily in modern furniture, so they have given little attention to our line. Customers like to buy where they can look over a large selection. You can have a much wider selection by adding our lines to your stock. To assure sales acceptance, each furniture line is consumer tested before it is introduced to our accounts. Our furniture is advertised in seven magazines: *House Beautiful*, *House and Garden*, *Better Homes and Gardens*, *Living for Young Homemakers*,

Good Housekeeping, for the southern market in *Southern Living*, and for the Texas market in *Texas Monthly*. We have a complete assortment of furniture—living room, dining room, and bedroom to match each of our lines. This helps you obtain a larger share of the Colonial Heritage business.

O'Keefe: All the brands I carry are mine exclusively in Waco. If I can have Colonial Heritage exclusively I'm interested. But I don't want it if it is going to be sold in any other store. My advertising and promotion would help Caswell's business. As long as Caswell has your brand, there is no advantage in my having it. With all my other brands, once a sale has been made on certain pieces of furniture in a line, it is more than likely that the customer will fill out their furniture needs with matching pieces in the same line in my store.

Leonard: I agree. I would close their account today if it were the right thing to do. But that would cause Caswell to have animosity toward you and toward Colonial Heritage. I would prefer dropping them more gradually. If you take on the line, I think it only fair for me to go to Caswell right away to inform them of the fact. If they want to discontinue handling my line, that will be fine for you and for me. If they decide to keep it, I will see that their name is removed from our mailing list, and I will not call on them personally in the future. Their only way of ordering will be by mail or at the furniture mart, and, since they will not be up to date on current information, merchandise, and prices, my line should die a slow death in their store. They will be anxious to close the account.

O'Keefe: I don't know what lines and pieces within lines would probably sell much better than others, and I don't want to tie up any money in slow-moving stock.

Leonard: I'll make an exception to company policy in your case and take back any items you find are not selling for the first six months. I want to do everything in my power to work with you and build up a fine trade for Colonial Heritage Furniture in Waco.

O'Keefe: Sounds fair enough to me, but if you want me to do a real selling job for Colonial Heritage, how about giving me some ideas for promoting your furniture? I've been using the same ads and displays over and over, year after year, and I'd like some new and different ideas on the display and promotion.

Leonard: It will be a pleasure, Mr. O'Keefe, to be of assistance to such an alert businessman. First of all, here is a promotional program directed at all new households in your community. It involves mailings to all new residents in the community, identified through arrangements with realtors, welcome wagons, and major employers, and to prospective brides, identified through engagement and wedding announcements. Second, is the development of card files on past customers with records of past purchases. Before Christmas, birthdays, and anniversaries, letters are written to each customer with catalogues and suggestions of fill-in purchases. We have standard letters for a number of occasions that can be typed on programmable typewriters for newcomers, brides to be, and so forth.

O'Keefe: I'd like a copy of each of the letters, and I think the purchase record cards are an excellent idea. If they're not overly expensive, I'd like to order a thousand.

Leonard: They're only 2 cents a card, or $20 for 1,000. Would you like that many? (Gives letters to prospect and puts order pad on counter.)

O'Keefe: By all means, they'll be very useful.

Leonard: Here is another idea introduced by Colonial Heritage Company. (Pulls an ad out of briefcase and places it on the counter.) This is a most effective way to advertise. It is similar to the testimonial ads featuring movie stars and athletes, but this one has a photograph of one of your own customers, with a write-up about the customer and a picture of an attractively furnished room in the customer's house that features your furniture. This tells readers where they can select their furniture—often with the hope that their pictures will get in future ads. Here are a few examples that some of my accounts have been using. (Shows additional examples.) If you like, you may keep these samples. (Hands samples to prospect.) They will give you an idea of the layout and copy of such an ad.

O'KEEFE: Now that's a very good idea. I've never seen anything like it. I'm sure we can make use of it in our ads right away.

LEONARD: I think it will be very attractive in the newspapers, and it should be an excellent way to keep your name in the public eye. We have a film in color, twenty minutes long, entitled, "Furniture and decoration make a home a Showplace," that you can borrow any time. It is a good movie to show at women's clubs, at high school sorority meetings, and at classes of home economics students. Perhaps you or one of your employees can introduce the film and answer questions after it is shown to each group.

O'KEEFE: I'll make a record of that. It could be useful.

LEONARD: Fine! Please give us a week's notice for delivery, if you decide to use it.

O'KEEFE: Thanks. I will.

LEONARD: Now here are some very effective booklets by B. J. Valenti, part of a series entitled "Sell Traditional Home Furnishings." (Hands booklets to prospect.) One is on the policies and history of the Colonial Heritage Furniture Company, another is entitled, "Planning Sales to Promote Furniture," one is called "Displaying to Promote Furniture," and one is a sales manual, "Modern Selling of Furniture." Those are my personal copies. Unfortunately, these are all out of print. If you and your employees would like to read them, I'll be happy to lend them to you. I'll pick them up the next time I call.

O'KEEFE: Well, I doubt if I'll have time to read them, but I would like the rest of my people to look them over. I'll see that you get them back on your next trip.

LEONARD: Thank you. There is a very good pre-Christmas coffee and end table promotion that you can probably use. I'll send you some literature on it in plenty of time for Christmas. The local brides-to-be are offered a free consultation by your decorator on their first home or apartment. This plan really helps you make a whale of a lot of sales. I suggest you give this careful consideration. It has been a real money-maker for many of our customers. With a good follow-up, I think it will bring in a lot of business.

O'KEEFE: It sounds interesting. I'll keep it in mind.

LEONARD: And now—last but not least—we have a truly wonderful plan, one that will establish your store permanently as Waco's leading furniture dealer. It is a time-consuming, costly promotion, but it is one that will bring you immeasurable good-will and future business. The plan I am referring to is a room decorating contest and exhibit. It is a contest in which you contact officers of all the local ladies' clubs and suggest that each group submit a winning room in a home. The various clubs compete for cash prizes to be given for originality, beauty, and style. This winning room is described and shown in pictures in the local newspaper. These furniture promotions have been tremendously successful all over the country. When and if you are ready to plan one, just call on me to help you organize it. I helped run the contest by Thompson and Randolph. Here is the photograph of the write-up of the winning room. (Shows photograph to prospect.) Their trade has really gone up since that contest. This booklet will give you many of the details. (Hands booklet to prospect.) It also suggests that you write to some of the furniture retailers who have used the promotion for their advice and suggestions. Well, what do you think?

O'KEEFE: That's certainly an original idea. Right now I don't think I want to plan anything that expensive. But, perhaps after Christmas, when business is slow, I can plan a room decorating contest.

LEONARD: Surely. Just call on all your sales representatives for assistance. I know they'll all be glad to help make it the success it should be. Now, about that opening order?

O'KEEFE: I don't know exactly what I want. What do you recommend?

LEONARD: If it's O.K. with you, I'll write my own order. It will be a small one. I'm more interested in repeat business than I am in loading you up with a large opening order. I can bring in a copy of the order I write the first thing tomorrow morning, and you can confirm it then. (Leonard looks at clock on store wall.) I see it's closing time, and I don't want to take any more of your time today. Besides, I want to decide carefully on the lines that should be the best for you.

O'KEEFE: That will be fine. I'll be seeing you in the morning any time after 9:30.

LEONARD: Thank you very much, Mr. O'Keefe. (Shakes hands.) It's been a pleasure talking to you, and I know you will always be pleased that you took on the Colonial Heritage line. Goodbye, see you in the morning.

Comment on the tactics used by Leonard to overcome what appeared to be initial antagonism on the part of O'Keefe.

Did empathy play a role in this sale? If so, where?

If O'Keefe had refused flatly to take on the Colonial Heritage line while Caswell still carried it, what should Leonard have done?

Should Leonard have shown O'Keefe some illustrations of the Colonial Heritage line? Why or why not?

At what points in the interview did O'Keefe voice objections? Analyze how each was handled by Leonard.

When did Leonard start to close? Would he have been wise to get the order approved before leaving the store?

CASE 1-11

Stanamer Corporation

Plumbing and Heating Company—Sales Force Expansion

The Plumbing and Heating Division of Stanamer Corporation made and sold plumbing fixtures and fittings, hydronic heating and cooling equipment, food-waste disposals, water softeners, and invalid bath lifts. The largest of seven corporate divisions, it operated fourteen plants from coast to coast. Toward the end of the year the general sales manager, J. B. Samson, was analyzing a problem concerning an increase in the size of the sales force. (See Exhibit 1 for Selling

EXHIBIT 1 Selling Section, Marketing Department

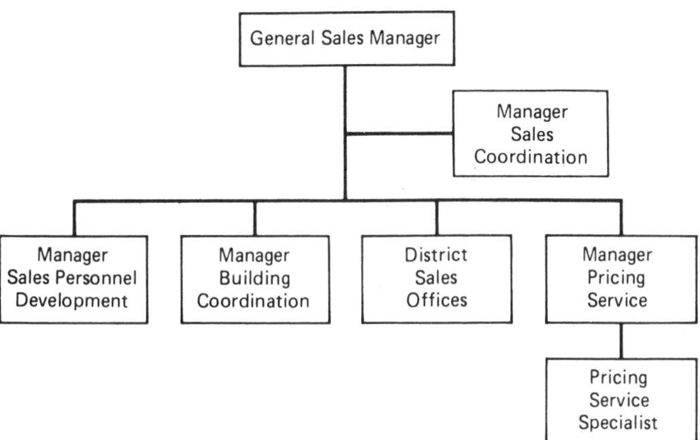

Section organization.) The budget for the next year provided funds for adding fifteen salespeople, and Samson compared two alternatives: (1) hiring sales personnel with previous sales experience in the field and (2) following the company traditional practice of hiring and training inexperienced persons.

Stanamer led the plumbing and heating industry in sales; its sales of $600 million were double those of the nearest competitor. Well known and respected, the company's market share was estimated at 50 percent. Although its position was enviable, company management recognized the dangers of complacency, particularly as competition stiffened and the market share showed signs of declining.

Activity in the home-building industry, the largest market for plumbing and heating supplies, had fallen off. There were predictions that new housing starts in the first half of the current year would be below the previous year's level; however, an upturn was expected. When new housing starts dropped, total demand for plumbing and heating products also declined; consequently, competition for available business increased. Most firms moved to hire additional sales personnel to provide more intensive market coverage. Samson's decision to hire fifteen additional salespeople was made for the short-term objective of reducing excess inventory. If housing starts recovered, top management might question the value of having fifteen extra persons, since in such circumstances Stanamer normally received sufficient business to support its full productive capacity.

The company's products were of high quality and as such commanded prices about 10 percent above those of competitors. All promotion emphasized the superior product quality. Company sales-training sessions, focusing on product information and selling techniques, also emphasized the price-quality relationship.

Stanamer's sales force sold exclusively through wholesale plumbing and heating distributors. The 250-person force called upon 1,400 wholesalers, who, in turn, sold through 50,000 contractors and plumbers. Sales personnel worked out of twenty-three sales offices located in some but not all of thirteen sales districts. (See Exhibits 2, 3, and 4 for the organizations of the various types of typical sales districts.)

District sales managers performed administrative duties and reported di-

EXHIBIT 2 Typical Sales District (Multiple Sales Offices): Selling Section, Sales and Marketing Department

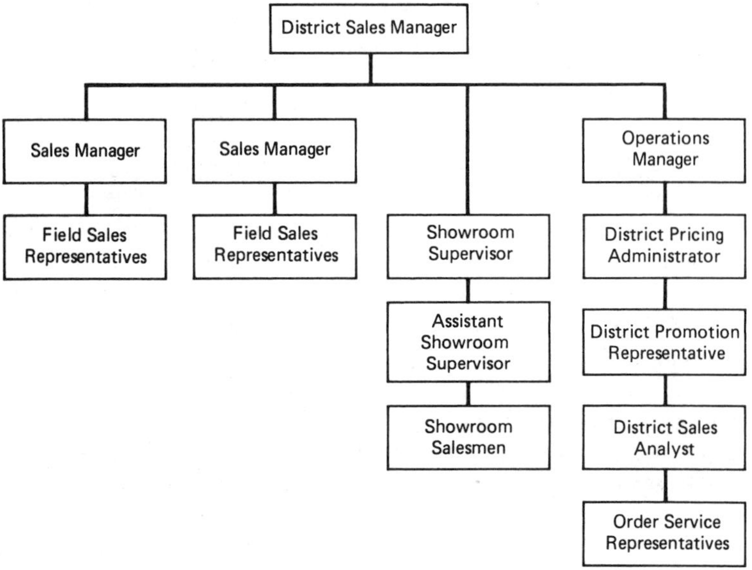

EXHIBIT 3 Typical Sales District (One Sales Office): Selling Section, Sales and Marketing Department

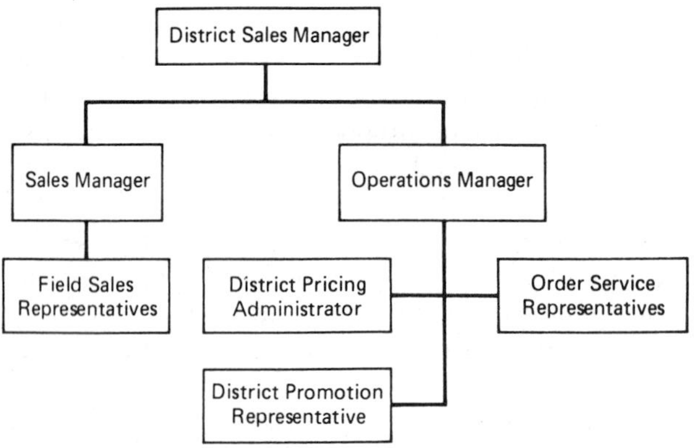

EXHIBIT 4 Typical Sales District (No Sales Office): Selling Section, Sales and Marketing Department

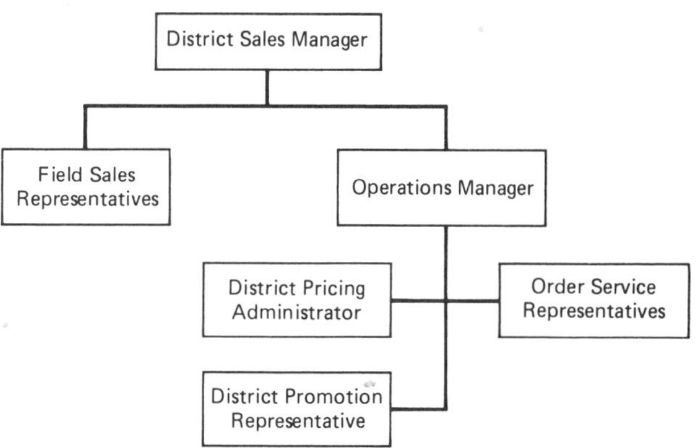

rectly to the general sales manager. Their responsibilities included recruiting and training of the sales staff. However, the general sales manager determined the number and the qualifications of those hired.

The average salesperson wrote orders totaling from $2,400,000 to $3,600,000 annually. Each received a straight salary of $20,000 to $50,000 per year. Sales personnel maintained contact with distributors and assisted them in inventory control, in the training of their sales staff, and in the use of company promotional plans, programs, and materials. Sales personnel also promoted the use of Stanamer products through their contacts with home-builder and contractor trade associations. In addition, they promoted the use of the division's products in talks with key personnel in hospital and school administrations, public utilities, and governmental agencies. They also inspected consumer products and made service calls.

Traditionally, Stanamer hired inexperienced people and put them through a six-month program. Sales recruits spent the first three months becoming acquainted with the company's products and policies. They then attended a formal three-month program emphasizing advanced product knowledge and sales techniques. Training costs amounted to approximately $2,500 per person. Once out of training, new salespersons generally became fully operational and productive in from three to six months. (See Exhibit 5.)

To lure salespeople with field experience away from competitors required starting salaries averaging $20,000 annually. Also, considerable recruiting time and effort were involved, and there was the danger that competition might reciprocate. People with previous field experience usually became fully operational Stanamer sales personnel in about one month.

Samson wanted to hire the fifteen additional people, but he was not certain whether he should concentrate on those with or without previous selling experience in the industry.

EXHIBIT 5 Sales Personnel Development Unit: Selling Section, Sales and Marketing Department

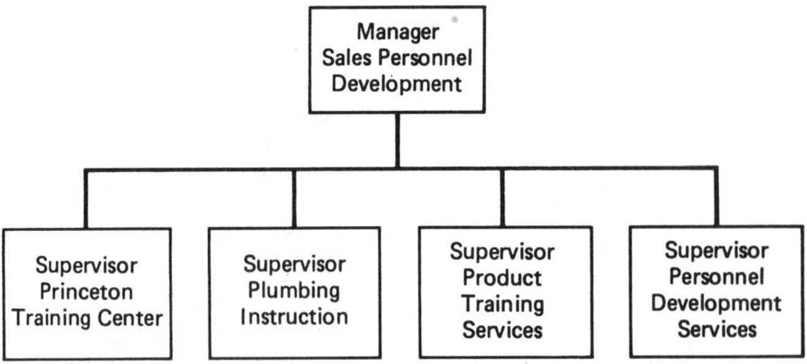

How should Samson have gone about implementing the decision to add fifteen new salespersons?

In alleviating the excess inventory situation, what other alternatives should have been explored?

Evaluate the appropriateness of Stanamer's various policies and practices relating to sales force management.

CASE 1-12

Piezo Technology, Inc.

A Manufacturer of Filtering Devices for Radios— Determining Sales Policies

The vice-president of sales for Piezo Technology, Inc., Mr. John Dinman, periodically examined copies of outstanding customer orders kept on file in his office. It was late September, and he was disturbed when he discovered that many of these orders were more than eight weeks old and there was no completion date in sight for most of them. While he realized that the company's recent move to new facilities could account for part of this backlog, Mr. Dinman felt that other factors must have been responsible. Prompt service had been an important element in building PTI's strong reputation, and Mr. Dinman was determined to find the reasons for the backlog and to take corrective action. He was convinced that something had to be done soon.

COMPANY BACKGROUND

PTI was incorporated about ten years ago as a manufacturer of a new type of crystal filter, the monolithic crystal filter, for VHF and UHF two-way radios, paging receivers, and land and marine mobile radios. PTI revolutionized this segment of the communications industry through the introduction of the first commercially produced monolithic crystal filtering device. Prior to 1970, all frequency filters were composed of many electronic components arranged in a package, called discrete-element crystal filters. These filters were large and very expensive due to the number of components and the technical skill required for their assembly. The introduction of the monolithic crystal filter by PTI enabled communications equipment manufacturers to produce smaller, less expensive, more reliable products. PTI's was a major innovation that helped change an entire industry.

In its first year of operation, PTI had sales of $1.5 million. In four years, sales volume nearly tripled to $4.1 million, and then it leveled off for two years owing to what Mr. Dinman called a "wrinkle in the industry's overall growth curve." Things improved, however, and for the current year the company expected to reach a sales level of at least $8.5 million, based upon the number of orders received during the first ten months. While sales had plateaued in the past three months, profits had increased dramatically as a result of a comprehensive cost-cutting program.

PTI was the dominant producer of monolithic crystal filters, with a market share of 70 percent. This market position was partially the result of the company's being the developer of the monolithic crystal filter and first onto the market. But Mr. Dinman felt a more significant factor was the reputation that PTI had developed for quality and service. PTI was willing and able to meet the requirements of customers for specially designed and manufactured filters. Because PTI was by far the largest filter manufacturer (PTI employed over 350 people), it was often able to produce large orders at a lower cost than their competitors. In addition, the company had always quoted firm delivery periods which seldom exceeded four weeks.

THE MONOLITHIC CRYSTAL INDUSTRY

Customers for monolithic crystal filters were categorized into three major groups. By far the largest market was that comprised of the manufacturers of paging receivers and land and marine mobile radios, which accounted for nearly 70 percent of all monolithic crystal filter production. The military purchased about 25 percent of industry output, while medical equipment manufacturers purchased the remainder.

PTI had a large number of very small competitors throughout the country. Most of the smaller companies concentrated their efforts on the military segment. PTI did not actively seek government contracts because of the volatility and intensive price competition which characterized the market for government contracts. Bids were required on every contract. Typically, the small companies would bid very low because the government would make progress payments that provided these small companies with additional cash flow. When it became evident that they could not fulfill the contract profitably (as often happened), they would seek to void it. Consequently, the government then turned to PTI, which reluctantly accepted the order. Almost 20 percent of PTI's business was generated in this manner. However, serious problems sometimes arose. The military contracts usually required many specification changes from the filters that PTI normally produced. Fast delivery was often an additional requirement.

The pager and land and marine mobile radio segment contributed 75 percent of PTI's sales. In this segment, Motorola accounted for 70 percent of the purchases, followed by GE with 15 percent. Mr. Dinman stated that Motorola was PTI's largest customer, accounting for over 20 percent of PTI's total sales. The Motorola account was particularly important because the company typically purchased large quantities of standard items, making long production runs possible. In addition, though, Motorola purchased significant numbers of the more specialized filters.

Recent technological advances in the medical equipment industry were increasing this segment's demand for monolithic crystal filters. Consequently, PTI was directing an increasing portion of its resources toward this market. PTI filters were currently being used in hearing aids and portable heart monitors, and Mr. Dinman felt that many similar products would require PTI filters in the future. He regarded this market segment as worth increased attention.

MARKETING AT PTI

PTI distributed its products through a network of twenty sales agencies. While most of these agencies operated in North America, PTI had representatives throughout the free world. Mr. Dinman maintained strict policies as to the selection of sales agencies. All agencies were "engineering oriented," and able to market effectively highly technical products and communicate the special requirements of PTI customers. Each handled only noncompeting lines of electronic components, and had established contacts in customer segments not currently served by PTI but that might be future targets.

The agencies retained by PTI were generally small, employing an average of four salespersons. The salesperson established contact with the purchasing and engineering heads of established, as well as potential, customers. During these meetings, he or she would distribute information about new developments by the company, obtain information about any problems encountered with previous purchases from PTI, and inquire about future plans which might mean additional business for PTI. The sales representative took orders only for standard or near-standard PTI products. If the customer required new or unusual filter specifications, this information was fed back to headquarters and the customer was contacted directly by PTI management. This procedure had been instituted because Mr. Dinman found that salespeople often took orders for "odd ball" filters that were either unnecessary or next to impossible to produce.

The highly technical nature of PTI's products led Mr. Dinman to be concerned that sales personnel may have been dealing directly with the engineering departments, thereby causing friction with purchasing departments. This was somewhat of a problem in the industry. Mr. Dinman recently had established a policy of distributing specification sheets containing the model numbers of all standard filters to the customer's engineering and purchasing departments. Model numbers also were assigned to new specialized filters. In this way, the customer's engineering department could specify a particular PTI product to the purchasing department.

PTI focused most of its advertising resources on trade publications. During the past year, the company spent approximately $30,000 in publications such as *Electronics* and *Electronic Engineers Master Catalog*. Advertisements emphasized the capabilities and reliability of monolithic crystal filters in general, as well as the particular qualities of PTI filters (such as low failure rate) compared with other brands. The advertising was designed to serve two purposes: first, the company sought to influence purchasing agents to look first to PTI for their needs, and, second, it was hoped that the ads would encourage engineers to design new products to be compatible with standard PTI models.

Problems and Prospects

Mr. Dinman felt that the market for monolithic crystal filters was likely to expand dramatically through the 1980's. The Federal Communications Commission was debating two issues of importance to the monolithic crystal filter market. The commission was considering a proposal already adopted in Great Britain that would cut all frequency band widths for mobile radios in half so that the number of channels could be expanded. Such a move would be a boon to the monolithic crystal filter industry because additional filters would be required in each radio to maintain the signal within the narrower band. The FCC was also considering a requirement for more stringent frequency control. The filters commonly used in citizen band radios allowed frequencies to overlap somewhat within each channel. A new ruling would make it necessary for manufacturers to use monolithic crystal filters in place of current filters.

While the prospects for the monolithic crystal filter industry appeared excellent, Mr. Dinman was worried that PTI's market share would decline as a result of PTI's growing inability to promise definite and timely delivery dates. The company could maintain its policy of fast service if it deemphasized the production of specially designed products. But Mr. Dinman wondered how PTI's customers would react to such a policy, many of whom seemed to depend on PTI for such custom-made products. For example, what would be Motorola's reaction? Would Motorola or other companies be tempted to integrate vertically if

PTI cut back on producing specialized filters? Would other filter producers fill the void? These and other questions were on Mr. Dinman's mind as he contemplated his next action.

What are Piezo Technology's alternatives? What course of action do you recommend? Why?

CASE 1-13

The Family Tree Manufacturing Company

A Producer of Brass Beds—Opportunity Analysis

Brass beds had been very popular at various times throughout the course of their history, most notably at the turn of the century and then the period following World War II. A resurgence of their popularity occurred in the 1970s. With antique brass beds in short supply and with many people in the market, some furniture stores and antiques dealers began selling reproductions of the old beds.

Five years ago, Sanford Patten, a businessman, and Jim Epps, an antiques dealer, decided to test the market for reproductions of antique brass beds in the southeastern United States. The partners established contact with a bed supplier in Pennsylvania, bought a truck, and began selling beds to any southern furniture or antiques dealer who would buy them. By the end of the first six months, more than 300 beds had been sold, mostly to antiques dealers.

Encouraged by their initial success, Mr. Patten and Mr. Epps began manufacturing the beds themselves to minimize transportation costs and control product quality and design. By the end of the second year of the partnership, The Family Tree Manufacturing Company had begun manufacturing brass bed reproductions in Colbert, Georgia.

The manufacturing process was very simple and required a relatively small investment in fixed assets. Brass tubing, imported from West Germany, was cut to desired lengths and polished with cutting rouges and compounds. Holes were drilled so that the parts could be easily assembled with screws and bolts. Soon, the company was producing approximately eight beds per day.

In addition to the line of brass beds, The Family Tree also sold a number of accessory items that were purchased from various sources. The most popular were brass spitoons, which were used as planters. Other items included oak china cabinets and chairs, reproductions of antique clocks, wrought-iron tables, and glassware. Though the margins were lower on the accessories, they were very valuable display and trade items.

PRICING

The price of the brass beds to dealers ranged from $200 to $500 per unit. Direct labor and materials costs were estimated at $130 to $230 per unit. Some discounts were allowed on large orders. Commissions were paid to sales personnel only on initial orders. Repeat business was noncommissionable. Profit on each bed ranged from $50 to $200.

THE MARKET

Northern antiques dealers were the primary outlets for the high-priced antique brass beds. These outlets generally refused to handle any kind of reproductions. In the South, however, where antique beds were in short supply, antiques dealers purchased pure brass reproductions such as those manufactured by The Family Tree. Some antiques dealers and furniture stores also purchased cheaper brass-plated beds. While antiques dealers remained the main outlet for brass beds, many manufacturers were seeking to gain distribution through the major furniture chains.

There were approximately thirty manufacturers of brass beds in the United States. In The Family Tree's trading area in the Southeast, there were only two manufacturers of pure brass beds. These competitors were located in Virginia and New Orleans. Because of its more central location, The Family Tree felt that it could achieve a dominant position in the southeastern market.

DISTRIBUTION

Approximately 95 percent of The Family Tree's output was sold through antiques dealers. The company, however, had initiated efforts to gain distribution through some major furniture chains. For example, Ethan Allen had recently agreed to carry The Family Tree line and had featured a Family Tree bed on the cover of its spring catalog. The company also sold a limited number of beds at retail directly from its manufacturing location, though at present, there were no plans to expand retail sales.

The company maintained the same sales and distribution strategy adopted at the company's inception. Two large trucks with samples of all the firm's products traveled throughout the Southeast, making calls on as many dealers as possible. The trucks returned to Colbert only when everything had been sold. At that time, any additional orders written while the trucks were on the trip would be delivered by the company. The Family Tree provided the truck and driver, while the customer paid for the gasoline.

The Family Tree had been able to sell all of its output to date. The company planned to double its manufacturing capacity in the next several months to meet demand. Management was very cautious, however. The market, while good for the past several years, could drop off at any time, as it had several times in the past. For the present, there was substantial demand. How long it would last was anybody's guess, according to Mr. Patten. Should The Family Tree go ahead and try to capitalize on the market demand? Were there other distribution strategies that might prove successful? Would a change in sales strategy be advisable? These were some of the questions that Patten and Epps were thinking about as they considered their next move.

What were the feasible alternatives for The Family Tree? What do you recommend for a course of action?

CASE 1-14

Parts Warehouse Company

An Automotive Parts Distributor—
A Variety of Problems in Sales Management

Mrs. Elizabeth Korn, owner and president of Parts Warehouse Company, spent considerable time during the summer reviewing the performance of her business over the past several years. While sales revenue for the auto parts distributor had grown steadily in recent years, Mrs. Korn was disturbed by the company's growing cash flow problems. Those problems, it seemed to her, resulted from certain sales and marketing policies that had been instituted with the hope that Parts Warehouse Company could provide faster and more complete service to its customers. This was regarded as very important in this competitive industry.

COMPANY HISTORY

Parts Warehouse Company was founded by Roger Korn, late husband of Mrs. Korn, in 1955. The company, operating out of a medium-size midwestern city, supplied retail auto parts outlets and repair shops with a wide range of automotive parts purchased from numerous national manufacturers. Each year, Mr. Korn plowed the bulk of company profits back into the business to build inventories and to expand PWC's market share in and around the city. This practice, as well as Mr. Korn's personal dedication to customer service, enabled PWC to become the dominant auto parts wholesaler in the area by the early 1970s.

Roger Korn's untimely death in 1972 left Elizabeth Korn with the responsibility of operating a business with which she was unfamiliar. Since the company's reputation was well established and with a willingness to educate herself in the ways of the auto parts wholesaling industry, Mrs. Korn decided to carry on with PWC. Mr. Earl Hemley, Jr., formerly PWC's sales manager, was appointed vice-president of sales and was given full responsibility for operation of the business. By 1976, Mrs. Korn's two sons had entered the business; one served as a salesman while the other became an assistant manager in the warehouse. Mrs. Korn by this time, had become the chief decision maker at PWC, although Mr. Hemley remained responsible for day-to-day operations and regularly was consulted by Mrs. Korn.

INDUSTRY STRUCTURE AND TRENDS

The auto parts industry was dominated by several large manufacturers who sold their products to parts wholesalers, like PWC, serving local markets. Wholesalers competed locally for the business of the large number of auto parts stores, service stations, and repair shops. Because retail outlets needed ready access to a vast array of parts for cars of various makes, models, and years, the wholesaler functioned as a local inventory and delivery service.

The market for auto parts had demonstrated impressive growth in recent years. Inflation and recession had prompted many consumers to put off purchases of new automobiles in favor of fixing their older cars. Moreover, inflation was expected to continue or worsen, promising the continued growth of the auto parts market.

PWC'S ORGANIZATION

The Warehouse Operation

PWC employed twenty-eight people. Four so-called "outside men" served as salesmen and were responsible for designated territories in and around the city. The other twenty-four people worked at the warehouse in a variety of jobs such as order packing, serving the counter trade, delivery, office work, and management.

The company maintained a parts inventory that was large by industry standards. Management sought to stock all items that had been purchased from PWC in the past year. Little effort was made to keep track of requests for new items. Mrs. Korn was concerned because the inventory turnover rate had declined from 6.2 on net sales of $2.1 million three years ago to a current rate of 4.3 on net sales of $2.4 million.

A little over a year ago, the warehouse operation was expanded to include a front counter aimed to handle emergency orders from customers unable to wait for their regular PWC salesman to call. Under this system, a buyer could telephone an order for delivery the next day, or could request that the parts be placed in a special bin set aside for the buyer's own driver to pick up. This procedure applied only to small orders; larger telephone orders were transferred to a back desk in the shipping room and processed as if the order had been sent in by a PWC salesman. Many buyers, however, did not consolidate their orders, preferring to call them in frequently throughout the day. Because PWC delivery trucks visited each buyer daily, it was only necessary for buyers to pick up rush orders personally. However, it was permissible for a buyer to walk into the warehouse and order parts over the counter.

The front counter concept had been enthusiastically received by PWC customers. However, Mrs. Korn noted some problems with the system. First, buyers tended to stock fewer parts, preferring to place frequent small orders with PWC. Second, the larger number of small orders required more personnel to fill them than when fewer numbers of large orders were being processed. Although these were serious problems, Mrs. Korn did not want to discontinue the front counter because it was a great convenience for customers and a major factor differentiating PWC from other auto parts wholesalers.

PWC maintained a liberal returns policy. A buyer could return any item for any reason and receive full refund. Parts manufacturers, however, limited returns to 5 percent of purchases and charged a 10 percent penalty for any returned parts. Although returns to PWC averaged 15 percent of sales, management felt that no costs were incurred because the items were simply returned to inventory. Mrs. Korn wondered, however, if there might not be hidden costs associated with these policies.

PWC priced in strict accordance with price sheets supplied by the manufacturer. Prices normally allowed the wholesalers a 20 percent margin on most items. Although there were two discount auto parts wholesalers in the market served by PWC, they were not considered important competitors because of PWC's location and service. Sales had increased at a rate of 3 to 4 percent over the past five years. Mrs. Korn expected net sales (after returns and allowances) to reach $2.75 million for the current year.

Profits had been averaging 3 to 4 percent of net sales. Although inflation had helped to spur sales, profits were beginning to suffer because, as PWC's average collection period increased, the firm's cash flow deteriorated. Consequently, the firm could not always take advantage of the 2 percent discounts offered by manufacturers for early payment.

The Sales Organization

Three of the four sales personnel employed by PWC covered the immediate metropolitan area, which generated 80 percent of the firm's sales. The fourth handled accounts in the outlying regions within 120 miles. The jobs of sales personnel involved two major responsibilities: (1) each existing account was to be called upon regularly and sold sufficient merchandise to maintain the inventory of that account at a certain level, and (2) new accounts were to be established in the sales areas. Quantity and composition of the inventories of the new accounts were left to the judgment of sales personnel.

Some Problems

Problems associated with management of the sales force and the compensation plan had surfaced recently. It was believed that personnel changes and territory redesign had contributed to these difficulties. The current sales manager, Richard Ziegler, had been promoted from his selling position three years ago. He had found it increasingly difficult to handle his management responsibility, and he attributed this mainly to the fact that he was still responsible for selling a group of accounts. His inability to perform either job adequately pointed to a further problem, this one with the compensation plan.

Originally, each person on the sales force was paid a commission of 2.25 percent of the total billings to their accounts, regardless of whether the order was placed through sales personnel or called in directly to the warehouse. Two years ago, the company began receiving repeated complaints from five large accounts—the salesperson, Richard Ziegler, was providing inadequate service. Management responded by placing those accounts with PWC's best salesperson and gave his accounts to the sales manager. The total billings from those five accounts, however, was not sufficient to provide the same income that the best salesperson had earned handling his former accounts. Management decided, then, to continue paying the best salesperson's commissions on his old accounts, while the sales manager was given a much lower rate on PWC's total billings so that his earnings remained the same.

These sales management and compensation problems gave rise to a more serious problem—motivation. Because business had been very good of late and because sales personnel were paid for any sales coming from accounts in their area, sales personnel were simply taking orders rather than aggressively promoting products to current and potential customers. Mrs. Korn was disturbed to see this happening. She knew each of these individuals to have been very competent, hard-working salespeople in the past.

The sales area outside the city represented PWC's attempt to expand its market. These accounts were not numerous and were widely dispersed. A system was set up in an attempt to afford them the same availability of service as provided to local customers. When additional parts were needed, the order could be telephoned to the shipping department and would be delivered within two days. If orders exceeded $250, there was no charge for delivery. The same $250 minimum for free delivery applied to the weekly orders taken by sales personnel.

The Current Situation

Mrs. Korn's appraisal of her company's performance in recent years led her to conclude that, while PWC was basically sound and could look forward to an expanding market and growing market opportunities, certain nagging problems required immediate attention. She was particularly concerned with PWC's deteriorating cash flow position and declining profitability. Why, she wondered, was inventory turnover continuing to fall? How could the company forecast future demand for PWC products? Why were PWC salesmen no longer motivated to push their products in an effective, professional manner as they once had? How should the company approach its growing market? Should the company aim to increase market share in its present market or work at penetrating markets in other areas? How about the compensation plan?

There seemed to be many things requiring attention, so many that Mrs. Korn did not know where or how to begin. She thought a starting point might be to sit down with the sales vice-president, Mr. Hemley.

Which problems were the most pressing for Parts Warehouse Company? What action should PWC have taken? What was the sales executive's job in this case?

CASE 1-15

Ecol Oil Company

A Major Petroleum Company—An Industrial Customer's Complaint

Don Ames was an Ecol Oil Company sales engineer. His primary responsibility was to market Ecol products to the industrial market. He had been informed by an Ecol distributor that one of his industrial accounts, North Machine Company, was having trouble with a machine lubricated with an Ecol lubricant. Since Mr. Ames had recommended the lubricant to the customer for the application, he visited North Machine Company on the following day to analyze the problem, attempt to offer the customer a solution, and determine if the Ecol Oil Company was liable for any damage to the machine resulting from their actions. He was very familiar with the account as a result of past activities with North Machine Company.

THE COMPANY

Ecol Oil Company was a fully integrated major petroleum company engaged in exploration, production, and refining and marketing. Its products included automotive fuels and lubricants and industrial fuels and lubricants. Total sales revenues were about $12 billion. Ecol's marketing organization was segmented according to customer groups. Products for the motoring public were generally marketed through dealer-operated service stations that were supplied by local commissioned distributors. Industrial users were supplied directly by the local distributor. Service station accounts were the responsibility of Ecol sales representatives while industrial accounts were the responsibility of Ecol sales engineers. For the industrial market, the United States was divided into five regions, each of which was subdivided into five areas. The sales engineers reported to an area sales manager who, in turn, reported to the regional sales manager. The southeastern region included nine states that were covered by sixty-three sales engineers. Mr. Ames's geographical territory was northeast Georgia and included twenty-one distributorships. He was compensated by a straight salary that was reviewed annually by management.

NORTH MACHINE COMPANY AND THE PROBLEM

North Machine Company, located in a Georgia town of under 25,000, manufactured small textile machinery. All its petroleum requirements were served by the Ecol Oil Company's local commissioned distributor. The account was one of Mr. Ames's smaller industrial consumers, accounting for $2,980 worth of lubricants in 1979. Although the sales volume was small, North Machine Company was one of three major industries located in its community, and the local Ecol distributor was responsible for acquiring the account when it began operation.

One year ago, Mr. Ames had made a survey of all mechanical equipment operated by North Machine Company to update lubrication recommendations. This was part of the service package offered by Ecol Oil Company to its customers. The machine that prompted the customer complaint—a Burns A-24 Surface Grinder—had been included in the Ames survey. The lubricants recommended by Mr. Ames conformed to the type recommended by the manufacturer of the machine. The recommendation is cited in Exhibit 1.

When Mr. Ames visited North Machine Company to investigate the machine problem, he met Mr. Peterson, who was a service engineer for Burns Company, the machine's manufacturer. Mr. Peterson explained that the machine was not functioning properly due to extreme wear of the slides and ways that supported the spindle and grinding wheel. These ways were lubricated under pres-

EXHIBIT 1 Recommended Lubricants

Equipment	Lubricant	Frequency
A 24 Burns Surf. Grinder		
Lubr. & Hydr. Syst. Reservoirs	#682	Ck. Wk. - Chg. 6 Mos.
Spindle, Hydr. Motors Sealed	None	
Fan motor Brgs. Hand Oiled	Harmony 53	3 weeks
#12 B. & S. Milling Machine		
Spindle Change Gear Case Reservoir	#682	Ck. Wk. - Chg. 6 Mos.
S Spindle Transverse Adj. Press. Gr. Fitt.	Flex A	Weekly
Table hand Adj. Press. Gr. Fitt.	Flex A	Weekly
Spindle head Elev. Scr. Hand oiled	Harmony 53	Monthly
Feed Change Gear Case Reservoir	#682	Ck. Wk. - Chg. 6 mos.
Arbor Yoke Reservoir	Harmony 53	AR
Spindle & feed motors Sealed	None	
#0–8 Cinc. Plain Auto Milling Mach.		
Hydr. Syst. & Table Drive Reservoir	Harmony 44	Ck. Wk. - Chg. 12 Mos.
Spindle Drive Parts Reservoir	Harmony 53	Ck. Wk. - Chg. 12 Mos.

sure with oil pumped from the hydraulic system. The machine was hydraulically controlled and had a closed combination hydraulic and lubrication system. The configuration of the machine and the worn parts were diagrammed in Mr. Ames' Technical Field Report. (The Technical Field Report is contained in Exhibit 2.) After the machine was disassembled and examined, both men agreed that the wear resulted from poor lubrication. However, they disagreed on the cause of the poor lubrication.

North Machine Company was operating four other Burns A-24 Surface Grinders of the same age in addition to the one that failed, and the other four machines were developing the same wear problem. After examining the machines, Mr. Ames and Mr. Peterson met with Mr. King, a manager and part-owner of North Machine Company, to discuss what caused the machine to fail and to determine who was responsible.

The total cost of repairs to the five machines was estimated at over $20,000. At the meeting, Mr. Peterson told Mr. King that he did not think the lubricant being used, Ecol Oil #682, had the required lubrication properties to lubricate the ways properly. He also pointed out that Burns Company had not had the wear problem with other A-24 Surface Grinders using another oil company's Vacuoline Oil #1405. Burns Company recommended the use of Vacuoline Oil #1405, but agreed that its equivalent or oils conforming to A.S.L.E. W-150 specifications could be used satisfactorily. Mr. Ames agreed that the problem appeared to result from poor lubrication; however, he felt that Ecol Oil #682 was not necessarily the cause of the problem. Mr. Ames claimed that other factors needed investigating, including (1) the operating condition of the lubricating system and (2) the condition of the used oil in the system. The lubrication system

EXHIBIT 2 Technical Field Report

TECHNICAL FIELD REPORT
PREPARE AND ROUTE COPIES IN ACCORDANCE WITH INSTRUCTIONS FROM REGION OFFICE.

DISTRICT	REGION	SAMPLE NO. (S)
ATHENS, GA	SOUTHERN	A94(A) used oil A94(B) new oil A94(C) deposit
SIGNATURE	APPROVED	TYPE OF ANALYSIS See Mr. Edwards A94(D) oimcool 5
DATE	DATE	

CHECK ONE

PRODUCT(S) 682 OIL/ STAINLESS METAL 41 COMPLAINT ☑ SERVICE ☐

CUSTOMER AND/OR SUBJECT NORTH MACHINE CO

ADDRESS Georgia

SAMPLES TAKEN (DATE AND SOURCE) A94(A) oil reservoir A94(D) reservoir

NO. OF HOURS ON SAMPLE 2/17 A94(B) opened 55 gal. RSD

A94(C) taken from the pipe of drum pump in 55 gal. RSD

FOR WHAT IS THIS PRODUCT USED AND IN WHAT EQUIPMENT? BURNS A24 Surface Grinder, single oil lubricates ways and functions as hydraulic oil

AGE AND CONDITION OF EQUIPMENT less than two years

WHAT IS TYPE OF SERVICE ON OPERATIONAL CYCLE? 8 hours/day

PLEASE INCLUDE ALL APPLICABLE INFORMATION—ADD ADDITIONAL WHERE NEEDED

BRAND NAMES:

GEL ______ OIL ______ GREASE ______

OIL CHANGE INTERVAL ______ GREASE INTERVAL ______ OIL FILTER ______ CHC. INT. ______

AIR FILTER TYPE ______ CHG. INT. ______ ANTIFREEZE, NOW ______ PREVIOUSLY ______

THERMOSTAT TEMP. RATING ______ OPERATING ______ PCV SYSTEM OPERATING ______ MANIFOLD HEAT VALVE OPERATING ______

IS SIMILAR EQUIPMENT OPERATED SATISFACTORILY BY SUBJECT USING SAME PRODUCTS? ______

SHOW LOT NO., FILLING DATE AND PACKAGE SIZE ______

LIST COMPETITIVE PRODUCTS AND ADDITIVES USED ______

IMPORTANT

GIVE DETAILS SURROUNDING REQUEST FOR SAMPLE ANALYSIS. GIVE OPINIONS OF INTERESTED PARTIES AND RECOMMENDATIONS MADE BY ECOL REPRESENTATIVES. ATTACH ADDITIONAL SHEET IF REQUIRED. IT IS MOST IMPORTANT THAT AS COMPLETE INFORMATION AS POSSIBLE BE PROVIDED. THIS WILL ENABLE THOSE ANALYZING THE TEST RESULTS TO PROVIDE MORE HELP AND SEPCIFIC RECOMMENDATIONS.

682 Oil was recommended for this application as being the same type oil as Mobil Vacuoline Oil 1405. The manufacturer has had good results with the Mobil product. The ways which support the spindle and grinding wheel on the machine in question are badly gouged and worn. These slides and ways are stationary for about ½ second while the work is passed under the wheel. The spindle is then moved forward or backward on the ways to position the wheel for a new pass. The ways and slides on the table are in good condition and show no signs of wear. North is operating 5 of these machines, and they all are developing the same problem. I believe there is too great of a load on these slides and ways to be lubricated by an oil of the Vis of 682 or Vacuoline 1405. Mr. R. J. Peterson, Burns Service Engineer, claims they have no problem with the Mobil product. Will you test this oil for contamination with the coolant and test the new oil to see if it meets specifications? The deposits included are of the type which are plated out on parts of the machine. What are they? Can you give me a comparison of the load carrying capabilities of ECOL 682 OIL and Mobil Vacuoline Oil 1405? BURNS may claim that the oil is responsible for this damage. I have told Mr. King and Mr. Peterson that the Ecol 682 Oil was recommended as having the lubrication properties and capabilities of the Mobil Vacuoline Oil 1405. If we show that this is true I believe we will have fulfilled our responsibilities.

Mr. Ames

was checked and adjudged to be functioning properly. Ames collected samples of the used oil for analysis as to physical properties and possible contamination.

During this meeting Mr. Ames questioned the design of the Burns A-24 grinder that used the same oil for hydraulic use and way lubrication. He believed that a higher-viscosity oil would be better suited for way lubrication, but this would have required a separate reservoir and other additional equipment. Mr. Peterson said that his company did make a surface grinder similar to the A-24 with a separate system for way lubrication, and it did require a higher-viscosity oil than the Vacuoline #1405. Mr. Peterson further stated that the hydraulic control systems were designed for an oil with the viscosity of Vacuoline #1405 and that machines with a combination hydraulic and way lubrication system had to use oil of that viscosity. He claimed that Vacuoline #1405 had an additive (fatty acid) that gave it the necessary lubrication properties to be used as both way lubricant and hydraulic oil.

At the conclusion of the meeting, Mr. King stated that he did not believe the failure was the result of poor service or maintenance practices by North Machine Company personnel. He said that he planned to meet with executives of Burns Company and to ask them to repair the machines at Burns' expense. He also stated that it was Ecol's responsibility to recommend the correct lubricant for North Machine Company's machinery and asked Mr. Ames to supply additional information on the Ecol Oil #682. Mr. Ames agreed to forward the results of the used oil analysis and the information Mr. King wanted on Ecol Oil #682. It was decided that if Mr. Ames' oil recommendation was in error, North Machine Company would then hold Ecol Oil Company liable for the repairs.

Several weeks after the initial meeting, Mr. Ames received the results of the sample taken at North Machine Company. Ecol Research and Development Laboratory made the analysis (two to three weeks were usually required to make the analysis and to report the findings). The analysis showed that the used oil taken from the reservoir contained particulate matter identified as sand. A sample of new oil taken from the opened drum at North Machine Company was shown to meet the manufacturer's specifications and to be similar in type to Vacuoline #1405. The analysis report is in Exhibit 3.

EXHIBIT 3 ECOL Oil Company-U.S. Technical Service

Customer's Name and Address	North Machine Co. Georgia
Type K Analysis	
Sample No.	A 94 (A)
Reference:	R 2313
Product Brand & Grade	ECOL 682 OIL (Stainless Metal 41)
Source	Hydraulic Oil System
Unit Make	Burns A 24 Surface Grinder
Unit Model	—
Unit Number	—
Unit Capacity: Gal.	—

EXHIBIT 3 (*Continued*)

Customer's Name and Address	North Machine Co. Georgia
Make-Up Oil Added: Gal.	—
Total Unit Service. Hr.-Mi.-Yr.	—
Sample Service: Hr.-Mi.-Mo.	—
Date Sample Taken & Received	2-18; 2-26
Inspection:	
Gravity, ASTM D 287: °API	27.1
Viscosity, SUV, ASTM D 88: Sec.	
100°F	164.5
210°F	42.6
Viscosity Index, ASTM D 567	57
Color, ASTM D 1500	L1.5
Appearance, 70–80°F, 498	Bright
Neutralization Value, ASTM D 664	
Total Acid No.	0.93
Insoluble Matter, ASTM D 893: % by Wt.	
n-Pentane	0.01
Benzene	—
Resins	—
Flash, OC, ASTM D 92: °F	350
Water, Qual., 797	Absent
Sulfated Ash, ASTM D 874: %	—
Microscopic Examination of Benzene Insolubles, 707	Insufficient Insoluble
Wear Metals: PPM	
Aluminum	3
Barium	L THN 1
Boron	L THN 1
Calcium	L THN 5
Chromium	2
Copper	33
Iron	2
Lead	L THN 10
Silicon	L THN 1
Silver	L THN 1
Sodium	4
Tin	L THN 1
Particulate Matter MG/L	582
Particulate Size Microns	
L THN 25%	100.6
Nature	Sand Carbonaceous
Type P	
Sample No.	A 94 (B)
Reference:	R 2314
Product Brand & Grade	NEW ECOL 682 OIL (Stainless Metal 41)
Source	—
Unit Make	—
Unit Model	—
Unit Number	—
Unit Capacity: Gal.	—

EXHIBIT 3 (*Continued*)

Customer's Name and Address	North Machine Co. Georgia
Make-Up Oil Added: Gal.	—
Total Unit Service. Hr.-Mi.-Yr.	—
Sample Service: Hr.-Mi.-Mo.	—
Date Sample Taken & Received	2-18; 2-26
Inspection:	
Gravity, ASTM D 287: °API	28.0
Viscosity, SUV, ASTM D 88: Sec.	
100°F	164.2
210°F	43.2
Viscosity Index, ASTM D 567	77
Flash, OC, ASTM D 92: °F	370
Pour, ASTM D 97: °F	−35
Color, ASTM D 1500	L0.5
Carbon Residue, Ramsbottom, ASTM D 524: %	0.06
Neutralization Value, ASTM D 664	
Total Acid No.	0.96
Sulfated Ash, ASTM D 874: %	—
Saponification No., ASTM D 94	7.6

COMMENTS: Sample analysis of used oil shows properties that compare favorably with the new oil. This oil like Mobil Vacuoline 1405 contains a fatty agent to provide mild E.P. properties. However, the used oil is very high in particulate matter. Sand was identified in this matter. This is abrasive, and most likely is the basic cause of your troubles and maybe coming from grinding process. System should be flushed and cleaned and new oil installed. Cleanliness is stressed to keep contaminants from hydraulic system. Also possible that the dirty oil is plugging lines to upper ways causing starved lubrication, indication of coolant contamination.

Sample No.	A 94 (C)
Reference:	R 2315
Product Brand & Grade	ECOL 682 OIL or STAINLESS 41 Deposit
Source	Pipe or Drum Pump
Unit Make	24 Surface Grinder
Unit Model	—
Unit Number	—
Unit Capacity: Gal.	—
Make-Up Oil Added: Gal.	—
Total Unit Service. Hr.-Mi.-Yr.	—
Sample Size	0.4 GMS
Date Sample Taken	2-18-70; 2-26-70
Inspection:	
Appearance	Light Gray Deposit

EXHIBIT 3 *(Continued)*

Customer's Name and Address	North Machine Co. Georgia
Insoluble Matter	
n-Pentane D893	55.7
Benzene	32.1
Microscopic Examination of Benzene	
Major	Light Gray Material
Ash, 599: %	7.87
Spectrographic Analysis 905:	% of Ash
Aluminum	0.6
Chromium	0.7
Copper	0.2
Iron	1
Lead	2
Magnesium	0.03
Manganese	0.07
Nickel	0.07
Potassium	0.02
Silicon	0.4
Sodium	0.4
Zinc	60

INFRARED ANALYSIS: The spectra of the deposit indicates the presence of a petroleum oil, small concentration of carbonyl ester material which probably is attributed to fatty oil in 682 oil, salt of an organic acid which has a spectra identical to zinc stearate.
COMMENTS: The major portion of the sludge deposit was a light gray material identified as a zinc compound. There is no zinc in Ecol 682 oil. The source of this contaminant should be determined.

Due to prior commitments, Mr. Ames could not visit North Machine Company the week he received the analysis from the laboratory. The analysis indicated that sand contamination was a probable cause of the worn ways and, realizing that the other four A-24 Surface Grinders were also possibly operating on oil contaminated with sand, Mr. Ames telephoned Mr. King to discuss the results of the analysis. As recommended in the laboratory report, Mr. Ames advised that they flush the reservoirs of all A-24 grinders and refill them with new oil to avoid further gouging and wear of the ways. Mr. King acknowledged the possibility of sand contamination of the oil, as he knew that the parts which were machined on the A-24 grinders were sand-cast before being machined. However, Mr. King was unwilling to accept Ecol Oil Company's theory that the micronic particulate matter, sand, was the cause of the problem. He further stated that he was negotiating with Burns Company, and until the problem was resolved they would operate the four remaining Burns A-24 Surface Grinders on Vacuoline #1405 oil at the request of Burns Company. He said that they would flush the machines and also determine how the sand entered the oil system. Written copies of the analysis and Ecol's comments were forwarded to Mr. King by Mr. Ames.

In the negotiations that followed, the Burns Company executives continued to claim that North Machine Company was using the wrong lubricant and that this was the cause of the wear of the ways. This attitude of Burns Company caused Mr. King to write Mr. Ames requesting written confirmation from Ecol Oil Company that its #682 oil was equivalent to Vacuoline #1405 for its application (Exhibit 4). Mr. Ames passed this letter to the director of Product Application, who answered Mr. King's letter. The director assured Mr. King that the #682 oil was the equivalent of Vacuoline Oil #1405 (Exhibit 5).

Mr. King later recalled Mr. Ames's remarks concerning the possibility of poor design of the Burns A-24 Surface Grinder. In a telephone conversation, Mr. King asked Mr. Ames if he believed that the ways in question could be lubricated satisfactorily by any oil of the viscosity of Vacuoline #1405 or Ecol Oil #682. In a subsequent letter (Exhibit 6), Mr. Ames reported to Mr. King that the ability of the ways to carry the necessary load under hydrostatic conditions was a function of several design factors: surface area of the ways, oil pump pressure, height of separation between surfaces, quantity of oil flow, and the viscosity of the oil. Mr. Ames stated that the machine should have been designed consider-

EXHIBIT 4

NORTH MACHINE COMPANY

PLEASE REPLY TO:
April 13

Mr. Ames
P.O. Box 1272
Athens, Georgia 30601

Dear Sir:

In order to complete our investigation of the galling problem on our Model A-24 Burns Surface Grinders, we are in need of written confirmation from Ecol that Ecol Oil No. 682 is equivalent to Mobil Vacuoline Oil No. 1405 in so far as being a suitable combination hydraulic & way lubricating oil, and that Ecol Oil No. 682 is recommended by Ecol for this application on the Model No. A-24 Burns Surface Grinders.

Your prompt attention to the above is requested and will be appreciated.

Yours truly,

Mr. King

EXHIBIT 5

ECOL OIL COMPANY - U.S.

April 22

Mr. King
North Machine Co.

Dear Mr. King,

This has reference to your letter of April 13, which was directed to Ecol Sales Engineer Mr. Ames in Athens, Georgia. Mr. Ames has requested that we answer your inquiry directly.

Ecol NO. 682 OIL is a compounded oil having a saybolt universal viscosity of 147.5 seconds at 100°F. Therefore, it is quite similar in formulation to the Mobil Vacuoline Oil No. 1405, and we feel that Ecol NO. 682 OIL is a suitable combination hydraulic and way lubricating oil.

We hope that this information will be helpful to you, but if you should require any additional data, please do not hesitate to contact Mr. Ames. We take this opportunity to thank you for the business which you have given our company, and we look forward to serving you in the future.

Sincerely,

ECOL OIL COMPANY - U.S.

Allan Johnson, Director
Product Application
Southern Region

cc:—Mr. Ames - Athens
Note: While this letter should satisfy Mr. King's requirements, we call your attention to the previous TSR's covering analyses of oils from this machine. It would appear that the failures which this account experienced were the direct result of poor housekeeping practices, as shown by the large amount of particulate matter in the oil. Neither lubrication nor machine design was indicated as a probable cause of failure.

ing only the design factors stated. If the system has been well designed, the additives (fatty acid) desired by Burns Company would not be necessary. Mr. Ames included the necessary calculations and formulas to determine if the oil of the viscosity of Vacuoline #1405 and Ecol Oil #682 was capable of supporting the necessary load. Burns Company would have to supply some of the data to complete the calculations. He advised Mr. King not to discount the possibility that the particulate matter present in the oil was the source of his difficulties.

Later, the Ecol Oil sales engineer in Boston, Mr. Wagner, met with the

EXHIBIT 6

ECOL OIL COMPANY - U.S.

May 14

Mr. King, Manager,
North Machine Company
Georgia

RE:—Burns A24 Grinder

Dear Mr. King

Mr. Allan Johnson's letter addressed to you on April 22 states that we believe that Ecol No. 682 Oil is a suitable combination hydraulic and way lubricating oil. To answer your question concerning the ability of a 150 second oil to lubricate the ways in question, several design factors must be investigated. The load carrying capacity of these ways is a function of surface area, oil pump pressure or pressure differential, height of separation between surfaces, the quantity of oil flow, and the viscosity of the oil. Additives are often effective in reducing wear when boundary conditions exist. These ways should be designed to operate hydrostatically and the effect of additives would not be considered in this design.

The attached formula and calculations can be used to estimate the load-carrying capacity of the ways under hydrostatic conditions. I have made several simplifying assumptions which are stated, Burns Co. should be able to supply you with the necessary data on the Model A-24 Grinder to complete these calculations.

The results of previous sample analysis should not be overlooked. The particulate matter present in the oil is a possible source of your difficulties.

If you have any more questions, please do not hesitate to contact me.

Yours very truly,

ECOL OIL COMPANY - U.S.

Mr. Ames
Sales Engineer

manager of Burns' service department, Mr. Green. Mr. Green told Mr. Wagner that he did not believe Ecol Oil #682 was the equivalent of Vacuoline Oil #1405 and, therefore, North Machine Company was not using the correct lubricant. Mr. Wagner contended that both Burns Company and North Machine Company had neglected to consider the contamination of the oil in their evaluations of the problem.

Burns Company claimed that it was not responsible for the damage to the A-24 Surface Grinders since North Machine Company was not using their preferred lubricant, Vacuoline #1405. Furthermore, Burns Company recommended that North Machine Company make a claim against Ecol Oil Company for the damages if Ecol could not prove that their oil #682 met the A.S.L.E. W-150 specifications, even though the specifications were not used by Burns Company as a means of evaluating lubricants until after the machines in question were bought and operating on the Ecol Oil #682. At that time Ecol Oil #682 had not been tested against A.S.L.E. W-150 specifications by Ecol since it had another oil that it offered against those specifications.

Whose side of the argument do you favor? Why? What should Ecol Oil do?

CASE 1-16

The Banner Company

Integrated Food Products Company—Solicitation of New Accounts

The Banner Company, which had annual sales in excess of $800 million, processed and distributed lines of dairy products, foodstuffs, and such specialties as glues and animal food supplements. These lines were marketed throughout the United States and Canada by five separate sales organizations departmentalized by products. Each of these sales organizations was further divided geographically by districts and branches. The Spokane branch of the Northwest District of the Ice Cream and Fluid Milk Division manufactured and distributed bulk and packaged ice cream, ice cream novelties, and fruit sherbets. Because sales depended to a large extent upon the number of outlets selling Banner ice cream, Mr. Shaw, sales manager of the Spokane branch, was considering ways to aid sales representatives in the solicitation of new accounts.

Banner ice cream was sold to three types of accounts. More than 60 percent of all ice cream sales were made to retail dealers, including soda fountains, drugstores, variety stores, independent grocers, chain supermarkets, and ice cream drive-ins. In the Spokane branch's territory, approximately 500 dealers handled all or part of the Banner line. Depending on the size of the account, deliveries to retailers were made once or twice a week. Approximately 20 percent of the sales of ice cream were made to restaurants, which were serviced two or three times per week. The remaining 20 percent were sold to industrial and institutional accounts, including manufacturing plants and schools, which used the ice cream in connection with the operation of cafeterias. Deliveries to industrial and institutional accounts were usually at the rate of four times per week.

In the Spokane branch there were two sales representatives and four route salespeople, all of whom worked under Shaw's direction. The job of the sales representatives consisted of the solicitation of all types of new accounts, the performance of "missionary" duties, and the changing of point-of-sale displays in retail stores. Each week, sales representatives devoted the first three days to calling on prospective accounts. Normally, a sales representative could make six to twelve calls during the three days allotted for this purpose. On Thursdays and Fridays, the sales representatives visited established accounts and changed displays. Each established account was visited at least once every four to six weeks, but some that demanded special attention were contacted weekly. All point-of-sale displays were changed six times a year. Sales representatives were required to submit daily written reports on their activities and to discuss their plans with Shaw each morning prior to making their first call.

The four route salespersons were primarily deliverymen. Since dealers ordered ice cream directly from the trucks, the route salespeople had to be skilled in the anticipation of dealer wants when they filled out their truckload orders. Although route salespeople did not solicit new accounts, frequently they turned over the names of prospects to sales representatives.

With the objective of obtaining an even pattern of retail distribution, each sales representative regularly made an informal survey of the assigned district. These surveys were conducted monthly during the summer and fall seasons, and bimonthly during the winter and spring. For these surveys, in areas with little or no distribution, the sales representative listed all stores selling ice cream. Each store was then rated as to location, cleanliness, and the like, with the purpose of detecting desirable new distributors for Banner ice cream.

The next step was for the sales representative to attempt the conversion of the best store in the area to a Banner dealership; sometimes, however, the company was satisfied to secure the second- or third-best store as its area outlet. After a sales representative had made the initial call, the new prospect was entered on a rating chart. After subsequent calls, sales representatives entered percentages on the chart, indicating the extent to which it was estimated that the prospects were now sold on the Banner line. All percentage estimates of this type were arrived at solely on the basis of each sales representative's experience in the solicitation of new accounts. For example, when a prospect expressed a real interest in such matters as pricing and terms of sales, the prospect was rated about 75 percent. But when a prospect allowed the sales representative only a few minutes of his time, the prospect was rated approximately 25 percent.

Although chart percentages were used mainly to answer the questions of route salespersons who had turned in the names of prospects, they also served as a general guide for the determination of the frequency of calls by sales representatives. Sales representatives made their second calls on prospects approximately thirty days after the first contacts. Thereafter, the following schedule was used:

Prospect Rating (%)	Indicated Call Frequency (or Action)
0–4	Drop the prospect
5–24	One call every two months
25–59	One call each month
60–79	One call every two weeks
80–100	Weekly calls

The conversion of a prospect into a Banner account took from one month to a year. The experience had been the same whether the outlet was selling a competitive brand or was not selling ice cream at all.

The Spokane branch distributed ice cream north to the Canadian border, east to the Montana-Idaho border, west to Wenatchee, and south to Clarkson, Washington, and Lewiston, Idaho. One sales representative was responsible for the northern and eastern segments of the branch's territory; the other worked the southern and western parts. Sales representatives were paid on a salary-plus-commission plan. Sales quotas were established on the basis of the previous year's sales, plus 10 percent. The arbitrary 10 percent annual increase in quotas was justified by the company on the basis that population in the Spokane branch territory was growing rapidly. Shaw was of the opinion that the size of the Spokane market area and its expanding population would soon mean that the addition of a third sales representative would be desirable and feasible.

Because sales representatives were burdened with a large amount of missionary and sales work, and because their operating territories were very large, they were unable to spend sufficient time in the effective solicitation of new accounts. Some means of making additional time available for this purpose needed to be found. However, Shaw was undecided about a specific approach to this problem.

In what ways could the distribution of Banner ice cream have been improved in the Spokane sales territory?

CASE 1-17

Harmon Business Forms

A Manufacturer of Business Forms— Problem in Obtaining New Accounts

Russ Demarest, general sales manager of Harmon Business Forms, was concerned about the company's sales picture. While the company had grown at a rapid pace during its first six years of operation, sales had leveled off in the last three years. In light of the fact that business form industry sales grew by an average of 12 percent during those same three years, Demarest was hard pressed to do something—Harmon sales had increased by an average of only 1.15 percent in that period. This was unacceptable from management's viewpoint, and Demarest knew that the situation required immediate action.

Harmon Business Forms was established nine years ago by L. C. Harmon following sixteen successful years as a salesperson for Moore Business Forms. The Kansas City–based manufacturer produced a complete line of business forms for virtually every type of user and use. Company sales were $6.5 million.

Harmon business forms were distributed by a field sales force of seventeen men and women, operating out of twelve branch offices located in five states (Missouri, Kansas, Illinois, Arkansas, and Oklahoma). Sales personnel were paid a combination salary and commission, with salary normally comprising over 90 percent of total compensation. The commission rate was 3 percent and was paid on all sales above quota, which was established by the branch manager in consultation with Mr. Demarest. In addition, each branch manager spent considerable time selling, usually to "A-1" accounts. Russ Demarest doubled as the KC branch manager. Branch managers received straight salaries.

Company products and services were competitively priced. Harmon advertised in two monthly magazines, *Data Processing* and *Business Forms*. Advertising was sporadic, as management believed that business forms and related services could only be sold on a personal basis.

Although Harmon produced quality business forms, the success of the company was largely attributed to its sales personnel and their competent, personalized service. Each salesperson was fully capable of working with a potential customer and determining the best "paper flow" system for that particular user. Experience showed clearly that customers stayed with them. Few accounts were lost to rivals, despite the intense competition. A problem, though, was the small number of new accounts. Mr. Demarest was sure that, once a new account was obtained, it would be kept. Company records proved this.

The sales training program, developed by Mr. Demarest, stressed product knowledge and the service aspects of helping a customer design a system that made paper flow in a logical and smooth way. The sales training consisted of two weeks of classes at the Kansas City office (the first KC week was spent learning about business forms, the second on specialized services) and one week with a veteran salesperson in the field. The recruit was then put into a territory. General instructions were given to the new salesperson to not overlook any kind of business because every business in existence had some need for business forms.

At a recent meeting, attended by the company president, vice-president, operations manager, major accounts manager, and Mr. Demarest, it was agreed that Harmon's inability to attract new accounts was a major factor in the company's sluggish sales picture. Among other things, it was suggested to Demarest that he devise a letter, to be sent to each salesperson, outlining the importance of generating new business and proposing methods for obtaining new business. Demarest believed, however, that such a letter would have negligible effect because, he said, each salesperson knew the importance of new business and that obtaining new customers was a simple matter of calling on non-Harmon users to present the Harmon sales pitch. He felt there was no single "method" that should be used; rather, the whole thing could be reduced to making random cold calls on prospective buyers. When questioned, he indicated he was not sure if sales personnel were making cold calls on prospects, so he did not know if they were making presentations. He said that the new-business problem was a general thing, but "two or three branches showed up much better than the others." He said, as far as he knew, that the Wichita and Tulsa branches had brought in about 80 percent of the new business in the past two years.

The major accounts manager, Joe Bailey, suggested that the easiest solution to the problem was to provide more incentive to the sales force to develop new accounts. He proposed that this might be achieved by substituting a commission on all new account sales instead of the present commission on sales above quota. Russ Demarest argued that a financial incentive of this sort would not be a strong enough motivator. Instead, he believed that what was needed was a better program of training in new account development for all sales personnel.

L. C. Harmon, at the conclusion of the meeting, asked Russ Demarest to draft a full-scale plan on how Harmon Business Forms sales personnel could generate more new business. Everyone agreed the opportunities were there; the big question centered on how Harmon could capitalize on them. Harmon asked Demarest to have the plan ready for discussion in two weeks.

Evaluate the divergent viewpoints of Bailey and Demarest.

Develop a plan whereby Harmon Business Forms sales personnel could have captured new accounts. For each part of the plan, provide your reasons.

CASE 1-18

Coggins Granite, Inc.

Manufacturer of Granite Monuments—Sales and Marketing Strategy in a Changing Environment

Frank Coggins, Jr., president of Coggins Granite, Inc., was faced with the task of formulating a marketing strategy for his company that had experienced declining sales volume in recent years. Coggins was a Georgia-based manufacturer of quality granite monuments that were distributed nationwide through a network of independently owned retail outlets. The company was founded shortly after the turn of the century in Elberton, Georgia, and had grown steadily to become one of the largest firms in the industry. In the mid-1970s, however, sales began to fall. Coggins' sales personnel reported that retailers were increasingly resistant to Coggins products and were turning to other suppliers. Although some complaints concerned product quality, the main problem appeared to be one of price.

Coggins had traditionally been one of the higher-priced firms in the southern segment of the monument industry. Retailers and consumers had accepted these higher prices as a reflection of prestige and the quality image associated with the Coggins name. The diminished purchasing power of consumers that had resulted from an inflationary economy had prompted these consumers to seek a lower-priced alternative to Coggins' products. Smaller producers in the Elberton area had taken advantage of the situation with lower-priced monuments. Coggins' market share began to erode.

Frank Coggins' brother, John, who had headed the sales organization for many years, recently left the business. D. Lee Eubanks, a former sales manager with a large New England monument firm, was hired as head of marketing and sales. Messrs. Coggins and Eubanks immediately set about re-examining Coggins' position within the monument industry. Their goal was to formulate a plan to improve the company's performance.

THE MONUMENT INDUSTRY

There were three centers of monument manufacturing in the United States: St. Cloud, Minnesota; Barre, Vermont; and Elberton, Georgia. Though Elberton was a relative newcomer to the granite industry, it had become the world's largest producer of granite monuments. The tremendous abundance of high-quality granite deposits around Elberton had enabled an ever-expanding number of firms to flourish in the area. Elberton's growth had met with determined resistance from northern firms who degraded the quality of stone and the workmanship of their southern competitors. This effort was so successful that, for many years, southern stone was not allowed in many northern cemeteries. Over the years, however, Elberton monuments came to be accepted as equal to or better than the northern product.

There were several granite companies doing business in the Elberton area, ranging in size from Coggins, with over 300 employees, to one-man backyard operations. Almost every granite company in Elberton was an outgrowth of Coggins Granite, Inc. The substantial profits achievable in the granite industry prompted many former Coggins employees to strike out on their own. These companies, in turn, spawned others. Because of the variety of heavy machinery required, the smaller companies participated in only certain stages of monument production.

In 1980, there were 115 Elberton companies doing business in granite and allied products. Their shipments totaled a record $45 million (wholesale value) in that year. During the 1970s, the volume of granite shipments had virtually doubled to 1.9 million cubic feet annually.

Monument Manufacturing

The monument manufacturing process began with granite quarried in open pits. The quarrying process removed rectangular blocks of granite from the walls of the pit. Blocks weighed as much as 50 tons. Various sawing techniques were then used to cut blocks into manageable pieces called slabs. Slabs were cut into smaller pieces for refinishing. Although the majority of monuments were of the same basic type, each piece was individually cut and shaped. A technique called "smoothing" was then used to polish the granite to a mirrorlike finish. The finished monument had to be handled with great care to avoid chipping around the edges.

Typically, a monument was an upright stone with a matching base, although there was an infinite number of ways to differentiate one from another. The buyer could custom order the monument at prices ranging from $75 to more than $100,000.

Monument Retailing

Monument retailers were an even more diverse group than their manufacturing counterparts. Retail outlets ranged from elegant, spacious showrooms to the living rooms of enterprising housewives. There were more than 5,000 retail firms throughout the country.

The typical retailer hunted the local obituary column for leads. Then a brochure was sent to relatives prior to a personal visit. If the prospect was interested, the retailer would help select the monument style and color. For use in the selling process, manufacturers provided a variety of sales aids, such as brochures. When the monument was delivered, the retailer was generally responsible for its erection. Retail prices were approximately 2½ times the wholesale price.

Women bought nearly 70 percent of all monuments. (On the average, women had a greater life expectancy than men.) And, generally speaking, people did not select a monument prior to the death of one's husband, wife, or loved one. The retailer, therefore, had a very delicate selling job. The widow worried about whether or not her choice of a particular monument was what her late husband would have wanted. She also was concerned about the financial implications. Normally, the purchase was paid for out of the insurance funds on which she would be dependent during her remaining years. Retailers found that these uncertainties could not be dealt with through "pre-need" sales because couples typically were hesitant to face the inevitable prospect of death.

COGGINS' MARKETING STRATEGY

Coggins' past marketing success was attributed to an image of quality and prestige. This image was built and reinforced through the use of the Coggins Stone Eternal seal and the Good Housekeeping seal. (Coggins was the only U.S. monument manufacturer with the Good Housekeeping seal.) The Stone Eternal seal was a private symbol used on some Coggins monuments as a guarantee of quality. For a nominal fee, the consumer could purchase this seal and an accompanying certificate that would guarantee the replacement, by Coggins, of a monument that proved to be flawed. While some retailers made extensive use of the Stone Eternal seal, many did not.

Coggins had occasionally used a limited amount of national advertising in family magazines and cooperative newspaper advertising with certain retailers. Since 1960, however, there had been little advertising because demand had exceeded the firm's manufacturing capacity.

To enhance customer service, Coggins had, on several occasions, attempted to build an inventory of basic stock items. This reduced delivery time by four to eight weeks. These experiments had been discontinued, however, due to the large number of Coggins' products and an inability to devote sufficient capacity to the building of inventories. There was a consensus among management that this policy could provide a significant competitive advantage for the company if the logistics could be worked out. Very reluctantly, Coggins had given up this practice.

Mr. Coggins was increasingly concerned about the quality of the company's retailers. Sales personnel had reported that some retailers had allowed their establishments to become run-down and did not maintain images consistent with that of Coggins. Coggins management had never been particularly selective in developing its retail network. Mr. Coggins said, "We've always sold to anyone who paid their bills." He did mention, however, that a northern firm had become very successful by restricting its sales to high-quality retailers.

Coggins' policy had been to set prices according to cost plus a percentage. In the past three years, costs had risen over 40 percent. To counteract sagging demand, and to get the company to full production, management had lowered the price on selected items. Sales personnel reported that retailers were pleased with these specials. Mr. Coggins stated that he wished he could compete on a price basis. However, the nature of monument production precluded any economies of scale. In fact, he said, Coggins' cost structure was higher than the smaller competitors, due to greater fixed costs and overhead associated with operating what essentially was a very large job shop producing a much wider variety of products than smaller companies. Innovations in the manufacturing process were being developed that would eventually narrow the cost gap between the large and small producers; however, the impact of these developments would not be felt for at least five years.

The Sales Force

Nine sales representatives were responsible for selling Coggins products to retailers throughout the United States. Individual territories ranged in size from the metropolitan New York area to a group of fourteen western states. The sales representatives were compensated through a combination of salary and commission, depending on the relative experience and the territory of the individual.

Each sales representative was responsible for two major selling functions: first, for convincing the retailer to maintain a representative selection of Coggins products, and, second, for providing the retailer with the incentive and means to promote Coggins products. As an aid to retail sales, Coggins provided retailers with binders containing descriptions of a wide selection of monuments, complete with transparent overlays depicting the many types of granite carving available. The company charged the retailer a modest fee for these sales aids.

After reviewing past marketing strategies, Mr. Coggins decided to go outside the company for a "fresh marketing approach." He contacted a local university that agreed to provide a group of graduate business students to aid Mr. Coggins and Mr. Eubanks in formulating a five-year marketing plan. Mr. Coggins said, "Our problem has always been one of capacity, not sales. With a changing environment and increasing competition, we've got to shift gears and develop a strategy by which we can successfully compete in this crazy market. I honestly never thought we would come to this."

What sort of sales and marketing strategy would you recommend for Coggins Granite? Is it wise to go "outside" for help? Why or why not? What are the advantages? The disadvantages?

CASE 1-19

Bil-Dry, Grip-On Corporation and Subsidiaries (A)

Manufacturer of Specialty Building Products— Formulating Personal-Selling Strategy

Bil-Dry, Grip-On Corporation and Subsidiaries manufactured specialty building products that were marketed to the building trade and retail consumers. During its twenty-year history, the company had enlarged its operations through plant expansion and acquisition to the point where annual consolidated sales exceeded $1.8 million. Bil-Dry and its subsidiaries[1] retained independent manufacturers' representatives who were responsible for all product sales, except for sales to several large retail accounts that were handled directly by Bil-Dry's marketing organization. Michael Baecher, president of Bil-Dry, had recently approved the hiring of a company salesperson. This person would be responsible for visiting the manufacturers' representatives to encourage them to promote Bil-Dry products more actively. Mr. Baecher was also considering the option of hiring additional company sales personnel to take over all of Bil-Dry's large retail accounts. In addition, a number of other things required attention, among them a decision on securing greater market penetration.

COMPANY BACKGROUND

Bil-Dry began operations twenty years ago in a three-story, 5,400-square-foot building in downtown Norfolk, Virginia. With the introduction of its Grip-On Ready-Mix Coating line eight years age, Bil-Dry moved to a new 26,000-square-foot location outside of Norfolk. Six years ago, Bil-Dry acquired the Stone Mountain Manufacturing Company in Lithonia, Georgia. At this time, the dry product segment of the original operation was moved to the Georgia location.

Acquisition of the Stone Mountain subsidiary enabled Bil-Dry to take part in the tremendous construction boom in Georgia. The rapid expansion forced Bil-Dry to relocate its Stone Mountain subsidiary three times in four years, when it finally purchased a 21,000-square-foot facility in Lilburn, Georgia, outside of Atlanta. During this period, Bil-Dry acquired the Plaxicrete subsidiary that was moved to the Georgia plant. Two years ago, the company acquired facilities in Fort Lauderdale, Florida, enabling Bil-Dry to reach more effectively the Florida and Caribbean markets.

The rapid sales growth had tailed off. A depressed market for residential

[1]For convenience, Bil-Dry, Grip-On Corporation and Subsidiaries is referred to as Bil-Dry. This abbreviation should not be confused with the Bil-Dry entity of the corporation.

construction caused a 16 percent sales decline for the Stone Mountain of Georgia and Plaxicrete subsidiaries. This decline was offset, in part, by increased sales of Bil-Dry and Grip-On products resulting from increased consumer spending in the "do-it-yourself"; market. Stone Mountain of Florida also achieved a healthy sales increase because a larger, more effective network of manufacturers' representatives had been retained. Although Bil-Dry's consolidated sales advanced by only 3.7 percent, the past year was a record year for profits. According to Bil-Dry's president, Michael Baecher, "Our acquisition strategy has begun to pay off. The marketing organization was stabilized and we achieved manufacturing and distribution efficiency by consolidating operations in our three locations in Norfolk, Lilburn, and Fort Lauderdale."

PRODUCTS

The Bil-Dry entity of Bil-Dry, Grip-On Corporation and Subsidiaries manufactured several products used to waterproof exposed concrete and masonry walls. The line included such items as cement coatings, water repellents, floor sealers, floor hardeners, dustproofing agents, hydraulic cement, patching and bonding compounds, and texture coatings. In addition to waterproofing, these products improved the appearance of buildings by adding various colors and textures to plain, unfinished walls. Bil-Dry and Grip-On products were designed for use by consumers for "do-it-yourself" home improvements. The Bil-Dry and Grip-On products accounted for approximately 39 percent of Bil-Dry's total consolidated sales.

The Stone Mountain subsidiaries in Georgia and Florida manufactured adhesives for the installation of ceramic tile products. The product line included a dozen different dry and ready-mixed grouts and mortars to satisfy users' requirements for most types of wall and floor tiling. These products were marketed through ceramic tile distributors to the building trade. Stone Mountain of Georgia and Stone Mountain of Florida contributed about 42 percent and 16 percent, respectively, to consolidated sales.

EXHIBIT 1 Six-Year Sales Growth Rate, Bil-Dry, Grip-On Corporation and Consolidated Subsidiaries

F/Y Ended February 28	% of Change	Bil-Dry	Stone Mountain	Plaxicrete	Stone Mountain-Fla.	Consolidated Total
Year 1	+72.8%	$305,212	$ 210,281			$ 515,493
Year 2	+26.0	356,202	293,628			649,830
Year 3	+29.1	361,567	477,540			839,107
Year 4	+48.0	500,207	715,522	$26,459		1,242,188
Year 5	+41.5	602,841	921,251	51,466	$182,240	1,757,798
Year 6	+ 3.7	710,413	775,238	42,899	294,279	1,822,829
Current Year (projected)	+24.5	755,011	1,054,063	24,044	437,199	2,270,317

The Plaxicrete subsidiary manufactured a variety of liquid resin–based products that, when sprayed onto a building, would appear much like stucco. This subsidiary contributed just over 2 percent of consolidated sales. (Product sales by individual entity are presented in Exhibit 1.)

MARKETING ORGANIZATION—BIL-DRY ENTITY

Bil-Dry's marketing organization was responsible for coordinating the marketing efforts for the Bil-Dry entity and the Stone Mountain and Plaxicrete subsidiaries. The marketing group was headed by the vice-president for sales and marketing. He was assisted by a major accounts field sales manager and a sales coordinator at each of Bil-Dry's three manufacturing locations.

Most of the Bil-Dry and Grip-On products were distributed directly to major retail chains on the east coast. The three most important accounts were Evans Products Company Retail Group (which owned Moore's and Grossman's), Lowe's Companies, Inc., and Diamond International. The Professional Sales Association of Asheville, N.C., had ten men servicing the entire Lowe's chain while Evans Paint Division personnel represented the Bil-Dry entity in the Evans Retail Group. The Bil-Dry entity also sold its products directly to a network of independent building material retailers and small regional chains through a group of eight manufacturers' representatives.

The Professional Sales Association and the Evans Paint Division personnel were responsible for conducting complete sales training programs and seminars for retailers' employees and administering promotional programs in addition to maintaining displays and adequate inventories. Because these sales personnel were responsible for a limited number of locations, they were able to provide these extended services. By contrast, the eight agents servicing smaller regional accounts simply maintained displays and inventory levels, because each was required to call on a large number of accounts located in several states.

To distribute directly to these retail outlets, the Bil-Dry entity had a policy of not selling directly to contractors or commercial users. This was consistent with the Bil-Dry entity's marketing strategy, which focused on the "do-it-yourself" retail customer. Bil-Dry further catered to these retail accounts by maintaining a fleet of delivery trucks, relieving the retailer of the responsibility for maintaining and stocking the Bil-Dry, Grip-On displays.

MARKETING ORGANIZATION—STONE MOUNTAIN ENTITY

Stone Mountain products were marketed through wholesale ceramic tile distributors who sold primarily to installers; with only a small percentage going directly to the "do-it-yourself" consumer market. The company did not sell directly to retailers and products were delivered by company trucks.

Sales and servicing wholesale distributors was the responsibility of five independent manufacturers' agents who covered the United States and Puerto Rico. Each agent, typically, was responsible for several states (except for the Florida representative).

Unlike the Bil-Dry entity, there was little advertising and promotional activity for Stone Mountain products. Only new products got aggressive promotional support.

The Future

John G. Briggs, Jr., vice-president of sales and marketing, wrote a memorandum describing some of the strategic issues that Bil-Dry, Grip-On Corporation and Subsidiaries faced:

> We've recognized the limitations of the Stone Mountain and Plaxicrete operations which stem from their vulnerability to the wide fluctuations in the residential construction industry. We, therefore, intend to focus our attention on expanding our business in retail markets by developing our current accounts to strengthen our base and finding new regional chains to improve our market penetration. This expansion will likely include some new product introductions, some expansion into new geographical markets, and very much expanded promotional activities.
>
> We've recently joined with Owens-Corning in a venture where Bil-Dry will manufacture a new fiberglass-reinforced cement. In addition to selling the product to Corning, we will be adding it to the Bil-Dry line where I expect it will do well with the "do-it-yourself" customer.
>
> The Bil-Dry, Grip-On "Silent Salesman" is an example of the innovative promotional programs that we hope to continue with in the future. The "Silent Salesman" is a permanent merchandiser which displays the entire line. It explains the products and answers many of a customer's potential questions so that the retailer's time is freed up. This is important to them.
>
> We're now looking at several new potential markets in other areas of the United States. Initial contacts and ground work have already begun in Chicago. We feel that we may want to market the Bil-Dry, Grip-On line through hardware distributors there, because we don't have the same kinds of contacts with big retail chains that we have here.
>
> Stone Mountain and Plaxicrete should rebound somewhat as the construction industry gets geared up again. We've expanded our distribution in Florida and Puerto Rico which will give us a boost. The critical need is to expand our customer base. We've just instituted a program of sales goals and quotas for our agents. We've never had anything like this before.
>
> You know, dealing with manufacturer's reps can be a frustrating experience because they're spread all over the map and we have no real control. We've had great results from sales contests, cooperative advertising, and other promotions with Evans and Lowe's. Even if I had the manpower, I'm not sure how I'd design or administer incentive programs with our reps.
>
> The big companies use their own sales force. This hasn't been feasible for us in the past, but I think the time is coming when I'm going to have to move in that direction. I've just hired one man who will be working with the reps and may take over some of the retail accounts that are now being handled by manufacturer's repre-

sentatives. If that doesn't poison our relationships with the reps that I want to keep, I may consider hiring some additional salesmen. We have some problems and many opportunities. We have to make the best of everything.

Identify the problems facing Bil-Dry, Grip-On Corporation and Subsidiaries. For each problem, list the alternatives, evaluate the options, and suggest a course of action, stating your reasons.

Should the company set up its own sales force? Why or why not? What would be the duties of company sales personnel?

CASE 1-20

The Kramer Company

Manufacturer of Men's Toiletries—Seeking Greater Sales and Profitability

Sales executives of The Kramer Company, manufacturer of a limited line of high-priced men's toiletries, were concerned that current sales of Forest Dew, the company's major product, was insufficient to support the present sales organization. Sales for Forest Dew had increased gradually during the past three years; however, the rate of increase was substantially below forecasted figures. At the same time, actual profits for Forest Dew were well below those projected, even for the existing level of sales. As a result, Kramer sales executives sought to conduct an overall analysis of the entire sales strategy underlying its primary product, with the twofold aim of achieving greater sales along with increased profitability to bring both figures closer to their desired levels.

The Kramer Company was a division of Mitchell Company, one of the leaders in the men's grooming-aids industry. The Kramer Company was set up by Mitchell Company as a means of entering the "prestige-price" market for men's personal products and to establish working relationships with department stores and specialty shops. Since its inception, Mitchell had catered to the mass market for men's grooming aids, with an extensive line of successful products. It was hoped that Kramer would permit Mitchell to achieve successful entry into the high-priced market for men's toiletries. Selling unique, high-quality products to a limited market through restricted distribution policy, Kramer also was to be an industry leader in new products and new packaging concepts.

Kramer's first marketing effort was Forest Dew, a shaving cologne. It was packaged in a colorful, uniquely designed bottle and sold in an attractive styrofoam case. Forest Dew was priced at $3.75 per ounce, as Kramer management felt that this price would enhance the prestige of the product. The shaving cologne segment of the men's toiletries market was highly competitive; the bulk of Forest Dew's competition came from such brands as Aramis, Braggi, Kanon, English Leather, and Brut.

The product was test marketed for the Christmas season in New York City and Los Angeles. In New York City, Forest Dew was sold in Lord & Taylor's, Gimbel's, and Macy's, and in Los Angeles it was sold in I. Magnin, May's, and The Broadway. With very favorable results in the test markets, Forest Dew was introduced nationally for the Father's Day and graduation gift seasons. On the basis of the test markets, Kramer estimated that department stores would account for 60 percent of sales, men's stores for 30 percent, and independent drugstores for 10 percent.

Kramer employed a sales force of thirty persons, all of whom were selected from the Mitchell Company and included some of Mitchell's best salespersons. There were three sales regions: New York, Chicago, and Los Angeles. The regions were broken down into districts, with offices in Atlanta, Detroit, St. Louis, Dallas, and San Francisco.

The national sales effort was under the direction of the general sales manager, who was headquartered in Philadelphia. The three regional sales managers reported directly to the general sales manager. Their major responsibilities were related to directing the sales effort in their respective regions. The district sales managers' duties included directing, hiring, and training field sales personnel. District managers had limited account responsibility, calling only on key accounts in their districts. Field sales personnel were required to handle all Kramer business within their respective territories. Salespeople were responsible for selecting the outlets in their respective areas.

The Kramer Company utilized a policy of exclusive distribution for Forest Dew. Management felt this was necessary if Forest Dew was to be a prestige item. No wholesalers were used, as Kramer preferred to deal directly with its exclusive retailers. Executives believed that the absence of wholesalers enabled the firm to control distribution and maintain the prestigious image for Forest Dew. Kramer realized that it could exercise more control over the selling price if retailers had exclusive rights to a territory and did not have price-cutting competition. It was generally recognized by Kramer's sales executives that elimination of wholesalers probably increased the total cost of marketing Forest Dew, since Kramer had to perform the wholesaling functions itself, but this was considered acceptable in light of the heightened image of the product.

Kramer advertising was designed to familiarize the public with the Kramer name and, specifically, the Forest Dew brand of shaving cologne. It was felt that effective advertising that presold the consumer would virtually eliminate the need for personal selling at the retail level. Advertising expenditures were divided among network and local spot television, magazines, and cooperative advertising. To promote a prestige image, Kramer advertised Forest Dew in *New Yorker, Esquire, Sports Illustrated,* and *Playboy*. Its television spots were carefully selected with the Forest Dew image in mind. Kramer engaged in cooperative advertising with some of its larger accounts on a fifty-fifty basis. Kramer's Forest Dew account was handled by the advertising agency of Doyle Dane Bernbach. The heaviest promotions came at Father's Day and Christmas, the seasons that Kramer estimated to account for 75 percent of its sales.

While Forest Dew was in its early stages of market development, Kramer introduced an entirely new line of men's cosmetics. The product was a popularly priced line of after-shave lotion and cologne called Male Image. The new product was intended for the mass men's market, and a policy of intensive distribution was followed. The advertising for Male Image, done by Ogilvy and Mather, used a variety of appeals and concentrated on a hard-hitting approach.

Many retailers that carried Forest Dew would not accept Male Image because of its popular price and because it was sold in K-Mart, Woolco, and a variety of discount department stores and drugstores. The Kramer philosophy was that the company had excluded itself from a segment of the men's-toiletries market and Male Image was introduced to fill that void.

It was too early to estimate the success of Male Image; however, it was clear that Forest Dew was experiencing disappointing sales and profitability. The sales picture of Forest Dew indicated that present sales volume could not support the company's present sales organization. As a result, Kramer was considering the possibility of introducing the Forest Dew line into more retail outlets, such as Penney's, Ward's, Sears, and various drug chains. Management believed that change in distribution policy and sales strategy would make it easier to gain dealer acceptance of its new Male Image line.

What alternatives did the Kramer Company have open to achieve greater profitability for the Forest Dew brand of men's shaving cologne? Analyze each alternative.

CASE 1-21

Martin Packaging Company, Inc.

Manufacturer of Packaging Products and Systems— Evaluation of Sales Strategy

Thomas Steeves, manager of the Marketing Research and Analysis Department of the Martin Packaging Company, Inc., faced the task of evaluating the marketing and sales strategy implications of the new "plasti-shield" bottle being tested by the soft drink industry. The plasti-shield bottle was a new soft drink bottle that had a plastic coating around the lower half of the bottle.

Martin Packaging Company was founded in 1852. The company originally produced only paper products; however, in the last thirty years, Martin purchased a majority stock interest in twenty-four companies and a minority interest in several others. As a result, Martin had a diversified product line. One of the twenty-four companies which Martin controlled was the Dixon Paper Company, a family-held firm.

Dixon was established in 1936 and produced corrugated boxes, folding boxes, dry-cleaning bags, and other types of plastic bags. During World War II, under a government contract, Dixon developed "V-Board" packaging, which consisted of solid fiberboard. V-Board was water-resistant and highly durable packaging that could withstand even the hardest handling abuse. It was used to ship goods across the ocean during the war.

After World War II, it was recognized that V-Board had considerable potential for use as a secondary packaging for soft drinks. Therefore, when Dixon developed the V-Board Coca-Cola carton, Dixon Paper Company grew so rapidly that it became the leader in paperboard packaging.

Martin Packaging Company also was involved with paperboard packaging; however, this part of its packaging line was not profitable. Consequently, when Martin was looking for further vertical integration through a merger, it was evident that Dixon Paper Company offered substantial promise, and Martin began to acquire Dixon stock. After the merger, Martin developed new packaging methods for the soft drink and beer industries. Martin also advanced into automated systems packaging. Net sales were approximately $1.1 billion.

Martin was organized into two divisions for producing and marketing paper and related products. The Martin Container Division produced folding boxes for frozen foods, dry goods, and hardware. It also made plastic Cluster-Packs for margarine and other dairy products. The Martin Packaging Division manufactured secondary packaging for soft drinks, beer, and wine.

The Packaging Division, for which Steeves' research and analysis was conducted, had a direct sales force of forty people. Martin management felt that the secondary packaging industry was changing from one in which the sales force simply took orders to one in which they had to provide "technical assistance" to the customer, as this was critical to success in the packaging industry. Martin's sales force needed an excellent working knowledge of the packaging industry, plus considerable knowledge of each customer's business.

The forty-person sales force was divided along both geographic and product lines. Martin believed it should deliver a total packaging system to its customers, and that to do this, ten salespeople made calls only on soft drink bottlers in major cities to explain the Martin automatic packaging system. The remaining thirty salespersons were assigned geographic areas within the Southeast. These salespeople handled all breweries as well as soft drink bottlers in their areas.

Sales personnel were compensated by salary, with no bonus system in effect, except "across-the-board" bonuses, the size of which was determined by overall company performance.

On the whole, Martin management was pleased with the performance of the sales force and it was regarded as a vital factor in the company's success. However, recently a question had been raised concerning the information-feedback function of the salespeople. Instances were cited in which communications had been either nonexistent or had broken down somewhere between the sales personnel and the management.

The Packaging Division was continually being evaluated because secondary packaging, especially for the soft drink industry, was highly competitive. The industry leaders that provided major competition were International Paper Company, Olin-Mathieson, and Federal Paperboard. Secondary packaging in the soft drink industry consisted of packaging, such as soft drink cartons and wrap-around plastic cartons, which Martin produced. This was in contrast to soft drink primary packaging, which referred to the bottles or cans that contained the soft drink.

Soft drink bottlers traditionally operated small-scale bottling plants in almost every U.S. city of any size. For years they made use of only returnable bottles. Martin was among the leading producers, in sales volume and profit, of the traditional cardboard carton for returnable bottles.

With the innovation of the canned soft drink, the investment capital necessary to bottle (can) soft drinks increased substantially. Bottlers began consolidating into large-scale operations to gain economies of scale. As the primary packaging changed, the secondary packaging changed also. The revolutionary "wraparound" carton was developed. However, Martin did not adopt this new method for several months after its introduction by a competitor, and thus lost its position as the leader in the secondary packaging of soft drinks.

When the nonreturnable bottle was introduced in the soft drink industry, Martin welcomed this innovation. The canned soft drink had reduced the requirements of secondary packaging, because the cans themselves performed much of the advertising, promotion, and protection functions. The nonreturnable bottle called for secondary packaging for promotion as well as for product protection and convenience in handling. Martin was among the leaders in developing cartons for the nonreturnable bottles. As sales of nonreturnable bottles grew, Martin again became the industry leader in secondary packaging in the soft drink industry.

But later, as sales of nonreturnable bottles began to slump, Martin speculated that people were becoming less willing to spend the extra money for nonreturnable bottles. To combat this slump, soft drink bottlers began to work on a new type of bottle that would have a plastic coating around the lower 50 percent of the bottle. This was called the "plasti-shield" bottle. As the industry began research on additional primary packaging, Martin began research on additional secondary packaging.

The plasti-shield bottle was born from interdivision rivalry at Owens-Illinois. Owens-Illinois invested over $40,000,000 in the project. The method of production used could produce up to 580 bottles per minute, with a future anticipated speed of 700 bottles per minute. Based on a forecasted market demand,

Owens-Illinois planned to establish between eight and ten production facilities in Boston, New York, Chicago, Los Angeles, and St. Louis for the manufacture of 10- to 16-ounce sizes of primary glass containers.

The plasti-shield bottle weighed 3.5 ounces less than the lightest nonreturnable bottle of any capacity. The plasti-shield rolls of polystyrene were decorated by printing with up to four colors, but factory production was limited by the number of bottles that could be plastic-wrapped in an "off-line" operation. Initially, machine lines applied the plasti-shield jackets at a rate of only 200 bottles per minute (B.P.M).

Plasti-shield bottles were available in colors of flint, green, and amber glass and were produced in five sizes: 10, 12, 16, 28, and 32 ounces. The plasti-shield container would have three convenience closures: the wide mouth, the aluminum ring-pull, and the narrow neck.

Owens-Illinois had begun work on plasti-shield several years ago, to combat the efficiencies of the 12-ounce can, with essential emphasis on a secondary packaging system to be developed that would handle at least 1,500 B.P.M. and having a packaging materials cost of less than $200 per thousand.

The current secondary packaging of the wide-mouth plasti-shield bottle used the "top-hold" principle in which paperboard cartons were used. Olin-Mathieson, Martin's leading competitor, had arranged for a 60-day delivery on a lease-only basis of a machine designed to run at about 250 B.P.M. This machine was being used in the test setup at Owens-Illinois. The Olin-Mathieson "top-hold" carton was priced at $19 per thousand for 2 by 4 blanks and $16 per thousand for 2 by 3 blanks.

Owens-Illinois expected the plasti-shield bottles, plus the secondary packaging "top-hold" principle, to develop into a major part of the soft drink container market. Owens-Illinois was going after the can market by offering high-speed filling lines and lower packaging costs. Olin-Mathieson had the competitive advantage in secondary packaging with its new system, and Owens-Illinois' market success with plasti-shield could bring Olin-Mathieson into some of Martin's volume accounts.

Steeves believed that it would be necessary to react fairly soon to the plasti-shield bottle and to the competitive threat posed by Olin-Mathieson. He also believed that any delay would seriously threaten Martin Packaging Company's position as industry leader. He believed that development of a sales and marketing strategy was essential to success with the plasti-shield bottle.

Develop a set of recommendations for the sales and marketing strategy that you believe to be necessary to respond to the plasti-shield bottle and to the competitive threat faced by Martin Packaging Company. Specifically, what role do you see for the Martin sales force in this strategy?

6 The Effective Sales Executive

The sales executive's job, like those of other line executives, is to make decisions and to see to it that others carry them out. However, in marked contrast to the jobs of other marketing executives, the job of the sales executive is more action oriented and less planning oriented. Not that sales executives are unconcerned about planning, because they are. But their plans cover rather short periods and concern near-term personal-selling objectives and how to attain them. It is not stretching things very much to say that the main concern of marketing management is the "future" and the main concern of sales management is the "present"—the "here and now." Ultimately, all marketing plans call for action in their implementation, and sales management's plans typically are near to the action point.

What qualifications must sales executives have to make decisions? They require a base of experiential and other knowledge, much of which may not be very explicit; this base provides a "feel" for problems and possible solutions. They need keen awareness of company and sales department goals—they must recognize the key features distinguishing the sort of company that top management is trying to build, and they must visualize the nature and type of contributions the sales department can make toward realizing that future "company image." They need the ability to conceptualize problem situations in areas where they have the main decision-making responsibility and in those where they contribute to decisions that have implications in other marketing areas and/or in other parts of the business.

The decisions that the sales executives are involved in may affect only the sales department, or they may have significant implications elsewhere in the organization. Sales executives, in performing their jobs, must know how to analyze information, how to combine its significance with their own experiential knowledge and judgment (and their willingness to accept a certain amount of risk), how to apply imagination in searching for alternative solutions to problems, how to predict the likely outcomes of different alternatives, and how to choose that alternative with the highest payoff.

NATURE OF SALES MANAGEMENT POSITIONS

The requirements of the sales executive's job vary from company to company and from position to position within companies. However, certain responsibilities are typically assigned to the same types of executives in different companies. It is possible, therefore, to generalize about the activities and responsibilities of sales managers, district sales managers, product managers, and other sales or marketing executives. Some companies have formulated concise statements of duties associated with various positions, known as job or position descriptions. Typical job descriptions for the jobs of sales manager and district sales manager follow.

Position Guide—Sales Manager

Reporting relationship. The sales manager reports to the vice-president of marketing.

Job objective. The primary objective is to secure maximum volume of dollar sales through the effective development and execution of sales programs and sales policies for all products sold by the division.

Duties and responsibilities. In working toward achievement of the primary job objective, the sales manager is expected to be concerned with

1. *Sales program.* The sales manager takes the initiative in establishing short- and long-range sales goals of the division and, in collaboration with other marketing executives, sets sales, profit, growth, market share, and other goals.

   The sales manager arranges for the development of detailed sales programs designed to improve competitive positions, reduce selling and other distribution expenses, and reach established sales goals.

   The sales manager reviews and approves sales policies, sales strategies, and pricing policies (to the extent that they impact upon sales goals) for all products to ensure that short-term operations are in accord with long-term profitability and do not jeopardize other phases of the company's operations.
2. *Organization.* The sales manager establishes an effective plan of organization, and methods of controlling the activities of members of the sales organization, that will provide sufficient time for carrying out the full line of departmental responsibilities.

The sales manager provides leadership both to immediate subordinates and all levels of the sales organization in establishing a sound basis for each individual's self-development, and in making certain that rewards are in line with responsibilities and performance.

3. *Sales force management.* The sales manager identifies promising sources for the recruitment of new sales personnel and sets standards for selection of the most promising recruits.

   The sales manager provides for the training of new personnel so as to achieve high-level performance in the shortest possible time. At the same time the sales manager provides for the training of veteran sales personnel, so as to improve their performance levels and to prepare them for possible promotion. The sales manager sees to it that there is an adequate supply of sales executive talent for replacements up through and including the sales manager's own position.

   The sales manager ensures that sales personnel are properly motivated, so as to achieve optimum sales performance.

   The sales manager establishes a system of sales supervision that controls waste and inefficiency and points sales efforts into the most profitable channels.

4. *Internal and external relations.* The sales manager develops effective working relations with other department heads and the general manager so that significant sales developments can be translated into appropriate courses of action.

   The sales manager develops and maintains relationships with key accounts that provide maximum long-term participation in their available business.

   The sales manager develops and maintains effective working relationships with sales, training, and other key personnel in the employ of customers to ensure that cooperation is beneficial to both parties.

5. *Communications.* The sales manager keeps the vice-president of marketing informed on sales results and future plans of operation.

   The sales manager establishes a system of communications with other sales personnel that keeps them informed of overall departmental sales objectives, results, and problems and keeps the sales manager informed of their needs and problems.

6. *Control.* The sales manager consults with the production manager so that production rates and inventories are geared as closely as possible to actual sales needs.

   The sales manager reviews and approves sales and expense budgets and evaluates periodically the performance of all sales activities in relation to budget and sales goals and takes such corrective actions as are required.

   The sales manager delegates authority and develops control records and performance standards to permit a proper balance of time spent on the various activities in this job description.

Performance criteria. The sales manager's performance is considered satisfactory when

The department's dollar and unit sales are equal to or exceed the quantities budgeted.

The profit contribution of the sales department is in line with plan.

The details of sales plans are in writing and are acceptable to marketing management.

The turnover rate of sales personnel is maintained at a level regarded as satisfactory by marketing management.

Position Guide—District Sales Manager

Reporting relationship. The district sales manager reports to the sales manager.

Job objectives. The primary objective is to secure maximum dollar sales of the company's products in the sales district in accordance with established sales policies and sales programs, within the limits of the sales budget.

Duties and responsibilities. The district sales manager is responsible for the effective deployment of selling efforts and the maintenance of good trade relations in the assigned district. In working toward achievement of the primary job objective, the district sales manager is expected to be concerned with

1. *Supervision of sales personnel.* The district manager evaluates the sales opportunities in the district and assigns territories that have equitable work loads and that permit minimum travel costs, so as to secure maximum dollar sales at minimum cost.

   The district sales manager directs, assists, and supervises sales personnel in maintaining and improving the company's competitive position and in handling special sales or competitive problems.

   The district sales manager rates sales personnel in the performance of all their duties, and at least annually discusses these ratings with them to direct their attention toward areas where improvement is needed.

   The district sales manager advises the sales manager on important personnel problems.

   The district sales manager evaluates the sales personnel's strategies for key accounts, helping each to plan strategy for all assigned accounts and to develop new accounts.
2. *Control.* The district sales manager forecasts short-term sales of the district and works with sales personnel in estimating future sales in their territories so that accurate sales budgets and sales quotas can be developed.

   The district sales manager prepares a periodic progress report on industry condition, forward plans, and the progress made toward sales objectives.

   The district sales manager reports on significant sales or competitive developments that may affect the company's future.
3. *Administration.* The district sales manager is responsible for the efficient

administration of the district office operations and warehouse and stock facilities in accord with established policies and procedures.

The district sales manager develops effective working relations with technical personnel, other district managers, and home office personnel so as to take full advantage of their help to achieve sales goals, reduce costs, and effectively carry out sales programs.

4. *Communications.* The district sales manager studies and analyzes the plans, programs, and policies originating in the home office and interprets them to the sales staff so that these plans, programs, and policies can be coordinated in the district's activities.

   The district sales manager communicates to the sales manager and top administration any information about customers and markets or about personnel that should be of interest to them.

   The district sales manager maintains membership in professional organizations whose activities are of interest and concern to the division so as to promote better customer relations and develop intelligence sources.

Performance criteria. The district sales manager's performance is considered satisfactory when

The district's dollar and unit sales are equal to or exceed the quantities budgeted.

The district's total expenses are no higher than the amounts budgeted.

The profit contribution of the district office and warehouse and stock facilities is in line with plan.

The turnover rate of district sales personnel is maintained at a level regarded as satisfactory by the (general) sales manager.

FUNCTIONS OF THE SALES EXECUTIVE

Many sales executives get promoted into their positions because of their previous performances as salespersons. In some companies, outstanding salespersons have an inside track when sales executives' jobs are being filled. The assumption is that outstanding salespersons will be outstanding sales executives. Nothing could be farther from the truth. The sales executive's job demands administrative skills much beyond those required of salespeople. Personal-selling experience is not unimportant, as sales executives manage people who do personal selling. But personal-selling experience and outstanding personal-selling performance are two different things—most companies can recount instances where an outstanding salesperson failed in a sales executive's job.

Basically, the sales executive has two sets of functions: operating and planning. The operating functions include sales force management, handling relationships with personnel in other company departments and with the trade (middlemen and/or customers), communicating and coordinating with other marketing executives, and reporting to some superior executive (such as the marketing vice-president). In addition, in some companies and fairly commonly in lower-level sales executive positions, the sales executive sells some accounts personally (to keep a "hand in" and to keep abreast of current selling problems and conditions).

The sales executive's planning functions include those connected with the sales program, the sales organization, and its control. The sales executive is responsible for setting personal-selling goals, for developing sales programs designed to achieve these goals, for formulating sales policies and personal-selling strategies, and for putting together plans for their implementation. Sales programs are put into effect through the sales organization, and the sales executive is responsible for designing and shaping the sales organization, for staffing it, for developing the skills of those who are part of it, and for providing leadership to it. Achievement of sales departmental goals requires controls over selling activities, sales volume, selling expenses, and the like. The sales executive is responsible for these and related control activities.

The relative emphasis that sales executives give to the operating and planning functions varies with (1) the type of products, (2) the size of company, and (3) the type of supervisory organization. Customarily, sales executives at all organizational levels devote more time and attention to sales force management than they do to any other single activity.

The significance attached to operating and planning functions varies with the product. If the product is a consumer good, sales executives attach the greatest importance to planning functions: development of sales programs, coordination of personal selling with advertising, and building and maintaining relationships with dealers and customers. If the product is an industrial good, sales executives attach the greatest importance to the operating functions—managing and directing the sales force, making calls with salespeople, and selling personal accounts. Consumer-goods sales managers, in general, spend more time on planning and less on operating than do their counterparts in industrial-goods companies.

The amount of the sales executive's time devoted to planning and operating functions is influenced by the size of the sales organization. Sales executives in small companies spend less time on planning and more on operating. As the size of the company increases, the sales executive devotes more time to planning and less to operating.

Exerting important influences on the way sales executives distribute their time and effort, too, is the type of supervisory organization. When the sales executive supervises the field sales force directly, he or she spends most of the time on operating functions. When the sales executive supervises the field sales force through subordinate sales executives, more attention is devoted to planning and less to operating. Sales executives who have high-caliber subordinates generally are more willing to delegate most of the performance of the operating functions to them and, consequently, have more time left for planning.

QUALITIES OF EFFECTIVE SALES EXECUTIVES

What qualities should sales executives possess? It is difficult to list "success" qualifications. Sales executives' jobs cover a gamut of products, markets, and marketing channels, and there would seem to be few, if any, qualifications in common. Nevertheless, five qualities (or abilities) common to effective sales executives, whatever their fields, can be identified:

1. *Ability to define the position's exact functions and duties in relation to the goals the company should expect to attain.* Sales executives calculate what is entailed in their responsibilities. Whether or not the company provides them with a job description, they draw up their own descriptions consistent with the responsibilities assigned by higher management. Revisions are necessary whenever changes occur in the assigned responsibilities or in company goals.
2. *Ability to select and train capable subordinates and willingness to delegate sufficient authority to enable them to carry out assigned tasks with minimum supervision.* Ability to delegate authority is a must. Effective executives select high-caliber subordinates and provide them with authority to make decisions. Within existing policy limits, decisions are made by subordinates; when an exception falling outside these limits occurs, the superior decides. The more capable the subordinates, the wider policy limits can be and the more the superior's time is freed for planning.
3. *Ability to utilize time efficiently.* The time of sales executives is valuable, and they budget it and use it carefully. They allocate working time to tasks yielding the greatest return. They arrive at an optimum division between office work and field supervision. Even the use of off-duty hours is important. Excessive work time and too little leisure reduces efficiency. Successful sales executives balance such leisure-time activities as community service and professional meetings against personal social activities, recreation, and self-improvement.
4. *Ability to allocate sufficient time for thinking and planning.* Able administrators make their contributions through thinking and planning. They know how and are willing to think. They recognize that reviewing past performances is a prerequisite to planning. They strive to gain new insight that will bring problems into better focus. Effective sales executives shield themselves from routine tasks and interruptions. Failing this, they retreat to Shangri-Las where surroundings are conducive to thinking and planning.
5. *Ability to exercise skilled leadership.* Competent sales executives develop and improve their skills in dealing with people. Although they rely to a certain extent on an intuitive grasp of leadership skills, they depend far more on careful study of motivational factors and shrewd analysis of the ever-changing patterns of unsatisfied needs among those with whom they work. Skilled leadership is important in dealing with subordinates and with everyone else.

RELATIONS WITH TOP MANAGEMENT

Effective sales executives are well above average in initiative and personal drive. Realizing the sales executive's potential, however, depends largely upon relations with top management. Sales executives should want to get ahead, for personal goals are as vital to them as the objectives they set for the sales department, but if they are to achieve these goals, not only must they know where they are going, but top management must be kept abreast of their progress.

Effective sales executives plan and implement their own self-development programs, and setting definite career goals is essential. They harmonize their own goals with those of the organization, this being important for maximum progress of individual and company alike. Whenever the sales executive and the company cease to move toward mutually compatible goals, friction causes both to fall short. When this happens, either the two sets of goals must be reconciled, or the executive should leave the firm. Sometimes, sales executives unilaterally reconcile such goal conflicts (usually by adjusting personal goals to fit those of the organization). More often, they reconcile them through interaction with company top management.

Effective sales executives accept responsibility for all activities related to their positions, but they avoid becoming indispensable. Indispensability is undesirable for both the executive and the company. For the sales executive, it means blocking opportunities for promotion; for the company, it means that too much is being staked on one individual. One way to avoid becoming indispensable is to practice and advocate delegation of authority, and effective sales executives place high priority on training their own replacements. Junior sales executives are well advised to learn and master the duties and responsibilities of the positions immediately above theirs. Promotions come to those prepared for them, and preparation consists of setting definite career goals and adhering to programs of continuing self-development.

Effective sales executives are highly qualified as problem solvers and decision makers. Consequently, sales executives guard against taking too many of their problems to top management. Asking for help in deciding problems is asking for closer supervision (and less authority). Competent sales executives do not require a close watch over their activities.

Effective sales executives keep top management informed on important decisions and the department's plans and accomplishments. They transmit all ordinary reports promptly, and special reports when appropriate. They exercise restraint in reporting their own activities, but they see that their superiors have all the information needed to evaluate their personal effectiveness. Their reports ensure that top management knows in broad outline the problems encountered in selling the company's products, the ways they are handled, and the results accomplished.

Effective sales executives pay attention to the manner in which they communicate with top management. They do not hesitate to give their superiors the benefit of their thinking, but, unless matters of high principle are involved, they are willing to modify preconceived ideas.

When the sales executive has a great idea, is absolutely sure of it, and top management is unconvinced, the sales executive must play the role of super-salesperson and "sell" to those with the authority to decide. When the facts do not speak for themselves—when those in authority fail to grasp their full significance—the sales executive, like any competent executive, should bring to bear his or her full powers of persuasion.

Effective sales executives listen and learn. They keep a dated record of important conversations. They refrain from voluntarily discussing the personal competence of fellow executives. They avoid relaying rumors. They control their executive contacts, never missing scheduled engagements without reason. Sales executives following such rules of conduct experience little difficulty in winning top management's confidence and respect.

RELATIONS WITH MANAGERS OF OTHER MARKETING ACTIVITIES

Sales executives spend most of their time on sales force management; they also are concerned with other marketing activities. The degree of responsibility over these activities, and the amount of time allocated to them, vary with the particular job, but sales executives are almost always concerned with products, promotion, pricing, and distribution. They may also have a role in achieving control over these activities and coordination among them.

Relation with Product Management

Product planning and the formulation of product policies requires numerous decisions. Periodically each product needs appraising in terms of its profitability and its ability to fullfill buyers' wants. Decisions are made on whether each should be retained, changed or improved, or dropped from the line. Other decisions are made on adding new products and on changes in product design and other features. Still other decisions concern product quality, services rendered in connection with sales, and packaging.

Product decisions are often the shared responsibility of marketing, production, research and development, and financial executives, operating as a product committee. Sales executives provide inputs for these decisions. Their contact with the market through subordinates and sales personnel provide them with feedback about product performance and acceptance generally not available from other sources.

Relations with Promotion Management

Chief marketing executives are responsible for setting promotional policies, but sales executives participate in their formulation. Their knowledge of the market and their control over personal-selling activity make sales executives a key source of information, and they occupy a strategic position in implementing promotional plans. Sales personnel are responsible not only for transmitting sales messages to prospects but for securing the use of point-of-purchase displays and for coordinating dealer efforts with advertising programs. Sales executives, because of their key roles in making and implementing promotional policies, must coordinate closely with other executives in the formulation and implementation of the promotional program.

Almost every product relies on personal selling as a promotional method at one or more points in the marketing channel. Personal selling's effectiveness traces to the use of personal contact in conveying the sales message to prospective buyers. But personal selling is the most expensive promotional method in terms of cost per sales message transmitted. The proportion of personal selling in the promotional mix generally must be limited, and it is the sales executive's responsibility to keep selling costs down.

The sales executive makes certain that salespeople keep abreast of current advertising compaigns. Sales personnel need briefing on specific advertising appeals, enabling them to adapt their selling approaches in ways that enhance the total promotional impact. The sales force should know which media are scheduled to carry advertisements for which products and the timing of each ad's appearance. Advertising personnel need access to the sales executive, since this executive is an important source of information about customers, their needs, behavior, and motives.

Sales executives play similar roles with respect to other promotional methods. Decisions regarding the usage of these methods in the promotional mix are normally made by the chief marketing executive or by other specialists. Besides serving as an important source of information, the sales executive secures coordinative efforts by the sales force to ensure that each promotional activity obtains optimum results.

Relations with Pricing Management

When major decisions on pricing policy are required, both the chief marketing executive and the sales executive occupy influential positions in top management councils. Relative to other executives, they generally have much clearer ideas of the prices final buyers are willing to pay, the sales executive because of close and continuing contacts with the market and the marketing executive because of access to pricing information gathered and interpreted by the marketing research staff.

In spite of the fact that these two executives are well qualified to speak with authority on pricing matters, price policies should be formulated and prices should be set by a group of executives. Each department affected should be represented, for pricing policymaking is, by nature, an interdepartmental activity. Included in the policymaking group should be representatives not only of the marketing department but also of such departments as production, cost accounting, credit, advertising, legal, and public relations. Pricing policies should result from the cooperative action of the group rather than from compromises among its members.

Once pricing policy is established, its implementation is the responsibility of the sales executive. For example, the pricing committee might adopt suggested list prices, but the sales executive is the one responsible for informing distributors and dealers and obtaining their conformance. Responsibility for administering prices should be assigned to the sales executive, because the sales department has the closest relationship with the market.

Relations with Distribution Management

Distribution policies are major determinants of the breadth and complexity of the sales department's organization and functions. Selection of a marketing channel, or channels, sets the pattern for sales force operations, both geographically and as to the classes of customers. It is also necessary to determine the number of outlets for the product at each distribution level, and this affects the size and nature of the manufacturer's sales organization and the scope of its activities. Furthermore, marketing management determines policies on the amount and extent of cooperation it desires with members of the distributive network—also influencing the size of the sales force, the nature of the salesperson's job, the need for sales supervision, and the like. Because of the impact of distribution policies upon the sales organization and its activities, sales executives play key roles in providing information needed for their formulation, since they are responsible for implementation of these policies.

COMPENSATION PATTERNS FOR SALES EXECUTIVES

Selling is often important to the success of a company, so it is not surprising that sales executives often command substantial compensation. The importance of selling is reflected in the compensation of top marketing executives who often earn six-figure annual incomes. Top sales executives have compensations averaging 70 percent of those of top marketing executives in the same companies. In large companies, as much as one-third of the top sales executive's compensation is in the form of bonuses. Financial rewards in smaller companies are less spectacular, but even here the top sales executives ranks among the highest-paid four or five company officials.

Sales executives at lower levels are paid less than their chiefs. Higher-ranking subordinates, such as regional or district sales managers, have median earnings approximating 90 to 95 percent of those of the top sales executive. Field sales managers, those on the first step of the ladder in the sales force executive hierarchy, receive median earnings about two-thirds of those of the top sales executives. Salespeople earn about half as much as the top executive.

Commonly, sales executives receive some of their pay as bonuses, commissions, or other "incentive" payments. These payments at higher executive levels are based upon relative profit performances and at lower executive levels upon sales volumes achieved relative to sales potentials. The prevalence of incentive payments of sales executives causes their earnings to fluctuate from year to year.

Most studies show that more than half of the top sales executives have stock options (granting them the right to buy company stock on advantageous terms) and receive some compensation in the form of an incentive bonus, profit-sharing plan, stock purchase plan, deferred compensation plan, or some combination of these. Other fringe benefits, such as retirement funds, company-paid insurance policies, and annuities, are common.

CONCLUSION

Sales executives' jobs vary from company to company and from position to position within companies, but all are responsible for making decisions and seeing to it that others carry them out. All sales executives, from the top sales executive down, spend most of their time managing personal-selling activities. Lower-ranking sales executives, such as branch managers, devote nearly all their time to direct supervision of salespersons. Thus, while sales executives need qualifications similar to those of effective executives in other fields, they must be adept at leading people. The higher their positions are in the organizational hierarchy, the more sales executives must work with decision makers in other marketing areas, since all marketing decisions impact on the personal-selling situation.

7 The Sales Organization

Effective sales executives insist upon sound organization. They recognize that the sales organization must achieve both qualitative and quantitative personal-selling objectives. Over the long haul, it must achieve qualitative objectives—those concerning personal-selling's expected contributions to achievement of overall company objectives. In the short run, it must attain the quantitative personal-selling objectives—not only sales volume but other objectives related to "profit" (such as keeping selling expenses within certain limits) and to "competitive position" (such as attaining given market shares). Achieving short-run quantitative personal-selling objectives precedes attainment of the long-run qualitative personal-selling objectives. The effective sales executive looks upon the sales organization both with respect to the "here and now" and to the "future." But the sales organization makes its major contribution in the present and the near term—recognizing this, the effective sales executive builds both sales-mindedness and profit-mindedness into the sales organization.

A sales organization is both an orienting point for cooperative endeavor and a structure of human relationships. It is a group of individuals striving jointly to reach qualitative and quantitative objectives, and bearing informal and formal relations to one another. Implicit in the concept of a sales organization is the notion that individual members cooperate to attain ends. The sales organization is not an end in itself but rather the vehicle by which individuals achieve given ends. Existence of a sales organization implies the existence of patterns of relationships among subgroups and individuals established for purposes of facilitating accomplishment of the group's aims.

Organizational defects often trace to lack of attention given to sales organization during the early existence of a company. When setting up a business, management is more concerned with financing and nonmarketing problems. Executives of new enterprises consider organization questions, but most often these relate to nonmarketing activities. In manufacturing, for example, as products are improved, production quantities increased, new products added, and production processes developed, the manufacturing organization is adapted to changed situations. Similar alterations in the sales organization are frequently neglected or postponed.

Sales organizations in many companies evolved without regard for changing conditions. The basic setup designed when the company was new remains, despite, for example, changes in selling style and size of sales force. The sales organization, after all, is the vehicle through which personal-selling strategy is implemented. A well-designed sales organization, like a well-designed automobile, accomplishes more, and more economically, than does one that is an artifact.

The sales organization should be adjusted to fit—ideally, to anticipate—changing situations. Shifts in marketing, in competition, and in other business factors call for changes in the sales organization. The ideal sales organization has a built-in adaptability allowing it to respond appropriately in fluid and diverse marketing environments.

PURPOSES OF SALES ORGANIZATION

In the ideally organized sales department, wasted motion and duplication of effort would be eliminated, friction would be minimized, and cooperation maximized. Dynamic characteristics inherent in marketing preclude the achievement of such perfection. But when sufficient attention is given to sales organization, the ideal is approached, if not attained, and personal-selling efforts increase in productivity.

Executive effort expended on sales organization need not, indeed should not, go exclusively to questions of design, that is, of the "formal" organization plan. How an organization works is more important than how it is supposed to function. Sales management should direct its main organizational efforts toward the "informal" organization. Through intelligent leadership and related "human relations" talents, the skilled manager moves both individuals and informal groups along lines that facilitate achievement of the purposes of formal organization.

To Permit the Development of Specialists

As a business expands, marketing and selling activities multiply and become increasingly complex. It is difficult to fix responsibility for performance of all necessary activities, particularly when executives are reluctant to delegate authority.

One purpose of reorganizing the sales department is to facilitate assignment of responsibility and delegation of authority. This often requires reshaping the structure so that it is easier for specialists to develop. In fact, specialization, or division of labor as economists call it, is the chief means through which the processes of organization and reorganization are effected. As tasks grow in number and complexity, they are broken down into manageable units and are assigned to specialized personnel. This involves fixing responsibility for specific tasks with specific individuals (or, occasionally, with certain groups). The assignments made are called "delegations of authority." This is conducive to the development of specialists.

To Assure that All Necessary Activities Are Performed

As a sales organization grows and specialization increases, it is increasingly important to perform all necessary activities. What is "necessary" changes over time. When jobs are highly specialized, danger exists that the organizational plan will not provide for supervision of all activities. Essential tasks may not be performed, simply because they are not assigned to specific individuals.

When a company is small, for instance, its executives are in close contact with users of the product. As a company grows, as marketing channels lengthen, and as the marketing area expands geographically, top executives become farther and farther removed from the customers. As soon as executives begin to lose their informal contacts with customers, an individual should be assigned responsibility for maintaining such relationships. If these contacts are highly important, responsibility for maintaining them should be assigned to an executive specializing in customer relations.

To Achieve Coordination or Balance

Good organization achieves coordination or balance. Individuals vary in competence, potential, and effectiveness. Particularly forceful executives may prevent a basically sound organization from functioning smoothly. Their personalities may be such that through assumption of authority, failure to delegate it, or both, their positions are magnified out of all proportion to their importance. Worse yet, total accomplishments of the organization are less than they could have been if, so to speak, greater advantage had been taken of the synergistic effect—when the sum of a combination effort exceeds the efforts of the same individuals working alone. By getting people to pull together as a team rather than as an assortment of individuals, the organization accomplishes more collectively than its members could independently.

Motivating individuals to work together toward common objectives is, then, important in achieving coordination. Individual goals are subordinated to, or reconciled with, organizational goals. Some of the means for accomplishing this are indoctrination and training programs, group meetings, supervision and guidance, and two-way communications. Throughout the sales organization different activities are kept in proper relation to one another in order that the greatest organizational effectiveness is realized.

As specialists emerge in a growing sales organization, management must guard against a tendency of each to search for ways to justify his or her own existence. One form of justification is to devise technical nomenclatures that nonspecialists in other areas have difficulty understanding. This, in turn, leads to increasing communications difficulties with other specialists and a reduction in overall organizational effectiveness. These instances of uncoordinated proliferation suggest that top sales executives should concern themselves continually with orchestration of effort. Modern organizational theory suggests that sales departments should be divided into small, freely communicating, face-to-face groups to decrease the possibility of uncoordinated proliferation.

To Define Authority

Sales executives should know whether their authority is line, staff, or functional. Line authority carries the power to require execution of orders by those lower in the organizational hierarchy. Staff authority is the power to suggest to those holding line authority the method for implementation of an order. Functional authority enables specialists in particular areas, such as in technical product service, to enforce their directives within a specific and limited field. Line executives make decisions on the need, place, and time of action over a wide range of matters. Staff executives advise line executives about methods but have no formal power to require or enforce the execution of their recommendations. Functional executives are specialists—experts in some aspect of the business—who assist executives holding general line authority. For example, such specialists advise on new product introduction. They do this by issuing orders, mainly on routine technical problems, directly to lower organizational levels. All executives should understand the nature of their authority with respect to each aspect of the operation; otherwise, friction develops. When, for instance, staff executives attempt to exercise line authority, they are headed for trouble with the line executives whose authority is usurped.

A sales organization receives directions from several sources. A salesperson, for instance, may get instructions on merchandising the advertising from an advertising specialist, directions for administering a questionnaire to customers from a marketing research technician, and general supervision and direction from the district sales manager. This conflicts with traditional organizational theory, which, in general, has said: No person should have more than one boss. The supporting argument is that, if individuals receive instructions from multiple sources, they may get conflicting and confusing directions. The argument is a good one, but the "one-boss" rule does not necessarily follow. Modern organizational theory points out, and rightly so, that the real problem is one not of avoiding the multiple-boss situation but harmonizing orders and directives from different sources. A smoothly operating sales organization has built-in ways of achieving harmony. Two important ways are continuing coordination of the work of different executives and free-flowing communications systems.

To Economize on Executive Time

As a sales department's operations and activities increase in complexity and number, additional subordinates are added. This permits higher-ranking sales executives to delegate more authority. It also allows for the more effective use of specialization, while higher executives devote less time to operations and more to planning. One purpose, then, of organization—and one often overlooked—is achieving economies in the use of executive time. Top sales executives need not concern themselves personally with all the sales department's problems and activities, particularly routine or technical ones, when they have capable and well-trained subordinates.

However, as sales executives gain subordinates, they must devote more attention, and probably more time, to coordinating their efforts. Unless the executive is an effective coordinator, subordinates may not work in harmony or discharge assignments in line with expectations.

In building the sales organization, then, the need for effective coordination limits the number of subordinates who report directly to certain executives. This limit is the "span of control." It is not possible to specify the proper number of subordinates. But the greater the abilities of the coordinator and of those reporting to him or her, the larger the number that can be effectively coordinated. Lower-level sales executives, however, those with salespeople reporting directly to them, have a wider span of control than higher executives devoting much time to planning and policy formulation and little to administrative and operating details. One must consider not only relative abilities of the coordinator and the subordinates, but the nature and importance of the coordinator's other duties. Furthermore, in deciding optimum span of control for a particular position, other factors are taken into account. The span of control is widened: (1) with improvements in the efficiency, speed, and reliability of the communications system; (2) when subordinates perform routine, similar, or repetitive tasks; and (3) when subordinates are concentrated at the same location as the executive.

SETTING UP A SALES ORGANIZATION

Not often is a sales organization built entirely from scratch, as some structure usually exists. Most problems of sales organization, in other words, are problems of reorganization—the sales organization exists and the goal is to make it more effective. It is appropriate, nevertheless, for the sales executive to approach the organizational problem, each time it arises, as though a completely new organization were being built. There are five major steps in setting up a sales organization:

1. Defining the objectives.
2. Delineating the necessary activities.
3. Grouping activities into "jobs" or "positions."
4. Assigning personnel to positions.
5. Providing for coordination and control.

Defining Objectives

The initial step is to define the sales department's objectives. Top management, of course, defines the long-run objectives for the company, and from these, the general, or long-run, objectives for the sales department are derived. Considered collectively, general objectives constitute top management's vision of the company at some future time. Top management, for instance, may want the firm not only to survive but to achieve industry leadership, develop a reputation for outstanding technical research, diversify its product lines, provide excellent service to customers, furnish investors with a generous return, establish an image of public responsibility, and so on. From such composites, sales management determines the implications for the sales department and articulates a set of qualitative personal-selling objectives. Quantitative personal-selling objectives, in turn, are set with an eye on the qualitative objectives. Survival, for instance, is the most basic qualitative objective of any enterprise as well as its sales department, and this requires, among other things, a continuing flow of sales revenue; so, securing a given level of sales volume is an important sales department quantitative objective.

Survival also requires profits. Hence, a second qualitative personal-selling objective is to produce profits, not only by making profitable sales but by controlling departmental costs and expenses. Furthermore, survival requires growth in both sales and profits; otherwise, in a growing economy the company is destined to fall behind competitors or even risk being forced out of business. It follows that a third qualitative personal-selling objective is to realize long-term growth in sales and profits. Therefore, three of the sales department's general objectives—all traceable to management's desire for survival of the firm—may be summed up in three words: sales, profits, and growth.

Qualitative personal-selling objectives are indispensable for long-range planning and must be kept in mind in short-range planning. Quantitative personal-selling objectives are required as operating guideposts. Thus, the qualitative personal-selling objective of producing profits may be translated into specific quantitative personal-selling objectives such as "to increase our market share of the hand-held calculator business to 20 percent by the end of the current year" and "to secure four wholesalers in Australia and one in New Zealand to introduce our vest-pocket calculators in those markets next year." People in the sales department, as those elsewhere, work more effectively, with less wasted time, effort, and money, when assigned definite goals. The sales department as a whole, similarly, operates more smoothly, and its activities are more purposeful, when it has specific quantitative objectives.

The qualitative objectives set for the sales department form the basis for the general policies governing its long-term performance. The quantitative objectives set are the foundations from which to develop day-to-day operating sales policies and programs. A thorough examination—perhaps even a restatement—of the qualitative and quantitative goals of the sales department is the logical place to begin the task of reorganization.

Determination of Activities and Their Volume of Performance

Fundamental to sound organizational design is recognition that activities are being organized. Only after determining all necessary activities and estimating their volume of performance is it possible to answer such questions as: What executive positions are required? What should be their relationships to other positions? What should be the duties and responsibilities of persons who fill these positions?

Determining the necessary activities and their volume of performance is a matter of analyzing the sales department's qualitative and quantitative objectives. Thorough examination discloses which activities must be performed in what volume. The activities involved in modern sales management are similar from firm to firm, and although individual sales executives think that their operations are different, most differences are more apparent than real. Almost every sales department carries on the same general activities; differences among departments are those of detail, of relative emphasis placed upon individual activity and in volume of performance.

Grouping Activities into Positions

Next, the activities identified as necessary are allocated to different positions. The planner must keep in mind that activities are aimed at achieving certain objectives—ultimately the composite provides the raw material from which job descriptions are compiled (in terms of reporting relationships, job objectives, duties and responsibilities, and performance measures).

Activities are classified and grouped so that closely related tasks are assigned to the same position. Each position should contain not only a sufficient number of tasks but sufficient variation to provide for job challenge, interest, and involvement. Only in very large organizations, where extreme specialization is practiced, should a position comprise only a single activity, and even here the burden of proof should be on those proposing such a move. Pressures of administrative economy are generally strong enough that most position holders are responsible for a number of diversified, although related, activities.

Certain activities are of crucial importance to success of the sales department, and this has implications for organizational design. For example, in a highly competitive field, product merchandising and pricing are assigned to positions high up in the organizational structure. Activities of lesser importance are assigned to lower-level jobs.

When a large number of positions is being set up, groups of related jobs are brought together to form departmental subdivisions. In most cases, a number of intermediate-level positions would, in turn, have to be coordinated by the top sales executive. Nevertheless, the planner should guard against building too many levels into the department. The smallest number of administrative levels that permits the organization both to perform its activities and to operate smoothly is best.

Assignment of Personnel to Positions

The next step is to assign personnel to the positions. This brings up the question of whether to recruit special individuals to fill the positions or to modify the positions to fit the capabilities of available personnel. This is a question that has long been controversial. Compromises are frequent. On the one hand, some position requirements are sufficiently general that many individuals possess the necessary qualifications, or can acquire them through training. On the other hand, some individuals possess such unique talents and abilities that it is prudent and profitable to modify the job specifications to fit them. Nevertheless, planners prefer, whenever the situation permits, to have individuals grow into particular jobs rather than to have jobs grow up around individuals.

Provision for Coordination and Control

Sales executives who have others reporting to them (that is, those with line authority) require means to control their subordinates and to coordinate their efforts. They should not be so overburdened with detailed and undelegated responsibilities that they have insufficient time for coordination. Nor should they have too many subordinates reporting directly to them—this weakens the quality of control and prevents the discharge of other duties. Thus, in providing for coordination and control, consideration must be given the span of executive control.

Control and coordination is obtainable through both informal and formal means. Strong leaders control and coordinate the efforts of their subordinates largely on an informal basis. Through sheer force of personality coupled with unusual abilities to attract and hold the loyalty of followers, the strong leader tends to make minimal use of formal instruments of control and coordination. But all sales executives, whether strong leaders or not, can improve their effectiveness through formal instruments of control.

The most important formal instrument of organizational control is the written job description. This instrument sets forth for each job: reporting relationships, job objectives, duties and responsibilities, and performance measurements. The most critical section is that of setting forth the job objectives—many planners argue that the job objective section should be the part emphasized and, to the extent possible, the person who holds the job should be allowed to determine how to achieve these objectives. This not only encourages position holders to use their own initiative but makes it clear that they are to achieve stated job objectives even if that requires performing duties and responsibilities beyond those contained in job descriptions. Few sales executives will dispute this argument, but most are also convinced that there is merit in detailing duties and responsibilities and in defining the measures for evaluating the position holder's performance.

Good job descriptions provide clear pictures of the roles job holders are to play in the sales organization, and are also useful in other situations. Written job descriptions find use in employee selection processes. They are used, too, in matching job specifications with applicants' qualifications—where recruits cannot be found with all desired qualifications, job specifications form the basis for training. Position holders, in addition, can use their job descriptions as yardsticks against which to appraise their own performances.

An organizational chart, another control instrument, shows formal relations among different positions. A chart reduces confusion about the individual's role. An organizational chart delineates formal relations and, because of this, rarely provides a true picture of how the organization actually works. Nevertheless, availability of an organizational chart enables members of a sales department to learn the nature of their formal relations with others, to know with whom they are expected to cooperate, and to clarify their formal roles.

An instrument of organizational control used increasingly is the organizational manual. It is an extension of the organizational chart. Typically, it contains charts for both the company and the departments, write-ups of job descriptions and specifications, and summaries of major company and departmental objectives and policies. The organizational manual brings together a great deal of information and helps its users to learn and understand the nature of their responsibilities, authorities, and relations with others.

BASIC TYPES OF SALES ORGANIZATIONAL STRUCTURES

If sound practices are followed in setting up the sales department, the resulting structure takes on features of one or more of four basic types: line, line and staff, functional, and committee. The grouping of activities into positions and the charting of relationships of positions causes the organization to take on structural form. The first two types (line and line and staff) are the most common. Functional and committee organizations are rare. Most sales departments have hybrid organizational structures, with variations to adjust for personalities and to fit specific operating conditions.

The sales department's structure evolves from the needs of the business. No two companies have identical sales organizations, because no two have identical needs. The customers, the marketing channels, the company size, the product or product line, the practices of competitors, and the personalities and abilities of the personnel are but a few of the factors affecting the organizational structure of the sales department. So numerous are the factors influencing the structure of individual sales departments that it is impractical to draw generalizations about the many possible "mixed" types; the discussion that follows is an analysis of the four basic types. Organizational planners should know the chief features of each type, and its respective merits and limitations. If they have this background and understand the other factors influencing the structure of the sales department, they are equipped to evaluate its appropriateness.

Lines Sales Organization

The line organization is the oldest and simplest sales organizational structure. It is widely used in smaller firms and in firms with small numbers of selling personnel—for instance, in companies that cover a limited geographic area or sell a narrow product line. The chain of command runs from the top sales executives down through subordinates. All executives exercise line authority, and each subordinate is responsible only to one person on the next higher level. Responsibility is definitely fixed, and those charged with it also make decisions and take action. Lines of authority run vertically through the structure, and all persons on any one organizational level are independent of all others on that level.

The line sales organization sees its greatest use in companies where all sales personnel report directly to the chief sales executive. In these companies this executive often is preoccupied with active supervision and seldom has much time to devote to planning or to work with other top executives. Occasionally, however, the line sales organization is used where more than two levels of authority are present.

Figure 7.1 shows a fairly large sales department organized on the line basis. The sales manager reports to the general manager, assistant sales managers report to the sales manager, and salespeople report to assistant managers. Theoretically, there is no cross-communication between persons on the same level. Contacts between persons on the same level are indirect and are effected through the next higher level. For example, the assistant sales manager of Divi-

FIGURE 7.1 Line Sales Department Organization

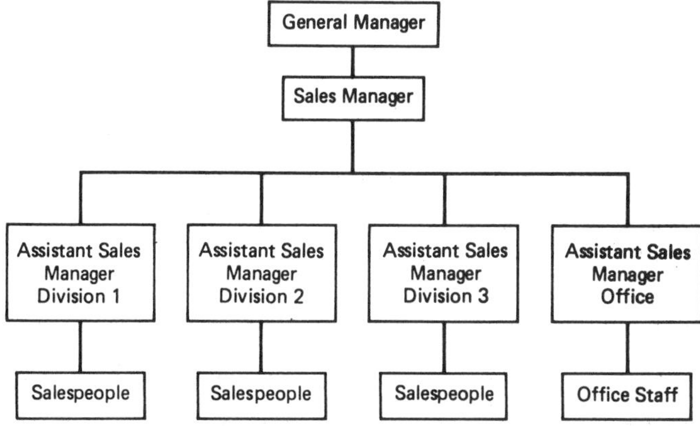

sion 1 arranges to confer with the assistant sales manager of Division 2 through the sales manager. Similarly, contacts by sales personnel with the office staff flow up through the organization to the sales manager and back down through the assistant sales manager in charge of the office to the office staff.

The basic simplicity of line organization is the main reason for its use. Because each department member reports to only one superior, problems of discipline and control are small. Lines of authority and responsibility are clear and logical, and it is difficult for individuals to shift or evade responsibilities. Definite placement of authority and responsibility saves time in making policy changes, in deciding new plans, and in converting plans into action. The simplicity makes it easy for executives to develop close relations with salespersons. With this working atmosphere, it is not surprising that executives who come up through a line organization are frequently strong leaders. As the typical line sales department has few organizational levels, administrative expenses are low.

The greatest weakness of the line sales organization is that so much depends upon the department head. The head needs outstanding ability and rare qualifications, and should be well versed in all phases of sales management, for there are no subordinates with specialized skills and knowledge. Even if the head is an all-around expert, there is insufficient time for policymaking and planning, since rigidity of the line structure requires that a great deal of attention be given to direction of sales operations. The head often must make decisions and take action without benefit of planning. Under such conditions, results are often disappointing.

For rapidly growing concerns and for those with large sales staffs, the line organizational structure is inappropriate. As the department grows, new layers of executives must be added to retain control. Orders and directions must be passed down through a growing series of administrative levels. Managerial effectiveness becomes impaired and results are less predictable, as directions become more and more distorted and garbled at each succeeding organizational level. Moreover, as growth proceeds, earlier advantages of close relations among executives and salespeople are sacrificed, and maintaining morale becomes a greater challenge.

Not many executives have the talents needed to manage a large-scale line sales department effectively, and line organization offers little opportunity for subordinates to acquire these skills. Ordinarily, the stakes are too high, except perhaps in the smallest companies, for management to gamble on the availability of a replacement at the time needed. Sound organizational practice dictates that trained understudies be ready to step into the shoes of their superiors. But more often than not, chief sales executives in line sales organizations fail to groom their own replacements.

Line and Staff Sales Organization

The line and staff sales department is often found in large and medium-sized firms, employing substantial numbers of sales personnel, and selling diversified product lines over wide geographic areas. In contrast to the line organization, the line and staff organization provides the top sales executive with a group of specialists—experts in dealer and distributor relations, sales analysis, sales organization, sales personnel, sales planning, sales promotion, sales training, service, traffic and warehousing, and similar fields. This staff helps to conserve the top sales executives' time and frees them from excessively detailed work. They make it possible for their chiefs to concentrate their efforts where they have the most skill. If the top sales executive is not equipped, through prior training or experience, to handle certain problems, staff specialists assist in increasing overall effectiveness of the department. Similarly, by delegating problems involving considerable study or detailed analysis to staff executives the top sales executive has more time for planning and for dealing with higher-priority matters.

Staff sales executives do not have authority to issue orders or directives. Staff recommendations are submitted to the top sales executives, who if they approve, transmit necessary instructions to the line organization. Departures from this procedure are occasionally made. For example, staff members may be authorized to deal directly with line executives regarding execution of plans and implementation of policies developed by the staff and approved by management. Although staff members act on behalf of line sales executives in these instances, they assume joint responsibility for results. This departure from the normal procedure is justified if it speeds the translation of staff plans into line action.

Figure 7.2 illustrates the line and staff sales organization. The general sales manager reports to the vice-president in charge of marketing as does the advertising manager and the manager of marketing research. Six subordinates report to the general sales manager, but only one, the assistant general sales manager, is a line executive. Four of the five staff executives have responsibilities in specialized fields; the fifth, the assistant to the general sales manager, is given more general assignments.

Note the difference between the *assistant to* and *assistant*. The *assistant to* is a staff executive who is given a broader operating area than those staff specialists with more descriptive titles. In contrast, the *assistant* has general line authority delegated by the superior. The assistant general sales manager is an understudy of the general sales manager who performs assignments of a line nature in the name of the superior. The assistant to the general sales manager carries part of the general administrative load that would otherwise be borne by the general sales manager.

The advantages of the line and staff organization are mainly those of specialization. The chief sales executive, being relieved from much detail work, can take a broader view of the department. Problems can be seen in clearer perspective, and connections between apparently unrelated problems are brought into focus. A pool of experts provides advice and assistance in specialized fields. Planning activities are subdivided and apportioned to staff members, and decisions and policies rests on a sounder base than in the line organization.

Meanwhile, the top sales executive can concentrate on control and coordi-

FIGURE 7.2 Line and Staff Sales Department Organization

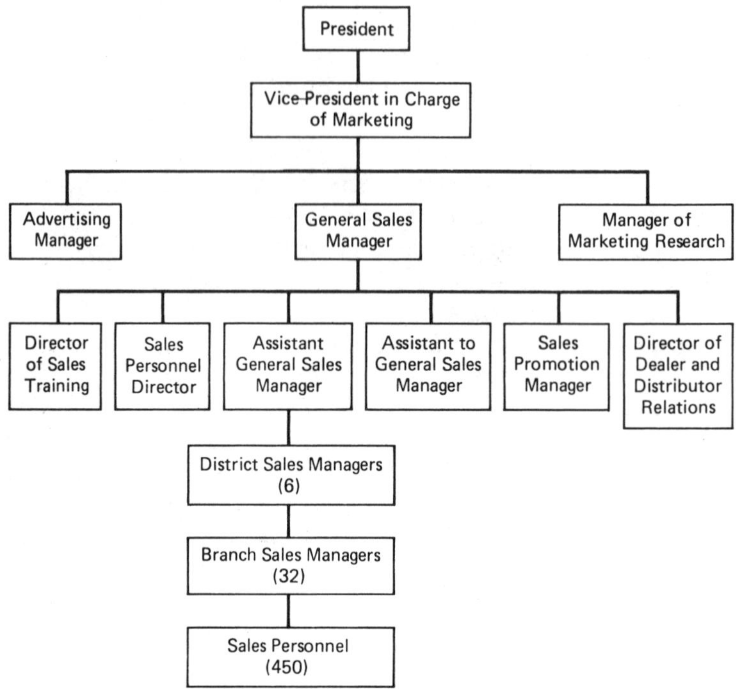

nation of subordinates. Staff members assume much of the burden of solving problems in their areas. Thus, the top sales executive can devote more attention to the human aspects of administration.

The specialization made possible by line and staff organization is also the source of its weaknesses. Work of the staff specialists must be coordinated, and this is costly. Other administrative expenses may also increase, unless the number of staff executives is kept in line with departmental needs. The staff should be expanded only when it can be shown that the contributions of new staff members will equal or exceed the costs of maintaining them.

Close control over staff-line relations is essential. If staff people issue instructions directly to line executives, it is difficult to prevent some persons from evading unwanted responsibilities. All areas in which line and staff executives share authority and responsibility should be noted in written job descriptions and in the organizational manual. All other areas of responsibility and authority should be delineated and assigned to specific individuals.

When the line and staff sales organization is used, the time between problem recognition and corrective action tends to widen. This results from giving staff executives time to study problems before making recommendations to the decision makers. This interval is reduced by permitting staff planners to assist in expediting the implementation of the plan. But, as already indicated, this may play into the hands of those wanting to evade responsibility. When time is important, though, it is wise to use staff people in this capacity. However, when salespeople take instructions from several sources, confusion may result, especially if experts overstep their authority. Then, too, problems in maintaining contact with individual salespersons are multiplied.

Functional Sales Organization

Some few sales departments use functional organization.[1] This type, derived from the management theory developed by Frederick W. Taylor, is based upon the premise that each individual in an organization, executive and employee, should have as few distinct duties as possible. The principle of specialization is utilized to the fullest extent. Duty assignments and delegations of authority are made according to function.

No matter where a particular function appears in the organization, it is in the jurisdiction of the same executive. In the functional sales department, salespeople receive instructions from several executives but on different aspects of their work. Provision for coordinating the functional executives is made only at the top of the structure; executives at lower levels do not have coordinating responsibilities. In contrast to the line and staff organization, all specialists in a functional organization have line authority of a sort—or, more properly, they have functional authority. Instructions, and even policies, can be put into effect with or without prior approval of the top-level coordinating executive.

A functional sales organizational structure is shown in Figure 7.3. The coordinating executive is the director of sales administration; all executives on the next level are specialists. As indicated, sales personnel receive instructions from six different executives.

The outstanding advantage claimed for the functional sales department is improved performance. Specialized activities are assigned to experts, whose guidance should help in increasing the effectiveness of the sales force. The sheer size of the sales force in many large firms makes the highly centralized sales operations of a functional organization impractical. This limitation is traced to the requirement in the functional model for a lone official to coordinate the specialists. Most large firms need more administrative levels when the marketing area is extensive, when the product line is wide, or when large numbers of selling personnel are required. It is possible to use modified versions of the functional model—versions providing for a modicum of decentralization and for more administrative levels—but in its pure form, at least, functional organization for the sales department is inappropriate.

The practicality of functional organization for the sales department is open to question. Small and medium-sized firms do not find it feasible, or financially

[1]Functional organization is seldom utilized for the enterprise as a whole. It is used principally in highly centralized departments, such as manufacturing. In departments that are by nature decentralized, such as the sales department, functional organization is little used.

FIGURE 7.3 Functional Type of Sales Organization

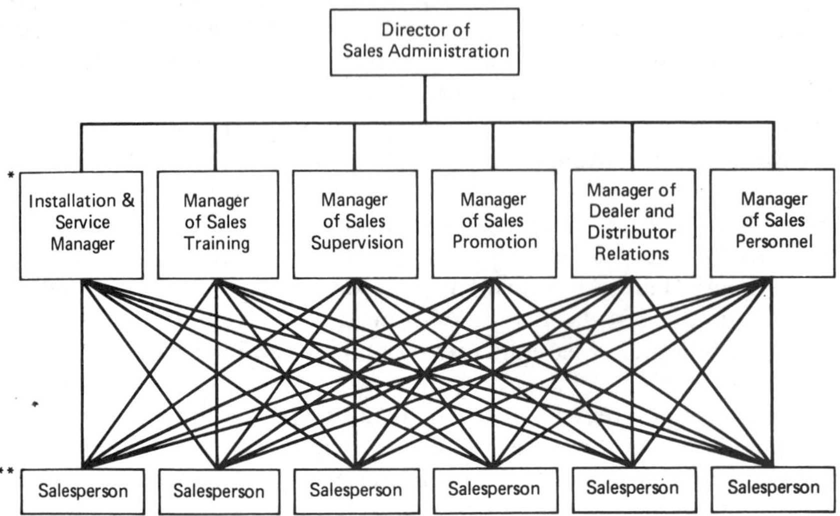

*In practice the number of executives on this level would be much larger, and their areas of functional responsibility would be broken down in much greater detail than is shown here.

**A sales department using the functional type of organization would undoubtedly employ more than six salespeople. Only six are shown in this example, because of the difficulties encountered in depicting lines of authority for larger numbers.

possible, to utilize the high degree of division of labor. It is sometimes contended that functional organization is suitable for large firms with stable operations and with opportunity for considerable division of labor; however, certain characteristics of functional organization cause it to be rejected even by most large firms. Large companies with stable selling operations are the exception rather than the rule.

Committee Sales Organization

The committee is never the sole basis for organizing a sales department. It is a method of organizing the executive group for planning and policy formulation while leaving actual operations, including implementation of plans and policies, to individual executives. Thus, many firms have a sales training committee (comprised of the general sales manager, his or her assistants, the sales training manager, and perhaps representative divisional or regional sales managers) that meets periodically to draft training plans and formulate sales training policies. Implementation of these plans and policies, however, is the responsibility of the sales training manager, if the company has one, or of the line and/or staff executives responsible for sales training in their own jurisdictions. Other committees found in sales organizations include customer relations, operations, personnel, merchandising, and new products.

The use of committees in the sales department has advantages. Before policies are made and action is taken, important problems are deliberated by committee members and are measured against varied viewpoints. Committee meetings, where ideas are interchanged and diverse opinions are present, promote coordination among members of the executive team. When problems are aired in the give and take of committee meetings, cooperation is likely to be better than under any other organization plan. However, unless decision making and policy formulation are left to specific individuals, it is impossible to fix responsibility. Committees render their most important service in providing focal points for discussion and for the making of suggestions, so many companies prohibit committees from making decisions or formulating policies. No committee should develop into a vehicle for the evasion of responsibility.

For committees to operate effectively, other precautions are necessary. The agenda must be planned and controlled to avoid wasting time of executives not directly interested in the topics considered. The tendency for committees to consume large amounts of time is counteracted if the chairperson keeps the discussion focused upon the subject at hand. But the chairperson should not dominate. Chairpersons should guide discussions within specified bounds, but they should not force their opinions on others.

FIELD ORGANIZATION OF THE SALES DEPARTMENT

Every growing company faces, sooner or later, the necessity for establishing a field sales organization. The sales manager can personally supervise field selling operations when a company is young, when only a few salespeople are employed, when the sales force travels out of the home office, and when the marketing area is small. As more salespersons are added, it is increasingly difficult to supervise and control them. If growth in sales volume is to parallel additions to the sales force, either the same marketing area must be worked more intensively or new areas must be penetrated. Both alternatives call for closer supervision and control of field sales personnel.

The field organization consists of all employees of the sales department who work away from the home office. All outside salespeople are included, as are traveling sales supervisors, branch and district managers, and clerical employees in branch and district offices. Also included are service, repair, and sales promotion personnel. Although not all are concerned directly with increasing the effectiveness of field selling operations, each makes contributions to that end.

The two main purposes of a field organization are (1) to facilitate the selling task and (2) to improve the chances that salespeople will achieve their goals. Sales personnel count on the field organization for assistance and support. Their jobs should be made easier because of it.

The makeup of the field organization is influenced by the organizational philosophy of the management. Companies that consider centralization desirable have complex supervisory organizations. Each salesperson is subjected to close supervision—hence the need for a considerable force of supervisors. Firms that believe in decentralization, in contrast, permit individuals in the field to operate more on their own.

Numerous factors influence the size of the field organization. The larger the firm, assuming similar sales-related marketing policies, the greater the required number of salespeople, supervisors, and regional, branch, and district managers. The relative emphasis placed on personal selling in the marketing program affects the size of the field organization. For example, the firm selling directly to retailers, ultimate consumers, or industrial users commits itself to the performance of a sizable personal selling task, and it requires a field organization of commensurate size. In contrast, companies using wholesalers find that their field organizations can be correspondingly smaller, since parts of the personal selling and other tasks are transferred to these middlemen. Other factors affecting the size of the field organization include desired frequency of sales calls, number of customers and prospects, and geographical spread of sales accounts.

CENTRALIZATION VERSUS DECENTRALIZATION IN SALES FORCE MANAGEMENT

In the centralized sales organization almost all activities, including sales force management, are administered from a central headquarters. The central sales office has full responsibility for recruiting, selecting, training, compensating, supervising, motivating, controlling, and evaluating the sales force. In the decentralized organization, in theory at least, all these activities are handled by field sales executives.

A decentralized sales organization is one in which there is decentralization in management of various selling tasks and in performance of certain important personnel management activities. For example, branch or district sales offices may do the recruiting, selecting, motivating, and supervising; the central headquarters may handle training, compensating, and evaluating; and the branches and the central headquarters may share responsibility, in proportions varying with the marketing situation and management philosophy, for other aspects of sales force management. It is rare, in other words, for sales force management to be either 100 percent centralized or 100 percent decentralized. Management's appraisal of relative costs and effectiveness results in some aspects being centralized and others decentralized.

Centralization in sales force management varies. Smaller companies that have few salespeople and confine their operations to a small geographical area, keeping the unit of sales high, the sales call frequency low, and the caliber of salespersons relatively high, incline toward centralized sales force management. Manufacturing firms relying almost entirely upon specialized wholesale middlemen for marketing of their products need only minimum sales forces and, therefore, tend toward centralization. Local wholesalers with restricted sales areas also have small sales forces and, by the nature of their operations, are highly centralized. The principal factor determining centralization, then, is a small size of sales force, but other marketing factors, such as those illustrated, also move a company in this direction.

High decentralization in sales force management is found mainly among companies with large sales forces. Likely to have considerable decentralization, for instance, is a manufacturing firm distributing a wide line of consumer products over a vast market area and selling directly to varied retailers—all conditions indicating the need for a large number of salespeople. Wherever marketing conditions require large sales forces, the economies and effectiveness of decentralization are more attractive than are those of centralization.

Other things being equal, there is a strong pull in the direction of sales force decentralization as a company grows. This is true even though decentralization requires at least one more level of sales management, and the maintenance of branch and district offices (or both) causes additions to other fixed operating costs. With growth, the advantages of decentralized sales force management increasingly outweigh the higher costs. Among these advantages are:

1. More intensive cultivation of the market and, consequently, a higher sales volume to absorb the higher fixed costs.
2. More effective control, improved supervision, and increased sales productivity resulting from the addition of at least one intermediate level of sales executives, and from reduction of geographical separation of executives and sales personnel.
3. Improved customer service stemming from more effective control of sales personnel.
4. Reduced need for and costs of territorial "break-in" time, since more salepersons are recruited from the areas to which they are assigned.
5. Improved sales force morale—there are more frequent contacts with executives, reductions in travel time, and fewer nights away from home.
6. Lower travel expenses—salespeople are dispatched from decentralized points, and fewer field trips by home office sales executives are required.
7. A "built-in" management development program—branch and district offices not only provide realistic training but serve as proving grounds for future high-level sales executives.

SCHEMES FOR DIVIDING LINE AUTHORITY IN THE SALES ORGANIZATION

As marketing operations expand, line authority and responsibility eventually become excessively burdensome for the top sales executive. There is an increasing number of people to supervise. Ordinarily, the first remedial step taken is to add a general line assistant, for example, an assistant general sales manager. As the burden of line administrative work continues to grow, it is necessary to provide additional assistants. These new subordinates are given line responsibilities narrower than those of the assistant general sales manager. Although they work with a variety of matters, their assignments cover a limited area of operations. Tasks of line administration are subdivided among these new assistants in one of three ways: (1) by geographic area, (2) by products, or (3) by customers or marketing channels.

Geographic Division of Line Authority

The large firm with far-flung selling operations is likely to subdivide line authority geographically (see Figure 7.4). This is particularly so if the characteristics of large numbers of customers vary by geographic location, if different selling problems are encountered in different areas, or if certain products are more strongly demanded in some regions than in others. But there is an even more compelling reason for dividing line authority geographically—as more customers are added and as a wider area is cultivated, the size of the sales task increases enormously. Setting up geographic divisions is a way of cutting the sales task down to manageable proportions. When centralized administration becomes too great a burden for the top sales executives, secondary line executives are delegated authority to conduct sales operations within smaller areas. Geographic division is usually made first into regions or divisions. These may or may not be broken down further into districts or branches.

When line authority is divided geographically, local problems are handled speedily. It is not necessary to wait for decisions from the home office; many questions of importance to customers can be answered by executives personally

FIGURE 7.4 Sales Department with Line Authority Subdivided Geographically

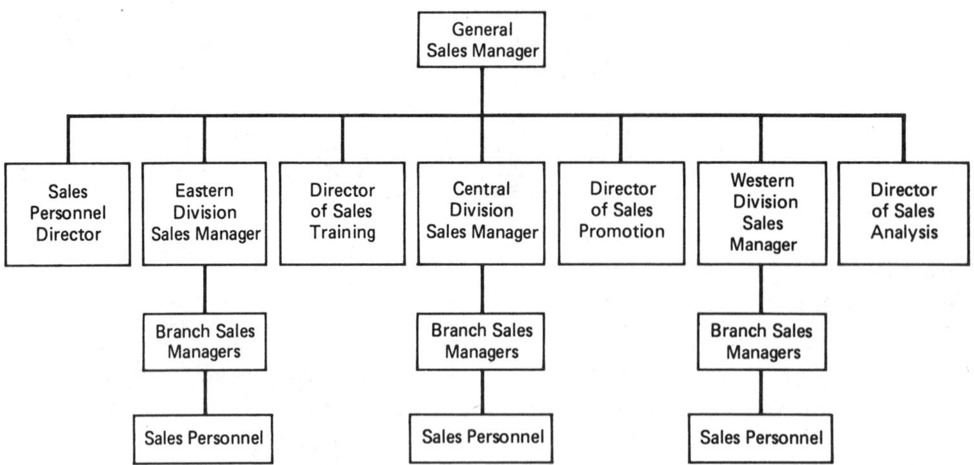

acquainted with local conditions. Shortening the lines of communication makes possible closer supervision of salespeople, which, in turn, helps in improving customer service. Local markets can be cultivated intensively, and tactics of local competitors can be met and countered in the field.

However, this system calls for multiple offices, so administrative expenses increase. Then, too, the top sales executive faces coordinating several regional operations. Unless this coordination is effective, conflicting policies may develop in different regions.

Product Division of Line Authority

A second scheme for dividing line authority is to split the sales task among subordinate line executives, each of whom directs sales operations for part of the product line. When authority is so divided, more than one sales force may be required. Some companies' product lines are too wide to be distributed economically by a single sales force. Others sell both highly technical and nontechnical products; thus some salespeople need specialized training and some do not. In still others, economies of a single sales force are reduced or eliminated because different products are marketed to different types of customers.

Figures 7.5 and 7.6 illustrate two schemes for dividing line authority by products. In Figure 7.5, the customary line and staff organization has been retained; in Figure 7.6, the primary division is on the basis of products, and each product sales manager has his own staff of specialists. The use of separate staffs, shown in Figure 7.6, is unusual. Often this is an intermediate stage resulting from a merger. Because of the expenses incurred in maintaining duplicate staffs, most companies, after mergers, gradually change the organization to its basic line and staff form shown in Figure 7.5. Unless there are strong reasons for retaining separate sales managers and sales forces, as will shortly be explained, line authority should be divided on some basis other than products.

FIGURE 7.5 Sales Department with Line Authority Subdivided by Products, but Retaining Basic Line and Staff Form

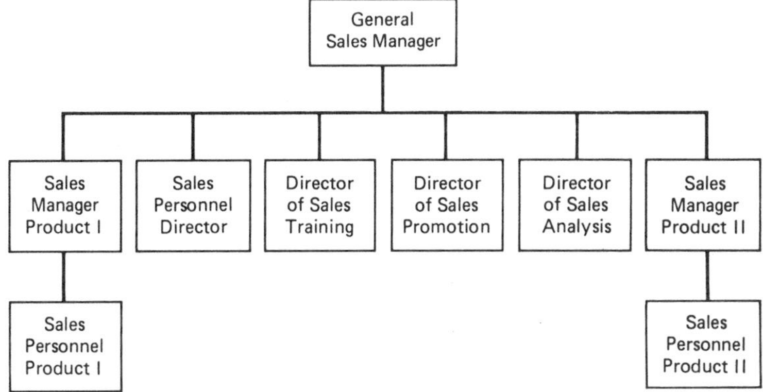

FIGURE 7.6 Sales Department with Line Authority Subdivided by Products Utilizing Duplicate Staffs

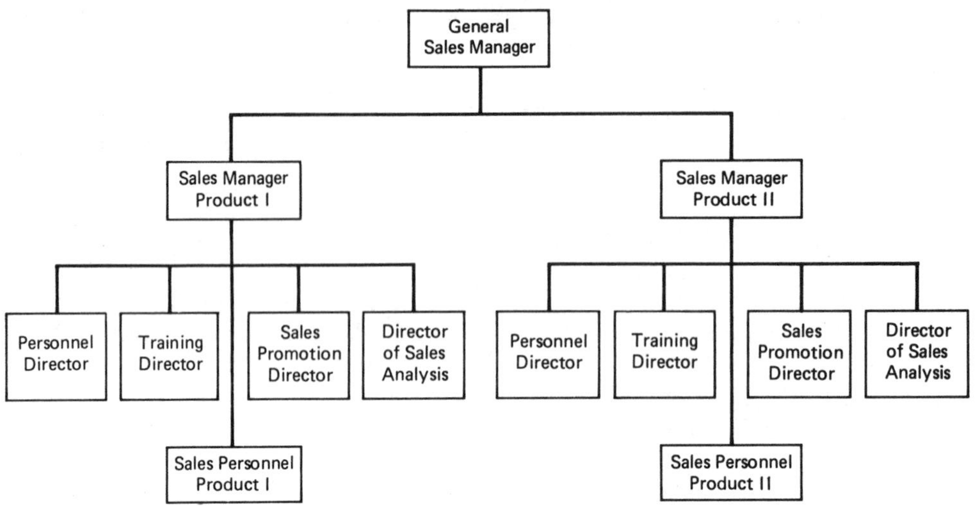

The decision to use the product type of sales organization should rest on whether the benefits of product specialization outweigh the additional expenses. If they do not, it is wiser to organize the sales force on some other basis. Gains associated with specialized salespersons, who concentrate on selling specific products, must be outweighed against increased expenses. Maintaining more than one sales force results in higher administrative and travel expenses. There are almost certain to be times when two company sales personnel selling different products make calls on the same customers. Although specialized salespeople may give more "push" to individual products, many customers object to multiple calls from the same company. The benefits of specialized sales forces are greatest for companies selling broadly diversified lines, reaching different markets with different products, and encountering unique selling problems for the various products.

Customer (or Marketing Channel) Division of Line Authority

The third scheme for subdividing line authority is by type of customer (Figure 7.7) or marketing channel (Figure 7.8). This is appropriate when nearly identical products are marketed to several types of customers and the problems of selling to each type are different. When the same, or similar, products are sold to a number of industries, they often find different applications in each industry. The company in Figure 7.7 sells its products to the lumber, construction, and mining industries. In each industry, the products are used for different purposes. Customers not only have different needs, they are influenced by different buying motives. Thus, special sales forces sell to each major type of customer.

FIGURE 7.7 Sales Department with Line Authority Subdivided by Type of Customer

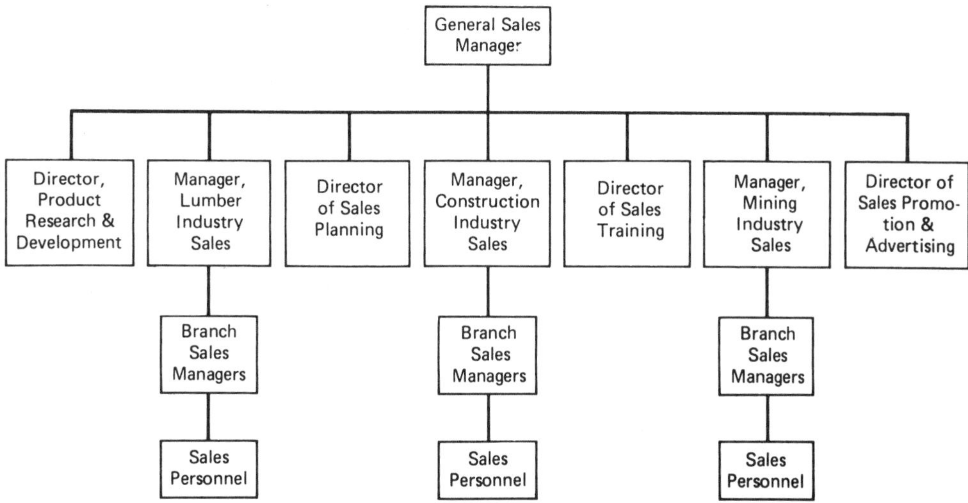

Other companies, especially in the consumer-goods field, pattern their sales organizations after the marketing channels. Although ultimate consumers may be substantially alike, they frequently must be reached in different ways (that is, they may buy the product in different types of outlets). Problems of distributing to chain stores are often unlike those of selling to independent

FIGURE 7.8 Sales Department with Line Authority Subdivided by Marketing Channel

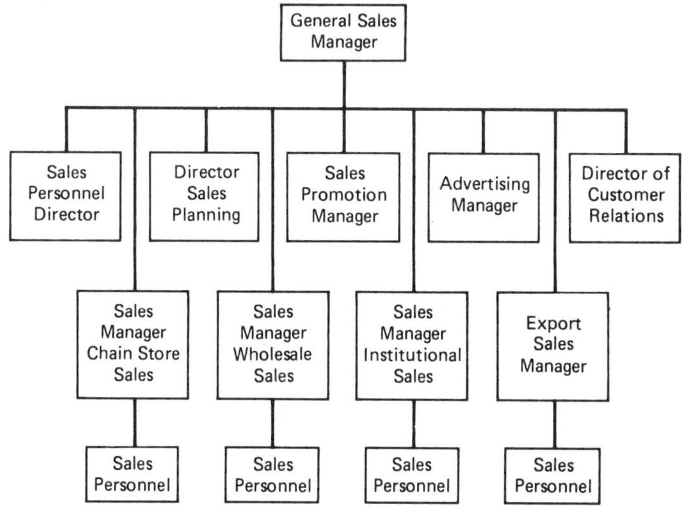

wholesalers and retailers, and specialized sales training programs are often required. In cases of this kind, the problems of selling vary more with the marketing channel than they do with the product or geographical location; consequently, line authority is subdivided according to marketing channels.

Dividing Line Authority on More than One Basis

Few companies use a single basis for subdividing line authority. Most use a combination, subdividing the selling task more than once, to permit greater specialization. Nearly every large sales department subdivides authority on the geographic basis at some level of organization, but this is done usually in combination with either the product or type-of-customer system. If geographical differences are more important than those of product or type of customer, the primary subdivision is geographical, and the next is at a lower organizational echelon according to one of the other bases. If geographical differences are of lesser importance, the procedure is reversed. The factor most important to the marketing success of the company should form the basis for the first subdivision, and less important factors should determine subsequent breakdowns at lower organizational echelons.

CONCLUSION

There is growing recognition of the need to apply sound principles of organization to the sales department. Organizational planning is a continuing activity, and the sales department structure is adjusted to changing marketing needs. This has evolved as less emphasis has been placed on securing orders and more attention has been paid to control of costs and expenses and the realization of net profits. These are trends of great importance. As they continue, an increasing number of sales organizations are structured more logically. Selling activities are performed with less waste effort, and total effectiveness of the sales effort is enhanced. These advances result in significant benefits to the firms achieving them, and to their customers.

8 Sales Department Relations

The sales department occupies a strategic position. It spearheads the organization's effort to supply customers with ever-increasing quantities of products at profitable prices. To the extent that this is achieved, the company's reputation rests upon a sound foundation.

Good products at competitive prices are not enough. Company success is affected by the dealings and associations of the sales department with customers and other publics. Sales department relations with other departments influences the company's reputation with many publics. Individual sales personnel, as well as the entire department, are in a position to add to or detract from the company reputation. It is important to assure that all are alert to their responsibilities for maintaining good relations.

In companies without separate public relations departments, sales executives frequently have additional responsibility for public relations. The main reason is that they have close relations with external publics. Even sales executives not assigned primary responsibility for public relations handle the public relations program as it pertains to the sales department. Under either arrangement sales executives consider the probable public relations impact when planning and administering department programs. They are responsible for maintaining satisfactory relations with all those with whom they or their subordinates come into contact.

INTERDEPARTMENTAL RELATIONS AND COORDINATION

Coordinating the activities of all departments so that maximum progress is made toward overall company objectives is top management's responsibility. Department heads, in addition to implementing top management's directives, harmonize their activities so that the tasks of all departments are accomplished effectively. Each understands the functions of other departments, and each is responsible for coordinating his or her department's activities to contribute to company success.

Although the primary responsibility of top sales executives is to manage the sales department, they know the operations of other departments. Sales executives understand how other departments influence and are influenced by the sales department. These are dynamic relationships, so a change in one department often has repercussions in others.

Formal Coordinating Methods

Formal coordination among departments is achieved by one or more of three methods. The first is to build coordination into the organization through grouping allied activities under a high-ranking executive. In most companies, chief marketing executives have reporting directly to them the heads of departments performing marketing activities, such as sales, advertising, marketing research, and service. Under this arrangement, marketing executives coordinate the operations of departments under them.

The second method is to achieve coordination through the general administrative officers—the president, executive vice-president, or general manager. Here the coordinating executive coordinates the operations of all company departments, not just those performing closely related tasks. This explains why the second method is most widely used in companies having only a small number of departments.

The third method is to use policy, planning, and coordinating committees made up of representatives of concerned departments. On the surface, this appears the weakest method, as no one executive has responsibility for coordination. But this arrangement often works out quite satisfactorily in practice.

Informal Coordination

Informal coordination is generally more important than formal coordination. Department heads may solve an interdepartmental problem informally while it is still being thrashed out through formal mechanisms. Informal coordination procedures are preferred in most companies, and solutions so developed may or may not be formally adopted later by a coordinating body. One thing is certain—unexpected problems with important interdepartmental implications should be handled with minimum delay, for to prolong their solution is to risk costly friction. Sometimes informal solutions are accepted as tentative and are subject to modification after review by the formal coordinating mechanism. To arrive informally at workable solutions to problems affecting the sales department, the top sales executive maintains satisfactory relations with heads of other departments; all think of themselves as members of the same team, cooperating in the effort to reach company objectives.

Sales executives report that informal coordinating procedures are more important than formal methods, particularly where frequent communication is required. A study of four companies revealed that a large amount of communication took place informally among executives responsible for marketing-related activities. Informal coordination was partly through voluntary exchange of informational copies of correspondence, but largely through informal, nonperiodic exchanges of information occurring when executives met, by chance or arrangement, in their offices, or over coffee or meals.[1]

The same study revealed that one individual, or occasionally more than one, served as a communication center for exchanges of information on each important decision area. These executives were either receivers or senders in almost every exchange of information that took place with respect to their interest area. All executives, acting as "centers," assumed the responsibility for providing a continuous flow of information regarding their areas to everyone in the company who they felt might need or could use the information. The top sales and advertising executives served jointly as communication centers for all activities that create demand, including personal selling, advertising, merchandising, sales promotion, and packaging.[2]

The informal communication network is important in coordinating marketing activities, but its existence poses several problems:

1. Marketing personnel must be made aware of the need for coordination. The traditional lack of close coordination among marketing-related activities makes this a difficult challenge.
2. Marketing personnel must be given the opportunity to understand the role and responsibilities of other marketing jobs and to know the people holding these jobs. This is especially important when personnel responsible for marketing decision areas report to different superiors.
3. Marketing management must establish a climate that encourages a continuous and free exchange of ideas and information.[3]

Sales department operations influence and are influenced by the operations of departments performing related marketing activities and of others, such as production, personnel, finance, and data processing, where influences are indirect. The following discussion focuses upon instances where cooperation and

[1]R. C. Anderson and E. W. Cundiff, "Patterns of Communication in Marketing Organizations," *Journal of Marketing*, 29, no. 3 (July 1965), p. 32.

[2]Ibid.

[3]Ibid.

coordination are essential and communications desirable for the top sales executive. It covers the main points of interdepartmental contact, but the dynamics and organizational peculiarities of an individual firm may require cooperation and coordination in other situations.

COORDINATION OF PERSONAL SELLING WITH OTHER MARKETING ACTIVITIES

Sales and Advertising

The sales and advertising departments work toward the same objective—the stimulation of demand—but they use different approaches. Personal selling techniques are the province of the sales department and nonpersonal selling techniques that of the advertising department. The two types of selling effort need skillful blending to achieve an "optimum promotional mix." This requires coordination of plans and efforts. The activities of the sales force are planned and directed along lines that increase advertising's impact, and advertising is geared to help salespeople where and when they need it most. The sales department assists the advertising department in selecting themes and media, in preparing schedules, and in securing dealers' support for cooperative advertising programs. The advertising department helps the sales department in such ways as furnishing sales aids for the sales force and for dealers and by providing sales leads. Advertising conserves the sales force's time, for prospects presold through advertising are easier to convert into customers. Proper timing and coordination of advertising and personal selling are essential, and promotional programs need skillful administration by executives who understand both types of selling effort.

Both departments work toward the same goals, so formal coordination is best achieved by having both department heads report to the same high-ranking executive, for example, the marketing vice-president. However, because so many matters are of joint interest and so many require frequent communication, most coordination between these two departments are on an informal day-to-day basis, with frequent interactions of department heads and subordinates.

Sales and Marketing Information

To obtain maximum returns per dollar spent for marketing information, the sales department works in close harmony with the department or departments producing marketing information. In some instances, this information is provided by marketing research, but in companies with sophisticated marketing information systems, marketing research is only one of the subsystems providing information inputs. Marketing information systems assist the sales department by gathering data needed for analyzing sales problems, assisting in determining sales potentials and setting quotas, measuring the effectiveness of the sales effort, assisting with sales tests, and in other ways. The sales department provides the information system with many of the raw statistics and other information needed for sales and market analysis and forecasting. Fairly often, although the practice is controversial, salespeople are made available to marketing research to do field interviewing. (See Figure 8.1).

As marketing information systems and marketing research become more sophisticated, the sales department works ever more closely with information personnel. Surprisingly little systematic research has been done in evaluating the relative effectiveness of alternative personal-selling appeals and methods of making sales presentations. When sales and information personnel address themselves jointly to these and related important topics, close cooperation becomes even more critical.

Coordination of the sales department with the information system and its data-processing capacity is important. The sales department provides the marketing information system with definitions both of its information needs (desired "outputs") and the information it has available (the "inputs"). The data-processing unit may or may not combine the sales department's own information inputs with inputs from elsewhere. Both in designing and operating a management information system, continuing formal and informal cooperation and communications are of the highest importance.

Improvements in data-handling activities have been significant. From the sales department's standpoint, for example, it has always been important to bill customers correctly and promptly. Automation of order processing not only has resulted in improvements in customer service but has produced as by-products data needed for making rapid changes in sales and production plans, and for inventory control.

Traditionally, sales volume and profit reports are used to measure the performance of the sales force. Computers turn out these reports quickly, fre-

FIGURE 8.1 The Role of the Sales Force in Gathering Research Data

Use Sales Force	All Respondents	Division Size: Large	Medium	Small
A great deal	36%	36%	29%	43%
Moderately	54	51	63	48
Not at all	10	13	8	9
Total	100%	100%	100%	100%
Base	(256)	(50)	(119)	(87)

SOURCE: Survey, School of Business, State University of New York at Albany, 1974.

quently, and in great detail. The computer's capabilities are so great that sales executives call for "exception reports" to avoid being buried in mountains of detail. These reports highlight things requiring attention; details are available but are held in reserve until the executive requests them. Among the exception reports are sales personnel failing to achieve quotas; sales activities exceeding budgeted expenses; territories in which the company is losing competitive position; customers with declining purchases; and product lines having slow sales movement, declining profit margins, or both.[4]

The distribution systems of many companies provide customers with automatic ordering procedures. Many apparel makers, for instance, have set-ups allowing store buyers to punch out their orders on in-store console teleprocessing stations linked to a central computer at the seller's plant or warehouse, which, in seconds, scans the customer's account for a credit okay, examines inventory records to see whether the styles, sizes, and colors can be supplied, discerns the age of the account, types out a shipping order, and stores the new inventory information in memory. This makes it convenient for customers to reorder and speeds up order processing, both improving relations with customers. The continuing need for developmental selling and for keeping in close touch with customers' problems means that the salesperson's role has been changed, not eliminated. Automatic reordering procedures are spreading and sales executives work with data-processing specialists both in setting them up and in monitoring their operations, adjusting them as required to meet changing customer requirements.

Sales executives have continuing need to maintain close relations with information and computer specialists. There is room for improved coordination and cooperation between the sales department and the information function. Probably the greatest opportunity lies in the development of closer informal relationships among personnel at all levels. Insofar as formal coordination is concerned, both marketing information and sales department heads generally report to the same superior.

Sales and Service

In companies manufacturing technical products or products requiring installation and repair services, cooperation and close contact of the sales and service departments are essential. Availability of service, such as technical advice on the installation of a new product, is a powerful selling argument, and there are implications for the service department in a salesperson's promises to buyers. Moreover, in many industries (commerical refrigeration, for example), the recommendations of service personnel often influence buyers' decisions, and in selling vacuum sweepers and other household appliances, service personnel act in a sales-making capacity.

[4]M. A. Jolson and R. T. Hise, *Quantitative Techniques for Marketing Decisions* (New York: Macmillan, 1973), pp. 117–18.

Where service is important in sales strategy, provisions for formal coordination are built into the organizational structure. When both sales and service departments are decentralized, the organization should provide for bridging the gap between the home office and the field. Sales and service should relate—usually by locating sales and service personnel in the same field offices, with regional managers responsible for both activities. Under both centralized and decentralized organizational plans, sales and service functions are coordinated at the department head level, most often by having both these heads report to the chief marketing executive. Under all organizational arrangements, the need for continuous cooperation between sales and service means that the great bulk of coordinating is informal, and between personnel on *lower* organizational levels.

Sales and Physical Distribution

Achieving effective coordination of selling and physical distribution operations is important. Most firms accept the notion that all business operations should be geared toward serving customers at a profit. This requires the maintenance of favorable relations between sales volume and costs of various kinds, including physical distribution costs.

Proper packing, accurate freight-rate quotations, and promptness in delivery—all physical distribution activities—are important in securing sales volume. Unless costs of performing these activities are kept under control, sales volume yields less profit than it should. Sales policies, such as those on delivery schedules, are coordinated with the capabilities of the physical distribution operation and its costs.

The benefits of effective coordination with physical distribution are significant. These benefits, all of which can help to generate additional sales volume and profit include the following.[5]

1. Minimize out-of-stock occurrences (helps to reduce sales lost because of "outs" and helps raise the level of customer satisfaction).
2. Reduce customers' inventory requirements. (If a company develops a more responsive distribution system than competitors, its customers obtain an economic advantage by doing business with it. This is a strong selling point.)
3. Solidify relations with customers (through integrating company delivery facilities with customers' receiving facilities, consignment of stocks to customers, and similar devices).
4. Allow greater concentration on demand creation. (Development of a well-organized physical distribution activity, in which a separate administrative group is set up to plan and operate the distribution system, can free marketing and sales personnel, allowing them to concentrate more on their basic responsibility—demand creation. In many companies this

[5]W. M. Stewart, "Physical Distribution: Key to Improved Volume and Profits," *Journal of Marketing*, 29, no. 1 (January 1965), p. 68.

has led to an increased number of warehouses, and a consequent reduction in total distribution costs.)

The most effective formal coordination of sales and physical distribution results from having the heads of both operations report to a common superior, such as the marketing vice-president. Even more important is the informal coordination of sales and physical distribution personnel, at all levels, on a day-to-day basis. Salespeople and their counterparts in the physical distribution department, for example, communicate directly and frequently, thus helping to ensure efficient processing of customers' orders.

COORDINATION OF PERSONAL-SELLING WITH OTHER DEPARTMENTS

Sales and Production

Coordination of sales and production activities is essential. Whereas at one time production was started only after orders were on hand, today most production is in anticipation of future sales. Similarly, although some products, such as defense materials for the armed forces, are manufactured to specifications established by buyers, most products today are manufactured according to specifications set within the company itself.

Coordination is important both in planning and operations. In planning, joint consultation is required when deciding the products to manufacture, the quantities to produce, the production schedule, inventories, and packaging. But even carefully made plans rarely work out as originally visualized. On the sales side, the sales estimate (on which production schedules are based) may prove in error, or the sales department may accept rush orders, necessitating reshuffling of production schedules, addition of extra shifts, or payment of overtime wages. On the production side, output may not conform to planned quantities because of labor difficulties, material shortages, adverse weather conditions, and the like. These and other operating situations require changes in plans that must be worked out jointly by sales and production personnel.

There is a natural tendency for the two departments to work at cross-purposes, and this makes coordination more difficult. Much has been written about the conflicting philosophies of "production-minded" and "sales-minded" executives. It is sufficient to say here that production executives are naturally concerned with such matters as product line standardization and simplification, and achieving manufacturing economies through long and continuous production runs. Sales executives are naturally concerned over "having something for everybody." Thus, their inclination is to argue for wide selections of products and models, adapted as nearly as possible to the preferences of individual customers. The marketing concept, however, rejects these extreme positions, and top management works to integrate both departments' interests into unified company policies.

The cooperation of the sales department helps the production department. Sales estimates, prepared by or with the assistance of sales executives, are needed for efficient planning of production and purchase schedules. The sales department has a reservoir of market knowledge that is invaluable to production executives seeking more efficient utilization of plant facilities. Sales executives keep production executives informed of changes in market demand for different products, and this increases the chances of attaining optimum production levels. Sales executives recommend elimination of slow sellers, addition of promising new products, and changes in product specifications. For all products, present and proposed, the sales department gives its appraisals from the standpoints of price and potential volume. Moreover, when inventories of raw materials, goods in process, or finished products are excessive, the sales department assists by pushing sales of the products affected.

The production department helps the sales department. It provides selling ammunition in the form of detailed technical information on products and assists in training salespersons in product information. When drafting promotional plans, sales executives draw upon production executives' know-how on such matters as manufacturing costs at different output levels, limitations of production facilities, and the practicality of building given characteristics into products. By relaying information on unused plant capacity and work-in-process to the sales department, the production department helps in stimulating sales personnel to greater efforts. The same information is useful for detecting the need to change the sales emphasis given different products.

Methods for achieving interdepartmental coordination vary, but, because sales and production are both of critical importance, top management generally retains the primary responsibility. If the company has a separate merchandising department, top management delegates to it the authority to coordinate many sales and production activities through staff channels. In other companies, merchandising committees with representatives from both sales and production obtain formal coordination. Formal coordinating mechanisms are valuable, but close informal contacts between personnel at many levels are important in handling many complex problems arising in the course of operations with minimum expenditure of executive time.

Sales and Research and Development

In large firms and in most firms oriented toward product innovation, research and development (R&D) is organized as a separate staff department. In smaller and more conservative firms, responsibility for R&D may be placed in the marketing or production department. Research and development work consists of scientific and engineering efforts to develop new products and to improve established products. It is related to merchandising, that is, structuring the product line and adjusting product features to fit customers' wants, which is of prime concern to the sales department as well as to the production department. Because engineering and design characteristics affect the salability of products, synchronization is required of research and development, sales, and production departments—all of which are involved in product innovation. Among the means of achieving this synchronization are

1. New Product Departments—charged with responsibility for developing new products through coordination of R&D, production, and sales and marketing personnel.
2. New Product Managers—one-person units responsible for developing new products through coordinating R&D, production, and sales and marketing personnel.
3. New Product Project Management Team—composed of persons home-based in other departments brought together to work on a new product.
4. Product Development Committee—similar to (3), but with a permanent existence and dealing with continuing problems of innovation relating to a given product group.

Whether main reliance is placed upon formal or informal mechanisms, coordination should take place at *lower* organizational levels. Department heads find it difficult to keep abreast of the multitude of rapidly changing factors that must be considered in the day-to-day process of developing new products. Specialists have the detailed knowledge of markets and technologies that enables them to make the frequent decisions innovation requires.

Sales and Personnel

Because of the unique problems in managing employees located away from company offices and facilities, most personnel departments are ill-equipped to service sales personnel. Sales departments ordinarily handle nearly all their own personnel problems, and the personnel department acts mainly in an advisory capacity. Personnel department specialists in job analysis, recruiting, selecting, training, and motivation often are consulted by sales executives. Some routine personnel work, such as maintaining records or personal data, is performed by the personnel department. The two departments cooperate in formulating policies on pensions, vacations, sick leaves, safety, health checks, and similar matters. Formal coordination is through top management, and there is significant informal coordination.

Sales and Finance

The sales department assists the finance department by furnishing sales estimates for the company budget, by developing the sales department's budget, and by assisting in control of selling cost. The finance department assists the sales department by providing rapid credit checks on prospective accounts, keeping sales people informed of customers' credit standings, helping locate prospective accounts, and providing credit information on candidates for sales positions. In some firms, salespersons represent the financial department in making collections and securing credit information. These interdepartmental activities require good communications, consistent policies, and close working relationships. Most organizational plans provide for formal coordination through budget and executive committees.

Coordination of sales and finance takes place informally by personal contact, in a mutual effort to overcome the natural conflict of interest in credit policy. Credit terms are significant factors in obtaining orders. Length of the credit period, size and nature of discounts, relative liberality in granting credit—all can be instrumental in persuading prospects to buy.

Good reasons exist for keeping control over credit policy and its implementation away from the sales department. Some sales executives, and far too many salespeople, are more interested in obtaining orders than in collecting amounts due, resulting in a tendency to grant credit to below-average risks. Furthermore, salespeople shy away from making collections, especially from slow-paying accounts, for fear of antagonizing customers.

But credit terms should be set to permit their use as selling points. And there is a need for tact in credit negotiations, both by salespeople and by credit personnel. When a customer's credit must be shut off, a situation arises requiring not only tact but coordination to avoid buck-passing and resultant loss of goodwill. Generally, the sales department, wanting to increase sales, favors liberalizing credit policies, whereas the credit department, wanting to control credit losses, favors tightening them. Close coordination and communication strike a balance between these inclinations to serve the best interests of the whole company.

Sales and Accounting

Traditionally the sales department relied upon the accounting department to bill customers, handle the department's payroll computation and disbursement problems, and provide data for sales analysis and marketing cost analysis. With development of companywide management information systems, performance of these functions shifted away from the accounting department. That department, however, may retain primary responsibility or even, organizationally speaking, have the centralized data-processing unit under its jurisdiction. More and more companies have set up such units, sometimes called "computer centers," to handle data-processing and analysis functions for all, or nearly all, departments.

Sales and Purchasing

The sales and purchasing departments cooperate in three main ways. First, the sales department provides purchasing with sales estimates so that adequate stocks of raw materials, fabricating parts, and other items can be procured in advance of scheduled production runs. Sometimes these data are furnished through an intermediary such as the production department or data-processing unit. Second, the purchasing department informs the sales department, again sometimes through an intermediary, of material surpluses and shortages, so sales emphasis can be changed with regard to products made from these materials. Third, data on sales department needs (for example, office supplies and fixtures, and company cars) are furnished the purchasing department so that purchases can be made on advantageous terms.

A fourth point of cooperation exists in companies where reciprocity is approved policy. The two departments coordinate their efforts, buying as much as possible from customers and selling as much as possible to suppliers. Coordination is achieved formally through top management and informally through personal contacts.

Sales and Public Relations

The sales department works closely with the public relations department. Public relations is consulted on any contemplated moves that might have public relations repercussions, and the sales department assists public relations personnel by relaying information, secured through its contacts with various publics, that has public relations significance. Relations between the two departments are normally informal and with frequent personal contacts, with formal coordination being the responsibility of top management.

Sales and Legal

Legislation regulating and affecting marketing activities makes effective coordination of the sales and legal departments imperative. Every sales department activity has, or can have, legal implications. Sales executives require legal advice on contracts with sales personnel, pricing, relations with competitors and trade associations, salesperson recruiting policy and practice, and disputes with customers. Sales executives and legal officers are in continuing communication to avoid costly litigation and unfavorable publicity. Formal coordination of the sales and legal departments is achieved through top management, but interdepartmental coordination on legal matters is informal.

SALES DEPARTMENT'S EXTERNAL RELATIONS

The sales department has important contact with six main external publics. In the remainder of this chapter, relations with five of these publics are analyzed: final buyers, industry and trade associations, governmental agencies, educational institutions, and the press. Because of the uniqueness of the sales department's relations with middlemen, discussion of distributive network relations is deferred to Chapter 9.

Final Buyer Relations

Final buyers, whether ultimate consumers or industrial users, are the most important public that any marketer strives to please. The competitive free enterprise system is based on the premise that customers' wants must be satisfied; individual companies prosper when their products contribute to this end. An analogous situation exists in politics. If candidates satisfy voters' requirements and win their confidence, they are elected; if politicians fail to maintain this support, they meet defeat at the polls. Manufacturers and their products are on trial with the final buyer public, but in business, the trial goes on each and every day—not, as in politics, just on election day. Satisfaction, or the lack of it, is recorded daily in sales order books and at the nation's checkout counters.

Buyer attitudes and behavior patterns, formed over time and crystalized by experience, are not easily changed. Manufacturers have a competitive edge when they are aware of attitudes and prejudices attaching to their products and organization, and know the reasons for them. Research among final buyer groups gathers the information required for planning ways to alter final buyer attitudes and behavior. Research also measures progress toward overcoming prejudices, determines prejudices against competitors and their products, detects the the need for product improvement, and evaluates middlemen's prestige.

Responsibility for good final buyer relations is not the sales department's alone. If the production department, for example, makes products that fail to meet final buyers' expectations, unsatisfactory final buyer relations result. In consumer goods fields, personnel policies are part of the consumer relations program, since employees are often customers and have contact with other customers. Dividend and other financial policies affect consumer relations, since stockholders and their friends may be customers. When suppliers of industrial products are also customers, final buyer relations are influenced by the seller's purchasing policies and procedures. Middlemen at all distribution levels mold final buyer attitudes toward manufacturers and their products. The effort of all departments need skillful blending with those of middlemen; in this effort, the sales department plays a key role.

Sales department personnel play major roles in formulating basic product service policies and in implementing them. These policies affect not only final buyer attitudes but the ease with which initial sales are made. For example, guarantees and service obligations should be honored promptly and cheerfully. If products fail to perform in the manner that final buyers have a right to expect, then adjustments, refunds, repairs, or replacements should follow. Instruction booklets should be clear and complete, not cluttered with technical jargon. Final buyers' requests for service or information should be answered without needless delay. Above everything else, all employees in contact with final buyers should be courteous, friendly, and competent in their jobs.

Industry Relations

Although trade associations have different objectives, two are of special interest to sales executives: (1) to interpret the industry and its problems to outside publics and (2) to encourage member companies to act in the public interest. Activities directed toward the first objective include trade association advertising, furnishing expert witnesses for legislative hearings, and disseminating industry news. Activities directed toward the second objective include studies of attitudes and opinions of final buyers toward the industry and counseling on public relations problems.

Trade associations have other functions meriting the attention of sales executives. Some serve as clearinghouses for industry production and sales statistics useful to individual companies for planning and controlling their activities. Others sponsor employee training programs; conduct management development programs; arrange for or conduct cooperative research; serve as vehicles for reaching the educational, governmental, and press publics; and provide consulting services. Where industry products are in strong competition, with those of other industries, it is not unusual for an association to coordinate advertising and other promotion aimed to stimulate primary demand. Finally, some associations plan, organize, and direct industrywide trade conventions attended by manufacturers, middlemen, and sometimes even final buyers.

The sales executive has additional contacts with competitors and other business executives through professional and service organizations. Chambers of commerce, manufacturers' associations, the American Marketing Association, and the American Management Association all furnish sales executives with excellent opportunities to exchange ideas. Participation in local business clubs and service groups is worthwhile. It is not essential to be a joiner, but most sales executives find it advantageous, professionally and personally, to maintain as many contacts as time permits.

Proper competitive conduct is difficult to describe, but the rules of common courtesy are good guides. Sales executives, as well as sales personnel, for example, should refrain from making disparaging remarks about competitors and their products. It makes better sense to play up the strengths of one's own company and its products.

The border line between what is right or wrong, good or bad, moral or immoral, is not clear-cut. Ethical criteria are qualitative and relative, not quantitative and absolute. Many practices are controversial—considered ethical by some, unethical by others. Among these are hiring sales personnel away from competitors, persuading suppliers not to sell to competitors, cutting prices in the hope of driving competitors out of business, and paying distributors' or dealers' employees to push the company brand.

Government Relations

Government lays down the rules and regulations under which businesses operate. Rules and regulations affecting the sales department are continuously modified with shifts in judicial and administrative interpretations. Effective sales executives are familiar with such basic pieces of legislations as the Robinson-Patman Act; the Civil Rights Act; the Age Discrimination Act; the Wool Products Labeling Act; and the Food, Drug, and Cosmetic Act. And they keep abreast of judicial and administrative interpretations of such laws. Proposed regulatory legislation is also of concern. To protect company and industry interests, they cooperate with, and appear as witnesses before, legislative committees investigating or holding hearings on industry problems and practices.

Many business executives think of government primarily as a source of regulation; for sales executives other aspects of governmental influence are more important. Federal and state governments affect the size of the market for many products through changing tax laws and rates. Over the past half-century, the effect has been to change the shape of the income distribution curve—relatively speaking, lower economic groups have had their disposable personal incomes raised, and higher groups have had theirs lowered. Most consumer incomes have been rising, and fewer people are in the extremely high, and low, income groups. The average consumer has more disposable income, and this has made possible significant expansions in the markets for many products.

Government influences sales department operations by controlling credit. Through the Federal Reserve System and the Treasury Department, the federal government has powers to expand or contract credit and thus to affect business conditions and the ease with which sales are made. Changes in the relative availability of credit expand or contract the market for such "big-ticket items" as automobiles, consumer durables, and housing. Credit policy of the federal government, therefore, is of considerable interest to sales executives in many fields.

Government affects the market for many products in still other ways. Governmental units are large buyers. During wars and other periods of national emergency, governmental purchases swell the sales of a long list of items. During peacetime, governmental purchases account for important shares of total sales for paper, office equipment and furnishings, automotive equipment and supplies, laboratory equipment and supplies, and computers and data-processing equipment. The armed forces are important customers for foodstuffs, optical goods, photographic equipment and supplies, clothing, chemicals, arms and munitions, aircraft, aerospace items, and communications equipment. Government contracts often lie behind the purchases made by contractors working for federal, state, and local governmental units. Government business is so important to many companies that specialized staffs are formed to negotiate and administer government contracts, and although these staffs may not be wholly under the sales department's jurisdiction, sales executives have a stake in their performance.

Effective sales executives recognize that the government provides income for millions of consumers—government employees and other millions who receive income from governmental sources, including retired government employees, social security recipients, holders of government securities, and disabled war veterans. The Medicare and Medicaid programs have brought additional widespread benefits and a major impact on sales of drugs, pharmaceuticals, and other health care products.

Many governmental agencies provide services or engage in activities that affect the sales executive. Federal and state governments compile and distribute statistical and other information useful for sales planning. Federal agencies help in promoting standardization of product characteristics. The Federal Trade Commission encourages the development of voluntary trade and competitive practice regulations. The federal government has taken up the cause of small companies, helping them through the Small Business Administration. Other governmental agencies protect legitimate business enterprises from commercial shysters and racketeers such as smugglers and bootleggers. From time to time, too, domestic firms find relief and protection from overseas competitors through tariff laws and other import regulations.

Sales executives assist in implementing government relations programs. They expedite the gathering of data needed by governmental statistical agencies. They see to it that the communication lines from the sales department to governmental agencies are open and clear. They lend their support to governmental units seeking appropriations for purposes of gathering information of interest and use to business, such as the U.S. censuses of business.

Educational Relations

The sales department has a sizable stake in educational relations. Future members of significant publics, including the final buyer public, receive their first, and usually most lasting, impressions of the business system and individual companies during their years in school. Schools serve as training grounds for future dealers, distributors, sales personnel, and sales executives. The schools are important customers for many products. There are both future and present payoffs in having good relations with educational institutions.

The educational world provides many services to sales executives. Collegiate schools of business, research bureaus and institutes, and individual instructors conduct studies on relevant problems and make the results available. The expertise of scholars often is brought to bear on problems of direct interest to sales executives, such as application of computer techniques to the design of sales territories and analysis of sales performance. Evening schools and extension divisions provide opportunities for developing sales department personnel. Many universities offer management development programs, providing occasions for sales executives to blend their own experiential knowledge with the thinking of scholars.

Sales executives often further the educational relations program. They assist in collecting and preparing teaching materials, and they help educators and students doing research. They recommend that their companies award scholarships, fellowships, and grants-in-aid to educators. They serve as guest speakers in such courses as marketing, sales management, and consumer behavior. Some companies provide summer internships for educators; others work with educational specialists in developing case materials and new research techniques. Company publicity generally is welcomed by the educational public, but the company preparing it should guard against making it overly commercial. Last, effective sales executives accept their responsibilities as public-spirited citizens. They take an active interest in the welfare of the schools and lend support to those seeking to improve the educational system.

One educational relations problem of special concern to sales executives is the widespread lack of student interest in selling as a career. Many students and teachers have unsavory stereotypes of selling positions, and certain selling jobs (e.g., the used-car salesperson) are definitely not role models. Few students and public schools teachers are aware of the nonmonetary, let alone the financial, rewards of selling careers. Sales executives concerned with building career interest in personal selling should do their homework. In contacts with students and teachers, they should determine the reasons for negative attitudes toward selling, decide what can be done about them, and act accordingly.

Press Relations

The press public consists of writers and editors of newspapers, magazines, trade journals, news services, radio and television stations, and other media. Unfavorable media comments about a company, its policies, products, or personnel not only damage a company's reputation but impede its selling efforts. Bad publicity makes it difficult to make sales and increases the cost of those made. Good publicity makes it possible to obtain sales at less expense.

Good press relations help in obtaining good publicity but will not alone ensure it. Press publicity should be planned as part of the promotional program; planned press releases complement or supplement other elements, such as personal selling and advertising. Skill in handling press relations and basic appropriateness of the publicity plan are the factors causing publicity to be good, bad, or indifferent.

Effective sales executives observe a few simple rules in managing press relations. One is that all stories given to the press have news value—a story has news value if it has human interest, or concerns a subject of interest to the audience reached. Newsworthy stories originating in the sales department relate to the introduction of new products and improvements, new models, promotional plans, additions to the sales staff, promotions of sales personnel, and retirements. A second rule is that press publicity is not unpaid advertising. Presenting the press with copy that amounts to advertising, which the press calls space grabbing, is a sure road to poor relations.

Pressure, influence, or threats to discontinue advertising if publicity is not obtained are avoided. If a news story is likely to present the company or its product in an unfavorable light, it is better to provide reporters the pertinent details than to ask that the story be suppressed. If interviews are on controversial subjects, or involve material that might be misunderstood, reporters are handed statements covering the situation; in other circumstances, prepared press releases are avoided.

Effective sales executives maintain an open-door policy with press representatives—all are treated fairly and courteously. Favorable publicity generated by preferential treatment to some is offset by bad relations incurred with others. The effective sales executive compliments reporters and editors responsible for well-written stories. Building and maintaining good press relations, in other words, is a matter of the sales executive's exercise of good judgment.

CONCLUSION

Good relations with other departments and outside publics are important to the sales department. Improved relations begin inside the company. Internal frictions and inefficiencies inflate costs and are reflected in deteriorating relationships with external publics. Smooth internal functioning of an enterprise requires more than adherence to formalized charted relationships. It requires people on different levels and in different departments to work effectively together.

There is no simple way to obtain a favorable working climate. Simply avoiding frictions, interpersonal and interdepartmental, is not enough. Top management, along with the management of each department, must promote cooperation among all company personnel.

Effective sales executives maintain formal and informal coordination. Formal coordination is secured through top management, which harmonizes the activities of different departments. Informal coordination within and among departments and their personnel is highly important to the smooth functioning of an organization.

The sales department occupies an especially strategic position. Of all company personnel, those in the sales department are in the closest touch with final buyers and middlemen. Sales department personnel also work closely with such key publics as the industry, the government, the educational world, and the press. How these representatives of the sales department conduct themselves with these publics affects the company's reputation. Good relations depend in large measure upon the skill with which personal selling programs are planned and executed.

9 Distributive Network Relations

Securing and maintaining harmonious working relationships with the distributive networks is as important as building and maintaining favorable reputations with final buyers. Distributive outlets are customers for the products, and collectively they bear responsibility for making the "payoff" sales to final buyers. Unless the supply of product flows through to final buyers, marketing channels clog, and all previous personal selling and other marketing efforts are wasted.

The distributive outlets handling the product, or assisting in its sales, are extensions of the manufacturer's sales organization. Often they are final buyers' only points of contact with the manufacturer. Confidence in individual outlets is frequently a crucial factor influencing decisions to buy or not to buy the manufacturer's product. Distributive outlets are the manufacturer's on-the-spot representatives; within their spheres of operation, their reputations are influenced by that of the manufacturer, its products, and its promotion. From the sales executive's standpoint, the importance of establishing and maintaining favorable relations with the distributive network can hardly be overstated, since they directly influence selling efficiency, costs, and profits.

SETTING UP COOPERATIVE PROGRAMS

To implement its overall marketing strategy, the manufacturer needs the cooperation of its distributive outlets. In consumer-goods markets, for instance, retailers must have adequate stocks of a product on hand prior to the launching of national consumer advertising campaigns. Retailers must provide support through tie-in displays and local advertising. Manufacturers of industrial goods look to their distributive outlets for similar support.

The initiative for establishing and maintaining cooperative programs almost always comes from the manufacturer rather than from the distributive outlets. Within the manufacturer's organization, the sales department is often the initiator of such programs and generally the implementer. The product is, after all, the manufacturer's product, and the manufacturer's sales department has the most direct interest in selling it.

Most manufacturers recognize their dependence upon their associated distributive outlets. However, many distributive outlets, perhaps the majority, do not recognize their parallel dependence upon any one manufacturer. They have contact with, and in most cases represent, other manufacturers, many times even those with competitive lines. Then, too, in most marketing situations, the manufacturer's organization is larger, more experienced, and better equipped to plan and administer cooperative programs. Therefore, the distributive outlets usually look to the manufacturer to set up and manage any cooperative efforts.

Some manufacturers achieve marketing success without the cooperation of the outlets handling their products. A few succeed even in spite of their distributive outlets' hostility and open resentment. Manufacturers of high-volume convenience goods, for example, sometimes achieve strong consumer preference through heavy expenditures for advertising, thus forcing the cooperation of dealers who recognize that they will miss opportunities for profit if they do not service the consumer demand. In such cases, although dealers may dislike the manufacturer and its products, they serve the manufacturer's interests, mainly because that is the profitable thing to do.

ROLE OF MANUFACTURER'S SALES FORCE

Distributive outlets regard the manufacturer's salespeople not only as sales representatives for the product line, but also as instruments through which the manufacturer's business philosophy is implemented. Their opinions of the company and its products are influenced by the conduct of its sales personnel. Salespeople need not be public relations experts, but they need skill in interpersonal relations. Training, retraining, and experience make salespeople competent in applying the manufacturer's sales policies and practices, but only skill in interpersonal relations equips them to get along with people. Unless customers receive favorable impressions of the manufacturer from their contact with its sales force, cooperative programs with the distributive outlets are not likely to succeed. Selecting basically good people for the sales force and developing their interpersonal relations skills are important.

Attitudes of distributive outlets are particularly influenced when manufacturers' sales personnel apply undiplomatic tactics. In one study, dealers stated that they resented salespersons who begged for business with personal hard-luck stories, became unpleasant when they did not receive orders, bragged about big orders they had written for other dealers, acted as though they were doing a favor for the dealer, carried gossip from dealer to dealer, hinted at great favors in the future, and acted as though they were entitled to business just for making calls. Such tactics are more common than many sales executives admit.

First-line communications with distributive outlets are initiated and maintained by the manufacturer's sales force, so the utmost care is needed in their selection, training, and supervision. Nothing damages the reputations of a company and its products more than a salesperson who fails to win and hold the respect and confidence of the customers. Sales management relies upon the salespeople to treat customers fairly. Good salespeople do not make promises that cannot be kept or that are later ignored. Good salespeople do not sell orders larger than the customer can handle—overselling causes poor relationships with distributive outlets.

Making lasting friendships for the company is as much a part of the selling job as securing orders. Effective sales management keeps salespeople supplied with up-to-date information of the products, their applications, and changes in sales and other policies (or their manner of implementation). With this information and skill in interpersonal relations, salespeople handle customer relations effectively.

OBJECTIVES AND METHODS OF MANUFACTURER-DISTRIBUTIVE NETWORK COOPERATION

The manufacturer and its distributive outlets share a common objective—to sell the manufacturer's products at a profit. To achieve this objective, manufacturers set more specific objectives. These objectives, of course, differ with the marketing circumstances, even though many variations of specific objectives fit into definite categories. Manufacturers undertake cooperative programs (1) to build distributive network loyalty, (2) to stimulate distributive outlets to greater selling effort, (3) to develop managerial efficiency in distributive organizations, or (4) to identify the source of supply for the product line at the final buyer level.

Methods used to achieve these objectives differ from manufacturer to manufacturer and from time to time, and some aim to accomplish more than one objective. The selection of methods of cooperation depends upon the manufacturer's particular problem(s). The following discussion identifies circumstances leading to the choice of specific objectives and methods of manufacturer-distributive network cooperation.

Building Distributive Network Loyalty to the Manufacturer

Whether distributive outlets actively promote, simply recommend, or just handle the product line depends upon their relationships with the manufacturer and its sales force. If they value these associations, the manufacturer's chances of securing active promotion are good. If they stock the product line merely for the convenience of their customers, it is more difficult for the manufacturer to capitalize on market opportunities. Occasionally, through heavy advertising and promotion to final buyers, the manufacturer pulls a product through the marketing channel despite adverse attitudes of distributive outlets. But if the outlets are forced to handle the product, marketing costs are often high. In the long run, it is less costly and more effective to have the cooperation of distributive outlets.

The most serious situations occur when distributive outlets are hostile to the manufacturer and its product. Many manufacturers who experience this difficulty have little personal contact, such as through salespeople, with the outlets handling their product. Some pull their products through marketing channels by liberal expenditures for advertising to final buyers. They believe that a product is certain to sell if a strong final buyer preference or recognition develops, but they underestimate the importance of having the goodwill of distributive outlets. Outlets stocking products only because the number of calls generated through advertising forces them to do so may give the product the least desirable shelf or counter positions, or even put it under the counter. They give competing products better shelf positions and more space, and they sell substitutions when final buyers ask for the manufacturer's brand. This circumstance is even more serious when the brand possesses few features that differentiate it from competitors' offerings.

In short, in many situations a manufacturer meets sales resistance from the distributive outlets. When this resistance evolves into obstructive tactics, the net result is a progressive deterioration in final buyer respect for, and confidence in, the manufacturer and its product. The manufacturer's problem is to inspire in its distributive outlets a feeling of mutual interest and trust and to convince them that it appreciates their contribution to the marketing success of the product. The sales department and the sales force play significant roles in solving such problems.

Any program designed to build or strengthen distributive outlet loyalty includes two important components. First, there must be appraisals of the manufacturer's policies and their manner of implementation, with a view to identifying the impacts on distributors' and dealers' attitudes. Second, there must be analysis of the communications system with the distributive network. In other words, most cases of disloyalty have their roots in the manufacturer's policies, which may be inappropriate or misapplied, or in shortcomings of the communications system.

Appraisal of the manufacturer's policies and their implementation. The manufacturer needs critical appraisals of the product, the services rendered in connection with it, and the policies and practices followed in its distribution and promotion. The manufacturer must determine the degree to which the product matches the distributive outlets' merchandising requirements and how the product conforms to "their" evaluations of final buyers' wants. Manufacturer-performed services, such as installation and repair, should be offered in response to the recognized needs of distributive outlets and final buyers. All the manufacturer's distribution and promotion policies and practices must be intelligently conceived, fairly applied, and fully understood by the outlets.

The interest of distributive outlets in improving relations with manufacturers varies from product to product. When the product is a mass-distributed convenience good, many manufacturers try to reach the ultimate consumer with similar products. Each competes for the attention of the same dealers, the majority of whom see little reason to favor one supplier at the expense of others—unless a particular supplier proves the benefits that it claims will accrue to the dealer. Since such products are generally distributed through multiple layers of distributive outlets, conditions do not favor the development of close relations with those selling to final buyers. Thus, the manufacturer, who sells through wholesalers, finds it difficult to develop close relations with retailers.

For shopping or specialty goods, some form of exclusive agency or selective distribution is generally used, and the manufacturer sells direct to the retail dealer. Dealers handling these products have as much, or almost as much, interest as the manufacturer in the success of cooperative efforts. Thus, in the consumer-goods field, programs for improving distributive network relations are most appropriate, and stand the greatest chance of success, when the manufacturer markets a specialty or shopping good through a limited number of outlets.

In the industrial-goods field, most manufacturers distribute their products directly to industrial users. Those who utilize nondirect marketing channels usually have opportunity to improve, and to benefit from, improving relations with their distributive networks.

Dealers often pursue obstructive tactics because of a manufacturer's unwise pricing practices. For example, when a manufacturer grants excessive discounts for large orders, the product may become a "price football" for large dealers competing on a price basis. This happens after a heavily advertised product becomes well known and is in strong demand. Smaller dealers may not even try to meet their larger competitors' resale prices. Instead, they promote substitutes for the manufacturer's brand. The underlying difficulty here, as in most cases of unwise pricing, is that some dealers believe that they are receiving inadequate compensation for handling the product. The price and discount structure should allow dealers, large and small, a reasonable gross margin. The solution to problems arising from unwise pricing practices is often to overhaul policies on marketing channels and distribution intensity. For this reason, an appraisal of pricing should accompany a close examination of distribution policy.

The manufacturer should appraise the impact of its promotional policies on the distributive network. These policies need evaluating to determine how well the manufacturer's advertising program is coordinated with the sales force's efforts, for instance, and to assess the effectiveness of coordination of the total promotional program with the network's efforts.

In appraising the manufacturer's policies, the manner in which each is administered deserves attention. The manufacturer should have sound and appropriate policies, and these should be applied fairly in all relations with dealers. The manufacturer, in other words, should abide by the rules that it itself has set up—it should refrain, for example, from allowing secret price concessions and furnishing special assistance to some dealers and not to others. But even though the manufacturer holds to its policies and refuses to make exceptions, dealer complaints arise. Some are without merit, but each should be acknowledged, investigated, and adjusted before it evolves into permanent resentment.

Favoritism among customers should be avoided, not just disapproved of officially. Sales personnel, and sometimes sales executives, play favorites when the product is in short supply. When final user demand expands more rapidly than the available supply of product, or when total demand is underestimated, salespeople and sales executives are bombarded with entreaties of important customers for increased orders. Those who submit to these pleas, and who thereby neglect smaller accounts, should realize that when normal conditions return, customers whose business was ignored are susceptible to competitors' selling arguments.

In attempting to avoid favoritism, some manufacturers go too far in the opposite direction. During periods of scarcity, they spread available supplies over as many accounts as possible. Unless adequate controls are provided, large customers receive allocations too small to be useful, and small customers more than they have ordered in the past. If this happens, relations with the best accounts, the larger ones, are affected adversely. Again, the likely consequence is a general weakening of the company's competitive position. Allocation policies should be based on the relative needs of all classes of accounts. Complaints of unfair treatment should be investigated, and inequities should be adjusted. Under conditions of short supply, it is impossible to keep every customer satisfied, but all should be convinced of the fairness of the policies in effect.

Analysis of communications system. Insufficient personal contact between distributive outlets and the manufacturer often contributes to disloyalty. When the marketing channel includes several layers of distributive outlets, when personal selling plays an insignificant part in the promotional program, or both, defects in the manufacturer's communications system with its distributive network are likely. Although its product, distribution, promotion, and pricing policies are sound, a manufacturer's remoteness, institutionally if not geographically, from outlets and their problems may mean certain policies are inappropriate for them. When competitors have closer relationships through their own salespeople with these outlets, the outlets may regard the manufacturer as too distant to deserve their cooperation. They may continue to handle its product, but mainly because of its already established demand. Before the situation can be improved, steps must be taken to improve communications.

Improvements in communications with the distributive network take many forms. Sometimes it is a drastic change in distribution policy, for example, a manufacturer switches from the use of wholesalers to direct-to-retailer selling and obtains closer contact with retailers. Or it is backing up wholesalers' efforts with a force of missionary salespeople. A program of occasional visits to distributive outlets by sales executives improves communications and cements relationships. Similar benefits accrue from company sponsorship of national or regional conventions for distributive outlets. Such inexpensive methods as personal letters or telephone calls from sales executives, the circulation of specially edited dealer magazines, or advertising to the trade are effective not only in improving communications but in building and retaining dealer loyalty.

Strained relations with distributive outlets result from ineffective handling of correspondence. When dealers request information, or when sales personnel relay their queries, responses should be prompt. To procrastinate is to irritate the customer and to risk losing goodwill. All messages from customers should be acknowledged, and if answers are not readily available, that fact should be communicated. Questions that cannot be answered usually relate to subjects that should command the attention of top-ranking sales executives.

Effective sales executives have many ways to keep track of customers' attitudes. In well-managed companies, salespeople report important changes that they observe taking place. Internal analysis of sales records detects shifts in the source and size of orders received; often these are symptomatic of changes in customers' attitudes. Studies by marketing research personnel reveal criticisms of company policies and practices and suggestions for their improvement. Ownership of a few outlets allows the firm to experiment with new merchandising and selling techniques that, if successful, are passed on to customers.

Stimulating Distributive Outlets to Greater Selling Effort

Dealer apathy is common. Some manufacturers invest millions of dollars in promotion, but dealers, outwardly at least, are not only unimpressed but unmoved. Many dealers fail to see why they should tie in with the manufacturer's promotion or provide extra push for the product. They feel, sometimes rightly, that the manufacturer wants more assistance from them than it is willing to extend—and frequently these feelings trace to inadequacies in salespeople's presentations. Under these circumstances, coordination of promotional efforts is difficult. The first step in overcoming dealer apathy is to identify the reasons lying behind it. The second step is to take positive action to increase dealer selling effort.

Changing policies. It may be that inappropriate or outmoded sales policies are the cause of dealer apathy. Alert competitors may have adjusted their policies to the changing situation, while the company, whose dealers are apathetic, may have lagged behind. Management may have clung to policies for sentimental reasons. Bringing policies into line with marketing conditions stimulates dealer effort.

For example, automobile manufacturers once charged dealers for transportation expenses that were often fictitious—transportation charges were billed on the assumption that each car would be shipped from a central plant when actually it came from an assembly facility closer to the dealer. These charges, known as "phantom freight," were much criticized by dealers. These charges were also responsible for the bootlegging of new cars, where unfranchised dealers purchased new cars from dealers close to the home factories and towed or hauled them to the Southwest or Far West, there to sell them in competition with franchised dealers. Several years later, the automobile manufacturers, partly because of a congressional investigation and partly because they recognized the growing dealer apathy, abandoned phantom freight charges. With much, or almost all, of the freight differential wiped out across the country, automobile bootlegging became less profitable, and the morale of authorized dealers improved.

Companies utilizing multiple marketing channels frequently encounter problems in obtaining support from distributive outlets in some channels. One consumer-products company, for instance, sells directly to large retailers such as corporate chains and through wholesalers to smaller retailers. Company salespeople are in personal contact with large retailers, and they gain the support of these dealers. But to gain the support of smaller retailers, the sales personnel must work through the intervening wholesalers, earning their support as well.

Particular attention should be given to pricing policy. Wholesalers, as well as retailers, expect that margins will be in line with the marketing tasks the manufacturer expects them to perform. But margins need setting, too, with an eye on the margins competing manufacturers offer. If distributive outlets believe that the manufacturer is asking for too much support and offering too little margins or if competing manufacturers expect less support and/or offer higher margins, the manufacturer's pricing policy must be brought into line.

Reformulation of other policies stimulates distributive outlets to greater selling effort. Policies on credit extension, service, advertising and selling allowances, and quantity and cash discounts should be scrutinized to determine if they provoke dealer apathy. Policies on marketing channels and distribution intensity sometimes need revising to stimulate the distributive outlets to greater effort.

A frequent reason for the indifference of distributive outlets lies in their previous experiences with promotional programs. Wholesalers and retailers are offered far more promotions than they can accept. Distributive outlets accept and push the promotions of those manufacturers with whose promotions they have had good experience in the past. If a manufacturer has had successful promotions in the past, then the distributive outlet has more confidence in the manufacturer's current promotion.

Sharing promotional risks with dealers. On analyzing the attitudes of dealers, the manufacturer sometimes finds that these outlets are not enthusiastic, because they are risking so little on the promotional program. Benefiting from the manufacturer's promotion over a long period, dealers come to depend upon the manufacturer to perform almost the entire selling task. They feel that it is the manufacturer's job to bring customers into the store and theirs to ring the cash register and pocket the profits. Other dealers consider it unfair to show enthusiasm for any one promotional program, since so many manufacturers' products are represented on their shelves.

To combat problems of this sort, manufacturers demonstrate considerable ingenuity in devising strategies to stimulate dealers to greater sales effort. In one widely used strategy, the manufacturer attempts to persuade dealers to invest time, effort, and money in promotional programs. Thus, manufacturers who would provide free point-of-purchase display materials to retailers charge for these materials, theorizing that retailers who risk their own funds will make good use of the displays and hence justify their costs. Similarly, manufacturers who inaugurate dealer-cooperative advertising programs in which expenses are shared with dealers commonly experience renewed dealer interest. Whenever dealers have a stake, even a limited one, in the final results of a promotional program, they work toward making it successful.

Using forcing methods. To stimulate distributive outlets, manufacturers may use techniques that compel them to provide extra push for the product. These techniques, known as "forcing methods," overcome distributors' indifference by providing additional incentives. These incentives appeal to the distributive outlets, their salespeople, or final buyers.

Incentives to the distributive outlet. Dealers are offered special prices on larger-than-average orders, or a free case of the product for every so many purchased. These offers persuade dealers to increase the size of their inventory investments, thus putting them under more pressure to promote the product. Other ways of accomplishing this result include offering premiums to dealers who make purchases above a specified minimum size, or packing premium coupons, redeemable for merchandise of the dealer's choice, in each shipping case. Sometimes the manufacturer awards the premium only after resale of the product, thus shifting the emphasis from building up the dealer's inventory to making sales to the final buyer.

Manufacturers sometimes combine dealer incentives with sales volume quotas set for individual dealers. If dealers meet or exceed their sales quotas within the sales campaign period, they receive prize awards—often in the form of trips for dealers and their spouses to exotic places like Acapulco, Casablanca, or Tahiti. In some instances, dealers are assigned sales volume quotas on a month-to-month basis and are awarded prizes monthly. Combining the dealer incentive with a sales volume quota often motivates dealer management to strive very hard to achieve manufacturer-set sales volume quotas.

Incentives to distributive outlets' sales personnel. To stimulate the sales personnel of distributive outlets, manufacturers use a wide variety of incentives. Special premiums and plans involving trading stamps (redeemable in merchandise of the winner's own choosing) are used extensively. In some fields, as in cosmetics and women's accessories, the manufacturer pays retailers' sales clerks a small sum (known as a "spiff" or "P.M.") for each unit of the product they sell.

One hosiery manufacturer, for instance, paid retailers' clerks 25 cents for each pair of its brand sold. Clerks, waiting upon customers not specifying brand, naturally push the brand on which they receive the P.M. Many retailers dislike P.M.s, however, because they weaken management's control over selling techniques used by clerks.

One widely used strategy is for the manufacturer to conduct a sales contest for dealers' or distributors' sales personnel. The automobile manufacturers, for instance, conduct incentive programs for their dealers' sales personnel. Prize awards are incentive trips and "prize-point checks" redeemable in merchandise. Typically, points are awarded for selling units of particular models and extra points for conversion sales (where a competitive model has been owned by the customer). There are thousands of dealerships for each make and tens of thousands of dealer salespersons, so these are large-scale contests. Because of the specialized planning and administration required, most manufacturers turn the planning and sometimes the administration also, over to firms specializing in sales incentive programs. E.F. MacDonald Company, for example, assists in developing campaign themes, designs promotion pieces, handles their distribution, arranges hotel and travel reservations, sets up special entertainment programs, and, in general, attends to all the details. The planning and administrative services of sales incentive agencies are made available to manufacturers at little or no cost–they make their profits from the markups on merchandise and travel used as contest awards.

Incentives to ultimate consumers. Manufacturers of convenience goods stimulate dealers indirectly by using forcing methods to promote purchases by ultimate consumers. These methods include couponing, sampling, consumer contests, premium plans, "cents-off" promotions, and special introductory offers. If a forcing method works out as the manufacturer intends, rapid movement of the product helps to overcome dealer lethargy. Numerous administrative details, however, must be handled effectively in successful implementation of these forcing methods. The manufacturer must see that its own sales force exerts the needed effort and obtains the required support from wholesalers and their sales personnel. Companies using numerous programs of this sort generally have a sales promotion manager, who is responsible for both planning and administration.

The manufacturer using a forcing method must not antagonize or burden its dealers. One survey of supermarket managers revealed that the majority favored discontinuance of cents-off deals by coffee roasters. Too frequent use of these deals caused problems in supermarkets of mixed inventory of coffee containers—some with and some without cents-off offers. Supermarket managers, too, are not generally entranced with coupons giving cents-off allowances to buyers of particular products—redemption of coupons slows down movement at checkout counters and creates extra bookkeeping problems. Continual use of forcing methods promotes footdragging by dealers.

Developing Managerial Efficiency in Distributive Organizations

To make its dealers more enthusiastic about its product, the manufacturer should consider increasing dealer efficiency. The dealer's primary concern is to make, or better yet, to increase, profits. The manufacturer, who frequently has access to superior managerial know-how, can search out improved methods for its dealers. It is not enough for the manufacturer to find better operating methods for the dealers to use; the manufacturer must see that they learn how to incorporate these methods into their operations. The manufacturer recognizes that an important key to success lies in how dealers operate their businesses. More efficient dealers move the manufacturer's products more rapidly through the marketing channel and produce larger sales and profits both for themselves and for the manufacturer.

Dealer training programs. Not all manufacturers benefit from providing dealer managerial training programs; payoff from these programs varies with the product. Management training programs for dealers are most beneficial when the products require considerable personal-selling effort. Such programs are less beneficial where final buyers buy as a matter of habit or on impulse. Dealer training programs are important, when the product's unit price is high, trade-ins are common, the final buyer's purchase decision is postponable, the product requires demonstrations, and dealers' recommendations play a major role in making sales.

Assistance in sales force management. To develop managerial efficiency in distributive organizations, the sales executive's role often is to improve dealer sales force management. Dealers are advised on sources and methods of recruiting new sales personnel, sales compensation plans, and supervision and control of sales personnel. Sometimes, dealers are provided with exhaustive "audits" of their entire personal-selling programs, together with recommendations for improvements.

Many manufacturers, particularly those marketing industrial items and big ticket consumer durables, provide sales training assistance to dealers. Sometimes this may be nothing more than manufacturer-prepared sales training material, including films and slide presentations. More often, the manufacturer's sales force, specialized training personnel, or sales executives conduct or participate in dealers' sales training programs. The manufacturer's main aim in assisting dealers with sales training is to make certain that dealers' sales personnel know the product's "talking points" and how best to present them. Other objectives include improvement of sales techniques used by dealer sales personnel, more effective prospecting, spreading the word on product uses and applications, and explaining cooperative advertising programs in terms of the roles of dealer sales personnel.

Dealer sales training programs should not be standardized throughout the entire market. Subjects included should vary and receive different degrees of emphasis depending upon problems confronting dealers in each area. With each clinic focusing on local problems, participants show greater receptiveness, and there is strong and immediate impact on sales of the manufacturer's product. Consequently, prior to planning a dealer sales clinic, the manufacturer's sales force should report fully on dealers' problems territory by territory.

Training of dealers' sales personnel generally is decentralized. Unless the manufacturer uses selective or exclusive agency distribution, dealers are reluctant to have their salespeople attend training sessions at the factory. However, if the product is an industrial good of high unit value, about which dealers' salespersons need considerable technical information, factory training schools are appropriate. When training is at the factory, the cost to the manufacturer is high, because usually the only costs borne by dealers are trainees' travel charges. Dealers object to having their sales forces away from their territories, and, if the trainees are paid partially or wholly on a commission basis, they dislike the financial sacrifice. For these reasons, as well as the fact that orientation to local problems is desirable, most training of dealer's sales personnel is decentralized; it may be conducted on the dealer's premises or, especially when each dealer has only a few salespeople, at hotel meeting rooms, convention halls, nearby resorts, or the manufacturer's branch sales offices.

Advice and assistance on general management problems. Another approach to improving efficiency of distributive outlets is to provide advice and assistance on general management problems. Dealers are counseled on store location, store layout, arrangement of fixtures and stock, accounting methods and systems, control of inventories and costs, advertising, credit and collection policies, and other matters. The manufacturer furnishing management advice usually expects the dealer to pay only for the actual cost of the service given, if at all. In some instances, the manufacturer regards the dealer advisory service as part of its own sales promotional program and absorbs the entire cost. One building products manufacturer, for example, has its marketing research department predict its dealers' sales from the building permits issued in each area and passes this information along to dealers for use in their business planning.

Many dealers do not manage their businesses soundly. They fail to reach sales volume and profit goals, even when the manufacturer provides them with well-planned promotion and selling support. Failures adversely affect the morale of both the manufacturer's sales force and the dealers. To avoid dealer failures, some manufacturers have programs for the evaluation and analysis of dealers and dealer selection processes. This pays off in reduced dealer turnover, dealer growth in profitability, and increases in sales of the company's products.

Shelf-allocation programs. Manufacturers of items sold through self-service retail outlets have a special interest in securing shelf space for their brands. One cereal company has a "shelf-allocation program," which purports to outline for retailers an ideal shelf-space arrangement for its entire breakfast cereal sections. Several large grocery manufacturers provide retailers with pamphlets describing inventory control and shelf-space allocation procedures for each grocery department. NABISCO performs shelf-allocation analysis for retailers on cracker and cookie displays, and its competitors offer comparable services.

A manufacturer's interest in receiving a reasonable share of available shelf space stems from a desire to minimize stockouts and to attract more impulse buyers. Some retailers overallocate shelf space to private labels and slow-selling items, putting the space squeeze on faster-selling, nationally advertised brands. Other shelf-space inequities develop because retailers stock excessive numbers of duplicate brands. Other inequities develop because of the effect of store manager–competitor sales force relations. A logical and "fair and unbiased" shelf-allocation program, intelligently merchandised to the dealers, can help assure reasonable space for the manufacturer's product on retail shelves. The manufacturer's sales force plays a key role in implementing shelf-allocation programs, especially in lining up the cooperation of store managers.

Missionary sales personnel. Another approach aimed toward making distributive outlets more efficient is to use missionary salespeople. In marketing consumer products, for instance, missionary salespeople work closely with wholesalers' personnel and make calls upon wholesalers' customers and prospects—the retailers. The missionaries check each wholesaler's inventory, make suggestions for increasing the effectiveness of wholesaler sales personnel, and assist in their training; they acquaint wholesalers with the manufacturer's advertising program and generally maintain close and friendly relations. In addition, they call on retailers in an effort to improve movement of the product at the retail level. Orders they obtain from retailers are turned over to the wholesalers for filling. In the drug and certain other fields, missionary salespersons are known as "detailers," and they also make calls on persons who influence, but do not make, purchase decisions, such as doctors, dentists, hospital administrators, and schoolboard members.

In marketing industrial goods, missionaries perform similar functions, but generally they give more emphasis to training distributors' and dealers' sales personnel on product characteristics, new applications, and sales fundamentals. In selling highly technical products with numerous specialized applications, they assist in analyzing customers' problems and consummating sales. In industries served by outside professionals, such as in building and construction, missionary salespeople acquaint engineers, architects, and other professionals with the technical characteristics and applications of the manufacturer's product.

Missionary salespeople provide services designed to improve relations with the distributive network. They perform an educational function as they acquaint distributive outlets and their personnel with new products and applications, while they keep alive the trade's interest in established products. Their effort supplements those of the distributive outlets' selling forces in translating this knowledge into greater sales volume. The role of missionary salespersons is particularly critical when they call on persons influencing but not making buying decisions, or when the consummation of sales demands greater product knowledge than the middlemen's sales force possesses.

Generally, missionary salespeople should not permanently assume functions that belong to the dealer. A manufacturer sets up a missionary sales force because its middlemen are not performing as it desires. The manufacturer attempts to obtain quick improvement by substituting direct action for the much slower, indirect effort to upgrade the overall management efficiency of distributive outlets. The outlets should understand that the missionary sales force is only a temporary way to fill the gap between the outlet's present capabilities and the manufacturer's expectations. However, some distributive outlets are constrained from attaining desired performance levels. An outlet stocking competing brands may be unwilling to promote one at the expense of the others, and a permanent missionary sales force is necessary to achieve satisfactory promotion. The manufacturer providing permanent missionary sales help should guard against continually increasing its range and allowing distributive outlets to pass on the blame for their own inefficiency.

Missionary salespeople are often unpopular with dealers. They are accused of playing off one dealer against another, selling to poor credit risks and expecting dealers not only to accept the resulting orders but to bear the likely losses, and interfering with the activities of dealer sales personnel. Therefore, it is advisable to restrict the activities of the missionary salespeople, as much as possible, to training dealer management and their sales force. The manufacturer should, with rare exceptions, expect its dealers eventually to resume functions performed by the missionary sales force. The more effective missionary salespeople are as developers of managerial and selling skills, the sooner they can be reassigned to other duties.

Identifying Source of Supply at Final Buyer Level

Many manufacturers make special efforts to ensure that final buyers can find the local outlets that handle their product and that, once in the right outlet, these buyers can locate the product with minimum difficulty. The significance of this problem differs with the product, the manufacturer's policy on distribution intensity, and the distributive outlets' operating characteristics. Consumer-goods manufacturers, owing to the greater length and complexity of their marketing channels, general have greater problems in this area than do industrial-goods producers.

For the manufacturer distributing its product through a limited number of dealers and/or distributors, publicizing the identity of outlets stocking the product is essential. Thus, for consumer products manufacturers using selective or exclusive agency distribution, the identification of local retail outlets is an important objective. These manufacturers generally also invest heavily in consumer advertising. But it does little good to presell through advertising unless consumers can find the product. The consumer is not often predisposed to spend a great amount of searching time in finding a store that stocks a particular item. If the manufacturer is to capitalize on the preconditioning of consumers through advertising, steps must be taken to assure that consumers can identify the proper retailers.

Local advertising. Manufacturers of consumer specialty and shopping goods achieve identification of their local outlets in different ways. Some buy space and time in local media and advertise over the names of local stores, occasionally with the stores paying part of the cost. Others list their dealers in national advertisements. Many list their dealers in local telephone classified directories, and some provide their retailers with appropriate store signs. Others persuade their retailers to feature the manufacturer's product in their own local advertising and make available ready-made advertising layouts or matrices.

Local advertising of the manufacturer's product, whether paid for by the manufacturer or retailer or jointly, not only adds local flavor to a promotional program but may increase its effectiveness. In individual market areas, dealers frequently know better than the manufacturer which types of advertising are the most effective. Because of regional variances, many manufacturers use prices only in local advertisements. The manufacturer desiring to advertise its product's price locally may use the same advertising to identify its local dealers.

Manufacturers of industrial products use advertising to final buyers to identify the sources of supply. Direct mail, listings in trade directories and industrial catalogues such as Sweet's, and national advertising in trade publications are all used to identify distributive outlets. On the local level, especially in important industrial centers, listings of dealers and/or distributors in the classified sections of telephone and business directories are used.

Point-of-purchase identification. Although the manufacturer of a consumer convenience good rarely attempts to identify all its dealers, it often takes steps to emphasize the in-store presence of its product. When the item is one that customers buy on impulse, the manufacturer's sales force secures point-of-purchase promotion. The only place in the entire marketing channel where the product and the ultimate consumer actually come into contact is in the retail outlet—at the point of purchase. The manufacturer has the best opportunity to make the "payoff" sale if the product is where consumers can find it. Counter and floor mechandisers, shelf makers, preprints and reprints of national advertisements, mass interior displays (often erected by the manufacturer's salespeople), special display cases, and easeled display cards, to mention only a few of the many sales promotion pieces, are all used to identify the product inside the retail store. Where the manufacturer's sales personnel call upon the dealers frequently, it is common for them to receive preferred shelf or counter positions for the product display. Self-service point-of-purchase pieces and preferred display positions (tied in with good packaging) are the only ways in which the manufacturer can influence consumer buying behavior in the store. Point-of-purchase materials take the place of clerks in providing information to prospective buyers and even in persuading them to buy. As self-service spreads to stores retailing specialty and shopping goods, point-of-purchase materials become even more important.

Careful attention should be given to the distribution of point-of-purchase display materials, and special precautions can assure their use by retailers. The most effective distribution method is to have the sales force (or a specialized display service company) both deliver and set up the displays in retail stores. When display pieces are distributed in shipping containers with the product, many, if not most, retailers (or their receiving clerks) discard them. To avoid the waste of display pieces, some manufacturers obtain distribution by publicizing their availability through direct-mail or trade-paper advertising; however, unless the display piece is most unusual, few dealers write in, or even ask salespersons for it. This seeming lack of interest by retailers does not necessarily reflect disapproval of these promotional devices—more often it reflects lack of understanding or inspiration in their use, inability to cope with the volume of materials received, or inertia.

To maximize retailers' use of display pieces, they are designed with retailers' problems in mind. A display piece should not be too complicated for the average retail employee to assemble, neither should it be too large nor too small for the space in which it will be erected in retail stores. The design should make it clear that the display piece will help retailers to make more sales. In gathering information for design purposes, the knowledge of retailers' problems and operating circumstances of the manufacturers' salespeople should be fully utilized.

DISTRIBUTIVE NETWORK CHANGES AND MAINTAINING RELATIONS

The evolution of new types of distributive outlets has been a recurring phenomenon. Over the years, many new marketing institutions have appeared and grown in importance—department stores, mail-order houses, corporate chains, cooperative and voluntary chains, producers' and consumers' cooperatives, supermarkets, rack jobbers, discount houses, and discount department stores, to name but a few. Older, better established types of distributive outlets proclaim loudly that each new institution is "illegitimate." They plead with manufacturers for protection against such unfair and unorthodox competitors. Consequently, the newborn institutions fight all the harder to make sales and even to secure sources of supply—perhaps that is why new institutional forms seem more virile than older ones. Whenever new types of distributive institutions have been successful, they have filled a market niche that went unfilled up to the time of their appearance. Manufacturers who do not allow their marketing channels to "freeze," those with truly dynamic marketing and sales policies, have less difficulty in maintaining adequate overall distribution. It may be appropriate occasionally for a manufacturer to assist its conventional outlets in coping with their new competitors, but the manufacturer must also ensure that its products are represented in the new outlets. Marketing history is full of instances of manufacturers who have clung too long to losing causes. The best policy is neither to assist nor to throw roadblocks in the way of the newer institutions. If research of broad underlying economic, political, and social trends indicates that newer types of outlets are capable of becoming important outlets for the product, changes in marketing channels and sales policies should be considered.

CONCLUSION

Both the manufacturer and the distributive outlets have much to gain from cooperation, and much to lose if it is lacking. Although cooperation is a two-way street, generally the manufacturer must initiate it. Those charged with planning, administration, and implementation of programs of cooperation with distributive outlets must consider the implications for personal-selling strategy and sales department operations.

No manufacturer's marketing program is complete if it lacks plans for securing and maintaining the cooperation of the distributive outlets. The fortunes of manufacturers rise and fall with those of their distributors and dealers. If distributors and dealers succeed in selling the product, the manufacturer also succeeds. If they fail, the manufacturer fails.

Cases for Part II

CASE 2-1

Donaldson Manufacturing Company

Electrical Products Manufacturer—Selecting a Top Sales Executive

The president of the Donaldson Manufacturing Company of Chicago faced the problem of selecting a new general sales manager. The company had annual sales in excess of $75 million and more than forty years of experience in manufacturing electrical safety switches, circuit breakers, regulators, manual and magnetic starters, and related products. These products, which were used in industrial and institutional markets, were distributed through nearly 250 electrical supply wholesalers. Four divisional sales managers directed field operations from offices in Chicago, New York, Houston, and San Francisco. Divisional managers each supervised from three to eight salespeople and were responsible for recruiting, selecting, and training the personnel under their control. Sales potential and quotas were determined by the general sales manager and an assistant but were adjusted after consultations with the divisional sales managers.

The need for selecting a general sales manager was occasioned by the impending retirement of Mr. Preston, who had been with the company since its inception. For many years, Preston had been an advocate of increasing decentralization in sales force operation and control. He felt that the central sales department should concern itself almost exclusively with planning and that the sales divisions should have maximum freedom in deciding how goals should be reached. Sales personnel in the field received little direction or control from the Chicago head office. Divisional sales managers administered their divisions like independent business people; they had grown accustomed to making decisions and to formulating policies for their own marketing areas. Little standardization existed in the sales operating policies followed in the four divisions.

Price competition in the industry was of secondary importance, the main basis being that of product development and design. Donaldson sales personnel spent a high proportion of their time calling on industrial and institutional users with the representatives of electrical supply wholesalers. Their principal function was to analyze the problems of the wholesalers' customers and to prescribe Donaldson equipment as a solution. If standardized products were not adaptable to customers' problems, sales force members often recommended that equipment be specially manufactured to meet users' requirements.

The twenty-five Donaldson salespersons all possessed degrees in electrical engineering or equivalent experience, and they had been trained under the personal direction of the divisional sales managers. Sales personnel were compensated on a straight salary basis, partly because of the great amount of time spent working with wholesalers' salespeople and partly because they were required to assist in installation of equipment and to make repairs in emergency situations.

Divisional sales managers were compensated on the basis of a minimum fixed salary plus a commission on the gross margin realized from sales originating within their respective divisions. The central office made decisions on changes in the salaries of divisional sales managers, but divisional sales managers made adjustments in the compensation of salespeople. Indeed, only recently had all divisions adopted the straight-salary plan for salespeople, a change insisted upon and pushed through by the company president.

It had been impossible to assign the sales personnel to nonoverlapping territories—each person worked with several wholesalers, and, in many instances, the same areas were cultivated by two or more wholesalers. However, it was unusual for more than one salesperson to make calls on the same industrial or institutional user.

Preston was responsible for setting sales quotas and determining sales potentials, planning promotional programs with the advertising agency, assisting in the setting of price ranges, developing the sales department budgets, and in formulating other basic marketing policies. He was also responsible for conducting the public relations program.

The president of the company, who had the support of the board of directors, felt that the time had come to centralize more of the operations of the sales department. He realized that any changes would have to be made gradually, but he was certain that greater control over the salespeople was essential. For example, the head office had little information on the performance of individual salespersons. It was often several months before the head office learned of personnel changes made in the sales divisions.

The president had been authorized by the board of directors to screen all applicants for the position of general sales manager, and to submit his selection for final approval. Because he believed in the basic soundness of a "promotion from within" policy, he first considered the four divisional sales managers and the assistant general manager. He decided that two of the divisional managers were incapable of assuming the increased responsibilities; the third, although competent, had expressed a desire to continue in his present capacity; the fourth was not only willing but anxious to assume the added responsibility. The assistant general sales manager was also in the running, and four other applications had been accepted. From the president's investigations, the following information was extracted:

1. Thomas G. Gunning

Personal information: Age 48; height: 6 feet 2 inches; weight: 225 pounds; fair health; divorced; three dependents by two ex-wives.

Education: Attended public schools in Denver, Colorado. Received B.S. degree in electrical engineering from the University of Colorado.

Experience: Past eight years divisional sales manager, Southern Division (Houston). One year as salesperson, Southern Division. Outstanding sales record.

Three years in military service as infantry officer. Served overseas, principally in staff positions. Also assigned as an instructor at the Infantry Officers' Candidate School.

Three years as salesperson, Southern Division. Average record.

Three years as salesperson, Fort Worth Electrical Wholesale Supply Co.

Two years employed as engineer on various government projects, chiefly in the Mountain States.

Six years as partner in electrical contracting business, Denver. Business was liquidated as a result of financial reverses.

2. Glen G. Parker

Personal information: Age 35; height: 5 feet 3 inches; weight: 150 pounds; good health; married; five dependents.

Education: Attended parochial schools in Syracuse, New York. Received B.S. degree in business administration from Syracuse University. Successfully completed three correspondence courses in electrical and mechanical engineering.

Experience: Past nine years assistant general sales manager. Works directly under Preston, who was responsible for hiring him. His principal duties have been to gather economic and marketing statistics and to assist in sales forecasting.

Three years as assistant store manager, Rochester, New York.

Stock boy in department store, Utica, New York, for one year after college.

While in college, worked as a waiter in a restaurant for three years.

3. Joseph Q. Brunzell

Personal information: Age 38; height: 6 feet; weight: 175 pounds; excellent health; married; two dependents.

Education: Attended public schools, Oak Park, Illinois. Attended Indiana University, majoring in European history. Left college after three years because of lack of funds and death of father.

Experience: Past seven years assistant sales manager of Logston Corporation, Chicago manufacturer of sound recording equipment. Is responsible for sales research work. Plans and conducts sales training programs and "training clinics" for company and distributors' salespeople.

Five years as salesperson, Chicago office supply firm. Work included the demonstration of various items of office equipment and the making of suggestions to customers on methods of simplifying office procedures.

Two years general work in chain grocery store, Oak Park, Il.

4. Sven A. Pelly

Personal information: Age 59; height: 5 feet 9 inches; weight: 165 pounds; good health; married; one dependent. Has son attending Princeton.

Education: Attended private elementary and secondary schools in Ohio. Received B.A. degree in political science from Princeton.

Experience: Past fifteen years account executive with New York advertising agency. Has participated in planning and executing promotional programs for several products, mostly in the consumers-goods field. Has had considerable experience in planning promotional budgets for large clients.

Ten years free-lance writer of promotional literature. Did work for a large mail-order house. Prepared some material, including sales portfolios, for companies manufacturing industrial goods.

Ten years employed by Cleveland stockbrokerage firm. At first was mainly a statistician, later became a customer contact man.

Comment: When interviewed, Pelly was extremely nervous.

5. Richard E. Black

Personal information: Age 34; height: 6 feet; weight; 180 pounds; good health; married; two dependents.

Education: Attended public schools in western Oregon. Received B.A. degree from University of Oregon. Received M.B.A. degree from Stanford University.

Experience: Past two years assistant sales manager of Morrow Electric Corporation. Has helped plan and execute marketing programs for several electrical products similar to those in Donaldson line.

Four years as market analyst, Morrow Electric Corporation.

Two years as instructor in marketing, Foothill College.

Two years as student, Stanford University.

Two years as office manager, Chrysler automobile dealership, Portland, Oregon.

Comment: Applicant has been active in community service organizations.

6. John H. Curtin

Personal information: Age 40; height: 5 feet 9 inches; weight: 175 pounds; married; no dependents.

Education: Attended parochial schools in Boston. Completed two years at Boston College.

Experience: Past eight years—owns and manages wholesale electrical supply house in western Massachusetts. Donaldson distributor for past five years.

Has completed preliminary negotiations for sale of his business.

Four years as production supervisor, Baltimore electronic plant.

Eight years as supervisor for a Boston electrical contractor.

Comment: Applicant appears to have substantial means. It is also rumored that his wife, the daughter of a wealthy New York banker, furnished the money that enabled him to go into business for himself eight years ago.

Which, if any, of the six applicants should have been selected?

CASE 2-2

Riverside Container Corporation

A Producer of Corrugated Shipping Containers—Position Guide for a Sales Manager

Riverside Container Corporation (RCC) was a newly formed manufacturer of corrugated shipping containers located in Augusta, Georgia. After four years working with Jack Anderson as sales manager, Henry Adams, president of Riverside, was faced with the job of hiring a new sales executive and, in the process, more carefully defining the duties of this job.

THE INDUSTRY

Corrugated boxes were the most common type of shipping container. Corrugated board came into existence around 1900. At first, it was used primarily as a cushion between bottles and other glass products. In 1914, the Interstate Commerce Commission abolished the premium rates that the railroads had previously been required to charge for the shipment of goods in corrugated containers. Subsequently, the industry showed impressive growth. By the end of World War I, there were 100 corrugated box plants in the United States, with an annual production capacity of 5 billion square feet. Currently, there were more than 1,350 plants producing 216 billion square feet of corrugated board with an annual market value of over $6 billion.

Corrugated board was made from two basic raw materials, linerboard and semichemical medium, both products or by-products of the pulp and paper industry. Semichemical medium (consisting of wood residue and hard-wood fibers) was used to make the crinkly interior which was sandwiched between layers of fiberboard. The fiberboard was manufactured from the linerboard (consisting of virgin kraft soft wood and soft wood fibers), which was shipped to the box manufacturer on huge rolls. The process by which raw materials were made into corrugated board was called converting.

The dominant forces in the corrugated container industry were the fully integrated national container manufacturers, such as Continental Can, Container Corporation of America, and the corrugated division of Owens-Illinois. These companies controlled every phase of corrugated board production from raw material supply to distribution of the end product. They owned their own woodlands, papermills, and converting plants. Non-integrated firms, like Riverside Container Corporation, depended upon large manufacturers to supply the raw materials.

COMPANY BACKGROUND AND OPERATIONS

Riverside Container Corporation was closely held, with the majority of stock being controlled by the William F. Jones family of Boston, Massachusetts. The Jones family had been in the corrugated box business since 1932, when it founded the J and J Corrugated Box Company of Fall River, Massachusetts. In the late 1950s, the Jones family became interested in opening a new corrugated container company to serve the rapidly industrializing South. In 1960, it established the Old Dominion Container Corporation in Martinsville, Virginia. This new plant proved successful, and the Jones family began conducting market research to find other potential locations.

A study conducted by the Augusta branch of the Industrial Development Division of Georgia Tech indicated a definite need for a corrugated box manufacturer in the Augusta area. The study revealed a number of potential markets for RCC within a 200-mile radius of Augusta. The area's major potential users of corrugated containers included textile manufacturers (fifty-nine plants), chemical producers (thirty-seven plants) and food producers and processors (sixty-eight plants). In addition, there were several other large corrugated container users in Augusta, including a synthetic detergent plant, a large manufacturer of refractory products, and a steel office furniture manufacturer. Of the corrugated users within a 30-mile radius of Augusta, only 2 percent were currently being supplied by corrugated box plants within 100 miles. On the basis of this research, Augusta was selected as the site for Riverside Container Corporation.

Although the Jones Family owned other corrugated box companies, Riverside was incorporated as a separate company. Henry Adams, general manager of a box company in San Francisco, was hired as president of the new company. His senior administrative staff included James Dreyfuss, production manager, Richard Bendix, comptroller, and Jack Anderson, sales manager.

Riverside planned to market its products within a 200-mile radius of Augusta. This distribution area permitted the company's delivery fleet to leave the plant and return in one day. Jack Anderson, the new sales manager, employed five sales representatives to cover this territory.

The marketing strategy developed by RCC management centered around price, largely because the company had no established accounts. Management believed that entry into the market could be achieved most effectively and quickly by competing on a price basis. RCC wanted to enter the market by offering products at prices well below the competition. After accounts were firmly established, the intention was to increase prices gradually up to the competitive market level. The company hoped that a strong emphasis on service and customer satisfaction would counteract any negative impact of the price increases.

The summer immediately preceding RCC's market entry was characterized by a serious depression in the corrugated box industry. It resulted from a series of dramatic price cuts by the large producers, who were using price to increase market shares. When RCC opened its doors in the latter part of the year, management felt compelled to set prices below the existing depressed prices to obtain market shares. While RCC was the only corrugated box manufacturer in the central Savannah River area, there were twenty-six competitive manufacturers in Georgia, South Carolina, and southern North Carolina. Because of the intense competition in the region and the depressed market prices, establishing new accounts proved difficult and progressed much more slowly than anticipated. The first year of operation provided a return on investment (ROI) of only 1.5 percent, far below expectations. Plant efficiency was poor. Many orders were small, resulting in a high ratio of direct labor to machine time. Many orders were so small that it took more time to set up the machines than it did actually to run the order.

During the first year, the sales force spent virtually all its time seeking new accounts. There were no established accounts to count upon to provide a certain amount of regular business. To make a sale, the salesperson had to spend time prospecting for the potential customer. Then it was necessary to seek out the persons authorized to make the purchase decision and convince them that RCC could provide more benefits than were being provided by the present supplier. The sales force did not have the support of any promotional program.

The second year of operation proved even less successful than the first. Competitive pressure within the industry became more intense. RCC reduced its prices even further in an effort to retain established customers and gain new accounts. The company began offering extra services such as warehousing, which was unprecedented in the industry. This enabled customers to reduce the amount of funds tied up in inventory. Other service innovations included packaging corrugated boxes for shipment on wooden pallets and coils, and the manufacture of special types, such as boxes with extra printing or perforated breakaway tops, at no extra charge. These services helped to attract additional accounts. However, in the second year ROI fell to 0.5 percent. Sales dollar volume actually declined, because of lower prices and a decrease in average order size.

RCC's performance in the third year was significantly improved over the previous two years, although the ROI was still only 2.7 percent. During the year, industry pricing began to stabilize. Company sales volume expanded with an increase in the number of orders and average order size. However, RCC was still plagued by plant inefficiencies tracing to the many short production runs.

RCC's sales force began allocating more time to existing accounts. The sales manager estimated that, whereas previously sales personnel had spent 80 percent of their time prospecting for new business and 20 percent servicing established customers, their time was now more evenly split between these two functions. Sales personnel became more efficient and were making more money. Customers' confidence in the sales force and the company increased. Sales personnel were doing a better job for the customers in less time, and relationships with customers were becoming firmly established.

The sales manager, Jack Anderson, anticipated that the sales force would soon be in a position to spend 40 percent of the time prospecting and 60 percent servicing established accounts. He further hoped that by next year, this time division would change to 20 percent and 80 percent, respectively.

A small number of RCC's accounts were very large users of corrugated products who spread their business among several box suppliers. Because these accounts enabled RCC to make long production runs, the sales manager hoped that RCC could attract a bigger percentage of their business by increasing the frequency of sales calls. He emphasized, however, that the competitive nature of the industry required the sales force to devote a substantial portion of its time to prospecting on a continuing basis.

In December of his fourth year with Riverside, Jack Anderson was offered a job as marketing vice-president of a container company with headquarters in Atlanta. Since the company was larger and well established and the salary offered was 50 percent higher than his present one, he submitted his resignation to Henry Adams. In his exit interview with Adams, he voiced several criticisms of Riverside policy. First, he believed that the company's emphasis on price as the major competitive approach was a mistake. Second, he believed the sales manager's job was made almost impossible by the firm's emphasis on production costs. It made it difficult or impossible for the salespeople to adapt to market needs. Third, he felt that his job description was too much sales oriented and not enough marketing oriented.

Since Riverside's upcoming year was a critical one, Adams was anxious to hire a new sales manager within ninety days or less. First, he felt it was necessary to define the job and its responsibilities more carefully. He also needed to rethink the role of sales and its relationship to other areas of the company.

Prepare a position guide for the marketing/sales executive of Riverside Container Corporation.

What characteristics would be important in the new sales manager?

CASE 2-3

Diamond Pump

A Manufacturer of Industrial Pumps—Sales Manager Performance

Homer Castleberry had held the job of vice-president of sales at Diamond Pump for five years. Lately he had had the feeling he was running on an endless treadmill, never getting anywhere. Returning from an extended trip visiting seven sales agents in the western states, a postponement of an eighth visit found him with two uncommitted days in Kansas City. For the first time in many months, he had the time to sit back and evaluate his job, his performance and his future.

Diamond Pump Company, a subsidiary of Greyson Industries, Inc., manufactured positive displacement pumps for use in the chemical, petroleum, and other industries. Diamond gear pumps, screw pumps, and progressive cavity pumps were sold through several hundred distributors. Distribution covered the entire United States, Canada, and most of the free world. In addition, Diamond sold specially designed pumps direct to original equipment manufacturers. Throughout its 118-year history, Diamond had been a strong competitor in the industrial market and enjoyed a fine reputation as a maker of quality pumps. The company had achieved a sales increase each year for twenty consecutive years. In spite of this success, management felt that the company could find better ways of handling certain nagging distribution problems.

INDUSTRY STRUCTURE AND PRICING

The industrial pump industry was dominated by several large companies, with Diamond among the largest. Because pumps were used in such a variety of applications, no one of these companies could provide the best pump for each application. Most companies, including Blackmer Company and Viking Corporation, two major competitors, produced only screw-type and gear-type pumps, respectively. Diamond, in contrast, offered a diverse standardized line that included both types. These standard pumps were purchased by a wide variety of users, primarily for process applications.

Original equipment manufacturers (OEMs) comprised the other major customer group, a group that had become an increasingly important market segment. OEMs included petroleum tank truck manufacturers, for example, who required specially designed pumps not offered in Diamond's standard product line.

Prices tended to be uniform among competing pump manufacturers. The customer's decision to buy was based mainly on the quality of service. The pump's performance characteristics were also important, and price played a limited role in the buying decision. While Castleberry tried to limit price increases to one a year, this objective recently had fallen victim to the escalating prices of raw materials, which comprised the major portion of costs, as well as to rising overhead costs.

Promotion

National advertising in trade journals comprised the bulk of the promotional effort. Castleberry and the advertising agency aimed at two important targets: the first consisted of petroleum tank truck manufacturers, petroleum storage operations, and the like. Diamond appealed to these potential buyers through *Fuel Oil News*, *Chemical Engineering*, and *National Petroleum News*. Inquiries resulting from these advertisements were turned over to the sales agent and distributor in the area from which the inquiry originated.

The second equally important target was comprised of engineers and product designers who determined what brands of equipment would be included in product specification sheets for new products. The jobs of sales personnel at the company and distributor level were made more difficult if the Diamond pump was not specified initially. Therefore, advertisements in trade journals such as *Design News* were placed to influence the design specifications.

Diamond also advertised in the Yellow Pages section of telephone directories in major metropolitan areas. These ads listed all Diamond sales agents and distributors in the metropolitan area.

Sales Agents—Distribution

Homer Castleberry achieved distribution through twenty-one commissioned sales agents who were responsible for marketing pumps in their respective geographic areas. While these sales agents personally called on OEMs in their territories, OEM accounts were serviced by distributors under the supervision of the sales agents. There were 425 Diamond distributors employing 2,000 sales personnel.

The sales agent was responsible for selecting Diamond distributors. Distributors were approved by Homer Castleberry, approvals being based on creditworthiness and ability to promote Diamond products. Castleberry insisted that distributors not sell competing lines. Additionally, the distributor was required to have a quality image, that is, sell high-quality complementary products and provide excellent service and technical advice.

Because customers for Diamond pumps required good fast service and competent technical help, the sales agent tried to ensure that distributor salespeople were well informed. This was done through periodic training. In addition, the agents often accompanied distributor personnel on sales calls. Installation of a Diamond WATS line enabled sales agents to get fast answers to technical questions raised by customers.

Sales agents were required to establish and maintain personal contact with current and potential OEM customers. This was difficult at times because individuals involved in deciding specifications for new products were often hard to identify. Agents, however, agreed that the results could be worth the effort. Recently, diligence led one sales agent to a contract under which Diamond supplied the pumps used to filter hot oil in Kentucky Fried Chicken's pressure cookers.

Distribution Problems

Despite success in increasing sales revenue and maintaining profitability, Castleberry felt that the company could be more efficient in handling certain nagging distribution problems. Attracting high-quality distributors was becoming increasingly difficult. Sales agents testified that distributors were reluctant to "change partners" even though the Diamond Company offered a broader line than did present pump suppliers. Agents also pointed out that distributor sales personnel were often unwilling or unable to seek individuals who had significant input to buying decisions; for example, engineers and production people. "If the purchasing agent says, 'no,' they just give up," said a Diamond sales agent. Another agent said there weren't enough hours in the day to supervise distributors and also work with OEM customers. Castleberry summed it up, "The numbers look good every month, but I get the feeling that we could do better. We need greater effectiveness in distribution."

In evaluating his performance as a sales executive, Castleberry decided that he had been spending all his time on operating responsibilities. He had been so busy putting out fires and handling day-to-day problems, he had neglected planning almost entirely. He wasn't even sure that he had done a very efficient job of handling operations.

Describe Castleberry's major operations responsibilities. How well is he carrying out each of these responsibilities?

What kind of planning activities should Castleberry be carrying out regularly? What planning areas need immediate attention?

How do you suppose Castleberry's time should be divided between operations and planning?

CASE 2-4

Frito-Lay, Inc.

Manufacturer of Corn Chips—Reorganization of Executive Structure

Frito-Lay, Inc., had recently undergone an extensive reorganization of marketing-related activities to provide more effective control in regional and district offices. Arch C. West, the vice-president of marketing, found it necessary to reevaluate his role and responsibilities under the new organizational structure, which had redefined his formal relationships with other executives.

Frito-Lay, Inc., with its home office in Dallas, Texas, was a national manufacturer of corn chips, potato chips, and related food products. Its sales accounted for about 75 percent of the national market for corn chips and a much smaller share for potato chips. It also produced a line of canned processed foods, the most important of which was chili and beans, under the Austex brand. Owing to the perishability of the corn and potato chips, the company had factories located throughout the United States close to major markets. Product perishability made it necessary to maintain a sales force that could sell and deliver direct to retailers. To serve retail food stores directly on a national basis, the sales force numbered in excess of 3,000 persons.

To provide communication with and control over its large sales force, Frito-Lay had developed a complex organizational structure, with three layers of geographical subdivisions of authority. The national market was divided into four zones, and these were subdivided into a total of fourteen divisions. The divisions were further divided into districts, each with a district sales manager and ten or twelve salespeople. The new organizational structure had placed the vice-president of sales under the line authority of the executive vice-president rather than under the vice-president of marketing. The position of vice-president of sales was a staff position, since the district and divisional sales managers were under the authority of their respective district and divisional managers. The relationships are shown in Exhibit 1.

Under the formal organizational structure, the vice-president of marketing was assigned a staff position with respect to the sales organization. In actual practice, he exercised considerable control over activities of the sales organization. For example, the subdivision of each district into individual sales territories, and reshaping of territories, was handled by West's office. The availability of detailed computer-derived information about each territory made it possible to make such decisions at a distance.

EXHIBIT 1 Organizational Chart of Frito-Lay, Inc.

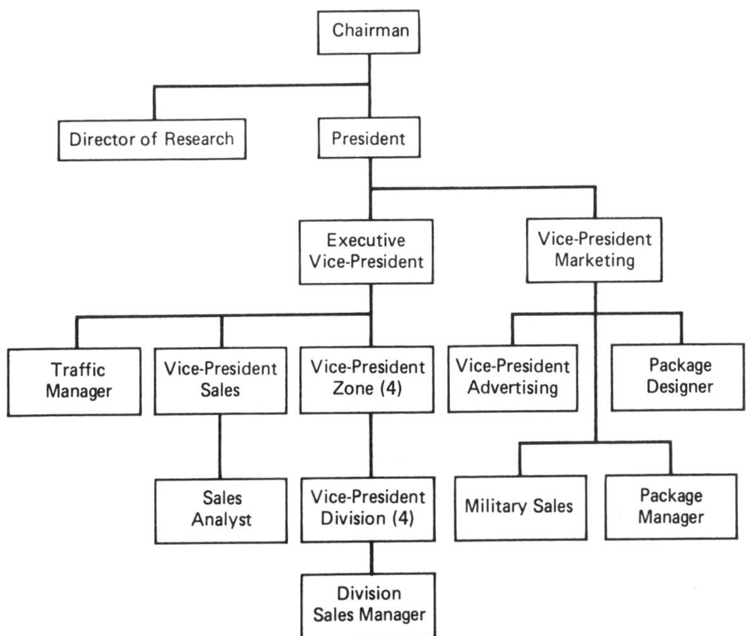

Explain how West can successfully deal with problems relating to the sales force when the formal organizational structure cuts him off from direct contact with them.

Under the Frito-Lay organization, what avenues are open to achieve coordination between various marketing related activities?

What individuals in the Frito-Lay organization should be involved in new-product planning and development?

CASE 2-5

Forbes Co., Inc., Heating Equipment Division

Wholesale Distributor—
Sales and Organizational Problems

It was the beginning of the new year, 1978, and Mr. Roger Matthews, the marketing manager of Forbes Co., Inc., was becoming increasingly concerned with the performance of the Heating Equipment Division (HED) of his company. Not only were sales declining, but the division was losing market share. Also, there appeared to be significant employee turnover and unrest. In seeking a solution to these problems, Roger realized that he would be hampered by strong and knowledgeable competitors as well as by internal personnel complexities. He decided to schedule a meeting with Tom Forbes, the manager of the Heating Equipment Division, to gain further insight into possible reasons for the sales and organizational problems. Roger believed this would lead to a more workable solution. Prior to the meeting he reviewed the background of the division, current and historical, to place it in the overall company framework.

THE COMPANY

Forbes Company was a wholesale distributor of heating and plumbing equipment. Its 1977 sales were approximately $20 million, 1978 sales were expected to top $22 million. The Heating Equipment Division sales were $1,596,000 in 1977 and were forecasted to be approximately the same for 1978. Exhibit 1 shows HED gross sales since 1974.

HED specialized in sales of heating equipment, such as furnaces and associated products. The parent company sold the entire range of plumbing equipment from simple home valves, washers, and so forth, to complete industrial plumbing installation; representing such manufacturers as Crane, American

EXHIBIT 1 Gross Sales of the Heating Equipment Division

Year	Total Sales	Monthly Average
1974	2,193,517	182,793
1975	1,906,909	158,909
1976	1,702,109	141,842
1977	1,595,875	132,989

Standard, and others. Customers were original equipment manufacturers as well as industrial users, such as plants, stores, and hospitals.

Forbes operated from its main headquarters in a medium-sized northeastern city. The Heating Equipment Division was located in the same town, although in a separate building. Forbes also had five other locations within a 50-mile radius of its headquarters. The company's major markets were within a radius of approximately 150 miles of the headquarters.

The company was family owned and had grown from its beginning in the 1940s to a position of prominence in its marketing area. The president and owner took a floundering company and directed it to its present position through hard work and business acumen. He was particularly concerned that HED not continue to reflect poorly on the entire operation.

The day-to-day activities of Forbes Company were supervised by an executive vice-president; the president concerned himself mainly with corporate financial affairs. Recently, the president's son, Tom Forbes, had taken a position with the company—manager of HED. Tom had worked for the company in various jobs during summer vacation from school and since graduation from college and had been in his present position for less than one year. As manager of HED, Tom reported to the executive vice-president of the main company.

Roger Matthews (marketing manager) joined the firm ten months ago as a salesman. Recently he was moved from his sales position to the newly created marketing manager's position. He was informed that the promotion was due to outstanding performance and his strong managerial capabilities. The HED "problem" was delegated entirely to Roger by the executive vice-president. His words to Roger were, "This is your baby; you are responsible for getting HED back on target. You have the authority to make whatever changes you feel are necessary."

THE MEETING

Roger scheduled the meeting with Tom Forbes for 3:00 P.M. one Tuesday afternoon—a time normally free of interruptions. The meeting was held at HED so that Roger would have a better chance to view the operation.

The meeting began with Roger explaining to Tom that he was aware that

HED sales were not satisfactory and that they needed to work together to resolve this problem. Therefore he wanted Tom to enlighten him as to why Tom felt that this problem had developed.

Tom stated that the present situation was somewhat due to the fact that two years ago the then manager of HED quit and opened his own business in direct competition with HED, taking with him four inside people, a secretary, and many important key customers. Since that time that competitor's business had prospered as had the businesses of other competitors in the area. Further, that competitor was recently bought out by a larger national firm that seemed to be intent on "buying" even more business in the immediate area. They now appeared to be selling at 5 percent less than other major suppliers in the area.

Tom noted that Forbes people (including HED) were compensated on a straight-salary basis. The former manager had wanted to switch to salary plus commission, but was not allowed to do so since other divisions were not compensated in this manner. He quit over this issue and because he felt he could make more money elsewhere. Evidently many of the staff felt the same since they went with him, and were compensated with salary and commission.

Tom also told Roger that the fact that HED was physically separated from the parent company appeared to be a cause of problems. Up until twelve years ago, all operated from the same building, but space pressures dictated a move to another building some distance away. Tom mentioned comments from the sales force such as, "Why is HED always left out?" and "What we do isn't that important to the overall operation."

Tom showed Roger an organization chart of HED (see Exhibit 2). The division employed fifteen people: three outside salesmen, Tom Forbes (manager), an office manager (also purchasing agent) and his assistant, inside/counter people, secretaries, and warehouse clerks. Most of the people had worked their way

EXHIBIT 2 Organizational Chart of the Heating Equipment Division

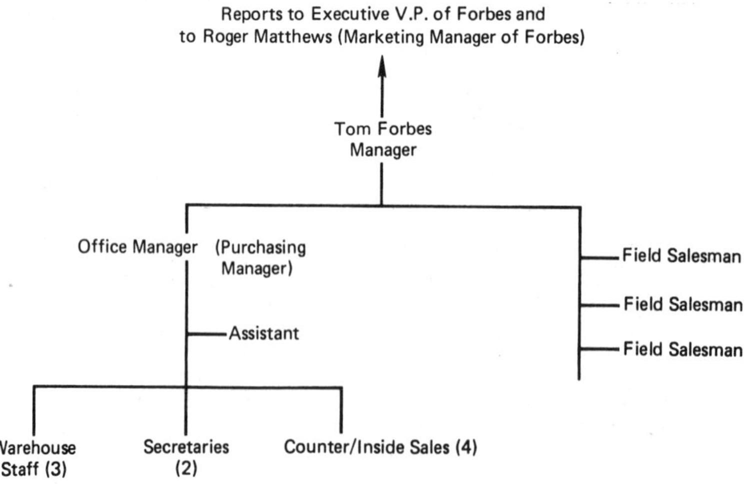

up through HED to their present positions, many having started as hourly help in the warehouse. All training was "on-the-job"; there was no formal training program.

Elaborating about the organization chart, Tom explained that he oversaw the entire operation of HED, performing the functions of division manager as well as sales manager. However, he noted that he really had more to do than he could handle since he wanted to travel with and train the sales force, yet he felt it necessary to supervise the inside operation.

Tom was aided by the office manager who was in charge of the internal operations of the division and also had responsibility for purchasing. Since purchasing was a new responsibility for him (it had been handled by another person who since had been promoted to outside sales) it distracted him from other duties. He also had responsibility for pricing orders for billing purposes, but the return of a former employee reduced the pressure here somewhat. The office manager had expressed an interest in moving into a field sales position because he felt that the chances for financial gain were greater, but this had been rejected due to a shortage of trained inside people. Further, the office manager seemed to resent his isolation (both in physical distance and status) from the parent organization across town.

Roger commented that inside-counter people had both phone sales and counter sales responsibility. Tom said that this frequently resulted in confusion over who should do what. In busy periods there was chaos, with either long lines or ringing phones, and time wasted in slack periods. During one such busy period Roger noted a warehouse worker and a secretary sipping soft drinks together, seemingly unaware of or uninterested in solving the overload problem. Tom and his assistant were too busy to notice this, and the secretary and warehouse worker didn't take any initiative on their own. When Roger mentioned this, Tom replied that each person in the organization appeared interested only in doing his or her own job; teamwork was not practiced.

Roger also noticed two outside sales representatives in the office during his Tuesday afternoon meeting. When questioning them about this, during a period when Tom was answering a phone, they said they wanted to be sure that the inside people did their jobs correctly. Therefore, they frequently came into the office to price orders, waited on the counter and checked the warehouse for product availability.

Tom told Roger that he worked with the sales force and the inside staff, as time permitted, to develop new business. However, his other duties and lack of experience in his managerial role limited his time and effectiveness as a leader for the field sales force. Although Tom was aware of the declining sales figures (shown in Exhibit 1), he felt they were about all that could be expected under the circumstances, particularly with the lack of teamwork and motivation. As a result, new customer prospecting was virtually nil and the sales force spent its time trying to maintain present business with old accounts, but even here there were problems.

ROGER'S DILEMMA

After the meeting, Roger was pondering the information given to him by Tom as well as that obtained through his own observations. Since this was his first real managerial problem as marketing manager, he felt that the president was watching closely to see how well he handled the matter. He felt there was much business to be acquired, both from old customers and new, and that present business must be maintained. He wanted to avoid any more turmoil due to turnover and wanted to improve morale and teamwork. He had come across certain trade data regarding industry price indices (see Exhibit 3), that gave him even more cause for concern.

EXHIBIT 3 Plumbing and Heating Industry Price Index

1974	+20.9%
1975	+7.2
1976	+6.7
1977	+8.8

Roger was trying to decide on a course of action. He knew that the resolution of the problems wouldn't be easy, but he was optimistic that he would be able to improve the situation at HED.

What would you do to reverse the sales decline?

What should be done about compensation?

Is the organizational layout appropriate? What changes, if any, are indicated?

How should HED go about achieving organizational teamwork and motivation?

CASE 2-6

Monrovia Oil Company

Petroleum Company—Decentralization of the National Account Department

Monrovia Oil Company, with head offices in New York City, was one of the largest producers of petroleum products in the United States. In his monthly meeting with Frank Spriegel, marketing vice-president, Jeff Gasden, vice-president of sales, recommended a reorganization to decentralize the national account department and bring its salespeople under the regional sales managers. The purpose was to achieve more coordination between the operations of the regional and division offices, which were engaged in direct marketing, and the national account department, which functioned as a sales contact group in handling special accounts.

The national account department, functioning as a separate sales organization, was responsible for distribution of gasoline, fuel oils, and industrial lubricants to approximately three hundred companies. These customers operated in industries where reciprocity was a major factor in the development of new business. This department was headed by a department manager, reporting directly to the vice-president for sales, Gasden. The department manager, Grant Newcomb, supervised six sales representatives. The purchasing department supplied the manager with a weekly report on all purchases amounting to $25,000 or more. The national account manager (Newcomb) kept the sales staff informed of all purchases made by Monrovia from accounts they were now selling and from sources to which sales had not yet been made. Sales personnel were responsible for the development of sales to each account assigned to them, and made weekly reports. The regional and division offices were notified when a salesperson sold an account, and it was their responsibility to service the account.

Regional and division offices were strategically located throughout the company's market area. Regional managers, who reported to Jeff Gasden, the vice-president of sales, were assigned five staff specialists. Each region was subdivided into three divisions. Under the division manager was a T.B.A. manager, a retail sales manager, a wholesale sales manager, an industrial sales manager, and a superintendent of operations (see Exhibit 1). Each division manager supervised from five to eight salespeople who called on all classes of trade in their territories, including national accounts after the initial contacts had been made.

The regional and division managers were critical of the national account department. They contended that the duplication of sales effort could be avoided by eliminating the department. On many occasions, salespeople from the division offices had quoted prices on fuel oil and gasoline that were different from those used by national account representatives. Since the division managers were responsible for the business developed by the national account department, they felt it should be their prerogative to quote prices advantageous to their own operations.

Gasden, the vice-president of sales, thought that more business could be obtained through decentralization of the national account department rather than through its elimination. He made the following proposals to the board of directors at the spring meeting: (1) the national account department should be decentralized, (2) the national account manager should be made an assistant to the vice-president of sales, (3) a national account salesperson should be assigned to each regional office to work with the division managers and their sales personnel, and (4) the activities of the national account salespersons should be coordinated with those of the division sales personnel by the regional managers.

Grant Newcomb, the national account manager, argued that the national

EXHIBIT 1 Sales Organization of the Monrovia Oil Company

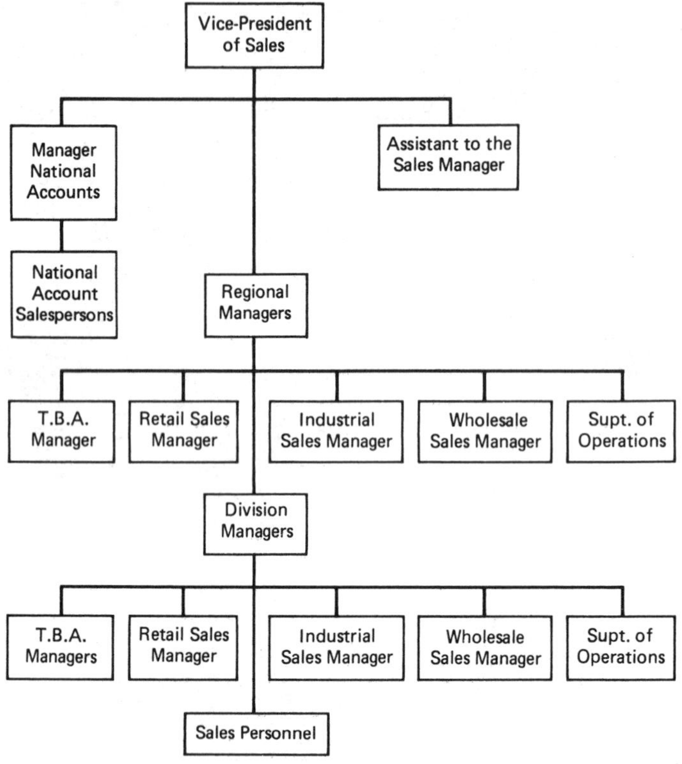

account sales force should continue to report directly to him: "National account salespeople are needed as 'blockbusters' or 'openers' to get the original purchase from a large account. In addition, the national account organization has a career planning advantage. These more prestigious sales positions provide a means of promotion and reward to capable salespeople who are not interested in sales management. Finally, because of their disproportionate effect on sales, operations, and profits, national accounts require special treatment (even on prices), and each treatment must be coordinated under a single head."

What changes, if any, would you recommend in the organization of the national account department?

CASE 2-7

Lindsay Sportswear

Manufacturer of Sportswear— Sales Department Reorganization

Although the current sales organization of Lindsay Sportswear had been effective for a number of years, recent changes in the marketing and distribution of sportswear, as well as changes in Lindsay policies and practices, indicated that a revision of the present sales organization was required. Arthur Lindsay, president of Lindsay Sportswear, was concerned with the apparent inability of Jim Frankfort's sales force to handle the various tasks assigned to it. His son, Arthur, Jr., who was registered in an MBA program at Dartmouth, suggested that a reorganization of marketing responsibilities in the firm might solve the problem. He explained that a vice-president of marketing could coordinate merchandising, advertising, and selling activities. He also suggested that product managers would ensure that each product got a fair share of the time of the sales force.

Lindsay Sportswear manufactured a wide line of men's and boys' sportswear, including sweaters, hunting coats, caps, gloves, sport coats, slacks, sport shirts, jackets, swimwear, walking shorts, and socks. Annual sales of $125,000,000 attested to the wide consumer acceptance of the "Lindsay Sportswear" brand. The sportswear was distributed directly to 8,000 men's and boys' shops and department stores. As Lindsay sales increased over the years, the sales organization evolved from a simple line type into a more complex organization, as shown in Exhibit 1.

The vice-president of sales was responsible for the administration of the sales department and was concerned with organizing, planning, directing, coordinating, and appraising the total sales operation. Regional sales managers were responsible for sales in their territories, field supervision of the branch sales offices, and implementing the sales policies. The sales branch managers spent the majority of their time in the field with the sales force. Ninety full-line salespersons operated out of twenty sales branch offices.

The directors of advertising, commercial research, and merchandising reported to the executive vice-president, as did the sales vice-president. The advertising director administered the $4,000,000 annual advertising appropriation and, in consultation with the sales vice-president, prepared the advertising budget and examined and approved all work done by the advertising agency. The commercial research director planned and conducted surveys for the sales vice-president as well as for other department heads. Surveys measuring the market potential for sportswear, the preferences of buyers, the frequency of purchase, the attitudes of dealers, and the like were used in establishing sales policies and strategies, setting sales quotas, determining sales territories, selecting dealers,

EXHIBIT 1 Sales Organization of Lindsay Sportswear

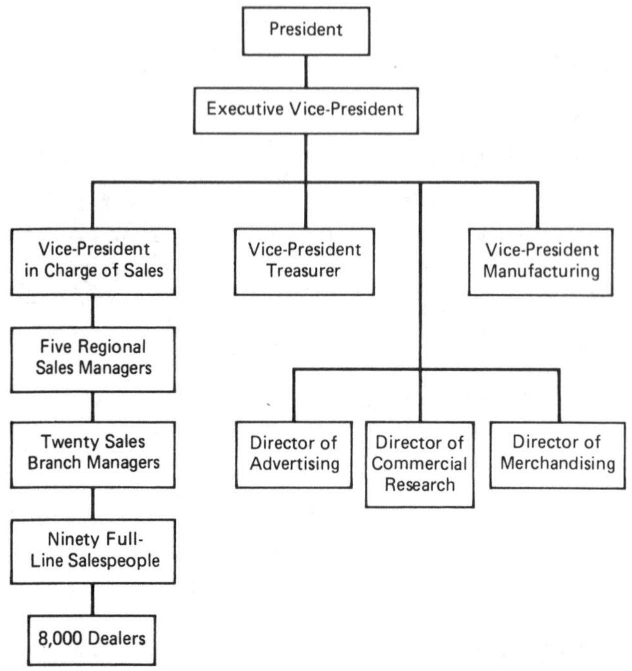

and evaluating sales performances. The merchandising director was responsible for coordination of manufacturing and sales, by taking demand preferences on the one hand and manufacturing costs on the other and working out a plan that balanced the two. His main function was to determine garment design and specifications and to make sure that dealers and consumers got what they wanted without building up excessive inventory.

One development that signaled a need for possible change in the sales organization was that sales of boys' sportswear had more than doubled due to a number of factors such as an increase in the number of individual children's shops and the growing interest of men's wear retailers in boys' wear. Thus, boys' sportswear became the largest seller in the Lindsay Sportswear line, a great change from just five years ago. One effect of the boys' wear sales increase was that Lindsay Sportswear sales personnel were devoting most of their efforts to the easier-to-sell boys' wear line, at the expense of the men's wear line.

Greater dealer and consumer interest in the color, style, and fabrics of men's sportswear made it necessary to give closer consideration to buyers' tastes and preferences. The salespeople, by virtue of being closest to the market, were in a position to suggest garment-style preferences to the merchandising department. One Lindsay salesperson suggested to the merchandising director that a panel of famous personalities be established as style consultants from which would come sportswear ideas the panel considered to be most fashionable. The initial panel consisted of several famous golfers. The sales of the sportswear selected by the style consultants were good enough to warrant investigation of a possible change in the Lindsay Sportswear sales organization that would permit closer cooperation between the merchandising staff and the sales department.

As the Lindsay line expanded, it became apparent that the ninety full-line salespeople were spending so much time introducing new seasonal lines and promotions that they were unable to serve dealers properly. Much important service work by salespersons was being neglected, such as assistance in stock control, pricing, point-of-purchase display, and training retail salesclerks. Neglect of dealer service duties resulted in the loss of some major accounts, who switched to competing lines of men's sportswear.

The sales manager, Jim Frankfort, argued that the current organizational structure reflected correct priorities because personal selling was the really important factor in the success of the Lindsay company. Sales were dependent on the strength and cooperation of retail outlets, and it was the sales force that achieved the cooperation of the retailers. His proposed solution to correct criticisms, therefore, was that the sales department be reorganized to solve three problems: (1) neglect of the full line of sportswear by salespeople who spent most of their sales attention on the fast-selling boys' wear, (2) the need to improve styling of the line by the merchandising department through closer cooperation with the sales department, and (3) neglect of dealer service by the sales force.

What are the relative roles of merchandising, advertising, and personal selling for Lindsay Sportswear? Should the sales force be relieved of some of its current responsibilities?

How should Lindsay Sportswear have reorganized the structure of its sales department to eliminate the problems outlined in the case? Draw a new organization chart.

CASE 2-8

Allen Specialty Company

Manufacturer of Writing Supplies—Coordination of Advertising, Sales Promotion, and Selling

Allen Specialty Company, located in Detroit, Michigan, manufactured a line of ballpoint pens, and mechanical pencils and, in the past five years, had added a line of stationery. Allen products were sold to stationery and office supply wholesalers and retailers, as well as to department stores, discount houses, drugstores, variety stores, and supermarkets. A field sales force of eighty-two persons operated out of six district sales offices. Allen management believed that a critical factor in the company's sales success was the coordination of its national advertising and the activities of Allen salespeople and dealers.

The sales promotion program was the responsibility of the sales promotion manager, Jack Biggerstaff, and his staff, in conjunction with the sales planning committee at Allen headquarters in Detroit. The sales planning committee consisted of the managers of merchandising, advertising, and marketing research. The sales promotion plan, for both new and existing products, described objectives; roles of salespersons and dealers; anticipated sales; the national, local, and trade advertising; and point-of-purchase displays, deals, premiums, and contest offers.

With approval of the sales promotion plan by the sales planning committee and the sales promotions manager, Jack Biggerstaff, the sales promotion department prepared sales promotion kits for the Allen sales staff. The kit included advertising proofs, product samples, illustrations of the point-of-purchase displays, samples of premiums offered, and a description of the special deal or contest featured in the promotion.

The sales promotion department prepared a timetable for each promotion plan, showing the date when each advertisement appeared in various media. The timetable was distributed to the sales force and dealers to enable them to time their sales and advertising to coincide with the national advertising, thereby achieving full impact from the advertising.

When the sales promotion plan was approved by headquarters, it was presented to Allen sales personnel at meetings in each of the six district sales offices. The sales promotion manager and the field sales promotion manager, who reported to the former and whose job was to work with Allen salespeople and dealers on sales promotion projects, made the presentation. Following the meetings, the field sales promotion manager trained the salespeople in proper presentation of the promotion and called on key dealers to enlist their support.

The sales promotion program used with a recent new product introduction was typical of Allen's efforts. In addition to the objectives and timetables, the sales promotion program included (1) selling tools for Allen sales people—circular letters describing the promotion, a visual presentation portfolio for making promotion presentations, product samples, reprints of consumer advertisements; (2) selling tools for Allen dealers—presentation kits for selling the new product to consumers, mail circulars for dealers to send to consumers, mailing folders for use by dealers, sample folders, and a considerable amount of prize money for dealers' sales personnel; and (3) advertising support for Allen dealers—advertising in national media and sample folders to be sent to consumers who responded to a coupon offer.

The sales promotion programs were presented one each week in the district offices in late November and December. When the schedule was announced, Mike Halloran, assistant sales manager in charge of the Pacific Northwest district called Jack Biggerstaff to complain that the sales promotion orientation session in his district had been scheduled for December 27 during the quiet week when many of his salespeople had found extra time to spend with their families and when several had customarily taken short skiing vacations, Biggerstaff explained that the promotion plan would not be completed until mid-November, and since these sales promotion meetings were conducted by home office personnel in the six sales regions, it was not possible to schedule more than one a week. It was tough, but Halloran's district had drawn the bad week this year.

Halloran responded that he thought the sales promotion sessions were a waste of time anyhow. His salespeople lost two productive days in these sessions, and, in his opinion, knowledge of details of the Allen Company's advertising and promotion plans didn't make the sales rep's job of selling to wholesalers and retailers any easier. Anyhow, it was the responsibility of the field sales promotion manager to work with the individual salespeople and call on key dealers. He also complained that when these sessions were scheduled in mid-November, they interfered with sales productivity in the busiest season of the year.

Evaluate the Allen Specialty Company's organization and plan for coordinating sales and advertising.

How should Biggerstaff answer Halloran's complaint?

CASE 2-9

Scripto, Inc. (B)[1]

Manufacturer of Writing Instruments—Relationship Between Sales and Marketing Research

At one time, Scripto, Inc., utilized the services of Audits and Surveys, a national marketing research firm, but, owing to budgetary restraints, Scripto eliminated marketing research and channeled its financial resources in other directions. As a result, the company had little of the data it required for important marketing decisions. For example, the company experienced great difficulty in securing comparative data for sales of its products and competitive products in retail outlets.

Determined not to let the void of data affect the 19¢er, Scripto management decided again to consider using marketing research. While management was in general agreement that marketing research was an essential ingredient in

[1]For background information, see Scripto, Inc. (A), pp. 95–100.

its marketing orientation and sales strategy, there were two viewpoints as to the type of marketing research needed. One group believed that market studies and data were most crucial to the success of the 19¢er; hence, they favored using the services of marketing-research companies, such as Audits and Surveys or A.C. Nielsen Company. Both Audits and Surveys and Nielsen prepared bimonthly reports measuring sales and movements of products through stores (the former was used by Papermate). The major differences between the two research companies were (1) cost and (2) type of retail outlet sampled. It would cost Scripto $20,000 to use Audits and Surveys and $25,000 to use Nielsen. Audits and Surveys recorded sales and product movement primarily of mass merchandisers (variety stores) and a relatively small sample of drugstores and grocery stores, while Nielsen sampled more drugstores and grocery stores than A and S but a smaller sample of variety stores.

Another group, however, preferred a different course of action—the use of a marketing research firm that specialized in consumer buying patterns rather than market studies per se. This group contended that consumer research was more instrumental in the future of the 19¢er. Such research was typified by the data generated by the National Consumer Panel of Market Research Corporation of America.

Decisions were required on (1) whether or not to again use marketing research; (2) if so, the type of marketing research most important for Scripto's 19¢er, market studies and/or consumer buying patterns; and (3) the relationship between sales and marketing research. Management was especially concerned about the relationship between sales and marketing research.

What is your position on the three problems that had to be solved by Scripto? Defend your arguments.

CASE 2-10

Owens-Illinois, Inc., Forest Products Division

Container Board and Corrugated Box Manufacturer—Tradeoff Between Advertising and Sales

As Roy La Fontaine, director of marketing for the Box Operations of Owens-Illinois' Forest Products Division, hurried down the hall for a meeting with the general manager, he reflected on the recommendation he was about to make concerning the marketing budget. There had been strong pressure from the managers of the box plants to increase the field sales force. The number of new sales personnel being considered was twenty-one, involving a salary, travel, and training expenditure of nearly $900,000. This decision would have been fairly straightforward under ordinary circumstances. However, the imposition of strict corporate limits on budget increases (6 percent) made the decision more difficult. These circumstances were forcing a trade-off between adding the sales personnel and reducing the advertising budget by $300,000 versus holding the line on the advertising budget and not increasing the field force quite as much. Some middle-ground alternatives were also possible.

COMPANY BACKGROUND

Owens-Illinois, Inc. (O-I), was one of the world's leading and most diversified manufacturers of packaging products. Within its two major operating units, the Domestic and the International operations, the company manufactured and sold a broad range of products. These included glass containers, containerboard, corrugated and solid fiber shipping containers, composite cans, multiwall paper and plastic shipping sacks, plastic shrink and stretch film, plywood and dimensional lumber, semirigid plastic containers, metal and plastic closures, metal containers, and disposable paper and plastic cups, tubs, lids, and plates. Another important part of O-I's business consisted of specialized glass products, such as television bulbs for color and black-and-white picture tubes; scientific and laboratory glassware; and tumblers, stemware, and decorative items for household and institutional use. In addition, some overseas affiliates manufactured flat glass and related products.

In 1976, O-I operated more than one hundred manufacturing and related facilities in twenty-seven states and employed more than 50,000 persons in the United States. In addition, foreign affiliates in which O-I had a fifty percent or more equity interest employed about 32,000 persons in twenty-one countries outside the U.S. These affiliates operated eighty-three plants and other facilities in Europe, Latin America, Canada, the Far East, the Caribbean, and Australia.

Owens-Illinois was organized into three lines of business: Packaging, Consumer and Technical, and International. Packaging included the Glass Container Division, Forest Products Division, Plastic Products Division, and Closure and Metal Container Division. Consumer and Technical included the Lily Division, Television Products Division, Kimble Division, and Libbey Glass Division. International was responsible for substantially all of Owens-Illinois' international operations and was organized principally on geographic lines—the European Division, Western Hemisphere Division, Far East/Pacific Operations, and Overseas Forest Products Operations. Owens-Illinois considered each major business segment to be a separate line of business.

The company had grown steadily in assets, sales, and profitability between 1972 and 1976. Net sales in 1976 were $2,572 million with $106 million in after-tax profits. The sales increase since 1972 had been just over 57 percent and after-tax earnings had grown somewhat faster, rising by 65 percent over this same period. (See Exhibits 1 and 2 for income statements and balance sheets.)

EXHIBIT 1 Corporate Income Statements

Five Years Ended December 31, 1976 Millions of Dollars	1976	1975	1974	1973	1972
Revenues:					
Net sales	$2,571.7	$2,273.2	$2,116.4	$1,856.9	$1,636.3
Other	54.1	56.8	47.7	44.6	32.8
	2,625.8	2,330.0	2,164.1	1,901.5	1,669.1
Costs and expenses:					
Manufacturing, shipping and delivery	2,123.3	1,895.9	1,741.3	1,525.9	1,332.0
Research, engineering, selling, administrative and other	285.9	248.5	238.3	216.5	198.2
Interest	42.6	43.7	38.0	31.6	26.7
	2,451.8	2,188.1	2,017.6	1,774.0	1,556.9
	174.0	141.9	146.5	127.5	112.2
Provision for income taxes	63.1	51.0	58.6	50.2	45.0
Minority shareholders' interests in earnings	4.2	3.6	4.4	2.8	2.6
Earnings before extraordinary items	106.7	87.3	83.5	74.5	64.6
Extraordinary items	71.6	—	—	56.4	4.4
Net earnings	178.3	87.3	83.5	130.9	69.0
Preferred and preference dividends	3.7	3.7	3.8	3.8	3.8
Net earnings applicable to common shares	$ 174.6	$ 83.6	$ 79.7	$ 127.1	$ 65.2

EXHIBIT 2 Corporate Balance Sheets

Millions of Dollars	1976	1975	1974	1973	1972
Assets:					
Current assets	$ 801.1	$ 635.0	$ 648.0	$ 581.9	$ 507.1
Investments and other assets	248.3	249.0	238.9	189.9	174.5
Property, plant, and equipment, net	1,145.8	1,063.9	958.4	870.7	816.3
	$2,195.2	$1,947.9	$1,845.3	$1,642.5	$1,497.9

EXHIBIT 2 (*Continued*)

Millions of Dollars	1976	1975	1974	1973	1972
Liabilities:					
Current liabilities	$ 391.2	$ 324.6	$ 312.6	$ 325.7	$ 238.9
Long-term debt	551.8	571.9	553.3	417.4	420.8
Reserves and other credits	206.2	168.1	161.1	141.2	126.2
Minority shareholders' interests	38.5	35.3	28.4	25.7	25.0
	1,187.7	1,099.9	1,055.4	910.0	810.9
Shareholders' Equity:					
Capital	214.2	142.5	144.1	144.6	149.3
Retained earnings	793.3	705.5	645.8	587.9	537.7
	1,007.5	848.0	789.9	732.5	687.0
Equity and liabilities	$2,195.2	$1,947.9	$1,845.3	$1,642.5	$1,497.9

CORPORATE MANAGEMENT

The philosophy of O-I's senior management was oriented toward a decentralized operation with a high degree of autonomy at the division level. The corporate organization included staff specialists in key functional areas, who interacted with the divisions on a policy and guidance level. From the standpoint of the corporation's marketing activities, there were four corporate staff departments that had a direct or indirect influence on the marketing decisions of the various divisions.

1. Department of Economic Research (ER) (headed by Elmer Lotshaw).
2. Department of Corporate Marketing (CM) (led by Benjamin Colosky).
3. Department of Business Analysis (BA) (under Richard Beck).
4. Advertising and Communications Department (AC) (directed by Thomas Weiss).

The first three of these functions were grouped together within the Department of Planning reporting to the director of planning (who was vice-president of the corporate staff).

1. Department of Economic Research (ER). This department was responsible for developing and maintaining industry statistics (shipments, capacity, price levels) as well as product line market share data on the major market areas served by O-I. ER also prepared and distributed three-month moving forecasts as well as long-range forecasts of these markets. This was accomplished both through corporate forecasting models as well as ongoing participation in the data gathering activities of the various industry trade associations.

2. Department of Corporate Marketing (CM). This department was responsible for consulting with the operating divisions in the development and implementation of their marketing strategies and plans. The director of CM was also a member of the Corporate Marketing Committee, which sought to increase the effective utilization of the corporation's marketing resources. A vital role performed by CM in its consulting role was to reconcile conflicting industry forecasts among operating divisions that served the same market segments with competitive products (e.g., Glass Container, Plastic Products, and Closure and Metal Container Divisions).

3. Department of Business Analysis (BA) and the planning process. This group was the guardian and coordinator of the planning process within O-I. The latter was a "bottom-up" process—from the product groups within the divisions, to the division manager, to the president—with the resulting plan ultimately presented for approval or modification to the Executive Policy Committee, which consisted of the chairman and CEO, three senior vice-presidents, and the presidents of Domestic Operations and International Operations. This annual effort was divided into three separate but interrelated stages.

The first stage was the strategic plan. It was prepared in June of each year and generally focused on the following questions: What is or will be happening in the product markets served by the division? How will these occurrences affect O-I and its competitors? What strategic responses are expected by competitors? And, finally, what strategic responses does the division plan to make? This was not intended to be a financial plan, but a description of the anticipated environment and responses to it.

The second stage was to convert these descriptions into financial plans. The latter were intended to spell out the financial implications of the environment and the strategies identified earlier.

The final stage, the annual plan, was prepared in the fall and laid out in detail the operating plans and programs for the coming year for each product line and division. These were developed in the context of corporate guidelines for profitability and expenditure levels established by the Policy Committee after evaluation of the strategic plans and their financial implications. It was at this stage that the detailed decisions about sales manpower and advertising expenditures were made. Divisional management was generally considered to have wide latitude in making these decisions provided the corporate guidelines were fulfilled. These plans were formally reviewed by the operating personnel at the six-month point to make any adjustments in light of changing circumstances.

BA analyzed the plans prepared by the divisions and made recommendations to the Policy Committee as well as suggesting changes to divisional management. BA's role was particularly significant in areas related to capital investment decisions and new product programs.

4. Corporate Advertising and Communications Department (AC). In 1972 this department became the locus of the advertising, print and audiovisual creative services, and trade show activities for a number of divisions and product groups (Packaging and International businesses, Kimble and Television Product divisions, as well as the Electronic Materials and Venture Marketing activities). AC provided assistance to these units in overall marketing communications planning as well as supplying creative resources both internally and from outside suppliers. AC also implemented two major corporate communications projects: a corporate advertising program in print media and a corporate identity program, which emphasized appropriate and consistent graphics on all O-I property and communications.

Together this represented a budget in excess of $7 million for advertising and related communications in 1976. The budget was broken down approximately as follows:

Activity	$'s (millions)
Corporate Advertising and Communications	1.8
Divisional Advertising and Promotion	5.2
Total	7.0

The director of AC identified the following decision elements that he thought reflected the key dimensions used in setting the advertising budget at both the corporate and divisional level:

1. Historical expenditure level (as a frame of reference)
2. General satisfaction with results of prior expenditures
3. Conformance with corporate expenditure and P&L guidelines
4. New product introductions
5. Promotable advantage(s) in the product
6. Number of market segments pursued
7. Sales potential of typical customer sought

The director of AC stated that no formal guidelines were used by his office in assisting the various divisions in establishing their advertising budgets. He did comment that the department had an important educational role in getting the divisions to consider the communications program (advertising, publicity, etc.) seriously as an integral part of the business and marketing planning process.

In pursuing this broad objective, the AC undertook a number of specific activities:

1. Established a task checklist that advertising could perform for the divisions and the corporation as part of the annual communications presentation.

2. Conducted readership and message recall studies to indicate the cost effectiveness of the advertising programs.
3. Conducted several image studies among the financial and business community to determine their attitudes and opinions of O-I.
4. Continual analysis of Starch readership reports to monitor and compare effectiveness of competitive advertising.

O-I FOREST PRODUCTS DIVISION

The Forest Products Division (FPD) was one of the country's largest fully integrated manufacturers of containerboard and corrugated boxes. Its integrated operations consisted of 1,300,000 acres of woodlands, three plywood and lumber mills, four containerboard mills, and twenty corrugated box plants. These activities were divided into three separate operating units within the division. Primary Operations, which was responsible for all forestry and papermaking activities through the production of containerboard, and Box Operations, which was responsible for the manufacture and marketing of corrugated boxes, were the principal volume producing arms. The third group, Special Products Operations, manufactured and marketed two other classes of packaging materials.

Composite cans. Spirally wound containers consisting of layers of paper in various combinations with foil and plastic. These cans were generally less expensive than metal containers, permitted better graphics, and had certain technical advantages over metal in competitive applications. Areas of application were snack foods, motor oil, and frozen citrus concentrate.

Bag and film products. This product area included multiwall paper bags, plastic shipping sacks, and polyethylene packaging films.

FPD's 1976 sales in total were approximately $450 million. These were roughly divided as follows:

Primary operations (including lumber operations)	$200 million
Box operations	175 million
Special products	75 million
Total	$450 million

The sales figures reported externally were lower (see Exhibit 3 for the FPD's five-year sales history), since a significant portion of the division's sales were internal to itself or to the glass container division.

EXHIBIT 3 Forest Products Division Sales

	1976	1975	1974	1973	1972	1971
Forest Products	385	318	380	316	245	211

Box Operations (BO)

Box Operations, which supplied corrugated shipping containers to over 4,000 customers, consisted of twenty corrugated box plants organized into three regional groups (southern, northern, and western).

Each plant served a highly localized geographic market generally encompassing customers within a 150-mile radius from the facility. This was the result of the high weight-to-value ratio of the product that created a competitive disadvantage due to shipping costs when the plant solicited business outside of the 150-mile range. The individual plants were organized to operate on a semi-autonomous decentralized basis, creating, as one manager put it, "twenty 'independent' medium-sized businesses." The general managers of the box plants, who were evaluated on their contribution to divisional/corporate profits, had wide ranging decision-making authority. For example,

1. Plant management was responsible for pricing (within broad guidelines established by the general manager of Box Operations), customer service levels, product lines offered, types of customers served, etc.
2. Each plant had its own sales organization, including a sales manager and a sales force of four to ten people. Plant managers determined the number, deployment, and compensation levels of this organization.
3. Each plant purchased its paper at an established transfer price from the paperboard mills of the primary operations.

By contrast, plant management had very limited involvement in other significant marketing decisions. Among the latter were determination of marketing strategy, developing marketing programs, organizing and providing sales training, establishing the nature and expenditure level for advertising and sales promotion programs, coordination of national account strategies, and providing customer services and technical support in package design as well as packaging systems.

These functions were the responsibility of the director of marketing (title changed from manager of marketing services) in Box Operations.

Marketing Activities

As noted, the marketing functions in BO were sharply divided. The individual plants controlled product, pricing, market selection, and personal-selling activities. The director of marketing, with assistance from the corporate advertising department, was essentially responsible for the strategy, communications, service, and support functions.

The personal-selling function was conducted by twenty separate sales organizations, each serving a limited geographic area, each headed by a sales manager, who reported to a specific plant manager. In total, 105 sales personnel were (1976) in the field, representing an expenditure of $10,500,000, or approximately 6 percent of BO's sales.

Advertising and sales promotion expenditures totaled $370,000 in 1976. These included $110,000 for literature and special presentations, and $260,000 for advertising in trade media.

The trade media used in the advertising campaign encompassed both horizontal packaging journals (two) and selected general business publications (two) which covered the most significant user markets served by O-I. See Exhibit 4 for a list of publications and the insertion schedule used in each.

In discussing the marketing communications effort by BO, Roy LaFontaine observed:

> Packaging is a custom product and the role of the salesman in getting business is extremely important. He interprets the customer's needs and translates them into a specific design. Of course, he has help from specialists, but he's the one the *customer* looks to.
>
> Advertising in trade media reminds customers that we exist and also tries to present a unified image. You know, when you have twenty independent businesses and you're trying to implement an overall strategy, these things are certainly needed. Also, we tend to emphasize in advertising our design, consulting, and support services, because those represent our competitive edge—particularly in relation to the smaller competitors. We also put a good deal of money into product literature and special presentations in support of the sales force. As I mentioned earlier, they are the vital link to the marketplace in this business.

The plan for 1977 called for an increase in sales from $175 million to $200 million. This 15 percent increase was expected to be achieved by a 7 percent expansion of physical volume (square feet of corrugated board) and an 8 percent general price increase, which had recently been put into effect.

The marketing program to accomplish this goal primarily involved a planned 20 percent increase in the field force, which had been projected to expand to 126 sales personnel over the year. To accommodate this growth, while remaining within the corporate guideline of a 6 percent overall expenditure increase from 1976, the planned advertising budget had been reduced to $80,000 for the year.

The director of marketing indicated that this initial plan grew from a conscious trade-off discussion in a meeting among himself, the general manager of the FPD, and the general manager of BO. The original impetus for a sales force expansion came from the individual plant managers, as part of the 1977 planning process. In arriving at their judgments concerning plant volume projections and sales force needs, the individual plant managers had available corporate expenditure guidelines, industry economic trends (volume, price levels, user segments affected) supplied by the BO marketing department, as well as detailed data on business mix, growth potential, and penetration within their own geographic service area.

In discussing these allocation decisions further, the director of marketing cited the following considerations, which he believed to be primary factors:

EXHIBIT 4 Trade Media Employed by Box Operations

Media	Number of Insertions	Insertion Schedule Jan.	Feb.	Mar.	Apr.	May	June	July	Aug.	Sept.	Oct.	Nov.	Dec.
Packaging Digest	6	X		X		X	X			X		X	
Modern Packaging	6		X		X		X		X		X		X
Purchasing	7	X	X			X	X	X		X		X	
Business Week (Industrial)	8	X		X(2)	X		X		X		X		X

1. Box Operations had not added any sales personnel since the early 1970s as a result of a series of headcount reduction programs.
2. BO had been losing market share.
3. There was insufficient sales coverage in two growing market areas: Texas and Wisconsin.
4. The division needed to improve the quality of its sales personnel. The addition of new people would provide greater opportunities to weed out marginal performers.
5. There appeared to be a need for more promotable sales manager(s).
6. A significant mill expansion was underway with an additional investment of $100 million expected to produce increased capacity in 1977 and in 1979–80.
7. BO's growth objective in its 1977 strategic plan was to expand sales at a rate 1 percent faster than the industry's current growth.
8. The discussion of the number of additional sales personnel was based on an annual sales volume guideline per *new* sales person of $500,000. This represented $10,500,000 of the $25,000,000 sales growth for the operation as a whole. (The sales volume produced by the operation's present sales force averaged $1,700,000 per field sales person.)

In addition to these factors, the basic framework of BO's marketing strategy also seemed to be reflected in these planned allocation decisions. According to the director of marketing, BO had been seeking to position itself as a high-volume, low-cost producer with the aim of supplying customers whose volume of corrugated purchases were at least $50,000 per year. Further, they preferred customers for whom the cost of corrugated packaging was a significant part of the product's value and characteristics. The management saw a competitive advantage stemming from its design, consulting, and support services, which had been directed toward the customer's production engineering and packaging specialists.

The operation served 4,000 customers nationwide on a direct basis, representing an average of 200 customers per plant location. The management estimated that some 20,000–30,000 potential customers, covering the spectrum of SIC categories, met their criteria for a prime customer target.

The process involved in these budgets was a "bottom-up" approach as detailed in the O-I corporate description. The budget was reviewed in progressively broader degrees of aggregation at each management level from the plant manager up to the Executive Policy Committee. The key marketing decisions for a product market area were generally made at the operations level within this division. The communications choices generally had not been made as formal trade-off decisions, but as individual judgments of responsible managers. These judgments were made with differing frames of reference and perspectives. The decisions made during the 1977 budgetary process reflected a conscious trade-off process, while at the same time they demonstrated the dominance of personal selling in the communications mix.

Corrugated Box Industry

The corrugated box industry was a large, mature, slow-growth, capital-intensive business involving a commodity product. In 1975, total sales were $5.6 billion, representing 194.3 billion square feet of corrugated containers. This was the equivalent of 18 percent of the dollar value of all packaging materials sold in that year. The compounded annual growth in unit volume of products sold from 1960–1975 had been 3.9 percent, and the growth rate in dollar volume over this period had been 7.9 percent. The latter figure reflected the effects of inflation over the past several years. (See Exhibit 5 for dollar shipments of the industry since 1960.)

The users of corrugated boxes covered the full spectrum of U.S. industry. The food and beverage segments dominated, totaling 36 percent of the corruga-

EXHIBIT 5 Corrugated Container Industry Shipments (dollars)

Dollars			
Year	Total	Corrugated	Solid Fibre
1923	$ 135,493,100*	$ 83,960,000*	$51,533,400*
1930	115,659,700*	80,088,300*	35,571,400*
1940	231,082,800	211,339,000	19,743,800
1950	1,054,502,400	995,154,100	59,048,300
1960	1,791,171,100	1,746,525,600	44,645,500
1961	1,820,090,000	1,777,068,100	43,021,900
1962	2,000,415,600	1,956,573,300	43,842,300
1963	2,067,429,400	2,027,179,900	40,249,500
1964	2,213,855,300	2,175,406,500	38,448,800
1965	2,406,758,600	2,367,541,000	39,216,700
1966	2,730,785,600	2,673,737,100	57,048,500
1967	2,814,803,600	2,761,635,200	53,168,400
1968	3,043,600,900	2,990,444,200	53,156,700
1969	3,320,521,800	3,268,934,500	61,687,300
1970	3,311,044,100	3,296,369,600	42,679,500
1971	3,463,680,200	3,422,262,100	41,118,100
1972	3,959,924,500	3,919,862,500	40,061,600
1973	4,862,056,300	4,815,186,600	46,569,700
1974	5,792,984,900	5,742,301,300	50,683,600
1975	5,623,765,200	5,578,612,500	45,152,700

*Estimated.

EXHIBIT 6 1975 Corrugated Shipments by Industry Segments

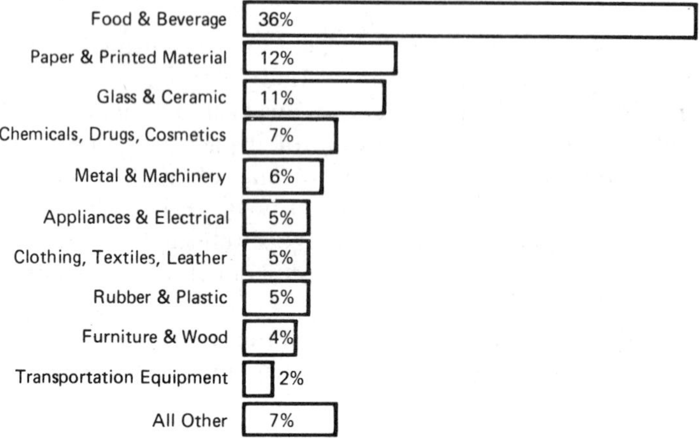

ted volume in 1975. The next largest segment, paper and printed material, only accounted for 12 percent of shipments. (See Exhibit 6 for the details of the remaining customer segments.) Industry shipments very closely paralleled the level of overall economic activity both on a national and a regional basis. (Exhibit 7 shows the breakdown of shipments by region in 1975 as well as the corresponding growth rates in each region since 1960.)

Competition

The industry was made up of 759 companies, operating 1,385 plants. The largest company in the industry, Container Corporation of America, had only a 7 percent market share. O-I, the number six company in the trade market (exter-

EXHIBIT 7 Corrugated Shipments by Region

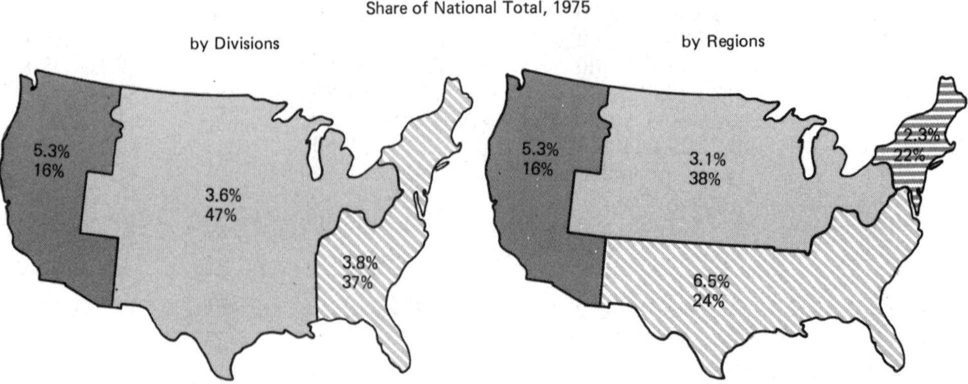

Source: Fibre Box Association

nal sales), had a 3.8 percent market share. The other major firms which fell in between included International Paper, Weyerhauser Corporation, Inland Container, and Horner Waldorf.

In spite of the large number of firms in the industry and the relatively small shares enjoyed by the major producers, the ten largest companies had a total market share of 43.9 percent in 1975. The next ten companies shared 21.2 percent of the market.

Another facet of the competitive structure related to the degree of vertical integration within the industry. In 1975, 78 percent of the industry's output was produced by firms supplying at least 50 percent of their own containerboard. In 1960, 67 percent of the output was from integrated firms, and in 1950, only 53 percent came from these sources.

Decision

Roy LaFontaine opened his presentation to the general manager with restatement of the alternatives he had been considering.

> Bill, I have been evaluating the alternatives with respect to next year's marketing budget. I believe there are three worth considering.
>
> We can keep the mix the same as last year with 105 salesmen and about a $400,000 ad budget for a total of $10.9 million.
>
> Or we can increase our field force by twenty-one people and cut our advertising and promotion expenditures by $300,000 to about $80,000 and increase the total budget to $11.4 million.
>
> Or possibly a third alternative would be to increase the salesforce by 10 and keep the advertising and promotion budget at about $400,000. This would produce a total budget of about $11.3 million. After careful analysis and evaluation, here's what I think we should do. . . .

Evaluate the alternatives open to O-I's Forest Products Division. What course of action do you recommend? Why?

CASE 2-11

Morris Machine Works

Manufacturer of Centrifugal Pumps—Relations with Dealers

Morris Machine Works, Baldwinsville, New York, was established in 1864 and was the first American company to manufacture centrifugal pumps. Morris pumps were sold to industrial users throughout the United States by thirty-two manufacturers' representatives, each of whom operated in an exclusive territory. Three representatives in Canada handled sales in that country, but all other foreign sales were made through export houses. The majority of Morris products were manufactured to users' specifications, and the company required its representatives to be technically trained. Consequently, most representatives either were engineers or included engineers on their staffs. The turnover among representatives was low, but the arrangement for splitting commissions on interterritorial sales had been a continuing source of friction. Although the sales manager did not consider this problem of major importance, he decided to review the entire situation.

Every Morris agent was required to sign an agreement governing his relations with the company (see Exhibit 1). This agreement included a general statement of company policy on the splitting of commissions. This statement did not provide specific rules for handling every situation that might arise. Consequently, the statement was not useful in handling many disputes among the manufacturer's agents.

The initiation, negotiation, and final installation involved with one contract occurred in three separate territories, illustrating the difficulties of reaching an agreement on the division of commissions. A large aluminum producer, whose main office was in Richmond, Virginia, was planning to build a plant in Corpus Christi, Texas, and a San Francisco firm was the contractor-engineer. Thus, three agents were involved: the Richmond agent who made the sale, the San Francisco agent who did the engineering, and the Corpus Christi agent who was responsible for installation and service. All three representatives incurred costs in connection with this sale; therefore, each should have received some compensation. The out-of-pocket costs of the Richmond agent were the lowest, but his influence was the deciding factor in the sale. The agent in Corpus Christi stood to profit from this installation in the future, since he would receive commissions on all repair parts. The commission split could have posed a problem for the sales manager, had not the three parties reached a mutual agreement independent of the home office.

Such problems were not always so easily solved, since disputing parties customarily looked to the Morris sales manager for a final decision. It was difficult to work out compromises satisfactory to all parties. Because representatives were not employees but independent business people, it also was difficult to enforce such decisions.

Two solutions had been suggested. One was to pay the entire commission to the representative into whose territory shipment was made, regardless of who originated, negotiated, or closed the sale. The second suggestion called for a fixed schedule of payments as follows:

10 percent for first quotation
10 percent for second quotation
15 percent to the territory in which equipment was installed
25 percent to the agent completing the purchase order
40 percent for influence on the sale

EXHIBIT 1 Standard Form used for Agreements with Manufacturers' Agents

Introduction

This Agreement has been adopted for governing the relations between the MORRIS MACHINE WORKS and it Agents, and between the different Agents of the MORRIS MACHINE WORKS in order to promote efficiency and cooperation.

It is realized that absolute and fast rules cannot be formulated to govern all conditions, but that fairness and justice must supplement all rules.

All questions as to interpretation of these rules or questions as to points not covered are to be passed upon by the Home Office, and its decisions are to be considered final.

In accepting the MORRIS MACHINE WORKS account, the Agent agrees to the provisions of these rules.

Definition of Agent

The term AGENT (Representative or District Manager) as employed herein is used to designate such individuals, partnerships, or firms who are regularly accredited MORRIS MACHINE WORKS representatives, who have a definite exclusive territory, who have prices and discounts covering a full line of MORRIS MACHINE WORKS equipment, or in some cases one complete line only of MORRIS MACHINE WORKS manufacture, who do not handle any competing product, and who are active in promoting the sale of MORRIS MACHINE WORKS equipment.

Definition of Territory

The term TERRITORY as used herein will designate only the area in which the Agent has exclusive rights to sell MORRIS MACHINE WORKS products, subject to such limitations and exceptions as are hereinafter specified. Only such an area will be assigned to an Agent as exclusive territory as he can actually cover; that is, in which the Agent can, and will, personally solicit business. Such territory as is not included in any Agent's exclusive territory will be open to all agents and to the Home Office; but to avoid complications, the Agents should communicate with the Home Office before quoting in the open territory.

Agents will not solicit in another Agent's territory except with that Agent's permission.

Prices, Price Lists, and Data

MORRIS MACHINE WORKS will quote the Agents its best agent's prices and discounts in all cases, and will furnish price lists, data sheets, drawings, and catalogues as required, and will assist the Agent in every way with information and data.

Price lists, drawings, etc., are the property of MORRIS MACHINE WORKS and subject to return upon request.

Detailed drawings will not be furnished except in special cases, and when furnished must not be allowed to pass out of the Agent's hands, and must be returned to the Home Office when their purpose has been accomplished.

EXHIBIT 1 (*Continued*)

Allocation of Inquiries and Orders

An Agent has exclusive rights to solicit and sell MORRIS equipment within his territory, and all inquiries and orders originating in that territory will be referred to, and credited to, that Agent except as provided hereinafter.

An inquiry received by an Agent from another Agent's territory is to be referred by him either to the Home Office or direct to the Agent for that territory.

Inquiries from dealers or from purchasing and engineering departments within an Agent's territory, for equipment destined to go into another Agent's territory, may be quoted on by that Agent, particularly if purchases are expected to be made in his territory; but a division must be made of the commission with the Agent into whose territory the equipment will go, as provided hereinafter.

Direct Quotations by the Home Office

The right is reserved by MORRIS MACHINE WORKS to quote and to deal directly, without commission, for any agent in the following cases:

1. On federal and state work that is publicly advertised and covered completely by the specifications.
2. To export houses, for shipment outside the United States or Canada.
3. To manufacturers, for resale as a component part of that manufacturer's equipment, to enable that manufacturer to quote competitive prices without the ultimate consumer having to pay two commissions.
4. On repair and replacement parts for equipment originally sold through other Agents or direct from the Home Office.

Commission

The Agent's compensation will be entirely through commissions on sales. The Agent will be credited the difference between the sales price and the Agent's prices.

Commissions will be paid the Agent as payments are received from the customer except as may be agreed.

Acceptance of orders is subject to approval by the Home Office.

The Agent, knowing his trade, is given the privilege to fix his commission and add same to the Agent's price. The right is reserved, however, by the Home Office to fix the amount of an Agent's commission in special cases in accordance with the price lists and discounts.

1. The full amount of commission will be paid the Agent on all sales made by him for shipment within his territory.
2. If the sale is made by one Agent for shipment into another Agent's territory, two-thirds of the commission will be paid to the Agent making the sale, and one-third to the territorial Agent.
3. If inquiry originates and is preliminarily negotiated in the Agent's territory into which shipment will go, but must be further negotiated and sale closed in another Agent's territory, commission will be equally divided.
4. If necessary to make a sale by the Home Office for shipment into an Agent's territory, that Agent is to receive one half of the Agent's commission.

EXHIBIT 1 *(Continued)*

5. No credit or commission will be given an Agent on orders placed in his territory but destined for shipment elsewhere, and which did not originate or were not negotiated in his territory.

Service and Cooperation

In accepting the MORRIS MACHINE WORKS account, the Agent is considered as having assumed an obligation to cooperate with other Agents and with the Home Office in promoting the sale of MORRIS equipment.

The Agent is to give assistance to prospective customers, regardless of what territory they may come from, in obtaining the required information, in making selections of equipment, in installing and operating MORRIS equipment, etc.

Duration of Contract

The duration of the contract is for one year, and it is self-perpetuating unless three months' notice to terminate is given by either party.

MORRIS MACHINE WORKS
By: ________
Date: ________

Accepted by: ________
Date: ________

Thus far, the sales manager had rejected both proposals.

Was the sales manager justified in rejecting both proposals? Why or why not?
How useful is the form agreement in settling disputes?

CASE 2-12

Delphic Corporation

Manufacturer of Appliances and Electronic Equipment—Distributor-Dealer Sales Training

The Delphic Corporation, St. Louis, Missouri, was a leader in the electronics and appliance fields. Its exclusive business was the design, manufacture, sale, and, for large jobs, installation of this equipment. The Modern Kitchen Division manufactured a broad line of kitchen cabinets, dishwashers, and garbage disposals for residential use. These products were sold throughout the United States and Canada by a distributor-dealer organization, which was expanding rapidly to meet the increasing desire for kitchen modernization. The sales training department of the division had developed a variety of training aids and was looking for additional ways to widen the scope and increase the effectiveness of its activities. Refrigerators and ranges were manufactured and sold by the Major Appliance Division.

The Modern Kitchen Division had sales of $38 million. No sales were made directly to ultimate consumers; all equipment was sold through franchised distributors and dealers by sixty salespeople who worked out of twenty-two branch offices. Delphic was one of the first to institute this type of distribution in the appliance industry, and executives were proud that many of the original dealers still handled the line.

Franchises were written for a specific product with an assignment of a definite territory, within which the distributor or dealer was responsible for the sale of that product. The distributor-dealer organization consisted of eighty distributors and two thousand dealers. Distributors were primarily merchandisers, promoting sales to their own organization of "associate" dealers, who were selected by the distributor, and controlled entirely by him. Dealers' territories were nonexclusive and were subject to change upon written notice. Technical and sales assistance were rendered by the distributor, aided when necessary by Delphic field personnel.

Associate dealers were mainly appliance stores, department stores, and hardware stores; but plumbing and electrical contractors were also included. When selecting associate dealers, the distributor considered the prospective dealer's location, both in the area and in the city, his credit standing, and his personal integrity. Delphic distributors met with keen competition for dealers from other manufacturers and had to offer more than just a franchise and a convenient warehouse location. The distributor had the Delphic reputation to offer but, in many cases, he was expected to finance the initial stock of equipment. Training in kitchen equipment sales and kitchen layout, and installation, were offered to dealers to enable them to become profitable.

Delphic's sales volume more than doubled in the previous five years, and the number of retail outlets (associate dealers) increased in about the same proportion. Training of newer dealers became important to the success of the distributors' expanded operations. Each distributor looked to Delphic for assistance, and much of the task of dealer training was shifted to the manufacturer.

Before the sales training department of the Modern Kitchen Division was organized, training was the responsibility of product managers. Under this arrangement, training was not given sufficient attention because of the pressing nature of other duties assigned to product managers—the design, development, manufacture, and sale of the various products, for instance. Although training was recognized as important, a comprehensive study of dealers' needs was not made, and the overall training program lacked organization.

After the sales training department was formed, an analysis was made of training methods and materials, and this department became the centralized source for all such aids. Sessions were held with distributors to determine their requirements, and there evolved a variety of packaged training courses, films, and a monthly informational service. A booklet entitled *Dealer Training* was published as a guide for planning a dealer training program.

It was decided that the sales training department could best satisfy distributors' needs for materials and methods for training dealers with a program that covered three areas of interest: sales, installation, and management, that is, "business development." Accordingly, a series of packaged courses was made available under the name "Business Development Program." Training courses were prepared for each of the three product lines sold through associate dealers: kitchen cabinets, dishwashers, and garbage disposals. Student packets were available for a nominal fee. Meeting guides were prepared to aid the instructor in emphasizing the important points and to indicate the amount of time and detail required for a particular phase of training.

One unit of the package training course on dishwashers was entitled "Selling Dishwashers." This dealt with problems encountered in selling home units and included selling fundamentals applicable to automatic dishwashing. The material was in looseleaf form, and a complete packet was provided for each trainee. The course was built around nine selling steps:

1. Get set to sell.
2. Spark interest.
3. Dramatize the need.
4. Make the survey.
5. Prepare the proposal.
6. Present the proposal.
7. Capitalize on objections.
8. Get the order.
9. Follow through.

Each step was elaborated on and detailed to apply to actual situations encountered in the sale of dishwashers. For example, step 7, "capitalize on objections," listed objections that prospects might voice, and each had a well-thought-out answer. A recommended procedure for handling competition and price objections was outlined, and sample letters for "getting back in" were exhibited. Also included were sales arguments and approaches for use with the consumer, architect, builder, and real-estate agent. Sample proposal and submittal sheets were added as examples of recommended practice. Finally, the packet included a brochure that illustrated advertising and promotional aids, along with booklets that reproduced, in printed form, two sound-slide films used for selling dishwashers. One was for showing to the home owner, the other for showing to builders and realtors.

To introduce the new training material, sales training department personnel presented the courses at meetings of Delphic sales personnel who presented the courses to distributor wholesale sales personnel, who then held meetings with dealer personnel for whom the material was primarily prepared. The first sessions were for the purpose of "training the trainer" and were considered highly successful. The printed material was supported by films and/or sound-slide films, attractively prepared to appeal to dealers. The intention was to "sell" the dealer while training him or her to sell the retail customer. Training was a continuing activity, and many distributors recognized the usefulness of weekly training. Sales training was not overlooked, often constituting the bulk of the weekly training, and materials from St. Louis were used to good advantage.

An important feature of Delphic's sales training program was the "Sales Planning Series," which was made up of eleven separate units with companion films. The series concerned practical procedures and was a digest of successful selling practices followed by Delphic equipment sales personnel. The eleven parts covered each of the nine steps in the sale, plus two preliminary steps, "Plan Your Time" and "Plan Your Sales." A student packet and meeting guide were available for each section. In the packet was a printed reproduction of the companion film, interspersed with self-improvement exercises that the student was to think out individually. The "Sales Planning Series," the backbone of the Delphic training program, provided basic selling instruction for the novice and for the experienced dealer's salesperson, and served as a means for evaluating and organizing one's sales practices.

Each month, a file folder called the "Business Development Service" was distributed. Issues contained samples of new training materials, successful selling ideas, information on competitive activities, reports from other distributors, tips on getting and handling dealers, hints on improving personnel performance, advice on where to obtain training aids equipment such as projectors and flannel boards, and always a "Lost Sale" quiz, a cartoon-type lesson from *Sales and Marketing Management* magazine.

One feature of Delphic's "Business Development" program was a sales control system for the retail salesperson. The system made it possible to simplify record keeping on prospect activity and selling schedules. It also provided the sales manager with information on the salespeople's progress.

Another development was being closely followed by the sales training department: the recent formation of the Atlanta Corporation. This wholly owned subsidiary of Delphic, staffed with personnel from the Delphic organization, took over the distributorship in Atlanta and had an organization of associate dealers. From Atlanta's experience, the home office executives expected to learn more about the problems of distributors to provide better sales, engineering, and management assistance. This subsidiary also was to be a proving ground for new marketing techniques.

Evaluate the methods used by the Delphic Corporation for training its distributors and dealers.

CASE 2-13

Hillman Products Company

Manufacturer of Power Tools—Distributor-Dealer Problems

James Weston, director of sales and marketing for Hillman Products Company, Springfield, Massachusetts, faced the problem of taking action to improve the company's distributor and dealer relationships, which had steadily worsened. The effect of the worsening relationships was reflected in the latest sales report, which recorded a 12 percent sales decline during the past year and a 17 percent decline over the past two years.

Hillman Products Company manufactured a wide line of power tools, such as saws, drills, and sanders, for use by the home handyman. Hillman products were distributed nationwide through ninety distributors, who, in turn, sold to more than 8,500 retail outlets. During the past two years, the number of distributors handling Hillman products had dropped from 115 to 90 and, while the number of retailers had remained about the same, sales per dealer had substantially declined.

Several factors combined to cause high turnover among Hillman dealers, as well as to contribute to declining sales for Hillman products. Locations of many Hillman dealers were unfavorable. Dealer sales personnel were untrained and poorly informed about Hillman products. Few dealers did any advertising for the Hillman line. Virtually all dealers carried competing lines and devoted little effort to selling the Hillman line. Many retailers bought in small quantities, often a single unit of each Hillman product, so sales were frequently lost to competitors because of stockouts.

Dealers showed little loyalty to Hillman products. They knew little and understood less of the company's history, policies, performance, or capabilities. The sole contact the dealers had with Hillman was through the distributors and their salespeople, who themselves were often poorly informed. Many Hillman dealers expressed dissatisfaction with the company and its distributors for actions such as overloading dealers with more products than they could ever hope to sell in a given period and, especially, for the lack of company support in local advertising.

Hillman distributors criticized dealers for what they claimed was deceptive dealer advertising and ignoring the manufacturer's suggested retail prices. Some distributors had dropped the Hillman line and taken on competing lines.

Weston believed that immediate action was necessary to prevent further deterioration of the situation and to improve distributor-dealer relations. Consequently, he proposed (1) establishing a distributor-dealer relations staff and (2) retaining a management consultant.

The distributor-dealer relations staff would determine attitudes toward Hillman and its policies and make recommendations for the improvement of relations. Weston hoped that this would result in better understanding between Hillman and its outlets and would improve communications. To help distributors and dealers sell more Hillman products, the distributor-dealer relations staff would plan and implement a program of sales development, promotion, and mechanical service assistance for dealers.

The management consultant would survey fifty of the most successful Hillman dealers to determine the best methods for merchandising products. Information from the survey would be used in designing and implementing the program of sales development, promotion, and mechanical service assistance.

Weston believed that these two measures would reverse the alarming situation of poor distributor-dealer relations and would pave the way for more efficient marketing.

Evaluate Weston's proposal for improving Hillman Products Company's distributor-dealer relations. Give the reasons for your position.

CASE 2-14

Bil-Dry, Grip-On Corporation and Subsidiaries (B)[1]

Manufacturer of Specialty Building Products—Distributive Network Relations

John G. Briggs, Jr., vice president for sales and marketing for Bil-Dry, Grip-On Corporation and Subsidiaries, stated that incentive programs for Bil-Dry's network of manufacturer's representatives would be expanded. These programs would become an important element in the strategy to increase market penetration and market share. In the past, numerous incentive programs had been instituted successfully at the retail level of Bil-Dry's distribution network. Now, however, Mr. Brigg's concern was to schedule incentive programs for manufacturers' representatives as well as for retailers and their personnel.

[1]For background details on Bil-Dry, Grip-On Corporation and Subsidiaries, see the (A) case on p. 160.

Through the Professional Sales Association of Asheville and the Evans Paint Division, Bil-Dry administered incentive programs for retail personnel in the Lowe's and Evans chains. Semiannually, Bil-Dry provided the retail stores with special discounts enabling them to run sales on Bil-Dry products. Promotional materials and layouts for special "sale" advertising were provided. Sales contests had also been very successful. Prizes (usually gift certificates as high as $250) were awarded to retail personnel exceeding sales quotas established by Bil-Dry.

Smaller retailers of Bil-Dry, Grip-On products, who were serviced by eight manufacturers' representatives, were encouraged to participate in a cooperative advertising program. Retailers were furnished ad layouts. Bil-Dry paid 25 percent of the advertising cost, while the retailer paid 75 percent.

Incentive programs had not been instituted for the manufacturers' representatives earlier because Mr. Briggs had felt that their administration would be too difficult with his limited staff. The recent addition of a new person to his staff caused Mr. Briggs to explore possible sales contests for the manufacturers' representatives.

He had a number of questions, however, about the advisability of contests. The matter of contest design also deserved consideration. Should contests continue for retail personnel? Would manufacturers' representatives respond favorably? What should be the basis for the contest? Would cash payments be more effective than merchandise or travel prizes? How often and how long should the contests be run? Mr. Briggs also wondered if there shouldn't be some differences in the contests among the manufacturers' representatives for the Bil-Dry entity and the representatives for Stone Mountain. He wondered too, if there were any other ways Bil-Dry could encourage manufacturers' representatives (and retailers) to push the product line more effectively. At this point, Mr. Briggs had many more questions than answers.

What should Mr. Briggs do to improve distributive network relations? Give your reasoning.

Personnel Management in the Selling Field

10

Managing the sales force involves the implementation of personal-selling strategy. The two key personal-selling strategic decisions are on selling style(s) and sales force size. These decisions result from planning how to achieve the sales volume and related company goals. The decisions on selling style(s) determine the range and nature of activities required for personnel management of the sales force. The decision on sales force size determines the magnitude of these activities. Implementing these strategic decisions is sales management's responsibility.

SALES FORCE MANAGEMENT

Sales force management is a specialized type of personnel management. Whether personnel management focuses upon sales, production, or office workers, the same set of problems needs considering, but each problem varies in nature and importance. It is impractical, for instance, to exercise close and constant supervision over sales personnel—at least not in the sense that one can supervise production and office workers. Furthermore, sales personnel work away from their coworkers and immediate superiors, so it is difficult to develop a spirit of identity with and loyalty to the company and to weld them into a unified team.

Sales personnel of necessity are given freer rein than are production or office workers. To a considerable degree, they are relied upon as individuals to plan and control their own activities. Most sales personnel visit the home office only infrequently, and centralized direction of their activities is mainly by phone and mail. The salesperson's job provides limited opportunity for face-to-face contact and supervision, so sales personnel often are referred to as "account administrators" or "territory managers."

Other unique conditions surround the selling job. Often the salesperson is away from home and family for extended periods. Selling success (or failure) depends upon prospects' and customers' actions and reactions; disheartening order turndowns and rebuffs from customers require the salesperson to repress normal responses and to suppress a natural tendency to become discouraged. The psychological effects of these conditions accentuate the need for sales management to pay continual attention to motivational factors.

The steps in sales force management are the same as those in general personnel management. Sales force management work, as shown in Figure 10.1, starts with job analysis—determining the job objectives, the component duties and responsibilities, performance criteria, and reporting relationships. The output of job analysis is the written job description that is used in deriving the necessary qualifications (job specifications) of the employee. Qualified job applicants must be found, and this requires decisions on recruiting sources and methods. From the supply of applicants, those meeting the job specifications are selected. After hiring, applicants undergo initial training and throughout their entire careers with the company—receive continuing training through diverse delivery systems. Compensation plans are designed to provide appropriate levels and methods of compensation.

FIGURE 10.1 Activities Involved in Sales Force Management

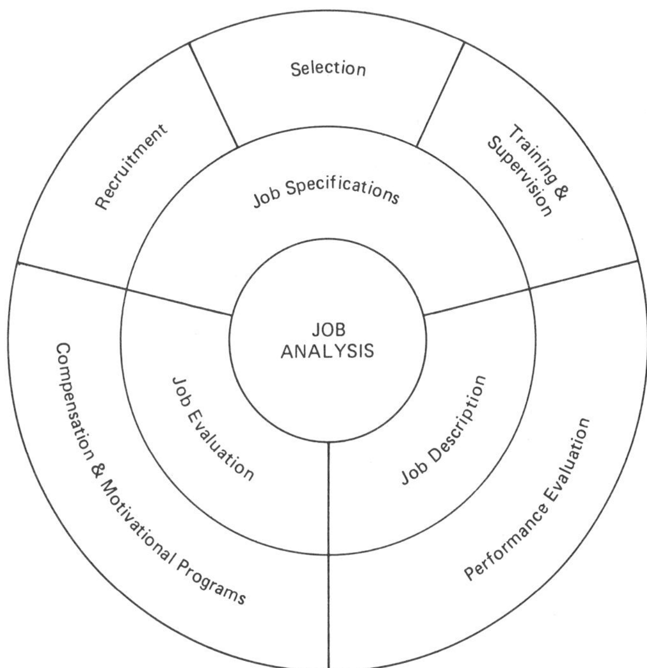

When the salesperson is assigned to the field, other personnel activities come into play. The salesperson is motivated to plan and make productive use of working time. To improve the effectiveness of sales calls, salespersons are counseled on working habits and methods. Controlling sales personnel requires analysis of selling records and evaluations of sales performance.

Sales force management activities mesh into a system. Faulty execution of any activity results in complications for other activities. If recruiting and selecting are sloppy, training tasks are magnified, supervision problems become greater, motivating and controlling salespersons is more difficult, and the turnover of sales personnel is accelerated. If training is inadequate, potentially good people fail to reach high productivity, the compensation system does not work as planned, supervision is ineffective, and there is excessive personnel turnover. Similar "bundles" of difficulty arise in cases of ineffective performance of other activities in the sales force management system.

Economies of Effective Sales Force Management

There are economies in effective sales force management. Assume that company X has ten salespersons, each making five calls per day, a total of fifty per day for the company. Assume further that four calls out of five result in sales and that the average sale amounts to $500. If through more effective management, each salesperson increases the number of calls to six per day, the company's daily total becomes sixty (an increase of ten), and eight more sales per day are made (8 x $500 = $4,000). This is equivalent to adding two new salespeople at the old call rate. If sales personnel are paid wholly, or partially, on a commission basis, their incomes are now higher and morale should be improved. Furthermore, because some selling costs are related to the number of salespeople, the company's average cost per call should be reduced.

There are two types of expenses of maintaining a sales force: fixed and variable. The fixed expenses are identical for all sales personnel regardless of their productivity, while the variable expenses are highest for the least productive sales personnel. Fixed expenses include sales salaries, traveling, equipment (autos, sales folios, sales manuals, and so forth), and advertising used to assist the sales force. Variable expenses include sales commissions, training, motivating, supervising, and controlling—these expenses are lower per unit of product sold for productive salespersons than for unproductive salespersons. In other words, when a company incurs variable expenses for maintaining its sales force, it receives its highest return from the most productive sales personnel. Total expenses per unit of product sold vary inversely with the productivity of the salesperson.

Rate of Sales Personnel Turnover

The rate of sales personnel turnover is a measure of the quality of sales force management. This is the ratio of separations per 100 salespeople. For example, a company employing a sales force of 250 persons and having twenty separations during the year has a rate of turnover of 8 percent.[1]

The turnover rate influences the total expenses of sales force management. Costs of recruiting, advertising, fees to employment agencies, and so forth often run to more than $500 per recruit. Interviewing costs are high, because companies interview several applicants for each selection. If an interview by an executive takes two hours, an executive's time is worth $25 per hour, and thirty people are considered for each vacancy, total interviewing costs amount to $1,500 per person hired. The costs of travel and time used for preparatory and follow-up training easily run $10,000 per person.

Some expenses are not readily calculated. For example, new recruits do not produce as much as experienced sales personnel, and the ratio of selling expenses to sales for a new person is likely to be excessive for at least the first year. A conservative estimate of the excess is $3,500 per new salesperson during the first year, and in some companies this excess is higher because it takes longer for a salesperson to get fully into stride.

The expenses of sales personnel turnover can account for a significant drain on profits. In a company with a sales force of 400 and an annual turnover rate of 25 percent, if the costs of replacing a single salesperson come to $10,000, the annual costs of turnover total $1 million—and this is only out-of-pocket cost. Other costs are increased expenses for supervision and motivation, lost business, decline in customer goodwill from mistakes of inexperienced salespersons, and miscellaneous expenses associated with taking on people who do not succeed. Few accounting systems measure the impact on profit of excessive sales personnel turnover. But profits are lower because inexperienced salespeople are assigned where turnover has occurred. Profits are not realized from sales not consummated.

All turnover is not bad, even though it seems costly. Sales executives report that most salespeople who leave a company have less than three years of service. If a person is proving unsuccessful, and is likely to leave eventually, it is desirable that the person leave immediately. The earlier the unsuccessful person leaves, the better off the company is, both in terms of dollar costs and effect upon other sales personnel. Too low a rate of turnover may indicate that the sales force is overloaded with veterans who do not produce as much as new personnel might. In this situation the entire system of sales force management may need overhauling. Some turnover is desirable. A sales force with no turnover may be growing stale, prospective new salespeople are not being attracted, and older ones are lingering on because of management laxity.

The age distribution among sales personnel should be analyzed for its impact on sales force turnover. It is desirable to spread salespersons' ages over a wide range. Otherwise, the productivity curves for all rise together, all reaching their peaks and declining together, and all reaching retirement at the same time.

[1]A convenient formula for calculating the rate of sales personnel turnover is

$$\text{rate of personnel turnover (expressed as a percentage)} = \frac{\text{number of separations} \times 100}{\text{average total sales force}}$$

Under these circumstances, it is necessary eventually to recruit an entire sales force almost at once, at considerable loss in market coverage and customer relations. Companies should establish an average length of service, which management considers desirable, before evaluating the turnover rate. If management believes the average length of service should be twenty years, then, assuming no errors in selection, the personnel turnover rate should be 5 percent—one-twentieth of the sales force should be replaced each year. Because even the best selection procedure is far from perfect, the actual turnover rate would run higher than 5 percent. In addition, many people do not take sales jobs with the intention of keeping them forever. A sales job is often the springboard to higher positions, and a company using its sales force as a source of managerial talent anticipates higher turnover.

Awareness of the current turnover rate is necessary for planning the operation of service functions. The personnel turnover rate is important in planning recruiting, selection, and training programs. For example, a company with a turnover rate of 25 percent is replacing its sales force every four years. It must organize its service functions to handle an annual volume of new recruits equivalent to one-fourth of its sales force. The costs and extent of the recruitment, selection and training programs largely depend upon the amount of turnover.

The personnel turnover rate is analyzed periodically to determine the causes. Analysis often uncovers areas where improvement is needed. A useful information source is an exit interview between the departing salesperson and either a line executive or a personnel consultant. This interview provides an opportunity to identify conditions contributing to personnel turnover. Identification enables management to modify or correct conditions within its control.

FIGURE 10.2 Causes of Turnover of Sales Personnel

Caused by Actions Controllable by Company	Caused by Actions Not Controllable by Company
1. Poor recruiting	1. Retirement
2. Improper selection and assignment	2. Death
3. Training deficiencies	3. Illness or physical disability
4. Inadequate supervision and motivation	4. Personal and marital difficulties
5. Breakdown in communications	5. Dislike for the job—travel, type of work, working conditions, etc.
6. Unsatisfactory performance—customer complaints, etc.	6. Military duty
7. Discharged for cause, e.g., alcoholism, conviction of a felony, dishonesty, etc.	7. Better position elsewhere
8. Cutbacks in personnel	
9. Transfer to another department	
10. Promotion to a higher position	

Causes of personnel turnover can be separated into two main groupings, as shown in Figure 10.2. Management should take corrective action when the causes are concentrated on the controllable list, particularly when turnover traces to reasons 1 through 7. Turnover resulting from reason 8 sometimes is unavoidable, and that resulting from 9 and 10 is usually desirable. Managerial action may be called for, even in the cases of some reasons appearing on the "not controllable" list; in fact, only reasons 2, 3, and 6 may be regarded as completely unavoidable.

INVOLVEMENT OF SALES EXECUTIVES IN SALES FORCE MANAGEMENT

Sales force management is a concern of sales executives at all organizational levels. For some sales executives, successful performance by sales personnel is the single most important responsibility. Sales supervisors, the level of administrators directly above the salespeople, devote the bulk of their energies to managing the sales force. Others spend less time on managing salespersons' activities but are concerned, nevertheless, with their effectiveness. Middle-level sales executives, such as regional sales managers, serve in line capacities managing lower-echelon sales executives who, in turn, manage the sales force. Other middle-level sales executives specialize either in some aspect of sales force management (for example, sales training) or in a phase of marketing (for example, brand promotion) that affects the salesperson's job.

At the top of the organizational structure, the chief sales executive has general responsibility not only for managing subordinate sales executives and through them for managing the sales personnel, but also for the management of other sales and marketing activities. Thus, as sales executives move to and through middle management levels, they retain their concern for management of the sales force. However, as they move up, added pressures cause them to ration their efforts among a growing set of responsibilities. They retain concern for sales force management but participate increasingly in long-range planning and forecasting, structuring the product line, setting prices, planning promotional programs, and managing marketing channels and physical distribution. Regardless of this, however, sales executives should never forget that the main reason for their own job's existence is to contribute to the effectiveness of the sales force.

Need for the Proper Setting

Programs for effective sales force management need installing in a favorable setting. Market exploration must have been carried to the point where management knows market and sales potentials, identities and locations of customers and prospects, the individuals in customers' organizations who influence buying decisions, and the best methods for reaching them. Product uses and applications must have been identified and different selling appeals evaluated. With this foundation of information, management is prepared to draft and implement appropriate programs for effective sales force management.

The Law and Sales Force Management

Two agencies, the Equal Employment Opportunity Commission (EEOC) and the Office of Federal Contract Compliance (OFCC), assist employers in implementing nondiscriminatory personnel policies (defined as policies that do not result in discrimination on the basis of race, color, religion, sex, or national origin).[2] The guidelines issued by the EEOC apply to all employers of twenty-five persons or more; those of the OFCC apply to firms with one hundred or more employees that contract with the federal government.

Both the EEOC and OFCC concern themselves with a broad range of personnel policies. Their regulations limit the use of ability tests to measure eligibility for hiring, transferring, promotion, training, and referral or retention. They apply particularly to all formal, scored, quantified, or standardized techniques used to assess job suitability, including specific qualifying or disqualifying personal history or background requirements, specific educational or work history requirements, scored interviews, biographical information blanks, interviewers' rating scales, scored application forms, and the like. These agencies require an employer using such techniques to have evidence of each technique's validity; this must consist of empirical data demonstrating that the technique is predictive of or significantly correlated with important elements of work behavior that comprise or are relevant to the job or jobs for which candidates are being evaluated. Basically, then, federal regulations require that employers using personnel administration techniques of this type for purposes of selecting from among candidates for a position or in making decisions on transfers, promotion, training, or dismissals must be prepared to prove that the techniques are used in a manner that does not discriminate on the basis of race, color, religion, sex, or national origin.

Companies that have a serious imbalance in the number of minority group members in their work force relative to the proportion who reside in the employment area are in noncompliance with the law. Although a company's hiring standards may be job related, for instance, those reflecting the norms of the white community or involving preemployment inquiries as to race or national origin are considered discriminatory.

Most violations of the Civil Rights Act involve discrimination on the basis of race and color, but an increasing number of cases relate to discrimination on the basis of sex. This has caused most companies to abandon certain long-standing practices. Today, it is rare to specify sex in help-wanted advertising. Similarly,

[2]See *Guidelines on Employment Selection Procedures* (Washington, D.C.: Equal Employment Opportunity Commission, August 1, 1970) and *Proposed Employment Testing and Other Selection Procedures* (Washington, D.C.: Office of Federal Contract Compliance, April 15, 1971).

most companies are recruiting women for sales positions that were formerly regarded as for men only. The EEOC recommends and some states require that help-wanted advertisements state that all applicants are welcome even though they may be labeled "Jobs of interest—male" or "Jobs of interest—female."

Discrimination on the basis of age is prohibited by the Age Discrimination in Employment Act. This act applies to employers of twenty persons or more in industries affecting interstate commerce and protects individuals aged forty to seventy against discrimination in hiring, discharging, or compensation. Small businesses (those with fewer than twenty employees) are exempted, but, as a practical matter nearly every business with more than twenty employees comes under the regulation as almost all affect interstate commerce. This act does not prohibit employers from asking job applicants to state their age or date of birth on application forms or in an interview. But it is unlawful to discriminate on the basis of age in hiring, discharge, or pay.

JOB ANALYSIS

Job analysis—assembling and analyzing factual information on specific jobs—is the basis for professional personnel management. Job analyses provide the data required for preparing written job descriptions, which, in turn, are used to derive job specifications (the qualifications and characteristics individuals need to perform given jobs). The job analysis, then, and its two derivatives, the job description and job specification, provide factual foundations for making decisions on hiring, transfers, promotion, training, and dismissals.

Sales Job Analysis

Sales job analysis is the critical first step in modern sales force management. Long the foundation for enlightened personnel management, sales job analysis has risen in importance since the Civil Rights Act brought pressure on sales executives to justify decisions on hiring, transfers, promotion, training, and dismissals. As a consequence, sales executives are concerned with making objective personnel decisions—basing decisions on facts, not upon hunches.

Sales job analysis requires systematic collection and study of information on particular sales jobs, such as that of territorial salesperson. It involves determining the job's objectives and what the person holding the job should do to reach them. It answers such questions as: To whom does this person report? Who reports to this person? What products does this person sell? To whom does this person sell? What information should this person gather? What reports should this person make and to whom? Sales job analysis, in addition, elicits details on specific duties and responsibilities, relations with customers, relations with other sales department and company personnel, and the like. The outcome of a thorough analysis of a salesperson's job is a detailed picture of the role(s) that the salesperson plays—as noted earlier (see Chapter 5), four basic selling styles cut, to a large degree, across industry and company boundaries: trade, missionary, technical, and new business. In analyzing the salesperson's job in a particular company, in most cases, we find that the job combines two or more of these basic styles.

Sales Job Description

The key output of sales job analysis is the job description. A sales job description is an organized factual statement covering (1) the reporting relationship of a particular job to other jobs, (2) the job objectives, (3) duties and responsibilities, and (4) job performance criteria. A sales job description tells to whom the sales jobholder reports, what has to be done, how it is done, and why and, in addition, describes the standards against which performance is measured.

Procedure for Sales Job Analysis and Preparation of Written Job Descriptions

Procedures for sales job analysis and preparation of written job descriptions vary from company to company, but four main steps are identifiable in procedures used in well-managed companies: (1) assembly of factual information about the job, (2) analysis of the information, (3) writing of the job description, and (4) as required, repeat the process. A suggested procedure is

1. Assemble factual information about the job:
   - 1.1. Clarify reporting relationships by questioning salespersons and those to whom they report.
   - 1.2. Prepare a questionnaire for sales personnel, asking them to list the job objectives, together with the major duties and what is involved in performing them, in doing the job effectively.
   - 1.3. Prior to receipt of the completed questionnaires, have sales executives and other executives interested in sales activities write down their conceptions of the salesperson's job objectives, the salesperson's responsibilities, and the duties they feel the salesperson should and should not perform.
   - 1.4. Survey customers to find out what they believe should and should not be the functions of a company salesperson.
2. Analyze the information gathered:
   - 2.1. Tabulate the information received.
   - 2.2. Reconcile differences revealed by the three viewpoints, write a concise statement of job objectives, and prepare a detailed list of duties that sales personnel are to perform.
   - 2.3. Classify the duties into major responsibility groupings, such as sales, service, territory management, sales promotion, executive, and goodwill duties.
3. Write the job description:
   - 3.1. Put the reporting relationships in writing.

3.2. Add the concise statement of job objectives.
3.3. Insert the detailed information on duties and responsibilities.
3.4. Develop a written statement of job performance measures.

4. As required, repeat the first three steps when changes in markets, customers' requirements, products, competition, the economic climate, and so forth require a review of job objectives, job duties and responsibilities, and/or performance measures.

An alternative approach to developing the "job duties and responsibilities" section of the job description is to use a checklist of activities and subactivities generally accepted as comprising salespersons' jobs. One checklist, originally put together for the U.S. Small Business Administration, is shown in Figure 10.3. This approach is helpful in preparing tentative descriptions of newly created sales jobs.

Preparation of Sales Job Specifications

Preparing a complete and accurate sales job description is simple compared to preparing a complete and accurate sales job specification. The "duties and responsibilities" portion of the job description is focused upon to determine the qualifications that an individual needs to perform the job satisfactorily. This set of qualifications is called the "job specifications." If the job description states, for instance, that the salesperson is to train dealers' sales personnel, then the salesperson must be qualified to conduct such training. What will the salesperson have to know about the products, their uses, and the dealers' customers? About dealers' operating methods and problems? About training methods? Will this require the salesperson to have a certain kind of education and/or special experience? Similar sets of questions must be answered about each of the duties and responsibilities in the job description.

There are differences among the qualifications that a new addition to the sales force may bring to the job, those that an individual may acquire through training and those that a person gains through field selling experience. Sales management decides which qualifications all new recruits should possess, and which should be provided through training. A company specifying somewhat higher entrance qualifications than another can expect, other things being equal, that its training program will have to accomplish less. But the first company is likely to encounter greater difficulty in finding as many recruits as the second company. A trade-off is made between recruiting persons with many qualifications, which reduces the need for training, and recruiting persons with few qualifications, which increases the need for training.

It is generally considered desirable for sales job specifications to set forth the required personality characteristics. These the salesperson must bring to the job, since sales training programs are not effective instruments for personality development. All sales personnel need certain traits: empathy and the ability to get along well with others; integrity and character; and maturity, in terms of a

FIGURE 10.3 Checklist for Compiling "Duties and Responsibilities" Section of a Sales Job Description

Sales:
Make regular calls.
Sell the line; demonstrate.
Handle questions and objections.
Check stock; discover possible product uses.
Interpret sales points of the line to the customer.
Estimate customer's potential needs.
Emphasize quality.
Explain company policy on price, delivery, and credit.
Get the order.

Service:
Install the product or display.
Report product weaknesses, complaints.
Handle adjustments, returns, and allowances.
Handle requests for credit.
Handle special orders.
Establish priorities, if any.
Analyze local conditions for customers.

Territory management:
Arrange route for best coverage.
Balance effort with customer against the potential volume.
Maintain sales portfolios, samples, kits, and so forth.

Sales Promotion:
Develop new prospects and accounts.
Distribute home office literature, catalogues, and the like.
Make calls with customer's salespeople.
Train personnel of wholesalers, jobbers, and so on.
Present survey reports, layouts, and proposals.

Executive:
Each night make a daily work plan for the next day.
Organize field activity for minimum travel and maximum calls.
Prepare and submit special reports on trends, competition.
Prepare and submit statistical data requested by home office.
Investigate lost sales and reason for loss.
Prepare reports on developments, trends, new objectives met, and new ideas on meeting objections.
Attend sales meetings.
Build a prospect list.
Collect overdue accounts; report on faulty accounts.
Collect credit information.

Goodwill:
Counsel customers on their problems.
Maintain loyalty and respect for the company.
Attend local sales meetings held by customers.

sensible self-perspective. Motivation is important—some sales jobs require their holders to be routine order takers only, but others serve as proving grounds for future managers. There is an optimum level of motivation for each job. If new salespersons are too strongly motivated, they may not be content for long with a routine job or one lacking in advancement opportunities.

Job specifications may stipulate minimum requirements with respect to education and product or technical knowledge, but *legally so only if* the company can prove that these requirements are significantly related to job performance. The importance of these requirements varies widely. Some selling jobs demand the detailed technical training offered only by colleges of engineering; others require only average ability to read, write, and do simple arithmetic; and there are all gradations in between. Graduation from an educational institution is tangible evidence that the job candidate has a certain level of ability. If a specified amount of formal education is set as an absolute minimum requirement, however, some otherwise qualified applicants are eliminated from consideration. Setting a specified amount of formal education as an absolute minimum requirement is dangerous on legal grounds—EEOC guidelines specify that the employer must prove that this requirement is significantly related to successful job performance and does not result in discrimination on the basis of race, color, religion, sex, age, or national origin.

Job specifications provide recruiters with a device for the conservation of time and energy—the set of minimum requirements to use in weeding out unqualified applicants. This usually takes the form of a list of negative factors, the presence of any of which automatically disqualifies an applicant. A set of minimum requirements, or preliminary screening standards, should be prepared only after a company analyzes its dismissals and should reflect the main reasons why a company's sales personnel fail. Companies must be prepared to prove that each minimum requirement is significantly related to successful job performance and does not result in discrimination on the basis of race, color, religion, sex, age, or national origin.

Because of difficulties met in developing a fully objective and accurate set of job qualifications for sales jobs, many companies do not formalize sales job specifications. Instead, sales executives and others interviewing prospective employees are provided with written sales job descriptions. Each interviewer has a set of desired qualifications (that is, a job specification) in his or her mind. Instead of a single set of qualifications (a standard specification) for the sales job, there are as many as there are users of the written job description.

CONCLUSION

Sales force management is personnel administration applied to the sales department. In its application, it requires adaptation to the special circumstances that surround the salesperson's job. Effective sales force management requires skill in setting up and operating the total system for sales force management—all the way from sales job analysis through the procedures used for evaluating and controlling sales personnel. Faulty sales force management results in high sales personnel turnover and excessive selling expenses, adversely affecting profit. The foundations for effective sales management are thorough sales job analysis, complete and written sales job descriptions, and meaningful sales job specifications.

11 Recruiting Sales Personnel

Fielding the sales personnel needed to service the company's customers and prospects is a key responsibility of sales executives. Discharging this responsibility requires that the sales executive implement personal-selling strategy in terms of both the kind and number of sales personnel. Implementation is by no means a simple process. Having determined the desired kind of sales personnel, implementation requires job analysis, the writing of job descriptions, and the deriving of job specifications so that recruiters will know the qualifications they should look for in prospective sales employees and sales trainers will know what additional qualifications they should aim to provide newly recruited sales personnel. Having decided the appropriate number of sales personnel, implementation requires recruiting that number initially and replacing those that are lost (for whatever reasons). Implementing personal-selling strategy, then, is a never-ending process—the nature of the selling job tends to change rather slowly (so changes in the kind of sales personnel desired are infrequent), but having and keeping the right number of sales personnel is a continual concern.

Recruiting and selecting sales personnel is an important part of implementing personal-selling strategy, but it is not all that is involved. Initial sales training is required to bring new sales personnel up to expected productivity levels, and continuing sales training is needed to maintain more experienced sales personnel at high levels of productivity. Motivational and supervisory efforts help in stimulating sales personnel to apply their skills effectively. It is one thing for sales personnel to know what they are supposed to know, but it is a different thing to get them to apply what they know.

Assuming that job analysis has been done, the sales job descriptions written, and the list of job specifications prepared, there are three main steps in recruiting and selecting a sales force. Step 1 is to evaluate the sources from which sales personnel with good potentials are obtainable. Step 2 is to tap the identified recruiting sources and build a supply of prospective sales personnel. Step 3 is to select those who have the highest probability of success.

ORGANIZATION FOR RECRUITING AND SELECTION

The organization for recruiting and selection of sales personnel varies from company to company. Company size, executives' personalities, and departmental structure all influence the organization used. Where the sales manager has a personnel staff assistant, recruiting and selection usually is handled entirely within the sales department. Companies with small sales forces sometimes assign sole responsibility for recruiting and selection of sales personnel to the company personnel manager, but this is unusual. It is more common for the personnel department to handle certain, but not all, aspects of recruiting and preliminary screening and for the sales department to handle other aspects of recruiting and screening and to make the hiring decisions.

Placement of responsibility for recruitment and selection of sales personnel in concerns with regional or district sales offices also varies. These functions tend to be centralized at the home office when the firm requires high-caliber sales personnel, such as those needed to do technical selling. Other factors, for example, size of regional and district organizations and location of training programs, make it difficult to draw further generalizations. However, decentralized recruitment and selection result in reduced interviewing costs and time, and facilitate the hiring of local applicants for sales work.

THE PRERECRUITING RESERVOIR

Because of uncertainties as to when new sales personnel will be needed, many companies have a prerecruiting reservoir. This is a file of individuals who might be recruited when the need arises. Figure 11.1 is a prerecruiting evaluation form one company uses in recording preliminary impressions of individuals whose names are being added to the reservoir.

The names of individuals added to the reservoir come from diverse sources. Some come from "volunteer walk-ins"—people who come by the sales department inquiring about job opportunities. Others come from chance remarks made by people with whom the sales executive comes into contact—at professional meetings, in conversations with customers, over cocktails at the club, seat partners on planes, and the like. Still others come from "centers of influence" that have been developed by the sales executive—the center of influence is a person who occupies a position in which he or she meets many individuals who have high potentials as possible sales personnel and who often are seek-

FIGURE 11.1 Prerecruiting Evaluation Form—Sales Personnel

Name ______________________________ Date ______________

Address ______________________________ Telephone ______________

Current Employer ______________________________ Current Job ______________

	Superior	Good	Acceptable	Fair	Poor
Poise					
Dress & Appearance					
Speech					
Personality					
Experience					
Education					
Health					
Interest in Selling					
Interest in Our Company					

Comments & Other Pertinent Information ______________________________

____

____

____

____

Possible References: ______________________________

____

____

Source of Contact: ______________________________

____
Signature of Person Completing this form

ing suitable job opportunities. Examples of centers of influence include the university professor of marketing and sales management, the trade association executive, the placement advisor of a university or community college, and vocational advisors in other educational institutions. Names in the prerecruiting reservoir should be reviewed periodically. Those that become badly dated should be culled.

SOURCES OF SALES FORCE RECRUITS

Recruiting Source Evaluation

One approach to evaluating the sources of recruits is to study those used in the past. Analysis of each source reveals the number of recruits produced, and the ratio of successes to failures. Each source, in other words, is analyzed quantitatively and qualitatively. One source may have provided numerous recruits but few successes; a second, fewer recruits but a high proportion of successes.

Consider the analysis in Figure 11.2. The source accounting for the largest number of recruits showed a success ratio only slightly more favorable than the ratio for all sources—but it did account for ten of the thirty-five successes recruited, and, for this reason, management might want to continue using it. Three sources had higher-than-average success ratios, and management should explore ways of increasing the number of recruits from them. Three other sources had very low success ratios, and management should use them sparingly in the future.

A word of caution: These results indicate the experience of only one company and should not be considered typical. Furthermore, the definition of success adopted by a particular management affects the analysis. Here success was defined as "demonstrated ability to meet or exceed sales quotas in two years out of three." Other managements might define success differently.

Another word of caution: Reliability of this sort of analysis depends upon

FIGURE 11.2 Source Analysis of Sales Personnel Recruited by an Electrical Products Manufacturer

Source	Number of Recruits	% of Total	Number of Successes	Ratio of Successes to Total
Recommendations by own salespeople	22	27.50%	10	0.455
Educational institutions	14	17.50	10	0.715
Sales personnel for noncompeting firms	12	15.00	2	0.167
Employment agencies	10	12.50	3	0.300
Personal acquaintances of executives	8	10.00	5	0.625
Customers' employees	6	7.50	1	0.167
Unsolicited applications	5	6.25	2	0.400
Competitors' salespeople	3	3.75	2	0.670
	80	100.00%	35	
Ratio of successes to total from all sources				0.437

the size of the group evaluated. More reliable conclusions can be drawn about the worth of a source producing twenty-two recruits than one producing only three recruits. However, even if only a small number of cases is available, the data may still serve as a helpful, although less reliable, guide in identifying promising sources of new salespeople.

Sources Within the Company

Company sales personnel. Many individuals apply for sales jobs because they know company sales personnel, and salespeople's recommendations may constitute an excellent source. Often such applicants already know something about company policies, and the fact that they apply indicates a favorable disposition toward the company. Salespeople have wide circles of acquaintances, since both on and off the job, they continually meet new people and have many friends with similar interests. Many of their contacts have potential as sales personnel—indeed, many now sell for other firms. However, some salespeople are not discriminating in their recommendations, and their recommendations need careful appraisal. Salespeople are a particularly valuable source of recommendations when jobs must be filled in remote territories; sales personnel in the same or adjacent areas may know more about unique territorial requirements and local sources of personnel than home office executives.

Company executives. Recommendations of the sales manager, the president, and other company executives are an important source. Sales executives' personal contacts may yield top-caliber people because of their understanding of the needed qualifications. Other executives' recommendations, by contrast, often are based upon personal friendships and represent less objective appraisals. Experience is the way to evaluate each executive's worth as a source of recruits, and the type of analysis shown in Figure 11.2 adapts easily for this purpose.

Internal transfers. Two additional internal sources are other departments and the nonselling section of the sales department. Employees desiring transfers are already familiar with company policies, and the personnel department has considerable detailed information about them. While little is known about their aptitude for selling, they often possess excellent product knowledge. Aptitude for selling, of course, can be tested formally or by trial assignment to the field. Transfers are good prospects for sales positions whenever product knowledge makes up a substantial portion of sales training, since it may be possible to accelerate field assignments.

Sources Outside the Company

Direct unsolicited applications. All companies receive unsolicited "walk-in" and "write-in" applications for sales positions. Some sales managers favor immediate hiring of applicants who take the initiative in seeking sales jobs, the reasoning being that this indicates selling aggressiveness. Others reject all direct applications because they believe the proportion of qualified applicants from this source is low. The most logical policy is to treat volunteer applications the same as solicited applications—applicants not meeting minimum requirements as set forth in job specifications should be eliminated; those meeting these requirements should be processed together with other applicants. The aim should be to recruit the best qualified applicants regardless of the sources from which they come. Direct unsolicited applications do not provide a steady flow of applicants; the volume fluctuates with changing business conditions.

Employment agencies. Sales managers traditionally regard employment agencies as unpromising sources. Many use agencies only after exhausting other sources. Many believe that good salespeople neither need nor will use an agency's services. Experience, unfortunately, tends to reinforce such attitudes, because frequently agency referrals fail to meet sales job specifications. Sometimes this traces to agency deficiencies (such as the overzealous desire to receive placement fees), but often the fault is that of prospective employers, who may be using unrealistically high job specifications, may not make the company's requirements clear, and so on. Experiences with individual agencies need reviewing periodically, using the pattern of analysis illustrated in Figure 11.2.

Whenever an agency is used, it should receive a clear statement of the job's objectives and a complete rundown of job specifications. The recruiter should meet with an agency counselor to assure that pertinent information is furnished and understood. Agencies need time to learn about an employing firm and its unique requirements—considerable gains accrue from continuing relationships with agencies. Agencies often administer batteries of tests, check references, and perform tasks otherwise done by the employer. Of interest to sales executives is the growing number of agencies that take the initiative in searching out promising job candidates, employed or not, instead of confining themselves to "volunteer" applicants.

Salespeople making calls on the company. The purchasing director is in contact with sales personnel from other companies and is in a position to evaluate their on-the-job performances. The purchasing director meets high-caliber salespeople for whom jobs with the company would be attractive both financially and in other respects. In well-managed companies, the purchasing director, serving as a "center of influence," contributes names to the prerecruiting reservoir.

Employees of customers. Some companies regard their customers as a recruiting source. Customers recommend people in their organizations who have reached the maximum potential of their existing jobs. Such transfers may have a favorable effect upon morale in the customer's organization. A customer's employees should be recruited only with the prior approval of the customer.

Sales executives' clubs. Many sales executives' clubs operate placement services. Salespersons seeking new positions submit personal data sheets that are duplicated and forwarded to members. At club meetings, sales executives have opportunities for informal discussion and exchange of placement information.

Sales forces of noncompeting companies. Individuals currently employed as salespersons for noncompeting companies are often attractive recruiting prospects. Such people have selling experience, some of it readily transferable, and for those who have worked for companies in related industries, there is the attraction of knowing something about the product line. For salespeople in dead-end jobs and those seeking to upgrade their employment, this source provides a channel for career advancement.

Sales forces of competing companies. Because of their experience in selling similar products to similar markets, personnel recruited from competitors' sales forces may require only minimal training. However, competing sales forces are costly sources, since generally premium pay must be offered to entice sales personnel to leave their present positions. Some sales executives, as a matter of policy, refrain from hiring competitors' salespersons—they feel that an individual hired away from one organization for higher pay or other enticements may be similarly tempted in the future. However, most sales executives will consider individuals who have worked previously for competitors even though they now are either working somewhere else or are unemployed.

In considering the recruitment of individuals currently employed by competitors, a key question to answer is why does this person want to leave his or her present position? When the new job will not improve the applicant's pay, status, or future prospects, the desire to change companies may trace to personality conflicts, or instability. But dissatisfaction with a present job may not mean that the fault is the applicant's. If the applicant has sound reasons for switching companies, there may be an opportunity to obtain a promising person who is ready for productive work.

Educational institutions. This source includes colleges and universities, community colleges, vocational-technical institutes, business colleges, high schools, and night schools. It is reasonable to expect that graduates have attained certain educational levels, the amount depending upon the type of school. Many have training in general business, marketing, and sales techniques. Schools are a fruitful source of new sales personnel at graduation time, and some maintain year-round placement services for their graduates. Recent graduates are new to the labor market and, consequently, need not be attracted away from other jobs.

Colleges and universities are important sources of sales and management trainees, and competition is keen for their graduates. Often the graduating senior is in a position to choose from among several job offers. Companies not maintaining close relations with the colleges are at a disadvantage, frequently being unable to obtain appointments on overcrowded campus recruiting schedules and finding it difficult to attract students away from companies better known to the college. Even better known companies face stiff competition in hiring the cream of the graduates. A few companies offer sales training programs to outstanding juniors during vacation periods. Thus, the trainee and the company have an opportunity to evaluate each other, and trainees who prove satisfactory are offered jobs upon graduating.

Older persons. The Age Discrimination in Employment Act prohibits discrimination in hiring decisions against persons forty to seventy years of age. Although discrimination against persons in this age group is outlawed, such individuals frequently have a difficult time obtaining jobs, so recruiters can select from a group for which there is little competitive bidding. Many people in this age group have years of selling experience and the maturity that is valuable in most selling situations. It is important, of course, to ascertain why an apparently good person is unemployed, but the reasons are often beyond the control of the individual. Assuming that an older person's qualifications compare favorably with job specifications, the hiring decision may hinge upon the amount of training needed for full productivity.

THE RECRUITING EFFORT

The sales personnel recruiting effort differs from one company to another, mainly as to the sources of recruits and recruiting methods, and stem from management's sizeup of the appropriate combination of selling styles. Different selling styles call for individuals with varying qualifications as to type and amount of education, other training, and experience. If trade selling is the basic style, the management seeks individuals with minimal or general education and little or no experience. If missionary selling is the basic style, management looks for higher-caliber individuals with specialized educations (as in science or pharmacy, if the job involves calling on physicians or hospitals) or equivalent qualifications, perhaps gained through experience in a similar job with another company. If technical selling is the basic style, management looks for even higher-caliber individuals with scientific or engineering educations and/or backgrounds. If the selling job also involves new-business selling, management looks for individuals with the required abilities to apply this selling style. Therefore, if the job specifications call for special talents, such as a knowledge of engineering or pharmacy, then management tends to emphasize educational institutions as sources of recruits and solicits applicants through personal contacts. Conversely, if trade selling ability is the main job qualification needed, management taps diverse sources and emphasizes indirect recruiting methods (for example, advertising in help wanted columns and responding to "situations wanted" advertisements in newspapers and trade publications).

The scope of the recruiting effort is influenced by the number of recruits desired, which, in turn, is influenced by the size and maturity of the sales organization itself, the sales personnel turnover rate, the forecasted sales volume, distribution channels, and promotional strategy. A large sales organization must recruit more new people just to maintain its average strength than is true of a smaller organization. Two firms of comparable size (as to sales volume) may have different-sized sales forces, often because one uses a different distribution channel or stresses advertising more in its promotional strategy. As might be expected, companies with high sales personnel turnover rates must do more recruiting than those with lower rates.

Personal Recruiting

College recruiting. Personal recruiting is used for recruiting graduates of educational institutions. Campus interviewing is often planned as a companywide affair, because this avoids much duplication of effort. Representatives of different departments do the interviewing, and the personnel department plans and coordinates the drive. In many companies an assistant sales manager shares the responsibility for interviewing students with the regional or district sales manager located nearest the specific campus. In other cases, home office sales executives rotate campus interviewing responsibilities among themselves; sometimes each returns annually to the same campuses, thus building long-term relationships.

College recruiting requires thorough planning. Statements of trainee requirements should be mailed to college placement officers early, preferably no later than January. The list of colleges, based primarily upon past interviewing experience, is updated, and interview dates are requested. The best months for recruiting June graduates are February, March, and April and March is the most in demand. If the visit comes too late in the spring, interviewers find that many of the best qualified graduates have already taken jobs. After visiting dates have been confirmed, colleges are sent letters specifying such details as salary, the training program, and starting date of employment. Some recruiters also send copies of promotional materials, company histories, and application blanks.

College placement officers schedule a 20- to 30-minute interview for each student. All interested students are granted interviews, the only screening device used. The most promising candidates are invited to company offices for follow-up interviews. However, some campus interviewers have the authority to hire if it appears that promising candidates will be lost through delay.

Recruiting direct-to-consumer sales personnel. One situation where personal recruiting sees widespread use is in the direct-to-consumer selling industry, crowded with companies that have a difficult time recruiting sales personnel. The type of selling, unattractive to many people, and the uncertainty of earning result in high sales force turnover rates. Experience has taught many of these companies that their best source of new salespeople is their own salespeople, so many (if not most) direct-selling companies offer bonuses (sometimes referred to as "bounties") for each new salesperson recruited.

Recruiting consultants. In many cities, independent firms operate as specialists in recruiting sales personnel for client firms. These consultants maintain contacts with diverse local organizations (for example, schools, churches, training specialists, salespersons' clubs, veterans' associations, and alumni associations) and have files identifying possible candidates for sales jobs. Some prescreen applicants through collecting personal histories, administering aptitude tests, and so on. Companies using recruiting consultants generally provide the appropriate job descriptions and job specifications. Sometimes, recruiting consultants are referred to as "headhunters," though this usually implies that the consultant has been commissioned to locate top-ranking executives.

Indirect Recruiting

City newspapers carry numerous advertisements publicizing openings for sales personnel. Such advertisements appear both in classified (want-ad) sections and as display advertising. So great is the number of prospective job candidates reached by a single advertisement that companies often try to reduce the volume of applications. If the employer publishes details about the company and job, fewer obviously unqualified persons will reply. Specific job details vary with the company and its situations, and these should be in the ad if it is to attract good applicants. Some ads give the compensation range of successful company sales personnel. Others explain that the person selected is to replace a regular salesperson in an established territory with active accounts. Still others specify that only highly qualified professional salespeople need apply. Information of this sort helps to convince promising applicants that the opening is legitimate.

Most sales managers favor open over blind advertisements, although mixed practice exists. An open advertisement reveals the company identity; a blind advertisement hides company identity behind a "box number, c/o this publication." The company name, if well known and respected, should be prominently featured to attract the best applicants.

Location of the advertisement in the publication is important. Newspaper advertisements on sports or financial pages are usually more productive but cost more per insertion than those in classified sections. Display ads on a sports page, for example, not only attract unemployed persons looking for work but employed ones who are not in the job market but who can be attracted by better jobs.

When direct-to-consumer sales organizations fail to recruit sufficient sales personnel through offering bonuses to their present salespeople, they generally use direct-mail recruiting, the mailing list often consisting of the names of former company sales personnel or names purchased from mailing list companies selling mailing lists. In addition, help wanted ads are placed in local newspapers or in publications such as *Specialty Salesman.* As a last resort, direct-selling companies, especially those with field supervisors, use cold canvass recruiting in open territories.

Recruiting Brochures

Some companies distribute brochures outlining sales career opportunities to applicants answering recruiting advertisements, as well as those contacted through such centers of influence as career counselors in educational institutions. Effective brochures are written from the viewpoint of the prospective sales recruit. Besides describing the company and its history, the brochure details the qualifications required for sales jobs, and the salesperson's duties, responsibilities, and advancement opportunities. Short write-ups on those who are and have been successful company salespeople are included. Effective brochures make liberal use of pictures, charts, diagrams, and other presentations—a few even give the telephone number of a "hot line" where the prospect can get more information.

CONCLUSION

Recruiting the right kind and the right number of sales personnel is an important responsibility of sales management. Recruiting sources need identifying, both those internal to the company and those external to it. Different selling styles influence both the sources of recruits and recruiting methods, because they call for individuals with varying types and amounts of education, other training, and experience. Personal recruiting is used for recruiting persons graduating from educational institutions and other recent graduates. Personal recruiting by present sales personnel is the main method of securing direct-to-consumer sales personnel, while personal recruiting by independent consultants is widespread in procuring new sales personnel in large metropolitan areas. Indirect recruiting, mainly through placement of advertisements in print media, is used to obtain replacement personnel when only one or a few individuals are needed and by direct-to-consumer sales organizations failing to recruit sufficient sales personnel through personal recruiting methods.

12 Selecting Sales Personnel

Selection systems for sales personnel range from simple one-step systems, consisting of nothing more than an informal personal interview, to complex multiple-step systems incorporating diverse mechanisms designed to gather information about applicants for sales jobs. A selection system is a set of successive "screens," at any of which an applicant may be dropped from further consideration. Figure 12.1 is an example—at any one of the seven steps in this system, a decision to drop the applicant may be made. Employment offers are extended to applicants surviving all seven steps. The order of use of the different screening mechanisms is related more to their helpfulness in terms of the information they secure than to the relative expense in using them.

Companies using multiple-step selection systems differ as to the number of steps and their order of inclusion. Each company designs its selection system to fit its own information needs and to meet its own budgetary limitations. A selection system fulfills its main mission if it improves management's ability to estimate success and failure probabilities. Management, in other words, because it has available the information gathered through the selection system, makes more accurate estimates of the chances that a particular applicant will succeed in a company sales position. As applicants "survive" through succeeding steps in the system, the additional increments of information enable increasingly accurate estimates of success and failure probabilities. Recognize, however, that no selection system is infallible; all eliminate some who would have succeeded and recommend hiring some who fail.

FIGURE 12.1 A Selection System

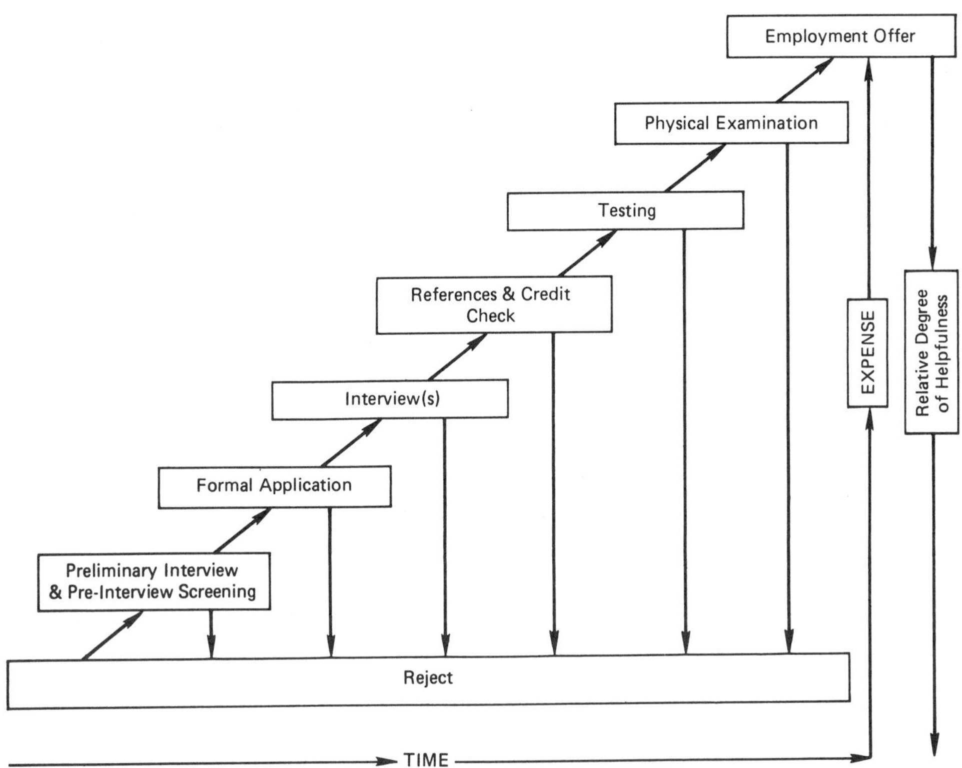

PREINTERVIEW SCREENING AND PRELIMINARY INTERVIEW

Preinterview screening is for the purpose of eliminating obviously unqualified applicants, thus saving the time of interviewers and applicants. The applicant is provided information about the company and general details about selling positions in it—a well-prepared recruiting brochure does this effectively and does not require an employee's time for anything other than to hand it to the applicant. Also most companies ask applicants to complete interview application forms, which obtain information on the applicant's basic qualifications, education, experience, health, and the like. No interview application form should be longer than two pages, and the applicant should be able to complete it in a few minutes. The interview application form fulfills its mission if it enables management to detect the presence or absence of predetermined minimum qualifications. Applicants not possessing these minimum qualifications do not receive appointments for interviews. The preliminary interview can be handled by a low-paid clerk or secretary, so this is generally the lowest-cost selection step.

The preliminary interview is short, perhaps no more than twenty minutes. Questions about the company and the job are answered while the company employee determines whether the applicant meets minimum qualifications. If this hurdle is passed and the applicant expresses interest, he or she is asked to fill out a formal application form, and an appointment is made for one or more formal interviews.

FORMAL APPLICATION FORM

The formal application form serves as a central record for all pertinent information collected during the selection process. A formal application is filled out after a preliminary interview indicates that a job candidate has promise as a company salesperson. The application form may be filled out by the applicant personally or by an interviewer who records the applicant's responses. In either case the completed formal application amounts to a standardized written interview, since most of the information that it contains could be obtained through personal interviews. Sometimes, sections are reserved for later recording of the results of such selection steps as reference and credit checks, testing, and physical examination. Figure 12.2 shows a widely used formal application form. Other standard forms from other sources are available. Ideally each company should prepare its own formal application form, since no two companies have the same information requirements—information significant for one may be useless for another. But if a company has only a small sales force, and recruits few people, the time and cost of preparing its own application form may warrant the choice of a standard form. Companies using standard forms ignore items inappropriate for them and obtain through interviewing needed additional information.

Certain items of information are always relevant to selection decisions, and these are assembled on the application form. Included are present job, dependents, education, employment status, time with last employer, membership in organizations, previous positions, records of earnings, reasons for leaving last job, net worth, living expenses, and length of job-hunting period.

Final decisions as to the items to include on the form should be based upon analysis of the existing sales force. The names of sales personnel should be arranged along a continuum, the best performer at one end and the worst performer at the other. This list is then divided into three or more parts, for example, good, average, and poor; if the sales force is large, finer subdivisions are justified. In measuring current qualifications, data are collected from sales records, supervisors' evaluations, and similar sources. The next step is to compare good and poor performers according to qualifications possessed by each at the time of hiring. This reveals any factors that differentiate the two groups, and these items should be included on the application form. The validity of this basis of evaluation depends upon the size of the individual groups, and no group should be smaller than thirty.

FIGURE 12.2 Application for Sales Position

APPLICATION FOR EMPLOYMENT—SALES

To the applicant: Thank you for your interest in our organization. Your application will receive consideration without regard to race, creed, color, sex, age, national origin or handicap. To enable us to properly and fairly evaluate your application, please answer all of the questions as carefully and completely as possible.

Do not write here

Personal Data

Name ______________________________

Address ______________________________

Telephone No.______________________ Soc.Sec.No.______________

In case of emergency, notify:

Name______________________________

Address______________________Telephone ______________

Position applied for:______________________________

Salary expected______________ When could you start? ______________

General Information

Previously employed here? _____Yes _____No. If so, what were the dates of your employment? From _________ to _________. Supervisor's name ______________

Your position ______________________________

Can you furnish proof of age, if necessary, to comply with legal restrictions? ________Yes ________No.

What prompted you to apply to our Company? ______________

Employment Record

Please provide information covering your employment history. Cover at least your last four jobs and at least the last 12 years. Include periods of military service, if any. Note any gaps in your employment. Begin with your most recent job and work back.

Current or most recent employer:

Name and address of Company	From		To		Starting Salary	Last Salary	Reason for Leaving	Name of Super.
	Mo.	Yr.	Mo.	Yr.				

In detail, describe your duties ______________________________

Tel. No._____ _____ _____

Type of business ______________________________

Name and address of Company	From		To		Starting Salary	Last Salary	Reason for Leaving	Name of Super.
	Mo.	Yr.	Mo.	Yr.				

In detail, describe your duties ____________________

Tel. No.____ ____ ____

Type of business ____________________

Name and address of Company	From		To		Starting Salary	Last Salary	Reason for Leaving	Name of Super.
	Mo.	Yr.	Mo.	Yr.				

In detail, describe your duties ____________________

Tel. No.____ ____ ____

Type of business ____________________

Name and address of Company	From		To		Starting Salary	Last Salary	Reason for Leaving	Name of Super.
	Mo.	Yr.	Mo.	Yr.				

In detail, describe your duties ____________________

Tel. No.____ ____ ____

Type of business ____________________

May we contact these employers? ______Yes ______No

List by name any previous employer you do not wish us to contact. ____________________

Is there anything further we should know about your employment history? Other jobs, skills, periods of unemployment, etc. ____

What specific kinds of selling experience have you had?

______Calling on the trade
______Retail (over the counter)
______Specialty (tangibles)
______Specialty (intangibles)
______ ____________________

______Delivery or route
______Missionary
______Technical
______"Big Ticket"

For each of the above where you had experience. List the firm, lines sold and amount of experience. ____________________

Education

Level	Name/city	Major field	Graduate?	Degree/certificate
Elementary				
High School				
College				
Bus Trade Technical				
Other				

Other activities: list past or present activities. Omit any organizations which reflect race, color, creed, sex, religion or national origin.

Type	Name/description	Active from	Active to	Offices/ dates	Still active?

Health

In the last five years, how much time have you lost from work due to health? ________________ When was your last physical examination? ____________ What was your physical condition? ________________________________

What is your present physical condition? ________________________________

Do you have any physical or mental conditions which might interfere with your ability to perform the job for which you have applied? _____ Yes _____ No. If so, please describe the condition ________________________________

____

If hired, would you be willing to take a physical examination at our expense? _____ Yes _____ No.

Personal References—do not list relatives or former employers

	Name	Address	Phone No.	Relationship
1				
2				
3				

Self-Assessment

What do you think are your greatest strengths as a salesperson?

____

____

____

What do you think are your greatest weaknesses as a salesperson?

____

____

____

What else could you tell us which might enable us to make a more accurate assessment of your qualifications to work for our Company? ____________________

____

____

____

Please read the completed application over carefully before signing it below.

The answers to the above questions are true and complete. I understand that any inaccurate or misleading information will cause rejection of this application or dismissal. I grant permission for the Company to investigate my references and I authorize my references to provide any information to the Company that they deem appropriate. I authorize the Company to make an investigative consumer report which may contain information obtained through personal interviews with my friends, neighbors and acquaintances. If made, this inquiry may include information as to my character, general reputation, personal characteristics and mode of living. I understand that I will have the right to make a written request within a reasonable period of time to receive additional information concerning the nature and scope of any investigative inquiry.

In consideration for my employment, I agree that my employment and compensation can be terminated with or without cause, and with or without notice, at any time at the option of either the Company or myself. Further, I understand that this agreement can only be modified by the Company President or Vice President, and only in writing.

Signature____________________ Date__________

Interview scheduled for____________________ at __________

Interview by____________________

Second interview _____ Yes _____ No

Scheduled for____________________ at____________________

Interview by____________________

Third interview _____ Yes _____ No

Scheduled for____________________ at____________________

Remarks____________________

____

____

SOURCE: Reproduced by permission of The Dartnell Corporation, Chicago, Ill. 60640. Further reproduction not permitted.

Objective Scoring of Personal History Items

The total profile, rather than any single item, determines the predictive value of personal history items. Considered singly, few items have value as selection factors, but individuals possessing all the personal history requirements are those most likely to succeed. However, many potentially successful salespeople do not possess all the requirements. One company found that most of its best salespeople were hired between the ages of thirty and thirty-five years, yet there were some as young as nineteen and as old as fifty-two. The significance of each personal factor is relative, not absolute. Although thirty to thirty-five may be the preferred age range, applicants outside this age range should receive consideration (since other factors may more than offset the fact that they are outside the desired age range).

Some firms with large sales forces establish objective measures for personal history items. A maximum possible score is assigned for each item, and the points assigned to a particular individual depend upon proximity to the ideal. In one firm fifteen personal history items are used as selection factors, at a maximum value of 10 points each. The maximum score is 150 points, and the cutoff is 100. Successful salespersons in this company all scored over 100 when hired, and the company automatically disqualifies all applicants with scores under 100.

The life insurance companies pioneered objective personal history scoring. Their sales forces were sufficiently large to permit establishment of trustworthy standards. The distortion of scores tends to increase in inverse proportion to the size of the sales force used for setting the standards. In line with requirements of the Civil Rights Act and the Age Discrimination in Employment Act, a company using objective personal history scoring must be prepared to prove empirically that the technique does not result in discrimination against applicants on the basis of race, color, religion, sex, national origin, or age. Further, they must prove that the scores above the cutoff point are predictive of or significantly correlated with important elements of work behavior that comprise or are relevent to the sales position for which applicants are evaluated. Effective sales executives use objective scoring of personal history items with caution, but they use "warning scores" to indicate the need for further investigation.

THE INTERVIEW

The interview is the most widely used selection step and in some companies it comprises the entire selection system. Some personnel experts criticize the interview as an unreliable tool, but it is an effective way to obtain certain information. No other method is quite so satisfactory in judging an individual as to ability in oral communication, personal appearance and manners, attitude toward selling and life in general, reaction to obstacles presented face to face, and personal impact upon others.

Good interviewers avoid covering the same ground as other selection devices. The interviewer reviews the completed application form before the interview and refrains from asking questions already answered. Perusal of the completed application indicates areas that require further questioning.

It is important to sell the applicant on the company, but there are more efficient ways of accomplishing this than through personal interviewing. One is by providing the applicant with a recruiting brochure. Another may be used when several applicants are to be interviewed consecutively, as in college recruiting: the interviewer meets with the whole group and describes general company policies. But it is still necessary to answer questions during interviews.

The job interview can be a trying experience for the applicant. Even for experienced salespersons accustomed to selling themselves and their products daily to strangers, the great importance attached to a job change and the unfamiliarity of the situation may cause nervousness. One way to relieve tension is for the interviewer to begin with questions on the person's family and educational background, subjects about which most people talk freely. One of the interviewer's tasks is to persuade the applicant that the firm is a desirable employer. Throughout the interview, pleasant rapport between interviewer and job applicant should be maintained.

Who Should Do the Interviewing?

The usual practice is for several persons to interview and evaluate each applicant. In large sales organizations, district or branch sales managers (or their assistants) handle the initial formal interview. Applicants surviving initial formal interviews are invited to the home office or—in a decentralized sales organization—to a regional office for subsequent interviews.

How Many Interviews?

The number of formal interviews varies with the selling style. One large steel company, which needs individuals to do highly specialized selling to important accounts, brings applicants to its home office for interviews by two assistant sales managers, the general sales manager, and the marketing vice-president—all four executives must approve a decision to hire an applicant. An office supply manufacturer that requires sales personnel for routine trade selling hires applicants after two interviews, one by a branch sales manager and one by an assistant branch sales manager.

Interviewing the Spouse

Many selling jobs involve frequent overnight travel. This leads some companies to require interviews with the applicant's spouse. For instance, if the spouse objects to having her or his mate out of town several days at a stretch, it seems unlikely that the applicant can succeed in a job requiring extended travel. An interview with a spouse need not be formal. Frequently, it amounts to nothing more than an impromptu dinner during which the executive can get a better idea of the spouse's attitude not only on travel but on other conditions inherent in the particular selling job.

Interviewing Techniques

Many companies provide specialized training for those doing interviewing. Scientifically designed rating scales and interview record forms help interviewers to guide discussions along productive lines. Interviews have become increasingly important sources of information about applicants and their reactions. The informal, unplanned interview has been giving way in most companies to newer techniques, some of which are described here.

1. *Patterned interview.* Here the interviewer uses a prepared outline of questions designed to elicit a basic core of information. A widely used patterned interview form for a sales position is shown in Figure 12.3. The interviewer may work directly from the outline, recording answers as they are given, but this may make the conversation stilted and the applicant nervous. Greater spontaneity results when the interviewer memorizes the outline and records the answers after the interview.
2. *Nondirective interview.* In this technique the applicant is encouraged to speak freely about his or her experience, training, and future plans. The interviewer asks few direct questions and says only enough to keep the interviewee talking. The nondirective interview does not provide answers to standard questions, and much time is spent on outwardly irrelevant subjects. Some personnel experts say that a nondirective technique yields maximum insight into an individual's attitudes and interests. Expert interpretation reveals much about the applicant—often including things of which the individual is not consciously aware. This technique's proponents claim that it is the best method for probing an individual's personality in depth. The main drawback is that administering the interview and interpreting the results demand specialized instruction.
3. *Interaction (stress) interview.* The interaction interview simulates the stresses the applicant would meet in actual selling and provides a way to observe the applicant's reactions to them. This interviewing technique has long been used by sales executives who, in interviewing prospective sales personnel, hand the applicant an ashtray or other object and say "Here, sell this to me." The objective is to see how the applicant reacts to the surprise situation and to size up selling ability.
   Interaction interviewing has become a more complex, and sophisticated, technique. In one version, two interviewers are required—one uses psychological techniques to set up the simulated situations, and the other, who is present but not an active participant in the interview observes and records the applicant's reactions. Because of their subtlety, the delicacy involved in their application, and the importance of expert

FIGURE 12.3 Patterned Interview Form—Sales Position

SALES APPLICANT INTERVIEW GUIDE

To the interviewer: This Applicant Interview Guide is designed and intended to assist you in selecting and placing sales personnel. When it is used for all applicants for an available position, it will help you judge among them and provide more objective information than you will obtain from unstructured interviews.

Because this is a general guide, not all of the questions may apply for each position. Skip those which do not apply and add any additional questions you believe to be necessary. Be sure to use the same questions for each applicant for the opening.

Federal law prohibits discrimination in employment on the basis of sex, race, color, national origin and, in most cases, age. The laws of most states also ban some or all of the above types of discrimination in employment, as well as discrimination based upon marital status, physical or mental handicap or disability, or ancestry. Interviewers should take care to avoid asking any questions which suggest that an employment decision based upon such factors may be made.

JOB INTERESTS

Name: ____________________

Position applied for: ____________________

What do you think the job involves? ____________________

Why do you think you are qualified for it? ____________________

____

What would your salary or earning requirement be? ____________________

What do you know about our Company? ____________________

____

Why are you interested in working for us? ____________________

CURRENT EMPLOYMENT STATUS

Are you currently employed? _____ Yes _____ No. If not, how long have you been out of work? ____________ What have you been doing? ____________ If employed, why are you applying for this position? ____________

____

When would you be available to begin work? ____________________

EMPLOYMENT EXPERIENCE

(Begin with the current or most recent position and work back in time. Account for all periods of time, for at least 12 years. Military service should be considered as employment.)

Current or last job:

Company name ____________________ Address/location ____________________

Starting date ____________ Date left ____________ Current or last job title ____________________

What are (were) the major duties of the job? (Be specific and complete)

____

____

____

Have you held the same job the entire time you have been with this Company? _____ Yes _____ No. If not, describe the various jobs you held, the dates of each and the duties of each of the jobs: ____

____

____

____

____

What was your starting salary? __________ What are you currently earning? __________ How much of that is salary? ______

Bonus _______ Commission _______ Other _______ Comments: ____

____

Name of your current or last supervisor: ____

May we contact him/her? _____ Yes _____ No.

What did you like most about this job? ____

____

What did you dislike most about it? ____

____

How well do you think you did on that job? How do you think your work compared with that of others in the same or similar work with that Company? ____

____

____

(If the applicant indicates that he or she did not do very well:) Why do you think you were not more successful? What accounted for that? ____

____

____

(If still employed) Why do you want to leave your current job? (If not still employed) Why did you leave that job? __________

____

____

Job before the current or last one:

Company name: ______________________________ Address/location ______________________

Started ____________ Left ____________ Last job title ______________________________

Duties of your job at the time you left: (Be specific and complete) ______________________________

____

____

What were you earning when you left? ______________ Please break that down between salary __________, bonus __________,

commission __________ and any other forms of compensation __________ Comments: ________________________________

____

Who was your last supervisor? ____

May we contact him/her? _____Yes _____No.

What did you like most about that job?____

What did you like least about it?____

Did you have other jobs with that employer before the last one? _____Yes _____No. If so, describe them, their titles, dates, and your duties. ____

____

____

How well do you think you did with that Company? Relative to others doing the same or similar jobs, how did you do? _______

____

____

(If the applicant indicates that he/she did not do well, ask for a further explanation.)________________________

____

Why did you leave that Company? ____

____

Any other comments about that Company or your job with them? ______________________________

____

____

Job before that one:

Company name: ____ Address/location____________________

Started ______________ Left ______________ Last job title ________________________________

Duties of your job at the time you left: (Be specific and complete)____________________________

____

____

What were you earning when you left? ______________ Please break that down between salary __________, bonus __________,

commission __________ and any other forms of compensation __________ Comments: ________________________________

____

Who was your last supervisor? ____

May we contact him/her? _____Yes _____No.

What did you like most about that job?____

What did you like least about it? ______

Did you have other jobs with that employer before the last one? _____ Yes _____ No. If so, describe them, their titles, dates, and your duties. ______

______

______

How well do you think you did with that Company? Relative to others doing the same or similar jobs, how did you do? ______

______

______

(If the applicant indicates that he/she did not do well, ask for a further explanation.) ______

______

Why did you leave that Company? ______

______

Any other comments about that Company or your job with them? ______

______

______

Interviewer: If the total length of employment in the last three jobs is insufficient, use additional sheets to go back further.

If there were any gaps in the applicant's employment history:
There is a gap between your employment at ______ and your employment at ______
of ______ months. Can you explain this? ______
______ What were you doing during this period to support yourself? ______
______

SALES EXPERIENCE

What kinds of sales work have you done? When, where, and for how long?

______ Retail ______
______ Door to door ______
______ Delivery or route ______
______ Missionary ______
______ Technical ______
______ Specialty: Tangibles ______
______ Specialty: Intangibles ______
______ Big ticket ______
______ Other ______

How do you feel about selling to:

Consumers ______
Jobbers/wholesalers ______
Retailers ______
Industrial users ______
Government ______

Do you have experience in:
(If the answer is yes, ask for details)

	Yes	No	Comments
Starting new accounts	______	______	______
Display work	______	______	______
Product demonstrations	______	______	______
Negotiating prices	______	______	______
Telephone sales	______	______	______

What types of sales work do you enjoy most?____

____

____

What types of sales work do you like least?____

____

Have you traveled in previous jobs? _____Yes _____No. If yes, how much? ____________________

Did you like travelling? _____Yes _____No. Did travelling create any family problems? _____Yes _____No. Comments: _____

____

If the job you are interviewing the applicant for has travel, ask the applicant how he/she would feel about it.______________

____

If applicant has indicated that some prior travel caused family problems, ask how these will be handled if he/she gets this job.

____

EDUCATION

What is your highest level of education? ____________________________________

If it is a college or graduate degree, in what area?_____________________________

Name of college or university ____

What scholastic awards or prizes did you receive?_______________________________

What activities did you participate in? (Caution applicant to omit those which indicate religion, race, color, sex or national origin.)

____

Further educational or training activities which might be pertinent to this job: ____________________

____

HEALTH

The purpose of this section is to help determine if you have any health-related problems which might interfere with your ability to perform this job.

How is your general health? ______________ In recent years, have you had any health-related problems? _____Yes _____No.
If you have such problems, please describe them ____________________________________
How much time have you lost from work due to health in the last five years? ____________ Do you have any physical or mental conditions which might affect your ability to perform the job for which you have applied? _____Yes _____No. If so, describe the problem ______________________ Have you had a physical examination recently? _____Yes _____No. When was your last physical? ____________ If employed, would you be willing to take a physical at our expense? _____Yes _____No.

CITIZENSHIP

Are you a U.S. citizen? _____Yes _____No. If not, what kind of visa do you have? __________ Are you legally permitted to work? _____Yes _____No.

MISCELLANEOUS

What off-the-job activities do you enjoy?

_____Part-time job	_____Clubs	_____(other)___________
_____Athletics	_____Reading	____________________
_____Spectator sports	_____Youth work	

PERSONAL

What do you think are your strong points? ______________________________

____

____

What do you think are your weak points? ______________________________

____

Interviewer: If there are any discrepancies between the employment application or resume and the interview, try to clear them up at this point. Ask the applicant about them. ______________________________

____

____

Before the applicant leaves the interview, the interviewer should explain the job in more detail and generally discuss the Company, the work location and other factors which might affect the applicant's interest in pursuing the position further.

_____Job details discussed

Interviewer's initials_________

Interviewer's impressions:

Personal characteristics—rate 1 to 4, with 1 being the highest:

	1	2	3	4	Comments
Neatness, cleanliness					
Dress					
Poise, manner					
Speech					
Cooperation with interviewer					
Job-related characteristics:					
Experience					
Knowledge of job					
Interpersonal relationships					

Overall rating for the job:

_____Superior _____Above average (Well qualified) _____Average (Appears qualified) _____Marginal (Barely qual) _____Unsatisfactory

Comments or remarks ______________________________

____

Interviewer__________________________ date_____________

SOURCE: Reproduced by permission of The Dartnell Corporation, Chicago, Ill. 60640. Further reproduction not permitted.

interpretation, the newer kind of interaction interviews should be planned, administered, and interpreted by a trained psychologist.

4. *Rating scales.* One shortcoming of the personal interview is its tendency to lack objectivity, a defect that is reduced through rating scales. These are so constructed that interviewers' ratings are channeled into a limited choice of responses. In evaluating an applicant's general appearance, for instance, one much-used form forces an interviewer to choose one of five descriptive phrases: very neat, nicely dressed, presentable, untidy, slovenly. Experience indicates that this results in more comparable ratings of the same individual by different interviewers. One drawback of the rating scale is that its objectivity restricts precise description of many personal qualities. It is good practice to encourage interviewers to explain ratings in writing. Companies using rating scales as a technique for assessing job suitability must keep in mind—in accordance with the guidelines issued by the EEOC and OFCC—that they need empirical data to demonstrate that the technique is predictive of or significantly correlated with successful job performance and does not result in discrimination on the basis of race, color, religion, sex, or national origin.

REFERENCES

References provide information on the applicant not available from other sources. Some employers deny the value of references, saying that references hesitate to criticize personal friends, or ex-employees. But the experienced employer reads between the lines, and sees where, for example, the weak candidate is not praised.

Personal contact is the best way to obtain information from references, since facial expressions and voice intonations reveal a great deal, and most people are more frank orally than in writing. When a reference is located at a distance, a telephone call may substitute for personal contact. Solicitation of written recommendations is the weakest approach and should be a last resort.

Applicants tend to name as references those on whom they can rely to speak in their favor. In addition, there is a tendency for references to be biased in favor of an applicant. These tendencies are partially offset by contacting persons not listed as references but who know the applicant. These people often are excellent sources for candid appraisals and fall into four classifications:

1. *Present or former employers.* These have observed the applicant under actual work conditions. However, many sales executives do not approach a present employer without the applicant's permission.
2. *Former customers.* If applicants have selling experience, their former customers are in a position to assess sales ability. It is advisable to contact these individuals without the applicants' assistance. This helps to avoid those who are personal friends of applicants.
3. *Reputable citizens.* If references suggested by the applicant are used, it is best first to contact those who are reputable, well-known persons. Such

people do not stake their reputations on those in whom they have little confidence.

4. *Mutual acquaintances.* Those who know both the applicant and the employer may give frank evaluations. What is even more important is that the employer is able to judge the worth of such evaluations.

CREDIT CHECKS

Many companies run credit checks on applicants for sales positions. Credit files are compiled by local credit bureaus, and special credit reports are provided by such organizations as Dun & Bradstreet. When a heavy burden of personal debt is found, it may indicate financial worries interfering with productivity, or a motivating factor serving to spur productivity—to determine which requires further investigation.

In analyzing the credit report, the executive looks for the danger signals—chronic lateness in making payments, large debts outstanding for long periods, or a bankruptcy history—any of which signal the need for additional probing. Financial irresponsibility may or may not be indicative of irresponsibility in meeting job obligations. Information on all aspects of the applicant's behavior, nonfinancial as well as financial, needs considering.

PSYCHOLOGICAL TESTS

In recent years, more and more companies have tended either to abandon or to rely less upon psychological tests as an aid in making selection decisions. One reason is the difficulty in validating psychological tests and in securing the empirical data to prove that results are predictive of or significantly related to successful job performance, and further that test results are being used in ways that do not result in illegal discrimination. When used, psychological tests are one of the last steps in the selection system, because of their relatively high cost.

The task of validating tests is complicated because different sets of behaviors or attributes can lead to successful job performance. Because of this, separate validity studies should be performed, for instance, for different ethnic groups. The different cultural experience and exposure of each group affects the relationship of test scores to job performance criteria.

Results of certain tests may underestimate the true abilities of disadvantaged applicants and cause tests that are valid for the advantaged to be invalid for the disadvantaged. White sales personnel, for instance, may make effective use of certain selling techniques with white customers that are different from those that black sales personnel find effective with the same customers. Tests can predict aptitude for using these selling techniques, but these are appropriate only for white applicants if they have not been validated for black applicants.[1] In

[1]W. C. Byham and M. E. Spitzer, *The Law and Personnel Testing* (New York: American Management Association, 1971), pp. 128–29.

some situations differential validity is found, in others not. Research is required to determine whether or not differential validity exists, and both the EEOC and OFCC emphasize the need to validate test results separately for minority group members.

Validation of Tests[2]

Because of the need to prove that a test is related to job performance criteria and because of the possibility that differential validity exists for different groups, it is important to understand test validation. All but the first three illustrations relate to validity studies of separate ethnic groups, but the same approach is used for other validity studies, such as for different age groups or for males and females.

Figure 12.4 is a scattergram of test scores and job performance indices; each dot represents an individual's score on both the test and the job performance criterion. The dots cluster in an elliptical shape, with more in quadrants 1 and 3 than in 2 and 4. This indicates a valid test, since people with high scores tend to have higher performance scores. However, the fact that dots are present in quadrants 2 and 4 indicates that the relationship is not perfect and that prediction errors will occur. If quadrants 2 and 4 contained fewer dots, the distribution would be more elliptical and the validity would be higher.

FIGURE 12.4 Scattergram: Test Scores and Job Performance Indices Showing Direct Validity

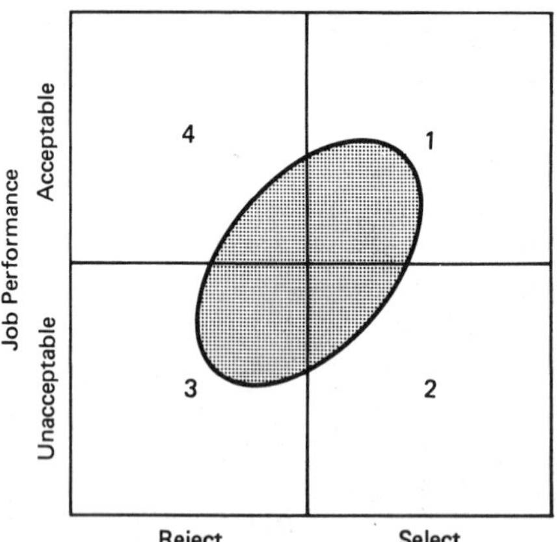

SOURCE: Adapted by permission of the publisher, from *The Law and Personnel Testing*, by William C. Byham and Morton E. Spitzer, pp. 31–40, © 1971 AMACOM, a division of American Management Association, New York. All rights reserved.

[2]Adapted by permission of the publisher, from *The Law and Personnel Testing*, by William C. Byham and Morton E. Spitzer, pp. 31–40, © 1971 AMACOM, a division of American Management Association, New York. All rights reserved. Byham and Spitzer credit Richard S. Barrett, City College of New York, for having provided the idea behind the types of illustrations.

Figure 12.5 also indicates a valid test because the dots are arranged in an elliptical shape. However, here there is an inverse relationship between test scores and job performance—persons with high test scores tend to have unacceptable job performance and those with low test scores tend to have acceptable job performance. In this case, the applicant with a low test score should be selected. In the situations illustrated in Figures 12.4 and 12.5, an applicant's test score is helpful in predicting job performance, but the direction of prediction is different.

If the cluster of dots is circular, as in Figure 12.6, the test has no validity. Regardless of how an individual scores, it is impossible to predict whether job performance will be acceptable or unacceptable. Use of this test for selection would lead to as many inaccurate as accurate predictions.

Next, consider some possible outcomes of studies of differential validity, that is, validity for different groups. Assume that a test has been given to a group of black and white applicants, with the results shown in Figure 12.7. The solid ellipse represents the test's validity for job performance for white applicants, and the dashed ellipse represents validity for black applicants. Black and white applicants do equally well on the test and performance measure, and the test is equally accurate in predicting the job performance of both black and white applicants. Consequently, the same selection instruments and selection standard can be used for both groups.

But what if the relationship of the test and the job performance criterion is as shown in Figure 12.8? The similarity of shapes indicates that the relationship between test scores and performance levels is about the same, but black appli-

FIGURE 12.5 Scattergram: Test Scores and Job Performance Indices Showing Inverse Validity

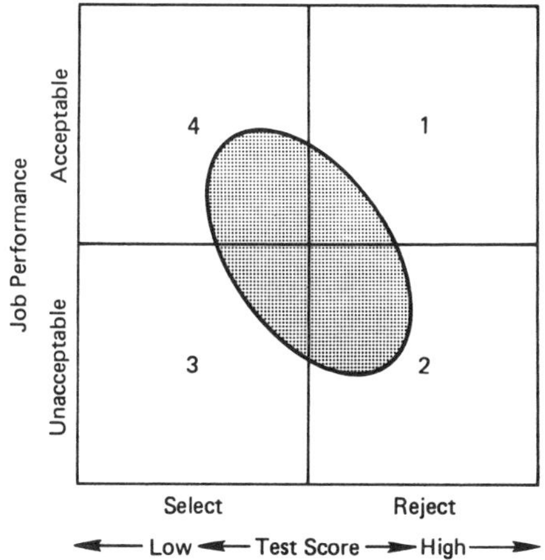

SOURCE: Adapted by permission of the publisher, from *The Law and Personnel Testing*, by William C. Byham and Morton E. Spitzer, pp. 31–40, © 1971 AMACOM, a division of American Management Association, New York. All rights reserved.

FIGURE 12.6 Scattergram: Test Scores and Job Performance Indices Showing No Validity

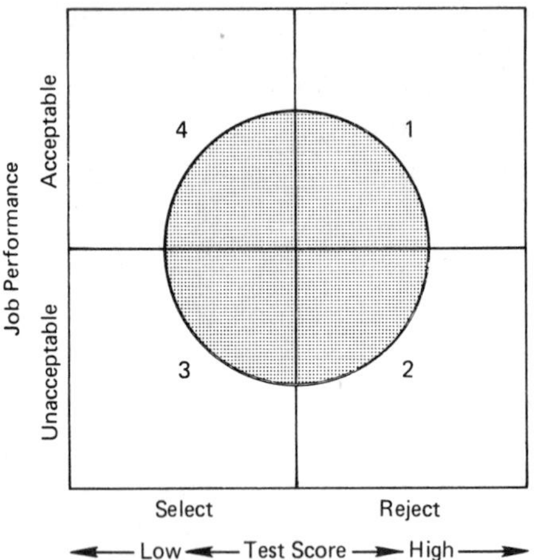

SOURCE: Adapted by permission of the publisher, from *The Law and Personnel Testing*, by William C. Byham and Morton E. Spitzer, pp. 31–40, © 1971 AMACOM, a division of American Management Association, New York. All rights reserved.

FIGURE 12.7 Scattergram Showing Equal Validity for Two Different Groups

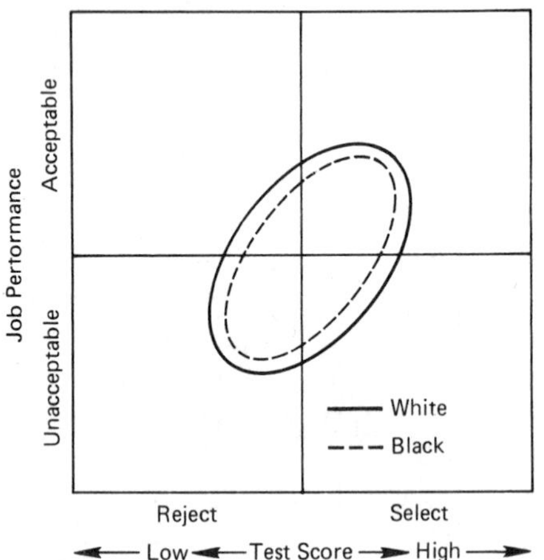

SOURCE: Adapted by permission of the publisher, from *The Law and Personnel Testing*, by William C. Byham and Morton E. Spitzer, pp. 31–40, © 1971 AMACOM, a division of American Management Association, New York. All rights reserved.

FIGURE 12.8 Scattergram Showing Differential Validity for Two Different Groups

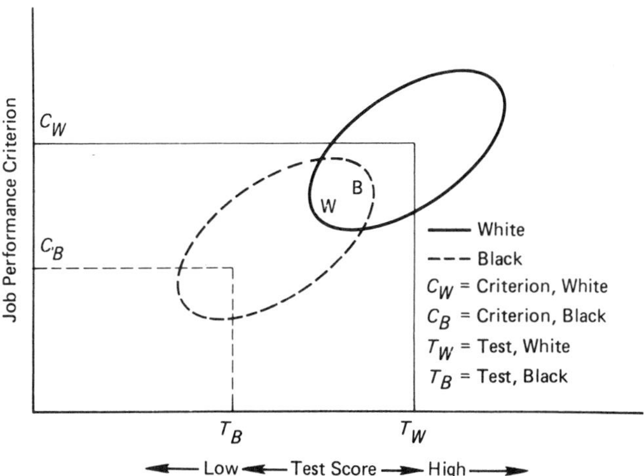

SOURCE: Adapted by permission of the publisher, from *The Law and Personnel Testing*, by William C. Byham and Morton E. Spitzer, pp. 31–40, © 1971 AMACOM, a division of American Management Association, New York. All rights reserved.

cants generally score lower on the test (T_B) and perform more poorly on the criterion (C_B). Evidently, in this situation the factors that depress test performance also depress job performance. Here a selection standard can be used that is not unfair or illegally discriminating. Blacks do poorer on what the organization regards as an important measure of job performance, and this is sufficient justification to hire a disproportionate number of them. But the legal requirement is that the hiring decision must be based on the test score, not on whether the applicant is black or white. When, for instance, a white and a black applicant are being considered for a job and the black's test score is higher than the white's, as indicated by the letters *B* and *W* in Figure 12.8, the black should be hired. Furthermore, the EEOC and OFCC require evidence that the measure of job performance is appropriate to the organization and is itself not subject to racial bias. These two agencies also want proof that some other factor, such as length of service, is not significant in producing the difference in job performance between black and white employees.

Figure 12.9 shows another possible relationship of test scores to a job performance criterion. The similarity of shapes indicates that the test is equally valid and predictive for both whites and blacks. Blacks as a group attain lower average test scores than do whites (T_B is less that T_W), but they achieve on the average the same level of performance (C_B equals C_W). If selection standards for all applicants are based on the test results obtained from the white group or from both groups combined, there is unfair discrimination against blacks. The fact that

FIGURE 12.9 Scattergram Showing Differential Validity for Two Different Groups

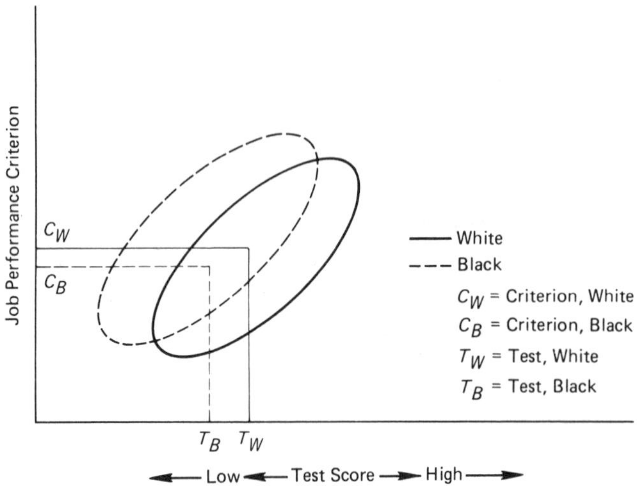

SOURCE: Adapted by permission of the publisher, from *The Law and Personnel Testing*, by William C. Byham and Morton E. Spitzer, pp. 31–40, © 1971 AMACOM, a division of American Management Association, New York. All rights reserved.

blacks, as a group, score lower on the test does not mean that they would have lower performance scores, so there is no reason to exclude a disproportionate number of black applicants.

If a differential validity study were not made and both groups were combined, the statistical estimate of validity would be reduced. In addition, fewer black applicants would be hired even though probabilities of success are equal to those of white applicants. That is the kind of practice that the EEOC and OFCC seek to prevent. Both agencies require data on the validity of the test for each group and data on average differences between the groups on the test *and* the job performance criterion. A company can use a test in these circumstances, but it must use the test differently—the test scores used as the selection standard (that is, the cutoff score) would have to be lower for the black group than for the white group. Of course, too, in a situation where whites scored lower on the test than did blacks, the whites would be subject to a lower selection standard than the blacks.

Now, consider a situation, as in Figure 12.10, in which a test is valid for one group but not for the other. The black and the white groups do equally well on the test and in job performance, but the test is valid only for the white group (as the scores of the black group form a circle). The test is usable as a selection instrument only for white applicants, since there is no evidence that the test predicts accurately the job performance of blacks. If an organization used this test to select from among all applicants, it would hire about the same proportion of ap-

FIGURE 12.10 Scattergram Showing Validity for One Group and No Validity for a Second Group

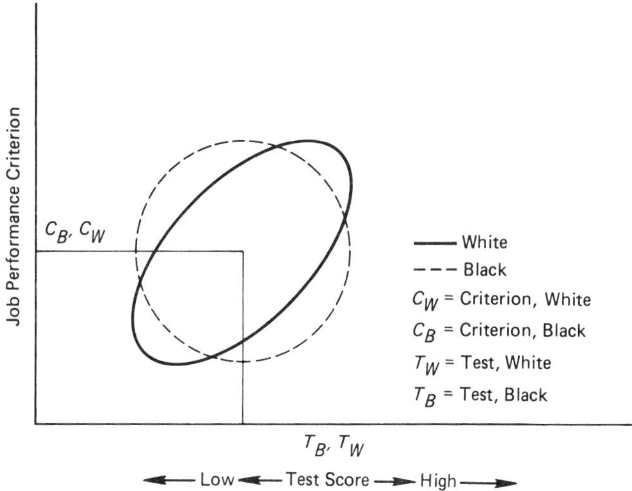

SOURCE: Adapted by permission of the publisher, from *The Law and Personnel Testing*, by William C. Byham and Morton E. Spitzer, pp. 31–40, © 1971 AMACOM, a division of American Management Association, New York. All rights reserved.

plicants from both ethnic groups. But a larger proportion of whites than of blacks would succeed on the job. When this type of differential validity exists, an employer should develop or seek other procedures that are valid for black applicants.

Evaluating psychological tests for selection purposes, then, requires considerable sophistication. There is a possibility that a test has differential validity, and the objectivity of tests leads many users to expect more validity and reliability in predicting selling success than the tests can offer. Some widely used tests are almost worthless for selection purposes, simply because they were designed for entirely different purposes; others are of questionable value even for measuring what they were intended to measure. More than a few testing "failures" are on the market, are even promoted and recommended by the publishers, and are used by executives unaware of the limitations. In addition, tests favor conformity rather than individual dynamics—they tend to rule out creative thinkers and imaginative, aggressive individuals who might be ideal for the job being filled.

Nevertheless, useful and reliable tests are available, and certain basically weak tests can serve as screening devices as long as their limitations are recognized. But it is important to determine whether or not differential validity exists. It is advisable for test users to employ a psychological testing specialist for purposes of selecting, administering, and interpreting tests.

Basis for Evaluation of Tests

Earlier discussion emphasized the importance of a test having validity—that it measures what it purports to measure—and of detecting whether or not differential validity exists. But even where statistical validity has been demonstrated, a test may not be valid in a particular instance. For example, a written intelligence test in English is not a valid measure of the *mental ability* of a Spanish-speaking person with an English language handicap. A low score does not necessarily indicate low intelligence; it may merely reflect poor understanding of English.

Test reliability is important. Reliability refers to the consistency of test results. If a test has reliability, an individual receives approximately the same score in subsequent retesting with the same or equivalent tests.

Test objectivity is important. If a test has objectivity, the scorer's opinion does not enter into the test results. Whenever a person giving or scoring the test can affect the test results, it is misleading to compare the results obtained by different testers.

Other criteria for evaluating tests are cost, time, and ease of administration. Wide variation in cost exists, and even small differentials are important if tests are given to large groups. There is little relationship between cost and quality, so it is sometimes possible to obtain quality tests at low cost. There is, similarly, wide variation in the time required to administer and score tests. Because time frequently is crucial in selection of sales personnel, the employer balances the time requirements of alternative tests against their relative merits. If the best available test consumes more time than can be spared, a mediocre test that can be given quickly may provide more effective screening than no test at all. Some tests can be administered and scored only by experts; others can be given and scored by persons with no special training. Employers balance the gains associated with more complex test against their costs in time and money.

Types of Tests

Three types of psychological tests are used in selection systems for sales personnel: tests of ability, of habitual characteristics, and of achievement. Tests of ability measure how well a person can perform particular tasks with maximum motivation (tests of best performance). Tests of habitual characteristics gauge how prospective employees act in their daily work normally (tests of typical performance). Achievement tests measure how much individuals have learned from their experience, training, or education.

Tests of ability. Tests of ability include tests of mental ability (intelligence tests) and tests of special abilities (aptitude tests). Tests of mental ability, or intelligence tests, are used in a wide range of applications and have higher validity and reliability than most psychological tests. However, they measure primarily abilities that make for success in educational or training situations, namely, language usage and comprehension, and abstract reasoning or problem-solving ability. They do not measure creativeness, originality, or insight. They are measures of mental aptitude, not of general intelligence. Because tests of mental ability are timed tests, they indicate an applicant's ability to learn quickly and to arrive at accurate answers under pressure.

Where there is no other evidence of ability, such as graduation from college, the test of mental ability serves as a screen to eliminate applicants falling below a predetermined level. A wide variety of mental ability tests is available.

Certain tests measure special abilities or aptitudes, such as spatial and perceptual abilities, speed and reaction time, steadiness and controlled movement, mechanical comprehension, and artistic abilities. Aptitude tests used individually aid in making selection for some industrial jobs, as illustrated, by the use of perception tests in selecting clerical personnel. But because selling requires diverse aptitudes, and sales job specifications differ even among competing companies, an especially designed battery of aptitude tests is needed for sales personnel.

The procedure for developing a battery of sales aptitude tests is straightforward. The test expert begins with the job specifications (derived, as you will recall, from the job description), checking them to assure that the abilities required for job performance are correctly identified. Then the expert selects existing tests and/or constructs new tests to measure each aptitude. Finally, the test expert develops a scheme for weighting and combining the scores of individual tests. Preparing—and later validating—a battery of tests is time consuming and costly, and calls for a psychologist's services. Only companies processing large numbers of sales job applicants can afford specially developed tests of sales aptitude. Tests not custom tailored for a particular sales job frequently have little validity, so companies with small sales forces find it impractical to include batteries of sales aptitude tests in their selection systems.

Empathy and ego drive are essential in good salespeople. Empathy is the ability to feel as others do, to put oneself in another person's shoes. The empathetic salesperson senses the reactions of customers and adjusts to these reactions. Ego drive makes the salesperson want to make the sale in a personal way. The salesperson's self-picture improves by virtue of conquest and diminishes with failure. The good salesperson has a proper balance between empathy and ego drive.

Tests of habitual characteristics. These include attitude, personality, and interest tests. Attitude tests are more appropriate as morale-measuring techniques than as selection aids. They ascertain employees' feelings toward working conditions, pay, advancement opportunities, and the like. Used as sales personnel selection devices, they identify abnormal attitudes on such broad subjects as big business, labor unions, and government. Their validity is questionable, since people often profess socially acceptable attitudes they do not actually have. Attitude tests do not measure the intensity with which particular attitudes are held.

Personality tests initially were used to identify people with psychotic tendencies—and certain tests are useful for this purpose. Subsequently, some have been used for measuring personality traits in normal individuals, for which purpose they have little or no validity or reliability. The basic limitation is the lack of uniform definitions for such traits as initiative or aggressiveness. The chief use of the personality test is as a screening device to identify persons with abnormal personalities.

Projective tests, of which the Rorschach is the best known, are a technique for personality measurement. However, they must be administered by skilled testers, and their results represent a subjective opinion rather than an objective measure. Further refinements of projective techniques eventually may provide useful personality measurements.

Interest tests. A basic assumption implicit in the use of interest tests is that a relationship exists between interest and motivation. Hence, if two persons have equal ability, the one with the greater interest in a particular job should be more successful in that job. A second implicit assumption is that interests are constant, that those of a person at age forty are the same as they were at twenty-one.

The interest test is useful for vocational guidance, but it is not a satisfactory selection device. This is because of the opportunity for faking responses—individuals may select answers overstating their interest in a particular field. Of two widely used interest tests, the Strong and the Kuder, the Strong uses the more indirect and subtle approach and is harder to fake, but because of its greater complexity, it is more expensive to score.

What proof is there that interest tests help in predicting selling success? Unfortunately, very little! Strong demonstrated that there is a positive but low correlation between interest scores and success in insurance selling. Significant variation has also been found in the interest test scores of successful and unsuccessful salespersons of accounting machines. Otherwise, there is little proof of the value of interest tests as devices for predicting selling success.

Achievement tests. Achievement tests seek to determine how much individuals know about a subject. Few standardized achievement tests are used by industry, because special job skills require different knowledge. Tests of clerical and stenographic ability are one exception, and civil service examinations are another. For the employer custom designing a test for sales applicants, achievement tests can assess the knowledge applicants possess in such areas as the product, marketing channels, and customer relations. However, as with other psychological tests, test designing is a job for an expert, not an amateur.

Conclusions on Testing

Besides the legal requirements that tests must not be used in ways that discriminate, there are other precautions to observe when incorporating psychological tests into a sales personnel selection system. It is essential to have accurate job specifications, derived from up-to-date and complete job descriptions. A qualified expert's services are required in selecting tests and in devising new ones when necessary, in determining test validity and in detecting differential validity, in administering the tests themselves, and in interpreting the results. Effective sales executives recognize that psychological testing, although capable of making a valuable contribution, is but one step in a selection system.

PHYSICAL EXAMINATIONS

Since good health is important to a salesperson's success, most companies require physical examinations. Because of the relatively high cost, the physical examination generally is one of the last steps. However, if physical condition is critical to job performance—such as the ability to carry a sales portfolio weighing 20 kilos—a physical examination is positioned early in the selection system. Even in companies requiring entrance physical examinations, poor health often accounts for some separations, but when the examinations are not compulsory, the number is higher.

CONCLUSION

Appropriate selection procedures, and their skillful execution, result in greater selling efficiency. A higher-grade salesperson is produced, and the advantages of having such employees make an impressive list—better work quality improved market coverage, superior customer relations, and a lower ratio of selling expense to sales. Good selection fits the right person to the right job, thereby increasing job satisfaction and reducing the cost of personnel turnover. Training costs are reduced, either because those hired are more capable of absorbing training or because they require less training.

The consequences of inappropriate selection policies are higher selling expenses. The misfit salesperson has a higher expense ratio because of lower sales, higher traveling costs, greater sales returns and adjustments, and inefficient distribution of working time. Because misfits rarely stay long with a company, the turnover rate rises along with hiring and training costs. Administrative costs go up, since low-grade salespeople require extra motivation and supervision. In short, the unsuccessful salesperson affects the profit picture adversely.

There are also hidden costs of poor selection, costs that cannot be expressed in terms of money. Customer relations deteriorate, as excessive turnover prevents establishment of close customer-salesperson relationships. Moreover, the effects of poor selection and resulting inadequate sales force performance spread to other departments. Costs rise throughout the business as work is disrupted in such departments as credit, accounting, advertising, and production.

13 Planning Sales Training Programs

The purpose of sales training is to achieve improved job performance. In the absence of training, job performance improves with experience. Training substitutes for, or supplements experience, so sales personnel given training reach high job performance levels earlier. In most companies, the rate of sales personnel turnover is higher for new personnel than for experienced people—often new sales personnel find themselves unprepared to perform their jobs satisfactorily, become discouraged, and leave the company. If sales training helps new sales personnel to perform their jobs satisfactorily, the rate of sales personnel turnover declines, recruitment and selection costs fall, and overall efficiency of the personal-selling operation climbs.

Considerable opportunity exists for improving sales force effectiveness through training. In most companies, training both new and experienced sales personnel is neglected. This is in marked contrast to the attention the majority of managements devote to developing reasonably effective systems for recruiting and selecting sales personnel. The existence of sophisticated recruiting and selection systems makes the opportunity for improving sales force effectiveness through training even greater. In other words, in most companies the marginal payoff from improvements in sales training exceed those from improvement in sales personnel recruiting and selection.

The overall efficiency of a company's personal-selling operation is influenced by the state of relations with customers and prospects. The sales force plays a crucial role in molding and maintaining these relations. Contrasted with inexperienced sales personnel, experienced sales personnel maintain better continuing relations with established accounts and make better impressions on prospects. Sales training contributes through accelerating (for the newly recruited sales personnel) the process of learning through experience.

The older generation of sales managers operated on the comfortable, albeit superficial, belief that good sales personnel are born, not made. Newly recruited sales personnel were given product descriptions, a territory, and an order book with instruction to "go out and sell!" These sales managers believed in "sink-or-swim" training and put new people into the field with scanty instructions and expected them to do their best, learning what they could in the hard school of experience.

Admittedly, then as now, there were and are some born or natural salespeople. But, given appropriate initial training, most recruits become productive sales personnel. Furthermore, continuing sales training improves job performances for both born and made sales personnel.

Modern sales executives, too, consider experience the most valuable road to improved job performance. But they also are convinced that sales training contributes to sales job performance. They regard training as a supplement to, not a total substitute for, experience.

BUILDING SALES TRAINING PROGRAMS

There are several types of sales training programs. The most comprehensive and longest is the training program for newly recruited sales personnel. More intensive and shorter programs on specialized topics, as well as periodic refresher courses (collectively known as continuing sales training), are presented for experienced sales personnel. In addition, many companies offer sales training programs for the sales personnel of their distributors and/or dealers. Some programs are designed to develop individuals as sales trainers (full or part time) or as junior-level sales executives (district or branch sales managers). Each type of program serves a different purpose, and its content reflects that purpose.

Building a sales training program requires five major decisions. The specific training aims must be defined, content decided, training methods selected, arrangements made for execution, and procedures set up to evaluate the results. Some sales training specialists refer to these decisions as the A-C-M-E-E decisions—aim, content, methods, execution, and evaluation.

DEFINING TRAINING AIMS

Regardless of the type of sales training program, defining its specific aims (the A in A-C-M-E-E) is the first step in its planning. Defining the general aim is not sufficient. Although, for example we may want to increase the sales force's productivity through training, we must identify what must be done to achieve increased productivity. General aims are translated into specific aims phrased in operational terms.

Specific aim definition begins with a review of general aims and the means currently employed to attain them. The process cannot be completed until sales management perceives the *training needs* from which specific training aims derive directly. Training needs, then, must be identified. The following discussion focuses on factors that management considers as it seeks to identify training needs for (1) initial sales training programs and (2) continuing sales training programs.

Identifying Initial Training Needs

Determining the need for, and specific aims of, an initial sales training program requires analysis of three main factors: job specifications, individual trainee's background and experience, and sales-related marketing policies.

Job specifications. The qualifications needed to perform the job are detailed in the job specifications. Few people possess all these qualifications at the time of hiring. The set of job specifications needs scrutinizing for clues to the points on which new personnel are most likely to need training. Other questions related to job performance need considering: How should salespeople apportion their time? Which duties require the greatest proportion of time? Which are neglected? Why? Which selling approaches are most effective? Answers to these and similar questions help in identifying specific training needs of newly recruited sales personnel.

Trainee's background and experience. Each individual enters an initial sales training program with a unique educational background and experience record. The gap between the qualifications in the job specifications and those a trainee already has represents the nature and amount of needed training. But it is not practical to adjust training precisely to individual differences. Time and money are saved by putting all recruits through identical programs. In some organizations, where training mechanisms are highly flexible, information about trainees' qualifications makes possible some tailoring of programs to individuals, increasing both trainee satisfaction and program efficiency. In all organizations, determining recruits' real training needs is essential to developing initial training programs of optimum benefit to company and trainee alike.

Sales-related marketing policies. To determine initial sales training needs, sales-related marketing policies must be analyzed. Differences in products and markets mean differences in selling practices and policies, which in turn, point to needed differences in training programs. For instance, selling a line of machine tools requires emphasis on product information and customer applications, whereas selling simple, nontechnical products demands emphasis on sales techniques. Differences in promotion, price, marketing channel, and physical distribution all have implications for initial sales training. In the case of promotion, for example, if advertising is not used or is used relatively little, sales training should prepare sales personnel to handle considerable promotional work, but if advertising is used extensively to supplement the sales force's efforts, new sales personnel need to learn how to coordinate their activities with advertising.

Identifying Continuing Training Needs

Determining the specific aims for a continuing sales training program requires identification of specific training needs of experienced sales personnel. Basic changes in products and markets give rise to needs for training, as do changes in company sales-related marketing policies, procedures, and organization. But even though products and markets change little and company policies, procedures, and organizations remain stable, sales personnel change, in some respects for the worse (as they develop, for example, careless or sloppy working habits).

Sales management must know a great deal about how sales personnel per-

FIGURE 13.1 Chart Useful in Assessing Nature of Training Needs for an Individual Salesperson

Date ____________19______

TRAINING STATUS CHART

Name of Salesperson ________________________ Name of Evaluator ______________

1 Key Elements of the job	2 Knows this, and needs no training	3 Knows this, but does not do it	4 Knows this, tries to do it	5 Does not know this, so does not do it	6 Training to be conducted by				
					Immediate Supervisor	Immediate Supervisor with help on how to do it	Training Specialist	Outside Program	
1)									
2)									
3)									
4)									
n)									

Note: Column 1 should list every key aspect of the job. In columns 2, 3, 4, and 5, check marks indicate the extent of training needed and column 6 indicates who is to conduct the needed training.

SOURCE: Suggested by Dr. Clyde E. Harris, Jr., Marketing Department, University of Georgia.

form to identify training needs and, in turn, to define specific aims. How does management gain this knowledge? Salespersons' reports are scrutinized for symptoms of needed training. Sales records are inspected to uncover performance weaknesses. Sales personnel are observed personally with a view toward detecting deficiences. And details contained in the sales job description are compared with the qualifications possessed by individual sales personnel. A clear picture is obtained by completing a chart similar to that in Figure 13.1 for each member of the sales force.

DECIDING TRAINING CONTENT

The content (the C in A-C-M-E-E) of a sales training program, whether an initial or continuing program, derives from the specific aims that management, after analyzing its training needs, formulates. Initial sales training programs are broader in scope and coverage than are continuing programs. Initial programs provide instruction covering all important aspects of performance of the salesperson's job; continuing programs concentrate on specific aspects of the job where experienced persons have deficiencies. Therefore, the following discussion relates to the content of initial sales training programs.

For an initial sales training program to contribute maximally toward preparing new sales personnel, it must cover all key aspects of the salesperson's job. Content varies from company to company, because of differences in products, markets, company policies, trainees' ability and experience, organizational size, and training philosophies. No two programs are, or should be, alike. However, different companies tend to cover the same general topics despite the fact that variations exist in exact content. Every initial sales training program should devote some time to each of four main areas: product data, sales technique, markets, and company information.

Product Data

Some product training is basic to any initial sales training program. Companies with technical products devote more than half their programs to product training. But in many situations, especially with standardized products sold routinely, new sales personnel require only minimal product training. In all cases, new salespeople must know enough about the products, their uses, and applications to serve customers' information needs. Product knowledge is basic to a salesperson's self-confidence and enthusiastic job performance.

Understanding product uses and applications is important. Trainees receive instruction on customers' problems and requirements and learn how company products can solve these problems and meet these requirements. Training provides them with full appreciation for buyer's viewpoints. New salespersons learn how to relate company products to the fulfillment of customers' requirements, thus equipping themselves for effective selling.

Many companies, especially those with technical products, include a period of initial sales training at the factory. Trainees observe and study the products during manufacturing and testing. They talk with or even work alongside factory personnel. The benefits are thorough product knowledge and increased confidence in demonstrating products to customers. Inordinate time, however, should not be devoted to technical production detail—such detail is important only insofar as it helps in actual selling.

Some training on competitors' products is desirable. Salespeople should know the important characteristics of competitors' products and their uses and applications. They should know the strengths and weaknesses of competitive products. Thus informed, salespersons gain a decided advantage. They can structure sales presentations to emphasize superior features of the company's products. Training on competitors' products must be continuous, the focus shifting as changes are made in both competitive and company products.

Sales Technique

Most new sales personnel need instruction in sales techniques. Some sales managers believe, however, that careful selection of sales personnel and product training are sufficient to ensure effective selling. They believe, in other words, that if an individual has an attractive personality, good appearance and voice, and reasonable intelligence and knows the product, he or she will sell it easily. But the predominant view is that new sales personnel need basic instruction in how to sell. This is reflected both in company sales training programs and in industrywide programs offered by such groups as the National Association of Food Manufacturers and the National Association of Machine Tool Builders.

Markets

The new salesperson must know who the customers are, their locations, the particular products in which they are interested, their buying habits and motives, and their financial condition. In other words, the salesperson needs to know not only who buys what but, more important, why and how they buy. When trainees are not given adequate instruction on the market, they take years to acquire the needed understanding. During this trial-and-error learning, through no fault of their own, productivity is low. In fact, left to their own devices, some trainees never gain important market information. For instance, a salesperson who is unaware of prospects' potentials as buyers may neglect completely to canvass them. Markets are always changing, so training in this area should be continuous, the content changing with market changes.

Company Information

Certain items of company information are essential to the salesperson on the job; others, not absolutely essential, contribute to overall effectiveness. The training program should include coverage of all sales-related marketing policies and the reasoning behind them. The sales person must know company pricing policy, for instance, to answer customers' questions. The salesperson needs to be fully informed on other policies, such as those relating to product services, spare parts and repairs, credit extension, and customer relations.

The initial training program must equip the salesperson to perform such tasks as recording and submitting customers' orders for processing and delivery, preparing expense and other reports, handling inquiries, following up on customers' requests, and so forth. Each firm develops its own systems and procedures. If trainees are to perform properly, the initial sales training program must provide the needed instruction. Otherwise, company systems and procedures are learned, if at all, through trial and error.

The sales department's personnel policies should be explained in the initial sales training program. Coverage should include selection procedures, training programs, compensation and incentive systems, advancement requirements and opportunities, savings and retirement plans, medical and insurance plans, and the like. Having this information contributes to employee morale and job effectiveness. Not having it shows up in employee uncertainty and excessive sales personnel turnover rates.

Contributing to the building of morale is "general company information." This concerns the company's history, its importance in the industry and economy, and its relations with stockholders, unions, competitors, government, and other groups. Knowing something about the personality, or image, of the company bolsters the recruits' confidence in its products, which they will shortly be selling.

It is worthwhile to provide formal training on general company information. But a common failing is that too much time is spent on company background, history, and prestige building. The challege is to provide sufficient general company information, but not to allocate instructional time disproportionate to its importance.

SELECTING TRAINING METHODS

The planners next select training methods (the M in A-C-M-E-E). There is a wide variety of methods, but the program content often limits those that are appropriate. If, for example, the content is a new policy on vacations and holidays, the training method almost certainly will be the lecture, supplemented, perhaps, with visual aids. In this instance, such methods as role playing and the demonstration would be ruled out. It is important to select those training methods that most effectively convey the desired content.

The Lecture

This ancient instructional method, in use before the invention of printing, is used extensively in sales training. Trainees mainly watch and listen, although some versions of lecturing permit questions. The lecture features passive, rather than active, trainee participation. Its main weakness is that teaching is emphasized more than learning. But a lecture can be effective, provided that the lecturer is able and enthusiastic and uses examples, demonstrations, and visual aids. Compared with other training methods, the lecture is economical in terms of time required to cover a given topic.

Many professional business teachers, perhaps most, regard lecturing as the least effective group instructional method. Professional sales trainers, by and large, agree. Estimates are that the average trainee can immediately recall less than 10 percent of what he or she hears in a lecture using visual aids. Furthermore, because of the absence of immediate participant feedback, no lecturer has any immediate or objective means for gauging the effectiveness of a lecture, but must rely on a personal appraisal of its reception, or on volunteered comments by participants.

Some lecturing in sales training is necessary. If initial sales training is brief, for instance, lecturing may be the only way to cover the desired content. It may be the only practical way to handle instruction when the training group is too large to permit constructive audience participation. Given longer training periods and smaller training groups, however, lecturing is most appropriate for introductory and orientation sessions and for providing summaries of major topics taught through methods such as case discussion and role playing. It is used, in continuing sales training programs for providing new information about the company, its policies, products, markets, and selling programs.

When using the lecture method, learning is improved through a multimedia approach. The room is equipped with two to six projectors and screens, and the entire lecture is projected visually on succeeding screens across the front of the room. Further support is provided by projecting illustrations, charts, and graphs and through sound effects. This version of the lecture increases attention, comprehension, and retention.

The Personal Conference

The potential of this method often goes unrecognized, because many people assume that learning occurs only in structured situations. However, learning occurs in structured and unstructured, formal and informal situations. In the personal conference, the trainer (often a sales executive or sales supervisor) and trainee jointly analyze problems, such as effective use of selling time, route planning and call scheduling, and handling unusual selling problems. Personal conferences are held in offices, restaurants, bars, motel rooms, and elsewhere. One version, the curbstone conference, takes place immediately after the trainee (accompanied by the trainer) has called upon a customer or prospect. The personal conference is an unstructured and informal method—it varies with the personalities of the trainer and the trainee and the topics discussed.

Demonstrations

The demonstration is appropriate for conveying information on such topics as new products and selling techniques. Demonstrating how a new product works and its uses is effective, much more so than lecturing on the same material. In initial sales training, demonstrating techniques to use in "closing sales" is more effective than is lecturing. Effective sales trainers use demonstrations to the maximum extent—since the beginning of time, showing has been more effective than telling! Demonstrations are generally used with other methods—they enliven an otherwise dull lecture, and they reinforce the interchange in a curbstone conference on, for instance, how to inform the next customer of an impending price increase.

Role Playing

This method has trainees acting out parts in contrived problem situations. The role-playing session begins with the trainer describing the situation and the different personalities involved. The trainer provides needed props, then designates trainees to play the salesperson, prospect, and other characters. Each plays his or her assigned role, and afterward, they, together with other group members and the trainer, appraise each player's effectiveness and suggest how the performance of each might have been improved.

In another version of role playing a training group is given information on, for example, a buyer's objection to a particular product and then is asked to extemporize a solution. Called a "sweat session," this provides individual trainees a chance to apply what they have learned. Post mortem critiques afford opportunities to reinforce what has been learned through participating in, or viewing, the role playing.

Role playing presents few problems, but there are some. Those playing roles must become actively and emotionally identified with the characters they portray; audience interest must be maintained throughout, even though spontaneous reactions are suppressed. Achieving these conditions is not easy. It is even more difficult when role players "ham it up" or when there is laughter or other involuntary audience reaction. Nonparticipants' comments should be saved for later, until role playing is completed, or during "cuts" called by the trainer. Note taking as the play unfolds distracts some players. This tendency, however, is overcome with repeated use of the method. These problems can be minimized by briefing trainees on what is and is not permissable, the group is limited to no more than ten or twelve, the trainer exercises discipline and control throughout, and role-playing assignments are realistic.

More than offsetting the problems are the many benefits of this training method. It provides realistic practice in applying what has been learned in other training or by experience. It is flexible and adapts to extreme diversity in role-playing situations. Role playing lends itself to training new personnel, experienced salespeople, or even mixed groups. Other benefits include the following:

1. Trainees learn to accept criticism from others, and the group soon recognizes that sound suggestions benefit everyone.
2. When a trainee criticizes another's performance, that individual has an incentive not to perform similarly later.
3. Role players practice introspection through participating in the appraisal of their own performances. Videotaping makes self-criticism even more beneficial and objective.
4. The free-wheeling nature of role playing is conducive to generating new ideas and approaches. Defects inherent in stereotyped solutions become apparent.
5. In role-playing sessions for mixed groups, junior people have a chance to learn valuable tricks, and experienced personnel are kept alert as a matter of personal pride.
6. Role players gain acting experience, which may help later in handling difficult selling situations.

Case Discussion

This method, originated by business educators as a partial substitute for learning by experience, is widely used in sales training. Write-ups of selling and other problems encountered on the job provide the bases for group discussion. Sometimes, the cases, particularly when they are long and complex, are assigned in advance—if this is the situation, then it is imperative that participants come prepared to the session—otherwise, valuable time is wasted in rehashing the situation. In most sales training situations, however, the cases used are short (one or two pages at most) and trainees are given ten or fifteen minutes to read them before group discussion starts. Each case either describes a real selling problem or is developed around a situation sufficiently real to stimulate emotional involvement by the trainees.

Trainees discussing a case should identify the issue(s), marshall the relevant facts, devise specific alternatives, and choose the one most appropriate. Most trainers believe that securing a thorough grasp of the problem situation is more essential to learning than the rapid production of solutions. To derive maximum benefit from case discussion, each session should conclude with the drawing of generalizations on lessons learned.

Impromptu Discussion

This method, sometimes called a sales seminar or buzz session, begins with the trainer, group leader, or some member of the sales force making a brief oral presentation on an everyday problem. General give-and-take discussion follows.

Group members gain an understanding of many problems that otherwise is acquired only through long personal experience. Many complexities and implications that might go undetected by individuals are revealed to all, and trainees learn a valuable lesson: fixed selling rules and principles are often less important than are analysis and handling of specific situations. Impromptu group discussion improves the salesperson's ability to handle problems.

Impromptu discussion differs from lecturing. The discussion leader assumes a less dominant role than the lecturer, trainees are active rather than passive participants, learning receives more emphasis than teaching, and the atmosphere is informal and relaxed. These are important advantages, and impromptu discussions are being increasingly used, chiefly in training programs for experienced sales personnel.

For maximum benefit from the impromptu discussion, certain conditions must be met. An effective leader or moderator is essential—otherwise, discussion drifts into extraneous subjects or becomes sterile. The discussion leader must command the trainees' respect, be skilled in dealing with people, and be well informed. The room arrangement is important—it helps in generating discussion, for instance, if all trainees can see each other. It is important, too, that someone draws conclusions at the close of the discussion.

Impromptu discussion requires considerable time. Most companies schedule sessions for at least a half-day or, more commonly, for a full day. If their aim is to maximize trainee learning of specific points in depth, the impromptu discussion—properly handled—is an effective training method.

Gaming

This method, also known as simulation, somewhat resembles role playing, uses highly structured contrived situations, based on reality, in which players assume decision-making roles through successive rounds of play. A unique feature is that players receive information feedback. In one game, for example, trainees play the roles of decision makers in customers' organizations, using data ordinarily available to make decisions on the timing and size of orders, managing sales forces and advertising efforts, and so on. The results of these decisions then are calculated by referees (using computers) and are fed back for the players to use in the next round of decisions.

Preparation of a game requires research to dig out the needed facts, the incorporation of these into a game model, development of detailed instructions for players and referees, and the writing of a computer program. Expertness and substantial investments in time and money, then, are required, but partially offsetting this is that, once prepared, a game may be used in many training programs.

Among the advantages of gaming are (1) participants learn easily because they involve themselves in game play; (2) players develop skill in identifying key factors influencing decisions; (3) games lend themselves readily to demonstrations of the uses and value of such analytical techniques as inventory and other planning models; and (4) games, with their built-in information feedback features, are effective in emphasizing the dynamic nature of problem situations and their interrelationships.

Among the limitations of gaming are (1) some minimum time is required for playing, usually three or four hours, to generate sufficient decision "rounds" to provide the desired learning experience; (2) since game designs are based on ordinary decision-making processes, their rules often prevent payoffs on unusual or novel approaches; and (3) players may learn some things that aren't so, a limitation applying especially to poorly designed games. These limitations are overcome through careful game design and administration.

On-the-Job Training

This method, also called the coach-and-pupil method, combines telling, showing, practicing, and evaluating. The coach, sometimes a professional sales trainer but more often a seasoned salesperson, begins by describing particular selling situations, explaining various techniques and approaches that might be used effectively. Next, accompanied by the pupil, the coach makes actual sales calls, discussing each with the trainee afterward. Then, under the coach's supervision, the trainee makes sales calls, each one being followed by discussion and appraisal. Gradually, the trainee works more and more on his or her own, but with continuing, although less frequent, coaching.

The instructional effectiveness of this method depends mainly upon the coach's qualifications. Given a qualified coach, the trainee starts off on the right foot, using appropriate selling techniques. Early deficiencies are corrected before they harden into habits. If, however, the coach is not qualified, the trainee learns the coach's bad habits as well as skills.

Many seasoned salespeople, otherwise qualified for coaching, are unwilling to spend the necessary time and effort. This is especially true when personnel are paid commissions on sales. The problem of recruiting coaches, nevertheless, is resolved through paying bonuses for each person coached, or "overriding" commissions on pupils' sales.

On-the-job training is an important part of most initial sales training programs. No more effective way exists for learning a job. This method is appropriate for developing trainees' skills in making sales presentations, answering objections, and closing sales. Training in these selling aspects requires practice, and this method provides expertly supervised practice.

Programmed Learning

This method breaks down subject matter into numbered instructional units called frames, which are incorporated into a book or microfilmed for use with a teaching machine. Each frame contains an explanation of a specific point, plus a question or problem for the trainee to use in testing his or her understanding. Trainees check answers by referring to another designated frame. If the answer is correct, the trainee is directed to new material; if it is incorrect, additional explanation is provided, and the trainee is retested on the point before going on to new material. Thus, trainees check their own progress as they work through the materials and move through them at their own speed. Companies using programmed instruction, however, regard formal examinations as necessary incentives for the trainees.

Programmed instructions has not been widely adopted for sales training. Most applications have been aimed at providing needed information. The Schering Corporation, for instance, provides programmed instruction on the clinical and pharmacological background of its drug products. This method is not used for training in sales techniques and market information because of difficulties in preparing appropriate programmed instructional materials. Preparation requires expert skills and thorough grounding in the psychology of learning.

Correspondence Courses

This method is used in both initial and continuing sales training. In the insurance field it is used to acquaint new salespeople with industry fundamentals and to instruct in basic sales techniques. Companies with highly technical products and small but widely deployed sales forces use correspondence courses to acquaint experienced salespeople with new product developments and applications. This method is used also to train noncompany sales personnel, such as distributors' salespersons, to improve their knowledge of the manufacturer's product line and selling techniques. Few companies use this training method exclusively.

Correspondence training is most appropriate as an interim training method when trainees are scattered geographically but are assembled periodically for lectures, seminars, role playing, and other instruction. Initial sales training, for example, might be by correspondence courses begun at different times and places; continuing, or follow-up, training might come later through group methods at a central location. Preparing a standardized correspondence course covering technical product data, general company information, selling techniques and markets presents few difficulties other than those of choosing, organizing, and writing up the material. In many companies, particularly in the insurance field, instructional materials are also taped for cassette players.

Successful use of the correspondence method requires administrative skill. The greatest problem is to motivate trainees to complete assignments on schedule. Not only are enrollees engaged in full-time work requiring that correspondence lessons be done after hours, but few have sufficient self-discipline to study without direct supervision. It is necessary to provide regular examinations, prizes for completing work on time, or other incentives. This method does not answer enrollees' questions; hence, successful users arrange for periodic face-to-face discussions. Similar problems are met in processing completed assignments, evaluating work, and correcting errors. Despite these administrative problems, correspondence instruction is a useful supplement to other sales training methods.

Group Versus Individual Training Methods

Of the ten training methods discussed, five are group methods, four are individual methods, and one can be either. Lecturing, role playing, case discussion, impromptu discussion, and gaming are group methods. The personal conference, on-the-job training, programmed learning, and correspondence course are individual methods. The demonstration is either a group or an individual method, depending on whether the audience is a group or an individual.

CONCLUSION

Three key decisions shape the nature of sales training programs. They are the A, C, and M decisions in A-C-M-E-E. Defining the aims is the first step in planning training, and this demands that sales management perceive the training needs, some of which groups of trainees share and others of which are unique to individual personnel. The decision on content derives from the aims, with initial training programs being more likely to feature content in the four main areas—product data, sales technique, markets, and company information—than continuing sales training programs, which focus upon specific job aspects where experienced personnel have room for improvement. The third decision—that on training methods—requires planners to select those that will most effectively and economically convey the desired content. The aim-content-methods decisions determine the essential formats of sales training programs and set the stage for other key decisions on program execution and evaluation (that is, the E-E in A-C-M-E-E).

14

Executing and Evaluating Sales Training Programs

Relating the A-C-M-E-E approach to sales training to Kipling's "six honest serving-men" brings the whole process into sharper perspective:

> I keep six honest serving-men
> (They taught me all I know);
> Their names are WHAT and WHY and WHEN
> and HOW and WHERE and WHO.
> —R. KIPLING, "The Elephant's Child," *Just-So Stories.*

Figure 14.1 shows the relationships. The aims, contents, and methods steps (A-C-M) are the why, what, and how, while the execution step (the first E) is the who, when, and where. The evaluation step (the second E) does not relate directly to the "six honest serving-men" but is the appraisal of results, that is, the extent to which the "whys" were accomplished. As indicated, evaluation requires comparison with program aims (note the feedback line).

The execution step (the first E) requires organizational decisions. Who will be the trainees? Who will do the training? When will the training take place? Where will the site of the training be? (Who, Who, When, and Where). The trainers—whether full time or on special assignment—must be notified, necessary travel reservations made, and living accommodations arranged. The "when" decision requires consideration of key time-related factors, and the "where" decision involves appraisal of factors bearing on the training site. In addition, instructional materials need preparing and training aids assembling. When these things are done, the stage is set for program execution.

Effective program execution depends upon instructional skills as well as

FIGURE 14.1 A-C-M-E-E Approach to Sales Training Related to Kipling's Six Honest Serving-Men

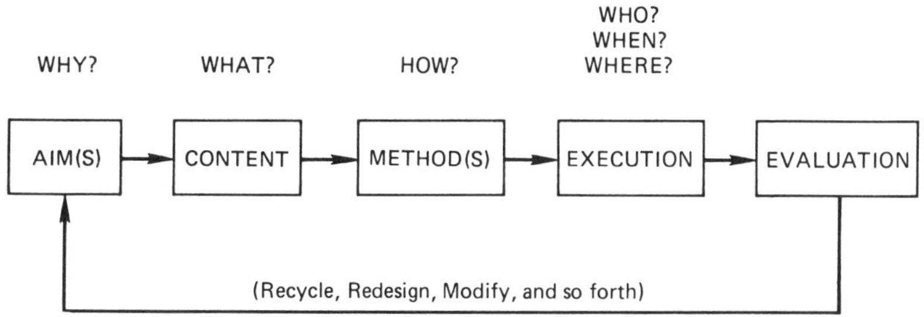

coordination of planning and housekeeping details. Program administration involves doing what can be done to produce a training atmosphere conducive to learning. Discussion in this chapter centers on (1) training philosophies, (2) organization for sales training, (3) timing of training programs, (4) their location, and (5) instructional materials and training aids.

PHILOSOPHIES OF SALES TRAINING

There are two philosophies of sales training, differentiated by the nature of the behavioral change they seek to bring about in trainees. The conditioned-response philosophy seeks to train sales personnel so that they will respond in standardized or programmed ways. The insight-response philosophy seeks to develop trainees' insight and analytical skills so that they respond appropriately, and in their own individualized ways. In a conditioned-response sales force, all individuals react in the same way to any given situation, while in an insight-response sales force, each person reacts in an individualized way.

Which philosophy is appropriate? The choice depends partly upon the predominant selling style the company expects its sales personnel to apply. If the predominant selling style is either trade or missionary, the conditioned-response philosophy is a natural choice—both the caliber of the persons in customers' organizations on whom calls are made and selling styles are low key, not requiring high-level technical training or ability, and programmed responses both conserve time and suffice for handling most situations. If the predominant selling style is either technical or new business, the insight-response philosophy is a natural choice—both of these selling styles are characterized by endless nonroutine situations, requiring either unusual knowledge (as in technical selling) or creativity and ingenuity (as in new business selling)—and appropriate responses need tailoring to highly individualized situations.

The choice of training philosophy is also influenced by other factors. If management regards the sales force as a source of future executive talent, then even if the predominant selling style is trade or missionary the insight-response philosophy is the more appropriate choice. The desired caliber of sales personnel generally is considerably higher than that required for performing rather routine job activities. The higher the caliber of sales personnel, the less likely it is that they will take kindly to conditioned-response training.

Similarly, the caliber of the persons in customers' organization upon whom calls are made influences the choice of training philosophy. If these are low-level people in low-level positions, conditioned-response training is the better choice. But if personnel in customers' organizations are high-level people in high-level jobs, insight-response training is the necessary choice.

How does sales training philosophy affect program planning, execution, and evaluation? Since *aims* will differ significantly, as will *content* and *methods*, planning is influenced. Training a new salesperson to sell housewares door to door (a field where sales personnel turnover rates are high) is most economically done according to conditioned-response philosophy—programmed responses to situations recurring with great frequency. Training a new salesperson to sell housewares to high-ranking buyers in supermarket chains, in contrast, calls for insight-response training. Thus, the aims are different, which, in turn, causes differences in training content and methods. The major portion of the execution phase (that is, the who, when, and where) influenced is the who—who will be the trainees—insight-response philosophy requires trainees of higher caliber than is true of conditioned-response philosophy. The part of execution consisting of the preparation of instructional materials and training aids is strongly affected—the conditioned-response philosophy requiring materials and aids designed to facilitate memorizing programmed responses while insight-response philosophy puts more emphasis upon materials and aids conducive to development of analytical skills and internalizing of responses.

The conditioned-response philosophy simplifies evaluation, if it consists mainly of determining the extent of accomplishment of training aims. Have the trainees learned the standardized responses? Among the ways of determining this are through written or oral tests, observing sales personnel on the job, and quizzing customers. By contrast, measuring the acquisition of insight and analytical skills (the general aim of insight-response philosophy) cannot be done precisely but are judgment evaluations. The results of conditioned-response training are measured objectively, those of insight-response training are appraised subjectively. For instance, a multiple choice test suffices to measure conditioned-response training, while an essay test is required to measure insight-response training.

ORGANIZATION FOR SALES TRAINING

The execution step of A-C-M-E-E (the first E) requires four key organizational decisions: (1) Who will be the trainees? (2) Who will do the training? (3) When will the training take place? (4) Where will the training site be?

Who Will Be the Trainees?

Identifying trainees is more complex for continuing than for initial sales training programs. A company identifies the trainees for its initial sales training program when it firms up sales job descriptions and hires sales job applicants. While continuing sales training programs are prescribed for all personnel in some companies, the general practice is to select trainees according to some criterion. Four criteria are in common use: (1) reward for good performance, (2) punishment for poor performance, (3) convenience (of trainee and trainer), and (4) seniority (the greater the seniority, the greater the opportunity for added training). Those selected for continuing training should be aware of the criterion used.

Who Will Do the Training?

Initial sales training. Initial sales training is a line function in some companies, a staff function in others. If a line function, responsibility for initial training is assigned to the top sales executive. If a staff function, responsibility for initial training is given to the personnel director, and sales management has an advisory role. Actually both executives should participate in initial sales training—the sales executives because of selling expertise and the personnel director because of training expertise.

How a particular company should decide placement of responsibility depends upon comparative costs. If much initial training of new sales personnel parallels that for other new employees, cost considerations cause the personnel director to have primary responsibility. If little of the initial sales training parallels other new employee training, the sales executive has primary responsibility.

Continuing sales training. Responsibility for continuing sales training resides with the top sales executive. Introduction of new products, adoption of revised sales policies, perfection of improved selling techniques, and similar developments call for training. The top sales executive is in the best position to recognize the need and design and execute appropriate sales training programs. Sales training is a never-ending process, and, regardless of who is responsible for initial training, the sales executive has continuing responsibility.

Sales training staff. Top sales executives usually delegate sales training performance to subordinates. Large sales organizations often have a sales training director, reporting to the top sales executive. The director conducts some training and coordinates that given on a decentralized (and usually part-time) basis by regional and district sales managers. In smaller organizations, some top sales executives handle some training themselves, but, in most cases, they rely upon others, such as assistant sales managers or district managers, to do the training. Companies without sales training directors often have full-time or part-time sales trainers, or both. The large sales organization makes efficient use of a full-time sales training director and sometimes even a full-time staff, but the small organization must rely on executives to train in addition to other duties. Because of specialized knowledge requirements, the tendency is for companies to train their own sales trainers rather than to recruit outsiders.

Training the sales trainers. No training program, however carefully designed, is more effective than the people conducting it. Consequently, many companies have a training program for sales trainers. The starting point is to identify the subjects that trainers should know thoroughly: the company and its policies, the products, the customers, and their problems, the salesperson's job, and sales techniques. If trainers are not experienced salespeople they are given field selling experience. Subjects presented formally should be handled by personnel already skilled as trainers, using the instructional techniques the trainers will use later.

Not only should sales trainers have expert and specialized knowledge, they must be effective teachers. Throughout their period of preparation, the theory and mechanics of teaching (and learning) are stressed. Trainers are required to master these, learn how to apply them effectively, preferably through doing practice training themselves. They also learn to plan and organize teaching materials for clear and effective presentation. Formal training alone does not prepare an individual for effective teaching, but a well-planned and well-executed program for sales trainers helps. For the most part, however, sales trainers develop their own teaching skills. To emphasize this point, management reminds them that

> If the trainee hasn't learned,
> the trainer hasn't taught.

Outside experts. Many companies hire outside experts to conduct portions of sales training programs, generally portions relating to sales techniques. Numerous outside training consultants present sessions on sales techniques (for instance, in prospecting, selling by telephone, or basic ways to meet objections) and, through broad and long experience, achieve high effectiveness. Other outside experts, including university professors and similar "moonlighters," also offer this instructional service. For the most part, outside experts are true professionals charging substantial fees, but when spread over several participants these fees are reasonable enough—a \$1,000 fee for two hours of instruction on sales techniques before a group of twenty amounts to only \$50 per trainee. The outside experts are under pressure to put on a good show; thus they provide something out of the ordinary, helping to maximize program benefits.

When Will the Training Take Place?

Timing group versus individual training. Opinion is divided as to the proper timing of group and individual training. Most sales executives contend that newly recruited trainees should receive formal group training before starting to sell. A sizable minority, however, assign trainees to selling jobs before sending them on to sales schools. In support of the minority view, three things can be said: (1) new personnel prove that they can sell before money is spent on their training; (2) new persons are not always, not even usually, hired in groups large enough to justify immediate formal training—people hired between programs can be put to work until the next school begins; and (3) on-the-job experience furnishes needed learning motivation and makes initial training more meaningful. The minority position, nevertheless, is inappropriate when highly technical products are sold to sophisticated buyers. In such cases, product training is not only important but is best provided through formal group instruction at the outset of trainees' careers.

When there are large numbers of new personnel, group training is the way to train at the lowest cost per person. In planning the curriculum and the sales school, however, management determines the content that should be taught in the field—group training is more effective when supplemented by individualized field training. To minimize overlap, and to maximize training results, there must be an integration of what is taught by group methods in sales schools: product data, company information, market information, and the theoretical and practical fundamentals of selling. Practical training in sales technique is best handled individually, in the field.

Individualized training is conducted in the field office or in the trainee's home. On-the-job training features personal conferences (of the trainer and trainee) and demonstrations (as the trainer explains "this is how to do it"). But not all field training is on-the-job training. In many companies, for example, trainees in the field are enrolled in correspondence and programmed learning courses. Both types of field training are supervised—on-the-job training by a supervisor in person and trainees participating in correspondence and programmed learning courses by mail, phone, or cassette correspondence (convenient for playing in the auto in between calls on customers).

Timing initial sales training programs. Timing of initial sales training depends upon the number of new personnel trained each year, and this, in turn, depends upon the size of the sales force, sales personnel turnover, and management's plans for changing sales force size. With a large number of new personnel, comprehensive highly structured programs are scheduled several times a year, dates being set after consideration of recruiting quotas and deadlines. When the number is small, initial training programs, if held at all, are infrequent. One company with a small sales force recruiting June college graduates schedules initial sales training to begin in late June or early July.

There is an optimum number of trainees who are effectively trained, in an initial sales training program. It depends upon training aims, content, methods, and the amount and availability of training talent. Individualized training is indicated in some situations; although it is expensive per individual trained, its timing can be flexible, depending only upon availability of trainees and trainers. In most situations, limitations of training funds and talent dictate training recruits in groups, programs being scheduled whenever the backlog of untrained people approximates the optimum. How large is an optimum-sized training group? Experience indicates that groups smaller than twelve to fifteen involve inordinately high costs, while those larger than thirty to forty incur heavy losses in training (that is, learning) effectiveness.

Timing continuing sales training programs. Effective sales management believes that training and learning must be continuous—new information must be assimilated and older concepts modified in the light of new developments. New products, new refinements of selling techniques, new product applications and uses, new customer problems, new selling aids, new selling suggestions—all these and other developments require that each salesperson's training continue as long as he or she is on the job. In some situations, sales personnel are kept abreast of new developments informally, perhaps through field distribution of information bulletins. But when new developments accumulate, are unusually important, or imply a need for substantial changes in salespersons' attitudes and behavior patterns, a formal retraining program is scheduled. Many companies integrate retraining programs into a series of sales meetings or a single sales convention.

Some but not all salespersons in any sales force have deficiencies that are correctable through training. If weaknesses lie in different areas, the practical and economical solution is on-the-job coaching. If several people are weak in the same area(s), it is both practical and economical to use group instructional methods in an organized formal program (often scheduled for an off-peak selling period).

Even when sales management has no clear indication of the need, regular scheduling of retraining programs is advisable. A survey of nearly 500 purchasing agents revealed that 60 percent felt that the majority of salespeople calling on them either had never learned or had forgotten how to sell. The same survey implied that continuing training provided sales personnel with more adequate product information and taught them how to present it in terms of user benefits.

Management should assume that sales personnel are eager to improve selling techniques; feel entitled to explanations of policy changes; want to learn how to tie in more closely with advertising programs; and are eager to learn about new products, model and design improvements, and market shifts. Continuing sales training programs are designed and "sold" as a means of helping salespeople do their jobs more effectively. If it is demonstrated that training results in more take-home pay and increased job satisfaction, salespeople are motivated. When salespeople see that these benefits are obtainable through the continuing sales training program, its chances of successful execution are enhanced.

Where Will the Training Site Be?

Some companies hold initial sales training programs at the central offices; others conduct separate programs at branch offices. Each practice has advantages and disadvantages. The centralized program generally provides better product training, but higher costs are incurred in bringing trainees to the central point. In many companies the small number of trainees does not justify decentralized initial training, and central location is a necessity. Numerous large companies, by contrast, have the option of decentralized initial training. They can train new salespeople near their future territories and acquaint them early with field selling problems. However, decentralized product training often requires the substitution of motion pictures, slides, and working models so it may be less realistic, less interesting, and less effective than centralized training. Decentralized programs have even more serious defects. Unless supervised by higher management, their execution tends to be poor, and the trainers, who have other responsibilities and regard training as a sideline, often turn in poor teaching performances. Except in a company with a vast pool of administrative and training skills, initial sales-training programs should be at central locations.

Retraining programs for seasoned sales personnel also are held either at centralized or decentralized points. These programs are often short, so the decision may hinge upon where the needed instructional talent is and whether it is more economical to transport and house the trainers or the trainees. If retraining programs coincide with sales conventions, they are held nationally (at convention headquarters), or regionally, on a decentralized basis.

Instructional Materials and Training Aids

Critical to successful execution of sales training programs are the instructional materials and training aids. These vary not only for different companies but for programs with different aims, contents, and methods. Pertinent features and uses of the main types of instructional materials and training aids are discussed in the following sections.

1. Manuals. Often known as workbooks, manuals are used in most group-type sales training programs. The best manuals contain outlines or summaries of the main presentations, related reading materials, statements of learning objectives for each session, orienting questions or thought provokers, cases and problems, plus directions for sessions involving role playing or gaming. Many include concise statements of selling, pricing, training of sales personnel, and other policies as well as details on company systems and procedures. Some contain information on the products and their applications. Discretion should be observed in selecting items for inclusion. It is easy to clutter up a manual with information of little value. Manuals often are designed with a dual purpose: to serve as study guides during training and as references later. Many are in loose-leaf form to facilitate additions and changes.

2. Other printed materials. These include company bulletins, sales and product handbooks, information bulletins, standard texts, technical and trade books, and industry and general business magazines and journals. Company publications are used chiefly to furnish field sales personnel with up-to-date and needed information. Keeping field sales personnel informed is also the reason many companies provide subscriptions to industry and general business magazines. Text, technical, and trade books supplement workbook materials, although trainees rarely read them thoroughly during formal training. The usual expectation is that the books will serve later as references.

3. Training aids. A training aid is an auxiliary device capable of transmission of sight and/or sound stimuli. The most used and indispensable is the blackboard—no training facility should be without one on which to illustrate points, summarize discussions, and the like, adding visual to vocal appeal. Modern substitutes for the blackboard (for example, the Vue-Graph projector, transparency roll, and screen) offer improvements such as making it possible for the trainer to face the class even while his or her writing appears on a screen, and conserving time through using prepared diagrams, charts, statistical tables, and so on. But there is no substitute for a blackboard, nothing so free of possible mechanical or power failure. Even when main reliance is placed upon some mechanically operated device, blackboard and chalk should be available for standby use, and to illustrate and explain points that arise in informal discussion. Mechanical training aids supplement or support the blackboard; none supplants it entirely.

The motion-picture projector and film are effective when the training is to explain complex situations. In conveying technical information on installation and operation of new machine tool models, for example, nothing short of actual demonstration is as effective as a movie. Substantial costs are incurred in producing training films, since cameramen, actors, a director, and special sets are needed. In deciding whether to produce tailor-made films, management appraises their probable effectiveness against the cost. Most sales training films seek to convey information on products and their applications, but some aim to refine sales techniques. One company, for example, used an amateur-produced (hence, low-cost) "candid-camera" film of its sales personnel in action as an aid to improving job performance. For the firm with limited funds, sales training films of varying quality, most relating to sales techniques, are available commercially. Any training film, whether company-produced or commercially produced, should be previewed before use.

Much of the motion picture's effectiveness is achieved at lower cost with still pictures projected from slides or filmstrips. A sound disk presents a commentary together with automatically timed changes in still pictures, or the trainer makes comments varying the change interval between pictures with a remote-control device. Many companies produce their own slides and filmstrips, but commercially produced items are available for purchase or rental.

Tape-recording and playback equipment is ideal for training in sales techniques. Actual or simulated sales presentations are taped and played back for individual or group appraisal. Miniature (sometimes concealable) cassette-type recorders make it easy for salespersons to tape their own sales interviews and play them back later. Thus, they gain greater objectivity in appraising their own effectiveness and in finding ways to improve performance. Larger recorders are used in formal training programs to tape group discussions and role-playing sessions, the tapes being played back with commentaries and appraisals by the participants and the trainer. Some trainers tape their own sessions routinely. Later playbacks help to improve teaching effectiveness and to conserve preparation time for repeat performances.

Closed-circuit television is used when timing is important. It is appropriate in decentralized programs, such as those in which new product lines are introduced to salespersons or dealer personnel. Other applications include the use of closed-circuit television in brief, decentralized retaining programs on policy changes, and as a substitute for training at national sales meetings.

4. Advance assignments. To conserve time, many programs require trainees to prepare assignments in advance. In some situations, these are reading assignments chosen to provide some minimum comprehension of subjects scheduled for coverage in formal sessions. In other situations, the assignment is to read a case and prepare a plan of action for use in a scheduled session. It is important that trainees understand the purposes of advance assignments and receive clear instructions (most expert trainers recommend *written instructions*). Trainees' motivations are strengthened when opportunities for feedback are built into advance assignments, for example, if trainees are required to submit a written precis of reading assignments and briefs of all cases scheduled. Advance assignments are used for groups as well as for individuals—in many companies, for instance, trainees are divided into groups and instructed to prepare specific individuals in the groups to play particular roles (note the built-in feedback feature).

Advance assignments serve another purpose. They consume time outside formal sessions, reducing trainees' inclinations to "go out on the town" or otherwise goof off. In addition, because they require extra time, advance assignments should convince trainees of the extraordinary opportunity—"you have to prepare for higher productivity."

EVALUATING SALES TRAINING PROGRAMS

The evaluation step (the second E in A-C-M-E-E) focuses upon measuring program effectiveness. A sales training program represents investments of time, money, and effort—sales management expects returns commensurate with the investment. However, measuring sales training effectiveness is not easy, but it is possible to gauge, somewhat roughly, program effectiveness.

The starting point is to compare the program's aims (the A in A-C-M-E-E) with the results, but the core of the measurement difficulty is in determining training results. Results, such as improved selling performance, for instance, may not show up until months later. Management approaches the measuring problem by making certain comparisons, such as the length of time new sales personnel (who have completed initial sales training) take to attain the productivity level of the experienced salesperson, the performance against standards of

FIGURE 14.2 Form for Trainee Rating of Sales Training Session

Session Review

A brief, candid review of this training session will help you evaluate what you have learned and help us in our efforts to improve the program. Please answer all questions. Do not sign your name; the results are anonymous.

Place an X where appropriate to describe your reactions to each of the following:

1. Material covered	Exciting	☐	☐	☐	☐	☐	☐	☐	Dull
2. Instruction	Excellent	☐	☐	☐	☐	☐	☐	☐	Poor
3. Worthwhileness of material	Great	☐	☐	☐	☐	☐	☐	☐	Little
4. Completeness of coverage	Very Complete	☐	☐	☐	☐	☐	☐	☐	Totally Inadequate

5. How might the session have been improved?

____

____

____

trained and untrained sales personnel, and the respective training histories of the best and worst performers. Some companies plot each salesperson's sales records on a before-and-after training basis, generally converting them to market share percentages.

However, any evaluation of training effectiveness based on sales records is an approximation. Territorial sales volumes are influenced not only by personal selling but by advertising, competitors' activities, economic fluctuations, and similar factors. No known analytical technique exists for precise isolation of the influence of these factors.

Other approaches to measuring program effectiveness are in use. Some companies use written tests (on a before-and-after training basis) to determine how much trainees have learned. This is appropriate for measuring improvements in amount and depth of product knowledge, for instance, but reveals little about the trainee's ability to apply this in the field. Other firms send observers to work with sales personnel who have completed training programs and to report the extent to which trainees are applying what was taught in programs. Still other companies solicit customers for their reactions to a salesperson's performance after training. None of these approaches produces precise evaluative data. They provide indications as to whether results are positive or not.

Management measures the effectiveness of training programs both while they are in progress and upon completion. The purpose is to obtain insight for improving the effectiveness of future programs. Tests and examinations measure trainee retention of materials presented, most appropriately when trainees are to memorize certain information, as product specifications and applications. There is little value in using tests and examinations for evaluating training in sales techniques; performance in role-playing assignments is a better approach.

Trainers in some companies rate each trainee's performance in role playing, panels, and other discussion. Necessarily, these are subjective ratings, but they provide learning incentives. Similarly, the practice of requiring trainees to rate each trainer's performance, either in each session or in the total program, is spreading. This may stimulate trainers to improve their effectiveness. Many sales executives, however, argue that trainees are in no position to judge the trainers' effectiveness until they gain additional field experience. Nevertheless, comment sheets similar to Figure 14.2 are used in numerous sales training programs. Many companies also ask trainees to evaluate training programs after they return to their territories.

CONCLUSION

The entire production and marketing process culminates in the making of sales, and management's objective in training sales personnel is improved job performance. Effective sales training also assists sales management in discharging its social responsibility for controlling marketing costs. When salespeople perform efficiently, cost savings show up in benefits to consumers as well as to the enterprise. A company's position in its industry is determined importantly by the performance of its sales personnel. Skillfully designed and executed sales training programs have potentials for helping sales personnel to achieve effective job performance.

15 Motivating Sales Personnel

The sales executive's job is to get results through company personnel—by making decisions and seeing to it that others carry them out. Put differently, the sales executive's performance depends upon the composite performances of the individuals making up the sales force. Small wonder, then, that sales executives are greatly interested in the factors influencing individual sales personnel to achieve given performance levels.

What causes a salesperson to achieve a given performance level? Native ability, or potential, has something to do with it—no one achieves more than they are capable of achieving. The skills that come with experience, education, and training influence performance—for the salesperson, this means knowing the job objectives and how to achieve them. The amount and effectiveness of effort expended by the individual impacts importantly upon performance.

Assuming that a salesperson has the requisite ability and the skills needed for satisfactory job performance, what causes that salesperson to expend the necessary effort? The answer is locked up in the behavioral concept known as motivation—what causes people to behave as they do. Behavioral scientists agree that motivation is goal-directed behavior aimed toward achieving given results, which, in turn, provide rewards in line with the goal.

High productivity in a sales force comes about neither naturally nor accidentally. Some sales personnel are self-starters, requiring little external incentive, but they are the exceptions. Most sales personnel require motivation to reach and maintain satisfactory performance levels.

MEANING OF MOTIVATION

Motivation is goal-directed behavior, underlying which are certain needs or desires. The term "needs" suggests a lack of something that reaching the goal could satisfy, while the term "desires" suggests positive ardor and strength of feeling. The complex of needs and desires stemming from within individuals leads them to act so as to satisfy these needs and desires.

Specifically, as applied to sales personnel, motivation is the amount of effort the salesperson desires to expend on the activities associated with the sales job, such as calling on potential accounts, planning sales presentations, and filling out reports. Expending effort on each activity making up the sales job leads to some level of achievement on one or more dimensions of job performance—total sales volume, profitability, sales to new accounts, quota attainment, and the like.

MOTIVATIONAL "HELP" FROM MANAGEMENT

Most sales personnel require motivational "help" from management to reach and maintain acceptable performance levels. They require motivation as individuals and as group members. As individuals, they are targets for personalized motivational efforts by their superiors. As members of the sales force, they are targets for sales management efforts aimed toward welding them into an effective selling team. Four aspects of the salesperson's job affect the quality of its performance. The following discussion focuses on these aspects, each is an important reason why sales personnel require additional motivation.

Inherent Nature of the Sales Job

Although sales jobs vary from one company to the next, sales jobs are alike in certain respects. Every sales job is a succession of ups and downs, a series of experiences resulting in alternating feelings of exhilaration and depression. In the course of a day's work, salespersons interact with many pleasant and courteous people, but some are unpleasant and rude and are difficult to deal with. They are frustrated, particularly when aggressive competing sales personnel vie for the same business, and they meet numerous turndowns.[1] Furthermore, sales personnel spend not only working time but considerable after-hours time away from home, causing them to miss many attractive parts of family life. These conditions cause salespersons to become discouraged, to achieve low performance levels, or even to seek nonselling positions. The inherent nature of the sales job, then, is the first reason that additional motivation is required.

[1]For an interesting discussion of frustration including examples of potentially frustrating situations in the sales force, see Alan J. Dubinsky and Mary E. Lippit, "Managing Frustration in the Sales Force," *Industrial Marketing Management*, 8, (1979), pp. 200–06.

Salesperson's Boundary Position and Role Conflicts

The salesperson occupies a "boundary position" in the company and must try to satisfy the expectations of people both within the company (in the sales department and elsewhere) and in customer organizations. There is linkage with four groups: (1) sales management, (2) the company organization that handles order fulfillment, (3) the customers, and (4) other company sales personnel. Each group imposes certain behavioral expectations on the salesperson, and, in playing these different roles, the salesperson faces role conflicts, such as

1. *Conflict of identification* arises out of multigroup membership. As the salesperson works with the customer, identification is with the customer rather than the company. On returning to the company, the salesperson drops identification with the customer and identifies with the company.
2. *Advocacy conflict* arises when the salesperson identifies with the customer and advocates the customer's position to other groups in the company organization. This may be important and may be encouraged by the sales management group, but the advocator is in a difficult position.
3. *Conflict is inherent in the salesperson's dual role as an advocate* for both the customer and the company and *the salesperson's pecuniary interest as an entrepreneur*. As an entrepreneur paid directly or indirectly on the basis of sales volume, the salesperson has an interest in selling as much as possible in the shortest time. However, the salesperson may uncover facts overlooked or unknown to the customer, indicating that difficulties in the customer's organization limit the product's usefulness. If the salesperson tells the customer about these conditions and that, in all probability, the product will not meet the customer's needs, the salesperson risks losing the sale and the income that goes with it.[2]

Not much can be done to reduce the role conflicts of sales personnel. Some evidence exists that experienced sales personnel perceive significantly less role conflict than do those with less experience. This suggests that a salesperson's perceptions of, and ability to cope with, role conflict are influenced not only by experience but by the effectiveness of sales training. It also suggests that those who become experienced sales personnel may cope better with role conflicts (that is, psychologically) than those leaving the sales organization earlier. So improving sales training effectiveness and revising selection criteria are two roads to reducing the impact of role conflict on sales force morale.[3]

Role conflicts traceable to the salesperson's linkage with groups that have divergent interests, then, is another reason why additional motivation is required.

[2]J. A. Belasco, "The Salesman's Role Revisited," *Journal of Marketing*, 30, no. 2 (April 1966), p. 7.
[3]Orville C. Walker, Jr., Gilbert A. Churchill, Jr., and Neil M. Ford, "Organizational Determinants of the Industrial Salesman's Role Conflict and Ambiguity," *Journal of Marketing*, 39 (January 1975), p. 38.

Tendency Toward Apathy

Some sales personnel naturally become apathetic, get into a rut. Those who, year after year, cover the same territory and virtually the same customers, lose interest and enthusiasm. Gradually their sales calls degenerate into routine order taking. Because they know the customers so well, they believe that good salesmanship is no longer necessary. Their customer approach typically becomes: "Do you need anything today, Joe?" They fail to recognize that friendship in no way obviates the necessity for creative selling and that most customers do not sell themselves on new products and applications. The customer's response, as often as not, is: "Nothing today, Bill." Later a competing salesperson calls on the same account, uses effective sales techniques, and gets an order. Many salespeople require additional motivation to maintain continuing enthusiasm to generate renewed interest in their work.

Maintaining a Feeling of Group Identity

The salesperson, working alone, finds it difficult to develop and maintain a feeling of group identity with other company salespeople. Team spirit, if present at all, is weak. Thus, the contagious enthusiasm—conducive to improving the entire group's performance—does not develop.

If sales management, through providing added motivation, succeeds in developing and maintaining team spirit, individual sales personnel strive to meet group performance standards. Few people who consider themselves members of the sales team want to appear as poor performers in the eyes of their colleagues. Providing the kind of working atmosphere in which all members of the sales force feel they are participating in a cooperative endeavor is not easy—nevertheless, effective sales management works continuously to achieve and maintain it.

NEED GRATIFICATION AND MOTIVATION

Behavioral research studies show that all human activity—including the salesperson's job behavior—is directed toward satisfying certain needs (that is, reaching certain goals). Patterns of individual behavior differ because individuals seek to fulfill different sets of needs in different ways. Some salespersons, in other words, are more successful than others because of the differing motivational patterns and amounts and types of efforts they exert in performing their jobs.

How particular individuals behave depends upon the nature of their fulfilled and unfulfilled needs modified by their environmental and social backgrounds. The motives lying behind any specific action derive from tensions built up to satisfy particular needs, some beneath the threshold of consciousness. Any action taken is for the purpose of reducing these tensions (fulfilling a need or needs to reach a goal or goals).

Needs are either primary or secondary. Primary needs are the inborn or physiological needs for food, water, rest, sleep, air to breathe, sex, and so on, the fulfillment of which are basic to life itself. Until primary needs are satisfied, other needs have little motivational influence. Secondary needs arise from an individual's interaction with the environment, and are not inborn but develop with maturity. Secondary needs include those for safety and security, belongingness and social relations, and self-esteem and self-respect.

Hierarchy of Needs

A. H. Maslow, a psychologist, developed a theory of motivation based on the notion that an individual seeks to fulfill personal needs according to some hierarchy of importance. He suggests the general priority of need fulfillment shown in Figure 15.1.[4] Maslow suggests that after an individual gratifies basic physiological needs, he or she proceeds to strive to fulfill safety and security needs, then belongingness and social relations needs, and so on—the individual's level of aspiration rising as needs on higher levels are satisfied. Not every individual and certainly not every salesperson, of course, establishes the order of priority of need fulfillment suggested by Maslow. Some sales personnel, for instance, appear to assign earlier priority to filling the esteem need (for self-respect) than they do to filling the need for social relations within a group.

After meeting basic physiological needs, it probably is impossible for most individuals to satisfy fully their needs on any higher level—needs seem to multiply along with efforts to satisfy them. As a particular need is satisfied, it loses its potency as a motivator, but other unfulfilled needs, some of them new, gain in

FIGURE 15.1 Hierarchy of Human Needs as Visualized by A. H. Maslow

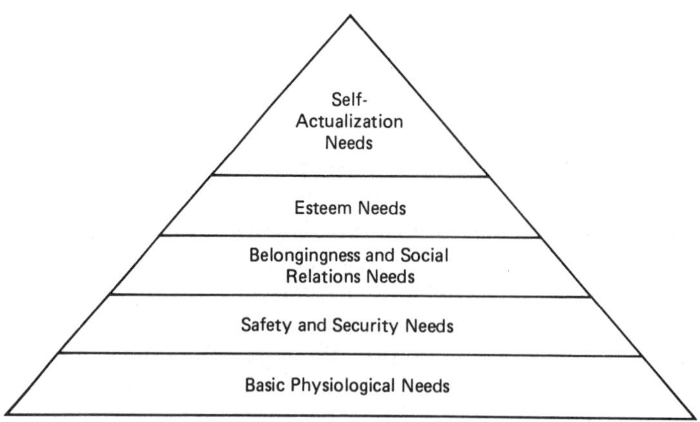

[4]A. H. Maslow, *Motivation and Personality,* 2nd ed. (New York: Harper & Brothers, 1970), Chapters 3–7.

potency. Individuals continually try to fulfill ever-larger portions of their need structures, and the unsatisfied portions exert the strongest motivational pull.

What, then, motivates salespeople? Salespersons' motives for working vary according to the nature and potency of the unsatisfied portion of their individual hierarchies of needs. We must also recognize, however, that some of the salespeople's needs are filled off the job as well as on it. One salesperson works because of the need for money to feed a family; another because the job is seen as a means for gaining esteem of others; still another because of a need to achieve (self-actualization) to the maximum of one's abilities, seeing job performance as a means to that end.

If sales management knew the makeup of the unsatisfied portion of a salesperson's hierarchy of needs at a particular time, it could determine the best incentives. The fact that an individual has needs causes him or her, consciously or not, to formulate goals in terms of them. If management can harmonize the individual's goals with those of the organization, then individual behavior is channeled along lines aimed at achieving both sets of goals. For a salesperson worried about providing for a child's education, an important individual goal becomes that of obtaining money to remove the uncertainty. If management sees how furnishing the salesperson with an opportunity to earn more money will also further the attainment of organizational goals (perhaps that of increasing the size of orders), then offering the salesperson the chance to earn more money for obtaining larger orders is a powerful incentive.

Money, however, loses its power as an incentive once the individual has gratified physiological needs and most safety and security needs. Other incentives (for example, a chance for promotion, which is one way to fulfill esteem and self-respect needs) become increasingly effective. The promise of more money becomes a weaker incentive the farther up in the hierarchy an individual's unfulfilled needs are pushed. Whatever power a larger income retains is related to unfulfilled esteem and self-actualization needs and the extent to which income can gratify them. Of course, too, the threat of receiving a lower income, a negative incentive, endangers the fulfilled part of an individual's need structure, and to the extent that this threat exists, money continues to have power as an incentive. Notice that whereas motives are internal to the individual, incentives are external. Sales management influences the behavioral patterns of sales personnel indirectly through the incentives it offers.

Motivation-Hygiene Theory

Frederick Herzberg and his co-researchers developed the motivation-hygiene theory. According to this theory the factors that lead to motivation and job satisfaction are not the same as those leading to apathy and job dissatisfaction. In other words, the contention is that job dissatisfaction is not the opposite of job satisfaction—two separate groups of needs are involved, one related to job satisfaction and the other to job dissatisfaction. While most needs have potentials for

FIGURE 15.2 The Maslow and Herzberg Models Compared

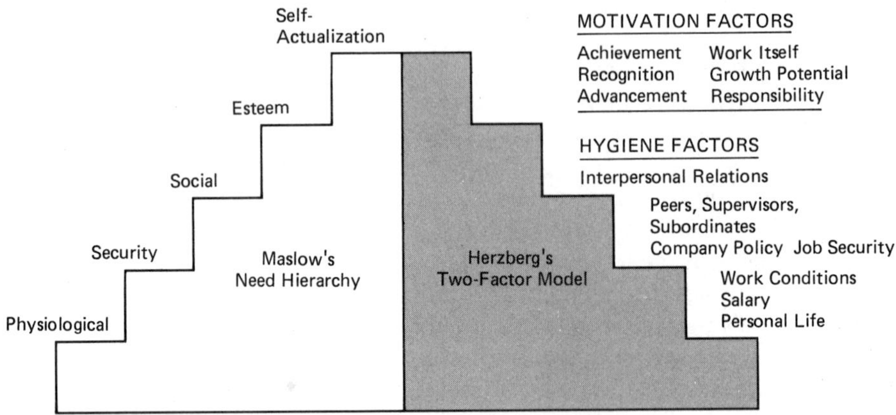

SOURCE: Adapted from James H. Donnelly, Jr., James L. Gibson, and John M. Ivancevich, *Fundamentals of Management,* sixth ed. (Plano, Texas: Business Publications, Inc., 1987) p. 302.

influencing both the relief of job dissatisfaction and the increase of job satisfaction, each need serves predominantly either a hygiene or motivator purpose.[5]

Deficiencies in fulfilling the hygiene needs cause job dissatisfaction. These needs relate to the working environment, compensation, fringe benefits, type of supervision, and other factors extrinsic to the job. Fulfilling the hygiene needs does not lead to job satisfaction, but in the achievement of a neutral point known as a fair day's work. Performance at this point does not result from motivation.[6]

At the "fair day's work" point, the individual is ripe for influence by the motivation factors, ones intrinsic to the job itself. These factors reflect needs for personal growth, including achievement, recognition, nature of the job itself, responsibility, and opportunities for advancement. The motivation factors represent needs that, when fulfilled, lead to job satisfaction.

Figure 15.2 shows the considerable similarity of the Maslow and Herzberg models. Herzberg's division of the need hierarchy into two factors—hygiene and motivational—implies that for many people, including most sales personnel, only Maslow's higher-order needs (esteem and self-actualization) are primary motivators. Yet even these people must satisfy the lower-order (hygiene) needs for maintenance of their job satisfaction.

Motivation-hygiene theory has two important implications for sales management. The first is that management must see that the job provides the conditions that prevent job dissatisfaction (to get a fair day's work from the salesperson). This means that management needs to provide an acceptable working environment, fair compensation, adequate fringe benefits, fair and reasonable

[5]Frederick Herzberg, *Work and the Nature of Man* (Cleveland: World, 1966).

[6]Donald Sanzotta, *Motivational Theories and Applications for Managers* (New York: Amacom, A Division of American Management Associations, 1977), p. 26.

supervision, and job security. The second implication is that management must provide opportunities for achievement, recognition, responsibility, and advancement (to motivate performance beyond that of a fair day's work).

Achievement-Motivation Theory

David McClelland, in association with other researchers, developed achievement-motivation theory. According to this theory, if a person spends considerable time thinking about doing his or her job better, accomplishing something unusual and important, or advancing his or her career, that individual has a high need for achievement (nAch). Those who have high need for achievement (1) like problem situations in which they take personal responsibility for finding solutions (ones in which the possibilities of reaching them are reasonable), (2) tend to set attainable achievement goals, and (3) want feedback on how they are doing.[7] In practical terms, nAch is a motivation to exceed some standard of quality in personal behavior—individuals who are self-motivated and who continually strive to improve their performance are in this category.[8] Many individuals like this are attracted to personal selling jobs, especially those where compensation is largely in the form of commissions—jobs characterized by opportunities to influence outcomes through personal efforts, challenging risks, and rapid feedback of results.[9]

What are the implications for sales management? If individuals with high nAch can be the best performers in the company's sales jobs, then management might target its recruiting toward such people. McClelland and his coinvestigators used the Thematic Apperception Test (TAT) in their research on achievement, so management might consider including the TAT in the sales selection system.[10] But management would want to make certain that the sales job environment was one in which high achievers flourish.

The fact that nAch drives individuals to act from an internally induced stimulus is noteworthy. People with high nAch are self-starters—they require little external incentive to succeed and constantly challenge themselves to improve their own performances. Such people do not require motivation by management other than that of providing the right kind of job environment. Understanding the concepts behind nAch, and the conditions that individuals high in nAch seek in their jobs, helps to explain and predict the behavior of sales personnel.

[7]David C. McClelland, "Business Drive and National Achievement," *Harvard Business Review*, 40 (July–August 1962), pp. 104–05.

[8]George H. Hines, *The New Zealand Manager* (Wellington, N.Z.: Hicks, Smith & Sons, 1973), p. 44.

[9]Stephen P. Robbins, *Personnel: The Management of Human Resources* (Englewood Cliffs, N.J.: Prentice Hall, 1978), p. 201.

[10]In the TAT, the subject is asked to tell stories about a series of pictures, while the tester records the stories and the subject behavior. Then the tester interprets the subject's personality in the light of the themes used in the stories related. See Harold J. Leavitt, *Managerial Psychology*, 4th ed. (Chicago: University of Chicago Press, 1978), p. 96.

Expectancy Model

The expectancy model, developed by Vroom, conceptualizes motivation as a process governing choices of behavioral activity. The reasoning is that the strength of a tendency to act in a certain way depends upon the strength of an expectation that the act will be followed by a given outcome and on that outcome's attractiveness to the individual. Put differently, an individual's desire to produce at a given time depends on that individual's specific goals and perception of the relative worth of performance alternatives as paths to attainment of those goals.[11]

An expectancy model, based on Vroom's, is shown in Figure 15.3. The strength of an individual's motivation to behave in a certain way (in terms of efforts) depends upon how strongly that individual believes that these efforts will achieve the desired performance patterns (or level). If the individual achieves the desired performance, then how strongly does the individual believe that the organization's rewards/punishments will be appropriate for that kind of performance, and to what extent will this satisfy the individual's needs (goals)?

The expectancy model raises motivational issues of concern to sales management. Does the company reward structure provide what sales personnel want? Do individual sales personnel perceive the kinds and amounts of effort management anticipates that they will make to attain set performance levels? How convinced are individual sales personnel that given performance patterns lead to given rewards?

Sales management, however, must recognize that this model is concerned with expectations. Sales personnel need counseling to view their own competencies realistically. They also need sales management's support in developing the skills that lead to improved performance.

FIGURE 15.3 An Expectancy Model of Motivation

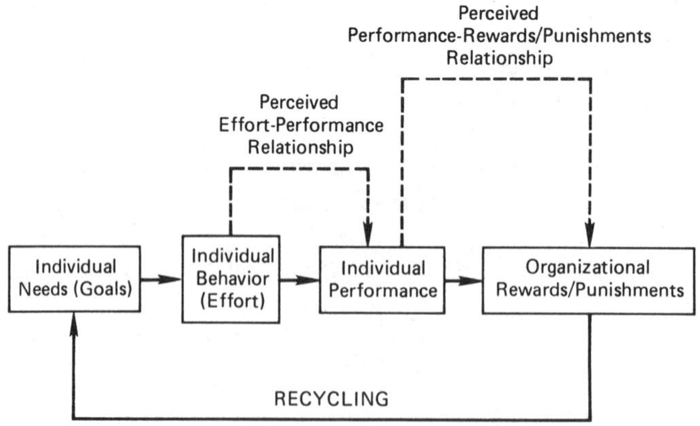

[11]V. Vroom, *Work and Motivation* (New York: John Wiley, 1964).

INTERDEPENDENCE AND MOTIVATION

In the formal organizational plan, each salesperson reports to someone higher up in the structure, a sales supervisor, a district sales manager, or, as in most small companies, to the chief sales executive. According to traditional theory, the superior has the authority to require that the salesperson take action, and the salesperson is obligated to carry out the superior's orders. This theory assumes that authority ("the formal right to require action of others") can be equated with power ("the ability to get things done"). Practical sales managers know that issuing an order to a salesperson or suggesting how he or she should act (that is, change a pattern of behavior) does not necessarily mean that henceforth the salesperson will change. On many occasions, of course, there is little problem in having orders and directions put into effect—as long as they are clearly stated and apply to simple tasks that are done quickly. However, if orders and directions require significant modification in the salesperson's behavior over an extended period, perhaps permanently, the salesperson's acceptance of the desired change is a great deal more unpredictable.

Whether or not orders and directions are accepted depends upon the relationship between the salesperson and the superior. In analyzing this relationship, the concept of interdependence, which explains how the appropriateness of authority varies as a function of dependence, is useful.[12] At one extreme, a salesperson is wholly dependent upon the superior, in which case he or she considers that superior's exercise of authority as fully appropriate; this situation, amounting to blind obedience, is rarely found in business.[13] At the opposite extreme, the salesperson and the superior are fully interdependent; that is, there is equal dependence both ways, a relationship comparable to that between close friends, and authority is useless as a means of control. This situation is also rare, but it seems desirable—in effect, the salesperson depends on the superior for reaching his or her individual goals. Thus, full integration of individual and organizational goals is possible.

The usual situation in sales force–superior relationships is one of partial dependence. The salesperson is partially dependent upon the superior and regards the latter's exercise of authority as appropriate in some circumstances and not in others; the superior is partially dependent upon the salesperson for help in reaching the organizational goals for which he or she is held responsible by higher management. Each salesperson, then, has a "zone of acceptance," a range over which he or she accepts directions from the superior, and each superior has a similar zone over which he or she honors requests from the salesperson. Within their respective zones of acceptance, too, both the salesperson and the

[12]L. Gulick, "Structure and Coordination," in J. A. Litterer (ed.), *Organizations: Structure and Behavior* (New York: John Wiley, 1969), pp. 107–11.

[13]The state of complete dependence is most closely approached, at least in the modern world, in the parent-child relationship found in authoritarian homes.

superior exhibit a "degree of acceptance" that varies according to the exact circumstances from grudging acquiescence to enthusiastic cooperation.

The sales manager should try to widen the zone and increase the degree of acceptance of each salesperson, but accomplishing this also means widening his or her own zone and increasing his or her own degree of acceptance. Actually this is only a fancy way of saying that effective supervision is prerequisite to improved performance. Through effective supervision, the sales manager satisfies many of the salespersons' needs and, at the same time, obtains fuller cooperation from them in striving for organizational goals by giving due credit for good work, by convincing each salesperson of his or her job's importance, by earning the sales personnel's confidence in his or her leadership, and by following other enlightened supervisory practices. Sales personnel under this sort of supervision work hard to earn praise and recognition and the resulting social approval, esteem, and self-respect. Effective supervision means, above all else, that salespeople are treated as human beings, as individuals in their own right, not as mere cogs in an impersonal industrial machine.

MOTIVATION AND LEADERSHIP

Effective sales executives are leaders, rather than drivers, of sales personnel. They earn the voluntary cooperation of members of the sales organization, motivating them, individually and as a group, to reach the sales department's goals. They know the motivations, desires, and ambitions of those they lead, and they use this knowledge to guide their followers into the necessary activities—whether they be learning or performing.

The effective sales executive sets a good example. The "do as I say, not as I do" approach is not effective in motivating sales personnel. The sales executive works with the same diligence he or she expects of sales personnel, and leads his or her life as he or she expects them to lead theirs. It is natural for subordinates to emulate their superior—the superior is, or should be, a symbol of success.

One aspect of leadership closely related to motivation has to do with the handling of relationships with sales personnel. Attaining skill in this area is not easy, but experience, maturity, and common sense are necessary attributes. Effective sales executives treat sales personnel fairly, particularly as to assignments, promotions, and changes in pay. They commend salespeople for jobs well done, but if performances are not up to par, they call that to the subordinates' attention privately. When discussing a salesperson's weakness, effective sales executives make it clear that they know the individual's strong points. Before making changes affecting salespeople's jobs, they consult those affected, helping to prevent the damaging impact of rumors upon morale. The sales force should be convinced, individually and collectively, that when right is on their side, the sales executive can be depended upon, if the need arises, to carry their case to top management. And, above all else, effective sales executives do not lose sight of the fact that they are managing the sales staff. They "sell" sales personnel on plans, policy changes, and anything else that affects them. Sales personnel are all the more sold on their jobs when sales executives apply good sales techniques in all their relationships with them.

MOTIVATION AND COMMUNICATIONS

It is important that good communications exist between each salesperson and his or her superior—unless it does, there is depressed morale and low productivity. The salesperson with pent-up grievances, real or imagined, displays both low morale and unsatisfactory performance. Similarly, the salesperson, like everyone else, comes up against personal problems, such as sickness in the family, inability to pay overdue bills, or marital troubles, all of which adversely affect morale and performance.

Good communications allow for free discussion of problems related to the salesperson's job and of any personal problems that, left unsolved, hurt job performance. For the salesperson, the existence of good communications means freedom of self-expression—freedom to talk over problems, business and personal, with the superior. For the superior, it means ease in talking with the salesperson, not only to determine what, if anything, is bothering him or her, but to provide assistance in solving any problems that come to light.

Interpersonal Contact

Interpersonal contact is an important way to communicate with and thereby to motivate sales personnel. Management uses contacts to make comprehensive evaluations of individual salespeople's morale. Interpersonal contacts provide opportunities for learning of financial, family, or other personal worries that have impacts upon job performance.

Sales executives at all levels have personal contacts with the sales staff. But at higher levels of sales management, contacts with salespeople are confined to conventions and sales meetings. Most of the individual salesperson's contact with management is with the immediate supervisor. Although supervisors have other important functions to perform, such as training, evaluation, and control, they also use their visits with salespersons for detecting personal or business problems, and for motivational purposes. Sales executives at all levels reserve some time for observing and conferring with sales personnel. District managers visit each salesperson on the job in the assigned sales territory. While it is impractical in large sales organization for top sales executives to visit personally all territories or even all sales districts, there are other ways to maintain personal contact with sales personnel. One is to arrange individual conferences between sales personnel and the top sales executive during regional or national meetings—the opportunity to visit with the "big boss" provides strong motivation.

Interpersonal contact is the best way to keep in touch with the sales staff, but other communications media sometimes are used. Not only is close contact with all sales personnel all of the time physically impossible, but the least effective salespeople demand the lion's share of the personal attention. When this happens, executive contact with the more effective salespeople is largely through written means. Confronted with this situation, many sales executives keep in touch with their better people not through letters, but through regular telephone calls.

On some occasions, sales personnel should be contacted personally, or by telephone, rather than by letter. A drop in performance that the executive suspects traces to family discord is not only difficult but awkward to discuss in writing. When a reprimand is necessary, a face-to-face meeting is better than a letter that could lead to further complications. Personal and disciplinary problems are best handled by interpersonal contact and not through the mail. In exceptional cases, a carefully phrased letter can avoid misinterpretations and misunderstandings, but the executive is still well advised to follow up with personal contacts.

It is difficult to motivate a salesperson whom the sales executive knows only casually. A special effort should be made to know each salesperson well, and to learn what is important to each. Effective sales executives develop empathy with their subordinates.

Motivational interviews. In progressive companies, sales executives set planned "informational" goals for personal visits with sales personnel. The executive attempts to find out about salespeople's patterns of need fulfillment and the order of priority assigned to each need. Insights are gained on individuals' motivational patterns, and guidance is furnished for choosing appropriate incentives. It is unlikely that a single interview can gather all this information, but after many interviews, the executive has the information to put together a comprehensive picture. Motivational interviews are a way to gather valuable information bit by bit.

Written Communications

Supplementing personal contacts, sales personnel are kept informed through letters, announcements, bulletins, and other mailed pieces. Written communications can become routine and deadening—increases in volume and frequency destroy their value. Some sales executives think nothing of spending hours planning a sales meeting but neglect to appraise the motivational impact of their correspondence. No single letter or bulletin has as strong a motivational effect as a sales meeting; yet the total impact of written communication, effectively used, can be much greater.

The effective executive writing personal letters and bulletins to salespeople avoids generalities and concentrates upon specific helpful suggestions. A letter to salesperson Brown, reporting that salesperson Jones wrote a $100,000 order last week, and instructing Brown to go out and do the same is not motivation. Describing how Jones succeeded in promoting a new use for the product to a certain kind of customer is motivation. Writing letters, especially those that cheer up and spur on salespeople in the field, is an art effective executives master.

A letter is superior to interpersonal contact to congratulate a salesperson for good work. A letter provides lasting evidence recognizing the salesperson's performance. Such letters have prolonged beneficial effect on morale, but, of course, they do not substitute for deserved promotions or compensation increases. A commendation letter is supported, whenever possible, by a personal expression that management recognizes, and is pleased with, the salesperson's performance.

UNIONIZATION OF SALES PERSONNEL

There are several reasons why unions have made little progress in organizing sales personnel. First, it is difficult to develop strong group identification in most sales departments because each person works alone and sees other members of the sales force infrequently. Little opportunity exists for mutual exchange of grievances. Second, in contrast to most employee groups, salespersons think of themselves as independent operators rather than as cogs in an industrial machine. Third, sales personnel have some control over their workday and workweek. If they work excessive hours, it is often to add to their compensation, and there are no time clocks. Fourth, the prospect of higher wages has never served as a strong organizing incentive for sales personnel, as sales personnel have been made to feel that low earnings are the result of personal ineffectiveness, not of the employer's niggardliness.

Only about one in ten salespersons belongs to a union. When unionization has occurred, it usually traces to a failure of sales management. Grievances stem from such failures as too many reports, competition of house accounts, inadequate expense allowances, poor territories, too many people on the sales force (which results in inadequate territories), and too many nonselling duties.

Unionization has made headway in industries where sales personnel are paid straight salaries, where they work together on the same premises (retail selling), and where the selling job is combined with that of delivery, as in the distribution of beer and soft drinks. Unions have made little progress in organizing sales personnel who sell directly to industrial users or those who make calls on middlemen. Sales personnel in these classifications, paid in whole or part according to productivity, frown upon union affiliation.

Many sales executives oppose unionization. Their opposition is based chiefly upon the effect that unionization has on the motivation and control of sales personnel and upon the limitations that union contracts place on management. Managerial action is circumscribed by the collective-bargaining agreement, and uses of incentive compensation are restricted. Commonly, unions object to sales contests and other devices for motivating the sales force; sometimes they insist that all additions to the sales force be recruited through the union, they discourage the use of quotas and other standards of performance, and a strict system of seniority is demanded.

Sales executives maintain that the organizational structure of unions does not harmonize with the demands of the selling job. Selling and sales management require more flexibility than does running a plant or an office. They argue that all salespeople are called upon at times for extra effort, this being the price paid for freedom from day-to-day supervision.

CONCLUSION

Motivating sales personnel is an important aspect of sales force management. Sales personnel require additional motivation because of inherent nature of the sales job, role conflicts, the natural tendency toward apathy, and difficulties in building group identity. The concepts of need gratification and interdependence assist in understanding the complexities of motivating sales personnel. Implementing motivational efforts requires that sales executives be skilled leaders, rather than drivers, of sales personnel. It demands that they be skilled in interpersonal and written communications. Satisfactory job performances develop out of deep understanding of motivational forces and processes, effective leadership, two-way communications, and effective handling of relationships.

Compensating Sales Personnel

16

Does money motivate sales personnel? Money, as our review of motivation theories in Chapter 15 showed, has limited potential as a motivator. In Maslow's hierarchy, money loses motivating power once an individual satisfies physiological needs and most safety and security needs, retaining only declining residual motivating power in fulfilling esteem and self-actualization needs (insofar as a larger income can fulfill them). In Herzberg's motivation-hygiene model, money is a hygiene factor, contributing to the prevention of job dissatisfaction but otherwise not motivating at all.

Nevertheless, the sales compensation plan is an essential part of the total program for motivating sales personnel. A sales compensation plan, properly designed, has three motivational roles: (1) provide a living wage, (2) adjust pay levels to performance, thereby relating job performance and rewards (in line with expectancy motivation theory), and (3) provide a mechanism for demonstrating the congruency between attaining company goals and individual goals (also in line with expectancy theory).

A properly designed sales compensation plan fits a company's special needs and problems, and from it flows attractive returns for both the company and its sales personnel. Sales and growth goals are reached at low cost, and profits are satisfactory. Sales personnel receive high pay as a reward for effective job performance, and *esprit de corps* is high.

Sales compensation plans are aids to, rather than substitutes for, effective motivation. No plan can be the entire motivational program, for it would be based on the naive hypothesis that sales personnel are totally mercenary. Nor should a compensation plan operate so as to conflict with what may be important motives—to conform, to be like others, to belong, to be liked by one's peers—for example, what do you suppose the motivational impact is of having a big earner branded as an apple polisher? The basic appropriateness of a compensation plan is important, and so is the way it is implemented and administered—it is not uncommon for a fundamentally poor compensation plan to work satisfactorily *when a skilled executive administers it.*

In established companies it is rarely necessary to design new sales compensation plans, and sales executives concern themselves mainly with revising plans already in effect. Most changes are minor, instituted to bring the plan and marketing objectives into closer alignment. If, for example, additional sales effort is needed for the factory to operate at optimum capacity, an adjustment in compensation may be required. This could mean paying bonuses on sales over the quota, paying additional compensation for larger orders or for securing new accounts, or revising commission rate schedules. Any change, of course, could be either temporary or permanent.

Major changes in the compensation plan are rare. Like most people, sales personnel resist sweeping changes, particularly when this requires them to alter accustomed ways of doing things. When a firm switches from paying straight salaries to straight commissions, for instance, many individuals have difficulty adjusting their living and spending habits.

Opinions vary as to how far-reaching changes, when required, should be implemented. Some executives think that introducing them gradually minimizes interference with established habits and elicits less resistance from sales personnel. Others claim that major changes should be made quickly, because continual changes erode salespeople's morale. Whether a change should be made in one step or in many depends upon the particular situation, and no easy generalization is possible. Explanation of impending changes is important, so careful orientation is a must.

There are two situations where total overhaulings of compensation plans are in order. One is the company whose sales force already has low morale, perhaps because of the current compensation plan. If the plan is at the root of the morale problem, drastic change is appropriate. A second situation calling for a complete revamping of the sales compensation plan occurs when a company is anticipating the cultivation of new and different markets. The problems in these two situations are like those in the newly organized company, which must build its sales compensation plan from scratch—in both cases management must consider many factors, the nature and number of which vary with the company and the situation, but usually include the types of customers, the marketing channels, characteristics of the products, intensity of competition, extent of the market, and complexity of the selling task.

REQUIREMENTS OF A GOOD SALES COMPENSATION PLAN

A good sales compensation plan meets seven requirements. First, it provides a living wage, preferably in the form of a secure income. Individuals worried about money matters do not concentrate on doing their jobs well. Second, the plan fits with the rest of the motivational program—it does not conflict with other motivational factors, such as the intangible feeling of belonging to the sales team. Third, the plan is fair—it does not penalize sales personnel because of factors beyond their control—within the limits of seniority and other special circumstances, sales personnel receive equal pay for equal performance. Fourth, it is easy for sales personnel to understand—they are able to calculate their own earnings. Fifth, the plan adjusts pay to changes in performance. Sixth, the plan is economical to administer. Seventh, the plan helps in attaining the objectives of the sales organization.

DEVISING A SALES COMPENSATION PLAN

Whether contemplating major or minor changes or drafting a completely new sales compensation plan, the sales executive approaches the project systematically. Good compensation plans are built on solid foundations. A systematic approach assures that no essential step is overlooked.

Define the Sales Job

The first step is to reexamine the nature of the sales job. Up-to-date written job descriptions are the logical place to start. If job descriptions are outdated, if they are not accurate, or if complete descriptions of the sales job objectives and work are not given, then a revision is in order. The effective sales executive asks: Does this description convey a realistic picture of what the salesperson is supposed to accomplish and to do? If there are no written sales job descriptions, they are prepared.[1]

Other aspects of company operations are considered in relation to their impact upon the sales job. Sales department objectives are analyzed for their effect on the salesperson's job. Sales volume objectives, for instance, whether in dollars, units of product, or numbers of dealers and distributors, are translated into what is expected of the sales personnel, as a group and individually. The impact of sales-related marketing policies are determined. Distribution policies, credit policies, price policies, and other policies affect the salesperson's job. Current and proposed advertising and sales promotional programs assist in clarifying the nature of the salesperson's goals, duties, and activities.

[1]See Chapter 10 for a discussion of sales job analysis and the preparation of job descriptions.

Consider the Company's General Compensation Structure

Most large companies, and many smaller ones, use job evaluation systems to determine the relative value of individual jobs. Job evaluation procedure is not scientific; it is an orderly approach based on judgment. It focuses on the jobs, without considering the ability or personality of individuals who do the work. Its purpose is to arrive at fair compensation relationships among jobs.

There are four job evaluation methods. Two are nonquantitative: simple ranking and classification or grading. The other two are quantitative: the point system and the factor-comparison method.

Simple ranking. In this inexpensive job evaluation method, widely used by small businesses, an executive committee sorts job descriptions in the order of worth. This is done without considering the individuals currently in the jobs or their compensation levels. No attempt is made to determine critical factors inherent in the jobs; only overall appraisals of the relative worth of different jobs are made.

Classification or grading. This approach utilizes a system of grades and grade descriptions, against which individual jobs are compared. The grades, sometimes called classes, are described in terms of job responsibility, skills required, supervision given and received, exposure to unfavorable and hazardous working conditions, and similar characteristics. Job descriptions are then classified into appropriate grades—this is done by an executive committee or by personnel specialists. The basic process is to compare job descriptions with grade descriptions. All jobs within a grade are treated alike with respect to base compensation.

Point system. The point system is the most widely used job evaluation method. It involves establishing and defining the factors common to most jobs that represent the chief elements of value inherent in all jobs. The specific factors chosen differ from one company to another, but generally include mental and physical skills, responsibility, supervision given and received, personality requirements, and minimum education required. Each factor is assigned a minimum and maximum number of points, different ranges being associated in line with the relative importance of the factors. Next, appraised factor scores are combined into a total point value. Finally, bands of points are decided upon and become the different compensation classes. Less arbitrary judgment is required than under the classification method; the use of point values makes it possible to determine the gap, or distance, between job classes.

Factor-comparison method. This method resembles the point system but is more complex. It utilizes a scheme of ranking and cross-comparisons to minimize error from faulty judgment. In a process similar to that used in the point system, the factor-comparison method employs selected factors and evaluation scales. However, the scale values are in dollars and cents, and no upper limit exists to the valuation that can be assigned to any one factor. A selected number of key jobs, typical of similar jobs throughout the company, are then evaluated, factor by factor. This is done by arranging them in rank order, from highest to lowest for each factor. As a check against this judgmental evaluation, the compensation dollars actually paid for each job are allocated to the factors; the allocation automatically establishes the relationship among jobs for each factor. The judgment ranking and the ranking by allocation of compensation are compared and differences are reconciled, or else the jobs are removed from the key list. On the basis of the dollar amounts assigned to the several factors making up key jobs, additional jobs are evaluated and their monetary values for each factor interpolated into the scale. This procedure is repeated until all jobs are evaluated.

Job evaluation and sales positions. Job evaluation occurs whenever decisions are made about the relative worth of jobs, and it is inescapable in organizational life. If, for example, the owner of an automobile dealership decides that the new car sales manager should be paid more than the service manager, the jobs have been evaluated. So *informal* job evaluation exists in firms not using formal job evaluation.

Traditionally, sales executives have opposed using formal job evaluations to determine the compensation levels of sales personnel. They contend that compensation levels for sales personnel are more closely related to external supply-and-demand factors than to conditions inside the company. Sales personnel enjoy greater job mobility than most other employees, and are in everyday contact with potential employers.

If a company has a formal job evaluation program that includes the jobs of sales personnel, there should be sales department representation on the committee that arrives at quantitative evaluations. If the job evaluation program does not cover sales personnel program or the company does not use formal job evaluation, it is important for the sales executive to establish the value of sales jobs relative to other company jobs. This helps assure that the monetary attractiveness of sales positions is no less than for comparable jobs elsewhere in the company. If the sales executive keeps informed on the relative differences between sales jobs and other company jobs, he or she is preparing for the day, which is probably inevitable, when sales positions are regarded as appropriate for inclusion in formal job evaluation programs.

Consider Compensation Patterns in Community and Industry

Because compensation levels for sales personnel are related to external supply-and-demand factors, it is important to consider prevailing compensation patterns in the community and industry. Management needs answers to four questions: (1) What compensation systems are being used? (2) What is the average compensation for similar positions? (3) How are other companies doing with their plans? and (4) What are the pros and cons of departing from industry or community patterns?

If there is a companywide formal job evaluation program, it should take into account the current rates for sales positions in the community and industry. A program for setting compensation of sales personnel is sound only if it considers the relation of external compensation practices to those of the company. Effective sales executives maintain constant vigilance against the possibility that the pay of sales personnel will get out of line with that paid for similar jobs in the community or industry.

Determine Compensation Level

Management must determine the amount of compensation a salesperson should receive on the average. Although the compensation level might be set through individual bargaining, or on an arbitrary judgment basis, neither expedient is recommended. Management should ascertain whether the caliber of the present sales force measures up to what the company would like to have. If it is too low, or if the company should have lower-grade people than those currently employed, management should determine the market value of sales personnel of the desired grade. Management weighs the worth of individual persons through estimating the sales and profit dollars that would be lost if particular salespeople resigned. Another consideration is the compensation amount the company can afford to pay. The result of examining these and other factors pertinent to the situation is a series of estimates for the total cost of salespeople's compensation. It is excellent practice to plot each cost estimate on a break-even style chart. When the several plots are compared with the company's cost goals, the sales volume needed to break even at each compensation level is revealed. The compensation levels for individual salespeople under the proposed plan also should be plotted in break-even style.

In some firms, companywide formal job evaluation programs are used to set compensation levels for sales positions. The procedure recommended earlier serves as a check on the compensation levels prescribed through job evaluations. Any discrepancies should be reconciled. When the job evaluation program is sound, there should be few, if any, discrepancies.

It is not unusual to find that two companies operate under similar selling conditions but with different sales compensation levels. Sales personnel in one company earn more than those who do essentially the same work in another company. Relatively speaking, the first group of salespeople is overcompensated. What explains such situations? Sometimes, management does not know the true worth of individual sales personnel. In other cases, management regards some sales personnel as indispensable, or managerial inertia prevents adjustment of the compensation level to changed selling conditions. In still other cases, sales managers are biased in favor of high compensation for selling jobs.

Provide for the Various Compensation Elements

A sales compensation plan has as many as four basic elements: (1) a fixed element, either a salary or a drawing account, to provide some stability of income; (2) a variable element (for example, a commission, bonus, or profit-sharing arrangement), to serve as an incentive; (3) an element covering the fringe or "plus factor," such as paid vacations, sickness and accident benefits, life insurance, pensions, and the like; and (4) an element providing for reimbursement of expenses or payment of expense allowances. Not every company includes all four elements. Management selects the combination of elements that best fits the selling situation. The proportions that different elements bear to each other vary. However, most companies split the fixed and variable elements on a 60:40 to an 80:20 basis.[2]

Special Company Needs and Problems

A sales compensation plan is no panacea for marketing ills, but it is often possible to construct a plan that increases marketing effectiveness. If a company's earnings are depressed because sales personnel overemphasize low-margin items and neglect more profitable products, it may be possible, despite the existence of other managerial alternatives, to adjust the compensation plan to stimulate the selling of better balanced orders. Specifically, variable commission rates might be set on different products, with the higher rates applying to neglected products.

Or, as another example, a firm might have a "small-order" problem. It is possible to design compensation plans that encourage sales personnel to write larger orders. Commission rates can be graduated so that higher rates apply to larger orders. However, it is desirable to supplement such a revised compensation plan with a customer classification and call scheduling system, enabling management to vary call frequency with account size.

As still another example, a company may want to obtain more displays or local advertising by retailers. The presence or absence of point-of-purchase displays can spell the difference between marketing success or failure. Securing retail displays is a task that sales personnel may neglect, especially if they are paid commissions based on sales volume. To overcome this tendency, an incentive payment for obtaining retail displays is often incorporated in the compensation plan.

Numerous other possibilities exist for using the compensation plan to help solve special company problems. Plans may assist in securing new customers and new business, improving the quality of salespeople's reports, controlling expenses of handling complaints and adjustments, eliminating price shading by the sales staff, reducing traveling and other expenses, and making collections

[2]*Marketing Times* (July–August 1978), p. 4.

and gathering credit information. Management, however, should recognize that other means exist for dealing with these problems, which are generally transitory in nature. Repeated tampering with the sales compensation plan frequently results in complex and difficult-to-administer plans.

Consult the Present Sales Force

Management should consult the present sales personnel, inasmuch as many grievances have roots in the compensation plan. Management should encourage sales personnel to articulate their likes and dislikes about the current plan and to suggest changes in it. Criticisms and suggestions are appraised relative to the plan or plans under consideration. But at this point, management compares the caliber of the present sales force with that of the people whom it would like to have. If the present salespeople are not of the grade that the company wishes to attract, their criticisms and suggestions are of limited usefulness. Since, however, nearly every sales force has some people of the desired caliber, more weight can be attached to their opinions than to those of others.

Reduce Tentative Plan to Writing and Pretest It

For clarification and to eliminate inconsistencies the tentative plan is put in writing. Then it is pretested. The amount of testing required depends upon how much the new plan differs from the one in use. The greater the difference, the more thorough is the testing.

Pretests of compensation plans are almost always mathematical and usually computerized. Past payrolls, perhaps for a year or two, are reworked to check operation of the proposed plan against experience under the old system. Analysts compare what happened with what would have happened had the new plan been in effect. If the sales pattern has shown considerable fluctuation, calculations are made for periods representative of average, good, and poor business.

Then a look is taken into the future. Utilizing sales forecast data, new and old plans are applied to future periods. The plan is tested for the sales force as a group and for individuals faced with unique selling conditions. Analysis reveals whether the plan permits earning in line with the desired compensation level. If deficiencies show up, the plan may not be at fault; weaknesses can trace to the way territorial assignments have been made or to inaccuracies in sales forecasts, budgets, or quotas.

To conduct a pilot test, several territories representative of different sets of selling conditions are selected. The proposed plan is applied in each one long enough to detect how it works under current conditions. Pilot tests are invaluable for spotting possible sources of trouble and other deficiencies.

Revise the Plan

The plan is then revised to eliminate trouble spots or deficiencies. If alterations are extensive, the revised plan goes through further pretests and perhaps another pilot test. But if changes have been only minor, further testing is not necessary.

Implement the Plan and Provide for Follow-up

At the time the new plan is implemented, it is explained to sales personnel. Management should convince them of its basic fairness and logic. The sales personnel are made to understand what management hopes to accomplish through the new plan and how this is to be done. Details of changes from the old plan, and their significance require explanation. All sales personnel should receive copies of the new plan, together with written examples of the method used for calculating earnings. If the plan is at all complex, special training sessions are held and aimed at teaching sales personnel how to compute their own earnings. If sales personnel do not understand the plan or certain of its features, such as quotas and variable commission bases, they may think that the company is taking unfair advantage of them. Inadequate understanding of the sales compensation plan is common and often a cause of low morale. No effort is spared to make certain that everyone on the sales force fully comprehends the compensation plan and its workings.

Provisions for follow-up are made. From periodic checkups, need for further adjustments is detected. Periodic checks provide evidence of the plan's accomplishments, and they uncover weaknesses needing correction.

TYPES OF COMPENSATION PLANS

The four elements of compensation are combined into hundreds of different plans, each more or less unique. But if we disregard the "fringe benefit" and "expense reimbursement" elements—as is entirely reasonable, since they are never used alone—there are only three basic types of compensation plans: straight salary, straight commission, and a combination of salary and variable elements.

Straight-Salary Plan

The straight salary is the simplest compensation plan. Under it, salespersons receive fixed sums ar regular intervals (usually each week or month but sometimes every two weeks), representing total payments for their services. The straight salary was once the most popular sales compensation plan, but it has been declining in importance. A recent study by Executive Compensation Service, Inc., shows that under 17.5 percent of all selling organizations use straight-salary plans. Such plans are more common among industrial-goods companies than among consumer-goods companies.[3] Firms that formerly used the straight salary

[3]*Sales & Marketing Management* (February 17, 1986), p. 57.

have tended to combine a basic salary with a variable element—that is, they have switched to combination plans.

In spite of the trend away from its use, sometimes the straight-salary plan is appropriate. It is the logical compensation plan when the selling job requires extensive missionary or educational work, when salespeople service the product or give technical and engineering advice to prospects or users, or when salespeople do considerable sales promotion work. If nonselling tasks bulk large in the salesperson's total time expenditure, the straight-salary plan is worthy of serious consideration.

Straight-salary plans are commonly used for compensating salespeople heavily engaged in trade selling. These jobs, in which selling amounts to mere order taking, abound in the wholesale and manufacturing fields, where consumer necessities are distributed directly to retailers. Frequently, too, the straight-salary method is used for paying driver-salespersons selling liquor and beverages, milk and bread, and similarly distributed products.

From management's standpoint, the straight-salary plan has important advantages. It provides strong financial control over sales personnel, and management can direct their activities along the most productive lines. Component tasks making up salespersons' jobs can be recast with minimum opposition from those affected, so there is flexibility in adjusting field sales work to changed selling situations. If sales personnel prepare detailed reports, follow up leads, or perform other time-consuming tasks, they cooperate more fully if paid straight salaries rather than commissions. Straight-salary plans are economical to administer, because of their basic simplicity, and compared with straight-commission plans, accounting costs are lower.

The main attraction of the straight-salary plan for sales personnel is that stability of income provides freedom from financial uncertainties inherent in other plans. In addition, sales personnel are relieved of much of the burden of planning their own activities (the practice of providing detailed instruction, for example, on routing and scheduling, generally goes along with the straight-salary plan). And, because of its basic simplicity, sales personnel have no difficulty in understanding straight-salary plans.

The straight-salary plan, however, has weaknesses. Since there are no direct monetary incentives, many salespeople do only an *average* rather than an outstanding job. They pass up opportunities for increased business, until management becomes aware of them and orders the required actions. Unless the plan is skillfully administered, there is a tendency to undercompensate productive salespeople and to overcompensate poor performers. If pay inequities exist for long, the turnover rate rises; and it is often the most productive people who leave first, resulting in increased costs for recruiting, selecting, and training. Other problems are encountered in maintaining morale, as arguments occur on pay adjustments for ability, rising living costs, and length of service. Because all the selling expense is fixed, it is difficult to adjust to changing conditions—a knotty problem during business downswings, when selling expenses can be reduced only by cutting salaries or releasing personnel. Moreover, during business upturns, there is difficulty in securing the company's share of rising industry volume, because salaried salespeople commonly are not disposed to exceed previous sales records by any large amount. However, many of the straight-salary plan's weaknesses are minimized through good administration.

In administering a straight-salary plan, individual sales personnel are paid, insofar as possible, according to their relative performance. The difficulty is in measuring performance. Management needs to define "performance" and the meanings of good, average, and poor performances. When management has these definitions and develops methods for performance measurements, it can set individual salaries fairly and intelligently. Users of the salary plan define performance as total job performance, not merely success in securing sales volume or in performing some other aspect of the job—and this is theoretically correct, because the payers of salaries assume they can exercise maximum control over the way salary receivers perform all job aspects. Some salary plan users attempt to measure performance by relating the salesperson's total selling expense (including salary) to total sales. While it is desirable to control total selling expenses, using the expense-to-sales ratio as the sole criterion of performance overemphasizes the importance of cost control.

In the absence of well-defined quantitative performance standards, and few companies have them, the sales job description, if up to date and complete, is the place to start in appraising job performances of sales personnel.[4]

All sales personnel need rating not only on their achievement of sales and cost goals but on their performance of each assigned duty. The total evaluation of an individual is a composite of the several ratings, weighted according to relative importance. Persons rated as average are paid average salaries. Salaries of below-average and above-average sales personnel are scaled to reflect the extent to which their performances vary from the average. Each individual's performance is regularly reviewed and upward adjustments made for those showing improvements, and downward adjustments made for those with deteriorating performances.

Straight-Commission Plan

The theory supporting the straight-commission plan is that individual sales personnel should be paid according to productivity. The assumption underlying straight-commission plans is that sales volume is the best productivity measure and can, therefore, be used as the sole measure. This is a questionable assumption.

The straight-commission plan, in its purest form is almost as simple as the straight-salary plan, but many commission systems develop into complex ar-

[4]Use of quantitative performance standards as part of an integrated system for controlling sales personnel is discussed in Chapter 19. The present discussion is related to organizations lacking such standards.

rangements. Some provide for progressive or regressive changes in commission rates as sales volume rises to different levels. Others provide for differential commission rates for sales of different products, to different categories of customers, or during given selling seasons. These refinements make straight-commission plans more complex than straight-salary plans.

Straight-commission plans fall into one of two broad classifications:

1. Straight commission with sales personnel paying their own expenses. Advances may or may not be made against earned commissions.
2. Straight commission with the company paying expenses, with or without advances against earned commissions.

There is a general trend away from the straight-commission plan, and today no more than 6 or 7 percent of all companies use such plans.[5] The straight-commission plan is used in situations where nonselling duties are relatively unimportant and management emphasizes order getting. Straight-commission plans are common in the clothing, textile, and shoe industries and in drug and hardware wholesaling. Firms selling intangibles, such as insurance and investment securities, and manufacturers of furniture, office equipment, and business machines also are frequent users of straight-commission plans.

The straight-commission plan has several advantages. The greatest is that it provides maximum direct monetary incentive for the salesperson to strive for high-level volume. The star salesperson is paid more than he or she would be under most salary plans, and low producers are not likely to be overcompensated. When a commission system is first installed, the sales personnel turnover rate accelerates, but usually the exodus is among the low producers. Those remaining work longer and harder, with more income to show for their efforts. Straight-commission plans, in addition, provide a means for cost control—all direct selling expenses, except for traveling and miscellaneous expenses (which are reimbursable in some plans), fluctuate directly with sales volume changes and sales compensation becomes virtually an all variable expense. The straight-commission plan also is characterized by great flexibility—by revising commission rates applying to different products, for instance, it is possible to stimulate sales personnel to emphasize those with the highest gross margins.

However, the straight-commission method has weaknesses. It provides little financial control over salespeople's activities, a weakness further compounded when they pay their own expenses. Salespersons on straight commission often feel that they are discharging their full responsibilities by continuing to send in customers' orders. They are careless about transmitting reports, neglect to follow up leads, resist reduction in the size of sales territories, consider individual accounts private property, shade prices to make sales, and may use high-pressure tactics with consequent loss of customer goodwill. Moreover, unless differential commission rates are used, sales personnel push the easiest-to-sell low-margin items and neglect harder-to-sell high-margin items; if manage-

[5] *Sales & Marketing Management* (February 17, 1986), p. 57.

ment seeks to correct this through using differential commission rates, it incurs increased record-keeping expenses. Under any straight-commission plan, in fact, the costs of checking and auditing salespeople's reports and of calculating payrolls are higher than under the straight-salary method. Finally, some salespersons' efficiency may decline because of income uncertainties. If a sales force has many financially worried salespeople, management may have to invest considerable time, effort, and money to buoy up their spirits.

Determining commission base. One important aspect of designing a straight-commission system is to select the base on which to pay commission. Company selling policies and problems strongly influence selection of the base. If obtaining volume is the main concern, then total sales is the base. If sales personnel make collections on sales, commissions are based on collections. If a firm has excessive order cancellations, commissions can be based upon shipments, billings, or payments. To control price cutting by sales personnel, some companies base commissions on gross margins. Other companies use net profits as the base, seeking simultaneously to control price cutting, selling expense, and net profit.

Drawing accounts. A modification of the straight-commission plan is the drawing account method, under which the company establishes separate accounts for each salesperson, to which commissions are credited and against which periodic withdrawals are made. Drawing accounts resemble salaries, since customarily individual sales personnel are allowed to overdraw against future earnings. If sales personnel become greatly overdrawn, they may lose incentive to produce, because earned commissions are used to reduce the indebtedness. More important, some sales personnel become discouraged with the prospects of paying back overdrawn accounts and quit the company.

To forestall quitting by overdrawn salespeople, some firms use "guaranteed" drawing account plans. These do not require the paying back of overdrawals. Sales executives in these firms are conservative in setting the size of guaranteed drawing accounts, for they are in effect combination salary and commission plans. Commonly, drawing account plans include a provision that covers the possibility of overdrafts. Legally, an overdraft cannot be collected unless the salesperson specifically agrees to repay it, or it is really a personal loan, or the salesperson has given a note acknowledging its receipt. Without a formal understanding, most courts hold that the relationship between the salesperson and the company is a partnership in which the company agreed to finance the salesperson and that the resulting loss is a normal risk incurred in doing business. Even if the company has an ironclad agreement with its sales personnel, there is a problem in collecting money that overdrawn sales personnel do not have.

Combination Salary-and-Incentive Plan

Salary plus commission. Most sales compensation plans are combinations of salary and commission plans. Most developed as attempts to capture the advantages and offset the disadvantages of both the salary and commission systems.

Where the straight-salary method is used, the sales executive lacks a financial means for stimulating the sales force to greater effort. Where the straight-commission system is used, the executive has weak financial control over nonselling activities. By a judicious blending of the two basic plans, management seeks both control and motivation. Actual results depend upon management's skills in designing and administering the plan. Unless there is skillful adjustment of salary and commission, weaknesses of both basic systems reappear.

Strengths and weaknesses of combination plans. A well-designed and administered combination plan provides significant benefits. Sales personnel have both the security of stable incomes and the stimulus of direct financial incentive. Management has both financial control over sales activities and the apparatus to motivate sales efforts. Selling costs are composed of fixed and variable elements; thus, greater flexibility for adjustment to changing conditions exists than under the commission method. Nevertheless, selling costs fluctuate some with the volume of business. There are beneficial effects upon sales force morale. Disagreements on pay increases and territorial changes are less violent than under a straight-commission plan. Further, if salespeople realize that the company shares their financial risks, a cooperative spirit develops between them and the company.

The combination plan, however, has disadvantages. Clerical costs are higher than for either a salary or a commission system. More records are maintained and in greater detail. There are risks that the plan will become complicated and that sales personnel will not understand it.

Sometimes a company seeking both to provide adequate salaries and to keep selling costs down uses commission rates so low that the incentive feature is insufficient to elicit needed sales effort. But, if the incentive portion is increased, salespeople may neglect activities for which they are not directly paid. Therefore, the ratio that the base salary and the incentive portion bears to the total compensation is critical. As mentioned earlier, most companies split the fixed and variable elements on a 60:40 to an 80:20 basis.

USE OF BONUSES

Bonuses are different from commissions—a bonus is an amount paid for accomplishing a specific sales task; a commission varies in amount with sales volume or other commission base. Bonuses are paid for reaching a sales quota, performing promotional activities, obtaining new accounts, following up leads, setting up displays, or carrying out other assigned tasks. The bonus, in other words, is an additional financial reward to the salesperson for achieving results beyond a predetermined minimum.

Bonuses are never used alone—they always appear with one of the three main sales compensation methods. If used with the straight salary, the plan resembles the combination plan. If used with the straight commission, the result is a commission plan to which an element of managerial control and direction has been added. If used with the combination salary and commission plan, the bonus becomes a portion of the incentive income that is calculated differently from the commission.

Certain administrative actions are crucial when a bonus is included in the compensation plan. At the outset, the bonus conditions require thorough explanation, as all sales personnel must understand them. The necessary records must be set up and maintained. Procedures for keeping sales personnel abreast of their current standings relative to the goals are needed. In addition, any bonus misunderstandings or grievances arising should be dealt with fairly and tactfully.

FRINGE BENEFITS

Fringe benefits, which do not bear direct relationships to job performance, range from 25 to 40 percent of the total sales compensation package. Some are required by federal and state law—for example, payments for social security premiums, unemployment compensation, and worker's compensation. Most, however, the company provides for other reasons: to be competitive with other companies in the industry or community, to furnish reasons for employees to remain in the company's service, and to comply with what employees expect as fringe benefits.

Fringe benefits, like monetary compensation, are not motivating factors. In the Maslow hierarchy, fringe benefits contribute to fulfillment of safety and security needs, although some (such as payment of country club dues) contribute to fulfillment of esteem and other higher-order needs. Since fringe benefits are given to all in the company's employ and do not vary with job performance, they help to prevent job dissatisfaction but do not add to job satisfaction (in line with Herzberg's motivation-hygiene theory).

Figure 16.1 shows fringe benefits currently offered by U.S. companies. As the variety of fringes has expanded, individual fringes have been added that appeal more to some groups than others—people with bad teeth are the ones most interested in dental insurance, while those with children are the ones most interested in plans for paying educational tuition fees for dependents. Similarly, given a choice between supplemental life insurance and increased retirement benefits from the savings plan, a fifty-nine-year-old probably would pick the latter, but a thirty-two-year-old father of five might opt for the life insurance.

An increasing number of companies offer a "cafeteria" approach to fringe benefits. In this approach, the company offers a core of basic benefits—the benefits required by law plus other traditional benefits, including paid vacations, medical, disability, and death benefits and a retirement program. Employees then use credits (based on age, pay, family status, and years of company service) to obtain optional benefits not included in the core; this lets employees select those benefits that best fit their needs. Because needs for benefits change, em-

FIGURE 16.1 Fringe Benefits—A Compendium of Types Available to Sales Personnel in Some Companies

Time
- Holidays
- Vacations
- Sick leave
- Personal leave
- Sabbaticals
- Pregnancy leave

Retirement Programs
- Social security (mandatory)
- Pension plan
- Profit sharing
- Salary reduction plans

Insurance and medical
- Physical examinations
- Medical payments and reimbursements
- Hospitalization insurance
- Dental insurance
- Disability insurance
- Life insurance
- Travel insurance
- Accident insurance
- Worker's compensation (mandatory)
- Unemployment insurance (mandatory)
- Cancer insurance
- Psychotherapy expense

Organization dues
- Trade association
- Civic clubs
- Country clubs
- Professional association

Miscellaneous
- Automobile
- Use of vacation spot
- Parking
- Dry cleaning and laundry
- Lunches (all or part)
- Secretarial services
- Employee stock purchase plan
- Company-provided housing
- Legal services
- Financial counseling
- Tuition for continuing education programs
- Financial support for dependents' education
- Credit unions
- Discounts for purchases of company products
- Child care payments
- Matching funds to charities and schools
- Company social events
- Company sports tournaments
- Retirement counseling
- Career counseling
- Payment of moving expenses

SOURCE: Developed at a Shirt-Sleeve Seminar, Atlanta Chapter, Sales and Marketing Executives-International.

ployees are given opportunities to change their selection of those benefits that best fit their needs. Because needs for benefits change, employees are given opportunities to change their selections. Companies using the cafeteria approach also have "awareness programs" aimed at making employees aware of the benefits available.

CONCLUSION

The sales compensation plan is an essential part of the total program for motivating sales personnel. Sales compensation plans play three motivational roles: (1) to provide a "living wage" (thereby contributing—in line with Herzberg's motivation-hygiene theory—to the lack of job dissatisfaction if not to job satisfaction), (2) to relate pay to job performance (in line with the expectancy theory of motivation), and (3) to demonstrate the congruency between attainment of company goals and goals of individual sales personnel (also in line with expectancy theory).

The basic sales compensation elements (salary, commissions and/or bonuses, or some combination thereof) should be in amounts large enough to provide the living wage and sufficiently flexible to adjust for changes in job performance. The fringe benefit elements, supplementary items not related to job performance and generally not payable in cash, need to be chosen and administered carefully—sales personnel, like other employees, increasingly look upon the fringes as customary and expected.

Appropriately chosen and skillfully administered sales compensation policies facilitate sales force management. They affect the relative ease of building and maintaining an effective sales force. They attract promising recruits and encourage satisfactory performers to remain on the job. This helps to hold down the sales personnel turnover rate, which, in turn, increases the return from sales training. The direction and control of sales force activities, in general, become increasingly more effective. In short, effective implementation of appropriate sales compensation policies and practices reduces time and effort devoted to other aspects of sales force management.

Managing Expenses of Sales Personnel

17

How a company manages the expenses incurred by its sales personnel is important. There are motivational implications, inasmuch as sales personnel who pay their own expenses look upon their jobs quite differently from those whose expenses are reimbursed fully or in part. Management's power to direct and control vary similarly, enjoying considerable power when expenses are reimbursable and little power when they are not. In contrast to other employees, sales personnel incur substantial expenses in the company's service, so effective sales executives regard their control and reimbursement as key features of the sales compensation plan. Generally, sales executives insist that policies for reimbursing and handling expenses of sales personnel be separate from reimbursement policies for other company personnel, such as those covering service and repair personnel or individuals on special assignments.

An idea of the size of sales expenses relative to sales compensation is obtainable from Figure 17.1. Notice that expenses as a percentage of the total of compensation and expenses range from a low of 9.3 percent in the electrical equipment industry to a high of 33.3 percent in the automotive parts and accessories industry. It appears, too, that sales expenses in most industries amount to from one-fourth to one-half of sales compensation; so, for instance, a salesperson with compensation of $50,000 annually is likely to have sales expenses in the range of $12,500 to $25,000.

Figure 17.2 shows how field selling expenses vary by the predominant selling style. Missionary selling incurs the lowest expense, probably because this selling style involves calling on customers (e.g., doctors, architects, lawyers, pharmacists, and hospital administrators) who are extremely busy people and have little

FIGURE 17.1 Sales Force Compensation, Expenses Incurred by Sales Personnel, and Total Sales Force Expenses in Twenty Industries, 1985

Industry	(1) Compensation (% of Company Sales)	(2) Expenses (% of Company Sales)	(3) Total Sales Force Expenses (% of Company Sales)	(2) ÷ (3) Expenses Total
Consumer Goods				
Durable goods	1.8%	0.7%	6.3%	10.4%
Ethical pharmaceuticals, surgical supplies and equipment, proprietary drugs and toiletries	3.4	1.6	6.9	23.2
Food	1.4	0.5	2.7	18.5
Major household items	1.8	0.6	5.8	10.3
Industrial Goods				
Automotive parts and accessories	2.2	0.7	2.1	33.3
Building materials	1.2	0.3	2.4	12.5
Chemicals and petroleum	1.6	0.5	3.1	16.1
Computers	1.5	0.4	2.9	13.8
Containers, packaging materials and paper	0.4	0.2	1.1	18.2
Electrical equipment	1.5	0.5	5.4	9.3
Electronics	2.2	1.3	4.2	31.0
Fabricated metals (heavy)	1.5	0.5	1.9	26.3
Fabricated metals (light)	2.0	0.7	6.4	10.9
Fabrics and apparel	2.1	0.7	4.5	15.6
Iron and steel	0.8	0.3	1.8	16.7
Machinery (heavy)	2.1	0.8	5.8	13.8
Machinery (light)	1.3	1.2	8.5	14.1
Office and educational equipment	8.2	1.2	10.4	11.5
Printing and publishing	5.5	1.1	7.0	15.7
Rubber, plastics, and leather	1.6	0.8	4.3	18.6

Note: Includes only salespeople's total compensation plus their expenses, that is, travel, lodging, meals, and entertainment.
SOURCE: *Executive Compensation Service, Inc.*, a subsidiary of the Wyatt Co.

FIGURE 17.2 Annual Field Selling Days, Annual Expenses, and Expenses per Day, Estimates for 1986 by Predominant Selling Style

Predominant Selling Style	Field Selling Days per Year	Annual Expenses	Expenses per Day
Trade	190*	$14,800	$ 77.89
Missionary	190*	11,000	57.89
Technical	141†	20,213	143.35
New business	190*	30,000	157.89

*Based on 5 days, 52 weeks per year, less 1 day per week office/nonfield work, less 6 holidays, and less 15 days for vacations and sickness.
†Based on 239 workdays less 2 days per week in office.
SOURCE: Estimates by the authors based on personal knowledge and figures reported in *Sales and Marketing Management's* 1986 Survey of Selling Costs.

time for entertainment. New business selling results in the highest selling expenses, since calls here are typically rather long and, because they are made on potentially large accounts, are ones where entertainment charges are regarded as "promising investments" by management. The technical selling style requires fewer days in the field than other selling styles but typically long calls on individual accounts, a situation often conducive to entertainment spending. The trade selling style generally involves making rather routine calls on a large number of accounts with relatively short times spent with each customer; so most of the selling expense here goes for travel and lodging and little for entertainment.

Keeping expenses of field sales personnel within reasonable bounds is important. Liberality, on the one hand, is desirable—to ensure that sales personnel have adequate funds to capitalize on market opportunities. The tendency to be too liberal, on the other hand, needs restraining to avoid having a profit less favorable that it need be. Sales executives are inclined to be too liberal rather than too stringent, and, it must be admitted, it is wiser to be overly liberal than to restrict salespeople's activities through insufficient expense reimbursement.

The degree of formal control over sales expenses varies a good deal from company to company. Some firms establish close budgetary controls and try to hold expenses within a planned total amount or to some percentage of sales volume of gross margin. Others control sales expenses only in a general way, such as by scrutinizing expense reports or through policy statements outlining the conditions under which expenses are reimbursable.

REIMBURSEMENT OF SALES EXPENSES—POLICIES AND PRACTICES

The two general policy alternatives on reimbursing sales expenses are (1) have sales personnel pay their own expenses or (2) reimburse sales personnel for all or part of their expenses. The first alternative is the simpler by far, but few companies choose it. Those that do are organizations, by and large, that regard sales personnel as independent businesspeople—most of these organizations also use straight-commission plans. The main advantage of the "pay-your-own-expenses" policy, from management's standpoint, is that no expense records are necessary inasmuch as sales personnel control their own expenses. In successful applications, the compensation level reflects the fact that sales personnel pay their own expenses. It is essential that their regular commission be sufficient to permit them to further the company's best interests. Even when the compensation level takes into account salespeople's probable expenses, some still skimp on expenses, to the company's detriment. They stay in second-and third-rate hotels; economize on meals, dry cleaning, laundry, and other traveling expenses; and avoid entertaining customers and prospects. Furthermore, they resist or ignore many of management's directives and instructions. Little management control can be exercised over their call and route schedules, especially in regard to accounts located in out-of-the-way places. Most sales personnel who pay their own expenses neglect nonsales-producing activities—they avoid missionary duties and follow up on sales leads only when no additional expenses are involved. They "high spot"; that is, they call only on large accounts, and they feel justified in adding "sidelines" (other manufacturers' products sold to the same classes of trade).

Most firms choose the second policy alternative—full or partial reimbursement. When expenses are reimbursable, sales management needs expense control. Funds used to defray sales expenses are deductions from gross profits. Many factors influence sales expenses, including territorial size and characteristics, caliber of sales personnel, nature and breadth of product line, managerial efficiency, intensity of competition, and mode of travel.

Two commonsense principles guide management in formulating expense-reimbursement policies: (1) reimbursable expenses should be large enough to permit the performance of assigned duties in the expected manner, and (2) all expenses incurred because sales personnel are away from home on company business should be reimbursable.

Expense reimbursement policies should take into account the customary living standards of the salesperson and the customers, with the emphasis on the latter. The salesperson should eat in restaurants and stay at hotels of the class patronized by the customers. In some instances, different salespeople in the same company should be allowed different amounts for expense, reflecting deviations in customers' living standards. Another reason for different-sized expense accounts is that actual expenses vary a great deal from one territory to another.

Reimbursement policies should keep expenses reasonable; they should not cause bad feeling among the sales staff. They should be economical to administer; that is, they should require only minimum supervision and record keeping. However, the desire for administrative economy should not result in arbitrary or unfair procedures.

Both in formulating reimbursement policies and in their implementation, effective sales executives guard against the tendency to overeconomize. Sales personnel are not forced to skimp to the point of impairing selling efficiency. Nor do they have to dip into their own pockets to pay legitimate expenses. Reimbursement policies and procedures are based upon the reasonable needs of those incurring expenses; enforcement relies largely upon each person's inherent honesty.

METHODS OF CONTROLLING AND REIMBURSING EXPENSES OF SALES PERSONNEL

Flat Expense Account

The flat expense account provides the salesperson with a stipulated sum to cover all expenses during a given period, such as a month or week. Allocation of this sum among different expense items is left to the individual's discretion. The majority of companies using flat expense accounts do so because this means there is no need to keep expense reports and no need to check expense accounts—two tasks many executives find onerous.

The flat expense account has several attractive features. It makes possible the advance determination of total sales expenses—so it is easy, at budget-making time, to appraise the reasonableness of total planned selling expenses relative to total planned sales. Sales personnel who have flat expense accounts are free to spend their allowances as they see fit, so there should be few arguments over expense accounts. The flat expense account forces sales personnel to control their own expenses, and, if they are guided properly by management, they plan route and call schedules so that each expense dollar is spent to the best advantage.

Successful operation of a flat expense account plan requires skilled administration. This plan works best either (1) when the exact amounts of expense accounts do not need changing often, as with companies whose sales personnel sell staple products in small territories, or (2) when expense allowances come up for frequent review and, possibly, revision. The amounts of the expense accounts should have flexibility built into them. If the plan is inflexible in a fluid marketing situation, sales personnel may not capitalize on sales opportunities requiring expenditures greater than the flat amounts. Even when marketing circumstances favor this plan, management regularly appraises each allowance for adequacy and appropriateness.

The great weakness of the flat expense account is the tendency of some sales personnel to overeconomize. These people come to think of the expense account as a regular addition to salary and do not spend all of it, preferring to save a portion for personal use. Careful sales supervision prevents situations of this sort.

Flexible Expense Account

The flexible expense account, sometimes known as the "exact" plan, is the most common reimbursement method. Its salient feature is that sales personnel are reimbursed for all allowable expenses incurred and reported. For this method to work, management must (1) know the total amount of sales personnel's probable expenses; (2) classify expenses into "allowable" and "nonallowable" categories, and furnish salespeople with clear descriptions of items under each heading; (3) set up a system and forms for the sales staff to use in periodic expense reporting; (4) establish procedures for checking itemized expense reports and for expeditious handling of reimbursements.

Figures 17.3 and 17.4 are typical expense reporting forms. The travel expense report form (Figure 17.3) provides space for reporting travel and hotel expense, meals, and incidentals. Note that the "meals section" is the space in which to report entertainment expense together with a written justification. Note, too, that expenses for incidentals (such as dry cleaning or laundry) must be explained. The "sales expense" report from (Figure 17.4) is used to report entertainment expenses.

The flexible expense account has attractive features. Because of the flexibility, sales opportunities are fully capitalized on as they arise. There is a basic fairness, because this method takes into account and makes payments for differences in territories, marketing conditions, and other factors. Therefore, management can exercise strong control over sales routes and call schedules. Finally, salespersons are under heavy obligation to perform all assigned activities, nonselling as well as selling.

The flexible expense account's unattractive features come out in its administration. Administrative costs are sizable, because of the large amount of clerical and accounting work in checking expense reports and making reimbursements. Similarly, clerical and accounting work requires a great deal of the salespeople's time, and many executives contend that good sales personnel are often poor record keepers. Without close control, some people spend the company's money too generously, this being further aggravated by the opportunity for expense account padding—and many disputes arise.

Honor System

Under the honor system, sales expenses are fully reimbursed. Sales personnel do not submit detailed, itemized lists of expenses but report only total expenses for the period. The implication is that management has complete confidence in the honesty of all sales personnel. The honor system is easy to administer and, compared with alternative reimbursement plans, savings occur in both accounting expenses and time. Arguments over questionable expenditures do not arise, and sales personnel do not envision management as parsimonious. Finally, at least in theory, the funds for territorial development are adequate; however, both the amounts and the ways in which they are spent are left to the sales personnel.

FIGURE 17.3 Travel Expense Report

TRAVEL EXPENSE STATEMENT

Name ______________________ Account No. ______________________

Destination and Trip Purpose ______________________

Residence ______________________ Date: from __________ to __________

TRANSPORTATION

CARRIER	FROM–TO	DATE	AMOUNT

MOTEL/HOTEL ACCOMMODATIONS

NAME	FROM	TO	DAYS	RATE	TOTAL

MEALS (INCLUDING TIPS)

DAY	AMOUNT*	DAY	AMOUNT*	DAY	AMOUNT*
B		B		B	
L		L		L	
D		D		D	
B		B		B	
L		L		L	
D		D		D	
B		B		B	
L		L		L	
D		D		D	

*Indicate name of guest (if any) and Business Affiliation (Refer to amount above)

DAY	MISCELLANEOUS (EXPLAIN)	AMOUNT

TOTAL AMOUNT

(Submitted by) (Date) (Approved by)

FIGURE 17.4 Sales Expense Report

SALES EXPENSE REPORT

SALES PERSON ______________________________

DEPARTMENT ______________________________

MAILING ADDRESS ______________________ DATE ____________

____

DESCRIPTION OF EXPENSE ______________________

____

____

____

____

____

DATE ____________________ LOCATION ____________________

AMOUNT (ATTACH RECEIPTS) $ ______________________

EXISTING CUSTOMER ☐

EXISTING AMOUNT OF SALES $ ______________ PER ____________

ACCOMPLISHED AS A RESULT OF THIS EXPENSE:

____

____

____

____

PROSPECTIVE CUSTOMER ☐

ANTICIPATED AMOUNT OF SALES $ ______________ PER ____________

ACCOMPLISHED AS A RESULT OF THIS EXPENSE:

____

____

____

____

____

APPROVED ______________________________ DATE ____________

With the honor system, management's control is weak, and this may cause problems. Some sales personnel evolve into free spenders, since detailed expense reports are not required. Others incur expenses from which the company has little chance of deriving benefit. Others appropriate company funds to their own use, for the system encourages people to regard expense accounts as sources of income. These abuses cause inequities in expense allowances, and this may adversely affect morale.

To avoid abuses, management, even though committed to the honor principle, should control individual salesperson's total expenses. One way is to establish maximum ratios of selling expense to sales. Another is to watch the trend of expenses; sudden and sizable increases in reported expenses, unless accompanied by parallel increases in sales, should be investigated. If dishonesty in expense reporting is detected, remedial action should be taken. In spite of the problems, the philosophy of the honor system lies behind the reimbursement policies and practices of many sales organizations.

Expense Quota

The expense quota is a compromise plan for reimbursing expenses. It controls sales personnel's total expenses over long periods but permits week-by-week variations in the amounts reimbursed. In setting up expense quotas, management first studies individual sales territories and estimates the sales volume each should provide and then establishes upper limits for each salesperson's total expenses over a specified period.

Under the expense quota plan, sales personnel receive prompt and full reimbursements, regardless of how allowable expenses vary from week to week. The budgeted figures are planned amounts only, and management does not hold rigidly to the upper limits. But because upper limits are established, sales personnel have a moral obligation to keep expenses under control.

The principal drawback of the expense quota is that the burden for controlling expenses is upon the sales personnel rather than upon management. As with all expense reimbursement plans, skillful administration is necessary for successful operation of the expense quota plan. Furthermore, unless sales and expense forecasts are accurate, and unless sales personnel are convinced that the upper limits are estimates only, they may curtail their activities toward the end of budgetary periods because of low balances left in accounts.

REIMBURSEMENT OF AUTOMOBILE EXPENSES

Companies using either flexible expense accounts or expense quotas *and* whose sales personnel operate their own automobiles (rather than company-owned or leased vehicles) need some system for determining the amounts of automobile expense reimbursements. Calculating "exact" automobile expenses is complicated. Three categories of expense are involved: variable, semivariable, and fixed. Variable expenses include costs of gasoline, lubricating oil and grease, and tires—all varying with the miles traveled. Fixed expenses include the costs of insurance coverage, license fees, and inspection fees. Semivariable expenses, which vary with the automobile's age and rate of usage, include charges for depreciation and obsolescence. Adding further to computation difficulties, expenses differ with the automobile make and model and expenses of ownership and operation, even for the same makes and models, differ from one territory to another, while differences in road and traffic conditions cause operating expenses to vary from territory to territory.

Complications in calculating exact automobile expenses cause most companies to settle for less exact procedures. Among companies using automobiles owned by sales personnel, more than 70 percent use the flat mileage rate system for reimbursing auto expenses. The rest use graduated mileage rates, fixed periodic allowances, combinations of fixed periodic allowances and mileage rates, the Runzheimer plan, or other systems.

Flat mileage rates. Most companies use a flat mileage rate system and reimburse automobile expenses at a fixed rate per mile traveled. Users of this system must set the mileage rate high enough to cover all expenses of automobile ownership and operation, yet low enough to permit the company to buy transportation economically.

Administering this system is simple. Sales personnel report mileages traveled, the flat mileage rate is applied, and reimbursement checks are issued. The system works satisfactorily when a company's sales force covers small territories (requiring little automobile travel) all in the same geographical area (incurring very similar expense amounts) and the mileage rate applied is on the generous side (eliminating arguments over actual and reimbursed expenses). Probably for these reasons, most local and regional wholesalers, among other small companies, favor flat mileage rates.

The flat mileage rate system has some fundamental shortcomings. It assumes that automobile expenses per mile vary at a constant rate at all operating levels. It ignores cost differentials arising from the use of various makes and models. It ignores territorial differences in expenses, for example, in prices of gasoline, oil, tires, insurance coverage, license and inspection fees, and even the automobiles themselves. Furthermore, in administering a flat mileage rate system, management often hesitates to adjust the rate, upward as well as downward, in line with changing actual expenses.

Graduated mileage rates. Under this system, different rates apply to mileages in different ranges, for example, 25 cents per mile up to 5,000 miles annually, 22½ cents per mile from 5,000 to 10,000 miles, and 20 cents per mile over 10,000 miles. Companies using this system recognize that the per mile costs of automobile operation are lower for long than for short distances; however, setting the cents-per-mile rates is difficult, since it is necessary to consider different operating levels in determining the mileages at which rates change. This system takes into account, almost mechanically, differences in sales territories, such as the length of route and frequency of calls. But, like the flat mileage rate system, it does not provide for cost variations resulting from operation of different makes and models and territorial expense differentials. Graduated mileage rate systems are appropriate when sales personnel travel long distances annually and serve concentrated geographic areas without significant regional expense differences.

Fixed periodic allowance. Some companies pay sales personnel a fixed allowance for each day, week, month, or other period during which they use their personal automobiles on company business. The fixed periodic allowance assumes that total automobile expenses vary with duration of use rather than mileage. Companies using this system tend to penalize sales personnel with large territories requiring extensive traveling for adequate coverage; unless the fixed periodic allowances is varied for individual sales personnel, it fails to reimburse for these differences. If allowances are uniform for all sales personnel, morale suffers because of the inequities. When the entire sales force faces similar driving conditions, owns comparable makes and models of cars, and has nearly equal-sized territories, each requiring approximately the same coverage, the standard allowance is defensible. It is unusual to have all these conditions present in the same situation.

Combination fixed periodic allowance and mileage rate. In this system a fixed periodic allowance (to cover fixed and semivariable expenses such as insurance premiums, license fees, and depreciation) is combined with a mileage payment (for operating expenses, including costs of gasoline, oil, and tires).

This plan recognizes that some expenses vary with automobile usage and some do not. In contrast to mileage rate systems, it provides for the expenses that do not vary directly with the operating level. In contrast to the fixed periodic allowance, it takes account of cost differentials arising from different operating levels. If sales personnel are granted identical fixed periodic allowances, this system, like the others, fails to consider territorial expense differentials and cost variations resulting from operation and ownership of different makes and models.

Some companies using combination systems accumulate reserves to cover depreciation on automobiles and reimburse sales personnel when they buy new cars. This assures that the salesperson can buy a new car without outside financing. Furthermore, this makes it unnecessary for the sales force to request company financial help in buying new cars. These reserves represent the withholding of some portion of expense allowances that otherwise would be paid periodically. When the reserve feature is not used, sales personnel often delay replacing old cars because of financial problems. The withholding feature assures that the sales staff will not drive dilapidated automobiles and risk embarrassing the company.

Runzheimer plan. The Runzheimer plan, originated by the consulting firm of Runzheimer and Company, is a combination fixed periodic allowance and mileage rate system. But it is superior to most combination systems in that it takes account of geographical variations by dividing the United States into twenty-nine "auto-use basic cost areas." (See Figure 17.5.) Allowances are on a per diem basis and include provisions for insurance premiums, state licenses, title and driver's fees, and depreciation. Mileage rates cover expenses of gasoline, oil, grease, washing, service maintenance, and tires. Runzheimer and Company recommends that certain expense items not provided for in the standard allowance be reimbursed as incurred and reported by sales personnel, such as local city license fees, property taxes, daytime parking, overnight parking away from home, and toll charges. Automobile depreciation allowances for travel in excess of 20,000 miles annually are adjusted, monthly or annually. In other words, the allowances are for 20,000 miles of average annual travel within each of the cost areas. The purpose of the depreciation adjustment is to enable high-mileage drivers to trade in cars when they reach the 60,000-total mileage point. Allowances are computed to allow for operation of different makes and models of cars. Since the plan was started in 1933, the service has been greatly extended and refined, and is now used by several hundred companies. More than 150,000 drivers of business automobiles are reimbursed over $500 million each year under the Runzheimer plan.

Runzheimer and Company also operate a living cost division. This division publishes a *Meal-Lodging Cost* index that measures meals, lodging, and public transportation costs in one hundred major U.S. cities. This division also tracks

FIGURE 17.5 The Runzheimer 29 Auto-Use Basic Cost Areas

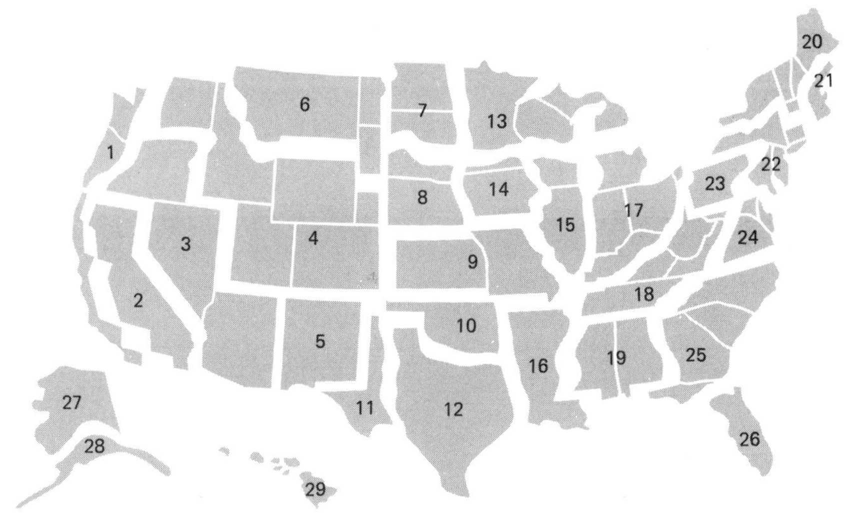

SOURCE: Runzheimer & Co.

housing costs on a geographical basis. The division combines standard costs for different components of living costs into *The Runzheimer Plan of Living Costs Standards,* which is a service prepared to offer companies comparisons of living costs for a few communities to hundreds, and for employees in different compensation ranges and with differing family sizes.[1]

CONCLUSION

Reimbursement of the expenses of sales personnel is part and parcel of the sales compensation plan. Like the basic sales compensation elements (salary, commissions and/or bonuses, or some combination thereof), expense reimbursements should be sufficient to contribute to Herzberg's "living wage" (thereby helping to prevent job dissatisfaction even though not resulting in job satisfaction). Effective sales executives see to it that sales reimbursement policies and practices are fair both to the sales personnel and the company, are sufficient to permit personnel to capitalize fully on profitable sales opportunities, and are administered in ways that prevent sales personnel from thinking of expense accounts as sources of additional income. Effective sales executives also set good examples by scrupulously adhering to established expense reimbursement policies and practices.

[1]Runzheimer and Company is headquartered in Rochester, Wisconsin, but operates multinationally with offices in London, Paris, Tokyo, Cairo, and Melbourne.

18 Sales Meetings and Sales Contests

What makes sales personnel strive for performance levels beyond "a fair day's work"? Some sales personnel, the real self-starters, are achievement motivated and need no extra push other than the challenge of the job itself. Most sales personnel, however, do not strive for performance beyond a fair day's work without additional motivation. Management provides the working environment, supervision, fringe benefits, expense reimbursement, and compensation (a "living wage")—these are the hygienic factors, whose fulfillment results in the lack of job dissatisfaction but, according to Herzberg, not job satisfaction. Performance at this level results merely from the desire to fulfill the hygiene needs. Sales personnel, at this level, are ripe for influence by the motivation factors—ones reflecting needs for personal growth including achievement, recognition, nature of the job itself, responsibility, and opportunities for promotion. The motivation factors represent needs that, when fulfilled, lead to job satisfaction. Sales management uses two main mechanisms for stimulating these needs: sales meetings and sales contests.

JOB SATISFACTION AND JOB PERFORMANCE

Think of the relationship of job satisfaction to job performance. According to Herzberg's motivation-hygiene theory, job performance leads to job satisfaction. Many managers believe exactly the opposite—job satisfaction leads to job performance. Most studies of industrial workers show a positive relationship between job satisfaction and job performance, but there is little agreement as to the direction of this relationship or the extent to which either satisfaction or performance or both are determined by other factors. It is misleading to assume that job satisfaction leads to improved job performance. Sales personnel who are "happy in their jobs" too often are people with little ambition and frequently report to managers who either misuse performance standards or do not know how to measure performance.

The motivational practices of many companies appear directed toward making sales personnel unhappy with their current performance in an effort to stimulate improved performance. Is there danger that this will decrease job satisfaction? Or is it possible—at least among some groups of sales personnel—that decreased job satisfaction stimulates improved job performance?[1]

In any event, then, we are better off focusing upon improving job performance rather than upon increasing job satisfaction. The purpose is to accomplish more than making sales personnel happier with their jobs. It is to improve job performances, regardless of the approach used.

SALES MEETINGS

Sales meetings are important both for communication and motivational purposes. When sales personnel are on the road without the day-to-day opportunity for employer communication and supervision, periodic group meetings are valuable for exchanging information and ideas. They also provide occasions for motivating individual sales personnel through group pressures. Most important, they provide occasions for management to stimulate the group to raise its standards as to reasonable and acceptable performance.

Planning and Staging Sales Meetings

Planning a sales meeting requires five major decisions: (1) defining the specific training aims, (2) deciding meeting content, (3) determining methods of conducting the meeting, (4) deciding how to execute (hold) the meeting, and (5) deciding how to evaluate the results. Thus, once again, the A-C-M-E-E approach also assures that sales meetings, like sales training programs, are fully planned and effectively staged.

Aims. In planning any sales meeting it is important to have clearly defined objectives. The underlying purposes, of course, are to communicate and motivate. But more specific aims, jokingly called "excuses for holding a meeting," are required. A new product may be about ready for introduction or research may have uncovered new insights on customer attitudes and behavior, and either of these could lead to meetings (of the sales training type) to communicate these matters to sales personnel and, it is hoped, to motivate them. Or supervisory re-

[1]Richard R. Still, "Sales Management," in Gerald Zaltman and Thomas V. Bonoma (eds.), *Review of Marketing 1978* (Chicago: American Marketing Association), pp. 265–66.

ports might have indicated that many sales personnel are deficient in applying sales techniques, and this could lead to a sales meeting, also of the training type, aimed to improve these skills. Or there may be new company policies or sales goals requiring explanation, and the meeting may aim not only to communicate but to use this important information to motivate the group. Running throughout all meeting purposes, of course, is the common aim of altering the attitudes of sales personnel so as to modify their behavioral patterns in ways leading to improved job performances.

Other specific aims of meetings include (1) improving the quality of sales force reports, (2) orienting sales personnel on the advertising program and showing how they can tie in their efforts with it, (3) increasing the effectiveness with which sales personnel use their time, and (4) introducing new services (such as inventory control assistance) for customers.

In setting a meeting's specific aims, the effective executive answers three important questions. (1) Are these aims clear and attainable? (2) Are they realistic in terms of time, audience, and other conditions? (3) Will the probable results justify the estimated costs?

Content. Determining a meeting's content is a matter of planning its agenda. An agenda, by definition, is a list or an outline of things to be considered or done during a meeting. Content, the C in A-C-M-E-E, derives directly from the meeting's specific aims. Say, for example, that there is an industry rumor that a strong competitor is about to introduce a fantastic new product and company sales personnel have high levels of anxiety. Thus, a meeting may be planned with the specific aim of reducing anxiety through informing sales personnel on what the company knows about the competitor's forthcoming new product and the company's plans for counteracting it. In this situation, content might include (1) what we know about X's new product, (2) what we think the trade's reactions will be and why, (3) what your company is doing, and (4) what you should do and how.

Method. The methods (M) used in conducting a sales meeting, of course, depend upon the aim and content as well as upon the time available and meeting place. Most local sales meetings, held rather frequently, are short and participative in nature; consequently, group discussion is generally used. Regional and national sales meetings, held less often, run for two or more days, have more ambitious aims and wider content, so they utilize a mix of methods.

Execution. The execution phase, the first E in A-C-M-E-E, is of key importance to meeting success. Decisions are reached on speakers, seminar leaders, meeting site, and time. Still other execution decisions, outwardly trivial, contribute significantly to a meeting's success or failure.

Among these seemingly trivial decisions is room arrangement. Most sales meetings, because of their underlying purposes of communicating and motivating, require active participation by attendees. The conventional classroom, as found in most educational institutions, is set up for the lecture method—seats in rows and columns. To stimulate participation, departures from the conventional arrangement are necessary. Figure 18.1 shows four popular arrangements. The herringbone breaks up the inhibiting influence of the conventional classroom arrangement—and is widely used when the presentation is basically lecture but

FIGURE 18.1 Four Popular Arrangements of Rooms for Sales Meetings

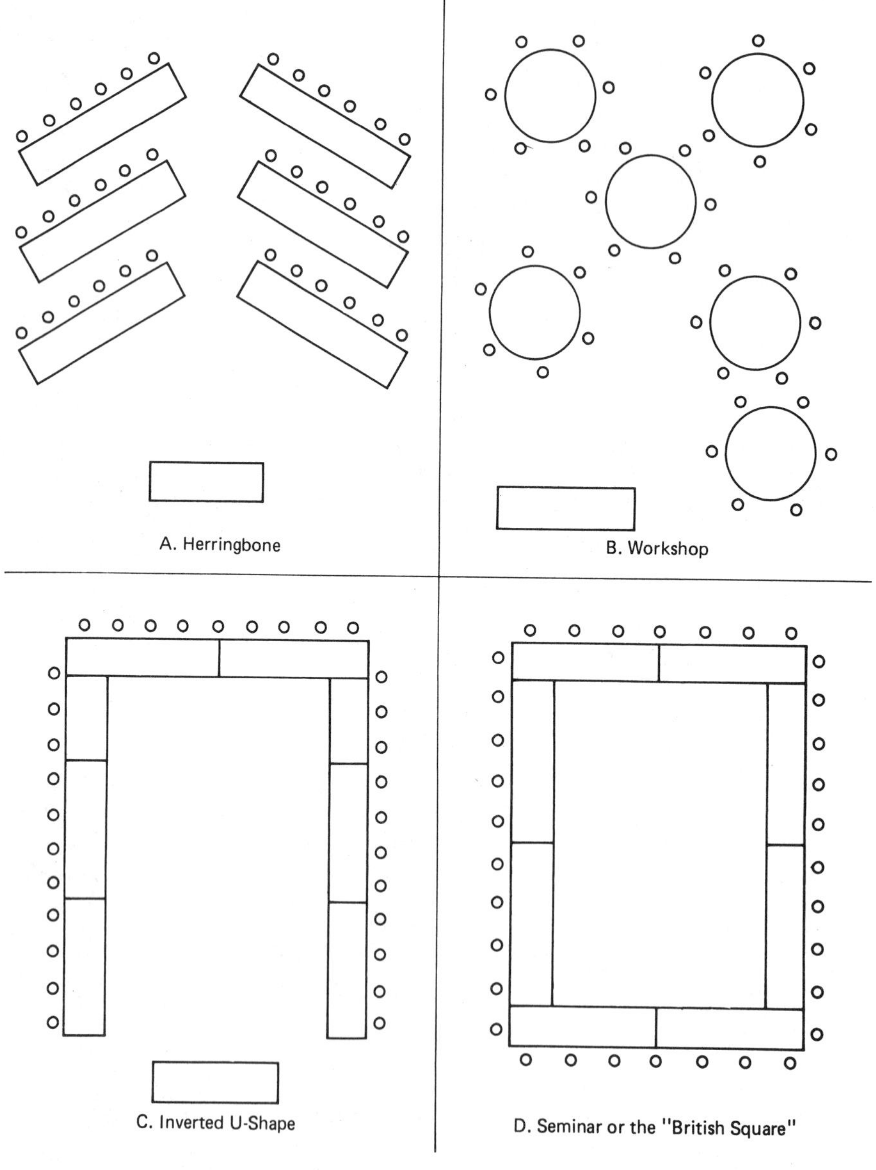

with some participation—with the herringbone, attendees see more of others attending than with the conventional arrangement. The workshop is appropriate when smaller groups are to hold buzz sessions on particular topics and report—round tables are preferred, but rectangular ones are also used. The inverted U-shape and the seminar or "British square" are used where considerable participation by the attendees is important.

Among other seemingly trivial execution decisions are those on audiovisual equipment and supplies, provision of materials to attendees (including pads and pencils), timing of breaks and refreshments, and starting time and closing time. Inappropriate decisions on any of these detract from a meeting's effectiveness.

Evaluation. The evaluation phase, the second E in A-C-M-E-E, is often neglected by meeting planners. Yet it is important, especially if management desires to improve meeting effectiveness. The basis for evaluation should be whether the meeting accomplished its aims. To determine this, participant feedback is necessary. Figure 18.2 is a sales meeting evaluation form. This form was designed to evaluate a seminar—other forms are needed to evaluate other types of meetings. The best practice is to design a new form to evaluate each sales meeting held.

National Sales Meetings

The costs of bringing the entire sales force to a central site are substantial, but national sales meetings are sometimes appropriate. If, for example, comprehensive changes in marketing or sales policies are being made, a national meeting can introduce these changes rapidly and uniformly, providing standardized explanations and answers to questions. Moreover, major executives attend a national meeting but not a series of decentralized meetings—and their attendance provides more stimulation than written or recorded messages at decentralized meetings.

There are other advantages in holding national sales meetings. Sales personnel meet informally with their counterparts from elsewhere and learn from the interchange of experience. On finding that others face and solve similar problems, sales personnel are encouraged to find their own solutions. Meeting home office personnel should result in better coordination between the office and the field. The size of the national meeting generates contagious enthusiasm. If the meeting is held at or near a factory, there is opportunity for product training and to acquaint sales personnel with technical manufacturing details.

The national sales meeting has drawbacks, in addition to the expense. It is difficult to find a convenient time for all sales personnel to attend, unless the product line is seasonal. Company routine is disrupted and competitors may cut into market share while sales personnel are away. However, more aggressive selling resulting from the national meeting should more than compensate for any temporary lapse in sales coverage.

FIGURE 18.2 Sales Meeting Evaluation Form

SALES MEETING – EVALUATION

In order to continue our efforts to improve the effectiveness of sales meetings, we need your answers to the following questions. You are under no obligation to sign this form. Thanks so much.

1. Did the seminar leader:

–know the subject? Yes ______ No ______

–present the subject practically? Yes ______ No ______

–speak clearly? Yes ______ No ______

–develop meaningful discussion from the group? Yes ______ No ______

–respond to your questions fully? Yes ______ No ______

2. The most important thing I got out of this meeting was ______________________________

3. How might this meeting have been improved? ______________________________

4. Anything else? ______________________________

Regional Sales Meetings

The trend is away from national and toward regional sales meetings. The reasons are several. Instead of the field sales force converging upon the central office, headquarters' sales executives and personnel attend the decentralized meetings, reducing total travel costs and lowering lost selling time. Headquarters' executives, brought into direct contact with field personnel, learn about current problems at firsthand. Each regional meeting may have a program designed to emphasize unique problems of that region. The smaller attendance should increase participation time per person attending.

Regional sales meetings have some disadvantages. Demands on executive time may be excessive; consequently, top sales executives often rotate attendance among regional meetings. The smaller percentage of the top management in attendance depreciates the meeting's importance in the eyes of the sales staff and, because total attendance is smaller, developing a spirit of contagious enthusiasm is more difficult.

The stimulating effect of the regional meeting is reduced further by the pressure to economize. The costs of conducting a series of meetings, for example, preclude using the top-flight speakers and entertainers featured at national meetings. Furthermore, the total costs of holding several meetings may equal or exceed those of one large national meeting, because much planning and organizational expense is not fixed but is incurred separately for each meeting.

Executive Opposition to National and Regional Sales Meetings

Many sales executives oppose both national and regional sales meetings. Some say that likely results do not justify expected costs, but they admit that many benefits, such as the effect on sales force morale cannot be measured in monetary terms. Other executives, especially those in industries without slack selling seasons, contend that they can ill afford to have sales personnel away from the field, even for a week. Still others object to the demands on their own time. In a few cases, sales executives oppose national or regional meetings because of a low sales force morale. They fear that sales personnel will use the meeting to compare complaints and to strengthen their convictions that the company is a bad place to work.

Local Sales Meetings

Local sales meetings are conducted weekly or biweekly by district sales managers and last from fifteen minutes to several hours. The strength of the local sales meeting is its informality, each salesperson having an opportunity to pose questions and to state personal views. Local sales meetings are occasions for sales personnel to get together, become better acquainted, and strengthen group identity.

Remote-Control and Traveling Sales Meetings

Certain forms of sales meetings retain the national sales meeting's advantages while reducing its cost and time expenditure disadvantages. Among these forms are meetings conducted by closed-circuit television, sales meetings by telephone, sales meetings at home, and the traveling sales meeting.

Closed-circuit television. Closed-circuit television enables a company to hold several sales meetings simultaneously. The program is "live" at one meeting site and is telecast to others, thus retaining much of the inspirational value of the live show without incurring costs and inordinate losses of selling time. Televised sales meetings are appropriate for companies with large sales forces or large dealer organizations. Many companies use televised sales meetings to introduce new products or to launch national sales campaigns.

Sales meetings by telephone. Telephone conference calls are used for small-group meetings and discussions. Users say the group should be no larger than twenty. The meeting is conducted like other small-group meetings: the sales manager welcomes the group and opens the discussion, which is guided by two rules—only one individual talks at a time, and speakers identify themselves and their cities. At the end of the call, the sales executive gives a brief summary. The telephone sales meeting saves time and money, and, of course, sales personnel lose little, if any, time away from their jobs.

Sales meetings at home. Seeking to reduce the time and costs of sales meetings, some companies mail recordings or printed materials to sales personnel at their homes. One format is to record an executive conference or meeting and to provide sales personnel with cassette copies. Another is to print an illustrated script of a home office meeting for distribution to sales personnel. Executives using these formats point to three advantages: (1) sales personnel receive the information at home, free from distractions; (2) they can review the information many times; and (3) there are savings in time and money.

Traveling sales meetings. Certain meetings require numerous physical props. For instance, a manufacturer introducing a new product line may want to display and demonstrate each new product. It is difficult in this situation to stage regional meetings because the displays must be transported to, moved in, and set up at each of several sites. Some companies overcome this by outfitting motorized vans and trailers with product displays and conference rooms. Thus, the sales meeting moves from city to city, and at each stop sales personnel and/or dealers come aboard.

SALES CONTESTS

A sales contest is a special selling campaign offering incentives in the form of prizes or awards beyond those in the compensation plan. The underlying purpose of all sales contests is to provide extra incentives to increase sales volume, to bring in more profitable sales volume, or to do both. In line with Herzberg's motivation-hygiene theory, sales contests aim to fulfill individual needs for achievement and recognition—both motivational factors. In terms of Maslow's hierarchy of needs, sales contests aim to fulfill individual needs for esteem and self-actualization—both higher-order needs. In addition, sales contests develop team spirit, boost morale (by making jobs more interesting), and make personal-selling efforts more productive.

Specific Objectives

Sales contests are aimed to accomplish specific objectives, generally one per contest, within limited periods of time. Most sales contests aim to motivate sales personnel:

1. To obtain new customers.
2. To secure larger orders per sales call.
3. To push slow-moving items, high-margin goods, or new products.
4. To overcome a seasonal sales slump.
5. To sell a more profitable mix of products.
6. To improve the performance of distributors' sales personnel.
7. To promote seasonal merchandise.
8. To obtain more product displays by dealers.
9. To get reorders.
10. To promote special deals to distributors, dealers, or both.

Contest Formats

Contest formats are classified as direct or novelty. A direct format has a contest theme describing the specific objective, such as obtaining new accounts—for example, "Let's go after new customers." A novelty format uses a theme which focuses upon a current event, sport, or the like, as in "Let's hunt for hidden treasure" (find new customers) or "Let's start panning gold" (sell more profitable orders). Some executives say a novelty format makes a sales contest more interesting and more fun for the participants. Others say that novelty formats are insults to mature people.

A format should be timely, and its effectiveness is enhanced if it coincides with an activity in the news. The theme should bear an analogous relationship to the specific contest objective—for example, climbing successive steps on a ladder can be made analogous to different degrees of success, experienced at different times—in persuading dealers to permit the erection of product displays. Finally, the theme should lend itself to contest promotion. Hundreds of themes for novelty formats have been used, most falling into one or another of the ten general categories shown in Figure 18.3.

Contest Prizes

There are four kinds of contest prizes: cash, merchandise, travel, and special honors or privileges. Cash and merchandise are the most common prizes. Many sales contests feature more than one kind of prize, for example, travel for large

FIGURE 18.3 General Categories of Themes for Sales Contests with Novelty Formats

1. Games:
   a. Team type—football, baseball, hockey, bowling, tennis doubles, tug-of-war, soccer, etc.
   b. Individual type—tennis singles, golf, wrestling, archery, fencing, broad jump, high jump, pole vault, hammer throw, discus throw, shooting match, javelin throw, bull fight, climbing the greased pole, etc.
2. Races:
   a. Team type—crew, cross-country, relay, bobsled, yacht, etc.
   b. Individual type—horse race, dog race, air race, soap-box derby, auto race, hurdles, dashes, marathons, dog sled, trotting race, swimming races, speedboat races, etc.
3. Card games—poker, pinochle, bridge, black jack, etc.
4. Hunting or fishing—treasure hunt, big-game hunt, uranium rush, gold rush, land rush, fishing derby, trapping contest, etc.
5. Travel—trip around the world, to Miami, to New York, to Hollywood, to Waikiki, to the moon, to space, etc.
6. Climbing—ladders, stairs, mountains, cliff scaling, ascent to the stratosphere, etc.
7. The rising thermometer, pressure, gauge, etc.
8. Building contests—skyscraper, other new buildings, tower, smokestacks, etc.
9. Military—naval battles, artillery engagements, bombing runs, invasions, interplanetary wars, etc.
10. Clothing contests (in one contest of this type, the salesperson earns one item of clothing at a time and appears at sales meetings clad only in those items earned up to that point).

awards and merchandise for lesser awards. Some contests give participants the option of accepting one prize rather than another.

Cash. The potency of cash as an incentive weakens as an individual's unfulfilled needs are pushed farther up in the need hierarchy. Once basic physiological needs and safety and security needs are satisfied, whatever potency money retains as an incentive relates to unfulfilled esteem and achievement needs. Noncash prizes fill these needs better than cash.

If the compensation plan provides sales personnel with sufficient income to meet basic physiological needs and safety and security needs, a cash prize is a weak incentive unless it is a substantial sum—say, 10 to 25 percent of an individual's regular annual income. A cash prize of $100 means little to most sales personnel, and they exert token efforts to win it. Another objection to cash prizes is that winners mix them with other income, and thus have no permanent evidence of their achievements.

Merchandise. Merchandise is superior to cash in several respects. Winners have permanent evidence of their achievement. The merchandise prize is obtained at wholesale, so it represents a value larger than the equivalent cash. For the same total outlay, too, more merchandise prizes than cash awards can be offered; hence, the contest can have more winners.

Merchandise prizes should be items desired by salespersons and their families. One way to sidestep this problem is to let winners select from a variety of offerings. From the psychological standpoint, people feel good when they are permitted to assert their individuality and take their choice. A number of "merchandise incentive agencies," some of them providing a complete sales contest planning service, specialize in furnishing prizes. Agencies issue catalogs with prices stated in "points" rather than in money.

Travel. Travel awards are popular. Few things can be glamorized more effectively than a trip to a luxury resort or an exotic land. The lure of a "trip of a lifetime" is a strong incentive, especially for the person to "escape" the job's routine. Travel awards generally provide trips for winners and their spouses, this being advisable both to obtain the spouse's motivational support and to avoid the spouse's opposition to solo vacation trips by the salesperson.

Special honors or privileges. This award has many forms: a letter from a top executive recognizing the winner's superior performance, a loving cup, a special trip to a home office meeting, or membership in a special group or club that has certain privileges. Winners, in addition, receive publicity through house organs and in hometown newspapers. These awards provide strong incentives, as, for example, they do with life insurance salespersons who push to gain membership in "the million dollar club."

The special honor or privilege award is used mainly by firms employing sales personnel who are almost "independent entrepreneurs." Such awards, however, are appropriate wherever management desires to strengthen group identity and build team spirit. This type of award appeals to the salesperson's belongingness and social relations needs, which, according to Maslow, an individual strives to satisfy after fulfilling basic physiological needs and safety and security needs. It also appeals to esteem and self-actualization needs (as do all other contest awards).

How Many Prizes and How Should They Be Awarded?

To stimulate widespread interest in the contest, it is a good idea to make it possible for everyone to win. This means that the basis for awards should be chosen with care. Contest planners recommend that present performance levels be taken into account—to motivate the average or inexperienced salesperson along with the star performer—and the basis of award be for improvement rather than total performance. Hence, total sales volume is less effective as an award basis than, for example, percent of quota achieved or percent of improvement in quota achievement. Many contests offer awards to all showing improvement, but the value of individual awards varies with the amount of improvement. The danger in offering only a few large prizes is that the motivational force will be restricted to the few who have a real chance of winning—the rest, knowing they have no chance to win, give up before they start.

Contest Duration

Contest duration is important in maintaining the interest of sales personnel. Contests run for periods as short as a week and as long as a year, but most run from one to four months. One executive claims that thirteen weeks (a calendar quarter) is ideal; another states that no contest should last longer than a month; still another points to a successful contest lasting six months. There are no set guides. Contest duration should be decided after considering the length of time interest and enthusiasm can be maintained, the period over which the theme can be kept timely, and the interval needed to accomplish the contest objective.

Contest Promotion

Effective contest promotion is important. To most sales personnel a contest is nothing new. A clever theme and attractive prizes may arouse interest, but a planned barrage of promotional material develops enthusiasm. A teaser campaign sometimes precedes the formal contest announcement; at other times, the announcement comes as a dramatic surprise. As the contest progresses, other techniques hold and intensify interest. Results and standings are reported at sales meetings or by daily or weekly bulletins. The sales manager dispatches telegrams carrying news of important developments or changes in relative standings. At intervals, new or special prizes are announced.

Management encourages individuals or groups to compete against each other. Reports of standings are addressed to spouses. If the prizes selected arouse the spouses' interest, continuing enthusiasm is generated in the home. The contest administrator should from time to time inject new life into the contest. From the start regular news flashes on comparative standings should be sent out, and, if initial contest incentives are not producing the desired results, the administrator adds the stimuli needed.

Managerial Evaluation of Contests

There are two times when management should evaluate a sales contest—before and after. Preevaluation aims to detect and correct weaknesses. Postevaluation seeks insights helpful in improving future contests. Both pre- and postevaluations cover alternatives, short- and long-term effects, design, fairness, and impact upon sales force morale.

The contest versus alternatives. If serious defects exist in key aspects of sales force management, a sales contest is not likely to provide more than a temporary improvement. Deficiencies caused by bad recruiting, ineffective training, incompetent supervision, or an inappropriate compensation plan are not counterbalanced, even temporarily let alone permanently, by a sales contest. The underlying purpose of all sales contests is to provide extra incentives to increase sales volume, to bring in more profitable volume, or to do both—this purpose is not accomplished if sales force management has basic weaknesses. Other avenues to improvement of selling efficiency need exploring and evaluating at the time that a sales contest is being considered. Probable results of pursuing these other avenues are taken into account in contest planning and in the post mortem evaluation.

Short- and long-term effects. A sales contest accomplishes its purpose if it increases sales volume, brings in more profitable volume, or does both in the short and the long run. No contest is a real success if it borrows sales from preceding months, succeeding months, or both. See Figure 18.4 for a visualization of the bunching-of-sales effect that so often occurs during a contest with a compensating fall-off after it is over. Successful contests increase both contest period sales and long-run sales (although there may be a temporary sales decline after the contest is over) because they inculcate desirable selling patterns that personnel retain. Furthermore, successful contests so boost the spirits of sales personnel that there is a beneficial carryover effect.

Design. A well-designed contest provides motivation to achieve the underlying purpose, while increasing the gross margin earned on sales volume by at least enough to pay contest costs. The contest format, whether direct or novel, should tie in directly with the specific objectives, include easy-to-understand and fair contest rules, and lend itself readily to promotion.

Fairness. All sales personnel should feel that the contest format and rules give everyone a fair chance of winning the more attractive awards. While the contest is on, all sales personnel should continue to feel that they have real chances of winning something. A sales contest is unfair if its format causes some to give up before it starts and others to stop trying before it is over.

Impact upon sales force morale. Successful sales contests result in permanently higher levels of sales force morale. If the contest format causes personal rivalries, it may have the counterproductive effect of creating jealousy and antagonism among the sales force. Even if sales personnel compete for individual awards, it is often advisable to organize teams and place the emphasis on competition among teams for recognition rather than among individuals for personal gain.

FIGURE 18.4 "Bunching-of-Sales" Effect During Sales Contests

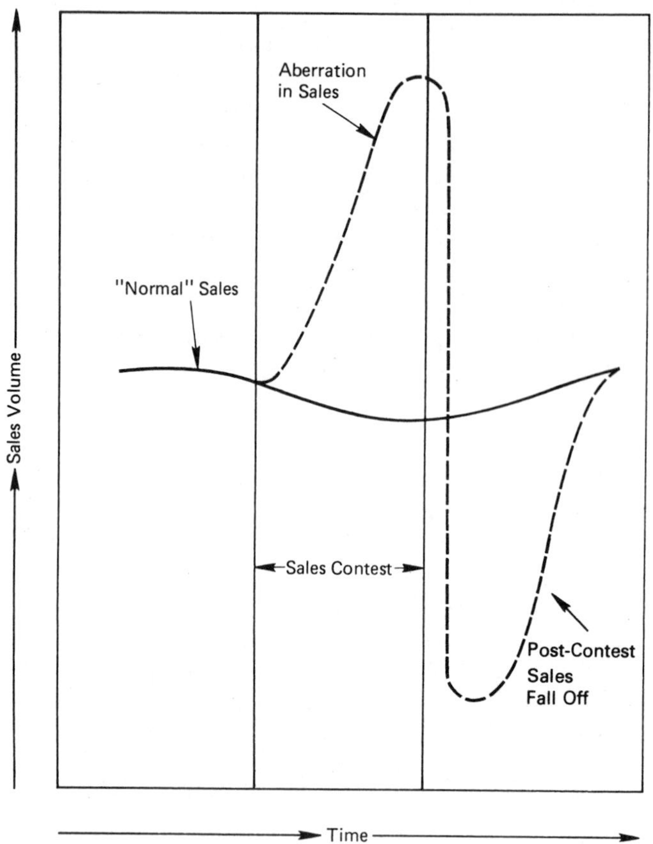

SOURCE: Adapted from H. Robert Dodge, *Field Sales Management* (Plano, Texas: Business Publications, Inc., 1973), p. 289.

Objections to Sales Contests

Only one in four sales departments use sales contests. Why? Among the standard objections are these:

1. Salespeople are paid for their services under provisions of the basic compensation plan, and there is no reason to reward them further for performing regular duties.
2. High-caliber and more experienced sales personnel consider sales contests juvenile and silly.
3. Contests lead to unanticipated and undesirable results, such as increased returns and adjustments, higher credit loss, and overstocking of dealers.

4. Contests cause salespeople to bunch sales during the competition, and sales slumps occur both before and after the contest.
5. The disappointment suffered by contest losers causes a general decline in sales force morale.
6. Contests are temporary motivating devices and, if used too frequently, have a narcotic effect. No greater results in the aggregate are obtained with contests than without them.
7. The competitive atmosphere generated by a sales contest weakens team spirit.

The first objection indicates misunderstanding of both personnel motivation and contest design, and the second may or may not be true in individual situations. All the other objections are overcome through good contest design, intelligent contest administration, and proper handling of other aspects of sales force management. Assuming that sales management is competent, thorough planning and effective administration of a contest can produce lasting benefits for both sales personnel and company. If a contest is used as a substitute for management, it is likely to have bad results.

Under some circumstances, nevertheless, sales contests are ill advised. When a firm's products are in short supply, for instance, it is ridiculous to use a contest to stimulate orders, but the same firm might find a contest appropriate to lower selling expense or improve sales reports. Companies distributing industrial goods (that is, raw materials, fabricating materials and parts, installations, accessory equipment, and operating supplies) do not find sales contests effective for stimulating sales—except, of course, where it is possible to take sales away from competitors. But, again, industrial-goods companies use contests to reduce selling costs, improve salespeople's reports, and improve customer service. Similarly, where the product is highly technical and is sold only after long negotiation, as with many industrial goods, sales contests for stimulating sales volume are inappropriate.

CONCLUSION

Sales meetings and sales contests are two means to stimulate sales personnel. Sales meetings provide opportunities for motivating and communicating with individual sales personnel and for strengthening group identification. Sales contests provide incentives to increase profitable sales volume and achieve more specific objectives. Sales meetings and sales contests require thorough planning and effective implementation. The judicious use of meetings and contests builds individual and sales force morale and helps to accomplish company goals.

19 Controlling Sales Personnel: Evaluating and Supervising

What part does controlling play in sales force management? To answer this, let's review what is involved in the management process. We'll do this in what is normally visualized, at least in the literature, as a sequence of activities performed more or less in chronological order.

The management process starts when top management makes known the company's goals, and department heads, including the top sales executive, use them to derive departmental objectives. For the sales department, the next step is to formulate policies and plans to achieve these objectives. Then, the sales management group maps out sales programs and campaigns, determines specific methods and procedures, and takes other needed actions, including making indicated changes in the sales organization to execute the policies and implement the plans. In performing these activities, sales executives coordinate the department's activities with each other and with related activities performed in other departments and by distributive outlets in the marketing channels. Up to this point, then, sales executives focus upon planning, organizing, and coordinating.

Four steps remain in the management process—some refer to it as the "management cycle." They are (1) establishing performance standards, (2) recording performances, (3) evaluating performances against the standards, and (4) taking action. These four steps constitute what is known as control.

Control, then, has both static and dynamic facets. The first three steps, all static, enable sales management to measure the progress toward achieving departmental objectives. If the fourth step in control—action—is not forthcoming, the three static steps cannot contribute maximally to sales management, despite the information they provide. Yet the "action" step, the dynamic facet of control, is frequently neglected. By taking the indicated actions, sales management keeps the department "on course."

Depending upon specific circumstances, sales management may decide (1) to take "no action" now, (2) to take action aimed to increase the degree of attainment of objectives, (3) to revise the policy or plan or the strategies used in their implementation to facilitate achievement of objectives, or (4) to lower or raise the objectives or the standards or criteria used for measuring their degree of attainment, to make them more realistic.

The managerial functions—planning, organizing, coordinating, and controlling—are not performed in an unchanging straight-line sequence. The order of performance is circular, and nowhere is this better illustrated than in the controlling phase. The decision to set sales performance standards (the first step in control) requires planning. Planning, in turn, means deciding where the sales department is going (that is, setting the objectives) and determining how the department is to get from where it is to where it wants to be. The initiation of control through standard setting is realistic only when the capabilities of the sales organization are taken into account; it does little good to set performance standards beyond the capabilities of the sales force. For control to reach maximum effectiveness, management must coordinate sale planning with sales efforts. After sales force control is set in motion, more planning, organizing, and coordinating are required. Indeed, the benefits of dynamic control, the initiating of action based on comparisons of actual performances with the standards, are not realized unless sales management takes further planning, organizing, and coordinating steps.

STANDARDS OF PERFORMANCE

Setting standards of performance requires consideration of the nature of the selling job. In other words, sales job analysis is necessary to determine job objectives, duties and responsibilities, and the like. These, in turn, depend upon selling strategy. In some companies, for example, the key problem is to obtain new customers. New-business selling requires skills different from those needed in companies whose main problem is that of servicing established accounts (that is, trade selling). Setting performance standards for new-business sales personnel requires different measures from those for trade-selling sales personnel. In companies relying upon dealer sales effort to push the product through the marketing channel, selling strategy calls for the manufacturer's sales personnel to devote major segments of their time to training dealers' sales personnel, assisting in the planning and preparation of dealer advertising, and securing "preferred" display space in dealers' showrooms. Performance standards are designed to measure the performance of activities that the company considers most important.

Some unique sales jobs exist. The mainframe computer "salesperson," for example, is both a management consultant and a system analyst—needing to know the decision-making approach appropriate to the particular industry or establishment buying the computer. Evaluating the job performance of a computer salesperson requires standards that measure not only skill in new-business selling but, even more basically, effectiveness as a management consultant and skill as a system analyst. It is important to recognize the nature of the selling job before selecting standards of performance.

Setting sales performance standards requires considerable market knowledge. It is important to know the total sales potential and the portion that each sales territory is capable of producing. Management needs evaluations of customers and prospects from the standpoint of potential profitability for each class and size of account. Marketing intelligence must provide evaluations of competitors' strengths, weaknesses, practices, and policies. Management must know the selling expenses in different territories. These items all bear on the setting of performance standards, especially quantitative standards.

Sales management takes still other factors into account in setting performance standards. Sales planning is reappraised to assure that it is the best possible under the circumstances. The policies and procedures being used to carry the personal-selling portion of the marketing program into effect are reviewed for appropriateness. Adjustments are made for the strengths and weaknesses of the individual sales personnel and for the differences in their working environments. Sales management puts together a combination of sales performance standards to fit the company's needs, its marketing situation, its selling strategy, and its sales organization.

RELATION OF PERFORMANCE STANDARDS TO PERSONAL-SELLING OBJECTIVES

Standards of sales performance facilitate the measurement of progress made toward departmental objectives. Specific objectives vary with changes in the company's marketing situation, but are reconcilable with the general objectives of volume, profit, and growth. For instance, a general objective might be to add $10 million to sales volume, a figure in itself of little assistance for operating purposes. But using this objective as a point of departure, management drafts plans to expand sales volume by $10 million. Through analysis of market factors, management may conclude that $10 million in additional sales can be made if two hundred new accounts are secured. Experience may indicate that 1,000 calls on prospects must be made to add 200 new accounts. Thus, in successive steps, the general sales volume objective is broken down into specific operating objectives. Performance standards are then established for the business as a whole and, ultimately, for each salesperson. These standards are used to gauge the extent of achievement of general and related specific objectives.

The first quantitative standard that any firm should select is one that permits comparisons of sales volume performance with sales volume potential. From the sales department's standpoint, the volume objective is the most crucial and takes precedence over the profit and growth objectives. Before profits can be earned and growth achieved, it is necessary to reach a certain sales volume level. It is entirely logical for sales management first to develop a standard to gauge sales volume performance.

Quantitative performance standards also measure success in achieving profit objectives. Profits result from complex interactions of many factors, so the modicum of control over profits provided through the standard for sales volume is not enough. Standards to bring some or all factors affecting profit under sales management's control should be set. Performance standards, then, are needed for such factors as selling expense, the sales mixture, the call frequency rate, the cost per call, and the size of order.

Setting quantitative performance standards to gauge progress made toward growth objectives is even more complex. Growth objectives are met to some extent through the natural momentum picked up as a company approaches maturity, but performances by sales personnel impact upon growth. In an expanding economy, where the gross national product each year is larger than that in the year before, it is reasonable to expect individual sales personnel to show annual sales increases. However, this assumes that marketing management keeps products, prices, promotion, and other marketing policies in tune with market demand and that sales management's efficiency is continuously improved. If these are logical assumptions, then the standards needed for individual sales personnel (besides successively higher sales volume and profit quotas each year) relate to such factors as increased sales to old accounts, sales to new accounts, calls on new prospects, sales of new products, and improvements in sales coverage effectiveness.

Quantitative Performance Standards

Most companies use quantitative performance standards. The particular combination of standards chosen varies with the company and its marketing situation. Quantitative standards, in effect, define both the nature and desired levels of performance. Indeed, quantitative standards are used for stimulating good performance as well as for measuring it.

Quantitative standards provide descriptions of what management expects. Each person on the sales force should have definitions of the performance aspects being measured and the measurement units. These definitions help sales personnel make their activities more purposeful. Sales personnel with well-defined objectives waste little time or effort in pursuing activities that do not contribute to reaching those objectives.

A single quantitative standard, such as one for sales volume attainment, provides an inadequate basis for appraising an individual's total performance.

In the past the performances of individual sales personnel were measured solely in terms of sales volume. Today's sales managers realize that it is possible to make unprofitable sales, and to make sales at the expense of future sales. In some fields—for example, industrial goods of high unit price—sales result only after extended periods of preliminary work, and it is not only unfair but misleading to appraise performance over short intervals solely on the basis of sales volume.

Sales personnel have little control over many factors affecting sales volume. They should not be held accountable for "uncontrollables" such as differences in the strength of competition, the amount of promotional support given the sales force, the potential territorial sales volume, the relative importance of sales to national or "house" accounts, and the amount of "windfall" business secured. Ample reason exists for setting other quantitative performance standards besides that for sales volume.

Each company selects that combination of quantitative performance standards that fits its marketing situation and selling objectives. If necessary, it develops its own unique standards designed best to serve those objectives. The standards discussed here are representative of the many types in use.

Quotas. A quota is a quantitative objective expressed in absolute terms and assigned to a specific marketing unit. The terms may be dollars, or units of product; the marketing unit may be a salesperson or a territory. As the most widely used quantitative standards, quotas specify desired levels of accomplishment for sales volume, gross margin, net profit, expenses, performance of nonselling activities, or a combination of these and similar items. When sales personnel are assigned quotas, management is answering the important question: How much for what period? The assumption is that management knows which objectives, both general and specific, are realistic and attainable. The validity of this assumption depends upon the market knowledge management has and utilizes in setting quotas. For instance, the first step in setting sales volume quotas is to estimate future demand for the company's products in each sales territory—hence, sales volume quotas can be no better than the sales forecast underlying them. When sales volume quotas are based upon sound sales forecasts, in which the probable strength of demand has been fully considered, they are valuable performance standards. But when sales volume quotas represent little more than guesses, or when they have been chosen chiefly for inspirational effect, their value as control devices is dissipated.

Selling expense ratio. Sales managers use this standard to control the relation of selling expenses to sales volume. Many factors, some controllable by sales personnel and some not, cause selling expenses to vary with the territory, so target selling expense ratios should be set individually for each person on the sales force. Selling expense ratios are determined after analysis of expense conditions and sales volume potentials in each territory. An attractive feature of the selling expense ratio is that the salesperson can affect it both by controlling expenses and by making sales.

The selling expense ratio has several shortcomings. It does not take into account variations in the profitability of different products—so a salesperson who has a favorable selling expense ratio may be responsible for disproportionately low profits. Then, too, this performance standard may cause the salesperson to overeconomize on selling expenses to the point where sales volume suffers. Finally, in times of declining general business, selling expense ratios inhibit sales personnel from exerting efforts to bolster sales volume.

Practice differs as to what is counted as selling expenses. If national advertising, home office sales department expense, and branch managers' and supervisors' salaries and other indirect expenses are included and allocated to each territory, sales personnel are accountable for expenses over which they have no control. But some sales executives argue that sales personnel influence the relation of indirect expenses to sales simply by putting forth some level of selling effort. In most companies, only expenses incurred directly by sales personnel, and controllable by them, are considered selling expenses. About one-half of all companies using this standard include the salesperson's salary and/or incentive compensation in the computation; the rest consider only selling expenses incurred directly by sales personnel in performing their jobs. In firms in which sales personnel pay their own traveling expenses, the selling expense ratio is calculated by simply dividing the salesperson's compensation by sales volume.

Selling expense ratio standards are used more by industrial-product companies than by consumer-product companies. The explanation traces to differences in the selling job. Industrial-product firms place the greater emphasis on personal selling and entertainment of customers; consequently, their sales personnel incur higher costs for travel and subsistence.

Territorial net profit or gross margin ratio. Target ratios of net profit or gross margin to sales for each territory focus sales personnel's attention on the needs for selling a balanced line and for considering relative profitability (of different products, individual customers, and the like). Managements using either ratio as a quantitative performance standard, in effect, regard each sales territory as a separate organizational unit that should make a profit contribution. Sales personnel influence the net profit ratios by selling more volume and by reducing selling expenses. They may emphasize more profitable products and devote more time and effort to the accounts and prospects that are potentially the most profitable. The net profit ratio controls sales volume and expenses as well as net profit. The gross margin ratio controls sales volume and the *relative* profitability of the sales mixture (that is, sales of different products and to different customers), but it does not control the expenses of obtaining and filling orders.

Net profit and gross margin ratios have shortcomings. When either is a performance standard, sales personnel may "high-spot" their territories, neglect the solicitation of new accounts, and overemphasize sales of high-profit or high-margin products while underemphasizing new products that may be more profitable in the long run. Both ratios are influenced by factors beyond the salesperson's control. For instance, pricing policy affects both net profit and gross margin, and delivery costs, which also affect both net profit and gross margin, and delivery costs, which also affect both net profit and gross margin, not only vary in different territories but are beyond the salesperson's control. Neither ratio should be used without recognition of its shortcomings.

The net ratio profit presents computational problems. Since allocations of indirect selling expenses to territories are arbitrary, the practice is to use contribution to profit, which takes into account only direct selling expenses identifiable with particular territories. Similarly, questions arise as to whether sales salaries and commissions should be included in calculating territorial net profit.

Territorial market share. This standard controls market share on a territory-by-territory basis. Management sets target market share percentages for each territory. Management later compares company sales to industry sales in each territory and measures the effectiveness of sales personnel in obtaining market share. Closer control over the individual salesperson's sales mixture is obtained by setting target market share percentages for each product and each class of customer or even for individual customers.

Sales coverage effectiveness index. This standard controls the thoroughness with which a salesperson works the assigned territory. The index consists of the ratio of the number of customers to the total prospects in a territory. To apportion the salesperson's efforts more among different classifications of prospects, individual standards for sales coverage effectiveness are set up for each class and size of customer.

Call-frequency ratio. A call-frequency ratio is calculated by dividing the number of sales calls on a particular class of customers by the number of customers in that class. By establishing different call-frequency ratios for different classes of customers, management directs selling effort to those accounts most likely to produce profitable orders. Management should assure that the interval between calls is proper—neither so short that unprofitably small orders are secured nor so long that sales are lost to competitors. Sales personnel who plan their own route and call schedules find target call frequencies helpful, inasmuch as these standards provide information essential to this type of planning.

Calls per day. In consumer-product fields, where sales personnel contact large numbers of customers, it is desirable to set a standard for the number of calls per day. Otherwise, some sales personnel make too few calls per day and need help in planning their routes, in setting up appointments before making calls (in order to reduce waiting time or the number of cases where buyers are "unavailable"), or simply in starting their calls early enough in the morning and staying on the job late enough in the day. Other sales personnel make too many calls per day and need training in how to service accounts. Standards for calls per day are set individually for different territories, taking into account territorial differences as to customer density, road and traffic conditions, and competitors' practices.

Order call ratio. This ratio measures the effectiveness of sales personnel in securing orders. Sometimes called a "batting average," it is calculated by dividing the number of orders secured by the number of calls made. Order call ratio standards are set for each class of account. When a salesperson's order call ratio for a particular class of account varies from the standard, the salesperson needs help in working with the class of account. It is common for sales personnel to vary in their effectiveness in selling to different kinds of accounts—one person may be effective in selling to small buyers and poor in selling to large buyers, another may have just the opposite performance pattern.

Average cost per call. To emphasize the importance of making profitable calls, a target for average cost per call is set. When considerable variation exists in cost of calling on different sizes or classes of accounts, standards are set for each category of account. Target average cost per call standards also are used to reduce the call frequency on accounts responsible for small orders.

Average order size. Average order size standards control the frequency of calls on different accounts. The usual practice is to set different standards for different sizes and classes of customers. Using average order size standards along with average cost per call standards, management controls the salesperson's allocation of effort among different accounts and increases order size obtained. Accomplishing this objective may require sales personnel to reduce the frequency of calls on some accounts.

Nonselling activities. Some companies establish quantitative performance standards for such nonselling activities as obtaining dealer displays and cooperative advertising contracts, training distributors' personnel, and goodwill calls on distributors' customers. Whenever nonselling activities are critical features of the sales job, appropriate standards should be set. Since quantitative standards for nonselling activities are expressed in absolute terms, they are, in reality, quotas.

Multiple quantitative performance standards. It is widespread practice to assign multiple quantitative performance standards. Figure 19.1 shows a form used by a company whose sales personnel are assigned nine different quantitative standards per operating period.

Qualitative Performance Criteria

Certain aspects of job performance, such as personal effectiveness in handling customer relations problems, do not lend themselves to precise measurement, so the use of some qualitative criteria is unavoidable. Qualitative criteria are used for appraising performance characteristics that affect sales results, especially

FIGURE 19.1 Form Used for Assigning Quantitative Performance Standards To Sales Personnel

ASSIGNED STANDARDS OF PERFORMANCE

SALES PERSON: . . . . OPERATING PERIOD: . . . .

1. Sales during period: . . . . (Quota: $ . . . .)

    STANDARD: Meet or exceed quota.

2. New accounts obtained during period: . . . .

    STANDARD: 5 per period.

3. Sales to new accounts during period: $ . . . .

    STANDARD: 10% of total sales.

4. Total calls during period: . . . . Average calls per day: . . . .

    STANDARD: 6 calls per day.

5. Percent of accounts called on one or more times during period: . . . . %.

    STANDARD: 100%

6. Total contacts during period: . . . . Average number of contacts per call: . . . .

    STANDARD: 2 contacts per call.

7. Proportion of calls on retail (R) accounts: . . . . %, wholesale (W) accounts: . . . .%.

    STANDARD: R 70%, W 30%.

8. Total sales meetings held: . . . . Attended: . . . .

    STANDARD: Attend all.

9. Customers entertained during period: . . . . Average per week: . . . .

    STANDARD: 1 or more per week.

over the long run, but whose degree of excellence can be evaluated only subjectively. Qualitative criteria defy exact definition. Many sales executives, perhaps most, do not define the desired qualitative characteristics with any exactitude; instead, they arrive at informal conclusions regarding the extent to which each salesperson possesses them. Other executives consider the qualitative factors

FIGURE 19.2 Form Used for Qualitative Analysis of Salesperson Performance

SALESPERSON PERFORMANCE ANALYSIS

NAME .... DATE ....

	PROBLEM	FAIR	AVER	GOOD	SUPERIOR
JOB FACTORS					
PRODUCT KNOWLEDGE					
AWARENESS OF CUSTOMER NEEDS					
RELATIONSHIP WITH CUSTOMERS					
NUMBER OF SALES CALLS					
QUOTA PERFORMANCE					
SERVICE FOLLOW-UP					
PERSONAL FACTORS					
PUNCTUALITY					
GENERAL ATTITUDE					
DRESS & APPEARANCE					
DILIGENCE					
COOPERATION					
ACCURACY					
ADAPTABILITY					
RELIABILITY					

STRONGEST POINT ....

....

WEAKEST POINT ....

....

COMMENTS ....

....

SIGNATURE

formally, one method being to rate sales personnel against a detailed checklist of subjective factors such as that shown in Figure 19.2.

Companies with merit-rating systems differ on the desirability of using numerical ratings. Most numerical scoring systems are in companies that rate sales personnel primarily for detecting needed adjustments in compensation. Companies that use merit rating primarily to improve and develop individual salespersons usually do not use numerical scoring systems.

Executive judgment plays the major role in the qualitative performance appraisal. Written job descriptions, up to date and accurate, are the logical points of departure. Each firm develops its own set of qualitative criteria, based upon the job descriptions; the manner in which these criteria are applied depends upon the needs of management.

RECORDING ACTUAL PERFORMANCE

Sales management's next task is to measure actual performance. Emphasis in this phase of control, in other words, shifts to gathering performance information. It is necessary to define information needs, determine the information sources, and collect the information.

The choice of performance standards dictates the information needed. However, with increasingly sophisticated management information systems, the choice of performance standards is based as much on information availability as on the desire to use certain standards. It is good practice to review periodically the sales performance standards in use and the availability of other information that might permit use of different or additional standards.

There are two basic sources of performance information: sales and expense records and reports of various sorts. Almost every company has a wealth of data in its internal sales and expense records, but this information frequently requires reworking, or reprocessing, before it is useful for sales control purposes. Reclassified according to sales management's information needs, sales and expense data contribute to the determination and measurement of actual performances.

Among the reports sales management has available are those from sales personnel and the lower echelons of sales management; these are discussed in the following section. In addition, companies using such quantitative performance standards as sales volume quotas and target share-of-the-market percentages require information contained in sales forecasts, which, of course, are prepared not only for sales management's use but for managerial planning throughout the enterprise.

The methods of obtaining needed information depend upon the sources. Internally generated information, such as that from the data-processing installation, is provided on a routine basis, or in response to requests for special tabulations. Information obtainable only from sales personnel or field sales management personnel is gathered through formal reports; such information is also obtained through personal observation—by trips to the field or through field sales supervisors.

System of Field Sales Reports

The fundamental purpose of field sales reports is to provide control information. Good communications require interaction between those preparing and those receiving reports. A good field sales reporting system provides both for communication from the field to headquarters and from the headquarters to the field.

Field sales reports provide sales management with a basis for discussion with sales personnel. They indicate the matters on which salespeople need assistance. The sales executive uses field sales reports to determine whether sales personnel are calling on and selling to the right people, and whether they are making the proper number of calls. Similarly, field sales reports assist in determining how to secure more and larger orders. Field sales reports provide the raw materials that sales management processes to gain insights on giving needed direction to field sales personnel.

A good field sales reporting system assists sales personnel in their self-improvement programs. Recording accomplishments in written form forces individuals to check their own work. They become their own critics, and self-criticism often is more valuable and more effective than that from headquarters. If this motivates sales personnel to improve coordination of their efforts with sales management's plans, the managerial process functions more smoothly.

Purposes of field sales reports. The purpose a report is to serve determines the nature of the information it contains and the frequency of its transmittal. The general purpose of all field sales reports is to provide information for measuring performance; many reports, however, provide additional information. Consider the following list of purposes served by field sales reports:

1. To provide data for evaluating performance—for example, details concerning accounts and prospects called upon, number of calls made, orders obtained, days worked, miles traveled, selling expenses, displays erected, cooperative advertising arrangements made, training of distributors' personnel, missionary work, and calls made with distributors' sales personnel.
2. To help the salesperson plan the work—for example, planning itineraries, sales approaches to use with specific accounts and prospects.
3. To record customers' suggestions and complaints and their reactions to new products, service policies, price changes, advertising campaigns, and so forth.
4. To gather information on competitors' activities—for example, new products, market tests, changes in promotion, and changes in pricing and credit policy.

5. To report changes in local business and economic conditions.
6. To log important items of territorial information for use in case sales personnel leave the company or are reassigned.
7. To keep the mailing list updated for promotional and catalogue materials.
8. To provide information requested by marketing research—for example, data on dealers' sales and inventories of company and competitive products.

Types of sales force reports. Reports from sales personnel fall into six principal groups.

1. *Progress or call report.* Most companies have a progress or call report. It is prepared individually for each call (see Figure 19.3) or cumulatively, covering all calls made daily or weekly. Progress reports keep management informed of the salesperson's activities, provide source data on the company's relative standing with individual accounts and in different territories, and record information that assists the salesperson on revisits. Usually the call report form records not only calls and sales, but more detailed data, such as the class of customer or prospect, competitive brands handled, the strength and activities of competitors, best time to call, and "future promises."
2. *Expense report.* Because most sales personnel are reimbursed for expenses and itemized expense records are required for income tax purposes, most companies have an expense report. From sales management's standpoint, the purpose is to control the nature and amount of salespersons' expenses. This report also helps the salesperson exercise self-control over expenses. The expense report reminds salespersons that they are under moral obligation to keep expenses in line with reported sales—some expense report forms require salespersons to "correlate" expenses with sales. The details of the report form vary with the plan for reimbursing expenses. A Weekly Expense Form is shown in Figure 19.4.[1]
3. *Sales work plan.* The salesperson submits a work plan (giving such details as accounts and prospects to be called upon, products and other matters to be discussed, routes to be traveled, and hotels or motels) for a future period, usually a week or a month (see Figure 19.5). The purposes are to assist the salesperson in planning and scheduling activities and to inform management of the salesperson's whereabouts. The work plan provides a basis for evaluating the salesperson's ability "to plan the work and to work the plan."
4. *New-business or potential new-business report.* This report informs management of accounts recently obtained and prospects who may become sources of new business. It provides data for evaluating the extent and effectiveness of development work by sales personnel. A subsidiary purpose is to remind sales personnel that management expects them to get

[1]For two other examples of expense forms, see Chapter 17, Figures 17.3 and 17.4.

FIGURE 19.3 Sales Call Report

CALL REPORT

Date ________________ 19 ______

Customer: ______________________________

Street: ______________________________

City: ______________________ State: ______________

Persons Contacted: ______________________ Title: ______________

______________________ Title: ______________

TYPE OF CUSTOMER

- ☐ Road Contractor
- ☐ Building Contractor
- ☐ Water and Sewer Contractor
- ☐ Governmental
- ☐ Industrial
- ☐ Utility
- ☐ Mining and Quarry
- ☐ Other ______________

SELLING STEPS TAKEN

- ☐ Catalogs
- ☐ Movie
- ☐ View Machine Demonstration
- ☐ Service
- ☐ Entertained
- ☐ Other ______________

INTERESTED IN

☐ NEW	☐ USED	☐ RENTAL
☐ Euclid ☐ Thew	☐ Gardner-Denver	☐ Pioneer ☐ Bros.
☐ Rogers ☐ Dynahoe	☐ Coastal	☐ Other ______

FOLLOW UP PLAN: ______________________________

Date of next call: ______________

REMARKS: ______________________________

Sales person: ______________________ ☐ Add to Mailing List.

WHITE-HOUSTON PINK-BRANCH YELLOW-SALESPERSON

new accounts. Comparing the information secured with data in company files, management evaluates the effectiveness of prospecting (see Figure 19.6).

5. *Lost-sales report.* This report provides information for evaluating a salesperson's abilities to keep customers and to sell against competition. Lost-

FIGURE 19.4 Weekly Expense Report

WEEKLY EXPENSE REPORT
CASH EXEPNDITURES

UNITED MARKETERS, INC.
MID-AMERICA OPERATIONS

Name ______________________ Week Ending ______________________

Date	From/To (or place at)	Meals (including) Self		Lodging		Enter-tainment		Miscellaneous			Daily Totals	
								Descript.	Amount			
M												
T												
W												
T												
F												
S												
S												
Expense Item Totals For Week												

Itemize below

Amount to be reimbursed ______

I hereby certify that the above expenses represent monies spent for legitimate business only

Approval ______________________

Signed ______________________

EXPLANATION OF ENTERTAINMENT EXPENSE (including meals, etc., others)

Date	Name Persons Entertained	Firm	Where	Nature and Purpose	Amount	
				Total		

FIGURE 19.5 Sales Work Plan

MEOW HOLDINGS, INC.

SALES WORK PLAN

Salesperson ______________________ Date ______________ Week of ______________

	Prospect	Location	Purpose of Contact
Monday			
Tuesday			
Wednesday			
Thursday			
Friday			
Saturday			

WEEKLY ACTIVITY REPORT

Salesperson ____________________

Branch ____________________

Week Ending ____________________

PROSPECTS

Customer	New or Used	Make and Model	Eng.	Sale	Rental Mos.	Pur. Opt.	Status

ORDERS PLACED

Customer	New or Used	Make and Model	Sale	Rental In Months	Remarks

LOST ORDERS

Customer	Machine Quoted	Purchased Make and Model	Sale or Rent	Reason

FIGURE 19.6 Weekly Activity Report on Prospects, Orders Placed, & Lost Orders

sales reports point the way to needed sales training, changes in customer service policies, and product improvements. The salesperson reports the reasons for the loss of the business; but receipt of a lost-sales report also causes management to consider further investigation (see Figure 19.6).

6. *Report of complaint and/or adjustment.* This report provides information for analyzing complaints arising from a salesperson's work, complaints by class of customer, and cost of complaint adjustment. This assists management in detecting needed product improvements and changes in merchandising and service practices and policies. These data also are helpful for decisions on sales training programs, selective selling, and product changes (see Figure 19.7).

Reports from field sales management. In decentralized organizations, field sales executives have an important part in setting sales performance standards. Branch and district sales managers and, in some cases, sales supervisors assist in establishing sales volume quotas for salespeople who, in many companies, also are consulted on their own quotas. Branch and district sales managers, in addition, play roles in breaking down branch and district sales volume quotas to quotas for individual sales personnel, and to products or product lines and/or to types of customers—occasionally, even to specific accounts. At the district level, especially in larger companies, profit and/or expense quotas are sometimes set for individual sales personnel and by product line.

The district sales manager's planning report is called a *district sales plan,* often prepared by compiling, with or without revisions, sales work plans, and covering the work or results that each district salesperson expects to accomplish during the month, quarter, or year ahead. Besides breaking down dollar or unit sales volume quotas by products or product lines for each salesperson, district sales plans include standards for number of calls, number of calls on each type of account or on individual accounts, and target number of new dealers and/or distributors. District sales plans usually require the district sales manager to suggest standards for appraising his or her own performance, for example, the recruiting of a certain number of new sales personnel and the carrying out of some amount of sales training. District sales plans are subject to review and to revision by higher sales executives.

Field sales executives have responsibility for reporting information on personnel performance. Since they are in the most frequent contact with the sales force, they are well placed to observe individual sales personnel in the field. Consequently, field sales executives prepare "sales personnel evaluation" reports, often of the merit-rating type, which gather information on qualitative sales performances. In some companies, this is called a "progress report" and includes qualitative information on personnel performance and data comparing individual performance to quantitative standards. See Figure 19.8 for a progress report. Sales personnel evaluation reports are prepared either periodically or each time a district sales manager or supervisor works with a salesperson. As companies increasingly utilize centralized data-processing facilities for processing

FIGURE 19.7 Customer Service Request

CUSTOMER SERVICE REQUEST

DATE ____________

CUSTOMER ____

ADDRESS ____

____________________________ PHONE: AC (   ) ____________

MERCHANDISE PROBLEMS

- ORDER NOT FILLED ☐
- DEFECTIVE ITEM ☐
- REPAIR PROBLEM ☐
- WRONG ITEM SOLD ☐
- AMOUNT CHARGED IN ERROR ☐
- CREDIT/REFUND NOT ISSUED ☐
- OTHER ____________________

DELIVERY PROBLEMS

- INCORRECT ADDRESS ☐
- CUSTOMER OUT ☐
- LOST IN TRANSIT ☐
- DAMAGED IN TRANSIT ☐
- MERCHANDISE MISSING ☐
- OTHER ____________________

REMARKS

DISPOSITION:

FIGURE 19.8 Monthly Sales Report Submitted by Branch Sales Managers

MONTHLY SALES REPORT

DIVISION ____________________ MONTH OF ____________

1. Sales Quota
   Monthly quota met or exceeded? Yes _____ No _____
   YTD quota met or exceeded? Yes _____ No _____
   Percent of quota achieved: __________ %

2. Sales Personnel who have met or exceeded monthly quotas:

Name	Percent

3. Sales Personnel who have not met monthly quotas:

Name	Percent

4. Action taken to correct deficiencies:

5. Dates of sales meetings held this month: ____________________

6. Subjects discussed at sales meetings: ____________________

7. Scheduled dates of meetings next month: ____________________

8. Subjects to be discussed at meetings: ____________________

9. Repeated complaints about the product? Yes _____ No _____
   Specify: ____________________

10. Competitors making inroads on company accounts?
    Yes _____ No _____ Specify: ____________________

FIGURE 19.8 *(Continued)*

11. General business activity in territory: ______________________________
____
____

12. Suggestions for improving products, sales, service:
____
____
____

13. Other comments: ______________________________
____

Sales Manager ______________

quantitative data, the role of the district sales office in gathering, collating, and reporting quantitative sales performance data has declined. But no good substitute method for gathering information on *qualitative* aspects of personnel performances has been found, and the district sales manager continues as the main unit for gathering such information.

The salesperson's immediate superior (a sales supervisor, branch sales manager, or district sales manager) usually is responsible for appraising his or her performance, but higher sales management reviews these appraisals. Review is necessary (1) to make certain that the appraisal form has been filled out properly, (2) to check against personal bias or errors in judgment, and (3) to rate the rater's ability to set performance standards and to evaluate sales personnel.

Number of reports. The optimum number of reports is the minimum necessary to produce the desired information. Holding down the number of reports is important, since they are generally made out after the selling day. Report preparation places demands on free time, and, unfortunately, the best people often have the least time. All reports are reviewed from time to time to determine whether the information is worthwhile. When a new report is proposed, the burden of proof of its need is upon its advocates. Information obtainable through other means at no higher cost should not be gathered through field sales reports. Some companies, in assessing the worth of a sales report, discontinue it without notice or insert intentional errors in the form, thus learning whether the report is essential and the use, if any, made of the information.

Design and construction of reports. Each field sales report should be as short as is consistent with its purpose. This is especially important for those submitted by sales personnel—whenever possible, the form should provide for easy checking off of routine informational items. Similarly, sales report forms should be of conveniently portable size and shape. More and more companies have adopted IBM or similar types of cards for call reports, which, incidentally, facilitates analysis. Where feasible, sales reports should include carbons so that the salesperson has copies. A minimum of clerical work, such as tabulations or comparisons, should be required of sales personnel.

Information on field reports should be so arranged that it can easily be summarized. There should also be set routines for transferring information onto other records. If original reports are not destroyed after a short time, there is needless accumulation of data.

Detail required in sales reports. The amount of detail required in sales reports varies from firm to firm. A company with many sales personnel covering a wide geographical area needs more detailed reports than does a company with a few salespeople covering a compact area. The more freedom that sales personnel have to plan and schedule their activities, the greater should be the detail required in their reports. However, and in apparent contradiction, commission sales personnel are asked for less detail in reports than are salaried salespeople, probably because management feels that it has less power to direct their activities. In general, the higher the caliber of sales personnel, the less is management's need for details. High-caliber people are expected to exercise self-control, thus reducing the need for detailed formal reporting.

EVALUATING—COMPARING ACTUAL PERFORMANCES WITH STANDARDS

The most difficult step in sales force control is the evaluation step—the comparing of actual performances with standards. This is more than a mechanical comparison; this step is difficult because evaluation requires judgment. The same standards cannot be applied to all sales personnel—there are differences in individual territories, their sales potentials, the impact of competition, and the personalities of sales personnel and their customers. It is possible to take territorial differences into account by setting individual performance standards for each territory, but it is not possible to adjust fully for differences in the personalities of the salesperson and the clientele. Furthermore, complications often develop in relating individual performances to standards, for example, when two or more salespersons work on the same account or when an account deals both with the salesperson and the home office.

Evaluating sales personnel requires both a comparison of performance with quantitative standards and an appraisal against qualitative performance criteria. Sales personnel with poor performances, as gauged by quantitative standards, may be making offsetting qualitative contributions. Individuals who do not reach sales quotas or keep to prescribed call schedules, for instance, may be building for the future by cementing relations with distributors and dealers. Evaluating performance of sales personnel requires judgment and deep understanding of market factors and conditions.

Judgment enters into the evaluation of sales personnel in still other ways. Performance trends, as well as the current record, are relevant—an individual showing improvement but with still substandard performance needs encouragement. There is always the chance, too, that something is wrong with a standard—when an individual continually fails to reach a standard, management should investigate whether the standard has been set too high.

In comparing actual results with projected results, the general procedure in scientific work is to set up tests that measure the variable under observation while taking account of the effects of other variables. In the evaluation of sales personnel it is not possible to set up such tests. Each salesperson's performance results from complex interactions of many variables, some beyond the control of either the salesperson or of management. The time element changes and so do the sales personnel, the customers, general business conditions, competitors' activities, and other variables. However, some companies measure the impact of particular variables on personnel performance through careful design of experimental and control groups.

TAKING ACTION—THE DYNAMIC PHASE OF CONTROL

The evaluations, or comparisons of actual performances with standards, tempered and adjusted by executive judgment, point the way to needed action. If performance and standards are in alignment the decision may be: no action needed. Otherwise, the three alternatives are (1) adjust performance to the standards, thus increasing the degree of attainment of objectives; (2) revise the policy and/or plan, or the strategies used for their implementation, to fit better the achievement of objectives; or (3) lower or raise the objectives or the standards and/criteria used in measuring their degree of attainment to make them more realistic. The actions resulting from these decisions, in turn, are conditioned by the executive's judgment, experience, knowledge of the situation, and administrative skill.

CONTROLLING SALES PERSONNEL THROUGH SUPERVISION

Management also controls sales personnel through supervision. Regardless of who does the supervising, the objective is to improve the job performances of sales personnel. The executive with supervisory responsibilities establishes working relations with sales personnel for purposes of observing, evaluating, and reporting on performance; correcting deficiencies; clarifying responsibilities and duties; providing motivation; informing sales personnel of changes in company policy; helping to solve business and personal problems; and continuing sales training. Clearly, sales supervision is concerned mainly with the action phase of control—action aimed at enhancing personnel contributions to the achievement of objectives.

How much supervision is enough? Too much is as bad as too little. It is difficult to prescribe how much supervision is enough, but there are some conditions under which supervision is needed. Among these conditions are:

Sales personnel turnover rate excessive in a branch, district, or other organizational unit.

High turnover of accounts.

Increased complaints from customers.

Mail or phone orders increasing for no known reasons.

Low ratio of orders to sales calls.

Total number of calls very low or very high.

Increasing ratio of selling expenses to sales in an organizational unit.

Low morale, as implied by negative attitude toward company, lack of enthusiasm, signs of restlessness, and job hunting.

These conditions can trace to the wrong kind of supervision as well as to too much or too little supervision. While this list is useful for appraising the effectiveness of sales supervision, those doing the appraising must recognize that many of these conditions may have their roots in deficiencies in other phases of sales force management. It sometimes happens, too, that a company upgrades the quality of its sales personnel and fails to adjust the pattern of supervision. The selling task in many companies has changed so that it is now high-level, key account selling, and this demands independent, self-reliant, highly educated sales personnel who can and must make their own decisions. When management brings in highly trained and self-reliant people to meet the new selling challenge, traditional supervision—and the attitudes that underlie it—stifles those whom management seeks to encourage. What worked for so long is wrong for the more dynamic assignment of the newer type of person. The type of supervision, in other words, should be adjusted to the type of person in the selling job—when the type of person changes, so should the type of supervision.

Who Should Supervise?

Depending upon the company and its organization, sales personnel may be supervised by home office personnel, branch or district managers, or field sales supervisors. Put another way, sales supervision may be either through executives as one of their job responsibilities, or through specialists whose jobs are mainly supervising. If the sales force is small and experienced, sales supervision is generally through the top sales executive or an assistant. Necessarily, control through home office supervision is minimal, but it may be enough, especially when the sales organization is small and permits the development of close relations among sales personnel and executives and when little sales training is required.

Companies having decentralized sales organizations sometimes assign the supervision responsibility to branch or district managers. Customarily promoted from the ranks, branch managers are presumably well prepared to supervise field sales personnel. However, even in companies with elaborate field sales organization, limitations exist on the amount of supervision that branch managers should exercise. In practice, the branch manager is often a local general manager more than a specialized sales executive and in this capacity is responsible for the local conduct of all the company's affairs, not only for managing sales personnel but for warehousing, extending credit and making collections, providing service, and performing other work. Branch managers spend most of their time attending to details, so it is unusual for them to devote much time to personal supervision of sales personnel. But they should spend some time. Especially when branch managers have large numbers of sales personnel under them, the time they can spend with each one is limited, and, as is true of supervision emanating from the home office, they rely mainly upon sales personnel to supervise themselves.

Qualifications of Sales Supervisors

Sales supervisors generally are selected from among the sales force, but besides having the qualifications required for selling success, they need other qualifications. They must be good teachers. They must recognize training needs, know how to train, be patient with those who have less skill, and be tactful in pointing out better ways of doing things. As vital links in the chain of communication—go-betweens for higher sales management and the sales force alike—they must understand the needs and problems of both and reconcile them in the field. They must be skilled in handling people and be equipped to deal with many complex situations. Beyond these supervisory duties, some companies expect sales supervisors to sell certain accounts personally, this being one way to motivate them to keep up to date on field selling techniques. The field sales supervisor's job is difficult and, in most companies, one with comparatively low pay. Nevertheless, many salespersons are eager for promotions to supervisory positions, since they often are stepping stones to higher positions.

CONCLUSION

Discussion in this chapter focused upon the part that control plays in the sales force management process. The following outline summarizes the different phases in this process.

1. Company goals are defined, and appropriate objectives for the sales department are derived.
2. To facilitate achievement of objectives, departmental policies are formulated and plans designed.
3. To execute the policies and implement the plans, promotional programs and campaigns are mapped out, specific methods and procedures are determined, and other needed actions, such as making indicated alterations in the sales organization, are taken.
4. Various sales department activities are coordinated with each other and with related activities performed by other organizational units and middlemen.
5. Quantitative performance standards are set, and criteria for appraising qualitative aspects of performance are selected.
6. Actual performance is recorded.
7. Actual performance is compared with quantitative performance standards and qualitative performance criteria, and judgment is reached on the significance of variations.
8. Indicated actions are taken after deciding
   a. To "take no action" at this time.
   b. To increase the degree of attainment of objectives.
   c. To revise the policy and/or plan, or the various strategies used in their implementation, to better fit the achievement of objectives.
   d. To lower or raise objectives or the standards and/or criteria used in measuring their degree of attainment, to make them more realistic.

In that they deal specifically with evaluating and supervising sales personnel, the last four steps comprise "control," the first three being static, whereas the action step (phase 8) is dynamic. Adoption and successful operation of appropriate control procedures for a sales department results in greater effectiveness, which ultimately shows up in greater sales volume at more profit and less cost per sales dollar.

Effective procedures for evaluating and supervising sales personnel assure that sales department objectives are reached with minimum effort. Evaluating and supervising are concerned with monitoring the balance between standards and actual performance. Both are instrumental in achieving sales force control.

Cases for Part III

CASE 3-1

Central CATV, Inc.

Community Antennas Television (CATV) Service—High Turnover of Sales Personnel

Thomas Wagner, sales manager for Central CATV, Inc., was concerned about a high turnover of sales personnel, as well as certain other problems that had surfaced recently. The average Central CATV salesperson stayed with the company for less than seven months. Although actual sales were close to projected levels, Wagner felt the need for immediate action. He believed that correction of the turnover problem would enable Central CATV to achieve higher sales.

Cable television was developed to alleviate signal reception problems in rural areas. Recognizing that people were willing to pay for variety in programming, CATV moved into cities that were receiving two or three channels and offered them between ten and twelve channels. Gaining acceptance in medium-sized cities, cable television went into large metropolitan areas and offered up to twenty-five television channels. CATV systems in the United States served nearly 13 million homes, or over 17 percent of the total homes with television sets.

The operational concept was simple. A large tower with antennas capable of bringing in signals from outlying centers was erected. The signals were then sent out via coaxial cables to subscribers' homes. Amplifiers were used to clarify and boost the signals along the cable network.[1]

Cable system start-up costs included construction of the master antennas, the cable network, and initial promotion. The initial outlay was relatively high and most cablevision companies did not earn a profit until the third year of operation. Once start-up costs were absorbed, generally there was excellent profit potential because of low operational costs.

For the previous three years, Central CATV had served a southern market comprised of over 60,000 persons, nearly 40 percent of whom were students at a large university. The company bought the cablevision system from the "pioneering" operator and immediately expanded the cable network from 100 miles to 200 miles and from six stations to ten stations. Central CATV charged an installation fee of $35 and a monthly service fee of $8.95.

Central CATV serviced nearly 30 percent of the TV viewing market in its operating area. The goal was to have 50 percent of the market by the end of the fifth year of operation. Wagner felt that was a realistic objective since, without the cable, it was possible to receive only two television channels.

[1]A more detailed description of the cable television system appears in the Scientific-Atlanta, Inc., case, pp. 111–112.

The only advertising Central CATV had sponsored occurred shortly after its takeover of the operation. There had been need to overcome the poor service reputation of the predecessor. Central used a three-month radio and newspaper campaign emphasizing the theme that "a new progressive company has taken over CATV." After this campaign, there was no further advertising. Wagner believed additional advertising unnecessary as most people were aware of CATV and the product "sold itself."

The sales force had one full-time and two part-time salespersons. Although the sales personnel reported directly to Wagner, his only "contact" with them, other than for occasional phone calls, were the billing invoices sent to the sales office after they had made sales. Sales personnel were paid straight commissions of $12 per sale. Management estimated that a full-time salesperson could earn up to $22,000 annually, although no person had ever been with Central that long. Part-time salespeople earned about $8,000. The personnel were not assigned territories, and there was no quota system.

Sales personnel attempted to close on the first call. They believed that most prospects already knew about CATV and had a predetermined opinion as to its value. Consequently, when salespeople could not close a sale on the first call, they generally did not make a callback.

In addition to the three salespeople, Wagner had an agreement with most local TV dealers. The dealers acted as cable television salespersons despite the fact that they competed with the cable service, since they sold rooftop antennas which were not needed with the cable hookup. Central paid dealers $15 for each sale made. The dealers liked this arrangement since, if they could not sell a customer a rooftop antenna, they usually succeeded in getting $15 commission for a cable system "sale."

During the past several months, three developments caused deep concern for Wagner: (1) a large number of subscription cancellations, (2) an increase in customer complaints, and (3) a great increase in the number of mail and phone orders for the cable service. In addition, there was the continued difficulty in retaining sales personnel. The subscription cancellations were over and above those associated with students leaving the university. The rapid turnover of accounts because of students leaving town was not a problem, according to Wagner.

Although sales were satisfactory, Wagner believed that investigation and correction of the problems, especially that of high personnel turnover, would enable Central CATV to attain and even surpass its projected sales goal. He could not understand why these problems had appeared simultaneously. He was not sure which problem to attack first but felt that the most important was the high personnel turnover.

Suggest what Wagner should have done to reduce personnel turnover and eliminate the other problems at Central CATV.

CASE 3-2

Norton Brothers, Inc.

Manufacturer of Men's Furnishings— Attempt to Reduce Personnel Turnover

Norton Brothers, Inc., of Rochester, New York, was a manufacturer of men's popular-priced neckwear sold under the brand name Snappy Cravats to small and large haberdashers and department stores. Joseph Norton, president and sales manager, was assisted by two people who were assigned primarily to office duties but who doubled as salespeople during the busy season. Three full-time salespeople covered the northeastern part of the United States, but other sections were reached by four side-line people. In addition, many orders were received direct and by phone and mail at the home office. Currently, Norton was faced with the problem of his salespersons' dissatisfaction with the high costs of traveling and of being on the road for extended periods.

One regular salesperson covered New York State, a second had the Pennsylvania territory, and the third was assigned to New England. The four side-line salespeople sold in distant territories; for instance, one was based in Puerto Rico. The regular salespeople, who reported directly to Norton, were paid on a drawing account plus commission basis. Commissions were 10 percent on regular merchandise, 7 percent on some lower-priced items, and 5 percent on close-out items. This method of compensation was widely used in the neckwear industry, and Norton was convinced that 10 percent was the maximum commission that his company could afford to pay. Although side-line salespeople did not have drawing accounts, they were paid the same commission rates as full-time salespeople and received credit for all orders shipped into their territories.

Norton had been concerned over the high turnover rate in his sales force, but the same condition existed throughout the industry. Norton stated that this was his most perplexing problem. Not only were experienced sales personnel being lost, but large amounts of time and expense were involved in training new people. Furthermore, he felt that the buyers, who were continually being called upon by new salespeople, were becoming more reluctant to place business with the company.

When new salespeople were recruited, Norton Brothers acquired them through the Men's Apparel Club, a national organization, or advertised in the "help wanted" columns of leading newspapers in the territories where the salespeople were to work. Occasionally, new sales personnel were hired from the ranks of customers' employees.

Because of the small size of the company, the training program was brief. The new salesperson spent two weeks at the factory becoming acquainted with the stock and general factory and office procedures. Then Norton or one of his assistants would go out on the road with the person, introducing him to the buyers and helping him to get started.

Norton recalled one case in which the expense of breaking in a new person was demonstrated. A new person out on the road with Norton finished making sales calls at 4:00 P.M. and wanted to quit for the day, even though there was time to make one more call that afternoon and to travel to the next city on the route. Norton felt that a veteran salesperson would have made the call and moved on, saving time and obtaining more business.

A manufacturer of noncompeting but complementary lines had proposed a plan whereby a number of firms would jointly share a salesperson's services. Each business would pay a certain portion of the person's drawing account and each would pay regular commission rates on whatever goods were sold in each company's line. Norton was undecided as to whether or not to enter split-draw deals of this type. He felt that it would be well to accept offers of this sort, provided that the salespeople were reasonably certain to work out satisfactorily.

Norton saw no immediate solution to his greater problem, that of keeping sales personnel who did not want to travel. A recent industry study had shown that the average neckwear salesperson was on the road forty weeks each year. The costs of traveling were high, and most people were dissatisfied when they were required to be away from home for long periods. Norton Brothers was attempting to hire only single people and was considering paying different commission rates according to the type of territory. The company had tried in every way to satisfy its sales personnel, but it could not decrease the turnover.

What should Norton Brothers have done to decrease the turnover of its salespeople? Should Norton have accepted the proposition involving split draws?

CASE 3-3

Thompson Corporation

Manufacturer of Equipment— Sales Job Analysis

Paul Hartgrave had only recently taken over as sales manager for the Thompson Corporation and was evaluating the systems and procedures of his predecessor. He found that there was no written job description or job analysis for sales personnel. The former sales manager, who had been in the job twenty-five years, had never reduced his definition of the job to writing. Realizing that a clear job description was a necessary starting point in making managerial plans and policy, Hartgrave also believed that a careful job description was necessary for operating within equal opportunity laws and regulations.

For forty years Thompson Corporation had manufactured and distributed a wide line of equipment for institutional, commercial, and light-industrial materials handling applications. The products included casters and wheels, equipment and food conveyers, inhalators, pallet trucks, wheelchairs, freight elevators, power lifters, and a variety of special engineered products.

In large metropolitan areas, Thompson maintained separate institutional and industrial sales personnel, but in other areas, sales personnel handled all types of accounts. Institutional customers included laundries, hotels, hospitals, schools, commercial buildings, department stores, bakeries, janitor-supply houses, government agencies, and institutional dealers. Industrial accounts were manufacturing plants, food processors, transportation lines, utilities, and industrial dealers.

The nearest thing Hartgrave found to a job description was the Salesperson Performance Appraisal form (Exhibit 1), which had obviously been designed on the basis of a job description of some sort. This form had been in use for twenty years. The district sales managers completed a Salesperson Performance Appraisal form after a thorough review of performance of each of the sales people in the district. After review by the sales manager, these appraisals were the subject of an individual review interview between the district sales managers and each sales rep. In these interviews, emphasis was placed on job aspects in which the salesperson should strive for improvement.

Since these performance appraisals were obviously based on both the sales managers' and the salespeople's current perception of what the sales job involved at Thompson Corporation, Hartgrave decided that they provided a logical starting point for preparing a job description for his sales personnel. Using these activities as a starting point, he then planned to prepare a rough job description, which would be sent to each of the district sales managers for suggested changes and clarification. Each district manager would then be requested to discuss the revised job description with a sample of his or her salespeople to identify further errors or omissions.

Hartgrave planned to send a copy of the final revised job description to each salesperson as a guide for future performance. In addition, he planned to use it in establishing criteria for recruiting and selecting new salespeople and as a basis for structuring sales training programs.

How effective do you think the Salesperson Performance Appraisal would be as a source of information in preparing a job description? What additional information would probably be needed?

What aspects of the job could be better described by the sales personnel rather than by sales managers?

EXHIBIT 1 Salesperson Performance Appraisal

Indicate achievement in the following areas of performance:	*Comments*
I. Obtaining Maximum Profitable Sales Volume *1. Calls on existing and prospective accounts with sufficient frequency.* *Inadequate* ... *Outstanding*	
2. Cultivates all purchasing agents, engineers, production personnel, and executives who influence the decision to buy. *Inadequate* ... *Outstanding*	
3. Plans for each call in advance to be well informed and ready for an effective presentation. *Inadequate* ... *Outstanding*	
4. Conducts sales interviews skillfully. Involves effective presentation, adept handling of objections, and ability to close. *Inadequate* ... *Outstanding*	
5. Services customers and prospects by expeditiously handling complaints and claims; providing development and engineering assistance; expediting orders; providing information relative to company policies, products, delivery schedules, and prices. *Inadequate* ... *Outstanding*	
II. Managing Time and Activities to Ensure Maximum Productivity and Efficiency *1. Organizes time and effort for most effective coverage of territory.* *Inadequate* ... *Outstanding*	

EXHIBIT 1 (Cont.)

2. Develops sales plans based on an analysis of each account in terms of sales objectives and sales-call effectiveness. *Inadequate — Outstanding*	
3. Submits required reports and keeps sales supervisor informed of conditions in territory. *Inadequate — Outstanding*	
4. Corresponds effectively with customers and appropriate offices within the company. *Inadequate — Outstanding*	
III. Knowledge of Company Products, Competitors, and Customers *1. Knowledge of company organization and policies.* *Inadequate — Outstanding*	
2. Knowledge of company products and related technical information. *Inadequate — Outstanding*	
3. Knowledge of competitor's policies, products, organization, and sales trends. *Inadequate — Outstanding*	
4. Knowledge of each customer's operation, personnel, products, and market requirements. *Inadequate — Outstanding*	

Indicate overall evaluation of performance.

Inadequate — *Outstanding*

COMMENTS OF REVIEWERS:

*Date*__________ *Signed*____________________ *(Salesperson)*

*Date*__________ *Signed*____________________ *(Sales Manager)*

*Date*__________ *Signed*____________________ *(Reviewing Manager)*

CASE 3-4

Holden Electrical Supplies Company

Manufacturer of Electrical Equipment—Recruiting Sales Personnel

Holden Electrical Supplies Company, Cincinnati, Ohio, manufactured a wide line of electrical equipment used in both home and industry. The sales force called on both electrical wholesalers and industrial buyers with the greater part of their efforts concentrated on industry buyers. The industrial products required considerable technical expertise upon the part of salespeople. Sales offices situated in twenty cities spread over the country had two hundred sales personnel operating out of them. In the past eight years sales volume increased by more than 50 percent, to a level of nearly $150,000,000. The fast rise in sales volume and the accompanying plant expansion created a problem in that more sales personnel were needed to keep up with the new accounts and to make sure the additional plant capacity was used profitably.

In addition, Holden's sales recruiting problem was compounded by a noticeable decline in the number of college seniors wanting a selling career. Holden recruiters had observed this at colleges and universities where they went searching for prospective salespeople. Another indication of the increased difficulty in attracting good young people into selling was aggressive recruiting by more and more companies. These factors combined to make the personnel recruiting problem serious for Holden; consequently, management ordered an evaluation of recruiting methods.

Virtually all Holden salespeople were recruited from twenty-five engineering colleges by district sales managers. Typically, Holden recruiters screened two hundred college seniors to hire ten qualified sales engineers. It was estimated to cost Holden $600 to recruit a candidate. Management believed the college recruiting program was deficient in light of the high cost and the fact that only 5 percent of the candidates interviewed accepted employment with Holden.

Evaluation of the college recruiting program began with the College Recruiting Division of the company asking district sales managers for their appraisals. Some district managers felt that Holden should discontinue college recruiting for various reasons, including the time required for recruiting, the intense competition, and the candidates' lack of experience. Other district managers, however, felt the program should continue with a few modifications, such as recruiting college juniors for summer employment more or less on a trial basis, concentrating on fewer schools, and getting on friendly terms with placement directors and professors.

Holden's general sales manager favored abandoning the college recruiting program and believed the company should adopt an active recruiting program utilizing other sources. He reasoned that, while engineering graduates had a fine technical background, their lack of maturity, inability to cope with business-type problems, and their lack of experience precluded an effective contribution to the Holden selling operation.

The general sales manager felt that the two hundred sales engineers currently working for Holden were an excellent source of new recruits. They knew the requirements for selling the Holden line and were in continual contact with other salespeople. By enlisting the support of the sales force, the general manager foresaw an end to Holden's difficulty in obtaining sales engineers.

The president preferred internal recruiting from the nonselling divisions, such as engineering, design, and manufacturing. He claimed that their familiarity with Holden and their proven abilities were important indicators of potential success as sales engineers.

A complete analysis of Holden's entire personnel recruiting program was in order, and, regardless of the approach finally decided upon, it was paramount that the company have a continuous program to attract satisfactory people to the sales organization.

Evaluate Holden's recruiting program, suggesting whether or not the company should have continued its college recruiting of sales engineers.

CASE 3-5

Arthur Tompkins—Shaklee Sales Distributor

A Sales Distributor—
Problems in Recruiting Salespeople

When Arthur Tompkins became a Shaklee sales distributor, his number one priority was to recruit a sales force. He felt that with unemployment above 10 percent in the Athens, Georgia, area, he would not have problems finding salespeople. However, six frustrating months later, he had only recruited one salesperson.

TOMPKINS'S BACKGROUND

Upon Mr. Tompkins's retirement from the military, he began to look for a suitable business opportunity in which to invest his time and money. The Shaklee organization was attractive to him because of its quality product line and progressive compensation plan. Mr. Tompkins felt that his previous experience in personal selling, even though limited, would enable him to develop a successful distributorship in a short period of time. For two years, prior to going into the service, Tompkins had worked as a salesman for a manufacturer of a line of hair grooming aids. He also spent six months as a research assistant in a North Carolina advocate organization.

Mr. Tompkins allowed himself one year to establish a strong distributorship in Athens. Then, he planned to retire permanently to Fayetteville, North Carolina, where he would apply the selling and recruiting techniques that he had learned to building a new sales force for Shaklee.

THE SHAKLEE CORPORATION

The Shaklee Corporation began as a door-to-door distributor of nutritional food supplements in 1956. Forrest C. Shaklee, Sr., developed the original product line after years of research into the nutritional requirements of the human body. His research provided the scientific knowledge that developed the products. To his achievements and experience were added the capabilities of his two sons: Forrest, Jr., contributed the financial skills, while Lee Shaklee, a highly successful sales executive, supplied the essential spark of marketing know-how and product promotion. From a modest beginning, Shaklee sales had grown to $190 million. An expanded line of food supplements still contributed the lion's share of the revenues, but the company had added lines of household products and cosmetics.

Shaklee pioneered the development of food supplements. The product line consisted of over 100 products, including items such as Alfalfa-Tabs, B-Complex, Herb-Lax laxative, Instant Protein drink mix, and assorted vitamin and mineral supplements. Food supplements contributed approximately 70 percent of Shaklee's total sales revenue.

During the 1960s, Shaklee added a line of concentrated cleaning products which the company felt offered advantages over store-bought brands. The products were biodegradable, safe, and economical to use. The company compiled data indicating that Shaklee products were approximately 33 percent less expensive than the leading brands of cleaning agents. Household products contributed 20 percent of total sales revenue.

The cosmetics, toiletries, and fragrances product line was Shaklee's most recent introduction, introduced six years ago. Although sales volume was still small, revenues had doubled in the past three years to approximately 10 percent of total sales revenue.

THE SHAKLEE SALES PLAN

Mr. Tompkins had been impressed by the earning potential and the opportunities for advancement which were provided by the sales plan. The major features of this plan were

1. A distributor earned immediate cash profits of 35 percent of sales based on manufacturer's suggested retail prices.
2. Additional bonuses of 3 percent and 22 percent of sales were earned according to Shaklee's suggested bonus schedule.
3. The distributor advanced to a position of supervisor once a monthly sales volume of $3,000 had been attained.
4. Supervisors who maintained a monthly purchase volume of $4,000 were provided with a company car.
5. Bonuses of up to 5 percent of sales were paid to supervisors who developed subordinates to the supervisor level.
6. A supervisor who developed four first-level supervisors was appointed to the position of coordinator, which made possible additional bonus earnings.

After studying the Shaklee sales plan, Mr. Tompkins decided that his first priority should be to recruit a group of sales distributors. His goal was to reach the level of supervisor within six months. To qualify for supervisor, he needed to sponsor a sales group that could maintain a monthly sales volume of $3,000.

TOMPKINS'S RECRUITING PLAN

Mr. Tompkins began to recruit a sales force in the Athens area. He described his efforts this way:

> I looked around me and saw all of these people out of work. Unemployment in the Athens area was over 10 percent at that time, so I didn't think I would have any problem in finding sales representatives. I started by running ads in the Athens newspaper for about a month. I received well over a hundred calls. But after I told a caller that it was commissioned sales and no guaranteed salary, I didn't get any farther most of the time. When I was able to set up an appointment for a face-to-face interview, the caller didn't show up. I finally decided that I was wasting my time.

Having abandoned his first recruiting scheme, Mr. Tompkins then sought the aid of local merchants. Because Athens was a university city, he felt that many merchants were approached by students interested in part-time selling jobs. He asked some merchants to hand out his business card to job-seekers. This technique also provided unsuccessful.

After six months, Mr. Tompkins had recruited only one distributor, a personal friend. Mr. Tompkins felt he had been beating his head against the wall and did not know how to proceed. He knew that Shaklee offered a quality product with excellent career opportunities for motivated individuals. He thought that if he could explain the opportunities with Shaklee on a personal basis, he could successfully sponsor one out of every three interested prospects. The problem, he believed, was that he had not been able to tell his story, a story he was sure would sell people on Shaklee. Arthur Tompkins was at a loss on what to do.

What kinds of people might be interested in selling Shaklee's line of products door to door? What methods might be effective in reaching prospective salespeople? Outline a specific recruiting plan.

CASE 3-6

Belton Industries, Inc.

Manufacturer of Toys and Bicycles—Selecting Sales Personnel

Albert Thompson, general sales manager for Belton Industries, Inc., faced a problem of high turnover of sales personnel. He was led to believe that something was wrong with the selection process and that the selection procedure should be evaluated.

Belton manufactured a wide line of children's toys and bicycles. Its sales organization consisted of 110 salespeople operating out of seventeen branch sales offices. The branch sales managers reported directly to Thompson. Belton products were selectively distributed to department stores, discount houses, toy stores, bicycle shops, and general hardware stores.

Belton Industries recruited its sales personnel from colleges and universities throughout the country, as well as from other sources. The branch sales managers performed the initial screening interview at college placement centers, and at the branch sales offices in the case of applicants from other sources. The preliminary interview served as an initial "screen" to eliminate obviously unqualified applicants. At the initial interview, applicants judged as "possibilities" were handed a standard application form requesting information such as personal history, education, previous experience, and the like. When the applicant returned the form, the branch sales manager contracted business and personal references by mail. As soon as references responded, a second interview was scheduled.

In the second interview, the applicant was given considerable information about the company, its history, organization, record, products, markets, and, in particular, the specific nature of the sales operation. The branch manager probed the applicant's habits, attitudes, and motivations and very often, to get a measure of an individual's ability to react to the unexpected, handed the applicant a pen, ashtray, or other handy object and asked him or her to make a sales presentation "on the spot." In addition, the branch sales manager fielded any questions that the applicant might ask.

Immediately upon completion of the second interview, the branch manager completed a rating sheet. At this time, he or she forwarded to the general sales manager all materials compiled on the applicant, including the application form, reference letters, rating sheet, and a statement recommending acceptance or rejection of the job candidate. The general sales manager decided whether or not to hire the applicant, then notified the branch sales manager, who, in turn, notified the applicant.

The general sales manager believed that the Belton sales force turnover rate was excessive and cited a recent study by a trade association that reported the industry's average sales force turnover was 15 percent, compared with Belton's sales force turnover of 25 percent. More specifically, Belton's turnover of first-year sales personnel was more than twice the industry average, which prompted the general sales manager to lay the blame directly on the selection procedure.

The general sales manager argued that the weakness could be corrected through psychological testing. He favored installation of a battery of tests, including intelligence tests, interest tests, personality tests, and sales aptitude tests. He thought that the tests would do more than correct weaknesses in the selection procedure, since they would provide an objective measure of a job applicant's true worth and probable future performance in a less complicated, less costly way. The results of each applicant's testing program could be compared with standards of achievement for sales personnel in the Belton company and in the entire industry. From these measures, the general sales manager contended, a sounder, more objective decision could be made.

The Belton president, John Wesley, disagreed. He contended that psychological testing had no place in the evaluation of a potential salesperson because testing was haphazard, it was highly theoretical and impersonal, and tests in no way could be substituted for experienced judgment as to the intangible human qualities possessed by an individual. He believed that many employers were using psychological tests as a crutch to avoid highly subjective selection decisions. Wesley contended that the selection process was not really the cause of the turnover problem. He suggested that if the sales department did a better job of training and motivating salespeople, job dissatisfaction and turnover would be reduced. Thompson agreed to abandon the idea of psychological testing and to concentrate more effort on training and motivation.

Two years later, a revised training program and a stronger program of sales incentives had not completely solved the turnover problem; sales force turnover, at 20 percent, was still well above the industry average. Albert Thompson explained this situation to John Wesley by stating that "you can't make a silk purse out of a sow's ear," that the first necessary step in reducing sales force turnover was to identify and recruit prospects with high potential for success. He had noticed that many successful salespeople seemed to have a strong internal drive for success. It was to identify such people that he had suggested using psychological testing. At this point, he sought the advice of an industrial psychologist, Dr. Claude Pfeiffer, who explained that personality types had been defined upon the basis of the needs of individuals to achieve. This need for achievement, or nAch as it was called by psychologists, results from the total environment of the individual from childhood and is essentially unchangeable in the adult. He suggested that Belton should be recruiting individuals with high need for achievement. High-nAch persons are successful in endeavors that require hard work and perseverance; they feel rewarded solely through their own efforts. Achievement is a means to fulfill their own self-system of values. They can be motivated by presenting challenges to them—each successfully met challenge tends to raise their own levels of aspiration. Such people are self-starters.

Only a small proportion of the population fall in this high-nAch category. Psychologists can assess the degree of nAch with tests and interviews, but laypersons might find it more difficult to identify this personality trait in the selection process. Dr. Pfeiffer suggested that answers to the following questions would help to identify high-nAch people. Do they use achievement words like success and accomplishment when talking about their work? Do they seem more concerned with results than with getting along with people? Do they have a track record of working independently? Are they moderate risk takers rather than impulsive reckless types? Do they seem to enjoy challenges or try to avoid them?

Dr. Pfeiffer recommended that Belton Industries concentrate its recruiting efforts on finding and hiring high-nAch salespeople. However, Thompson had reservations about seeking out and using such people in his sales force.

What is your opinion of the earlier decision on the use of psychological tests in selection?

What reservations might there be about the suggestion of recruiting high-nAch people for the Belton sales force?

What changes, if any, do you suggest in the selection procedure at Belton Industries?

CASE 3-7

American Machine and Foundry Company

Industrial Manufacturer—
Proposed Establishment of Formal Training Program

R. R. Woodruff, vice-president of marketing of the Bowling Products Division of American Machine and Foundry Company, was faced with a decision regarding a proposed new training program for bowling products sales personnel. American Machine and Foundry Company, an old established manufacturer of several lines of industrial products, had gotten into the bowling market early through the acquisition and manufacture of the first commercially practical automatic pinspotter. The introduction of the automatic pinspotter resulted in a revolution in the bowling industry. Pin boys had always presented a managerial headache for bowling center operators. Unskilled and low-paid, they were unreliable and inefficient employees with a high rate of absenteeism and job turnover. Elimination of pin boys through the use of automatic pinspotters solved an enormous managerial problem and made it possible for bowling center management to expand the size of the typical establishment and devote more time to improving customer service.

During the 1950s and into the early 1960s, the bowling industry increased enormously in size, and bowling became a major American participation sport. Then, the expansion of the new centers reached a peak, and although expansion continued, it was at a slower rate. As the bowling industry developed and changed, the role of AMF in the industry also grew and changed. AMF gradually broadened its bowling product line to include bowling lanes, seating and other bowling center furnishings, and a complete line of balls, pins, and other items of equipment for the bowler.

The only major competitor in the industry, the Brunswick Corporation, was three years behind AMF in getting an automatic pinspotter on the market; this delay had allowed AMF to capture about half the market. As the market for new bowling installations moved toward saturation and sales of basic equipment dropped to a somewhat lower level, competition became increasingly aggressive. Even so, bowling products still generated about one-third of the company's $400 million annual sales and more than half the $20 million earnings.

Until recently, bowling division products had been sold by two groups of sales personnel. Equipment, including pinsetters, bowling lanes, and furniture, was sold by bowling equipment salespeople. These people spent part of their time seeking new sources of capital that could be sold on the profitability of building new bowling centers, but they also called regularly on existing lanes to sell equipment for modernization. Supplies, including pins, balls, bowling shoes, lane finishes, and the like, were sold by supply sales personnel who called on bowling centers. Both groups of sales personnel operated out of district sales offices under the direction of district managers. In turn, the fifteen district managers reported to five regional sales managers. In recent years the bowling industry had ceased to be a growth industry, and a larger share of AMF booking sales was concentrated in supplies instead of equipment. As a result, the two sales forces were reorganized into a single sales force of one hundred, with all sales people responsible for selling both equipment and supplies.

At the time of the reorganization, it became necessary to provide a program of retraining for the new combination salespeople. Many of the former equipment salespeople had started as supply salespeople, so they needed only a brief review of the current supply line. Most of the ex-supply salespeople, however, were almost completely unfamiliar with the equipment line. Many items of equipment were complex, and their sale or lease required extensive negotiation. For these reasons it would not be easy for the salespeople to train themselves on the new line.

G. Lindsay Crump, vice-president of marketing development, arranged for the development of a two-week retraining program for all sales personnel. This was scheduled in several sessions at the training center in Fort Worth, Texas. This well-equipped training center had originally been established to provide training in bowling center operation for owners and managers of centers. It was located in the same building with a company-owned bowling center, which provided a laboratory for the training program.

Crump suggested to Woodruff that it was time to develop a formal training program for new sales personnel. AMF had never provided formal training for newly hired people. When the company first moved into the bowling business, there was no time to develop salespeople; capable people, experienced ones when available, were hired and started immediately on the job. Informal training was provided by sales executives and other experienced sales staff. The sales force had grown so large that normal turnover required the annual indoctrination of enough new salespeople to make it possible to offer formal training classes at least twice a year. In addition, the product line had become so complex that formal training offered an efficient way of presenting product information to large numbers of new persons. Top management agreed with Crump's suggestion and asked him to submit a proposal for the training program.

Before he could arrange for the actual development of the new program, Crump needed to make several broad decisions. These included reaching answers to the following questions:

1. What should be taught? What information and skills should be provided in the formal training program, and what should be a part of informal training?
2. How long should the formal program last?

3. Should formal training be preceded by some sort of indoctrination?
4. Who should teach in the formal program? (Alternatives included experienced salespeople, sales managers, and professional teachers.)
5. What teaching methods should be used?
6. Should the formal program be followed by a period of apprenticeship? How might this be achieved?
7. How should coordination be achieved between the formal program and on-the-job training?

Soon after the problem was recognized, Crump arranged a meeting with the director of the training center and with the sales manager, Howard Smith, to prepare a proposal including answers to the questions he had posed.

What, in your opinion, should this group have recommended?

CASE 3-8

Holmes Business Forms Company

Distributor of Office Supplies—
Centralized versus Decentralized Training

Holmes Business Forms Company was founded in Chicago, Illinois, in 1923 by Arthur K. Holmes to sell bookkeeping forms and office stationery. Gradually, the line of products was broadened and the market was expanded to the entire American market. The company distributed an extensive line of business office products such as various types and grades of papers, envelopes, forms, ribbons, pens, pencils, tapes, staplers, and small office machinery such as transcribers, paper collators, and electronic stencil makers. Holmes products were sold to retail stores and business offices throughout the country by 150 salespersons operating out of thirty district sales offices. Although the sales training program had been considered effective, it had been many years since it had been evaluated.

The prospect of hiring ten additional sales personnel to keep up with increasing sales volume led Holmes' general sales manager, Frank Ireland, to suggest that this was an appropriate time to appraise the training program. Any changes could be implemented in time for training the new recruits who were to be hired within the next ninety days. Specifically, he wanted to determine whether Holmes should continue with decentralized sales training or switch to centralized sales training.

Under the current program, new sales staff received a twelve-week sales training course at the Holmes district sales offices where they were employed. This training was under the direction of the district manager. The first six weeks were devoted to intensive training covering company history, organization, operations and policies, the salesperson's job, sales techniques and methods of making sales presentations including answering objections and demonstrating the product, and, finally, personal development. Among the sales training techniques used were lectures, discussions, and role-playing sessions. Examinations were given at the end of each two weeks of training.

The last six weeks of the training program were spent in the field. Arrangements were made for the trainee to spend the six weeks with at least two retailers so that he or she might gain firsthand knowledge of the problems involved in retailing business office products. The trainee worked as both a salesperson and a buyer at the retail level. Upon completion of the trainee's work in each store, the retailer forwarded to the district sales manager a thorough evaluation of the trainee's performance. After successful completion of the twelve-week sales training program, including passing several examinations along the way, the sales trainee was ready to take over a Holmes sales territory.

Frank Ireland, the general sales manager, felt that the sales-training program should be conducted at company headquarters by an experienced trainer under his personal direction. In addition, he also believed that headquarters' officials, such as the president, treasurer, production manager, advertising manager, and general sales manager should play active roles. He gave four reasons for favoring centralized training: (1) better quality training should result, with a full-time sales training specialist and top executives participating; (2) more uniform training should result, since each trainee would receive identical training; (3) better facilities at headquarters should provide an atmosphere more conducive to effective training; (4) centralized training should hold higher prestige in the trainees' minds.

However, the company president, Will Holmes, and several other executives maintained that decentralized training should continue. Their arguments were that (1) training in the field provided the trainee with a more realistic and more valuable experience that could not be duplicated in a headquarters classroom, (2) the district sales managers should do the training since they were responsible and accountable for the performance of salespeople, and (3) it was less expensive to conduct sales training at the decentralized district sales offices.

While disagreement existed over whether sales training should be centralized or decentralized, all agreed that a decision had to be made before the ten new sales personnel were recruited and selected. This group would be the first affected by any change in the sales training program. Consequently, management set up a task force to investigate and to recommend either centralized or decentralized sales training.

Should Holmes Business Forms Company have adopted a centralized sales training program, or should it have continued with its decentralized sales training program? Why?

CASE 3-9

Westinghouse Electric Corporation

Manufacturer of Distribution Transformers—Training Sales Personnel

Bob Ray, marketing manager for the Overhead Distribution Transformer Division (OHDT) of Westinghouse Electric Corporation, was concerned about his field sales engineers. It had been four years since OHDT had initiated any sort of formal training program directed at the field sales force. Company information revealed that the sales force had an annual turnover of 10 percent. His concern for the newer salesperson's depth of training was paralleled by his conviction that the veteran sales engineers would benefit from more exposure to product knowledge, especially in light of recent innovations. Interpretation of direct and indirect feedback revealed that both groups were reaching for more depth in product knowledge.

THE CORPORATION

Westinghouse was the world's oldest and second largest manufacturer of electrical apparatus and appliances. Founded by George Westinghouse in 1886, the corporation marketed some 300,000 variations of 8,000 basic products ranging from a simple piece of copper wire to a complex commercial nuclear power plant. The firm employed over 145,000 men and women in laboratories, manufacturing plants, sales offices, and distribution centers from coast to coast and around the world. Over 1,800 scientists and engineers were engaged in research and development activities. The corporation had more than 160,000 stockholders.

Westinghouse was organized into four operating companies: Power Systems; Industry and Defense; Consumer Products; and Broadcasting, Learning and Leisure Time. Each company was headed by a president, who had full responsibility for designing, building, and selling the company's products and services throughout the world. Each had its own staff of specialists. It also could draw on corporate resources for additional specialized support in marketing, manufacturing, engineering, design, research, personnel and public affairs, finance, and law.

The basic organizational unit of the company was the division, each with its own line of products and services. Each division, in turn, was grouped with a number of other divisions with related products and services, such as major appliances, construction products, or power generation equipment.

Combined annual sales before taxes were $5.1 billion. The Power Systems

Company was the leading contributor to income after taxes with a 43 percent contribution. The Power Systems Company was divided into: the Power Generation Group and the Transmission and Distribution Group, which contained the Overhead Distribution Transformer Division located in Athens, Georgia.

OVERHEAD DISTRIBUTION TRANSFORMER DIVISION (OHDT)

OHDT considered itself first in facilities, developments, and service; it had led the nation in overhead distribution transformer sales since 1971 with a consistent market share of about 23 percent. Industry sales were projected at $900 million by the early 1980s.

Since 1958, all Westinghouse overhead distribution transformers had been designed and manufactured in the Athens plant. OHDT was particularly proud of its engineering leadership—Westinghouse had expanded its staff and facility when others were cutting back. Bob Ray was instrumental in making this crucial marketing decision and was later honored with the Corporation's highest award, "The Order of Merit," given to only three employees a year. In the capacity over demand ratio, the company had been 131 percent, 85 percent, and 88 percent, respectively, for the past three years.

Competition

Westinghouse had long been recognized as the primary innovator in the distribution transformer industry. Four competitors, each with active R & D facilities, were considered major innovators: General Electric, RTE, Allis Chalmers, and McGraw-Edison. Other strong companies among the twenty-nine national competitors were Wagner, Kuhlman, and Colt. The Westinghouse product was generally ranked tops in its field. Some competitors though, had succeeded in promoting less expensive products.

The Customer and Pricing

Electric utility companies were the consumers of distribution transformers. There were three major classes: investor-owned utilities, rural electric cooperatives, and municipalities. The approximately three hundred investor-owned utilities accounted for 80 percent of consumption. The co-ops and municipalities numbered about 920 and 2000, respectively, and together accounted for 20 percent. With increasing migration of population and industries to metropolitan outskirts, the co-ops were expected to increase their share of the consumption.

There were about 33,000,000 overhead distribution transformers across the nation. Sales in this market represented about 60 percent change-outs (i.e., replacements in an area where power consumption had increased) and 40 percent new development units.

The major utilities negotiated year-long purchasing commitments during November–December of each year. Fierce price competition was prevalent among the investor-owned utilities and large discounts off list price were normally expected. Pricing for the co-ops and municipalities was more stable with smaller discounts from list being offered. The method of negotiation was small orders throughout the year for smaller utilities and the sealed bid method for publicly owned companies.

Promotion

Westinghouse advertised its electrical transmission, generation, and distribution equipment in leading trade journals. Additionally, it was a member of National Electrical Manufacturers Association (NEMA), which set standards for the industry. NEMA issued monthly reports to its members including total market volume and member market share information. Distribution was by a field sales force selling direct to customers.

MARKETING MANAGEMENT

The OHDT marketing department consisted of a marketing manager, a marketing services manager, and four area sales managers who were assisted by a staff of their own. Sales areas were divided geographically. Almost all marketing personnel had engineering backgrounds, considered a must in this field. Department personnel were particularly proud that Westinghouse had been number one in market share of transformer sales each year since 1971. Exhibit 1 shows organization of the marketing department in Athens.

The Field Sales Force

Overhead distribution transformers were sold through two Westinghouse companies: the Power Systems company and the Industry and Defense company. Each had its own sales network, as shown in Exhibit 2.

Over three hundred Westinghouse corporate field sales engineers, district managers, and zone managers throughout the country handled OHDT accounts. In addition to being loaded with OHDT products, sales personnel were responsible for selling other Westinghouse utility products. For example, they represented the Electrical Relay Division, Circuit Breaker Division, and the Electric Meter Division, each of which was managed through other corporate channels. The field sales engineers, in serving several product divisions, reported to district managers for product loading.

Area sales managers and their staffs (of OHDT) served the field sales engi-

EXHIBIT 1 Marketing Department—Athens

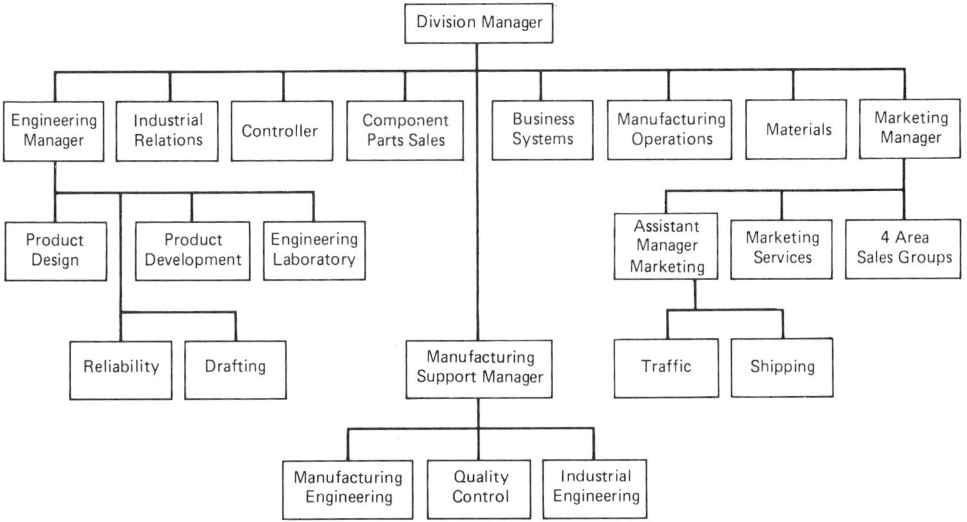

neers by taking and expediting product orders, answering product questions, and collecting feedback. Additionally, they held field training seminars and assisted sales personnel on important sales. Bob Ray often helped follow through with especially important customers.

Training a Field Sales Engineer

Westinghouse sales engineers were required to have a Bachelor of Science in engineering. The new sales recruit was first sent to Pittsburgh for a basic three-week orientation to Westinghouse. The recruit was then assigned to a corporate "graduate studies program" which lasted from three to twelve months, depending on individual skills. Upon completion, he or she was assigned to the field as an assistant sales engineer to serve a training tenure of from six to twenty-four months, depending on individual requirements. During this period, the recruit would travel for a two-week period visiting the various manufacturing plants he or she would later serve. Each plant presented a two-day training and orientation seminar. Ideally, sales engineers returned to these parent manufacturing divisions annually for refresher training. Additionally, they attended district or zone training seminars put on by representatives of the parent divisions.

A sales engineer, depending on experience and length of service, drew a base salary averaging $35,000 a year, not including bonus. The number of calls made and the type of customer served was established according to the individual's ability, experience, and product loading. It took roughly $500,000 worth of sales to support a field sales engineer.

EXHIBIT 2 Sales Organization Chart

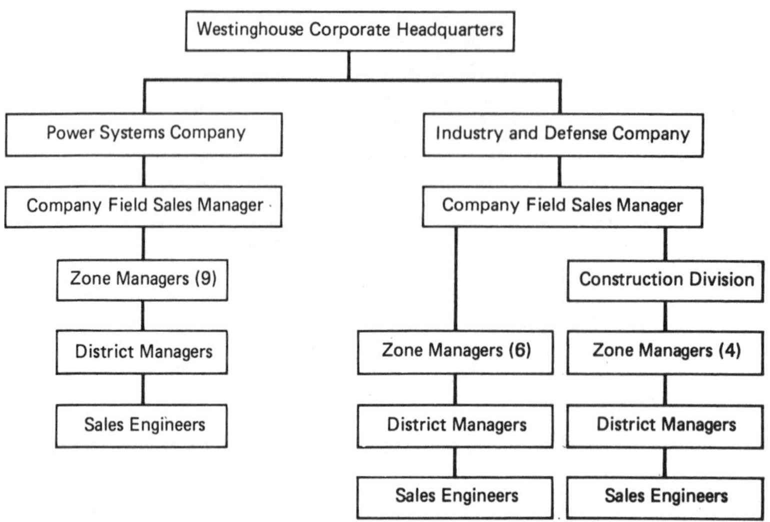

Thoughts of an OHDT Area Sales Manager

Marvin Jones was one of four area sales managers for the OHDT division. Prior to his present assignment, he was a field sales engineer for twelve years. Reflecting back, he recalled the difficulties involved in attending the training seminars of the various divisions. Sales personnel recognized that training was essential, that effective selling required sound training and that a person's potential (not to mention the quota) could not be realized without training. However, getting a salesperson to a training seminar was difficult, because, "when there was a sale to be made, there wasn't time for training." Attendance at refresher training was more or less left to the discretion of the individual sales engineer.

The Need to Train

Bob Ray was concerned about the field sales force's depth of knowledge about overhead distribution transformers, especially in light of recent innovations. He knew Westinghouse had become the leading producer of transformers, but he attributed this more to excellent engineering and excessive demand than to the expertise of his department. As questions were coming in to the area sales managers at a higher-than-normal rate, he pinpointed the problem as training. He also knew that the economy might be expected to take a slight decline. With the growing threat that demand might slacken soon, he felt that competition would get rough. In addition, he realized that an unprepared sales force might not fare well when the time came to give more in-depth and high-quality sales presentations. And it had been a while since Athens had a formal training program. The previous program, considered a success, consisted of a campaign to inform the sales force about the overhead distribution transformer and, as a gimmick, miniature transformer parts were sent to the salespeople.

A salesperson's time was a valuable commodity, and Bob Ray knew it. Training was one of the most difficult tasks to pull off effectively, even when the trainees were geographically close to management, but the Westinghouse field sales force was scattered across the nation. Making training even more burdensome was that the sales engineers were responsible for more than just the OHDT account. Athens would have to compete for both time and attention.

FROM IDEAS TO ACTION

With the facts on the table, Bob Ray called on Larry Deal, who headed Marketing Services, and his assistant, Glynn Hodges, who at that time was involved with marketing communications. Hodges was sent to Pittsburgh a few times to work jointly with Earl Swartz, the corporate contact to Westinghouse's ad agency. By June, Hodges had the layout completed for the proposed solution to the training problem—a training campaign called "The Problem Solvers," Bob Ray liked it. It was estimated that the campaign would cost about $20,000, a large slice of the OHDT marketing budget. Exhibit 3 gives an idea of the estimated costs.

EXHIBIT 3 "Problem Solver" Promotion for Westinghouse Overhead Distribution Transformers

General

This document summarizes various elements of the "Problem Solver" promotion. The costs are based on quotations from suppliers who have seen initially prepared layouts.

Puzzles

Five puzzles will be purchased directly from supplier by Westinghouse.

Shipping Boxes for Puzzles

Four hundred each of five different sized boxes plus one 6″ × 6″ envelope (for crossword puzzle and brochure mailing). Each to be printed in two colors using the same "Problem Solver" design (suggestion: each box to have a different color on the design).

Delivery time: six weeks from receipt of order.

Cost (including converting boxes, design preparation, color plates and printing): $2,500.

Crossword Puzzle

To be completed by salesperson and submitted with photo to get personalized jigsaw puzzle prize.

Timing: six weeks from receipt of words and clues from Westinghouse. Puzzles to be printed in simple four-page format and inserted in envelope along with cover letter and brochure.

Cost: $800.

EXHIBIT 3 (*Continued*)

Jigsaw Puzzle

One 11″ × 14″ puzzle will be sent to every salesperson submitting photo along with completed crossword puzzle. Photos will be held and sent in bulk to puzzle manufacturer, who will then send completed puzzle directly to each salesperson along with the original photo.

Timing: four weeks delivery from receipt of photographs.

Cost: $1,300.

Cover Letters

Total of five (one for each puzzle mailing), four hundred copies of each.

Cost (including artwork for masthead, copy editing, type setting, and printing): $600.

Brochures

One brochure will accompany each of the five puzzle mailings. Each brochure will focus on one aspect of the overhead transformers. The cover will have a full color cover of the puzzle being sent: inside pages will be black and white and use existing line art. Cost (including photos, type setting, tissue layout and key art, copy editing and production supervision for five 20-page booklets): $12,000.

Total Cost

Up to $20,000.

About the Problem Solvers Campaign

An overview of "The Problem Solvers" appears in Exhibit 4, which contains the background, program objectives, program implementation, elements of the program (stages 1 and 2), and a summary of elements and timing.

To catch the salesperson's attention, the proposed campaign would consist of expensive and eye-catching adult games emphasizing puzzle problems. The

EXHIBIT 4 The Problem Solvers: Westinghouse Overhead Distribution Transformers

I. BACKGROUND

The total market for overhead distribution transformers is very good. For Westinghouse, it is excellent.

While Athens is producing at full capacity and the current problem is meeting demand, there still remain several conditions with which Athens must cope if it is to achieve its long range potential:

1. Many Westinghouse and agent salespeople do not understand the advantages of Westinghouse transformers.
2. There are competitors who manufacture and sell transformers at a cheaper price. These transformers are inferior to those of Westinghouse. The Westinghouse story, which must be communicated through sales personnel to customers, is a *value* story.
3. The present sales boom cannot be expected to continue indefinitely, and the sales force must be prepared to conduct tougher, more effective sales presentations.

EXHIBIT 4 (*Continued*)

II. PROGRAM OBJECTIVES

To make Westinghouse and agent sales personnel more effective, representatives for Athens . . . by showing them why Westinghouse is the value leader and by giving them the information and tools needed to make more effective presentations.

By accomplishing these objectives, the sales representatives will become more confident of their abilities—and the Westinghouse line. This growing confidence will, in turn, create even greater success.

III. PROGRAM IMPLEMENTATION

This is a two-stage program.

The Stage 1 phase, the most important, is directed to the Westinghouse sales force and includes: an explanation of the program; a summary of the transformer market (and the profit contribution made by Westinghouse transformers); and detailed instruction on transformers (using the theme, "The Problem Solvers," along with unique mailings.)

The Stage 2 phase is the person-to-person contact between salespeople and customers. Having been effectively indoctrinated into the advantages of Westinghouse transformers, the salespeople are now supplied with effective sales presentation material, which will make contact between sales representatives and customers more productive for the Athens division.

IV. ELEMENTS OF PROGRAM—STAGE 1

1. Cover letter #1 from Mr. Meierkord (General Manager, OHDT) or Mr. Ray spelling out the theme "The Problem Solvers," and the purpose of the program.
2. Instruction brochure #1 on Cover and Bushing Assembly . . . along with puzzle.
3. Cover letter #2 from Meierkord or Ray.
4. Instruction brochure #2 on Tank Assembly . . . along with puzzle.
5. Cover letter #3 from Meierkord or Ray.
6. Instruction Brochure on Core & Core & Coil Assembly . . . along with puzzle.
7. Cover letter #4 from Meierkord or Ray. Letter to state that crossword puzzle answers are found in instruction booklet. If salesperson returns completed crossword puzzle along with any photograph of his or her choice. Athens will return a custom-made jigsaw puzzle made out of the photo.
8. Instruction brochure #4 on CSP (completely self-protected transformer) Features . . . along with crossword puzzle. Crossword puzzle will contain such clues as:
   "CSP Transformers (OUTLAST) conventional types by 60%."
   "CSP arresters (LOWER) discharge voltage on high-surge current."
   "After overload trips breaker, breaker can be reset to (*TEN*) percent more capacity."

V. ELEMENTS OF PROGRAM—STAGE 2

After salespeople have studied the four bulletins, they are now better prepared to make more effective presentations to their customers. To help them in their calls, they will be furnished with the following:

1. Cover letter (#5) again from Meierkord or Ray, reiterating the profitability of transformers, that they are great "Problems Solvers," and that the salespeople

EXHIBIT 4 (*Continued*)

(the ultimate "Problem Solvers") are now well prepared to communicate to their customers why Westinghouse transformers are truly the tops in the field. Cover letter will dwell on the importance of customer presentations, preparation, and follow-through.

2. Flipchart presentation entitled "Westinghouse Distribution Transformers: 'The Problem Solvers.' "
   The presentation will summarize the most important "Features/Functions/Benefits" from the four technical bulletins. The presentation will be designed in a horizontal format, so that the pages are adaptable for photographic slide or strip film reproduction.
3. Customer booklet to be prepared using same text and artwork from the presentation flipchart.
   Booklet will be left with the customer as a reminder of what was presented and as a source document for later reference.
4. Capabilities brochure, about to be produced, can be an added ingredient to the presentation. While it emphasizes Athens' manufacturing capability—as opposed to the engineering emphasis of the presentation—the booklet is prestigious and will reflect Westinghouse distribution transformers as being a value line.
   If not used as part of the presentation, the capabilities brochure would make an impressive mailing to the customer . . . along with a "thank you" letter for listening to the presentation.

VI. SUMMARY—ELEMENTS AND TIMING

Stage 1

First Mailing: Cover Letter #1 (Program Summary) Bulletin #1—Cover and Bushing Puzzle #1 (Adult Game) Master Crossword Puzzle

Second Mailing: Cover Letter #2

(two months later) Bulletin #2—Tank Assembly
Puzzle #2

Third Mailing: Cover Letter #3

(two months later) Bulletin #3—Core and Core and Coil Assembly
Puzzle #3

Fourth Mailing: Cover Letter #4

(two months later) Bulletin #4—CSP Features
Puzzle #4

Stage 2

Fifth Mailing: Cover Letter #5 (Customer Presentations)

(two months later) Flipchart Presentation
Presentation Summary for Customer
Athens Capability Brochure
Puzzle #5

games would cost $4–$5 each; a good example was a three-dimensional Tic-Tac-Toe game made of three clear plastic decks mounted on top of each other. Each player was represented by either clear blue or yellow marbles about an inch in diameter each. The game could be won horizontally, vertically, or diagonally.

Along with the mailing of each game would be a cover letter and an information bulletin emphasizing a particular feature of the overhead distribution transformer. As the salesperson read each information bulletin, he or she would fill in "clues" to a master crossword puzzle. When the mailings were completed, the salesperson would send in the completed crossword puzzle and a picture of himself or herself (along with the rest of the family, if desired) to the Marketing Department in Athens. Athens would have the picture made into a jigsaw puzzle and return it to the participant a few weeks later.

The Marketing Services Division—A Special Project

Larry Deal's Marketing Services division had the responsibility for supporting the ad agency by providing technical information necessary for turning the Problem Solvers idea into a manageable campaign. Brian Kennedy, assigned to marketing communications, and assistant, Jody Unsler, had been asked to design the instruction brochures and crossword puzzle. Coordination with Earl Swartz had resulted in the initial selection of a container for the adult games. The container was a cardboard box with a design of jigsaw puzzle parts; each part had a letter on it, with the total spelling being "The Problem Solvers." Kennedy put in some long hours working on the instruction brochures. In explaining the various components of the transformer, he had decided to set up a conversational sales presentation scene between a Westinghouse salesperson and a purchasing agent. The salesperson who was "Mr. Problem Solver" or "Ms. Problem Solver" was smoothly answering the questions asked by a purchasing agent, who was appropriately labeled "Mr. A. Gent" or "Ms. A. Lady."

Early November

One morning in early November, Bob Ray, relaxing at his desk, was sipping a cup of coffee. He was thinking about the "The Problem Solvers" campaign. Things were moving along pretty well. At the present rate he would be able to meet the January 15 target date for the first mailing. He knew $20,000 was a lot of money to spend on a training campaign of this type, but he was confident in the overall idea and felt it was the best way to reach such a broad and isolated target. However, a few decisions remained. There was some question about the two-month interval between each of the five mailings. He definitely wanted the sales force ready for November–December when the big utilities would negotiate year-long contracts. He wanted the campaign to last a good while, as it represented a big chunk of the budget, but he wondered whether the field sales force's attention could be held over such a long period. He also wondered about the effectiveness of the campaign's feedback mechanism. He remembered Glynn Hodges saying he anticipated a 65 percent response. Another point undefined in the campaign was the stand OHDT should take on future newcomers to the field sales force. Since the previous campaign, new sales personnel learned through OJT (on-the-job training) and sales materials, as well as picking up what they could from OHDT bulletins. This provided only short range coverage and would break down in the long run, or when making sales got tough. This had been one factor contributing to the present situation.

With those thoughts in mind, Bob Ray decided to call a division head meeting the same afternoon.

What is your opinion of "The Problem Solvers" campaign? Will it solve the training problem faced by Westinghouse? Why or why not?

CASE 3-10

Kalo Laboratories

Pharmaceutical Company—
Sales Manager Training

Stephen Young, manager of personnel development, Kalo Laboratories, was planning the fall Sales Executive Seminar (SES) for district sales managers. This was to kick off a new program of continuous training for district managers. In Young's opinion, training sales managers was Kalo's main problem. Dennis Baily, recently promoted from district sales manager, was to assist in setting up the SES and in conducting it. Young awaited Baily's arrival at the home office so that the fall program's planning could begin.

Kalo Laboratories of Trenton, New Jersey, produced ethical drugs and certain pharmaceuticals. It was a subsidiary of Standard Products Company, a conglomerate, whose sales exceeded $400 million, with Kalo accounting for $80 million. Kalo had four sales divisions: (1) hospital, (2) pediatric, (3) physician, and (4) government.

There were three groups of Kalo sales personnel: (1) "detail men," who called exclusively on either physicians or pediatricians, explained product features and uses, and urged the prescribing of Kalo products; (2) salespeople who called on hospitals, performed "detail" tasks, and wrote orders; and (3) salespeople who visited veterans' hospitals, military medical facilities, and large government installations and were skilled in negotiating and bidding on large contracts.

Each of sixty district managers supervised from eight to twelve of Kalo's 650-person sales force. Each reported to one of twelve regional managers. The company adhered to a promotion-from-within policy, and all district managers had prior experience in ethical drug and pharmaceutical sales. The sales organization manual outlined district managers' duties in seven areas:

1. *Office procedures.* General reports, correspondence, inventory of supplies, and supervision of office personnel.
2. *Field supervision.* Improvement, training, evaluation, demonstration, assistance, and personal supervision of the field sales force.
3. *Personnel improvements.* Determination of need and organization of a personal improvement plan for each salesperson. Relate to appraisal and evaluation.
4. *District progress.* Accountable for territorial profit and service.
5. *Reporting function.* Preparation of general and specific reports and communication with the regional manager and the home office.
6. *Personnel selection.* Recruiting, screening, interviewing, and assisting the regional manager in the final selection of applicants.
7. *Special duties.* Conducting sales meetings, attending annual SES, terminations, policing expense accounts, and other special assignments.

Recently, Kalo adopted a new sales training philosophy stressing customer orientation, the buyer-seller communication process, and advanced selling methods. Implementing this new philosophy involved using the latest developments in individualized training and participation techniques. Therefore, a new personnel center, complete with modern conference rooms and equipped with the latest and most advanced audiovisual equipment, was built in Trenton. All sales personnel received training there before assignment to sales districts. Young gave his evaluation by saying, "I believe the initial sales training program is good, but our continuous training is suffering a breakdown, as our district managers still stick to outdated techniques and continue to emphasize a product-oriented approach. We must do a better job of training the trainer." He believed that they should coordinate and conduct on-the-job sales training continuously rather than sporadically. Young also voiced concern for the district managers' performance in field supervision and personnel improvement.

The district manager training program consisted of intensive study of the sales organization manual, exposure to topics covered by past seminars, case studies, problem solving, and general discussion. The annual SES constituted the only continuous training program for district managers. In December, Young asked Jerry Chambers, a district manager from the southeastern region, to appraise the current state of district manager training and to submit a proposal for its improvement (see Exhibit 1). No decision on this proposal had been reached, since Young was awaiting Baily's arrival. The forthcoming SES included a computerized marketing game emphasizing bidding, pricing, budgeting, and certain aspects of marketing. Young wondered if this game should be replaced with a different type of program. He faced the twofold problem of training both new and old district managers and of organizing the SES.

Should Chambers's proposal have been accepted and implemented?

What further recommendations for training the district sales managers would you have made?

EXHIBIT 1

FROM: J. L. Chambers
TO: S. H. Young
DATE: December 18
SUBJECT: Proposal: New and Senior District Manager Training

PROPOSAL: New and Senior District Manager Training

I. Objective. The implementation of this program will minimize the maturation time of the early appointed District Manager and maximize the managerial capabilities of Senior District Managers.

II. Procedure

A. *Field Contact.* Rather than a formal introductory meeting, the District Manager will meet his personnel through scheduling himself into their respective territories. Since this contact will be made prior to a review of personnel records or Regional Manager counseling on this subject, the new District Manager will not have preconceived opinions of his sales force's capabilities. The resultant atmosphere will be conducive to open, candid discussion allowing both parties to meet on common ground.

B. *Orientation with Regional Manager.* After completing the above step, a thorough personnel discussion will also be reviewed at this time. Selected confrontations will then be shown the new District Manager. Because he will view his knowledge inadequate to handle the situations depicted, he will be motivated to search out the necessary information. Based on his recognition of those areas that require primary effort, the District Manager will outline a course of study with the Regional Manager which will be encompassed by the seven categories enumerated below. Case histories from former seminars and tape-recorded discussions of those topics listed below the categories mentioned will provide a reservoir of applicable information.

1. Office Organization—Procedures
   a. Value of basic organization
   b. Preparation for field contact
   c. Report evaluation
2. Field Supervision
   a. Training new personnel
   b. The hospital salesperson—hospital penetration
   c. Personnel evaluation techniques
   d. Capturing government business
   e. Drug and wholesale working
   f. The pediatric salesperson
3. Personnel Improvement
   a. Understanding the salesperson—application of drive patterns and motivational interviews
   b. Motivation of senior salespeople
   c. Counseling techniques

EXHIBIT 1 (Cont.)

4. District Progress
   a. Gathering distribution data—territory construction procedures—pool allocations
5. Reporting
   a. Written communication techniques
   b. Field contact report construction
6. Personnel Selection
   a. Applicant screening—sources of candidates—interviewing the applicant
7. Special Duties
   a. Organization of district meetings

The Regional Manager orientation session will require approximately two weeks. Upon completion, the Regional Manager will contact other District Managers of the region and arrange for a one-day introductory visit, with each manager, for the new District Manager.

C. *Personnel Central*
1. *New District Manager.* The new District Manager will participate in a two-week training period in Trenton. During his stay, he will occupy the District Office, which has been established at Personnel Central. Since this office has been organized to be representative of a typical district office, he will have an opportunity to become acquainted with systems and procedures applicable to his new position. Upon entering training, the District Manager will be requested to bring personnel files relative to his sales staff. These records will be valuable in conducting routine district business while in training, as well as providing search material for confrontation assignments. Training will proceed in accordance with the steps enumerated below.
   a. *Video Confrontations.* Two video confrontations will be completed on primary district problems. Through telephone contact with the Regional Manager, the District Manager counselor will explore specifics required for role-play setting. On completion, the counselor will suggest search of similar case histories, confrontation, and a review of personnel records involved before rescheduling further tryouts.
   b. *Sensitivity Training.* The District Manager will participate in sensitivity training through being assigned two salespeople upon their entering the course. He will occupy the third chair, counsel the salespeople assigned, and, in turn, discuss his progress with the District Manager counselor.
   c. *Recruiting, Screening, Hiring.* The District Manager will be required to complete confrontations as well as select four candidates for hiring. Basis for selection of personnel will be discussed with District Manager counselor.

EXHIBIT 1 (Cont.)

d. Time remaining, the District Manager will complete selected confrontations as suggested by the Regional Manager during the phone call previously mentioned, or through selection by the District Manager counselor.

e. The District Manager will complete the confrontations mentioned in (a) above and accept as his Back Home Commitment the completion of these confrontations with the personnel involved.

2. *Senior District Manager.* The senior District Manager will complete steps (a), (b), (d), and (e) as listed under New District Manager training. The exception will be that he need only bring those records pertaining to the personnel that form the basis for confrontations listed under (a). Since emphasis will be devoted to primary areas of weakness, the District Manager counselor should thoroughly discuss these with the Regional Manager prior to commencement of training. Concentration in these areas can then be implemented as outlined in (d). Senior District Manager training should require one week.

III. **Materials Required.** As stated in IIB, Confrontation Capsules, selected case histories from former seminars, and the seventeen taped topics listed under subheadings 1–7 will require duplication and distribution to the Regional Managers. As well, each Regional Manager will require one Fairchild projector. The majority of our Regional Managers currently have facilities to implement Regional Personnel; those that do not will be required to secure adequate additional office space.

IV. **Implementation.** Implementation of this program depends upon several factors. First, a District Manager counselor must be appointed to fulfill this new responsibility in Personnel Central. Second, as stated, regional office facilities must be approved and secured by those who currently do not have such space available. Finally, reproduction of those materials noted will have to be accomplished. It is anticipated that all three requirements can be accomplished to institute this program by January 15. At that time it is recommended that a continual rotation schedule be developed that will allow simultaneous training of four District Managers. Since Personnel Regional will be instituted coincident with this date, the Regional Manager will then have adequate decentralized training aids to augment the proposed central program.

V. **Conclusion.** The need for formalized managerial training has long been recognized. Implementation of this program not only fulfills current requirements, but offers an excellent base for future meaningful expansion in areas helpful in maximizing managerial skills. It is felt that an early decision to implement this program, by the date suggested, will further insure our continued progress in the years ahead.

J. L. Chambers

CASE 3-11

Fletcher-Fielding, Inc.

Manufacturer of Office Equipment and Systems—Training Sales Personnel

Tony Walker, director of Sales Training for Fletcher-Fielding, Inc., had been asked by his boss, Grayson MacDonald, vice-president of sales, to suggest some ways of reducing the high costs of refresher training for the sales force. The Fletcher-Fielding Company, located in Pittsburgh, Pennsylvania, was formed in 1937 to manufacture mimeograph-type duplicating equipment. The line now included dry copiers, word processors, and other items comprising a complete office system. Sales in 1985 were $65,000,000. The sales force of 1,000 called directly on office managers of potential buyers.

Training programs were conducted at the training facility located in a rural area a few miles south of Pittsburgh. The location was chosen to minimize urban distractions for the trainees. The threshold training program for new salespeople lasted for eight weeks and covered technical information about the product, office systems, the market for office equipment, company systems, and personal selling. As a part of the program, trainees visited the manufacturing facility in Pittsburgh. New sales trainees spent the first three to four months learning initial selling skills in the branch office where they were hired, and they were then sent to the training center for formal training sessions. Classes were offered three times per year. On completion of formal training, the new salespeople were assigned to territories of their own.

The training in salesmanship focused on the psychology of the buyer. The market for office equipment was a sophisticated one, and salespeople were trained to concentrate on the dynamics of the buyer. The salesperson had to understand the buyer's motivation to be able to close a sale; he or she had to recognize that there was a personal side and a business side to the buyer. Salespeople were trained to answer questions such as, Is the buyer seeking ego satisfaction? Is he or she primarily concerned with cost reduction? Is he or she trying to impress the boss with his or her problem-solving abilities? Most of the training staff were people who were high sales producers in the field, because Walker believed they had higher credibility with the trainees and could do a more effective job of coaching.

The How to Sell portion of the training program was designed by Xerox Learning Systems in Stamford, Connecticut. It was called "Professional Selling Skills III" and was a highly integrated system covering basic sales skills, follow-up, coaching, and group application seminars. One component of the Xerox system was a series of video tapes of common sales situations. The tapes were designed to allow the instructor to pause at various points and ask the audience to provide solutions to the problems described. The tape then continued and showed the correct solution. The entire process was then reinforced by replaying. Walker described the system as a sales communications course. The course helped the trainees to handle the difficult parts of selling such as talking to strangers and handling rejection. The entire training program was based on the belief that the art of selling was learned.

As a part of the continuing refresher training program for all Fletcher-Fielding salespeople, sales personnel were brought back to the Pennsylvania training facilities in groups of one hundred every two years for a one-week program. The costs of bringing a national sales force back to Pennsylvania and housing them for a week were high, and Grayson MacDonald had instructed Walker to find a less expensive alternative that would serve the same need.

Tony Walker had investigated the possibility of providing retraining programs that could be conducted in the ten regional sales offices, perhaps by district personnel. One possibility was the use of commercially prepared training films. NFL Films in Mt. Laurel, New Jersey, rented out a series of action-packed films that translated the winning strategies of sports to the business world. They were motivational films designed to inspire salespeople to strive for success. They varied in length from 2 minutes to 15 minutes and showed how to plan strategy, execute tactics, and outperform the competition. The films were designed to catch the audience's interest and make them sit up and take notice.

Another firm that rented out films for sales trainers was Producers International Corporation in Indiana. These films were designed to inspire success and achievement. The seven films in the company's product line boosted morale, improved productivity, and provided motivation. Each film was accompanied by a discussion guide with suggested questions to pose to the audience to reinforce the material covered in the film. In addition, wallet-sized reminder cards were provided for each participant containing summaries of the key points covered. These cards enabled the salesperson to review what he or she had learned at convenient places and times. Producers International described its films as providing a supportive way for a company to show its sales force that it wanted its salespeople to be the best they can be.

The use of films such as these would make it possible to provide refresher training in the regional offices under the direction of the regional sales managers. This would save the cost of bringing all sales personnel to the Pennsylvania training center and would also reduce the amount of lost productive selling time away from the job. However, Tony Walker was concerned that the commercially prepared films would not provide the same learning experience as programs specially tailored to Fletcher-Fielding salespeople. He was also concerned about the willingness of regional managers to allocate sufficient time of their own and their sales personnel's time to retraining to make it work. Also, conducting such programs amidst the activities and distractions of the regional office might be far less effective than in the purposely isolated training center.

MetraVideo, a New York city–based telecommunications transmission and programming firm, had proposed another alternative to the retraining sessions in Pennsylvania—the transmission of a video conference simultaneously from the home office to several locations around the country by satellite. MetraVideo not only provided its clients with networking equipment, but also helped to locate hotel rooms for its reception sites, wrote the scripts for the video conference and provided the catering for meals. MetraVideo made a strong pitch for the medium of video conferencing. They claimed that you can put out twice the information in one hour than you can with a full day of live meetings. And electronic graphics conveyed information faster with a higher retention level because of the attractiveness of the screen. The costs of producing a video conference were considerably higher than the use of training films, but they were still less expensive than bringing all sales personnel to Pennsylvania.

Evaluate the relative merits and limitations of the alternatives of decentralized versus centralized refresher training.

What changes can you suggest that might make either or both of the decentralized methods of training more successful in this company?

CASE 3-12

Motorola Canada

Manufacturer of Electronic Equipment—Training Sales Personnel

The director of sales training for Motorola Canada believed that the emphasis and approach to sales force training in the Canadian Division should be refocused. Motorola Canada was a subsidiary of Motorola, Inc., an American-based multinational engaged in the production and marketing of a broad range of electronic equipment and components. Total international sales in 1984 were in excess of $4.3 billion. The product line included two-way and other electronic communication systems, semiconductors, military and aerospace communication equipment, and high-speed modems, multiplexers, and network processors. The company had 78,000 employees worldwide. The communications division of Motorola Canada made and sold two-way radios and other forms of electronic communications equipment for customers that included governments, hospitals, airlines, construction, and telecommunications companies. Because of a continuing deterioration of the Canadian economy in the 1980s, sales management believed that greater attention had to be paid to sales performance.

The sales manager's office believed that the way to counteract an economic downturn was to increase pressures and incentives for improved sales performance. If the sales force could be persuaded, through additional incentives to work harder, the result should be an increase in sales volume. Ian Forbes, a sales training consultant, disagreed with this view. In his view, the members of the sales force needed new selling skills that with the same amount of effort would produce more sales volume. The training department had been experimenting with new productivity techniques and had evolved three basic principles that should guide any future activity aimed at increasing productivity among the sales force. First, productivity would be increased, not by policy or edict, but by directly influencing the behavior of the salespeople during their calls. Second, selling skills were considered to be more important than level of activity. If salespeople were not achieving a satisfactory level of sales, it was because they were doing the wrong things, and increasing their level of activity would simply mean that they would be doing the wrong things more often. So, management needed to improve sales skills rather than push sales personnel to more activity. Third, the company needed to identify the sales skills needed to achieve satisfactory sales and to develop these skills through training.

Forbes recommended an experiment to test the effect of improved training on sales performance. As a consequence, Huthwaite, Inc., was brought in to conduct a three-month experiment. A pilot group of Motorola sales managers was chosen to participate in Huthwaite's Sales Productivity Program—developed following an analysis of 6,000 sales calls in seventeen countries. This program taught managers to coach selling skills in the field and was backed up with computerized tracking of individual progress and a final analysis. Huthwaite personnel worked for weeks with each manager in the field—its system was based on retraining the salesperson on the job. The sales manager accompanied each salesperson on his or her sales calls. The system required hard work and lots of practice on the part of sales personnel.

To test the effectiveness of the program the sales personnel in the territories involved were divided into experimental and control groups. The control groups were matched with the groups receiving training, but they received no additional training. At the end of nine months, the trained groups showed a 5.3 percent increase in orders while the control groups showed a decline. This difference in performance was consistent both for new orders and for total sales. These differences are illustrated in Exhibits 1 and 2.

At the end of the experiment the director of sales training recommended that the new Sales Productivity Program be adopted throughout the sales organization, citing the expected increase in sales performance. However, several of the sales managers in the experimental group had complained about the extraordinary demands on their time required by the program. They claimed that they had neglected other aspects of their jobs to carry out the time-consuming one on one training program in the field.

EXHIBIT 1 Average Total Sales

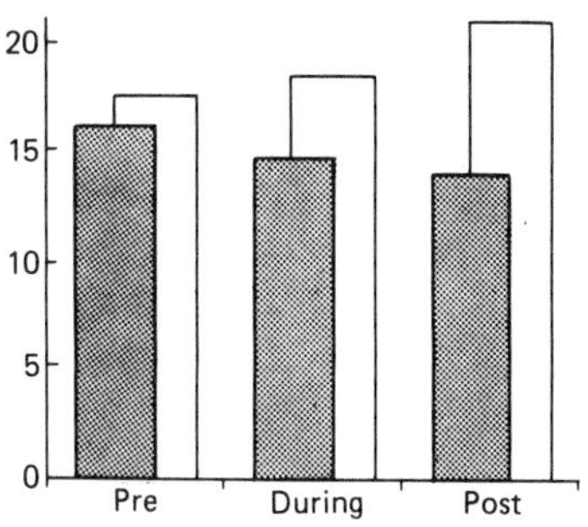

Control group*
(n = 42)
Total orders: – 13%
New orders: – 16%

SOURCE: Motorola Canada

EXHIBIT 2 Average New Sales

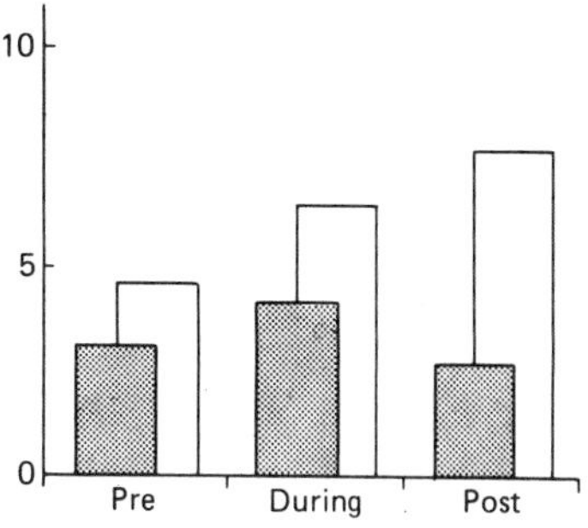

SPIN group
(n = 42)
Total orders: + 17%
New orders: + 63%

SOURCE: Motorola Canada

The sales manager admitted that the Sales Productivity Program had demonstrated the importance of good training in how to sell, but he questioned whether there might not be a more efficient method of achieving such training. He also raised the question as to whether better motivation and control might more than compensate for a somewhat less complete program of sales training.

How would you rate the relative importance of methodology over motivation in the performance of a salesperson?

What action should the sales manager take in this case?

CASE 3-13

Grady Tire Company

Tire Manufacturer—
Motivating Sales Personnel

James Bruce, sales vice-president of the Grady Tire Company, wanted to improve personnel attitudes to increase productive sales efforts. The Grady Tire Company was a manufacturer of auto, truck, and other tires, plus a number of other rubber products. Executive offices were in New York City, with manufacturing plants in Cleveland, Newark, and Los Angeles. The sales force of 295 persons was divided into four geographic divisions, each under a division sales vice-president.

Bruce was well aware that personnel attitudes influenced sales efforts since the way personnel felt about the company and the job affected enthusiasm in tackling selling. In the tire industry, where product differentiation was small, attitude constituted one of the strongest competitive differences between companies. It was only after reading an article on the effects of negative attitudes that Bruce thought seriously about the attitudes of his own sales staff. (An extract from this article is presented in Exhibit 1.) His conviction that such conditions existed within his own company was strengthened when he found that sales

EXHIBIT 1 Hazards of Poor Attitudes by Sales Personnel

Poor attitudes on the part of salespeople lead to low morale, which in turn provides a number of hazards to management:

1. Salespersons without enthusiasm are content to take orders; they are not creative thinkers.
2. They rarely inspire customer confidence or goodwill; they radiate dissatisfaction.
3. They tend to accept the customer's point of view that prices are too high, product quality low, or deliveries delayed.
4. They credit the competition with more ability and know-how than they have; their confidence falters.
5. They will complain to management that their salaries and commissions are too low, their expense accounts inadequate.
6. They will blame a poor sales record on ineffective advertising or poor leadership, never their own lack of effort.
7. Their negative attitudes will rub off on fellow salespeople.
8. They will ultimately leave the company.

policies had sometimes undergone considerable alteration by the time they filtered down to the customers. This represented either a failure in communication or resistance on the part of the sales force to management direction; Bruce was inclined toward the latter explanation.

In a meeting with John Rogers, vice-president of marketing, Bruce suggested that a firm of outside specialists be hired to conduct an attitude survey among the sales force. In justifying his request, he explained, "Every sales executive recognizes the existence of situations and conditions that prevent salespersons from doing their best work, but many do not care enough to try to find out what these conditions are. Most assume, I think, that adequate compensation cures all ills. They raise salaries or commissions every so often and let it go at that. The fact is that salespeople are just as concerned, if not more so, with other aspects of their job." He pointed out that members of the field force, because of their physical separation from the home office, are in an excellent position to evaluate the company—compensation, management, sales training, the products they sell, their territories, and customers. Once Bruce knew how salespeople viewed these conditions, he could eliminate areas of weakness and improve attitudes and hence motivation.

Bruce believed there was a need for a formal study of salespeople's attitudes. Informal impressions based on personal meetings with the sales staff were not objective and were influenced by the fact that management was asking the questions. A research firm specializing in attitude studies would have two things his staff lacked—the time and the know-how to develop a survey. Such a firm would not have preconceived opinions and could make an objective, meaningful analysis of results. Rogers approved the proposed survey.

Field management and sales personnel were informed of the impending arrival of a questionnaire a week ahead of time in a letter from Bruce. He wrote: "Your thinking and opinions will be considered with those of your fellow salespeople to give us a clear and broad picture of how our sales staff views the things we are doing and ways in which we might improve our total sales effort and field support. No one in the company will ever see the individual questionnaires, so express yourself freely and honestly." The questionnaire, consisting of one hundred questions in nineteen attitude areas, was mailed to the homes of sales personnel. Each question could be answered "yes," "no," or "don't know." A stamped envelope was provided, and thirty days after mailing (the cutoff date), 87 percent of the questionnaires had been returned.

The survey firm compared the results with a national average curve based on previous responses to the same questions from over 8,000 salespeople. The results provided the Grady management were as follows:

1. Attitudes toward sales work, home and job, sales helps, sales training, and communications were substantially more favorable than the national average. Satisfaction with territory and customers was high.
2. Attitude toward the company was slightly under the national average.

3. Sales personnel manifested a stronger fear of competition than did respondents in other companies.
4. The general attitude toward middle and top management was much less favorable than the national average. Salespeople felt that middle management often failed to provide sales ideas, did not go to bat for them with top management, and did not give credit where it was due. Top management, they indicated, was less progressive than in competitive companies. Eight percent said that the home office was not fully aware of their problems.
5. Suggestions drew greater-than-average negative reaction. Salespersons complained that they never knew whether their suggestions reached the home office or what happened when they did: that management gave no recognition to the people who submitted them.
6. Many salespeople were dissatisfied with their salaries and felt that other companies paid their field forces better.
7. The attitude toward job stability and opportunity for personal progress was more unfavorable than the average. Almost half the sales force felt that who you knew in the company was more important than what you knew, and that the real producers did not move ahead. Only 68 percent felt there was a better than average future for them within the company.
8. The opinion of other departments was low. Most of the sales staff felt that other department heads were uncooperative, failing to meet their requests and needs promptly.
9. Salespeople were not sold on company products. More than half saw no more customer benefit than those offered by competition.

Results were also broken down into regions to help management pinpoint the trouble areas and direct corrective action with the greatest efficiency. Another breakdown compared the opinions of salespeople with those of the field management staff. In presenting the report, the survey company noted that honest answers might not reflect reality. A salesperson who thought his or her company paid lower salaries would act in certain ways; it did not matter what the truth of the matter was—his or her attitude was based on what he or she thought.

One week after the survey results were in, Bruce held a meeting with the four division sales vice-presidents and the corporate industrial relations manager to determine what action to take.

What remedial action should have been taken as a result of the survey finding?

How could the survey results be used to improve personnel motivation?

CASE 3-14

Hammacher Company

Manufacturer—
Use of Sales Incentives

Wallace Bain, sales manager of the Hammacher Company, was considering whether or not to make some basic changes in the annual end-of-the-year travel incentive campaign. Many companies used travel incentives; Hammacher Company had used this incentive for almost twenty-five years. The method of operation had been polished and perfected so that sales personnel were motivated to greater and greater effort. Sales records were broken every year, and sales last year had been 12 percent better than the year before.

The main incentive for sales personnel meeting their quotas was an expense-paid "holiday" at a glamorous resort. Last year's meeting had been at the Hotel Fontainbleau in Miami Beach, Florida, in April. Although theoretically every salesperson had the opportunity to attend this convention, last year only 275 of the 500-person sales force had earned an invitation. Hammacher also awarded prize points to all sales personnel in accordance with their sales records. These were redeemable for merchandise selected from a prize catalogue. Despite the merchandise prizes, Norton Dowdy, sales vice-president, thought that nothing made the sales staff sell quite so well as the chance at that free four-day vacation. He described it as a grand holiday, more in the nature of a reward than anything else. At the Florida convention, business meetings had been scheduled on only two mornings, a total of six hours. These sessions were conducted primarily by home office executives and were of an inspirational nature. The remainder of the time was set aside for recreation and pleasure. Among the activities available were boating and fishing, swimming, golf, sightseeing, entertainment, and fine dining.

The Hammacher annual sales incentive program was scheduled from October 1 through December. Each salesperson was assigned a campaign quota derived from his or her sales volume during the year, his or her years of experience, and his or her market potential during the contest period. The sales staff was then divided into five groups with approximately equal quotas, to ensure that each person competed with others whose personal quotas were comparable. Branch managers formed a sixth group. All sales personnel selling their quotas received invitations to the convention.

A still stronger incentive was provided by the opportunity to earn membership in the Hammacher sales leadership club, a very exclusive honor organization. To become members, sales personnel had to sell a specified volume above their contest quotas, or a specified volume of business for the entire year. The highest honor of all, designation as an officer and board member of the club, was given to sales personnel with the highest percentage of sales above campaign quotas. These officers received an additional award—eligibility to attend a special two-day meeting just before the regular convention. Branch managers became eligible for the same honor by achieving their branch quotas during the campaign.

Wallace Bain, who was responsible for the incentive campaign, began the promotional program in August. The goal was to build suspense and interest through a barrage of notes and letters. He started by sending branch managers an August reminder to make preliminary preparations for the campaign. This was followed by detailed campaign instructions in September. Then, in late September, he provided a pep talk for managers to use for their group kickoff meetings with the sales personnel on October 1.

In July, when Bain met with Norton Dowdy to plan the campaign for the coming fall, he asked about the possibility of considering modifications. He pointed out that in any contest the average sales team is divided into three parts: one-third who say confidently that they will win, and usually do; one-third who think they can, and try hard to do so; and one-third who give up before the start because they are sure they cannot win. Hammacher had always tried to make the incentive good enough to motivate the top third to sell even more, to increase the number of winners in the second group, and to convince members of the third group that they at least had a chance to win if they tried. Nevertheless, Bain believed that the annual campaigns were not really getting a satisfactory increase in effort upon the part of the third group.

In addition, Bain wondered whether the company was getting value for the money spent. Did the chance to attend a convention where company business was discussed really motivate anyone, or were sales personnel working harder because of the honor and prestige attached to being invited? Would the same money invested in travel or merchandise incentives that could be selected by the winners (and that allowed the salespeople's spouses to participate in the reward) provide stronger motivation? Should the prizes or rewards be forthcoming sooner than four months after the end of the campaign? Dowdy believed that they shouldn't rock the boat. Past campaigns had continued to increase sales performance.

What changes, if any, do you think should have been made in the Hammacher Company's annual sales incentive campaign?

CASE 3-15

Office Supplies and Services Company

A Business Products Distributor— Stimulating Sales Personnel

The Office Supplies and Services Company distributed business products including office furniture and supplies, drafting and engineering supplies, and business forms. It also offered drafting, engineering design, and printing services. Sales were $26 million. While OSSCO's sales manager, Bob Brown, had been pleased with the performance of the sales force in terms of product sales, he felt that they had neglected the sale of OSSCO's services. The service end of the business was not contributing its share to overall company profit. Because Mr. Brown felt that the drafting, engineering, and printing services differentiated OSSCO from its competitors, he set a goal of doubling revenues from the sale of services for the next fiscal year. The competitors were mostly small suppliers who did not offer the same services as OSSCO.

The printing services ranged from letterheads and business cards to silk screening and lithography. Drafting services were connected with decoration. The full-time designers, employed by the furniture department, visited customers' premises and drew layout plans. Customers were able to visualize the end result and could make changes before incurring actual expenses. Business offices, banks, schools, and colleges were among the customers serviced.

OSSCO was headquartered in St. Louis and operated in several surrounding states. The area outside St. Louis was split into sixteen territories, with a subsidiary distribution center in each. OSSCO had six distribution center locations in the St. Louis area besides the central office. Fifty-five percent of the company's sales came from the St. Louis territory.

Each territory maintained its own sales force, which was supervised by the subsidiary center manager. Sales personnel were classified as general line or retail. Hiring was done by the combined efforts of the sales manager and the field trainer. New sales personnel were recruited from local areas through newspaper advertising. Once prospective sales personnel successfully completed the interview and testing procedures, they went through a six-week training program, which consisted of supervised work in each of the company's departments. Then each trainee was assigned to the field for six months to work under guidance of the field trainer. New recruits were paid salaries during training.

After completing training, new personnel became general-line salespersons and received straight commissions with drawing accounts. Each individual was assigned a section of the subsidiary distribution center's territory and assumed responsibility for selling all products and services in that territory. All general-line sales personnel were supervised closely by the center manager, who maintained a list of the active accounts for each salesperson. Each salesperson was required to call on each account at least once each week. To monitor performance, the manager reviewed call reports daily. Call reports listed all sales calls made and the dollar volume of products and services sold. The daily call report also specified the number of cold calls made on potential customers. (See Exhibit

EXHIBIT 1 Job Description

PURPOSE: To establish the rights and obligations that a salesperson has in connection with a listed account.
EFFECTIVE DATE: January 1. This supersedes and cancels all prior bulletins on this subject.
PROCEDURE: A listed account is a customer or a potential customer of Office Supplies and Services Company who is assigned to an outside representative of OSSCO for special solicitation of sales.

1. When assigned to an outside person for solicitation, the outside person then receives certain special privileges applicable only to the assigned account. They are:
   a. The privilege of selling the account all our lines.
   b. Receiving full and all commissions on sales to the account except sales made
      (1) In our 60 Lindbergh distribution centers, or any Service Center, where no commission is paid to salesperson listing the account.
      (2) On the 221 Ivy Furniture Floor by inside personnel, either by phone or personal appearance, where the commission will be split equally between the salesperson and the inside personnel.
      (3) When prior agreement has been arranged between department manager and salesperson for less than full commission to be paid on a specific sales transaction.
2. In return for the privileges granted under an account listing program the outside program agrees to certain requirements which are as follows:
   a. To contact the account by prescribed solicitation at least once a week.
   b. To treat as a listed account each separate buying department of an organization or a customer and contact them as required above.
   c. To treat as a separate buying entity each department of city, county, state, and federal government agencies, which have the authority to purchase or requisition merchandise.
   d. To prepare and keep current an accurate listing of the accounts showing the correct name, address, etc., and to work out a definite schedule of calls.
   e. To call on the accounts as scheduled on a regular daily basis and to prepare each day an accurate report of the day's work. Such a report to be submitted *each evening before the close of business.*
   f. To present continuously to all buying departments of the listed account the advantages of *each* of our individual departments.

---

1 for the job description for general-line sales personnel.) Each salesperson's performance was evaluated monthly, relative to the assigned quota. Quotas varied each month according to sales fluctuations. Monthly sales meetings were conducted and meeting schedules prepared one year in advance. (Exhibit 2 illustrates a typical series of monthly sales meetings.)

Despite the control procedures for monitoring sales performance, the central office sales manager had had little success in stimulating the sale of OSSCO services. Sales to direct commercial accounts, constituting 80 percent of all sales, were regarded as the most logical market for printing, engineering, and drafting services. However, sales results indicated lack of selling effort with respect to the aforementioned services. While Bob Brown recognized that a salesperson was motivated to sell those items that could most readily be turned into commission dollars, he insisted that by selling OSSCO's drafting, engineering design, and printing services, product sales would increase, almost automatically. Mr. Brown said, "We offer drafting and engineering design services so the customers can be provided with a comprehensive design plan for office renovation. Our service people will look at the customer's location and show exactly what we envisage in terms of making the office space more attractive and functional. A salesperson who takes the time to show the customer the benefits of these services will find it easy to sell a lot more than an occasional desk and file cabinet."

Regarding special incentive programs to push OSSCO services, the sales manager stated further, "We've run a number of month-long sales contests on specific products with pretty good success. Contest incentives have included cash prizes, merchandise, and travel. All contests have always been judged on the basis of dollar sales volume. But I haven't been able to think of a way to apply that kind of incentive to services for a couple of reasons. Perhaps the most important is that it's tough to get the store managers pumped up about services because they don't have much to do with them. And the salespeople themselves are very product oriented. They know that they can spend a certain amount of time and sell a particular dollar volume of a specific product. Selling services requires a lot more time, patience, and expertise and you really don't know what that effort is going to net in terms of dollars."

EXHIBIT 2 Sales Meeting Schedule

January 19	KICK-OFF MEETING
February 7	FURNITURE
March 6	FURNITURE
April 10	QUICK COPY
May 7	WRITING INSTRUMENTS
June 4	DATA PROCESSING
July 9	BUDGET FURNITURE
August 6	CALENDARS/AMCO
September 11	PRINTING
October 9	PRINTING
November 6	FILING & SUPPLIES
December 4	BUDGET STRETCHERS AND CALCULATORS

Mr. Brown had talked with a number of management people at OSSCO, but so far, this had not resulted in any concrete suggestions for stimulating sales of the services. His inclination was to have a contest, although others at OSSCO did not agree. He was not convinced that a contest was the only solution; yet, it was all he could come up with for now. It was time to do something, but Mr. Brown was not sure just what.

What should Office Supplies and Services Company have done? What were the alternatives? Was a contest the answer? Why or why not?

CASE 3-16

Universal Automotive, Inc.

Manufacturer of Automotive Parts and Accessories— Motivating Sales Personnel with a Sales Contest

Joseph Mahoney, general manager of Universal Automotive, Inc., Chicago, recommended a sales contest to improve declining sales performance. This was his response to first-quarter results that saw sales fall substantially below quota. Mahoney believed that a sales contest would, among other things, provide the incentive to get sales up to or beyond territorial quotas.

Universal manufactured and distributed a complete line of automotive parts and accessories. Its sales force of sixty persons operated out of nine district offices located throughout the United States. The sales force's compensation plan consisted of a base salary and a bonus. The bonus was based upon the territorial quota, which was set by the general sales manager in consultation with the branch sales manager.

Mahoney proposed a sales contest that he believed would motivate sales personnel to achieve their quotas. He felt that the salespeople's spouses should be involved in the contest. The proposed contest would run thirteen weeks, and each salesperson would be assigned a weekly sales volume quota, determined by the general sales manager and the district manager. In addition, each of the nine sales districts would have a district sales volume quota.

Each week, a $200 cash bonus would go to the sales personnel exceeding their quota by the greatest percentage, although Mahoney had seriously considered using total sales volume instead of a percentage. Each salesperson achieving quota for the thirteen-week period would get a $300 bonus. The person exceeding the thirteen-week quota by the greatest percentage would receive an additional $400, with $250, $200, and $100 bonuses for salespeople in second, third, and fourth places, respectively.

Spouses would also participate in the sales contest proposed by Mahoney. For each $100 worth of bonus earned by a salesperson exceeding his or her weekly or quarterly bonus, the salesperson's spouse would receive five chances to win a merchandise prize.

All quota-making salespeople and their spouses would attend a three-day convention at the Chicago headquarters. The three days would mix business and pleasure, culminated by a gala dinner dance and drawing for the merchandise prize.

In the competition among the sales districts, the district exceeding quota by the greatest percentage would receive an $800 prize with the money to be divided among that district's salespersons. Second, third, and fourth places for the districts would be worth $600, $400, and $200, respectively.

When Mahoney formally proposed his plan for a sales contest, several criticisms were voiced. Objections centered around the disappointments and frustrations of those people who did not win, the overaggressiveness that might result from ambitious salespeople striving to win at all costs, the disruption of normal activities caused by the convention, and the temporary nature of the stimulation provided. Several executives opposed the contest, arguing that the negative aspects outweighed the possible benefits.

Mahoney countered that a contest would help correct a poor sales performance, it would appeal to the sales force's competitive spirit, it would enable salespeople to earn some recognition, and it would raise the morale of the entire sales force.

In spite of the lack of agreement, Mahoney scheduled a meeting of his staff of eight people to discuss the advisability of conducting a sales contest.

Should Universal Automotive, Inc., have held a sales contest to motivate its sales personnel to better sales performance? Why or why not?

What is the purpose of including spouses in the contest? Would working and nonworking spouses be likely to react differently?

CASE 3-17

P.F.V., Inc.

A Plumbing Supplies Distributor— Sales Meetings

Grady Dethridge, assistant sales manager of inside sales personnel, of P.F.V., Inc., was concerned with the effectiveness of his staff sales meetings in motivating the internal sales force. He had just returned from a half day conference on Personal Communication Within the Sales Organization put on by the Atlanta Chapter of Sales/Marketing Executives International. An important focus of the meeting was the use of sales meetings and one-on-one interviews to motivate sales personnel. As a result, Dethridge proposed a change in format for his sales meetings to his boss, Ralph Turner, the sales manager.

P.F.V. was incorporated in Atlanta fifteen years ago as a plumbing supplies distributor specializing in pipes, valves, and fittings. The company had gradually expanded its operations to twelve southeastern states with sales offices in Atlanta, Georgia; Chattanooga, Tennessee; Charleston, South Carolina; and Greensboro, North Carolina. Warehouse facilities were maintained in Atlanta and Greensboro. Annual sales revenue had reached $16 million. P.F.V.'s success was attributed to the company's ability to hire and retain an experienced, knowledgeable and loyal core of sales and purchasing personnel. The "family" environment that P.F.V. management had worked so hard to develop was threatened recently by a serious internal conflict between one of the company's top salespersons and the Greensboro office manager with whom the salespeople worked very closely.

Plumbing supply distributors provided construction contractors and supply houses with a broad inventory of plumbing supplies. These customers typically could not afford to keep on hand the myriad types and sizes of plumbing products required. So distributors, in effect, were inventory risk takers. Because the distributor's investment was high, careful attention to the margin between the purchase and sale price for each item was crucial.

P.F.V. had numerous competitors in its trading area. To maintain an adequate return on investment, P.F.V. specialized in pipes, valves, and fittings. This allowed the company to stock a particularly deep inventory in these items. This made rapid delivery possible and enabled P.F.V. to charge slightly higher prices than if the company offered a full line.

With the necessity of maintaining strict control over the purchase schedules and selling prices, the organizational structure and training program was geared to facilitate communications among P.F.V. employees. When a sales trainee was hired, he or she spent one or two years working in the warehouse to acquire a comprehensive knowledge of the product line.

The salesperson then spent six to eight months working for the office manager at the billing desk to learn the procedure for price quotations. The office manager was responsible for monitoring inventory levels, interacting with manufacturers' representatives to purchase inventory at the best possible prices, and setting minimum selling prices for P.F.V. salespeople.

The trainee then spent two to five years as an inside salesperson. The inside salesperson handled house accounts and repeat purchases from established accounts, and expedited orders written by outside sales personnel. Each inside salesperson handled the accounts of one or two outside sales personnel so that good communications between the inside and outside sales personnel and the customer were maintained. Inside sales personnel were paid straight salaries.

After gaining inside experience, the salesperson was eligible to become an outside salesperson. On the firm's organizational chart, outside salespersons were considered as equals to the inside sales manager. They traveled a specific geographical territory, calling regularly on existing accounts with supply houses and contractors, as well as seeking new accounts. Because plumbing products were high-priced items, customers looked to the P.F.V. salespeople for advice on what and how much to buy. Considerable product knowledge was needed, because the salesperson frequently was asked to quote on items needed in huge construction projects. Outside sales personnel were paid a 10 percent commission and were responsible for setting product prices, subject to minimums determined by the office manager.

The "family" environment at P.F.V. was enhanced by regular formal and informal meetings. Twice monthly, manufacturers' representatives sponsored seminars to disseminate product information. The inside salespeople met each week to discuss products and operations with the inside sales manager and the office manager. Outside salespeople met monthly for the same purpose. Each outside salesperson met with his or her inside "partner" regularly to discuss their accounts.

The focus of the regularly scheduled meetings of both the inside and outside sales personnel was almost exclusively product training. Grady Dethridge, assistant sales manager of inside sales personnel, proposed to Ralph Turner that 25 to 50 percent of the time in each meeting be devoted to activities designed to motivate the sales force to greater and more effective effort. Motivation-increasing activities might include demonstration sales, description of "success stories," review of selling techniques, and information on comparative performance. Turner's response was that no time could be spared from product training—the line was large and complex and the P.F.V. sales force had established a reputation in the market for its knowledge of the product line and how it could best serve customer needs. Turner said that the 10 percent commission, combined with personal exhortation by the sales executives on a one-to-one basis should provide adequate motivation. Dethridge responded that his inside sales force were not at present eligible for commissions—only the outside sales force earned commissions. With an inside sales force of seven, he did not feel that he had time to motivate that many people on a one-to-one basis. In addition, he believed that group motivation activities were often more effective because of the competitive team spirit engendered. He was not trying to tell Turner how to conduct his meetings with the eight-person outside sales force, but he would like to include motivational material in his own meetings. Turner did not immediately approve the proposed change, but he promised to take the matter under advisement.

Evaluate Dethridge's and Turner's viewpoints with respect to the role of sales meetings at P.F.V.

Would you consider motivational subject matter more or less important as a part of the sales meetings of the outside sales force?

CASE 3-18

Bristol Laboratories

Pharmaceutical Company—
Sales Contests

Bristol Laboratories, a division of Bristol-Myers, was one of the world's largest manufacturers of antibiotics and pharmaceuticals. It had 725 salespeople deployed throughout the United States. With a sales organization of this magnitude, Bristol faced managerial problems in motivation and in balancing the selling emphasis given its product lines. Sales force management used sales contests to motivate and direct the sales staff. These ran continuously each month throughout the year.

Bristol's major brands included Tetrex, Saluron, Syncillin, Kantrex, Naldecon, Polycillin, Staphcillin, Prostaphlin, and Salutensin. Hospitals and drug wholesalers purchased direct from the company. Ultimate consumers bought Bristol's products from retail druggists on doctor's prescriptions.

Bristol's sales force was organized into ten regions containing sixty-five sales districts. Sales personnel were distributed within districts according to the sizes of individual territories and relative sales potentials. Their duties included calling on doctors, hospitals, and drug wholesalers, and making service calls on retail drugstores. Each salesperson visited an average of 120 doctors, ten hospitals, and two wholesalers per month.

The sales force compensation plan consisted of a relatively small salary plus a relatively generous 5 percent commission on territorial sales volume. K. J. Ryan, sales manager, believed that his salespeople were among the highest paid in the drug field. They averaged over $23,000, the top person earning over $49,000.

Through its sales contests, Bristol sought to direct salespersons toward emphasizing all products in the line instead of only the high-commission, easy-to-sell items. While contests ran continuously, different products received emphasis each month. Ryan thought money was less important than merchandise and travel awards, especially to a highly paid sales force. Salespersons competed against territorial sales goals; management believed that other bases for contests would have caused morale problems, as salespeople worked different territories and had varying selling abilities. In all contests, the closer a salesperson came to established targets, the greater was the reward.

Maritz, Inc., a firm specializing in organization and operation of sales-incentive campaigns, planned and administered Bristol's contests. Four different drugs were promoted each month. In December these were Polycillin, Tetrex, Kantrex, and Naldecon. The marketing department estimated dollar sales and the percentage of each drug that should comprise a salesperson's total effort. December's target mix was 65 percent Polycillin, 23 percent Tetrex, 9 percent Kantrex, and 3 percent Naldecon.

The contest scoring system involved awarding prize points in two categories: (1) total sales of the four drugs and (2) performance relative to the target sales percentage mix. For each dollar of total sales, one half of one prize point was awarded (for example, $20,000 total sales = 10,000 prize points). Points awarded in the second category "mix points," were based on performance relative to the target sales mix. For example, salesperson X had actual sales in December as follows:

Product	Target Mix (%)	Target Sales	Actual Sales	Performance Rating (%)
Polycillin	65%	$ 9,750	$14,700	150%
Tetrex	23	3,450	2,475	72
Kantrex	9	1,350	540	40
Naldecon	3	450	540	120
Total	100%	$15,000	$18,255	

If X's sales had equaled the target sales, all the performance ratings in the last column would have been 100 percent. This column represented the percentages of drugs sold relative to the mix goal. Prize points ("mix points") were calculated by multiplying the lowest performance number by the "sales factor" established by management (see Exhibit 1). X's mixpoint total was 11,000 points (40 × 275 = 11,000). The lowest performance number was used in an effort to motivate sales personnel to make sales proportionate to management's target percentages. Total prize points earned by X were:

total sales of promoted drugs ($18,255 ÷ 2) = 9,128 points
performance relative to target (40 × 275) = 11,000 mix points
total = 20,128 prize points

EXHIBIT 1 Memorandum

The contest items, product mix, and payoff for the sales month of December are as follows:

	Payoff	Mix (%)
Polycillin	$5,100,000	65
Tetrex	1,852,500	23
Kantrex	727,500	9
Naldecon	330,000	3
Total detail sales	$8,010,000	100
Total sales estimate		$10,125,000
Total budget estimate (0.9% of sales)		91,125
Less ½ point per $ sales		25,313
Mix payoff dollar budget		$ 65,812
Mix payoff in points ($0.005 × dollar budget)		13,162,500
Total detail items		8,010,000
60% of detail items*		4,806,000

$$\frac{4{,}806{,}000}{100} = \text{sales factor} = 48{,}060$$

$$\frac{\text{mix points}}{\text{sales factor}} = \frac{13{,}162{,}500}{48{,}060} = 275 \text{ points/sales factor}$$

*Determined by management.

Had X sold the exact targeted product mix, his mix-point would have been 27,500 and his total prize points 47,628.

"Prize-point" checks were mailed monthly and were exchangeable for merchandise described in the Maritz catalogue. Each prize point was worth $0.005 (20,128 points = $100.64). Management withheld the proper income tax each month. Points could be exchanged for almost any item imaginable, from airplanes to pearls. Travel awards consisted of trips to such places as London, Casablanca, and Tel Aviv.

Should Bristol have used sales contests? As many as it did?

What improvements, if any, might Bristol have made in its program for motivating and directing sales personnel?

CASE 3-19

Archer Stationers

Office Supply Company—Sales Compensation Problems

John Archer, owner of Archer Stationers, was troubled about the high rate of turnover among outside sales personnel; he wondered if the compensation system might be a contributing factor. Archer Stationers was started by John Archer in 1948 as a small stationery store in Oklahoma City, Oklahoma. The business had expanded continuously, adding lines such as office supplies and equipment. It grew from a small store to the largest office supply company in Oklahoma. The product lines included office supplies, stationery, office machines and equipment, desks, files, engineering supplies, and accounting systems. The engineering supplies and the accounting systems lines were the newest. An outside salesperson sold the engineering line by calling on various engineering firms in the market served by Archer. The accounting systems, ranging upward in price from $70, were sold similarly through an outside salesperson.

Archer employed a total of twenty-nine people. Of these, seven were outside salespeople who called on businesses throughout Oklahoma and the Texas panhandle. Outside sales territories were divided according to product line. Al Caines, the company's number one person on the sales staff, Mary Satterly, and Cecil Grey sold exclusively items pertaining to the office. Jack Rubin and Bill Westerfield were the engineering salespeople, and Otto Olsen and Mike Sanchez sold accounting systems. Al and Cecil had been with the company for many years, but Otto and Jack had been hired just six months ago to replace two outside salespeople who had quit. The remaining three had been with the company approximately one year. With the exception of Al and Cecil, the company had experienced high turnover in its outside sales force. The rate was particularly high with new salespeople. Archer had found that if a salesperson remained for a year, the chances were good that he or she might stay several years.

The outside sales force was paid on a commission basis, with a $1,500 monthly drawing account. Thus, if in one month a salesperson did not earn commissions in the amount of $1,500, he or she would be paid that amount anyway. However, a salesperson who failed to earn $1,500 in any month was obligated to pay back the difference between the amount earned and the amount paid; this was subtracted from earnings in excess of $1,500 in succeeding months.

The compensation system was initiated because Archer felt that commissions were the best way to stimulate real effort. He thought the drawing account was good since it provided a steady salary in bad months yet kept the salesperson from depending on this guarantee by requiring repayment of advances. In his opinion, the commissions paid were good (10 percent of gross profit), and he felt that anyone who would work hard and stick with the company could earn at least twice the drawing account. As examples, Archer pointed to the performances of the two senior salespeople. Al, with the company for twelve years, was making $44,000 yearly. Cecil, with the company for eight years, was still increasing his sales and, hence, his income from commissions ($36,000 last year). Earnings of all the salespeople are presented in Exhibit 1.

Otto Olsen, one of the systems salespersons, had yet to earn more than his drawing account in his five months on the job. He explained that the type of systems he sold were of little value to a company with less than fifteen employees, accounts receivable numbering less than eighty, and accounts payable numbering less than one hundred. Consequently, most of his time was spent trying to locate eligible customers, with little left for actual selling. Otto spent the best part of his time on the telephone trying to locate and make appointments with potential customers. The company visited often turned out to be too big or too small, or had its headquarters in another city. In Otto's opinion, this inefficient method of prospecting was the main reason he had not made enough sales to cover his drawing account. Mike Sanchez, with Archer Stationers for three months, was also having difficulties getting established with the accounting systems. Both salespeople seemed discouraged because they couldn't make wages in excess of their drawing accounts. The three remaining newer salesmen managed in less than six months to exceed drawing accounts, but they were all in debt to the company for past draws.

Was the existing compensation plan for Archer Stationers salespeople contributing to the high turnover?

What changes, if any, would you recommend in the compensation plan?

Are there other factors that might be contributing to the high turnover of sales personnel?

EXHIBIT 1 Sales Force Earnings

	No. of Months Employed	Commissions Earned					
		Jan	Feb	Mar	Apr	May	June
Office Supplies							
Al Carnes	144	$4,100	$4,250	$4,400	$3,000	$3,600	$2,950
Cecil Gray	96	2,900	3,150	3,200	2,800	2,975	2,675
Mary Satterly	5	—	870	1,025	1,185	1,450	1,545
Engineering Materials							
Jack Rubin	6	900	980	1,075	1,290	1,510	1,755
Bill Westerfield	4	—	—	875	1,015	1,240	1,580
Accounting Systems							
Otto Olsen	5	—	850	1,210	1,075	1,115	1,425
Mike Sanchez	3	—	—	—	910	1,160	1,340

CASE 3-20

Kroeger Company

Manufacturer of Industrial Products—Proposed Compensation Plan

The Kroeger Company was a manufacturer of glass-lined steel tanks and alloy steel equipment sold directly to the industrial market. The chief consuming companies were engaged in brewing, distilling, and chemical manufacture. Sales in the United States and Canada were obtained through a fifteen-person sales force working out of the home office in Milwaukee, Wisconsin. Foreign markets were not contacted by the American firm, but manufacturing subsidiaries in West Germany and Japan made sales throughout the rest of the world. Sales amounted to approximately $44 million, three-fourths accounted for by the parent company. All domestic sales personnel reported directly to the general sales manager, who was also vice-president of sales and advertising.

Sales personnel, who were graduate mechanical or chemical engineers, were given a year's training at the factory and home office before they were assigned to a territory. During training they received a salary of $2,000 per month; as soon as they reached their assigned territories, compensation was on a straight-commission basis. The annual earnings of the salespeople normally ranged from $27,000 to $60,000. Company sales, however, varied greatly from year to year, since demand was influenced significantly by the demand for products manufactured by Kroeger customers. Only a few low-priced items, such as replacement parts, were manufactured for inventory. Most Kroeger products were custom built to the user's specifications. Consequently, the earnings of salespeople were subject to wide fluctuations. With a downturn in business, sales force morale slumped, and newer salespeople left the company for greater stability elsewhere.

The high sales force turnover rate resulted in high training expenses during periods of increasing demand. At the same time, when sales were booming, other employees complained about the inflated pay that sales personnel were receiving. After several months' study of the problem, the general sales manager sent draft copies of a proposed sale compensation plan to the sales personnel. He requested that they read and digest it thoroughly and submit their comments and suggestions to the home office. The plan is summarized below:

> Because of the gross inequities that have existed in our sales compensation plan in the past, and to eliminate the periods of hardship that many of you have experienced, we are proposing that each salesperson be given a base salary. This is to be roughly 60 to 70 percent of total take-home pay, with commissions making up the remainder. Since commission payments will make up only about one-third of the total compensation, you will enjoy much greater security than in the past.
>
> We will attempt, with the assistance of the marketing research department, to estab-

lish potentials for our various sales territories by analysis of published data on the industries we serve, modified by our own experience, which is determined from averages of prior years' sales. Through the medium of the relation between the base salary and the base sales credit (sales necessary to reach the base salary), we will try to equalize territorial potential and incorporate other elements, such as seniority.

Above this base sales credit, 3 percent commission will be paid on the first $50,000; 1.5 percent on the next $50,000; 1 percent on the next $100,000; 0.5 on the next $100,000. The commission scales rise to 0.75 percent on the next $100,000; 1 percent on the next $100,000; it drops to 0.5 percent on the next $300,000; and finally is 0.25 percent on all sales over this amount.

The proposed plan is based on sales credits rather than actual dollar sales. Full credit equal to the dollar sales will be given on an order that is sold and shipped into the area of the salesperson writing the order.

If an order is sold by one salesperson and shipped to another salesperson's territory, each will receive half credit. This is because we feel that it is important to have the salesperson contact the plant where our equipment is being installed to make certain that it is handled properly and given good service after the installation.

To offset partially the effect of "windfall" orders, and to even out the compensation, credits will be scaled down on large orders. Full credit will be given on the first $100,000, 50 percent credit on the next $50,000, and 10 percent credit thereafter.

Commissions will be paid on the basis of orders received rather than on shipments made. Our manufacturing cycle normally involves a period of three to six months, and we feel that it is important that you receive your compensation at the time of the sale—not later, when you may have forgotten that you booked the order. Cancellations of orders for any reason, therefore, will be charged back to the salesperson involved and shown as an adjustment on the next commission payment.

Each salesperson will receive credit on the above basis for all sales made in his or her territory. It is our intention, if this plan is adopted, to eliminate all house accounts. The total volume of business coming out of each territory will be taken into consideration in planning the take-home pay of the salesperson.

Sales credits will be established by the sales correspondent at the time of entering an order. These data will then be entered on the regular IBM order card so that the accounting department can run off quarterly reports. You will know exactly what you are receiving and where it comes from.

As in the past, we will continue to pay all legitimate traveling expenses in accordance with standard procedures.

Should the proposed sales compensation plan have been adopted?

Appraise the plan from the standpoint of the individual salesperson.

What part should timing have played in the introduction of the new plan, assuming that the sales personnel approve it?

develop a proposal recommending changes to bring Christopher's selling expenses into line with the industry.

After compiling and analyzing expense records over a six-month period, the sales manager decided to recommend that the company adopt a flat expense account plan. He was convinced that company sales personnel had abused the current system under which all sales expenses were reimbursed and which required them only to submit their total expenses for each period instead of a detailed itemization.

The sales manager proposed the following flat allowances for controllable expenses for all salespeople: room, $40.00–45.00 per day; meals, $4.50 for breakfast, $6.00 for lunch, and $12.00 for dinner while on the road; entertainment, $30.00–40.00 per week; communication, including telephone calls, $9.00 per day; and travel, 30 cents per mile while on business.

To permit a smooth transition from one expense plan to another, the sales manager suggested that district managers discuss the flat allowances with each of their sales personnel individually. This would give the sales staff opportunities to react to the new plan and to suggest modifications based upon unique territorial conditions. Minor revisions of the basic plan could be authorized by the district managers.

Under the sales manager's plan, each week salespeople would submit their daily expenses on itemized forms for approval by district managers and for payment by headquarters. For the first week under the new plan, the salespeople would receive an allowance of $200, and adjustments would be made weekly to account for the previous week's expenditures. Any salesperson spending more than the flat allowance would have the excess amount deducted from his or her annual bonus.

The marketing vice-president decided to discuss the proposed new expense plan with the district managers. There was no clear-cut majority opinion regarding the proposal. Some district managers felt that the flat-expense-account plan was equitable, since the district managers could modify the basic plan according to territorial differences. Other district managers opposed the proposal, arguing that it was essentially inflexible, would encourage salespeople to overeconomize, and would prevent them from capitalizing on sales opportunities requiring greater expense outlays. One district manager said that salespeople should pay their own expenses out of their salaries, thereby relieving management of the accounting and control problems.

The marketing vice-president recognized the validity of some of the objections raised by the district managers. However, he felt that the flat allowance was not only fair to all salespeople, but also the best way to cut selling expenses, which, in turn, would affect company profits favorably.

Should the Christopher Candy Company have adopted the flat expense allowance plan proposed by the sales manager? State your reasons.

CASE 3-23

Carter Oil Company

Manufacturer of Petroleum Products—Evaluating Performance of Sales Personnel

Carter Oil Company was a regional producer of oil products located in Midland, Texas, selling gasoline, fuel oil, and related products under the Carter brand. Total sales in 1985 were in excess of $1 billion. Carter's sales organization was comprised of full-line sales personnel who sold in five districts throughout most of southern and southwestern United States. The full-line salespeople sold to oil wholesalers, distributors, commercial users, and domestic fuel oil consumers. The sales force was responsible for developing all new accounts. Carter sales personnel were evaluated according to a single criterion—sales volume.

District sales managers determined each salesperson's volume from the weekly sales reports. Each report showed the previous week's sales, both in amount and percentage of total purchases by name of account. The district managers summarized the sales reports into monthly and annual summary sales reports. The amount and percentage of gain or loss was shown on both the monthly and annual reports. In addition, each salesperson's sales volume performance was compared with that of other sales personnel in the district and region. Finally, each salesperson's sales volume was compared with his or her output the previous year, and the trend of his or her sales volume was shown over the past several years.

Jack Binswonger had recently been promoted from manager of the New Orleans district to vice-president of sales. When he was district manager, he had believed that the method of evaluating sales performance based solely on sales volume was an inaccurate appraisal of a person's effectiveness. He felt it was especially unfair to the salespeople who spent a portion of their time assisting dealers with problems such as special promotions, inventory control, merchandising, and administration activities that had no direct effect on sales. He also believed that evaluation based on sales volume alone ignored some fairly wide differences in the sales potential of individual territories. He found support for his long-held opinions in an article in the May 1985 edition of the *Journal of Marketing Research,* which reported that sales executives in a sample studied tended to evaluate their salespeople solely on the basis of effort exerted with no adjustment for differences in the difficulty of the task (as measured by differences in territorial potential).

As a result of the deficiencies he saw, Binswonger suggested that the present method of personnel evaluation should be supplemented by a merit-rating plan. This plan would incorporate such factors as work habits; effectiveness in merchandising work; cooperation with management, dealers, and other sales personnel; promotability; and differences in territory potential. The merit-rating plan, its objectives and procedural aspects, was presented to all the district managers at a meeting in Dallas in June.

The district managers would rate the salespeople semiannually; then Jack Binswonger would review the ratings. The numerical scores assigned to each performance factor (which had not yet been determined) would be totaled to yield a merit score for each salesperson. Finally, district sales managers would discuss this appraisal with each salesperson, counseling on strengths and weaknesses and making suggestions for improvement. And, before the plan was put into operation, each district manager would explain the new evaluation method to the salespeople in the district.

Reaction to Binswonger's proposal was mixed. Bill Schultz, manager of the Atlanta district, was strongly opposed to the idea. He thought the new method of evaluation was too complex and, hence, too time consuming for the district manager. He also thought the sales personnel would be unhappy with an evaluation system that was based on so many subjective factors. He argued that salespeople would feel that ratings were based on personal favoritism and other nonobjective factors over which they had no control.

Was the Carter Oil Company's present method for evaluating personnel performance adequate?

How can Binswonger answer Schultz' objections?

Should the proposed merit-rating plan have been adopted? Justify your position.

Develop an appropriate instrument for evaluating performance.

What are the most important performance factors that management should be seeking to measure? Why?

CASE 3-24

Dewey Dressing Company

Food Products Manufacture—Role of Sales Supervisors

Gary Graydon, general sales manager of the Dewey Dressing Company, was reevaluating the role of district sales managers. The Dewey Dressing Company produced a broad line of salad dressings and related products, sold in forty states under the Dewey name. The company was founded in Los Angeles when Lawrence Dewey, a successful restaurant operator, was persuaded to market commercially the salad dressings that were so popular in his restaurant. The

Dewey products were well accepted, and within twenty-five years, the company had achieved almost complete national distribution. Distribution was through food wholesalers, but an important job of the sales personnel who serviced these wholesalers was to call regularly on large retail outlets for promotional purposes.

The Dewey market was divided into seven regions, each under the direction of a regional sales manager, each reporting directly to Graydon. The regions were subdivided into districts, under the control of district sales managers. There were forty sales districts, and the entire sales force comprised five hundred individuals.

Each district sales manager had direct supervision over from ten to eighteen salespeople. Each was expected to spend at least one half day per month with each salesperson, during which time he or she observed the salesperson's performance and made demonstration sales. The district sales manager was responsible for recruiting the sales personnel in the district, since management believed that salespeople would be happiest working near home. The most important source for new recruits was classified advertisements in newspapers. After screening by the district sales manager, selection of new sales personnel was by the regional manager.

New sales personnel were assigned to working territories immediately. Normally, the district sales manager worked with a new salesperson during the first week on the job, but sometimes conflicting demands on the time of the district manager made it impossible to provide threshold training immediately. In such instances, the salespeople had to learn by doing. New salespeople were classified as trainees for the first six months, during which the district sales manager was expected to have several short sessions with each new person, in addition to the one-week threshold training. Continuing training was provided for all sales personnel in weekly sales meetings held by each district sales manager on Monday mornings.

District sales managers had normal administrative report work, checking and forwarding salespeople's reports, and submitting their own weekly reports. In addition, each had five to ten personal accounts to service. The Dewey Company followed a policy of promotion from within in selecting its district sales managers. Thirty-nine district managers were former salespeople, and the remaining manager had worked in the home office. No formal training was provided for district sales managers.

Recently, Gary Graydon was asked to cooperate in a national study of sales supervisors by Z. William Koby of Houston, Texas. One purpose of the study was to assess the role of first-line supervisors in American sales organizations. The Dewey Dressing Company was one of twenty-one large national organizations that participated in the study. A year later, Graydon received a summary of the results from Koby. These results were based upon detailed responses from top marketing executives, sales supervisors, and sales personnel. There were approximately 300 responses from supervisors and 1,500 from salespeople. Summarized extracts from this report are shown in Exhibit 1. Fifteen of the firms were industrial-goods manufacturers; the rest were consumer-goods manufacturers.

Evaluate the role of first-line sales supervisors in the Dewey organization. Do you think that Graydon should have made any changes in light of the findings?

EXHIBIT 1 Activities of Sales Supervisors

Selling:

The typical sales supervisor spends about 50 percent of the time in direct supervision. When a sales supervisor works with one of the sales staff, the major emphasis is on selling, which activity normally takes between three and one-half to five hours in a typical day. Approximately three-fourths of the sales supervisors in this study indicated that they handle personal accounts. These two factors suggest that selling activities are generally the major activities of first-line sales supervisors, on the basis of the amount of time spent in the activity.

Discussing Salesperson's Problems:

The most time-consuming nonselling supervisory activity is discussing problems with the sales staff. Typically, this takes somewhere between one and one-half to two hours of a supervisor's time when he or she spends a day working with a salesperson. The responses indicate that, as a firm gets larger, the supervisor spends less time in this activity.

Administrative Activities:

The performance of administrative activities by first-line sales supervisors was almost universal. As a firm gets larger, the amount of administration performed at the first-line sales supervisory level decreases.

Recruiting and Hiring:

Approximately 50 percent of the supervisors recruit sales personnel. Generally, their recruiting activities are centered around initial contact or screening of applicants, but first-line sales supervisors do not seem to have much final authority in hiring the sales staff. Sales supervisors in firms selling industrial products have somewhat more recruiting responsibility than do those in firms selling consumer products.

Training:

Training sales personnel is an activity performed by almost all supervisors in this study, but very few supervisors indicated that they felt this to be one of their more important duties. The training is predominantly on-the-job in which the supervisor and the salespeople actually make sales calls. The other major type of training at the supervisor's level occurs at the branch office, where emphasis is placed on acquiring product knowledge. Typically, supervisors give new sales personnel about three weeks of training.

Reporting:

The number of reports submitted by first-line sales supervisors and to first-line sales supervisors indicates that supervisors in firms that sell industrial goods have somewhat more authority in approving sales expenses.

Branch Meetings:

Holding meetings seems to be considered important by the first-line supervisors of al-

EXHIBIT 1 (*Continued*)

most all companies. Ninety-six percent of the supervisors included in this study indicated that they hold sales meetings for staff under their supervision. The average number of meetings is eighteen per year. Smaller firms hold meetings less often than large firms.

MISCELLANEOUS FACTORS OF SALES SUPERVISION

Source of Sales Supervisors:
The most usual route to the position of first-line sales supervisor is by promotion from within the company. The responses indicate that less than 10 percent of all first-line sales supervisors were hired from outside sources. Firms selling consumer products promoted 93 percent of their supervisors from the sales force.

Training for Supervisors:
Only one of four first-line supervisors received specific training for their current positions. There is some evidence that this situation is changing, since almost half the top marketing executives indicated that they train their sales supervisors. The most usual type of training offered is as assistant to another supervisor.

Span of Control:
The typical span of control for sales supervisors is between seven and eight salespeople. Firm size does not appear to be a significant factor when span of control is considered. The individual companies varied from a span of five to sixteen salespeople.

Supervisory Time and Salesperson Satisfaction:
Sales personnel are more content with the sales supervision they receive if their supervisor spends more than a token amount of time with them. The average time that supervisors spend with each salesperson is slightly more than one day per month. The sales staff who would like their supervisors to do things that are not now being done are most numerous among the group whose supervisors spend the least time in direct supervision.

SOURCE: Extracted from Z. W. Koby, *An Analysis of the Function of First-Line Sales Supervisors* (Austin: The University of Texas Press), pp. 128–35.

CASE 3-25

Matthews-Martin, Inc.

Manufacturer of Packaging Materials—Supervision of Sales Personnel

Greg Hendrix, the new sales manager of Matthews-Martin, Inc., was considering the possibility of more carefully structuring the program of sales supervision carried on by the district managers.

Matthews-Martin, Inc., manufactured a broad line of paper products used for packaging. Its products were sold to packagers by a field sales force of sixty-two salespeople operating out of eleven district sales offices. Each district office had a sales supervisor responsible for both group and individual supervision.

Group supervision for all sales personnel in each district office consisted of monthly half-day sales meetings. These meetings covered topics such as sales force reports of their activities, special problems, review of the district's sales performance, new business outlook, competitive and price conditions, and advertising and sales promotion comparisons (prepared by the headquarters' staff). Some meetings featured a film on a new product or a new application. Each closed with a statement by the district sales manager on sales progress and problems in the district.

Semiannually, a one-day group meeting was held at each district office. Various regional managers participated by talking about new product introductions, new applications, maintenance problems, deliveries, production schedules, and credit problems. Salespeople were instructed in vital areas of sales techniques, communicating with customers about company policies, handling customer complaints, and assisting customers with their operating problems. Sales personnel were encouraged to express their views, to make suggestions, and to ask questions. Generally, these one-day meetings generated considerable enthusiasm among the sales staff.

Individual supervision of the sales force at each district office was the responsibility of the district sales supervisor. Normally, he or she talked on the phone with each salesperson at least twice weekly. Salespeople made weekly sales reports, credit reports on delinquent customers, and special reports as requested by the sales supervisor.

Every ninety days, the supervisor met with each salesperson at the district office. The supervisor reviewed the salesperson's performance and sales and service activities. Customers were analyzed. A review was made of the salesperson's success in securing new customers. Sales of specific products were analyzed. Special customer problems were investigated. In short, the meeting was a comprehensive appraisal of the sales activities of the previous three months.

The district sales supervisor occasionally visited the salespersons in their homes to discuss individual selling problems. In addition, each salesperson was invited frequently to the supervisor's home for a strictly social get-together.

About 60 percent of the district sales supervisor's time was spent in the field observing sales personnel, giving them on-the-job training, and assisting them with sales problems. The supervisor rode with each member of the sales staff in their territories, listened as the salesperson made presentations, and, between calls, reviewed the previous calls and previewed the next call.

Hendrix's predecessor had laid down general ground rules for supervision of the sales force and given each district sales manager considerable flexibility in carrying them out. As a consequence, there was considerable variation in how the salespeople were actually supervised. He was concerned that some district managers were doing a far less effective job of supervising than others. To overcome this variation in actual practice, he designed a standardized sales personnel

EXHIBIT 1 90-Day Professional Sales Personnel Performance Evaluation

NAME ____________________

DISTRICT MANAGER ____________________ DISTRICT NO. __________

Instructions: Please check the appropriate box indicating the level of performance relative to company standards using the following phrases as a guide:

1. Totally Unsatisfactory —Individual's performance shows significant limitation(s) and is not likely to improve sufficiently to justify a satisfactory rating in the future.
2. Less than Satisfactory —Individual's performance is below job requirements but with anticipated improvements the employee will meet the requirements of the job.
3. Satisfactory — Individual's performance fulfills normal requirements, has some strong points.
4. Above Average — Individual performs well beyond normal requirements, outstanding in some respects.
5. Outstanding — A level of performance attained by few, usually means immediate promotion.

If any subject is checked "Totally Unsatisfactory" or "Less than Satisfactory," please comment in the section "Areas Needing Improvement or Development."

	Totally Unsatisfactory (1)	Less than Satisfactory (2)	Satisfactory (3)	Above Average (4)	Outstanding (5)
1. Customer or prospect approach					
manner	______	______	______	______	______
interest	______	______	______	______	______
2. Selling ability					
identifying needs	______	______	______	______	______
presenting merchandise	______	______	______	______	______
closing sales	______	______	______	______	______
3. Communication of product knowledge to customers	______	______	______	______	______
4. Knowledge and use of selling technique	______	______	______	______	______
5. Personal appearance and adherence to dress regulations	______	______	______	______	______

6. Working relationship with company personnel	______	______	______	______	______
7. Reliability in carrying out instructions and following through on assignments	______	______	______	______	______
8. Planning and use of time	______	______	______	______	______
9. Accuracy and completeness of weekly reports	______	______	______	______	______
10. Ability in performing nonselling customer services	______	______	______	______	______
11. Overall sales production by departmental standards ($ sales per week)	______ Below 10%	______ 20–40%	______ 50–70%	______ 70–80%	______ Above 80%
Total overall rating					

______	______	______	______	______
Totally Unsatisfactory	Less than Satisfactory	Satisfactory	Above Average	Outstanding

Strengths ______

Areas needing improvement or development ______

Rater recommends this person for promotion to district management. Why or why not? ______

Individual's comments about the program of sales supervision ______

Rated by ______ Date ______
Reviewed by ______ Date ______

evaluation form (presented as Exhibit 1) to be filled out quarterly for all sales personnel in each sales district.

The proposed new sales personnel evaluation procedure was introduced to the district sales managers in a special meeting at the home office. Reaction was mixed. John Samuelson, manager of the Pacific Northwest district, claimed that the form added nothing new to the process of supervision and evaluation he was already carrying out. He believed that this was an interference with his prerogatives as a manager. The reactions of the other managers was less specific and hostile, but Greg Hendrix had the general impression of resistance to his proposal.

What is your opinion of the methods Matthew-Martin, Inc., used to supervise its sales force?
Does the Hendrix proposal provide the potential for improved supervision?
How can Hendrix handle the reluctance of the district managers to accept his proposal?

CASE 3-26

Hopkins Management Service

Automobile Maintenance and Delivery Service—Year-Long Selling Process Evaluated for Efficiency

J. J. Hopkins, president of Hopkins Management Service, complained to Gary Sommerfeld that the sales force took too long to make the average sale. He admitted that some prospects needed more selling than others, but he didn't believe that it should take a year or more to make most sales. One sale, consummated the year before, had been under negotiation for thirteen years. "Our sales personnel are highly paid, and their time is too valuable to be wasted in overly long sales campaigns," was Hopkins opinion. "Something must be done to increase our selling efficiency." Sommerfeld, the marketing vice-president, disagreed, explaining that they were selling management service with contracts often running as high as $100,000 and occasionally to $1 million. Such sales required a great deal of sales research and engineering. Yet, every effort was made to get quick action. When Sommerfeld had received a recent tip on a prospect, within one day he had alerted the salesperson, mailed immediately available information on the prospect to the salesperson, and started a complete research job on the prospect. Hopkins replied that he had no complaint with home office support procedures. It was the actual negotiation and closing of the sales that seemed to take too long.

Hopkins Management Service provided automobile maintenance and delivery service to businesses on an annual contract basis. When Gary Sommerfeld joined the staff thirteen years ago, he became the entire sales force. He got the job because the president had become too busy to do the selling. Sommerfeld had developed a sales force of eleven, working out of eleven branch offices.

Each prospective sale started with procurement of the name of a new prospect. This lead might come from the sales force, from company officers, or a newspaper clipping. Before sales personnel were allowed to visit a new prospect, preliminary research was launched at the home office. The first requirement for the prospect was size: it had to be large enough to yield Hopkins a minimum return of $10,000 annually. The second requirement was good credit standing. If these two hurdles were passed, the researchers looked for additional information useful to the sales staff, including the name of the right person to approach, whether Hopkins had had any dealings with the prospect at other locations, whether any of the prospect's clients were also Hopkins' clients. When the research was completed, the file was turned over to the appropriate salesperson for solicitation.

Hopkins sales personnel were trained to use a five-step selling process designed by Sommerfeld. Each step was a sort of separate sale in itself. The first was to persuade the prospect to grant an interview. This was usually difficult, and it was one point where the research in advance was particularly useful. It might enable the salesperson to mention a person, a company, or a job having enough meaning to the prospect to obtain agreement on a meeting.

During the interview, in addition to selling the prospect on further action, the salesperson had several other things to accomplish. First, he or she had to decide whether he or she was dealing with the right person, the one who could make the decision on Hopkins' service. If not, an interview had to be arranged with the decision maker. The salesperson relied upon answers to certain key questions, as well as general observation of matters denoting the individual's status, to answer this question. Then, the salesperson made a final evaluation of the prospect to determine whether Hopkins could handle the account profitably. This was important, because selling costs rose rapidly at the second selling step.

When the salesperson decided the prospect was a good one, work began on the second step: selling the prospect on a survey. The survey was a necessity, both to Hopkins and the customer, because it determined whether or not Hopkins could do the job the most efficiently. Hopkins operated on a cost-plus-fixed-annual-fee basis. Returns in excess of these figures were paid to the client as profit, but returns less than these figures obliged the client to make up the difference. In the latter case, it was better for the prospect to continue to operate its own auto maintenance and delivery service. The sales appeal used was that Hopkins, not knowing if it could be of value to the customer, was willing to gamble the time and money involved in a survey to find out. The customer was also assured that it would receive a copy of the report for its own use.

If the prospect could be convinced of the value of a survey, the salesperson embarked on the third step, the survey. The survey covered everything that might have a bearing on the problem. The salesperson was responsible for doing the survey but got help from the closest Hopkins regional office, the office that would eventually be responsible for servicing the account. The information in the survey was used to prepare a proposal for the prospect. The salesperson got help on drafting the proposal; the legal department, treasurer's office, and operating department checked the figures, and company officers approved the proposal before its submission to the prospect.

Then, the salesperson was ready for the fourth step, selling the proposal to the prospect. The proposal was presented in an attractive form, with four-color pictures and charts and a handsome cover. If the proposal was well presented, it was not too difficult to convince the prospect. The preselling job on the survey would have aroused the prospect's interest, and if the results looked financially sound, little effort was needed to complete the sale. As a matter of fact, the prospect was often so sold on the service by this time that the contact assumed responsibility for the fifth step, that of selling top management. If the contact was not completely sold on the Hopkins service, it was virtually impossible to sell top management. Therefore, the Hopkins salesperson was particularly concerned with providing a total package that was attractive to the contact and would make him or her look good in the eyes of his or her bosses when he or she presented it to them as a cost and time-saving service.

Completing the five-step process of selling the Hopkins service took, on the average, one year; and often, a particular sales campaign ran into several years.

Evaluate the sales methods used by Hopkins sales personnel. Do you agree that the entire sales process was too slow?

20 The Sales Budget

The sales budget is a blueprint for making profitable sales. It details who is going to sell how much of what during the operating period, and to which customers or classes of trade. Simply defined, a sales budget consists of estimates of an operating period's probable dollar and unit sales and the likely selling expenses. These two estimates are related to predict net profit on selling operations. The sales budget, then, is a projection of what a given sales program means in terms of sales volume, selling expenses, and net profits.

Figure 20.1 shows how sales budgets fit into the personal-selling effort. Both the sales volume and selling expense portions of the sales budget have their roots in the personal-selling objectives, which, as you recall, trigger two key decisions on personal-selling strategy: (1) the kind of sales personnel and (2) sales force size.

The sales forecast is the source for the sales volume portion of the sales budget. The sales volume objective derived from the sales forecast is broken down into the quantities of products that are to be sold, the sales personnel or sales districts that are to sell them, the customers or classes of trade that are to buy them, and the quantities that are to be sold during different time segments in the operating period. Making these breakdowns requires complex sequences of planning decisions. After these breakdowns are made, the selling expenses that will be incurred in implementing this sales program are estimated.

The sales budget, then, starts with the sales volume objective as a point of departure and, as we have noted, that objective traces to the sales forecast. Consequently, the extent of involvement of the top sales executive in the early phases of budgeting (for the entire company) depends upon the degree to which this

FIGURE 20.1 Personal Selling as Part of the Promotional Program

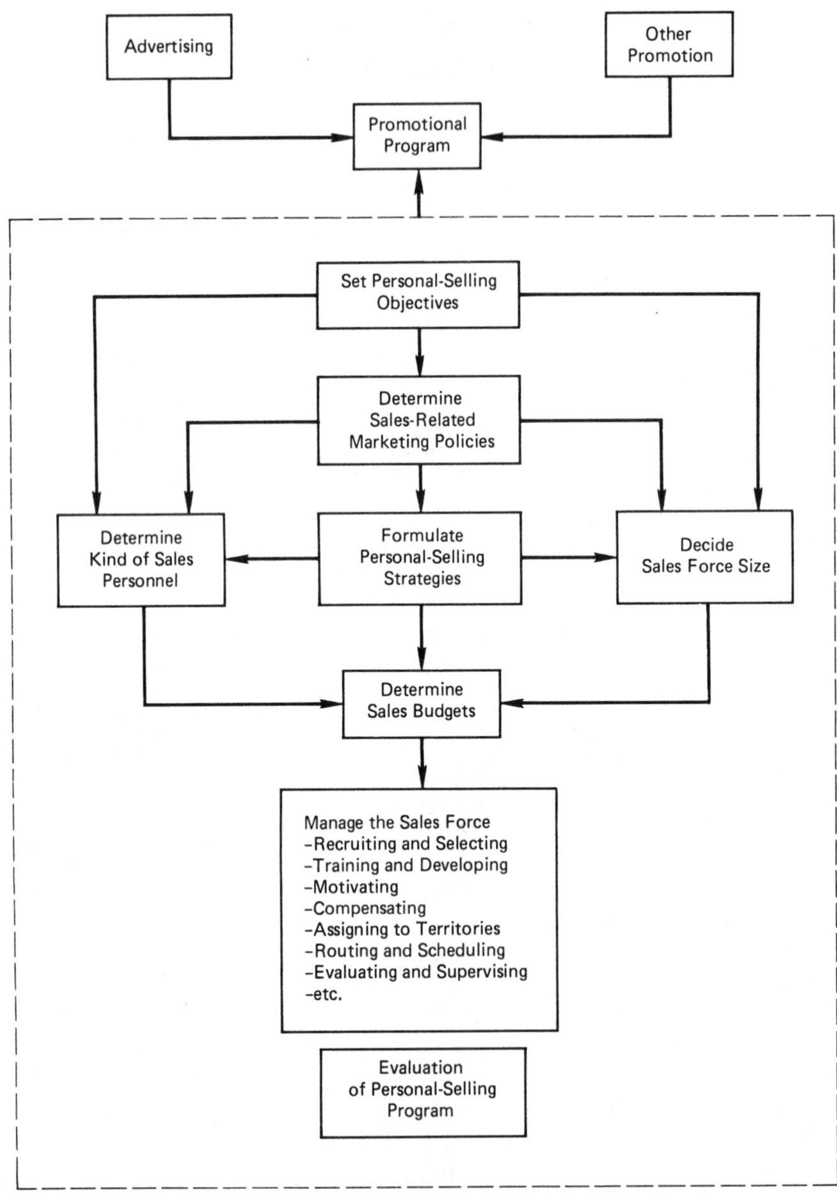

executive participates in forecasting. In some companies, top sales executives play leading roles in sales forecasting, while in other companies, they have passive roles (contributing advice and informed opinions). But in nearly every company, the primary responsibility for preparing the selling expense portion of the sales budget is the top sales executive's—since he or she controls the major portion of these expenses.

PURPOSES OF THE SALES BUDGET

Mechanism of Control

Control is the primary orientation in sales budgeting. The completed budget, which is a composite of sales, expense, and profit goals for various sales units, serves as a yardstick against which progress is measured. Comparison of accomplishments with relevant breakdowns of the budget measures the quality of performance of individual sales personnel, sales regions, products, marketing channels, and customers. These evaluations identify specific weaknesses in operating plans, enabling sales management to make revisions to improve performance. The sales budget itself, since it is a master standard against which diverse aspects of performance are measured, then serves as an instrument for controlling sales volume, selling expenses, and net profits.

Computerized information processing has enormously increased the effectiveness of control through the sales budget. Management is provided daily with details of actual performance compared with budgeted performance. With current and complete information on sales volume and selling expenses, the sales manager spots variations from the budget and takes corrective action before they get farther out of line.

Instrument of Planning

The budgeting process requires complex sequences of planning decisions. The sales forecast shows where it is possible for the business to go, and during the budgeting process planners determine ways and means for the business to get from where it is to where it wants to go. The sales forecast reveals data on sales potentials, and the budget planners calculate the expenses of converting forecasted sales into actual sales.

The sales budget planners formulate the sales plan so that both sales volume and net profit objectives are reached. Showing how to achieve the targeted sales volume is not enough. The planners show how the targeted volume can be reached, while keeping selling expenses at a level that permits attainment of the targeted profit. Sales budgeting requires the drafting of alternative sales plans and selection of the one most appropriate for serving the company's sales volume and net profit objectives.

SALES BUDGET—FORM AND CONTENT

The completed sales budget is a statement of projected sales revenues and selling expenses. The so-called "summary" of the sales volume section of the sales budget is both in dollars and cents and product units, so that budgeted figures are readily adjustable for price changes. The budget section on planned sales volume is presented in considerable detail. Not only are total unit sales shown but so are unit sales of each product, unit sales by sales territory (and/or region), unit sales by quarters or months, and unit sales by class of account (or type of marketing channel). For instance, Figure 20.2 shows unit sales of products A, B, and C by sales regions for 1988. Figure 20.3 take the breakdown one step farther and shows unit sales of the three products in the northeast region by quarters. Figure 20.4 carries the breakdown another step farther and shows unit sales of the three products in the northeast region for the first quarter by class of account. Computerized marketing information systems, of course, have the capability of calling up for display on desk-top consoles these and other breakdowns. Not every company uses the same breakdowns, each selecting those appropriate to its own planning, directing, and controlling of sales efforts.

FIGURE 20.2 Unit Sales by Sales Region, 1988

Product \ Region	Northeast	Midwest	West	South	Total
A	80	90	70	80	320
B	60	60	50	75	245
C	45	35	25	30	135

FIGURE 20.3 Unit Sales, Northeast Region by Quarters, 1988

Product \ Quarter	I	II	III	IV	Total
A	25	20	15	20	80
B	15	15	15	15	60
C	7	8	15	15	45

FIGURE 20.4 Unit Sales, Northeast Region, First Quarter, by Class of Account, 1988

Product \ Class of Account	A	B	C	Total
A	15	8	2	25
B	9	3	3	15
C	4	2	1	7

Estimating Budgeted Selling Expenses

The sales budget is drafted with a view toward obtaining an optimum net profit for the forecast sales volume. Note that it is the *optimum*—not the *maximum*—net profit that is the short-run profit objective. Profit maximization is the objective over the long run, but other considerations including the necessity for providing "business building" customer services, and for scheduling calls on prospective new accounts, make profit optimization the short-run goal. In other words, some selling expenses would not be incurred if management did not look beyond the current budgetary period. A forward-looking management considers these expenditures as investments that return sales and net profit dollars during succeeding budgetary periods. Management reasons that certain expenditures made during the period just ahead permit future savings in similar expenditures.

Thus, both immediate- and long-run sales plans are taken into account in arriving at estimates for the selling expense items included in the sales budget. Indeed, the immediate sales plan is an integral part of the plan covering a longer period. However, sales plans for the period just ahead are drafted in sharper outline than are those for longer periods, such as those covering five, ten, or twenty-five years. For the immediate budgeting period, plans cover the types and amounts of personal-selling efforts required to attain the sales and profit objectives. If the sales volume goal for the coming budget period calls for an additional $1 million in sales, sales management identifies the activities needed for reaching this goal. In turn, these activities, which may be stated in such terms as the numbers of new dealers needed in various classifications, are translated into estimates of the expenses incurred in performing them.

Therefore, after sales management expresses its plan for the forthcoming budgetary period in terms of required activities, the next step is to convert these into dollar estimates for the various items of selling expense. If the plan calls for sales personnel to travel a total of 500,000 miles in the year ahead, and the company pays a straight mileage allowance of 18 cents per mile, $90,000 to cover mileage allowances is included in the selling expense section of the sales budget. The paying of 18 cents a mile for sales travel, a previously established practice, aids in estimating the costs of reimbursing sales personnel for travel, but management determines the total number of miles sales personnel are to travel. In budgeting items of selling expense, then, management (1) estimates the volume of performance of the activity and (2) multiplies that volume by the cost of performing a measurable unit of the activity.

Using standard costs. When the total cost of performing a specific activity is analyzed and the cost of performing one measurable unit of the activity is determined, the first step has been taken toward establishing a standard cost. The second step is to compare the historical cost of performing one unit of the activity with what the cost should be, assuming standard performance, and considering the effect of changed conditions on costs. A standard cost, in marketing as well as in manufacturing, is a predetermined cost for having a standard employee perform under standard conditions one measurable unit of the activity.

The techniques for determining standard costs of distribution are less refined than are those for standard costs of production. Some companies have developed standard distribution costs accurate enough to provide a means for appraising the relative efficiency of performance of personal-selling activities. The executive compares current costs against known yardsticks. Standard costs of distribution simplify the estimating of individual items in the selling expense portion of the budget. Any predicted volume of sales, or any division of sales among the various products, classes of customers, or territories, are convertible into selling expense estimates through the application of standard costs.

Other estimating methods. Some companies that do not have usable standard distribution cost systems employ other methods for estimating selling expenses. Some simply add up selling expenses over a recent period and divide by the number of units of product sold, thus arriving at an average cost per unit sold. This figure is then multiplied by the forecast for unit sales volume, to obtain an estimate for the total budgeted selling expenses. Some adjust the average cost per unit sold for changes in the strength of competition, general business conditions, the inflation rate, and the like. Other companies calculate for past periods the percentage relationship of total selling expense to sales volume. This percentage, which may or may not be adjusted for changes in conditions, is applied to the dollar sales forecast to estimate budgeted selling expenses.

Finally, some companies *build up* their estimates for total selling expenses by applying historical unit cost figures to individual selling expense items. This is not a true standard distribution cost method, but it does focus upon individual expense rather than upon the total. Consequently, the expense estimates in the budget possess greater accuracy than if total selling expense percentages or total selling expenses per unit of product are used.

BUDGETARY PROCEDURE

Company budgetary procedure normally begins in the sales department. After all, the sales department in nearly all companies is the main department generating inward flows of revenues. The nature and amount of the predicted flows of sales revenues impact directly upon the activities of other departments. Therefore, once top management receives and gives tentative approval to the sales budget, other departments prepare budgets outlining their plans. For instance, the production department takes its cue from the sales budget in preparing budgets for manufacturing expense and inventory, as well as in planning production schedules. Similarly, the financial department uses the sales budget as the starting point in preparing budgets for capital expenditures, earnings and cash position, and administrative expenses. It should be noted that the production department is mainly interested in the budgeted *unit sales,* whereas the financial department is concerned chiefly with planned *dollar sales.*

Planning Styles and Budgetary Procedures

There are two basic planning styles—top-down and bottom-up. In top-down planning, top management sets the objectives and drafts the plans for all organizational units. Top-down planning goes along with the Theory X philosophy of management whose key assumptions are that people dislike work and responsibility and prefer to be told what to do and when.[1] By contrast, in bottom-up planning, different organizational units (generally departments) prepare their own tentative objectives and plans and forward them to top management for consideration. Bottom-up planning goes along with the Theory Y philosophy of management, whose key assumptions are that people like work and responsibility and commit themselves more strongly to objectives and plans that they have participated in formulating.[2]

Sales budgetary procedures differ from company to company with most differences tracing to difference in basic planning styles. If the predominant planning style is top-down, the head of each organizational unit in the sales department (for example, a regional sales manager) receives his or her sales and profit objectives from the next level above and makes plans to fit those objectives. Adjustments in objectives are made if subordinates raise questions regarding their fairness or soundness, but the tendency in a top-down organization is for subordinates to accept the objectives passed down by their superiors.

If the predominant planning style is bottom-up, the heads of even minor organizational units, such as branch sales managers, sometimes even individual sales personnel, assist in determining sales and profit objectives and in making plans to accomplish them. Most budgeting experts recommend planning at least partially in the bottom-up style, arguing that participation in planning at all levels helps to maximize benefits from sales budgeting.

Democratic administration (management based on Theory Y assumptions) requires the widest participation in planning, and participation, from the organizational standpoint, is as much a vertical as a horizontal concept. It is as important to have participation from each organizational level, from the lowest to the highest, as it is to have the overall company budget represent the best thinking from all divisions. The following discussion assumes that the head of even the most minor organizational unit not only participates in setting sales and profit objectives, but has a voice in drafting plans to accomplish these objectives.

Actual Budgetary Procedure

The preparation of the sales budget normally starts at the lowest level in the sales organization and works upward. The lowest level in this budgetary process is a profit center. Thus, each district sales manager estimates district sales volume and expenses for the coming period and the district's contribution to overhead. This budget includes rent, heat, light, secretarial costs, and all other expenses of operating the district office. It includes the salaries of the sales personnel and the

[1]Douglas McGregor, *The Human Side of Enterprise* (New York: McGraw-Hill, 1960), pp. 33–34.
[2]Ibid., pp. 47–48.

district manager, and all selling expenses incurred by the district. These district budgets are submitted to the divisional or regional office, where they are added together and are included with the divisional budget. In turn, divisional budgets are submitted to the sales manager for the particular product or market group. At the end of this chain of subordinate budgets, the top sales executive compiles a companywide sales budget.

While the top sales executive and the subordinates have been preparing budgets, the staff departments in the marketing department have been doing the same, showing credits for work they expect to perform for the sales department during the year. The office of the top marketing executive prepares its own budget, and this is then combined with the budgets of the sales department and the staff marketing departments, to give a total of sales revenues and of selling and other marketing expense for the company.

Each management level within the sales department approves the budgets for which it is responsible, incorporates them into its own budget, and submits this consolidated budget to the next higher level for approval. In each instance, a detailed description of the units' plans for the coming period are submitted as support and justification. Without this information, there is little basis for evaluating the budget submitted. When changes are made in the sales budget, corresponding changes are made in the plans. For example, a cutback in funds requested for sales personnel might necessitate a reduction in the planned number of new "hires."

Other departments use the same preparation period to compile their budgets, with the sales and profit objectives as their points of departure. The production department goes through a similar process of building up an expense budget from each operating subdivision and combining these until a total department budget is prepared. The comptroller's division, research and development, personnel, and all other departments are simultaneously going through the process of budget preparation. These departmental budgets are all submitted to the president, who in turn submits a final total budget to the board of directors. Just as in the preparation of the sales budget, the process of preparing a total company budget may require modifications and changes in plans.

At each step in the budget-making process, an effort is made to reduce the detail to be passed upward to the next step, so that the final company budget is relatively simple and undetailed. The approved budget is then distributed downward in the organization in a process exactly the reverse of that used in its preparation. Each subordinate budget is revised to reflect changes in the company budget. At each step downward, details previously deleted are added back. The lowest operating unit receives a final budget that is as detailed as the one originally submitted, even though it may be considerably changed.

Handling Competition for Available Funds Within the Marketing Division

The top sales executive must argue effectively for an equitable share of funds from the marketing division. The sales executive, like the advertising manager, marketing research manager, customer service manager, product managers, and other staff executives in the marketing department, submits a budget proposal to the chief marketing executive. From these proposals, the chief marketing executive selects those that are of the greatest potential benefit and that the company can afford to implement. In discharging this function, the chief marketing executive checks to assure that the plans presented are the result of careful study, that the proposed expenditures will enable the subordinate to carry out the plans, and that the forecasted sales are attainable.

The amount of money finally allocated to the sales department depends upon the value of the individual budgetary proposals to the company as a whole. The sales executive keeps this in mind in dividing the sales department's budget among subordinate departmental units. If a bottom-up planning procedure is in place, each subordinate has already prepared his or her own sales objectives and an estimate of expenses, thus simplifying the tasks of dividing up sales objectives and budgeted selling expenses.

"Selling" the Sales Budget to Top Management

The chief sales and marketing executives recognize that every budget proposal they make to top management competes with proposals submitted by other divisions. Top management receives more proposals than it is financially able to carry out simultaneously. In appraising proposals, top management looks not only at intrinsic merits but at the probable value to the whole organization. Consequently, it is necessary to sell the sales budget to top management. The budget is presented to top management just as a salesperson makes a presentation to a prospect. It is safe to assume that top executives are at least partially ignorant of the problems faced by the sales department, and of the many problems faced in putting together a sales program.

As in any other selling task, the starting point is a careful assessment of the wants and needs of the prospect. For the top executive, the major want is benefit to the company. How does the company, and incidentally the top executive, stand to gain from the proposed sales budget? To top management, the budget is a proposal to spend money to bring in profit. Top management divides the available funds among the departments, and the share each receives depends on the ability of the department head to sell his or her boss on the benefits to accrue from the plan.

Using the Budget for Control Purposes

Once approved budgets are redistributed to all organizational units, budgetary control features go into operation. Individual items in each budget serve as "quotas" or "standards" against which management measures performance. From here on, each level of management compares performance against standards.

For control purposes, each sales manager receives budget progress reports.

This report may be prepared monthly, but control is more effective if progress reports are weekly. In this way, corrective action is initiated before actual performance moves too far from budgeted performance. The report shows actual sales and expenses for the week, the month to date, and the year to date; budgeted sales and expenses; and the difference between the two. Sales performance figures are broken down further in ways useful to the executives using them, for example, by product, by package size, by sales territory, or by customer.

When performance shows a variance from budgeted performance, two courses of action are available. The first is to determine whether the variance is a result of poor performance by the sales group. It might be that a salesperson's travel expenses are out of line because of inefficient territorial coverage. In this case, steps would be taken to ensure that the salesperson organizes traveling more carefully, so that budgeted expenses are brought back into line. However, if it turns out that travel expenses increased because of calls on new customers not previously covered, the second course of action would be the choice—revise the budget to reflect changed conditions.

The budget is not an end in itself, merely a tool. Every effort is made to bring performance into line with budget estimates, but if unanticipated conditions occur, there is no hesitation about revising the budget. At the same time, the budget is not changed too readily. If it is changed too much, it becomes a mere record of sales and expense.

Effect of Errors in Budgetary Estimates

Operating conditions sometimes differ from those assumed at the time of budget preparation. Sales volume, expense, and net profit objectives prove too high or too low, either because of changes in the demand or because of changes in price levels. Particularly when estimates of the number of units to be sold differ from the number of units actually sold, significant variations occur in some expense items. Overhead and certain other expenses do not vary with volume, but some expenses, such as sales force commissions, vary directly with volume. Still other expenses, such as sales supervisory expenses, are semivariable, fluctuating with changes in volume, but not directly. If estimated unit sales volume is incorrect by much, the usefulness of budgeted selling expense figures as standards of performance is impaired. The budget may still be useful as a point of departure in appraising performance, but there remains the puzzling matter of determining how to allow for changed conditions.

Flexibility in Budgeting

If sales budget estimates are consistently, or even frequently, greatly in error, it may be that more time should be spent in budgetary planning. Perhaps sales forecasting methods are misapplied or are inappropriate for the budgeting situation. Experience shows that in most fields sales can be forecast for a sufficiently long period, and within limits of accuracy that are sufficiently close to serve the purpose of stabilizing production. If it is possible to forecast sales within the limits needed to stabilize production, it is possible to forecast sales within the limits of accuracy required for purposes of budgeting selling expenses.

Some companies, either intentionally or because of difficulties in securing accurate sales forecasts, use budgetary procedures without definite forecasts. One way is to prepare alternative budgets, based on different assumptions about the level of sales volume. Thus, efficiency can be evaluated, even though wide variation exists between expected volume and actual volume. "Low-volume" and "high-volume" forecasts are prepared on break-even style charts and interpolated to adjust for the difference between the two alternative budgeted sales figures and the actual operating level.

However, "flexible budgeting" is the subject of considerable criticism, because whenever it is used, plans must be made on the basis of a wide range of probabilities. Some experts refer to flexible budgeting a a crutch for weak executives who have not absorbed the art of forecasting. Most writers on sales management argue that some flexibility is desirable. Companies cannot authorize a year ahead expense appropriations so inflexible that there is no need later to review or revise them. Full advantage of new market opportunities must be taken as they appear. If competitors initiate actions not foreseen at budget-making time, funds must be allocated to counteract them. A realistic attitude toward the dynamic character of the market is part of effective sales budgeting.

When the budget is in error because of faulty sales forecasting and badly set sales and profit objectives, the accepted procedure is to alter estimates by applying standard ratios of costs to the adjusted volume figure. This system, known as "variable" budgeting, is used by most businesses.

CONCLUSION

The sales budget is a statement of projected sales revenues and selling expenses. The projected sales revenues are, in effect, the sales volume objectives derived from the various sales forecasts. The projected selling expenses are determined by the different organizational units within the sales department and are based on assigned sales and profit objectives. The sales budget is best prepared in an atmosphere where the bottom-up planning style predominates, with each echelon preparing a tentative budget of revenue and expense. During the period in which the budget is in effect, items in the approved budget are compared with actual sales and expenses, and action is taken to bring the two into alignment. In reality, the sales budget is a composite of quotas—for sales, profits, and expenses—and is a valuable tool for control.

21 Quotas

Quotas are quantitative objectives assigned to sales organizational units—individual sales personnel, for instance. As standards for appraising selling effectiveness, quotas specify desired performance levels for sales volume; such budgeted items as expenses, gross margin, net profit, and return on investment; selling- and nonselling-related activities; or some combination of these items. Sales management sets quotas for organizational units, such as individual sales districts and sales personnel. In some companies, sales management sets quotas for middlemen, such as agents, wholesalers, and retailers. Quotas set for sales regions, or other marketing units on higher organizational levels, are customarily broken down and reassigned to lower-level units like sales districts, or to individual sales personnel. All quotas have a time dimension—they quantify what management expects within a given period.

Quotas are devices for directing and controlling sales operations. Their effectiveness depends upon the kind, amount, and accuracy of marketing information used in setting them, and upon management's skill in administering the quota system. In effective systems, management bases quotas on information derived from sales forecasts, studies of market and sales potentials, and cost estimates. Accurate data are important to the effectiveness of a quota system, but, in and of themselves, they are not sufficient; judgment and administrative skill are required of those with quota-setting responsibilities. Soundly administered quotas based on thorough market knowledge are effective devices for directing and controlling sales operations.

OBJECTIVES IN USING QUOTAS

The general objective that sales management has in mind in using quotas is to control the sales effort. Sales control is facilitated through setting quotas to use in appraising performances of sales organizational units, such as a sales region or an individual on the sales force. Sales control is tightened through setting of quotas on expenses and profitability of sales volume. A skilled management uses quotas to motivate personnel to achieve desired performance levels. When management sets quotas, it firms up its performance expectations; when these expectations are communicated to those who are to perform, motivational forces are put into operation that, it is hoped, result in the required effort.

To Provide Quantitative Performance Standards

Quotas provide a means for determining which sales personnel, other units of the sales organization, or distributive outlets are doing an average, below-average, or above-average job. Territorial sales volume quotas, for instance, are yardsticks for measuring territorial sales performance. Comparisons of quotas with sales performance identify weak and strong points, but management must dig deeper to uncover reasons for variations. A well-designed quota system combined with sales analysis helps, for example, in assuring that a bad showing in selling one product in a territory is not hidden by good showings in selling other products. Sales performances vary product by product, territory by territory, and salesperson by salesperson. Quotas identify the strong and weak points; additional analysis of performance data uncovers reasons for performance differentials.

To Obtain Tighter Sales and Expense Control

Control over expenses and profitability is tightened through quotas. Some companies reimburse sales expenses only up to a certain percentage of sales volume, the expense quota being expressed as a percentage of sales. Others set dollar expense quotas and appraise sales personnel, in part, by their success in staying within assigned expense limits. Still others establish quotas for dollar profit or profit percentage on sales. These "budget" quotas shift the emphasis from making sales to increasing profitability. Budget quotas are particularly appropriate when additional sales volume is obtainable only at increased expense; thus profits increase only with improved selling efficiency (lower selling expenses or more profitable sales).

To Motivate Desired Performance

Quotas motivate sales personnel, distributive outlets, and others engaged in the sales operation to achieve assigned performance levels. Some managements use quotas solely for inspirational purposes, basing them almost entirely upon what they think individuals can be inspired to achieve. Because of the high degree of subjectivity in such quotas, they frequently turn out high, thus losing inspirational value. Most sales executives agree that quotas should be attainable goals, achievable with justifiable pride. The salesperson should believe so strongly in the quota's attainability that he or she will not give up with the excuse that it cannot be reached. Sales personnel should feel that they must reach assigned quotas, and they should be confident that management will recognize their achievements. One study revealed that most sales personnel are "quota achievers" rather than "dollar maximizers."[1] Motivation of sales personnel declines with easily attainable quotas. The decline may, in fact, be so great that sales personnel are less likely to achieve easy quotas than difficult quotas.

For maximum effectiveness in motivating desired performance, quotas cannot be based solely on judgment or on sales potentials. Past sales experience and analysis of the sales potential in a territory, for example, may appear to indicate that the sales volume quota of the salesperson assigned there should be increased by 50 percent over the previous year's record. Psychological factors may make the much higher quota inadvisable. Most sales personnel are hopelessly discouraged to learn that management expects their sales to rise by 50 percent in a single year. Consequently, in instances of this sort, management generally settles for raising the quota a small percentage each year until finally it is brought up to the desired level.

To Use in Connection with Sales Contests

Companies frequently use "performance against quota" as the main basis for making awards in sales contests. Sales contests are more powerful incentives if all participants feel they have a more or less an equal chance of winning. By basing awards on percent of quota fulfillment, the desired "common denominator" feature is built into a contest. Adjustments are made for differences among territories (as in coverage difficulty and competitive position) and for differences among sales personnel (as in experience with the company and in the territory). Generally, contest quotas are designed solely for contest use, "special quotas" to stimulate special effort, causing average sales personnel to turn in above-average performances.

QUOTAS, THE SALES FORECAST, AND THE SALES BUDGET

Relationships among quotas, the sales forecast, and the sales budget vary from company to company. Relationships depend not only upon the procedures used in forecasting, budgeting, and quota setting but upon how the planners integrate these three procedures. The greater the integration, the more effective quotas are as devices for controlling sales efforts. Planning a company sales ef-

[1]L. Winer, "The Effect of Product Sales Quotas on Sales Force Productivity," *Journal of Marketing Research,* 10 no. 2 (May 1973), pp. 180—83.

fort begins with a sales forecast and evolves naturally into a sales budget, thus setting the stage for the controlling phase, which involves, among other things, determination of quotas for use as performance standards.

A review of the sales planning process is in order. Basically, a sales forecast is a sales estimate tied to a marketing program and assuming certain environmental factors. When management arrives at the sales estimate, it has, in effect, decided the sales volume objective; then, after determining the expenses of obtaining this sales level, management computes the net profit contribution, brings all these figures together into a sales budget, and sets the objective for net profit. Management now decides how much of the estimated sales volume should come out of each territory, how much expense should be incurred in each, and how much profit contribution each should produce. Here management determines quantitative objectives, such as quotas, to assign to individual sales personnel (or to other organizational units of the sales department, or to distributive outlets). However, as is made clear later, setting quotas is not a matter of simply dividing companywide estimates into smaller parts.

TYPES OF QUOTAS AND QUOTA-SETTING PROCEDURES

Differences in forecasting and budgeting procedures, management philosophy, selling problems, and executive judgment, as well as variations in quota-setting procedures, cause each firm to have somewhat unique quotas. Ignoring small differences, however, quotas fall into four categories: (1) sales volume, (2) budget, (3) activity, and (4) combination. Differences in procedures show up mainly in the setting of sales volume and budget quotas.

Sales Volume Quotas

The sales volume quota is the oldest and most common type. It is an important standard for appraising the performances of individual sales personnel, other units of the sales organization, and distributive outlets. Sales volume quotas communicate managements' expectations as to "how much for what period." Sales volume quotas are set for geographical areas, product lines, or marketing channels or for one or more of these in combination with any unit of the sales organization, the exact design depending upon what facets of the selling operation management wants to appraise or motivate.

The smaller the selling unit, the more effective a quota is for controlling sales operations. Setting a sales volume quota for a sales region, for example, obtains some direction and control, but setting sales volume quotas for each sales territory in the region obtains much more. Setting sales volume quotas for smaller selling units makes it less likely that good or bad sales performance in one aspect of the selling operation will be obscured by offsetting performance in other aspects. The same holds for sales volume quotas on products or time periods—more direction and control are secured by setting quotas for individual products rather than for entire product lines, and for short periods rather than long.

Sales volume quotas see extensive use. Sales executives set them and the sales volume objective dominates other objectives. Before profits are earned, some sales volume level must be attained. It is entirely logical for sales management first to set standards for sales volume performance. Sales personnel readily grasp the significance of sales volume quotas. However, sales management should not deemphasize earning of profits or conserving on selling expense. Sales volume alone, although important, is not sufficient—profits are necessary for survival.

Dollar sales volume quotas. Companies selling broad product lines set sales volume quotas in dollars rather than in units of product. These companies meet complications in setting unit quotas and in evaluating sales performance for individual products. A key advantage of the dollar terminology is that the dollar sales volume quotas relate easily to other performance data, such as selling expenses, through ratios or percentages. In addition, when products have no established prices, and sales personnel have discretion in cutting prices, either dollar volume quotas or combined dollar and unit volume quotas assure that sales personnel do not cut prices too deeply to build unit volume.

Unit sales volume quotas. Sales volume quotas in units of product are used in two situations. One is that in which prices fluctuate considerably; in this situation, unit sales volume quotas are better yardsticks than are dollar sales volume quotas. If a product is now priced at $80 a unit, 600 units sold means $48,000 in sales, but if the price rises by 25 percent (to $100 a unit), only 480 units sold brings in the same dollar volume.

The second situation occurs with narrow product lines sold at stable prices. In this situation, dollar volume and unit volume quotas might both appear appropriate, but, especially if unit prices are high, unit quotas are preferable for psychological reasons—sales personnel regard a $1 million quota as a higher hurdle than a forty-unit quota for machines priced at $25,000 each.

Point sales volume quotas. Some companies use sales volume quotas expressed in "points." A company using point volume quotas might consider each $100 sales as worth 1 point, it might value unit sales of product A at 5 points and of product B at 1 point, or it might convert both dollar and unit sales into points. Companies use point volume quotas because of problems in using dollar or unit volume quotas. Porter-Cable Machine Company, for instance, once used dollar volume quotas, but sales personnel often attained most of their quotas through selling only one or two easy-to-sell products. Management initiated a program whereby products were put into eight different categories, according to relative profitability. Then individual point volume quotas were set for each category, and bonus points were awarded for sales over quota in each category. Sales personnel had to meet all the point volume quotas before becoming eligible for bonus points. In appraising performance, management regarded a 150 percent total point volume attainment with 4 bonus points as less meritorious than a 120 percent point volume attainment with 5 bonus points. The new quota system led to a more profitable sales mixture.

Procedures for Setting Sales Volume Quotas

Sales volume quotas derived from territorial sales potentials. It seems logical that a sales volume quota should derive from the sales potential present, for example, in a territory. A sales volume quota sums up the effort that a particular selling unit should expend. Sales potential, by definition, represents the maximum sales opportunities open to the same selling unit. Many managements derive sales volume quotas from sales potentials, and this approach is appropriate when (1) territorial sales potentials are determined in conjunction with territorial design or (2) bottom-up planning and forecasting procedures are used in obtaining the sales estimate in the sales forecast.

If sales territories are designed and sales personnel assigned according to procedures recommended in Chapter 22, management is justified in setting sales volume quotas by calculating the percentage relationship between each territorial sales potential and total sales potential and using the resulting percentages to apportion the company sales estimate among territories. If, for instance, territory A's sales potential is 2 percent of the total, and the company sales estimate is $20 million, then the sales volume quota for territory A is $400,000. Assuming that no further adjustments are needed, the summation of all territorial sales volume quotas equals the company sales estimate. However, total sales potential is generally not equal to the total sales estimate, even though the two figures are related. Sales potentials, for companies as well as for territories, are the sales volumes reachable under ideal conditions, whereas sales estimates and sales volume quotas are the sales levels management expects to attain under somewhat less than ideal conditions.

If bottom-up planning and forecasting procedures have been used, management already has considered such factors as past sales, competition, changing market conditions, and differences in personal ability, as well as contemplated changes in prices, products, promotion, and the like—if it has, then the final revised estimates of territorial sales potentials become the territorial sales volume quotas. However, in spite of what has just been said, further adjustments are generally advisable because sales volume quotas related directly to territorial sales potentials depend upon statistical data underlying estimates of sales potential; in other words, the tempering of experienced judgment is needed for realistic sales volume quotas to result. Rarely does a company achieve an ideal territorial design, and to the extent that territorial differences (in coverage difficulty, for instance) have not been taken into account previously, compensating adjustments are made when setting sales volume quotas.

Few companies achieve an ideal assignment of sales personnel to territories, so, in setting quotas, differences in anticipated personnel effectiveness because of age, energy, initiative, experience, knowledge of the territory, and physical condition require adjustments. Moreover, sales volume quotas motivate individual sales personnel in different ways—one is thrilled to learn that next year's quota is 50 percent above this year's, a second is hopelessly discouraged by similar news—and quota setters adjust for such differences. Then, too, some companies provide financial motivation by linking compensation to performance against quota; this generally means that volume quotas are set lower than sales potentials.

Sales volume quotas derived from total market estimates. In some companies, management has neither statistics on nor sales force estimates of territorial sales potentials. These companies use top-down planning and forecasting to obtain the sales estimate for the whole company; hence, if management sets volume quotas, it uses similar procedures. Management may either (1) break down the total company sales estimate, using various indexes of relative sales opportunities in each territory, and then make adjustments (such as those described in the previous section) to arrive at territorial sales volume quotas; or (2) convert the company sales estimate into a companywide sales quota (by taking into account projected changes in price, product, promotion, and other policies) and then break down the company volume quota, by using an index of relative sales opportunities in each territory. In the second procedure, another set of adjustments is made for differences in territories and sales personnel before finally arriving at territorial quotas.

Note that these choices are similar, the only difference being whether adjustments are made only at the territorial level, or also at the company level. The second alternative is the better choice. Certain adjustments apply to the total company and to all sales territories; others apply uniquely to individual territories. The two-level approach assumes that both classes of adjustments receive attention.

In companies with more than two organizational levels in the sales department, additional rounds of adjustments are necessary. For instance, consider the company with both sales regions and sales territories. One round of adjustments takes place at the company level, and another at the regional level. Most regional sales managers would want a third round of adjustments before setting territorial sales volume quotas, as territorial sales volume quotas should not be set finally until after consulting sales personnel assigned to territories. The regional sales manager ordinarily calls in each salesperson to discuss the territorial outlook relative to the share of the regional sales volume quota that each territory should produce; then the regional manager sets territorial sales volume quotas. Quotas developed in this way are more acceptable to the sales staff, because each has participated in setting them, and each has had the opportunity to contribute information bearing on the final quota.

Sales volume quotas based on past sales experience alone. A crude procedure is to base sales volume quotas solely on past sales experience. One company, for instance, takes last year's sales for each territory, adds an arbitrary percentage, and uses the results as sales volume quotas. A second averages past sales for each territory over several years, adds arbitrary amounts, and thus sets quotas for sales volume. The second company's procedure is the better of the two—by averaging sales figures, management recognizes that the sales trend is important. The averaging procedure evens out the distorting effects of abnormally good and bad years.

Companies using past sales procedures for determining sales volume quotas assume not only that past and future sales are related, but that past sales have been satisfactory. These assumptions may or may not be valid, but one thing is certain: companies making them perpetuate past errors. If a territory has had inadequate sales coverage, basing its sales volume quota on past sales ensures future inadequate sales coverage. Furthermore, the average-of-past-sales method has a unique defect in that average sales lag behind actual sales during long periods of rising or falling sales. Thus, during these periods quotas always are set either too low or too high. Quotas based solely on past sales, moreover, make poor performance standards, as previously poor performances go undetected and are built into the standards automatically. Two individuals, for example, may receive identical sales volume quotas, even though one realized 90 percent of previous territorial sales potential and the second only 30 percent. Neither knowing nor considering the true sales opportunities in each territory, management perpetuates past inequities. Past sales experience should be considered in setting territorial sales volume quotas, but it is only one of many factors to take into account.

Sales-volume quotas based on executive judgment alone. Sometimes, sales volume quotas are based solely on executive judgment. This is justified when there is little information to use in setting quotas. There may be no sales forecast, no practical way to determine territorial sales potential. The product may be new and its probable rate of market acceptance unknown; the territory may not yet have been opened, or a newly recruited salesperson may have been assigned to a new territory. In these situations, management may set sales volume quotas solely on a judgment basis. Certainly, however, quotas can be of no higher quality than the judgment of those setting them. Judgement, like past sales experience, is important in determining quotas, but it is not the only ingredient.

Sales volume quotas related only to compensation plan. Companies sometimes base sales volume quotas solely upon the projected amounts of compensation that management believes sales personnel should receive. No consideration is given to territorial sales potentials, total market estimates, and past sales experience, and quotas are tailored exclusively to fit the sales compensation plan. If, for instance, salesperson A is to receive a $1,000 monthly salary and a 5 percent commission on all monthly sales over $20,000, A's monthly sales volume quota is set at $20,000. As long as A's monthly sales exceed $20,000, management holds A's compensation-to-sales ratio to 5 percent. Note that A is really paid on a straight-commission plan, even though it is labeled "salary and commission."

Such sales volume quotas are poor standards for appraising sales performance; they relate only indirectly, if at all, to territorial sales potentials. It is appropriate to tie in sales force quota performances with the sales compensation plan, that is, as a financial incentive to performance, but no sales volume quota should be based on the compensation plan alone, for that is "putting the cart before the horse."

Letting sales personnel set their own sales volume quotas. Some companies turn the setting of sales volume quotas over to the sales staff, who are placed in the position of determining their own performance standards. The ostensible reason is that sales personnel, being closest to the territories, know them best and therefore should set the most realistic sales volume quotas. The real reason, however, is that management is shirking the quota-setting responsibility and turns the whole problem over to the sales staff, thinking that they will complain less if they set their standards. There is, indeed, a certain ring of truth in the argument that having sales personnel set their own objectives may cause them to complain less, and to work harder to attain them. But sales personnel are seldom dispassionate in setting their own quotas. Some are reluctant to obligate themselves to achieve what they regard as "too much"; others—and this is just as common—overestimate their capabilities and set unrealistically high quotas. Quotas set unrealistically high or low—by management or by the sales force—cause dissatisfaction and low sales force morale. Management should have better information; therefore, it should make final quota decisions. How, for instance, can sales personnel adjust for changes management makes in price, product, promotion, and other policies?

Budget Quotas

Budget quotas are set for various units in the sales organization to control expenses, gross margin, or net profit. The intention in setting budget quotas is to make it clear to sales personnel that their jobs consist of something more than obtaining sales volume. Budget quotas make personnel more conscious that the company is in business to make a profit. Expense quotas emphasize keeping expenses in alignment with sales volume, thus indirectly controlling gross margin and net profit contributions. Gross margin or net profit quotas emphasize margin and profit contributions, thus indirectly controlling sales expenses.

Expense quotas. The setting of dollar expense quota plans for reimbursing sales force expenses were analyzed earlier,[2] so discussion here focuses on using expense quotas in appraising performance. Hardly ever are expense quotas used in lieu of other quotas; they are supplemental standards aimed toward keeping expenses in line with sales volume. Thus, expense quotas are used most often in combination with sales volume quotas.

[2]See Chapter 17.

Frequently, management provides sales personnel with financial incentives to control their own expenses. This is done either by tying performance against expense quotas directly to the compensation plan or by offering "expense bonuses" for lower expenses than the quotas. Expense quotas derive from expense estimates in territorial sales budgets. But to reduce the administrative burden and misunderstandings, expense quotas are generally expressed not in dollars but as percentages of sales, thus directing attention both to sales volume and the costs of achieving it.

Setting expense quotas as sales volume percentages presents some problems. Variations in coverage difficulty and other environmental factors, as well as in sales potentials, make it impractical to set identical expense percentages for all territories. Then, too, different sales personnel sell different product mixes, so some incur higher expenses than others, again making impractical the setting of identical expense percentages. But most important is that selling expense does not vary directly with sales volume, as is implicitly assumed with the expense percentage quota. Requiring that expenses vary proportionately with changes in sales volume may reduce selling incentive. It may happen, for instance, that selling expenses amount to 3 percent of sales up to $700,000 in sales, but obtaining an additional $50,000 in sales requires increased expenses of $2,500, which amounts to 5 percent of the marginal sales increase.

Clearly, management should not arbitrarily set percentage expense quotas. Analysis of territorial differences, product mixes in individual sales, and expense variations at various sales volume levels should precede actual quota setting. Furthermore, because of difficulties in making precise adjustments for these factors, and because of possible changes in territorial conditions during the operating period, administering an expense quota system calls for great flexibility.

The chief attraction of the expense quota is that it makes sales personnel more cost conscious and aware of their responsibilities for expense control. They are less apt to regard expense accounts as "swindle sheets" or vehicles for padding take-home pay. Instead, they look upon the expense quota as one standard used in evaluating their performance.

However, unless expense quotas are intelligently administered, sales personnel may become too cost conscious—they may stay at third-class hotels, patronize third-class restaurants, and avoid entertaining customers. Sales personnel should understand that, although expense money is not to be wasted, they are expected to make all reasonable expenditures. Well-managed companies, in fact, expect sales personnel to maintain standards of living in keeping with those of their customers.

Gross margin or net profit quotas. Companies not setting sales volume quotas often use gross margin or net profit quotas, shifting the emphasis to making gross margin or profit contributions. The rationale is that sales personnel operate more efficiently if they recognize that sales increases, expense reductions, or both, are important only if increased margins and profits result.

Gross margin or net profit quotas are appropriate when the product line contains both high- and low-margin items. In this situation, an equal volume increase in each of two products may have widely different effects upon margins and profits. Low-margin items are the easiest to sell; thus sales personnel taking the path of least resistance concentrate on them and give inadequate attention to more profitable products. One way to obtain better balanced sales mixtures is through gross margin or net profit quotas. However, the same results are achieved by setting individual sales volume quotas for different products, adjusting each quota to obtain the desired contributions.

Problems are met both in setting and administering gross margin or net profit quotas. If gross margin quotas are used, management must face the fact that sales personnel generally do not set prices and have no control over manufacturing costs; therefore, they are not responsible for gross margins. If net profit quotas are used, management must recognize that certain selling expenses, such as those of operating a branch office, are beyond the salesperson's influence.

To overcome these complications, companies frequently set quotas in terms of "expected contribution" margins, thus avoiding arbitrary allocations of expenses not under the control of sales personnel. Arriving at expected contribution margins for each salesperson, however, is complicated. Even if a company solves these accounting-type problems, it faces further problems in administration. Sales personnel may have difficulties in grasping technical features of quota-setting procedures, and management may spend considerable time in ironing out misunderstandings. In addition, special records must be maintained to gather the needed performance information. Finally, because some expense factors are always beyond the control of sales personnel, arguments and disputes are inevitable. The company using gross margin or net profit quotas assumes increased clerical and administrative costs.

Activity Quotas

The desire to control how sales personnel allocate their time and efforts among different activities explains the use of activity quotas. A company using activity quotas starts by defining the important activities sales personnel perform; then it sets target performance frequencies. Activity quotas are set for total sales calls, calls on particular classes of customers, calls on prospects, number of new accounts, missionary calls, product demonstrations, placement or erection of displays, making of collections and the like. Before setting activity quotas, management needs time-and-duty studies of how sales personnel actually apportion their time, making additional studies to determine how sales personnel *should* allocate their efforts. Ideally, management needs time-and-duty studies for *every* salesperson and sales territory, but, of course, this is seldom practical.

Activity quotas are appropriate when sales personnel perform important nonselling activities. For example, activity quotas are much used in insurance selling, where sales personnel must continually develop new contacts. They are also common in drug detail selling, where sales personnel call on doctors and hospitals to explain new products and new applications of both old and new products. Activity quotas permit management not only to control but to give recognition to sales personnel for performing nonselling activities and for maintaining contacts with customers who may buy infrequently, but in substantial amounts.

While there is a large amount of clerical and record-keeping work, the main problem in administering an activity quota system is that of inspiring the sales force. The danger is that sales personnel will merely go through the motions and not perform activities effectively. Activity quotas used alone reward sales personnel for quantity of work, irrespective of quality. This is less likely to happen when activity quotas are used with sales volume or expense quotas; still adequate supervision and close contact with sales personnel are administrative necessities.

Combination and Other Point System Quotas

Combination quotas control performance of both selling and nonselling activities. These quotas overcome the difficulty of using different measurement units to appraise different aspects of performance (for example, dollars to measure attention given to developing new business). Because performances against combination quotas are computed as percentages, these quotas are known as point systems, the points being percentage points.

Figure 21.1 illustrates how performances, or point scores, are determined under a system incorporating both sales volume and activity goals. In this system, each of four different aspects of the sales job is weighted according to management's evaluation of its relative importance. Column 1 shows the four quotas making up the combination, and column 2 records actual performance data. Column 3, indicating the percentage of quota attained, is multiplied by the weighting factor in column 4 to yield the weighted performance in column 5. Finally, the column 5 total is divided by the column 4 total to determine each salesperson's overall performance rating. Thus, Snyder's rating is 87.145 percentage points (that is, 87.145 percent of the combination quota) and Thompson's is 85.143. Combination quotas may also be designed without attaching different weights to the various components (which, of course, is the same as equally weighting all components), but in most cases, different weights are justified because all components are rarely of equal importance. In the example, had different weights not been used, management would have appraised Thompson's performance as better than Snyder's: 91 versus 88 percentage points. The reversal emphasizes the importance of selecting weights with care.

Combination quotas summarize overall performance in a single measure, but they present some problems. Sales personnel may have difficulties in understanding them and in appraising their own achievements. Combination quotas also have a built-in weakness in that design imperfections may cause sales personnel to place too much emphasis on one component activity. Suppose that

FIGURE 21.1 Determination of Point Scores Under a Weighted Combination Quota System

Salesperson: *T. Synder*

	(1) Quota	(2) Actual	(3) Percent Quota	(4) Weight	(5) Quota × Weight
Sales volume	$75,000	$67,500	90	3	270
New accounts obtained	20	15	75	2	150
Calls on prospects	50	50	100	1	100
Displays erected	150	135	90	1	90
				7	610

$\frac{610}{7}$ = 87.145 (Snyder's point score)

Salesperson: *J. Thompson*

	(1) Quota	(2) Actual	(3) Percent Quota	(4) Weight	(5) Quota × Weight
Sales volume	$90,000	$63,000	70	3	210
New accounts obtained	30	27	90	2	180
Calls on prospects	90	100	111	1	111
Displays erected	200	190	95	1	95
				7	596

$\frac{596}{7}$ = 85.143 (Thompson's point score)

Snyder or Thompson, in the previous illustration, decides to erect twice as many displays as the quota specifies and to do almost no prospecting. The possibility that some sales personnel may try to "beat the system" in this or other ways indicates that, as with other complex quota systems, continual supervision of the sales force is essential.

Another widely used point system is the full-line quota, which is designed to secure some desired balance of sales among various products. Figure 21.2 illustrates a point system quota. Two members of the sales staff, Ed O'Reilly and Debbie Johnson, sell three products, A, B, and C. Products A and B are low-margin items and easy to sell; product C is a high-margin item that takes extra effort to sell. Sales management has set a quota for each product and established weights reflecting relative sales difficulty and profitability. By some coincidence, perhaps unrealistic but revealing, O'Reilly and Johnson were assigned identical quotas and, by an even greater coincidence, their performances resulted in equal sales volumes. However, Johnson receives the higher point score and therefore is the better performer. Why? She places more emphasis on selling product C and obtains a better balance in selling the three products.

FIGURE 21.2 Appraising Performance with a Full-Line Point-Quota System

Salesperson: *Ed O'Reilly*

Product	Sales Volume Quota	Actual Sales	Percent Attained	Weight	Percent Attained × Weight
A	$20,000	$20,000	100	1	100
B	20,000	20,000	100	1	100
C	10,000	4,000	40	2	80
Total	$50,000	$44,000		4	280

$\frac{280}{4}$ = 70.0 (O'Reilly's point score)

Salesperson: *Debbie Johnson*

Product	Sales Volume Quota	Actual Sales	Percent Attained	Weight	Percent Attained × Weight
A	$20,000	$16,000	80	1	80
B	20,000	18,000	90	1	90
C	10,000	10,000	100	2	200
Total	$50,000	$44,000		4	370

$\frac{370}{4}$ = 92.5 (Johnson's point score)

ADMINISTERING THE QUOTA SYSTEM

Skill in administering the quota system is basic not only to realizing the full benefit for control purposes, but to securing staff cooperation in making the system work. Most critical is securing and maintaining acceptance of the quotas by those to whom they are assigned. Few people take kindly to having yardsticks applied to their performance. Constitutionally, most sales personnel oppose quotas, and anything that makes them doubt the accuracy, fairness, or attainability of those quotas makes them less willing to accept them, thus reducing the system's effectiveness.

Accurate, Fair, and Attainable Quotas

Good quotas are accurate, fair and attainable. Obtaining accurate quotas is a function of the quota-setting procedure: the more closely quotas are related to territorial potentials, the greater the chances for accuracy. But, in addition, regardless of the type of quota—sales volume, budget, activity, or combination—

sound judgment is important in analyzing market data, adjusting for contemplated policy changes (and for conditions unique to each territory), and appraising changes in personnel capabilities, as well as in setting the final quotas. Accurate quotas result from skillful blending of planning and operating information with sound judgment. Setting a fair quota involves determining the proper blend of sales potential and previous experience.

Admittedly, whether quotas are fair and attainable depends not only upon the quality of management's judgment but upon the capabilities and motivations of sales force. Sometimes, perhaps even usually, the extent to which a salesperson's quota is fair and attainable can only be ascertained after performance has been recorded. Even then, management must exercise care in appraising variations from the quota—to what extent are they attributable to quota inaccuracies and to what extent to salesperson inadequacies? After all, quotas are not *absolute* performance standards, and errors are made in setting them.

If management believes that its quota-setting procedure produces accurate quotas and is confident that fair quotas are being assigned, then they should be attainable. Most quota-setting errors are those of judgment, most traceable to setting quotas above each salesperson's expected performance to provide an incentive for improvement. Quotas that some sales personnel fail to attain are not necessarily unfair—whether they are or not depends on who fails to attain them. One executive offers this general rule. "You have set equitable quotas if your weaker people fail to attain them, and if your better people either reach or slightly exceed them." Thus, in ascertaining fairness, management faces a possible dilemma because the quotas themselves are the performance standards most used for appraising the quality of sales personnel. Clearly, subjective evaluations of sales personnel according to qualitative performance criteria are required to ascertain whether quotas are fair.

Securing and Maintaining Sales Personnel's Acceptance of Quotas

Management must make certain that sales personnel understand quotas and the quota-setting procedure. Conveying this understanding is a critical step in securing staff acceptance of quotas. If sales personnel do not understand the procedure used in establishing quotas, they may suspect, for example, that the quotas are a technique to obtain extra effort from them at no cost to the company. This attitude destroys the quota's effectiveness as an incentive. It is important that sales personnel understand the significance of quotas as communicators of "how much for what period," but, if they also understand the quota-setting procedure, they are more likely to consider their quotas accurate, fair, and attainable. The quota-setting method should be simple enough for sales personnel to understand, yet sufficiently sophisticated to permit acceptable accuracy. Sometimes, this means that management, faced with choosing between two quota-setting procedures, may choose the less sophisticated because it can be more easily explained to, and understood by, the sales staff. More sophisticated procedures should not be ruled out, but managements using them must explain them to the sales force.

Participation by sales personnel in quota setting. If sales personnel participate in quota setting, the task of explaining quotas and how they are determined is simplified. With sales personnel helping to set their own quotas, management has more assurance that the procedure will be understood. How much staff participation is solicited depends upon management philosophy, types of quotas, information available, sophistication of the quota-setting procedure, and the caliber of the sales force. It is not advisable to turn the whole quota-setting job over to the sales staff, but some sales force participation can obtain more accurate and realistic quotas. Sales personnel have some information about their territories that management does not have, and it can contribute to quota accuracy. Furthermore, when sales personnel participate in quota setting, they are more easily convinced of the fairness of quotas.

Keeping sales personnel informed. Effective sales management keeps sales personnel informed of their progress relative to quotas. Sales personnel receive frequent reports detailing their performance to date. This permits them to analyze their own strong and weak points and take corrective action. Of course, sales personnel need encouragement, advice, and occasionally, warnings, in deciding to take measures to improve their performance. Reaping full benefits from keeping sales personnel informed requires frequent personal contacts by supervisors, as well as regular reports.

Need for continuous managerial control. In administering any quota system, there is a need for continuous monitoring of performance. Arrangements must be made to gather and analyze performance statistics with minimum delay. Charts recording each salesperson's performance against quota on a monthly, or even weekly, basis facilitates this analysis. Figure 21.3 is a typical chart for comparing sales quotas with actual performances. Not all sales executives agree that charts should be posted for all to see, but most provide each person with information on his or her performance. Keeping sales personnel informed at frequent intervals, at least monthly, requires subdividing the year. Generally, the annual quota is divided by the number of reporting periods, but, of course, this can be misleading, when random fluctuations in sales occur. For products with seasonal sales patterns it is more logical to apportion annual quotas relative to either the proportion of sales made in each reporting period during the previous year, or the proportions made in "normal" years.

Functioning quota systems can almost always be improved. An alert management continually appraises operation of the system and makes needed changes. Continuous managerial review and appraisal are required, since, for example, a quota that was accurate, fair, and attainable at the beginning of an operating period can prove totally unrealistic in view of changing selling conditions. Flexibility in administering the system is important—if a quota is proving unrealistic, it should be adjusted. Administrative flexibility is desirable, but not

FIGURE 21.3 Sales Quota and Actual Performance for Month, Year

Salesperson	*Current Month*				*Year to Date*			
	Quota	*Sales*	*Percent*	*Rank*	*Quota*	*Sales*	*Percent*	*Rank*
A								
B								
C								
D								
E								
F								
G								
H								
I								
J								
K								
L								
M								
N								
O								
P								
Q								
R								
S								
T								
U								
V								
W								
X								
Y								
Z								
Total								

too much. Small changes can be ignored; important changes call for adjustments. One company, for instance, adjusts dollar quotas in the event of a *significant* price change, or any change of 5 percent or more in their industry forecasts. Balance is needed between flexibility to every slight change and inflexibility regardless of changes.

REASONS FOR NOT USING SALES QUOTAS

Some companies do not use quotas. In certain industrial-goods categories, for instance, it is difficult to obtain accurate sales estimates; thus, quotas, if used, are based on subjective judgments. Numerous executives prefer not to use quotas if it means basing them on "guesstimates." In other situations, it is possible to obtain accurate sales estimates, but executives, perhaps wrongly, contend that obtaining and analyzing other data necessary for quota determination means inordinate expenditures of time and money. No quota should cost more than it is worth, but it is difficult to visualize a situation in which accurate quotas coupled with good administration would not increase selling efficiency.

In some companies, the fact that quota determination requires using statistical techniques is the reason given for nonuse of quotas. The fear is that sales personnel will not accept quotas prepared by hard-to-explain techniques. In other instances, there are difficulties in arriving at fair weights for territorial potential, competitive position, coverage difficulty, and salesperson ability. Thus, when quotas are tried, they may be set too high, which could cause high-pressure selling, or too low, which could provide insufficient incentive.

Some executives oppose quotas on the grounds that they place too much emphasis upon making sales. This may be a legitimate criticism of sales volume quotas, but not of all quotas. Other executives object to the word "quota," which they say has negative connotations, and prefer to assign "objectives." These executives, in other words, use quotas but under another name.

One situation exists where quotas, in the normal sense, are not appropriate. It occurs when a product is in short supply. In such cases, most managements believe that it is wise to divide the available supply equitably among customers. In sellers' markets, the allocation substitutes for the quota, which characteristically is appropriate for use only in buyers' markets.

CONCLUSION

Quotas are quantitative objectives assigned to sales personnel and other units of the selling organization. They are intended both to stimulate performance and to evaluate it, through communicating management's expectations and through serving as performance measures. In successful quota systems, special pains are taken to tie in quota-setting procedures with sales potentials and planning data from the sales forecast and sales budget. Sound judgment is required for adjusting tentative quotas both for contemplated policy changes and for factors unique to each territorial environment. Continuous managerial review and appraisal and balanced flexibility in making changes in quotas and improvements in quota-setting procedures characterize successful quota system. When based on relevant and accurate market information, and when intelligently administered, quotas are effective devices for directing and controlling sales operations.

22 Sales Territories

Establishment of sales territories facilitates matching selling efforts with sales opportunities. Sales personnel are assigned the responsibility for serving particular groupings of customers and prospects and provide contact points with the markets. Territorial assignments lend direction to the planning and control of sales operations.

In establishing sales territories, management is taking an important step toward accumulating knowledge on the company's strengths and weaknesses in serving different markets. Through utilization of this knowledge in planning sales operations, managerial efforts to improve competitive position become increasingly effective.

Realistic sales planning is done on a territory-by-territory basis. Characteristics of customers and prospects vary from one sales territory to another, and sometimes even from one county to the next. The territory is a more homogeneous unit than the market as a whole.

Breaking down the total market into smaller units makes control of sales operations more effective. Assigning responsibility for achieving specific objectives to subordinate line executives and individual sales personnel brings selling efforts into alignment with sales opportunities. Direction is lent to gathering information on individual performances, and comparisons of performances with sales opportunities present in each territory provide sound bases for appraisal.

THE SALES TERRITORY CONCEPT

The emphasis in the sales territory concept is upon customers and prospects rather than upon the area in which an individual salesperson works. Operationally defined, *a sales territory is a grouping of customers and prospects assigned to an individual salesperson.* Many sales executives refer to sales territories as geographic areas, for example, the Southern California territory or the Michigan territory. But, in contrast, in some companies, particularly those in which the technical selling style is predominant, geographical considerations are ignored and sales personnel are assigned entire classes of customers, regardless of their locations. Whether designated geographically or not, a sales territory is a grouping of customers and prospects that can be called upon conveniently and economically by an individual salesperson.

To emphasize the point that designations of territories should not be solely along geographical lines, consider the following situations. When sales personnel sell mainly to personal acquaintances, as in selling property insurance, investment securities, and automobiles. little logical basis exists for dividing the market geographically. Similarly, in selling real estate, where the market is localized and where the customer usually seeks out the firm rather than the salesperson, geographically defined territories are meaningless. In these cases, sales personnel are, for the most part, inside order takers; customers seek out the supplier. But even, as in life insurance selling, where sales personnel are outside order getters and seek out prospects, the personal and localized nature of the market makes geographical assignments of territories inappropriate.

Other situations exist in which sales territories are not designated geographically. Certain companies have highly specialized sales personnel, each with responsibility for serving customers who need his or her special skills. For instance, one maker of complicated machinery has only five salespersons, each specializing either in part of the product line or in particular product applications. In other companies, it is common to have more than one salesperson assigned to work in the same city or metropolitan area, and it is difficult to divide the area among them, not only because of the scattered locations of accounts but because "leads" furnished by established customers often require calls in different parts of the city.

Small companies, and companies introducing new products requiring the use of different marketing channels, often do not use geographically defined territories at all or, if they do, use rough divisions, such as entire states or census regions. In these instances, there is no reason to assign territories, since existing sales coverage capabilities are inadequate relative to sales potentials.

In most marketing situations, however, it is advantageous to "assign" sales personnel to territories. Determining the territorial assignments requires consideration of customers' service requirements and the costs of providing service. Geography affects both a company's ability to meet customers' service requirements and the costs of meeting them. Even when territorial boundaries are geographical, each salesperson's assignment is a grouping of customers and prospects, and only for reasons of convenience and economy a geographical cluster—the emphasis is on the customers, not on their locations.

House Accounts

A house account is an account not assigned to an individual salesperson but one handled by executives or home office personnel. Many are extremely large customers, most of whom prefer—indeed, sometimes demand—to deal with the home office. Frequently, house accounts are responsible for significant shares of a company's total business. When house accounts are excluded from territorial assignments, adverse effects upon sales force morale are possible—if sales personnel feel that the company is depriving them of the best customers.

Most companies prefer to minimize the number of house accounts. However, some large customers refuse to do business any other way. Companies in which sales personnel understand that their territories are particular groupings of customers and prospects—rather than specific geographical areas—find that house accounts have little adverse effect on sales force morale.

REASONS FOR ESTABLISHING OR REVISING SALES TERRITORIES

Sales territories are set up, and subsequently revised as market conditions dictate, to facilitate the planning and control of sales operations. More specifically, there are five reasons for having sales territories: (1) to provide proper market coverage, (2) to control selling expenses, (3) to assist in evaluating sales personnel, (4) to contribute to sales force morale, and (5) to aid in the coordination of personal-selling and advertising efforts.

Providing Proper Market Coverage

Sometimes a company loses business to competitors because it does not have proper market coverage. Sales management has not matched selling efforts with sales opportunities effectively, competitors have a better match, and they obtain the orders. To overcome problems of this type, generally management must establish sales territories, if the company does not have them, or revise those that it has. If sales territories are set up intelligently *and* if assignments of sales personnel to them are carefully made, it is possible to obtain proper market coverage. Note that mere establishment or revision of the sales territories is not enough. The design of the territories should permit sales personnel to cover them conveniently and economically. Territories, in other words, should represent reasonable work loads for the sales staff while assuring that all prospects who are potentially profitable can be contacted.

Good territorial design allows sales personnel to spend sufficient time with customers and prospects and minimizes time on the road. This permits them to become thoroughly conversant with customers' problems and requirements. Successful selling is based upon helping customers solve their problems, not just upon making sales or, even worse, upon taking orders. Well-designed sales territories, combined with appropriate sales force assignments, result in calls upon different classes of customers and prospects at needed frequencies. Call regularity is important in selling products purchased on a repeat basis, and persistence turns many a prospect into a regular account.

Controlling Selling Expenses

Good territorial design combined with careful salesperson assignment results in low selling expenses and high sales volumes. Sales personnel spend fewer nights away from home, which reduces or eliminates many charges for lodging and food; at the same time, cutting travel miles reduces transportation expenses. These savings, plus the higher sales volumes from increased productive selling time, reduce the ratio of selling expenses to sales. In fact, even if dollar selling expenses remain unchanged, the sales increase produced through proper market coverage reduces the selling expense percentage.

Reduced selling expense ratios do not, however, follow automatically. If territorial planning is unsound or is not combined with appropriate assignments of sales personnel, selling expense ratios increase. If the planner, for instance, ignores normal travel routes and geographical barriers, sales personnel spend time travelling when they could be calling on customers; this results in higher selling expenses and lower sales volumes.

Nor should management overlook the possibility that dollar selling expenses may have to go up to obtain a lower selling expense ratio. To secure larger sales volumes, sales personnel may have to incur additional expenses. Securing larger orders may require more frequent sales calls, which increases selling expenses. Well-designed sales territories and appropriate assignments of sales personnel increase the total time available for contact with customers and prospects, thus preparing the ground for improved sales volumes.

Sales management's problem in controlling selling expenses is not to minimize them but to obtain the best relation between dollar selling expenses and dollar sales volumes. Short-term reductions in the selling expense ratio are not always desirable; the long-term result is important. Rises in selling expenses may not be followed immediately by increased sales volumes and higher sales volumes in the future. The intelligent setting up or revising of sales territories is one step management takes to see that selling expense dollars are spent to the best advantage.

Assisting in Evaluating Sales Personnel

Well-designed sales territories assist management in evaluating sales personnel. Selling problems vary geographically, and the impact of competition differs widely. When the total market is divided into territories, analysis reveals the company's strengths and weaknesses in different areas, and appropriate adjustments can then be made in selling strategies. Through analyzing the market territory by territory and pinpointing sales and cost responsibility to individual sales personnel, management has the information it needs to set quotas and to evaluate each salesperson's performance against them.

Contributing to Sales Force Morale

Good territorial designs help in maintaining sales force morale. Well-designed territories are convenient for sales personnel to cover; they represent reasonable-sized work loads, and sales personnel find that their efforts produce results. All are responsible for achieving given levels of performance within their own territories, so all know what management expects of them. Results that come from each sales territory are correlated with the efforts of individual sales personnel. Good territorial design plus intelligent salesperson assignment help to make each person as productive as possible and make for high earnings, self-confidence, and job satisfaction. Morale is high also because there are few conflicting claims of sales personnel to the same accounts—when sales territories are not used, there are numerous conflicts. Even with well-designed sales territories, some conflicts arise, because some customers transact business in more than one territory, but well-designed territories reduce the magnitude of the problem. Finally, sales force morale is high because excellence in planning territories and making territorial assignments causes sales personnel to spend minimum time on the road.

Aiding in Coordination of Personal Selling and Advertising

Management may set up sales territories or revise existing territorial arrangements to improve the coordination of personal selling or advertising efforts. In most situations, personal selling or advertising alone cannot accomplish the entire selling task efficiently or economically. By blending personal selling and advertising, management takes advantage of a synergistic effect (the "2 + 2 = 5" effect) and obtains a performance greater than the sum of its parts.

Sales personnel play key roles in capitalizing upon synergistic opportunities. Prior to launching an advertising campaign for a new consumer product, for example, sales personnel call upon dealers to outline the marketing plan's objectives, provide them with tie-in displays and other promotional materials, and make certain that adequate supplies of the product are on hand in the retail outlets. Territorial assignments make every dealer the responsibility of some salesperson, and proper routing ensures that sales personnel contact all dealers at appropriate times relative to the breaking of the consumer advertising campaign. In some cases, the manufacturer's marketing plan calls for dealers to share in the costs of advertising the product; here, again, sales personnel "sell" such cooperative programs to dealers. In situations where sales personnel do work related to the advertising effort, the results are more satisfactory if the work is delegated on a territory-by-territory basis rather than for the entire market.

PROCEDURES FOR SETTING UP OR REVISING SALES TERRITORIES

In setting up or in revising sales territories, there are four steps: (1) selecting a basic geographical control unit, (2) determining sales potentials in control units, (3) combining control units into tentative territories, and (4) adjusting for coverage difficulty and redistricting tentative territories.

Selecting a Basic Geographical Control Unit

The starting point in territorial planning is the selection of a basic geographical control unit. The most commonly used control units are counties, Zip code numbers, cities, standard metropolitan statistical areas, trading areas, and states. Sales territories are put together as consolidations of basic geographical control units.

There are two reasons for selecting a *small* control unit. One reason is to realize an important benefit of using territories, the precise geographical identification of sales potential. If the control unit is too large, areas with low sales potentials are hidden by inclusion with areas having high sales potentials, and areas with high sales potentials are obscured by inclusion with those having low sales potentials. The second reason is that these units remain relatively stable and unchanging, making it possible to redraw territorial boundaries easily by redistributing control units among territories. If, for example, a company wants to add to Jones's territory and reduce Smith's adjoining territory, it is easier to transfer county-sized rather than state-sized control units.

Counties. In the United States, the county is the most widely used geographical control unit. The county is small enough to prevent the obscuring of areas with high and low sales potentials, and statistical information on the more than 3,000 counties in the United States is readily available. This makes it inexpensive to develop market and sales potentials on a county-by-county basis. Furthermore, the county typically is the smallest unit for which governmental sources report statistical data. The county is a smaller market division than the typical sales territory, so a company using counties as control units can build up or revise sales territories without collecting new data on potentials.

Zip code areas. A basic geographical unit increasingly used by U.S. companies is the Zip code area.[1] There are more than 33,000 Zip code areas in the United States, so the typical Zip code area is smaller than the typical county.

Using Zip code areas as the basic geographical units has advantages. The Zip code areas generally reflect economic characteristics of the areas—in marked contrast to counties, cities, and states, which represent political subdivisions. The Zip code system permits a precise definition of markets according to economic and demographic characteristics. Each Zip code area is a convenient unit for which to collect data on market and sales potentials.

Cities. When a company's sales potential is located entirely, or almost entirely, in urbanized areas, the city is used as the control unit, although, in some cases, both the city and the surrounding county (or counties outside the city) are used as "twin" control units. The city rarely is fully satisfactory as a control unit, inasmuch as most grow beyond their political boundaries. For many products, suburbs adjacent to cities possess sales potentials at least as great as those in the cities themselves, and, in addition, they can often be covered by the same sales personnel at little additional cost.

Metropolitan statistical areas. Companies whose markets have expanded beyond city limits and into suburbs and satellite cities find the Metropolitan Statistical Area (MSA) a good choice for basic geographical control unit. An MSA is a geographic area with a large population nucleus together with adjacent communities that have a high degree of economic and social integration with that nucleus. MSA designations follow a set of standards set by the Federal Committee on MSAs (these standards are revised after decennial censuses). Under 1980 standards, an area is designated an MSA in one of two ways: (1) if there is a city of at least 50,000 population or (2) if there is an urbanized area of at least 50,000 population with a total metropolitan population of at least 100,000. In addition to the county containing the central city, the MSA may include additional counties with close economic and social ties to the central county. MSAs are defined in terms of entire counties, except in the six New England states, where towns and cities are the units of definition because of the absence of county governments. As of mid-1986, there were 316 MSAs that, in total, accounted for over 76 percent of the U.S. population, over 76 percent of the

[1]The Zip code is a five-digit geographic code that identifies areas within the United States and its territories (including Puerto Rico, the Virgin Islands, Guam, and military installations worldwide) for purposes of simplifying the distribution of mail by the U.S. Postal Service. The Zip code alignments do not necessarily adhere to boundaries of cities, counties, states, or other jurisdictions. The first digit divides the country into ten large groups of states numbered from 0 in the Northeast to 9 in the Far West. Within these areas, each state is divided into smaller areas, identified by the second and third digits of the Zip code. The last two digits identify a local delivery area. Similar coding systems for postal services are in use in the United Kingdom, Canada, and Australia, among other countries.

households, over 81 percent of the effective buying income, and over 81 percent of the retail sales. These statistics emphasize the highly urbanized nature of the national market and explain why an ever-growing number of companies assign territories consisting of metropolitan areas to most sales personnel and either use "country salespersons" to cover nonmetropolitan areas or do not cover nonmetropolitan areas at all.

Because the MSA definition is in terms of counties, the tremendous amount of statistical data available for the counties themselves may also be tapped. If the planner is willing to accept the definition and boundaries for each metropolitan statistical area, it is easy to secure data for use in estimating sales potentials. In fact, because the definition is in terms of whole counties, the planner is free to add to or subtract from the official roster of metropolitan statistical areas.

For some companies, MSAs are too large to serve as basic geographical control units. These companies deal directly with large numbers of customers in urban areas, and commonly they assign two or more sales personnel to the same MSA. In such cases, companies use either minor political divisions of cities—precincts and wards, or clusters of contiguous census tracts—or city blocks as control units. The main problem in using these control units is the difficulty encountered in obtaining market statistics, although statistics are obtainable by census tract.

Trading areas. A logical choice for a geographical control unit is the trading area, since it is based upon the natural flow of trade. Formally defined, a trading area consists of the geographical region surrounding a city that serves as the dominant retail or wholesale center or both for the region. The trading-area concept recognizes that consumers, retailers, and wholesalers pay scant attention to political boundaries in deciding where to buy. Consumers, for example, regard convenience and the merchandise selection available as key factors in deciding where to shop. People living in suburban Connecticut or New Jersey, for instance, may reason that the best selection of the desired type of product is in New York City, conclude that New York is reasonably convenient to get to, and subsequently shop and buy the item there. Shopping across political boundaries is common, especially where population concentrations are close to state lines and where suburban areas have spread into counties surrounding cities.

Many consumer products, including most specialty and shopping goods, are available almost entirely in large regional shopping malls. So residents of small towns and rural areas must travel to these malls (or, of course, order by mail or phone). Increasingly, too, residents of the older areas of cities, when they are in the market for these items, go to outlying shopping malls. Where large cities are few and widely separated, as in the Rocky Mountain states, larger towns, often the county seats, are trading centers for surrounding smaller towns and rural districts.

It is difficult to define the limits of trading areas, as they vary from product to product. But because trading areas are based on natural trade flows, they are considered in planning sales territories even though they are not selected as geographical control units. The main problems in using trading areas as control units are defining them and estimating sales potentials.

Depending upon the product, both retail and wholesale trading areas vary in size and shape and change over time. Rural consumers buy work clothes and routine supplies in the nearest small towns, but they go to regional shopping malls or larger cities to shop for dress clothing, and even farther to buy expensive furniture or jewelry. Each such location is the focal point for a trading area, at least for products customarily purchased there. Trading areas for products purchased frequently and routinely are much smaller in size, and consequently more numerous, than are those for luxury products.

Trading area maps for general product classifications are available. Rand-McNally, for example, publishes a map of the United States showing 494 Basic Trading Areas and 50 Major Trading Areas. The Basic Trading Areas radiate out from centers important for shopping-goods sales, and the Major Trading Areas are combinations of Basic Trading Areas but in larger groups. Major newspapers, television and radio stations, and other advertising media provide maps of their circulation areas and related market data from which it is possible to delineate trading areas. Similarly, the U.S. Department of Commerce and several wholesale trade associations from time to time publish maps of trading areas. The trading areas identified in publicly available maps are approximations of the trading-area boundaries for broad categories of product at a given time, so their main interest for territorial planners lies in the general pictures they convey.

Precise delineation of trading areas requires primary research into, and quantification of, customers' buying habits and preferences. Considerable expense is involved in dividing market and sales potentials for counties or other political subdivisions among two or more trading areas. Consequently, most companies using trading areas as control units adjust trading-area boundaries to county lines.

Other features of trading areas limit their usefulness as control units. Every trading area has at least one city as a focal point, but it may be far from the area's geographical center, complicating the planning of routes and call schedules for sales personnel. Many trading areas contain both areas of high population density and of thinly settled forest, desert, or farmland, so care must be taken to prevent obscuring of areas with high and low sales potentials. Some trading areas are circumscribed partially by impassable geographical barriers and partially by the relative trading importance of neighboring areas, both of which change with highway construction projects and the development of new shopping malls. Sizes and shapes of trading areas even fluctuates seasonally; climatic conditions, such as snowfall in intervening mountainous areas, cause some cities to have separate summer and winter trading areas.

Some companies, however, identify trading areas for their own products. Knowledgeable executives rough out trading areas from sales statistics available in company files and from governmental sources, later refining them using data secured through interviews with customers and sales personnel. The most difficult problem is to allocate sales potential data among trading areas. This causes some executives who recognize the basic logic of the trading-area concept nevertheless to use other control units, such as counties or standard metropolitan statistical areas. They feel that the greater realism obtainable through identifying and delineating trading areas for their company's products is not worth facing the problem of allocating sales potential data.

States. States, as basic geographical control units, provide a rough basis for subdividing the national market. There are two situations in which the fixing of territorial boundary lines along the borders of states is justifiable. One is the company with a small sales force covering the market extensively rather than intensively; there are only a few customers and prospects, but they are all across the nation. The other situation is the company first seeking national distribution, which assigns its sales personnel to territories consisting of one or more states as a temporary expedient. As soon as feasible, a change is made to a smaller control unit. The main difficulty in using states as basic control units is that they are political rather than economic subdivisions. A Kentucky-Ohio boundary, for instance, ignores the fact that numerous consumers and middlemen in north central Kentucky do their buying in Cincinnati, and a Kansas-Missouri boundary ignores the fact that many Kansas consumers and other buyers trade in Kansas City, Missouri.

Determining Sales Potential Present in Each Control Unit

The next step is to determine the sales potential present in each central unit. The territorial planner needs some way to measure sales potentials, which, you will recall, represent the maximum possible sales opportunities open to a specific company selling a good or service during a stated future period to particular market segments. For the present purpose, substitute "a particular control unit" for "a particular market segment", in other words, each control unit is a particular *geographical* market segment. Geographical market segments, like all market segments, are made up of present and prospective customers, so the territorial planner must identify the buyers of the product as precisely as possible. A vague identification such as, "Our product is bought by women," is not sufficient. But if it can be determined that "Our product is bought almost entirely by middle-aged, lower-income women living in cities," a more precise description of the buyers comprising the market is obtained. Formal market identification studies may be necessary.

Sometimes, sales personnel supply information, but it is not necessarily usable. For example, a sales force calling only on wholesalers has little contact with retailers or consumers. Even when sales personnel sell to final buyers, as in marketing many industrial goods, they may neglect certain classes of prospects and be able to provide only partial identification of possible buyers. When there is no direct contact with final buyers, formal marketing research studies obtain precise identification of all classes of final buyers. Whether or not this process should be carried as far as identification of *each* possible buyer depends upon the product being marketed. In consumer goods, it is unnecessary and too expensive to go to this extreme. In industrial goods, where often there are only a few possible buyers, exact identification is desirable and feasible.

Having identified potential buyers, the planner next determines the sales potential in each control unit. The planner ascertains how many potential buyers in each class there are in each control unit and the units's total market potential. Then the planner estimates the portion of the unit's market potential that the company has an opportunity to obtain (that is, the sales potential).

Market potentials are generally converted into sales potentials by analyzing historical market shares within each control unit, adjusting for changes in company and competitors' selling strategies and practices, and arriving at estimates. Having made these estimates, the territorial planner ascertains those control units with sufficient sales potential to justify sales coverage. For the manufacturer with mass distribution, this is not a problem. Mass marketers provide sales coverage in every control unit, regardless of how little sales potential it represents, because maximum sales exposure is crucial to marketing success. Many manufacturers, however, provide sales coverage only in those control units containing sufficient sales potential to assure profitable operations, and for most manufacturers, there are some control units where selling costs are excessive. This is true of numerous industrial-goods producers, such as those selling machine tools and mining equipment. (Studies of industrial-goods markets show that over 90 percent of U.S. manufacturing is done in approximately 650 of the 3,000 counties.) It is also true of most producers of consumer shopping and specialty goods; the bulk of the market lies in a small number of market areas.

Combining Control Units into Tentative Territories

The planner next combines units into *tentative* sales territories. This is only a tentative arrangement because, as explained later, subsequent adjustments must be made for relative coverage difficulty. At this stage, the planner assumes that no significant differences in the physical or other characteristics of individual control units exists. The purpose is to obtain a "first approximation" of sales territories, by combining contiguous control units into tentative territories, each containing approximately the same sales potential.

At this point, however, the planner decides the number of territories, and this, assuming that all sales personnel are of average ability, is identical to deciding sales force size. Basically, the planner estimates the percentage of total sales potential that the average salesperson should realize. Analysis of past sales experience helps in making this estimate, which, once made, is used to determine the number of territories. In effect, the planner estimates the sales productivity per sales personnel unit and divides it into the total estimated sales potential, thus arriving at the number of sales personnel units—and territories—required. Assume that management estimates that an average salesperson should realize $2,500,000 of a total sales potential of $25 million—ten territories and ten units ($25,000,000/$2,500,000) of sales personnel are required. When these estimates and this calculation have been made, contiguous control units are combined into tentative territories of roughly equal sales potential. To simplify this step, sales potentials for control units are expressed as percentages of total sales potential. In the example, then, control units are grouped into ten tentative territories, each containing, about 10 percent of the sales potential. Throughout this grouping process, the planner combines only control units contiguous to each other; individual control units are not split into different territories, even if this results in tentative territories with different total sales potentials.

Territory shape. The planner now considers territory shape. The shape of a territory affects both selling expenses and ease of sales coverage. In addition, if the shape of a territory permits the salesperson to minimize time on the road, shape contributes to sales force morale. Three shapes are in wide use: the wedge, the circle, and the clover leaf (see Figure 22.1).

The wedge is appropriate for territories containing both urban and nonurban areas. It radiates out from densely populated urban center. Wedges, of course, can be in many sizes (up to just under 360 degrees). Travel time among adjoining wedges can be equalized by balancing urban and nonurban calls.

The circle is appropriate when accounts and prospects are evenly distributed throughout the area. The salesperson assigned to the circular-shaped territory is based at some point near the center, making for greater uniformity in

FIGURE 22.1 Shapes of Sales Territories in Wide Use

frequency of calls on customers and prospects. This also makes the salesperson nearer to more of the customers than is possible with a wedge-shaped territory.

The clover leaf is desirable when accounts are located randomly through a territory. Careful planning of call schedules results in each cloverleaf being a week's work, making it possible for the salesperson to be home weekends. Home base for the salesperson assigned to the territory is near the center. Clover-leaf territories are more common among industrial marketers than they are among consumer marketers and among companies cultivating the market extensively rather than intensively.

Adjusting for Differences in Coverage Difficulty and Redistricting Tentative Territories

The final step is to redistrict the tentative territories through adjusting for coverage difficulty. The tentative territories each contain approximately the same sales potential, but, almost certainly, territories with nearly equal sales potentials require different selling efforts and, in turn, selling expense totals. Now it is time to remove the unrealistic assumption that no differences in the characteristics of geographical control units exist. Significant differences in physical and other characteristics make providing sales coverage more difficult for some control units than for others. Certain large cities, for instance, have greater sales potentials for most products than some states, but the time required to contact customers and prospects in cities is much less, and the same is true of selling expenses. The optimum territorial arrangement is reached when incremental sales per dollar of selling expenditures are equated among all territories.[2] In working toward this ideal, both sales potential and coverage difficulty are taken into account. And, as J. G. Hauk writes, "It is only coincidental if equal potential territories achieve the optimum."[3] As the planner adjusts for differences in coverage difficulty, control units are taken away from some tentative territories and added to others. The final territorial arrangement almost certainly is one in which different territories contain different sales potentials.

Differences in coverage difficulty represent differences in work loads. The planner ascertains how large the maximum work load—the largest work load for any salesperson—should be. All work loads need not be the same size, since sales personnel vary in ability as well as in drive, and some can safely be assigned larger work loads. However, since there is an upper limit to the "desirable work load," and this also limits a territory's maximum geographical extent. When final adjustments for coverage difficulty are made, sales territories have varying amounts of sales potential and different-sized work loads, but none exceeds the maximum desirable work load. The work load method was discussed in Chapter

[2]H.R. Wellman, "The Distribution of Selling Effort Among Geographic Areas," *Journal of Marketing*, 3, no. 3 (January 1939), pp. 225–41.

[3]J.G. Hauk, "Research in Personal Selling," in G. Schwartz (ed.), *Science in Marketing* (New York: John Wiley, 1965), p. 238.

5 as one approach to determining sales force size. Here, the same concept, with minor modifications is used for redistricting.

Redistricting to adjust for coverage difficulty (that is, differences in work loads) is a seven-step procedure:

1. *Determine number, location, and size of customers and prospects in each tentative territory.* Customers are identified and located through sales records; prospects through trade directories, subscription lists to trade publications, classified directories, and credit-reporting agencies. Size is measured in terms of sales potential.
2. *Estimate time required for each sales call.* This varies from account to account and from prospect to prospect, so customers and prospects are classified into groups, estimating an average time per call for each group. Time and duty analyses of sales personnel are used to check these estimates.
3. *Determine length of time between calls, that is the amount of time required to travel from one customer to the next.* This varies among regions, depending on the density of customers and prospects and the condition of roads and transportation facilities. Particular attention is paid to physical characteristics. Large rivers, lakes, mountains, and other barriers to travel make natural and necessary territorial boundaries. The number of places where a large mountain range can be crossed by automobile are limited and often considerable time is consumed in the crossing. The same is true of large rivers, lakes, bays, and so forth. Transportation facilities are as important as physical characteristics. If travel is by automobile, territories are planned so that driving is mainly on primary, all-weather roads, with minimum cross-tracking. If public transportation facilities such as commercial airlines are used, territories are planned with an eye on locations of air terminals. The planner interrelates and balances differences in sales potential, physical geographical characteristics, and transportation facilities and routes. After sketching in on a map the tentative territorial division according to roughly equal sales potentials, the planner makes adjustments after superimposing maps showing topographic and transportation features.
4. *Decide call frequencies.* Within certain control units, some or all customer and prospect classes require call frequencies that differ from those in other control units. Differences in the strength of competition require variations in call frequency rates. Similarly, call frequency rates are influenced by the market acceptance of the product line within control units. Cost studies on minimum profitable order sizes also provide input to the decision on call frequencies.
5. *Calculate the number of calls possible within a given period.* This is a matter of simple arithmetic. To determine the number of calls per day in a certain control unit, the average amount of time required for each call is added to the average time between calls and divided into the number of working hours in the day. Adjustments are made when call lengths vary for different classes of customers and prospects.
6. *Adjust the number of calls possible during a given period by the desired call fre-*

quencies for the different classes of customers and prospects. This results in an estimate for the total work load represented by the control units in each tentative territory. Further adjustments are made to assure that the work load in any territory is not larger than the allowable maximum and that selling expenses are within budget limits. The planner shifts control units among different tentative territories, adding units to some by taking them away from adjacent territories. Each shift brings the territorial arrangement closer to the optimum—that is, closer to one in which incremental sales per dollar of selling expenditures are equated among all territories.

7. *Finally, check out the adjusted territories with sales personnel who work or who have worked in each area, and make further adjustments as required.* Personnel familiar with customer service requirements, competitive conditions, and the topography, roads, and travel conditions may point out weaknesses not obvious to the planner. These cause further shifting of control units from one territory to another, each shift bringing the final territorial arrangement a little closer to the optimum.

Deciding Assignment of Sales Personnel to Territories

When the arrangement is the best obtainable, it is time to assign sales personnel to territories. Up to this point in territorial planning, an implicit assumption has been that all sales personnel are "average," that is, that all are interchangeable, each capable of producing similar results at similar costs regardless of territorial assignments. Clearly, this is an unrealistic assumption, adopted only for territorial planning purposes, and one that is discarded when sales personnel are assigned to territories. Few sales personnel are average—they vary in ability, initiative, and effectiveness as well as in physical condition and energy. What constitutes a reasonable and desirable work load for one individual may not be appropriate for another person. Furthermore, salesperson's effectiveness varies with the territory assigned. One person is outstanding in one territory and a failure in a second, even though territorial sales potentials and coverage difficulty factors are almost identical. Performance, moreover, is conditioned by customer characteristics, customs and traditions, ethnic influences, and the like. Dyadic interactions, with customers and prospects, in other words, vary in their outcomes from one territory to another depending on many factors, most of them outside the salesperson's control.

In assigning sales personnel to territories, management seeks the most profitable alignment of selling efforts with sales opportunities. The territories, containing varying sales potentials, represent different amounts of sales opportunity. The sales personnel, differing in ability and potential effectiveness, represent the range of available selling talent. Management should "*Assign each salesperson to the particular territory where his or her relative contribution to profit is the highest.*"[4]

[4]Hauk, "Research in Personal Selling," pp. 241–42.

The general guide for assigning sales personnel to territories is not universally applicable because the discretion that management has in making these decisions differs from company to company. At one extreme, some companies display great reluctance to transfer sales personnel to different territories, management fearing not only sales force resistance but the consequences of breaking established salesperson-customer relationships. These companies adhere to a "no transfer" or "infrequent transfer" policy and build restrictions on shifting sales personnel into territorial designs. The planner expands or contracts territorial boundaries, adding to or subtracting from individual territorial sales potentials, until territories contain sales potentials appropriate to the abilities of assigned sales personnel. These companies, in effect, design sales territories around, and to fit, the abilities of sales personnel.

At the opposite extreme, management in a few companies is free to assign any salesperson to any territory, designing territories (according to procedures like those discussed earlier) and closely aligning salespeople's ability levels with territorial sales opportunity levels. Management shifts sales personnel to predesigned territories where their relative profit contributions are maximized.

The situation in most companies is somewhere between the two extremes. For various reasons, some totally outside management's control, certain sales personnel are not transferable, but others are freely moved from one territory to another. This means that management designs some sales territories to fit the ability levels of nontransferable sales personnel while reassigning other sales personnel with ability levels appropriate to sales territories redesigned according to the suggested procedures.

Illustration of Assigning Sales Personnel to Territories. Now let us work through several situations involving assignment of sales personnel to territories, our purpose being to demonstrate that, where practical, effective sales management assigns each salesperson to the territory where his or her relative profit contribution is maximized.

First, consider the situation in which territories have equal sales potential and coverage difficulty, but the sales personnel differ in ability. Figure 22.2 depicts this situation. Predicted sales are obtained by multiplying each territory's

FIGURE 22.2 Assignment of Sales Personnel to Territories of Equal Potential

Territory	Dollar Potential	Salesperson Assigned	Ability Index	Predicted Sales	Predicted Profit Contribution (25% of sales)
A	$ 500,000	1	1.0	$ 500,000	$125,000
B	500,000	2	0.8	400,000	100,000
C	500,000	3	0.7	350,000	87,500
Total	$1,500,000			$1,250,000	$312,500

dollar potential by the ability index of the salesperson assigned. Predicted profit contributions are assumed to amount to 25 percent of predicted sales. The total profit contribution is $312,500, the maximum attainable here regardless of how the sales personnel are assigned.

Now suppose that these territories are redesigned so that their sales potentials vary in direct proportion with the ability of the sales personnel assigned, with the same total dollar potential as before ($1.5 million). The results of this assignment pattern are shown in Figure 22.3. Redesigning territories so that sales potentials are directly proportional to abilities of assigned sales personnel increases the predicted profit contribution by $7,000 (from $312,500 to $319,500).

But what is the predicted profit contribution if total sales potential is divided some other way? After all, the number of possible ways of dividing it is very large. Consider Figure 22.4, which shows a different division of the $1.5 million sales potential; sales personnel, however, are still assigned territories in rank order of their respective abilities.

Again there is an increase in the predicted profit contribution, this one even more impressive than in the preceding example. However, it is unlikely

FIGURE 22.3 Assignment of Sales Personnel to Territories Containing Sales Potentials Proportionate to Salespersons' Abilities

Territory	Dollar Potential	Salesperson Assigned	Ability Index	Predicted Sales	Predicted Profit Contribution (25% of sales)
A	$ 600,000	1	1.0	$ 600,000	$150,000
B	480,000	2	0.8	384,000	96,000
C	420,000	3	0.7	294,000	73,500
Total	$1,500,000			$1,278,000	$319,500

FIGURE 22.4 Assignment of Sales Personnel According to Ability to Territories Containing Different Sales Potentials

Territory	Dollar Potential	Salesperson Assigned	Ability Index	Predicted Sales	Predicted Profit Contribution (25% of sales)
A	$1,000,000	1	1.0	$1,000,000	$250,000
B	300,000	2	0.8	240,000	60,000
C	200,000	3	0.7	140,000	35,000
Total	$1,500,000			$1,380,000	$345,000

that this is a feasible territorial division and salespersons assignment plan. The coverage difficulty and associated work load now involved in covering territory A would likely exceed salesperson 1's capacity to perform; thus, 1's ability index should be lowered. Similarly, territories B and C now have such greatly reduced sales potentials (which means that their coverage difficulty is less than before) that probably neither would represent sufficient work loads for salesperson 2 or 3.

There are upper and lower limits to the amount of sales potential to incorporate in any one territory. These limits are set by coverage difficulty and the size of the work load that it is reasonable to expect any salesperson, regardless of ability, to assume. Then, too, selling expenditures do not fluctuate directly with predicted sales volumes throughout all sales volume ranges. They may rise more or less in proportion to sales volume increases, but after a certain point is reached, the rate of rise accelerates greatly (that is, as the difficulty of making sales becomes increasingly greater), and they may decline proportionately to sales volume decreases until a minimum level is reached (where potential sales are no longer large enough to support needed selling expenditures). Work load restrictions, in other words, confine the uniformity of variation of selling expenditures within fairly narrow limits.

The optimum territorial arrangement is reached when the *incremental* sales produced per dollar of selling expenditures are equated among all territories. After a sales territory reaches a certain size in terms of sales potential, adding successive increments of sales potential is feasible only up to the point at which the last dollar of selling expenditures just brings in sufficient sales to provide a dollar of profit contribution. A company seeking the optimum territorial arrangement generally concludes that it is wise to cut off additional selling expenditures before reaching this "point of feasibility." This is because the best condition requires the equating among all territories of the incremental sales produced by the last dollar of selling expenditures in each.

Thus far, an implicit assumption has been that ability indexes do not change with assignment of sales personnel. However, sales personnel have different degrees of effectiveness in different territories, because environmental forces condition selling performance. It is not realistic, in other words, to assume that ability indexes for individual sales personnel are fixed regardless of the territorial assignment.

Consider, then, a situation where sales personnel maintain their rank order according to ability indexes as they are switched among territories but where the indexes change. With the assignment pattern 1A, 2B, 3C, the respective ability indexes might be 1.0, 0.8, and 0.7 (as in Figure 22.3, for example), but with the assignment 1B, 2A, 3C, the respective ability indexes could be 1.0, 0.9, and 0.7—salesperson 1 in this situation performs better than salesperson 2 regardless of the assignment. Using the basic data in Figure 22.3, the results of the 1B-2A-3C assignment are shown in Figure 22.5. This assignment pattern results in a higher total profit contribution than that secured by assigning sales person-

FIGURE 22.5 Assignment of Sales Personnel to Territories where Ability Indexes Vary with the Assignment

Territory	Dollar Potential	Salesperson Assigned	Ability Index	Predicted Sales	Predicted Profit Contribution (25% of sales)
A	$ 600,000	2	0.9	$ 540,000	$135,000
B	480,000	1	1.0	480,000	120,000
C	420,000	3	0.7	294,000	73,500
Total	$1,500,000			$1,314,000	$328,500

nel to territories strictly in accord with their abilities (that is, $328,500 versus $319,500). Thus in some territorial designs, the best salesperson should not necessarily be assigned to the territory with the highest sales potential, and in some, a salesperson should not necessarily be assigned to the one territory where his or her profit contribution is higher than that of any other salesperson who might be assigned to the same territory. *Each salesperson should be assigned to the territory where his or her relative contribution to profit is the highest.* In Figure 22.5 salesperson 1 could make a higher dollar profit contribution than salesperson 2 in territory A, but 1 contributes more, relative to 2, when assigned to territory B. Similarly, salesperson 2's inferiority relative to salesperson 1 is less when 2 has territory A, not territory B.[5]

Ability indexes change with different assignment patterns; consequently, management estimates ability indexes for each possible assignment pattern. The large number of possible assignment patterns makes complex the task of achieving an ideal assignment. When twelve salespeople are to be assigned to twelve territories, for example, there are 12! (that is 479,001,600) possible patterns. It would be possible, although not practical, to write down all 479,001,600 assignment patterns and select the one providing the maximum profit contribution; fortunately, however, the assignment linear programming technique and the computer afford a rapid and less laborious way to find the solution. But even this technique requires estimates for the probable net profit contribution for each salesperson for each possible assignment pattern, and this requires not only knowledge of the nature and peculiarities of each territory, but insight on how each salesperson might perform in each territorial environment.

[5]Strictly speaking, of course, the planner might now reapportion the total sales potential among the three territories in direct proportion to the revised ability indexes of the sales personnel assigned to each, thus obtaining a still further increase in the total profit contribution. The perceptive reader will see that this reapportionment would involve making territory B a higher-potential area than territory A. The resulting personnel assignment pattern, then, would be one in which the best salesperson (no. 1) would have the territory with the highest sales potential (now territory B), but note carefully that each salesperson still would be assigned to the territory where his or her relative contribution to profit is the highest.

ROUTING AND SCHEDULING SALES PERSONNEL

Routing and scheduling plans aim to maintain the lines of communication, to optimize sales coverage and minimize wasted time. When management is informed at all times of salespersons' whereabouts in the field—or at least knows where they should be—it is easy to contact them to provide needed information or last-minute instructions. Chances are good that sales personnel will be where they are supposed to be.

Routing and scheduling plans improve sales coverage. The mechanics of setting up a routing plan are simple, but in working out the plan, detailed information is required on the numbers and locations of customers, the means and methods of transportation connecting customer concentrations, and desired call frequency rates. Detailed maps are needed showing not only towns and cities and transportation routes but trading-area boundaries, mountain ranges, lakes, bridges, and ferry lines. If sales personnel are to travel by air, airport locations need spotting. The route, or routes, finally laid out should permit the salesperson to return home at least on weekends.

If the route planner considers the desired call frequency rate for each customer on the route, the call schedule is a by-product of setting up the route. In most cases, however, making up the call schedule is more than planning the route. Customers and prospects are segregated according to the desired call frequency rate. Using detailed maps, the planner identifies the locations of members of each customer and prospect group and reconciles the route with these locations. Hence, often the salesperson has a different route each time he or she travels the territory, to achieve the desired call frequencies and to incorporate new customers and prospects into the itinerary. Furthermore, because changes occur in account classifications, prospects, competitive activity, as well as in road conditions, it is impractical to set up fixed route and call schedules good for long periods.

Routing and scheduling plans reduce wasted time by sales personnel. Much backtracking, travel time and other "nonselling" time is eliminated, and scheduled call frequency is to fit customers' needs. Effective routing and scheduling automatically builds up the size of the average order.

In scheduling sales personnel, some firms not only designate the customers to call upon each day but prescribe the time of day to make each call. Detailed scheduling is coupled with a system for making advance appointments. Companies not using scheduling plans usually suggest advance appointments, but often salespeople ignore this suggestion. For effective detailed scheduling the scheduler needs current information on time required for each call, probable waiting time at each stop, travel time between calls, and the probable time with each customer. This information is difficult to collect and update. Detailed scheduling is most feasible when customers give their full cooperation. Most firms allow their sales personnel "time cushions" to allow for the many variations met on each selling trip.

Companies, almost without exception, benefit from systematic routing and scheduling, but not all find detailed scheduling feasible. The petroleum marketing companies, and other firms with combination driver-salespersons, use detailed routing and scheduling plans successfully, as do several large pharmaceutical manufacturers. Less detailed routing and scheduling plans are used by wholesalers of groceries, drugs, and hardware. Detailed scheduling plans are appropriate in trades typified by frequent calls, great homogeneity among customers, short travel time between calls, and highly standardized products not requiring large amounts of creative selling time—that is, in situations where trade selling predominates.

Routing, scheduling, and control. The routing plan, the scheduling plan, or both assist sales management in obtaining closer control over sales personnel's movements and time expenditures. The routing and scheduling plans are integral parts of the overall process of establishing sales territories and assigning sales personnel. Any routing or scheduling plan should have frequent checkups to detect needed adjustments. Call reports are compared with route and call schedules to determine whether plans are followed. Variations or discrepancies are noted and sales personnel asked for explanations. Adherence to the plans is also enforced through frequent and unannounced visits to the field by supervisors or branch sales managers.

CONCLUSION

Setting up sales territories facilitates the planning and control of sales operations. Well-designed territories assist in attempts to improve market coverage and customer service, reduce selling expense ratios, secure coordination of personal-selling and advertising efforts, and improve the evaluation of personnel performance.

Good territorial design is based upon thorough knowledge of sales potentials and differences in coverage difficulty. The steps in setting up or revising sales territories are (1) selecting a basic geographical control unit, (2) determining sales potential, (3) combining control units into tentative territories, and (4) adjusting for coverage difficulty and redistricting tentative territories. In assigning sales personnel to territories, management seeks the best alignment of selling efforts with sales opportunities, and systematic plans for routing and scheduling sales personnel help in accomplishing this. Since sales personnel vary in individual effectiveness with the territories to which they are assigned, management develops ability indexes for each possible assignment pattern.

Sales Control and Cost Analysis

23

Sales executives are responsible for many activities. They participate in setting selling and profit objectives, formulating sales-related marketing policies, and designing personal-selling strategies. They build and develop a sales organization to carry the sales program into effect. They integrate the sales organization with the distributive network and other company marketing units (such as advertising, sales promotion, and physical distribution).

In discharging these responsibilities, sales executives sometimes pay inadequate attention to selling and profit objectives. Caught up in the maze of everyday activities—many related to individual sales personnel and customer problems—sales executives neglect longer term matters. This is exactly the type of setting in which the installation and operation of control techniques pays off handsomely!

Appropriately designed and skillfully implemented control mechanisms increase the chances that the sales organization will focus upon achieving selling and profit objectives. The sales budget is the key control mechanism, and quotas (sales volume, profit, activity), properly set and administered, stimulate sales personnel to achieve sales and profit objectives. In setting up sales territories, management makes the control of sales operations more effective.

Still other control mechanisms contribute to the effectiveness of the personal-selling effort. Among these are the sales audit, sales analysis, and cost analysis. These control mechanisms help sales executives to monitor profitability of the operation.

THE SALES AUDIT

A sales audit is a systematic and comprehensive appraisal of the total selling operation. It appraises integration of the individual inputs to the personal selling effort and identifies and evaluates assumptions underlying the sales operation. More specifically, *a sales audit is a systematic, critical, and unbiased review and appraisal of the basic objectives and policies of the selling function and of the organization, methods, procedures, and personnel employed to implement those policies and achieve those objectives.*

Proponents of the sales audit stress the importance of focusing on overall selling strategy and methods for implementing it rather than examining individual components piecemeal. Sales executives, for example, may become so involved in programs to reduce sales personnel turnover or some new technique for motivating sales personnel that they lose sight of some key objective, which might be, for instance, to increase the profitability of small accounts. Existing sales personnel may do a poor job in working with small accounts, yet management focuses more on retaining these sales personnel than on making them more effective with small customers. Worse yet, the new motivational technique may be counterproductive—it may be encouraging sales personnel to concentrate upon getting the "cream of the business from the largest customers." Sales audits detect situations of this type.

A sales audit uncovers opportunities for improving the effectiveness of the sales organization. An audit identifies strengths and weaknesses—strengths have potential for exploitation, weaknesses have potential for improvements. While "audit" implies an after-the-fact evaluation (a carry-over from financial usage), a sales audit provides information useful for planning sales strategy.

Sales audits have no standardized formats. Each company designs a sales audit to fit its needs. Every sales audit examines six main aspects of selling operations:

1. *Objectives.* Each selling input should have clearly stated objectives, related to desired outputs. For example, a firm might have the objective of raising its market share from 15 to 20 percent without reducing per unit profit.
2. *Policies.* Both explicit and implicit policies are appraised for their consistency in achieving the selling objectives. If, for example, a policy of promoting only from within prevents management from finding a district manager capable of bringing district A up to a 20 percent market share, the policy is reevaluated.
3. *Organization.* Does the organization possess the capabilities for achieving the objectives? Are planning and control systems appropriate? If an organization is understaffed, or staffed with incompetents, there is little likelihood of achieving ambitious objectives or ensuring proper control.
4. *Methods.* Individual strategies for carrying out policies must be appropriate. For example, it is futile to attempt upgrading quality and price if

the company has already established a strong consumer image for low quality and price.

5. *Procedures.* The steps in implementing individual strategies should be logical, well designed, and chosen to fit the situation. The procedures should allocate responsibility for implementation to particular individuals and explain how the goals are to be achieved.
6. *Personnel.* All executives playing key roles in planning sales operations and strategy, as well as those responsible for implementation of sales programs, are evaluated as to their effectiveness relative to stated objectives, policies, and other aspects of sales operations. Too often an executive is evaluated in terms of ability to increase sales or profit rather than success in reaching predeterminded objectives, such as increased market share.

In making a sales audit, too, a company examines both its markets and its products. Fundamentally, in examining markets, the sales audit seeks answers to four questions:

1. Who is buying what, and how?
2. Who is selling what, and how?
3. How is the competition doing?
4. How are we doing?

SALES ANALYSIS

Sales analysis is a detailed study of sales volume performance to detect strengths and weaknesses. If sales management depends solely on summary sales data it has no way to evaluate its own activities and those of the sales force. The fact that sales increased by 2 percent over last year but profit *decreased* by 1 percent would be a cause for concern but of no help in determining how to reverse the profit decline. Sales analysis provides additional information, for example, that the increased sales volume came from products carrying a lower-than-average gross margin.

Through sales analyses, management seeks insights on strong and weak territories, high-volume and low-volume products, and the types of customers providing satisfactory and unsatisfactory sales volume. Sales analysis uncovers details that otherwise lie hidden in the sales records. It provides information that management needs to allocate sales efforts effectively.

Allocation of Sales Effort

In most businesses, a small percentage of the territories, customers, products, or orders brings in a high percentage of the sales; conversely, a large percentage of the territories, customers, products, or orders brings in a low percentage of the sales. A sales executive for a carpet manufacturing firm, for example, found that

80 percent of the customers accounted for only 15 percent of the sales. Comparable situations exist in most companies. These are examples of the "iceberg principle"—only a small part of the total situation is above the surface and known while the submerged part is beneath the surface and unknown. Sales analysis detects such situations, alerting management to opportunities for improving operations.

Iceberg-type sales patterns do not always mean unprofitable operations, but they frequently result in profits lower than necessary. Why? Simply because sales efforts, and hence selling expenses, ordinarily are divided on the basis of customers, territories, orders, and so forth, rather than on the basis of sales potentials or actual sales. It usually costs as much to maintain sales personnel in poor territories as in good ones, almost as much to promote a slow-selling product as one that sells "like hotcakes." It costs as much to have sales personnel call on customers who give small orders as on those who place large orders. Commonly, a large proportion of the total spending for personal-selling efforts brings in a small proportion of the total sales and profits. Sales analysis detects these situations.

Data for Sales Analysis

Companies vary in the data they have available for sales analysis. At one extreme, some have no data other than the accounting system records as sales are made, and, of course, copies of sales invoices. At the opposite extreme, some maintain detailed sales records and have data readily available for use in making all types of analyses.

The original sources of data for sales analysis are the sales invoices. In a company with a good information system, detailed data from sales invoices are transferred to computer tapes or data-processing cards. The information on each transaction identifies the customer (name, geographical location, and so on) the salesperson (name, territory, and so forth) and includes such sales data as order date, products sold and quantities, price per unit, total dollar sales per product, and total order amount. With information stored in this detail, sales analyses are performed quickly and at low cost.

Illustrative Sales Analysis

The southeastern sales manager of a carpet manufacturing firm has just learned that the region did not reach its quota for the second quarter. The region did not miss by far, achieving nearly 97 percent of its quota. However, the sales manager would like more details: Where did we fall down? Are we universally missing the target? Are there any bright spots?

Consequently, the sales manager asks for a sales analysis of the southeastern region by sales areas. Figure 23.1 shows this analysis. The good news is that Atlanta and Jacksonville exceeded their quotas. The bad news is that Charlotte and New Orleans missed their targets by considerable margins.

FIGURE 23.1 Sales Analysis by Sales Area Dollar Sales, Southeastern Region, Second Quarter (in 000s)

Sales Area	Quota	Actual	+/−	% of Quota
Atlanta	$ 3,400	$ 3,640	+240	107.1
Charlotte	3,300	2,960	−340	89.7
Jacksonville	2,700	2,830	+130	104.8
New Orleans	2,500	2,100	−400	84.0
Total SE Region	$11,900	$11,530	−370	96.9

The sales manager wants more details about the Charlotte and New Orleans situations. It is decided to probe the New Orleans sales area first, as it had a sales deficit of $400,000, greater than the deficit for the entire region ($370,000). The first sales analysis furnished details on the four members of the sales force assigned to the New Orleans area (see Figure 23.2). Edwards and Scott are responsible for the area's poor quota performance.

Edwards missed the mark by the largest amount (though Edwards' performance against quota was better the Scott's), so the sales manager next asks for a breakdown (sales analysis) of Edwards' sales by class of account (A = large accounts, B = medium-sized accounts, and C = small accounts). Figure 23.3

FIGURE 23.2 Sales Analysis by Sales Personnel Dollar Sales, New Orleans Area, Second Quarter (in 000s)

Salesperson	Quota	Actual	+/−	% of Quota
J. Bonin	$ 750	$ 770	+ 20	103.7
D. Comeau	660	665	+ 5	100.8
H. Edwards	650	410	−240	63.1
R. Scott	440	255	−185	58.0
Total N.O. Area	$2,500	$2,100	−400	84.0

FIGURE 23.3 Sales Analysis by Class of Account Dollar Sales, Salesperson H. Edwards, Second Quarter (in 000s)

Class of Account	Quota	Actual	+/−	% of Quota
A	$350	$210	−140	60.0
B	150	95	− 55	63.3
C	150	105	− 45	70.0
Total	$650	$410	−240	63.1

shows this sales analysis. Edwards' sales performance by class of account indicates the most success in selling smaller accounts, but across the board it has been below par.

The sales manager next asks for a sales analysis of Edwards' sales by product line. Figure 23.4 shows this analysis. Edwards has poor performance in the DeLuxe and Standard lines, but goes over quota in the Economy line.

FIGURE 23.4 Sales Analysis by Product Line Dollar Sales, Salesperson H. Edwards, Second Quarter (in 000s)

Product Line	Quota	Actual	+/−	% of Quota
DeLuxe	$240	105	−135	43.8
Standard	300	150	−150	50.0
Economy	110	155	+ 45	140.9
Total	$650	410	−240	63.1

Purposes of Sales Analyses

Sales analysis detects sales strengths and weaknesses, and each type of sales analysis sheds light on a different aspect. Analysis of sales territories answers how much is being sold *where*. Analysis of sales by products answers how much of *what* is being sold. Analysis of sales by customers answers *who* is buying how much. All sales analyses relate to *how much* is being sold, but each answers the question in a different way. Sales analyses identify different aspects of sales strengths and weaknesses, but they cannot explain *why* strengths and weaknesses exist. Answering the "why" question is up to sales management.

Sales analysis answered four of the sales manager's questions. First, it revealed sales areas with good (Atlanta and Jacksonville) and poor (Charlotte and New Orleans) performances. Second, it showed that salespersons Bonin and Comeau were above quota, while Edwards and Scott were below. Third, it indicated that Edwards' performance improved as accounts got smaller, but was unsatisfactory with all sizes of accounts. Fourth, it showed that Edwards' performance was unsatisfactory in selling the DeLuxe and Standard lines and above par in selling the Economy line. The sales manager, in other words, learned where sales were weak and strong, which salespersons were performing above or below quota, which classes of accounts were buying, and which products were being sold. No "why" questions were answered. It is up to management to explain why, and this could lead to reappraisals of the sales efforts, quotas relative to potentials, selling against the competition, which accounts buy which product lines and why, training salespersons to sell balanced sales mixtures, sales compensation, and sales support (for example, local advertising, sales promotional pieces, and dealer incentive campaigns).

MARKETING COST ANALYSIS

Marketing cost analysis analyzes sales volume and selling expenses to determine the relative profitability of particular aspects of sales operations. The first step in marketing cost analysis is sales analysis by territories, sales personnel, products, class of account, size of order, marketing channels, and other categories. Having broken down sales volume, for instance, by sales territories, the next step is to break down and assign selling expenses by sales territories. The outcome indicates relative profitability of the sales territories. Marketing cost analysis searches for ways to improve profit performance through exposing relative strengths and weaknesses.

Purposes of Marketing Cost Analysis

Marketing cost analysis determines the relative profitability of particular aspects of sales operations. In a given case, the specific objective is to suggest answers to questions such as: Which sales territories are profitable and which are unprofitable? What are the profit contributions of individual sales personnel? What is the profitability of the different products? What is the minimum size of a profitable account? How small can an order be and still be profitable? Which marketing channels provide the most profit for a given sales volume?

Marketing cost analyses only suggest the answers to these and similar questions. They indicate aspects possibly requiring managerial action, but not the nature of the action. Answers to more complex questions, requiring cross-analysis of expense allocations, are also suggested. If the expenses of selling different products, for instance, are cross-analyzed with the expenses incurred by individual sales personnel, insights are gained on how sales time should be allocated among products. But, here again, a complete answer to the question (on how to improve sales time allocation among products) requires consideration of other factors—among them, sales potentials for each product in each sales territory.

Marketing cost analysis produces data useful in defenses against price discrimination charges. The Clayton Act, as amended by the Robinson-Patman Act, prohibits any direct or indirect price discrimination by a seller among different purchases of commodities of like grade and quality, where the effect is to injure competition. The law prohibits price discrimination, but it permits certain price differentials—proving that a price difference is justified requires the kind of data generated by marketing cost analyses. Specifically, a marketing cost analysis performed for this purpose would aim to show that the difference in prices was no greater than the difference in selling expenses incurred in servicing the two customers.

Marketing Cost Analysis Techniques

Classifying selling expenses. Marketing cost analysis requires the classification of selling expenses as either separable (direct) or common (indirect). A separable expense is one traceable to individual sales personnel, sales territories, customers, marketing channels, products, or the like. A common expense is one that is not traceable to specific sales personnel, sales territories, customers, marketing channels, products, or the like.

Whether a given expense is a separable or common expense may depend on company policies or aspects of the operation under study. If sales personnel are paid salaries, for example, the outlay for salaries is a common expense as far as selling individual products is concerned. But if sales personnel are paid commissions, sales commissions are a separable expense of selling individual products and of selling particular categories of account or individual customers.

Converting accounting expense data to activity expense groups. Conventional accounting systems record expenses according to their immediate purpose. For instance, typical account titles include sales salaries, sales commissions, sales travel expense, branch sales office rent, advertising expense, general selling expense, general and administrative expenses, and bad-debt expense. In marketing cost analysis, accounting expense data are converted into activity expense groups, for instance, all the expenses related to field sales operations are grouped together (including sales salaries, sales commissions, sales travel expense, and branch sales office rent) to determine total expense for this activity.

Bases for allocating common expenses. Selection of bases for allocating common expenses is troublesome. In contrast to the analysis of production costs, where a single allocation basis, such as number of machine hours, is used for allocating all manufacturing expenses, some forms of marketing cost analysis require the allocation of selling and marketing expenses on several bases.

Allocation bases are factors that measure variability in the activities for which specific expenses are incurred. Allocation bases permit logical assignment of portions of common expense items to particular aspects of sales operations. Some expenses, such as credit and collection expenses, can be allocated according to a logical basis in any type of marketing cost analysis. But other expenses, such as sales salaries, can be allocated to sales territories or to customers but not usually to products, unless available data show the allocation of sales time among different products.

For most marketing cost analyses, no attempt is made to allocate all common expenses, only those that can be allocated on logical bases. Marketing cost analyses determine *relative* profitability, not net profitability, of particular aspects of sales operations. There is no need to allocate *all* common costs.

Contribution margin. Because marketing cost analyses focus upon separable expenses and those common expenses allocatable on logical bases, relative profitability is measured as a contribution margin. By definition, contribution margin = net sales - cost of goods sold - (separable expenses + common expenses allocatable on logical bases). Put differently, contribution margin is the dollar amount available to cover unallocated common expenses and profit (if any).

FIGURE 23.5 Salesperson Performance Reports and Marketing Cost Analyses for the Fiscal Year Ending December 31, 198X

	Sales Budget: Type A Territory			Territory #9: Ben Lomand			Territory #11: Nancy Hanks		
	Plastic	Metal	Total	Plastic	Metal	Total	Plastic	Metal	Total
Sales in units	24,000	16,000	40,000	24,000	17,000	41,000	20,000	20,000	40,000
Sales in dollars	$288,000	$320,000	$608,000	$288,000	$323,000	$611,000	$240,000	$380,000	$620,000
Cost of goods sold (st. costs)	144,000	240,000	384,000	144,000	255,000	399,000	120,000	300,000	420,000
Gross margin	$144,000	$ 85,000	$224,000	$144,000	$ 68,000	$212,000	120,000	$ 80,000	$200,000
Separable expenses									
Salary			$ 8,000			$ 8,000			$ 8,000
Commissions			18,240			18,330			18,600
Employee benefits			3,936			3,950			3,990
Travel and entertainment			13,500			12,000			15,000
Total separable expenses			$ 43,676			$ 42,280			$ 45,590
Allocatable common expenses									
Sales management and promotion									

Regular orders	$ 22,800	$ 20,000	$ 23,200
Special-handling orders	2,400	1,600	4,800
Packing and shipping	24,000	25,000	20,667
Credit and collection expense	3,000	2,600	3,200
Total allocatable common expenses	$ 52,000	$ 49,200	$ 51,867
Total separable and allocatable common expenses	$ 95,676	$ 91,480	$ 97,457
Contribution margin	$128,324	$120,520	$102,543
Other performance data			
Travel miles		32,000	28,000
Sales calls		1,200	1,000
Number of regular orders		1,250	1,450
Number of special-handling orders		50	150

Marketing Cost Analysis—An Illustration

The J. M. Dull Company prepared monthly and annual Salesperson Performance Reports for each of its twelve salespersons. The annual performance reports for two salespersons—Ben Lomand and Nancy Hanks—are shown in Figure 23.5. J. M. Dull Company classified its twelve sales territories into three types (A, B, and C), according to characteristics such as travel required, customer demographics, and product prices. A territory budget was formulated for each of the three types of territories. Lomand and Hanks were assigned to type A territories.

The Salesperson Performance Report had two purposes: (1) to compare the salesperson's performance with the budgeted performance, and (2) to show the salesperson's contribution margin. All expenses that could be associated with the salesperson's effort to generate and produce sales were included. Sales management and promotion expenses (including salaries) were charged to the salesperson according to the number of regular and special-handling orders sales personnel wrote. Special-handling orders required approximately twice as much administrative effort as regular orders; consequently, the charge for special-handling orders was double the charge for regular orders ($32 versus $16). The 198X rate was determined by dividing the amount budgeted for sales management salaries and sales promotion costs ($320,000) by the estimated total orders (regular, 18,000; special-handling, 1,000) weighted by the amount of administrative effort. Special-handling orders were approximately 5 percent of the total orders handled. The bases for allocating allocatable common expenses are shown in Figure 23.6.

Who is the better salesperson—Lomand or Hanks? The marketing cost analysis (Figure 23.5) shows that the contribution margin for Lomand is over $18,000 higher than that for Hanks, neither reaching the budgeted contribution margin (evidently because the realized price for metal units was $19/unit rather than the budgeted $20/unit). If the budgeted price for metal units is adjusted to

FIGURE 23.6 Bases for Allocating Common Expenses—
J. M. Dull Company

Expense	Allocation Basis for Analysis by Sales Territory
Sales management and promotion	
Regular orders	$16/Order (see text)
Special-handling orders	$32/order (see text)
Credit and collection expense	$2/order (total est. credit and collection expense divided by total est. # orders)
Packing and Shipping	Weight times number of units
Metal = 9 lb	
Plastic = 3 lb	

FIGURE 23.7 Comparative Performance Analysis

	Ben Lomand	Nancy Hanks
Gross margin (%)	34.70%	32.26%
Expense (%)	14.97%	15.72%
Contribution margin (%)	19.73%	16.54%
Average order size	$470	$388
Average cost per sales call	$100.43	$102.54
Travel and entertainment expense per sales call	$ 10.00	$ 15.00
Miles per sales call	26.67mi.	28mi.
Special handling/regular orders	4.00%	10.34%

$19, Lomand's contribution margin exceeds that budgeted by over $8,000 while Hanks's falls short by nearly $10,000.

What else can be said about the comparative performances of Lomand and Hanks? Figure 23.7 shows eight calculations of the sorts that interest sales executives. The gross margin, expense, and contribution margin percentages, all derived from the territory sales analyses, again demonstrate Lomand's superiority over Hanks. Lomand, too, sells larger orders per sales call at a lower cost per call and with less travel and entertainment expenses. Lomand travels fewer miles per sales call (this could imply room for improved route planning by Hanks). Lomand generates a smaller proportion of special-handling orders than does Hanks—special-handling orders require more managerial effort than do regular orders. These calculations and comparisons illustrate how to enrich the findings of marketing cost analyses.

CONCLUSION

Appropriately chosen control techniques contribute to the effectiveness of sales management. Periodic sales audits provide comprehensive appraisals of the total personal-selling operation, identifying areas of strength with potential for further exploitation and areas of weakness with potential for improvement. Sales analyses also detect strengths and weaknesses and are valuable for identifying situations where weaknesses (or strengths) are obscured by surface strengths (or weaknesses), that is, for analyzing iceberg situations. Marketing cost analysis goes beyond analysis of sales volume and probes selling expenses to determine relative profitability of particular aspects of sales operations. Sales audits, sales analyses, and marketing cost analyses are not "final ends" in themselves—the results of each are enriched by combining them with other techniques, such as ratios and percentage calculations. Effective sales executives continually scan the personal-selling operation for opportunities to exploit strengths and overcome weaknesses—control techniques contribute to scanning productivity.

Cases for Part IV

CASE 4-1

Midland Office Engineering

Manufacturer of Office Partitions and Equipment—Establishment of a Sales Budgeting Program

Fred Abbott, sales manager of Midland Office Engineering, was having difficulty convincing his boss, General Manager John Racklin, to accept his proposed sales budget. Although sales had increased 1 to 2 percent each of the past five years, Midland had experienced a steady decline in net profits. Abbott believed that it was his responsiblility to improve profits through cutting expenses and increasing efficiency, and he proposed the establishment of a sales budget to curb selling expenses, which he contended had gotten out of line. Although the company currently had no formal sales budgeting program, Abbott firmly believed that one was absolutely necessary if the sales operation was to contribute to the overall improvement of the firm's net profit picture.

Midland Office Engineering was started in Kansas City, Mo., in 1972 by Edward Hawkins, an architect/interior designer. He found that the materials available for office modernization and restructuring were inadequate in terms of flexibility, price, and appearance. Modular office partitions and furniture offered tremendous savings in down time and loss of productivity for the users of the offices and flexibility in terms of future changes. Existing modular materials were unimaginative and too expensive, in the opinion of Hawkins, so he designed his own line of equipment and established the Midland Company to produce and market it with co-founder John Racklin. The company had experienced an annual growth rate in sales of 15 to 20 percent during its first ten years. However, sales had stabilized somewhat over the past three years, averaging about 2.5 percent growth each year. During the same three years, net profits declined by more than 6 percent. In 1985 sales amounted to $12.4 million and yielded net profits of $243,00, or 1.96 percent of sales. This was down from a high of 8.4 percent profit in 1982.

Midland products were sold in twenty-eight states by a sales force of twenty-three persons who operated out of five branch sales offices. The sales force was paid on a straight-commission basis. Earnings ranged from $20,000 to over $35,000, with the average just under $26,000. Midland's sales force sold in forty-eight of the fifty largest metropolitan areas in the United States. The company estimated that it had captured 10 percent of the office modular equipment market.

Abbott's plan for establishing a sales budgeting program for the Midland sales department consisted solely of forecasts of sales expenses. He planned to determine the expenses involved in selling Midland products by scrutinizing the records of the branch offices and headquarters. He proposed to ask each of the five branch managers to submit itemized records of salespersons' salaries, traveling expenses, overhead and maintenance, clerical costs, and the costs of branch management and supervision. Abbott suggested that the itemized records include expenses for the previous year, the average for the past five years, and a forecast of expenses for the coming year. Combined with the branch office sales operating expenses were to be the expenses of the headquarters sales staff and sales management salaries and expenses, and all other costs attributable to the sales effort. The forecasts of the branch office and headquarters expenses for the coming year were to be combined to form the sales expense budget.

Abbott proposed to limit the sales budget exclusively to forecasts of sales expenses for at least three years. At that time, he expected to develop forecasts of sales volume and combine them with expense forecasts into a complete sales budget or projected statement of income and expense. It was Abbott's contention that the sales budgeting program must proceed slowly to gain acceptance and cooperation from everyone affected. Hence, he suggested a three-year interval between establishment of the sales expense budget and the sales budget complete with sales volume forecast.

The general manager, John Racklin, opposed having the company adopt any kind of sales budgeting procedure. He argued that sales budgets were nothing more than unreliable guesses and did not constitute a valid basis for executive action. He claimed that so many variables affected the forecasts of expenses and sales volume that the accuracy of any estimate was questionable. He also felt that any attempt to curb sales expenses through budgetary procedures would result in a reduction in the overall sales effort, harming both the company's sales and profits.

Abbott knew it was a complicated matter to establish a sales budget program. However, he felt it should and could be done despite the general manager's reluctance to accept the idea of a sales budget.

Whose side of the argument do you favor? Why?

Evaluate critically Abbott's proposal for a sales budgeting program for Midland Office Engineering Company.

CASE 4-2

Hanna File Corporation

Manufacturer of Filing Equipment—Variance Between Actual and Budgeted Performance

Michael Hanna was becoming increasingly concerned with his company's inability to keep within budgeted sales expenses. Hanna File Corporation manufactured and distributed a line of filing equipment and systems. The product line consisted of mechanized filing equipment, storage files, lateral files, insulated files, document conveyors, visible record cabinets, rotaries, posting trays, record safes, and file folders. The company had been organized in December 1982 by Michael Hanna, who had fifteen years' experience in a management capacity with one of the nation's leading office equipment makers. In each of the first three years of the company's existence, there had been considerable variation between budgeted sales expenses and actual expenditures.

During the nearly four years of operation, Hanna had increased the sales force as rapidly as qualified people could be hired so as to achieve a profitable volume of sales. At the end of 1983, Hanna File Corporation had six salespeople and a year later ten salespeople. By December 1985, a sales force of fourteen persons sold Hanna equipment over a six-state area (Pennsylvania, Ohio, West Virginia, Virginia, Indiana, and Kentucky). All the sales personnel reported directly to the company headquarters in Pittsburgh. Management planned to increase the market coverage gradually, with a ten-year goal of serving every state east of the Mississippi. Hanna was generally pleased that his firm was able to return a modest profit after only four years in operation, although it was slightly below his projected figure (see Exhibit 1). He foresaw an improved profit picture with each year's experience gained in managing the enterprise.

However, while things had been progressing reasonably well, one aspect of the business did cause considerable concern for Hanna, who served as company president, general manager, and chief financial officer. That concern related to the sales budget. For each of the first three years, actual performance varied markedly from budgeted performance. In each year, actual sales expenses were much higher than budgeted sales expenses. The magnitude of the variance was never known until the close of the fiscal year, at which time each performance center, including the sales department, submitted its report detailing actual performance data. These data then were compared with budgeted performance; as shown in Exhibit 1, Hanna suspected that the fourth fiscal year would again show a similar variance, although he would not know definitely until he received the final sales report. He believed that the sales manager should be held responsible for keeping actual sales performance in line with budgeted performance. He planned to arrange a conference with the sales manager for purposes of dis-

EXHIBIT 1 Hanna File Corporation
Sales Expense Budgets

	1983		1984		1985	
	Budget	Actual	Budget	Actual	Budget	Actual
Sales	4,000,000	2,892,003	6,500,000	4,985,500	9,000,000	7,214,998
	(100.00%)	(72.30%)	(100.00%)	(76.70%)	(100.00%)	(80.20%)
Sales compensation	120,000	118,450	195,000	191,203	270,000	265,213
	(3.00%)	(4.10%)	(3.00%)	(3.84%)	(3.00%)	(3.68%)
Sales bonuses	40,000	19,628	65,000	32,112	90,000	44,787
	(1.00%)	(0.68%)	(1.00%)	(0.64%)	(1.00%)	(0.62%)
Fringe benefits	17,600	16,977	28,600	27,514	40,000	38,975
	(0.44%)	(0.59%)	(0.44%)	(0.49%)	(0.44%)	(0.54%)
Travel expenses	56,000	58,429	91,000	93,743	125,000	132,045
	(1.40%)	(2.02%)	(1.40%)	(1.88%)	(1.40%)	(1.83%)
Sales administration	66,400	67,646	107,900	108,093	150,000	150,090
	(1.66%)	(2.34%)	(1.66%)	(2.17%)	(1.66%)	(2.08%)
Total selling expenses	300,000	280,948	487,500	452,665	675,000	631,110
	(7.00%)	(9.72%)	(7.50%)	(9.08%)	(7.50%)	(8.75%)
Net profit	400,000	(83,210)	650,000	(118,655)	900,000	370,130
	(10.00%)	(−2.87%)	(10.00%)	(2.38%)	(10.00%)	(5.13%)

cussing this situation prior to the preparation of the next sales budget. However, Hanna admitted that he did not know how to improve the situation.

The normal procedure for setting the sales budget was for Hanna first to estimate the probable dollar and unit sales and the expenses involved in obtaining them. Then, he called in the sales manager, Farah Benson, went over the budget with her item by item, giving his reasoning behind the estimates. Then, he asked the sales manager for comments and suggestions. Since she had not participated in the preparation of the budget, Benson found it difficult to make specific suggestions about details. The result of this meeting between Hanna and the sales manager was the final budget for the next fiscal year.

Benson felt that she should have the responsibility for establishing the sales budget. She complained that the several general suggestions she had made each year during the budget review meeting with Hanna had subsequently been ignored. According to the sales manager, the fact that each year the selling expenses were considerably higher than those budgeted by Hanna resulted from poor estimates that did not accurately reflect market and selling conditions. Benson believed that if she was to be held accountable for keeping actual performance in line with budgeted performance, she should have some voice in the setting of the budget. At the upcoming meeting, she planned to demand some authority in preparing the initial sales budget, subject to review by a budget committee, which she would recommend be established.

Does an examination of the budget figures provided in Exhibit 1 provide explanations for selling expenses above budget that may have been beyond the control of Benson, the sales manager?.

Evaluate the budgetary procedure employed by the Hanna File Corporation. Whose position do you favor? State your reasons.

CASE 4-3

Martin Packaging Company, Inc.[1]

Manufacturer of Packaging Products and Systems—
Use of Standard Costs

George Hannibal, manger of the Sales Department of the Martin Packaging Company, Inc., faced the task of evaluating the marketing and sales strategy implications of the proposed new method of using standard costs in budgeting sales costs. Because the averaging method currently in use provided very poor

[1]For background information, see Case 1-21 Martin Packaging Company, Inc. (A), pp. 166–169.

estimates for budgeting purposes, Grady Winkler, the Martin comptroller, proposed the adoption of standard costs.

MARTIN'S COST-CONTROL PROGRAM

Because of the very strong competition in the packaging and bottling industries, Martin management had found that careful cost control provided the difference between competitiveness and noncompetitiveness. To keep costs in line Martin had operated under fairly rigid budgets for the past decade. A continuing problem in the budgetary process had been the difficulty in estimating the various elements in selling costs. In the past, the accounting department had estimated selling costs by adding up the total selling costs in past months and dividing the total by the number of units of the product being sold. The resulting budgeted selling expenses bore little relationship to the actual expenses incurred and provided a continuing source of friction between George Hannibal and Grady Winkler. Winkler claimed that Hannibal and his sales force made little effort to stay within budgetary guidelines; Hannibal claimed that actual costs varied widely between salespeople in different regions. He argued that too rigid conformance to budget limits would reduce the ability of some of the salespeople to achieve sales goals.

Hannibal pointed out that he really had two sales forces, one selling in major urban areas to soft drink bottlers only, and another selling in all other markets to a broader group of bottlers. The selling expenses per dollar of sales for the thirty people in the nonurban sales force were higher than for the ten urban salespeople. Costs also varied with the size of the accounts being solicited. For these reasons variation from the budgeted averages was so great that the budget was of little value.

Winkler admitted that average costs had proven to be unsuitable for budgeting selling expenses. As an alternative he suggested using standard costs. Hannibal was highly suspicious of standard costs because of their apparent inflexibility in times of changing costs. However, he agreed to a test. After carefully observing the various tasks of salespeople in different markets, Winkler developed a set of standard costs that allowed for variations according to degree of urbanization and size of customer. The resulting budgeted expenses provided figures that were, in some cases, widely in variance from past performance of salespeople. As a consequence, Hannibal was doubtful of his ability to secure sales force cooperation and acceptance.

Explain why the new budgeted standard costs might be fairly accurate and yet vary from previous budget estimates.

What are the limitations of attempting to use standard costs in budgeting selling expenses?

How can George Hannibal explain the standard cost method to his sales force so as to obtain their acceptance of the proposed new method?

Evaluate Hannibal's claim that selling expenses change so rapidly that standard costs would always be out of date.

CASE 4-4

Driskill Manufacturing Company

Maintenance Equipment Manufacturer— Use of Quotas

Jack Dixon, sales manager, and Henry Granger, director of marketing research, of the Driskill Manufacturing Company, were in complete disagreement about the current method of preparing sales quotas.

The Driskill Manufacturing Company marketed a line of maintenance equipment used all over the country, in a variety of businesses, and had attained considerable prestige in the field. The company was comfortably successful, and its marketing effort showed no great sign of weakness. But the management, aware of external trends in motivation and control of sales personnel, and also aware of some internal friction among the sales staff, decided to scrutinize its motivation and compensation methods. Desiring the advantages of up-to-date knowledge and an unbiased point of view, Driskill engaged a management consulting firm specializing in selection, evaluation, compensation of employees, and management development to make a study of its existing practices.

The consulting firm discovered that Driskill's current compensation and motivation practices were the result of adjustments to meet change almost on an emergency basis rather than a result of long-term planning. The original plan, adopted a number of years ago, had been continually amended piecemeal, and adequate consideration had not been given to the effect of amendments upon other provisions or upon the plan's overall ability to promote the achievement of objectives. The result was a patchwork of policies, not an integrated program; it worked to the advantage of some sales personnel while inadvertently penalizing others.

Driskill knew that there was some dissatisfaction among the field sales force with its current practices and policies, but it did not know how strong this feeling was or how much it might affect sales. Recognizing that any new program was more likely to succeed if the sales force was given an opportunity to participate in its preparation, management emphasized that the private study would not be followed by a general announcement of sweeping changes. Instead, the study was to be based upon general cooperation and interest, involving carefully worked out changes.

The sales force welcomed the chance to have a say, and indicated approval of management's interest in their opinions. Many of the staff brought not only a spirit of interest but lists of subjects to discuss, having given considerable previous thought to the matter. Dissatisfactions were minor, often even unrecognized. The sales force generally agreed that the company's prices were competitive and that the product was one of quality, superior to competitors' in design and workmanship. Commission rates were generally satisfactory. Persons on straight commission felt, however, that an increase in commission rates on the new higher-priced equipment was due because of the greater selling effort required. But the staff on salary plus commission, who sold more of the lower-priced equipment, were not greatly concerned with the matter. The salary-plus commission personnel were mostly people with less than five years service with the company.

Approximately one-third of the sales force was paid on a straight-commission basis, receiving 7 percent on all sales and paying all their own expenses. These were the older salespeople, who had been with the company longest. The other salespeople were paid on a salary-plus-commission basis. New sales recruits were started at a salary of $18,000 and received semiannual increases on a merit basis. The average salary was $25,500. Every salaried salesperson was given an annual quota and received a commission of 4 percent on all sales above the quota. In addition, Driskill paid all selling expenses incurred by the salaried sales personnel; expenses averaged $700 per month per salesperson.

Earnings of the sales staff on a salary-plus-commission basis averaged $21,000. For example, R. C. Andersen, who had been selling for Driskill for five years, had a quota of $355,000 and received a salary of $18,500. Since his actual sales were $415,000, he earned a commission of $2,400, or a total income of $20,900. R. A. Scott, who had been selling for Driskill for fifteen years, was paid on a straight-commission basis. His gross earnings were slightly in excess of the average of $29,500 in gross income earned by the commission salespeople.

Since the commission sales personnel were generally more experienced, and since their incomes were directly related to their productivity, management had never felt it necessary to give them specific quotas or volume goals. Quotas for the salaried staff members were based on a running three-year average of each person's past sales. Arbitrary figures were selected for sales personnel who had not yet been three years on the job; these quotas represented a compromise between the experience of the salespeople formerly in the territory and the level of experience of the new person. Jack Dixon, the sales manager, believed that the basis for determining quotas was a satisfactory one. During the past ten years, 85 percent of the salaried sales staff had managed to exceed their quotas and earn some commission. In Dixon's opinion, therefore, the motivation was satisfactory to achieve maximum selling effort on the part of the sales force.

Henry Granger, the newly appointed director of marketing research, was less satisfied with the existing quotas. He claimed that any good salesperson could have exceeded quotas under conditions prevailing in recent years in the industry. He also believed that the existing system, based on past sales, merely tended to perpetuate past weaknesses. He suggested that future quotas be based upon a division of the annual forecast of sales among the individual territories and that the basis for division should be other than past sales.

Dixon supported the existing system, claiming that past sales had been an adequate basis for the establishment of quotas in the past. He held, furthermore, that if any new establishment of quota preparation were adopted, it should be based primarily on the buildup of sales estimates by the individual salespersons for the coming year.

If you were acting as a consultant for the Driskill Company, what recommendations would you make with respect to the preparation of quotas for the sales force?

How would you evaluate the arguments of the sales manager and the marketing research director?

CASE 4-5

Allied Board and Carton Company

Manufacturers of Containers—Difficulties with Quotas

The Allied Board and Carton Company manufactured and distributed cardboard boxes, cartons, and other packaging materials. The sales force of twenty-five persons, assigned to territories thoughout the United States, made calls directly on purchasing agents of manufacturers of industrial and consumer products. During the previous eighteen months, operating losses had been experienced, and a firm of management consultants had been retained to investigate the situation. The findings of the consulting firm indicated that the losses did not stem from manufacturing inefficiency, as previously believed, but rather from the fact that selling costs per order were significantly higher than for comparable companies in the industry. The problem, then, was to find ways to step up selling efficiency; management began its task by reviewing the methods used for compensating sales personnel, with a view toward uncovering a possible solution.

Salespeople were paid a base salary of $1,200 per month and a commission of 3 percent on sales over quota. The monthly quota was determined by adding the individual salesperson's expenses for the previous month to the $1,000 base salary and multiplying the result by 20. Since management was of the opinion that sales personnel would keep their expenses down to gain from the next month's lower quotas and increased expenses, this system of quota determination was designed to minimize selling expenses. Salespersons drove their own automobiles, but their expenses of operation were reimbursed at the rate of 25 cents per mile for the first 100 miles, 20 cents per mile for the next 100 miles, and 16 cents per mile for all miles over 200 travelled in any one month. Salespeople were not required to submit bills and receipts for expenditures made for rooms, meals, and incidentals. Reimbursements were made at the end of each month. Salespeople were allowed to draw monthly on anticipated commissions, and overdrawals were automatically wiped off the books at the close of the fiscal year.

At the close of each month, sales personnel submitted a report detailing the number of calls made, the number of presentations, and the number of orders written. At the same time, the monthly report of expenses was submitted. The credit department was responsible for approving all orders, but commissions were charged back against the salespersons when customers failed to pay their accounts.

Upon completing the review of the method of quota determination, management concluded that its effect was to increase, rather than decrease, selling expenses. As shown in Exhibit 1, a salesperson who managed to reduce his expenses by $200 in one month received an increase of only $120 in commissions the next month. Thus, sales personnel could make more money by increasing their expenses and quotas than they could by reducing expenses and working with lower quotas. Consequently, a new method of quota determination was adopted. The base for the new monthly quota was the previous year's sales for the corresponding month; this was adjusted to reflect changes in territorial potential, degree of competition relative to the previous year, and the salesperson's past performance.

At the same time, the expense-reimbursement procedure was changed. Now, before salespeople could receive reimbursements, they were required to substantiate their expenses by producing all bills and receipts. In addition, each

EXHIBIT 1 Effect of Method of Quota Determination on Sales Expenses

	Normal Expenses	Salesperson Receives		Increased Expenses
Salary	$ 1,000*	$1,000*	$1,000*	$ 1,000
Expenses	400	400	600	600
Total	1,400			1,600
	×20			×20
Quota	28,000			32,000
Monthly sales	36,000*			36,000*
Quota	28,000			32,000
Excess over quota	8,000			4,000
Commission rate	.03			.03
Commissions	$ 240	240	120	$ 120
Total income to salesperson		$1,620	$1,720	

*Constants used for purposes of illustration.

salesperson was provided with a predetermined amount each month, to be used for incidental expenses. Finally, the method of paying commissions was changed, with the objective of avoiding large fluctuations in the size of monthly paychecks. Salespeople were paid the same amount each month, based on the previous average monthly earnings of the individual. At the close of the year, total payments to sales staff were compared to the amounts actually earned through salary and commission. If actual earnings were in excess of the total paid to the salesperson, a check was made out for the difference. In the event that actual earnings were less than the amount paid, the salesperson was not required to make up the difference; his or her monthly check, however, was adjusted to reflect the new earning rate.

Evaluate the changes made in the method of quota determination of reimbursing sales expenses.

CASE 4-6

Goodtime Equipment Company

Manufacturer of Playground Equipment—Complaints About a Quota System and Proposal for a New Bonus System Based upon Quotas

The Goodtime Equipment Company, Minneapolis, was a medium-sized manufacturer of playground equipment. The company produced an extensive product line and marketed its products nationwide. The field sales force numbered thirty-five persons, who were paid on a salary basis. In addition to the salary plan, Goodtime Equipment Co. had a bonus program for its sales personnel, whereby they could earn extra pay for achieving and surpassing their quotas. Over the past several months, R. J. McNeil, the sales manager, had received two recurring complaints from salespeople dissatisfied with certain elements in the existing bonus program. The staff complained about their bonuses being paid on a once-a-year basis, preferring instead to have the payments spread out over the year. And, although roughly 80 percent of the sales force had received bonuses in the past, some complained about the difficulty in achieving quotas. Specifically, the salespeople felt that their assigned quotas were set too high, keeping them from earning larger bonuses.

McNeil believed that the complaint about the quota limit was probably nothing more than the usual griping from salespersons who thought that their quotas were too high. As a matter of company policy, the sales manager, in collaboration with the branch managers, set the quotas. Even though the sales staff were not consulted about the quota limits, McNeil felt strongly that the quotas were not only generous but also extremely fair. In defense of the fairness, he pointed out that each person's quota was set individually, based upon conditions unique to the territory. Therefore, he contended that the managers were bending over backwards to accomodate the sales staff.

Regarding the number of bonus payments to the salespeople, McNeil agreed that they had a legitimate complaint. Consequently, he carefully studied the situation, in consultation with his branch managers, and came up with what he believed to be an equitable solution. He prepared the following communication, designed to announce the new bonus program to the sales force.

PROPOSAL FOR NEW QUOTA-BONUS PROGRAM

It has been determined that our present bonus program is unsatisfactory. The new bonus program outlined below will take effect in time for the next fiscal year and will provide three major changes:

1. It will enable sales personnel to receive a bonus each quarter instead of yearly.
2. It will provide an extra incentive to exceed 100 percent of quota.
3. It will increase the payoff amount by $10 in each category.

To show the difference in the programs, the old program should be explained first.

Under the *old* program, each salesperson would receive a bonus at the end of each year if he or she exceeded 80 percent of yearly quota. The payoff was

1. 80–100% of quota = $30 per percentage point.
2. 101–110% of quota = $40 per percentage point.
3. 111–120% of quota = $50 per percentage point.
4. 121% and over of quota = $60 per percentage point.

Example

1. 95% of quota = 15 × $30, or $450.
2. 105% of quota = 20 × $30 = $600 + 5 × $40 = $200, or $800.
3. 115% of quota = 20 × $30 = $600 + 10 × $40 = $400 + 5 × $50 = $250, for a total of $1,250.

The *new* bonus program will have a payoff of

1. 80–100% = \$40.00 per percentage point.
2. 101–110% = \$50.00 per percentage point.
3. 111–120% = \$60.00 per percentage point.
4. 121–over% = \$70.00 per percentage point.

In addition to the higher rate of payoff, the bonus will be paid on a quarterly basis. This will be done on a quarterly averaging basis. An example of how this works is as follows.

1st quarter

146% of quota =	80–100%	= 20 × \$40.00	=	\$ 800.00
	101–110%	= 10 × \$50.00	=	\$ 500.00
	111–120%	= 10 × \$60.00	=	\$ 600.00
	120–146%	= 26 × \$70.00	=	\$1,820.00
				\$3,720.00

\$3,720.00 yearly bonus ÷ 4 = \$930.00 per quarter.
\$930.00 bonus paid for first quarter.

2nd quarter

114% of quota: to determine average rate, we add 146% + 114% = 260% ÷ 2 = 130% for two-quarter average.

130% of quota =	80–100%	= 20 × \$40.00	=	\$ 800.00
	101–110%	= 10 × \$50.00	=	\$ 500.00
	111–120%	= 10 × \$60.00	=	\$ 600.00
	121–130%	= 10 × \$70.00	=	\$ 700.00
				\$2,600.00

\$2,600.00 yearly bonus ÷ 4 = \$650 per quarter
\$650 × two quarters = bonus due for first two quarters of \$1,300. Since payment of \$930.00 was made in first quarter, we owe \$1,300.00 − \$930.00, or \$370.00 in second quarter.
\$370.00 bonus paid in second quarter.

3rd quarter

143% of quota: to determine average rate, we add 146% + 114% + 143% = 403% ÷ 3 = 134% average for three quarters.

134% of quota =	80–100%	= 20 × \$40.00	=	\$ 800.00
	101–110%	= 10 × \$50.00	=	\$ 500.00
	111–120%	= 10 × \$60.00	=	\$ 600.00
	121–134%	= 14 × \$70.00	=	\$ 980.00
				\$2,880.00

$2,880.00 yearly bonus ÷ 4 = $720.00 per quarter. $720.00 × three quarters = $2,160.00
$2,160.00 − $1,300.00 paid = $860.00
$860.00 bonus paid in third quarter.

4th quarter

138% of quota: to determine four-quarter average, we add 146% + 114% + 143% + 138% = 541% ÷ 4 = 135%. The yearly average is the same as it would have been under the old system.

135% of quota	=	80–100% =	20 × $40.00 =	$ 800.00
		101–110% =	10 × $50.00 =	$ 500.00
		111–120% =	10 × $60.00 =	$ 600.00
		121–135% =	15 × $70.00 =	$1,050.00
				$2,950.00

$2,950.00 is the yearly bonus. Fourth-quarter payment is $2,950.00 minus previous payments of $2,160.00, or $790.00.
Fourth-quarter bonus is $790.00
As an additional incentive, we are making an extra bonus available to those who exceed 100 percent of their quota. The payoff for this extra bonus will be

100–110% = $10 per percentage point
111–120% = $15 per percentage point
121% or over = $20 per percentage point

An example of this is as follows:

135% of yearly quota =	100–110% =	10 × $10.00 =	$100.00
	111–120% =	10 × $15.00 =	$150.00
	121–135% =	15 × $20.00 =	$300.00
			$550.00

This $550.00 will be paid in addition to the $2,950.00, for a grand total of $3,500.00 This shows an increase of $1,100.00 over the previous bonus program. It is roughly estimated that this new program will cost an additional $40.00 per $100.00 spent under the old system. Bonus payoffs under the new program are as follows:

Percent of Quota	Regular Bonus	Extra Bonus	Total Bonus
81	$ 40.00	—	$ 40.00
82	80.00	—	80.00
83	120.00	—	120.00
84	160.00	—	160.00
85	200.00	—	200.00
86	240.00	—	240.00

Percent of Quota	Regular Bonus		Extra Bonus		Total Bonus
87	280.00		—		280.00
88	320.00		—		320.00
89	360.00		—		360.00
90	400.00		—		400.00
91	440.00		—		440.00
92	480.00		—		480.00
93	520.00		—		520.00
94	560.00		—		560.00
95	600.00		—		600.00
96	640.00		—		640.00
97	680.00		—		680.00
98	720.00		—		720.00
99	760.00		—		760.00
100	800.00		—		800.00
101	850.00	+	$210.00	=	1,060.00
102	900.00	+	220.00	=	1,120.00
103	950.00	+	230.00	=	1,180.00
104	1,000.00	+	240.00	=	1,240.00
105	1,050,00	+	250.00	=	1,300.00
106	1,100.00	+	260.00	=	1,360.00
107	1,150.00	+	270.00	=	1,420.00
108	1,200.00	+	280.00	=	1,480.00
109	1,250.00	+	290.00	=	1,540.00
110	1,300.00	+	300.00	=	1,600.00
111	1,360.00	+	315.00	=	1,675.00
112	1,420.00	+	330.00	=	1,750.00
113	1,480.00	+	345.00	=	1,825.00
114	1,540.00	+	360.00	=	1,900.00
115	1,600.00	+	375.00	=	1,975.00
116	1,660.00	+	390.00	=	2,050.00
117	1,720.00	+	405.00	=	2,125.00
118	1,780.00	+	420.00	=	2,200.00
119	1,840.00	+	435.00	=	2,275.00
120	1,900.00	+	450.00	=	2,350.00
121	1,970.00	+	470.00	=	2,440.00
122	2,040.00	+	490.00	=	2,530.00
123	2,110.00	+	510.00	=	2,620.00
124	2,180.00	+	530.00	=	2,710.00
125	2,250.00	+	550.00	=	2,800.00

R. J. McNeil

What is your position regarding the way the quota limits were established?

Critically evaluate the proposal for a new bonus system. What changes, if any, would you suggest?

CASE 4-7

Augsberg-Wiesel, Ltd.

Manufacturer of Tableware—
Establishment of Sales Territories

COMPANY BACKGROUND

Augsberg-Wiesel, a manufacturer of fine chinaware since 1823, was located in Dortmund, Germany. The company was started by Herman Wiesel, formerly a potter for the court of Bavaria. The firm was operated by succeeding generations of the family until 1957 when it went public. Until the mid-twentieth century, Augsberg-Wiesel manufactured only products of china. Its fine chinaware and ceramic figures were known and admired throughout Europe. After the Wiesel family gave up control of the firm, the new management embarked on a program of broadening product lines and markets. Although the lines of figurines and the traditional patterns of chinaware were retained, new product lines were introduced to serve new markets. Several contemporary patterns of chinaware were developed to compete in a market formerly largely served by Scandinavian firms. In addition, a line of stainless steel tableware and hollowware in contemporary designs was introduced to support the contemporary china.

COMPANY SALES OPERATIONS

Prior to 1965, Augsberg china tableware was distributed only in major German markets, although individual importers had purchased parts of the line for sale in several other European markets. In 1965 the company moved aggressively into other markets. Sales offices were established in London, Paris, Amsterdam, Rome, and Madrid. By 1975, the line was available in most major European cities. Management had consistently followed a policy of selective distribution, restricting outlets to only the most prestigious retailers of such products in the major cities and, usually, to only a single outlet in smaller towns and cities.

In 1982, Augsberg made its first formal entry into the American market. An American marketing subsidiary was opened in New York City in March 1982 under the management of Wilfred Frank, formerly regional sales manager of Syracuse China of Syracuse, New York. He was chosen from among a number of applicants because of his familiarity with the American market for chinaware. He launched a promotional campaign designed to achieve national distribution within two years. By December 1984, Frank had hired six salespeople, two working out of the New York office and one each in Chicago, Dallas, San Francisco, and Atlanta. Following the home office policy of selective distribution, the American sales force sought out leading retailers of fine china and flatware among the department stores and specialty stores in each important metropolitan area. Frank's goal was to achieve distribution in all of the fifty largest markets in the United States. During 1984 the sales representatives concentrated their efforts on markets close to their operating bases, but by mid-1985 dissension had begun to arise over territorial jurisdiction. Until this time no territorial boundaries had been established. Bill (Tex) Jackson, the Dallas representative, was an aggressive salesperson, and by June had opened accounts in Tulsa, Oklahoma City, and Kansas City. Greg Watson, the Chicago representative, complained that Kansas City was clearly a part of the Chicago territory. Tex had also expanded eastward into Little Rock and Memphis to the dismay of the Atlanta representative.

The complaints from both the Chicago and Atlanta sales reps that Tex Jackson was infringing on their territories convinced Frank that something should now be done about establishing clearly defined territories. He felt that the six salesmen were about right to cover the American market, but the problem was to divide it so as to give each salesperson an approximately equal opportunity. The two salespeople covering the Northeast both operated out of his New York City office. They had essentially dividied the market into the area north and south of New York City, but customers in the city and many others in the close vicinity had been chosen on a first-come, first-served basis with Frank acting as a referee. Frank believed that Atlanta, Dallas, Chicago, and San Francisco were located fairly centrally for their respective regions.

A bigger problem, after roughly dividing the national market into six territiories, was to decide where the dividing lines should be set between the territories. Mr. Frank identified four territorial characteristics that he believed should be taken into consideration in establishing territories: potential, work load, concentration, and dispersion. Ideally, he felt that each territory should have approximately the same sales potential, that is, the number of retail outlets and potential customers should be equal. The territory work load was defined operationally as the number of accounts to be serviced. It should take the sales rep approximately the same amount of time to service a small retail account in Dayton, Ohio, as to service Marshall Fields in Chicago. Concentration, or the degree to which potential is available in the larger accounts in the territory, should in Frank's opinion have a significant positive relationship to sales performance.

Wilford Frank recognized that the impact of each of these factors could vary with the circumstances. Although the potential might be the same between two markets, regional preferences might give Augsberg products a decided advantage or disadvantage over competitive products. Work load between apparently similar accounts might vary because one account expected less service than the other. A retailer located in Spokane, Washington, simply was not accustomed to as frequent service as an account located in San Jose, California. Also, the fact that some accounts were concentrated in densely populated urban areas would mean that all the competitors were spending more time in servicing these accounts, and the sales rep willing or able to service the more dispersed accounts might get better results from the time spent. Also, the more widely dispersed accounts might be serviced at least partially through the use of telephone or other indirect approaches.

Is the present rough division of the American market for Augsberg products satisfactory? What changes might be made?

Evaluate the relative importance of the four territory characteristics to the market for Augsberg products? How could you weight them in importance?

CASE 4-8

McKay Clothing Company

Manufacturer of Work Clothes and Outerwear— Determination of Sales Territories

The McKay Clothing Company of Dallas, Texas, a regional manufacturer of work clothes and outerwear, had marketed its product line profitably since 1887 and had gradually obtained sales in the Southwestern states of Oklahoma, Arkansas, Louisiana, and New Mexico. Bryant A. Meeks, the sales manager, had become concerned with the allocation of sales territories among the sales personnel; he asked Jim Carsdale, his assistant, to study the potential of the company's market and recommend an improved system.

McKay's work clothes accounted for approximately 65 percent of total sales volume. Dungarees, several styles of overalls, and items such as aprons were produced and sold under the McKay label. Both the company and its retailers considered the work clothes line to be complete. The company offered its retailers more than thirty styles of dungarees, most of which had extremely good consumer acceptance, primarily because of the company's policy of producing a quality, full-cut product that would not bind or pinch the wearer. Attention to style was also considered to be a contributing factor in the company's success with work clothes. A portion of the line was restyled each year and distinctive features, such as bib pockets and elastic straps on carpenter's overalls, were stressed on each garment. In spite of competition from four other regional and two national producers, many of the McKay lines were estimated to have between 30 and 40 percent of the market within their sales area.

Outerwear, lightweight jackets, ski clothes, and hunting attire constituted the remaining 35 percent of the company's sales volume. The lightweight jackets were suitable for casual wear and could easily be distinctively modified for club and group use. The line of hunting clothes, which included a complete selection of gunning apparel, was made in weights that would be comfortable in the generally warm Southwest. The outerwear line tended to be more highly styled than the work clothes, although primary attention was given to quality, comfort, and practicality. McKay had more national and regional competitors in the outerwear field, but some of the company's products held a sizable share of the market in its selling area.

The company relied heavily on its reputation with consumers to sell its products. Both the work clothes and outerwear lines were promoted exclusively through point-of-sales material. However, promotion of the two lines had been differentiated because of the two separate consumer groups who purchased them. Point-of-sale material for work clothes typically stressed ease of upkeep, distinctive features, durability, and union label. Outerwear promotion emphasized comfort, workmanship efficiency, and consumer satisfaction. When styling a new product, the company usually made the garment and then priced it. However, if it became apparent that a new garment could not be produced at a competitive price without stinting quality and comfort, it was never marketed.

McKay sold its products exclusively to individual retailers and small chains. The company's accounts varied in size from small country stores to metropolitan department stores, and when establishing accounts, the company's principal concern was the buyer's credit standing and potential sales volume. Samples were shown to retailers, and the orders were then placed with the factory. The company shipped all merchandise F.O.B. factory. Work clothes were stocked at the factory, and delivery time was typically forty-eight hours. Outerwear, however, usually had to be manufactured to order, requiring a delivery time of one to three months. Consequently, dealers usually placed large orders at the beginning of the season. Service was considered important by the retailers, and the company tried to arrange its sales territories to provide it.

In the opinion of Meeks, the present sales force of five was clearly inadequate to give the kind of service demanded by retail customers. The present sales territories had been set up somewhat arbitarily as the company's market grew. One salesperson was assigned to New Mexico and West Texas, one to northern Texas, one to southern Texas and the Gulf Coast area, one to Louisiana, and one to Arkansas and Oklahoma. The market potential, and therefore the work load, for the sales personnel in the five territories was very unequal. Meeks wanted to add three additional salespeople and redivide the market into territories of approximately equal potential.

The first decision facing Jim Carsdale in setting up new territories was the selection of a basic geographical unit. Metropolitan areas seemed inappropriate for the sparsely populated area in the western section of the market. Therefore, it seemed sensible to use either trading areas or counties. He was somewhat troubled to discover the variation in size of counties in the states involved. For example, New Mexico, with 121,000 square miles of land area, had only 32 counties, whereas Texas, with only slightly more than twice the land area (262,000 square miles), had 254 counties. Finally his recommendations to Meeks were that the company use counties as the basic geographical unit, and that they use the *Sales and Marketing Management* Annual Index of Buying Power to measure the market potential in each county.

Do you agree with Carsdale's choice of a basic geographical unit?

Does the Sales and Marketing Management Index of Buying Power include all the important factors necessary to measure the market potential for work clothes and outerwear?

Using a current Index of Buying Power, divide the McKay market into eight territories, taking into consideration geographic and other pertinent influences.

CASE 4-9

Marquette Frozen Foods Company

Manufacturer of Frozen Foods— Design of Sales Territories

The Marquette Frozen Foods Company manufactured a wide line of frozen foods sold directly to all types of food stores. The company's 100 salespeople worked out of thirty-five district sales offices located throughout the United States. Annual sales were nearly $50 million. Although the sales picture was quite favorable, certain recent developments indicated a possible need for redesign of sales territories.

Sales territories were established using population as the base and were composed of one or more counties, depending on each county's population. The aim was to assign each salesperson to a territory containing about 1 percent of the country's total population. Since total population was approximately 205 million (exclusive of Alaska and Hawaii), an attempt was made to assign each person a territory consisting of about 2,050,000 people. Population statistics were obtained from the U.S. Bureau of the Census and were modified according to local area statistics.

The method of territory design was illustrated by the Northeast I sales territory, including Maine, New Hampshire, and part of Massachusetts. The Northeast I territory included the following Maine counties, along with their populations: Aroostook, 95,000; Piscataquis, 16,000; Penobscot, 125,000; Androscoggin, 91,000: Cumberland, 193,000: Franklin, 22,000; Hancock,

35,000; Kennebec, 95,000; Knox, 29,000; Lincoln, 21,000; Oxford, 43,000; Sagadahoc, 23,000; Somerset, 41,000; Waldo, 23,000; Washington, 30,000; and York, 112,000. Maine population: 994,000.

The following New Hampshire counties and their populations were included: Belknap, 32,000; Carroll, 19,000; Cheshire, 52,000; Coos, 34,000; Grafton, 55,000; Hillsborough, 224,000; Merrimack, 81,000; Rockingham, 139,000; Stratford, 70,000; and Sullivan, 31,000. New Hampshire population: 737,000.

Finally, the following Massachusetts towns were included to increase the sales territory population to the desired figure (the first six towns listed were in Essex County, while the last two were in Middlesex County); Amesbury, 13,000; Newburyport, 18,000; Haverhill, 46,000; Lawrence, 67,000; Salem, 41,000; Marblehead, 21,000; Tewksbury, 23,000; and Lowell, 95,000. Massachusetts population: 321,000. Total population in Maine, New Hampshire, and parts of Essex and Middlesex counties in Massachusetts: 2,055,000.

Analyses of population statistics were made every three years. When warranted by population changes, sales territories were redesigned; however, most changes were minor. The company supplied each salesperson with a detailed map showing the counties in his or her territory, the cities and towns, population, and the exact territorial boundaries. This was done to prevent misunderstandings as to territorial assignments and to ensure a salesperson's exclusive rights to a given territory.

The Marquette sales manager had proposed and received acceptance of this method of determining sales territories several years ago. He favored this procedure because it guaranteed equal territories and similar sales opportunities for all company sales personnel and therefore eliminated an important cause for poor morale. With total population divided evenly, it was easy to compare relative performances of the sales force. Total population was an accurate estimate of potential demand, according to the sales manager, because everyone was a potential customer for frozen foods. In addition, he said that the simplicity and economy of this approach made it even more desirable.

Careful analysis of a number of call reports, however, confirmed the sales manager's suspicions that many salespeople were "skimming the cream" or concentrating on the larger and easier-to-sell accounts, neglecting altogether a substantial number of prospects. Consequently, he concluded that territorial coverage was unsatisfactory. He believed that this situation could be remedied by reducing the size of the territories, permitting more intensive coverage.

The sales manager was aware that there were many reasons why reduction of the size of sales territories was difficult to implement. First, the sales personnel would feel that something was being taken away from them; in some cases they would lose accounts they had cultivated over a long period. The result was a possible morale problem. Second, high costs were involved in redesigning sales territories. Third, there would be a need to hire additional salespeople to cover the new sales territories. Fourth, someone would have to convince the sales force that the changes were in the best interests of the sales staff, the company, and the customers. It would be essential to secure the sales force's acceptance of the new plan.

Since substantial problems were associated with reducing the sizes of the sales territories, the Marquette sales manager was still undecided whether to redesign the present sales territories.

Evaluate Marquette's method of designing the sales territories—strengths and weaknesses. Should the company reduce the size of its territories?

CASE 4-10

McBride Electric Corporation

Manufacturer of Electric Equipment Accessories— Need for Revision of Sales Territories

McBride Electric Corporation, headquartered in Detroit, was a large producer of electrical equipment and accessories. Organized in 1910, McBride grew steadily and became one of the major U.S. suppliers of electrical products. McBride sold some of its products direct to a few large accounts, but most of the product line was sold through a nationwide network of distributors. The thirty-five person field sales force, working out of eight district offices, was assigned territories that had been established along county lines. In recent years, it had become increasingly clear that a need existed for redesigning the sales territories.

Sales personnel had been assigned responsibility for covering a varying number of counties in a way that gave each as close to one thirty-fifth of the total number of distributive outlets as possible. Management had adopted this procedure for establishing sales territories because of a desire to assure equal sales opportunity for each salesperson. Management had also been convinced that this procedure would facilitate comparisons among salespeople's performances.

With the expansion of McBride's business, there was no modification in the design of the sales territories. Some salespeople, as a result, found themselves with so much sales potential in their territories that it was impossible for them to provide adequate sales coverage. Although this situation had come to management's attention several years ago, essentially nothing had been done to improve territorial design. Management, however, had submitted a revision plan to the sales force a few years ago. This plan, which would have resulted in increasing the size of some territories and decreasing the size of others, caused so much friction among the sales staff that management backed off in the interest of maintaining high sales force morale.

Recent analysis showed that this situation was becoming increasingly serious. Investigation into the coverage of representative territories revealed that salespeople were concentrating on the easy-to-sell, high-volume accounts and were neglecting numerous good prospects. Consequently, many potential orders were going unwritten. Thus, McBride's competitors were gaining accounts that, under normal circumstances, the company should have secured. Furthermore, most territories were receiving uneven sales coverage.

Several factors had combined to create this situation. The nature of competition had changed substantially from area to area. In some territories, previously competitive environments became a salesperson's dream as competition disappeared for one reason or another. In other territories, ones where competitors in the past had been weak, other competitors had become firmly rooted, thereby making it necessary for McBride sales personnel to cover those areas more intensively and more frequently to just maintain a token share of the business. Therefore, some areas in certain territories received virtually no coverage by the McBride sales staff. Besides shifts in the strength of competition, economic conditions had changed from territory to territory making certain once-desirable territories considerably less profitable for the salespeople to cover. These market influences indicated that management should expand some territories and shrink others.

The vice-president of sales and the sales manager agreed that the situation had gotten out of hand. They both believed that the present territorial setup needed reviewing and possible revision to improve sales efficiency and sales control. They also agreed that more appropriate territorial design could help to minimize the friction among sales personnel that would, in all likelihood, appear when management announced its intention to revise sales territories. Both executives had further agreed that the two criteria for an improved territorial design pattern would be (1) lower selling costs and (2) increased sales volume.

Should McBride Electric Corporation have revised its sales territories? Why or why not? If you feel that the company should have changed its sales territories, outline in detail the procedure that should have been followed.

CASE 4-11

Burton Computer Technology

Computer Supply Firm— Marketing Cost Analysis

Ann Jackson, the new sales manager of Burton Computer Technology, was concerned that the sales force was not making the most efficient use of its time. Burton manufactured and sold a line of computer supplies and support equipment in Chicago and the surrounding area. The most important items in the line were floppy disks and computer paper. However, the line included almost any kind of supplies needed by the user of microcomputers. The sales force, consisting of six people, called directly on commercial users of computers and on computer supply stores. Jackson's predecessor had exercised almost no control over the activities of sales personnel. The market had been roughly divided into six sales territories, and each sales rep was given a sales quota, but no attempt had been made to direct sales efforts among prospective customers and between products in the line.

One of Jackson's first actions was to set up a marketing planning committee to review sales operations and to formulate a sales plan for the coming year. The committee's first order of business was to conduct marketing costs analyses according to size of account and type of product. The product line consisted of four broad categories: paper, disks, computer furniture and support equipment, and a new line, electronic boards used to increase the capacity of personal computers. Jackson believed that marketing cost analysis was essential because it permitted determination of the relative profitability of various aspects of the company's sales operations, and it also covered areas in which changes made in the new sales and marketing plan could result in improved performance.

At the request of the marketing planning committee, the accounting department made available the data presented in Exhibits 1-4.

EXHIBIT 1

Size of Account (annual purchases)	Number of Accounts	Number of Orders	Total Sales
Under $500	610	2,300	$ 338,000
$501–$1,000	1,540	6,500	595,000
$1,001–$2,000	830	5,400	957,000
Over $2,000	290	3,600	1,120,000
Total	3,270	17,800	$3,010,000

EXHIBIT 2

Size of Account (annual purchases)	Sales by Product				
	Paper	Disks	Furniture	Boards	Total Sales
Under $500	$ 98,000	$ 126,800	$ 78,100	$ 35,100	$ 338,000
$501–$1,000	170,000	206,200	131,200	87,500	595,000
$1,001–$2,000	320,100	335,000	195,800	106,100	957,000
Over $2,000	375,000	385,500	227,000	132,500	1,120,000
Total	$963,200	$1,053,500	$332,100	$361,200	$3,010,000

EXHIBIT 3

	Paper	Disks	Furniture	Boards
Cost of sales	$491,232	$558,355	$303,408	$266,152
Advertising	$ 50,000	$ 53,000	$ 48,000	$ 35,000
Number of shipping units sold	481,600	263,375	63,210	18,060
Weight per shipping unit	6 oz	6 oz	6 oz	7 oz

EXHIBIT 4 Selling and Administrative Expenses

Sales salaries	$205,129
Sales traveling expenses	69,078
Sales office variable expense	20,077
Sales commissions (3.2 percent of sales)	96,320
Warehousing	15,008
Packing and shipping	31,542
Credit management	35,871
Direct-mail advertising	92,000
Billing and miscellaneous bookkeeping	70,665
General selling, administrative, and other expenses	450,000
Total	$1,086,390

Develop a statement of profit and loss with analysis of selling costs by size of account. Do the same by type of product.

Analyze the data and develop a set of recommendations for Burton Company management to improve its profit picture with respect to account size and product lines.

CASE 4-12

Magnet Covet Barium Corporation

Producer of Oil Drilling Mud— Sales Region Ceases to Contribute Adequately to Profit

Magnet Covet Barium Corporation (Magcobar), a producer of oil drilling mud, was having trouble with the performance of its Midwest region. The products sold by Magcobar were used by oil producers to aid in drilling oil wells. The line consisted of over twenty-five mud products. On its role of customers were such big corporations as Exxon, Gulf, Texaco, and Mobil. It also sold its products to smaller companies, such as Hunt Oil, Sunray DX, Adams Petroleum Corporation, and even to smaller operators, such as drilling specialty firms located close to a concentration of oil fields.

Magcobar had experienced a steady growth in its twenty-five-year history. Its products were sold nationally as well as in many foreign countries. The American market was organized into regions, and the foreign market was under a separate import-export division.

The basis used for dividing the United States into regions was the concentration of oil production in various areas. For example, there was a large amount of oil-producing activity in southern Louisiana, and this area constituted the company's largest region from the standpoint of sales, warehouses, and inventories. The following table lists the company's nine regions and indicates the general coverage of each:

Region 00—Independent dealers	4 districts
Region 10—Texas	3 districts
Region 20—Illinois-Ohio area	3 districts
Region 30—Midcontinent (Oklahoma, Arkansas)	3 districts
Region 40—Kansas-Missouri	3 districts
Region 50—California-Alaska	3 districts
Region 60—Rocky Mountain area	3 districts
Region 70—South Louisiana	2 districts
Region 80—Foreign division	4 districts

These regions and districts covered the major areas where mud products were needed because drilling activities were being carried on there. Each region was divided into districts, and within each district the company maintained its own warehouses or leased space in public warehouses. The division into districts was based upon the number of ultimate users of the product, expected sales, and the number of warehouses needed to cover the area. A regional manager was in charge of each region. The district managers, who were responsible to the regional managers, were in charge of sales engineers and warehousers. The sales engineers advised customers on the right type of Magcobar product needed to drill each oil well successfully and without complications. Since these requirements varied from well to well, the sales engineers found it necessary to visit the drilling sites frequently.

The warehouses were the distribution points that maintained stocks of mud for quick delivery to users. Magcobar management believed adequate warehouse facilities were a very important element in the success of their business. Transporting their product long distances overland resulted in very high transportation costs. It was necessary to locate within a short distance of the concentration of the oilfields. The actual number of warehouses within a district or region depended upon the concentration of oil activity. Each warehouse kept an adequate inventory on hand to supply the needs of customers immediately—usually all twenty-five products were stocked, in varying quantities. The company considered an inventory turnover of four to be average. The inventory section of the accounting department at the home office kept monthly records of stock on hand in each region, district, and warehouse. The warehouses sent in monthly stock reports of material on hand and monthly records of sales receipts. Each region, district, and warehouse was visited at least once a year by an auditor, who checked inventory on hand against the records at the home office.

At the end of the current fiscal year, the company was faced with a regional problem. Region 40, the Kansas-Missouri area, was incurring high costs and disproportionately low sales. However, inventory turnover in the region was above average. Magcobar was servicing many accounts in the area but was not making a very good profit. In previous years the region had done well in inventory turnover, sales, and efficiency of operations. But in the past two years, sales declined to the point where operating costs in the region were not even covered. The marketing manager could not understand what was happening, because inventory turnover was still quite adequate. The company had important accounts in the region and did not want to abandon it; large capital investments were also tied up in the area. The personnel in charge of the region had been with the company for some time and were very upset about the recent trends.

In addition to the Magcobar warehouses, there were a number of independent dealers. These dealers were specialty firms, and they were supplied with mud products by Magcobar. They, in turn, sold these products to the drilling companies. These dealers made up a large part of the regional volume.

Magcobar was faced with a major decision, since management did not want to continue serving a region that was showing an inadequate contribution to profit. The sales manager felt that there were three alternative solutions: (1) they could shut down the area and write off the loss, (2) they could supply the independent dealers but shut down the company warehouses, and (3) they could merge Region 40 with another adjoining region to reduce overhead expenses.

The decision required a balancing, not only of monetary factors, but of human factors as well.

In your opinion, what decision should Magcobar have made concerning Region 40. Can you think of an alternative?

CASE 4-13

Arlington Paper Mills

Manufacturer of Paper Products—
Decision to Discontinue Sales to Accounts
with Unacceptable Profit Margins

John W. Ireland, sales manager for the Baby Products Division of Arlington Paper Mills, manufacturer of baby diapers and other baby products, faced a decision on what to do with a number of baby-diaper accounts that had fallen below the "acceptable" profit margin. Since most of the accounts in question returned some profit, he was reluctant to write off these customers just because they did not reach the level of return desired by management. In the past, he had been willing to discontinue sales to those accounts that fell below the acceptable profit margin, but his position had changed during the past year because of the decline in demand for Arlington Comfy diapers. Ireland had strong opposition in this matter from Maurice Conte, vice-president of sales, who had been the prime mover in establishing return-on-profit criteria four years previously.

Arlington Paper Mills, founded in late 1910, was located in Tuscaloosa, Alabama. Over the years, Arlington had acquired three paper companies and grew to an annual overall sales volume of $75 million. Originally, the company had produced only paper bags, but, through acquisitions, it had expanded the product line to include a large array of paper items. The Baby Products Division, organized in the 1950s, manufactured and sold a line of baby diapers, crib linens, bibs, and related items. Baby diapers constituted the single biggest item in the Baby Products Division product line, accounting for $16 million of the division's total sales of $21 million.

Arlington made diapers on machines that had been developed and patented by the company. The company had been an industry leader in the development of moisture proof and absorbent materials for diapers.

Arlington Paper diapers were distributed nationwide by a sales force of twenty-four persons plus one selling agent. The twenty-four company salespeople sold directly to retail outlets and hospitals. The company sales personnel were salaried and averaged about $22,000 in earnings, excluding bonuses. In addition to distributing its products to retailers and hospitals, Arlington also sold its diapers to Army and Air Force exchanges and Navy ship stores. These sales were handled by a commission selling agent who sold exclusively to the military.

The major competition for Arlington's Baby Products Division came from Procter and Gamble's Pampers Division and Scott Paper Company. Both promoted their lines of baby products heavily. In addition, there was competition from numerous other manufacturers in the baby products line. Arlington's prices were roughly the same as its competition. Selling prices to retailers averaged 16 percent over production cost.

During the past year and a half, an investigation had been made of the profitability of baby-diaper accounts. This investigation was part of an overall revenue cost analysis in the Baby Products Division, and its starting point had been the baby-diapers product line, which accounted for the largest sales volume in the division. The investigation revealed that over 18 percent of the company's 3,215 baby-diaper accounts (585) fell below the profit goal set by management. Of these 585 accounts, 68, or about 12 percent, were clearly unprofitable (this represented a fraction over 2 percent of the total 3,215 baby-diaper accounts). The remaining 517 accounts, although yielding a profit, were nevertheless below management's profit return standards and therefore were considered accounts with unacceptable profit margins.

Although company policy dictated the dropping of all accounts with unacceptable profit margins, Ireland contended that certain factors made it logical either (1) to revise the acceptable-unacceptable profit margin standards in view of changing market conditions or (2) to make exceptions to the policy for a period of time to combat the decline in demand for baby diapers. He pointed out that something had to be done soon, because overall demand for baby diapers had declined and Arlington had lost nearly 200 accounts in the past two years.

The two major reasons for the drop in demand were, according to Ireland, the declining birth rate and the stiff competitive pressures in the disposable paper diapers industry, led by names such as Pampers and Kimbies. The birth rate and competitive factors combined to lead the firm's economic experts to project a drop in demand over the next five years. Besides these conditions, Ireland argued that, regardless of any idealistic standards desired by management, the simple fact that an account was profitable should be sufficient reason to keep it, even if it was below the desired level. There was always the opportunity to do something about increasing the profitability of accounts. Discontinuation of an account, however, meant the loss of this opportunity.

Conte, the vice-president, was adamant in his opposition to Ireland's suggestion for some sort of change in the profit margin policy. He thought that a program for discontinuing accounts with unacceptable profit margins should be initiated without delay. He maintained that the profit margin policy had resulted from his spending a great deal of time and effort in a thorough analysis of the situation. And he argued that under no circumstances should the policy be changed after being in effect such a short period of time. He also said that he was not at all convinced that the outlook for market and economic conditions was as gloomy as Ireland believed. Consequently, he indicated that he would strongly oppose any attempt by Ireland to have the profit margin policy changed.

Thoroughly evaluate the arguments of Ireland and Conte. Whose position do you favor? Why?

Should Arlington Mills have discontinued sales to baby-diaper accounts with unprofitable margins even though they yielded some profit? Justify your stand.

CASE 4-14

Alderson Products, Inc.

Packaging Equipment Manufacturer— Control of the Sales Effort

Alderson Products, Inc., a $15 million company, had recently become a wholly owned subsidiary of National Beverage Corp. of Baltimore, Maryland. National had purchased 100 percent of Alderson stock. The acquisition brought with it a number of problems common to such ventures, with the most pressing problems centering around the control of the sales effort.

Alderson Products, Inc., produced and sold packaging equipment exclusively to the soft drink industry. The company, located in Detroit, was established in 1951 by the Alderson brothers, Jim and Frank, both of whom had worked for General Motors for several years but who wanted to be in business for themselves. After a five-year search while they were still working at GM, they decided to enter the packaging equipment industry when an opportunity came up to buy out a small bottle capping machine producer. For the first year of operation, Alderson produced only a limited line of bottle capping machinery. However, gradually at first and then more rapidly, the Alderson product line was expanded to include capping machines, decapping machines, bottle lifters, case painters, case rebanding equipment, parts, lubricants, blenders, fillers, water-coolers, carbonators, saturators, packers, decasers, washers, water treatment systems, conveyors, rinser load tables, warmers, water chillers, and refrigeration units. Most of the equipment bearing the Alderson name was manufactured by the company itself. Some equipment was purchased from other makers: the cappers and decappers came from the Zalkin Corp. (France), the bottle washers from Firton Manufacturing (Pennsylvania), rinser and warmers from Southern Tool (Louisiana), water chillers from Dunham Bush (Georgia), and the refrigeration units came from Vilter Manufacturing Company (Wisconsin).

The products offered by Alderson came in several different sizes to match the various different applications in the soft drink industry. In addition to the new products manufactured or purchased by Alderson, the company sold used equipment and machinery. The company got into used equipment after finding that a large number of its customers were too small to afford new equipment and could not perform extensive maintenance and repairs on their present equipment.

The market for used equipment grew to the point where it contributed 30 percent of Alderson's net sales. Most of the used sales were from rebuilt machinery. Alderson bought the used machinery from bottlers, brought it to Detroit, reconditioned it, and sold it. Other used machinery was sold "as is." This was machinery that was bought in acceptable operating condition and required minor modifications or repairs. Usually, the "as is" machinery was transported to the buyer directly from its original location.

The "rebuilt" phase of the business called for the customer to make a 25 percent deposit on the order before the particular unit went through the shop. Once in the shop, the equipment was dismantled to its basic components and parts were added as required. The customer ended up with a "like new" machine or piece of equipment. Savings to the customers were typically about 30 percent compared with a new unit. Alderson's rebuilt equipment carried a warranty. As an additional service, Alderson tried to maintain an adequate stock of spare parts for older units, even if the original manufacturer no longer made them available. There was some concern among management as to the future of the rebuilt equipment part of the business. About two years ago, the company began experiencing difficulty in acquiring used equipment that could be rebuilt. The supply of older units was dwindling, and competition for the used equipment was forcing prices up considerably. Alderson also found that more and more bottlers were reconditioning their own units. Although it constituted a profitable segment of the overall operation, there was some thought that it might be best for Alderson to get out of the used equipment business and concentrate on its growing business for new machinery and equipment.

Alderson served only the soft drink industry, despite the suitability of the company's products and services for other industries, such as the beer or fruit juice producers. No attempt had been made to branch out into the other markets, largely because the Alderson brothers felt they knew the soft drink industry best. The company served primarily local and regional bottlers; however, plans were underway to increase coverage to national and, possibly, international markets. Future expansion plans did not include markets outside the soft drink industry.

Distribution of Alderson products was through two company salespersons and six manufacturers' representatives. Both salespersons were paid straight salaries. One salesperson spent about one-fourth of his time appraising and procuring used equipment. The other salesperson spent about one quarter of his time piloting the company airplane. The representatives received a commission for their services, according to the following schedule: 5 percent for the first $50,000, 2.5 percent for the next $50,000 (up to $100,000) and 1 percent for anything over $100,000. This was based on individual sales. The representatives received a sales commission on any sale in their territory, regardless of whether the company (Alderson) or the representative closed the sale.

In addition to using personal selling, Alderson promoted its products through advertising, trade conventions, and direct mail. Alderson advertised in six trade publications, averaging one insertion every two months in each of the journals. The direct mail consisted of a newsletter, "Alderson's News," mailed to current and potential customers.

With the takeover complete, National sent its auditors to Alderson Products for a routine evaluation. Among other things, it soon became apparent that Alderson had been very lax in its sales control efforts. In particular, there was no evidence that a sales budget was used and there had been no attempt at a sales analysis. The sales manager, who had been in his position for two years after four years as a salesperson with Alderson, said there had been no sales budgeting or sales analysis effort for three years prior to his becoming sales manager. He did mention that a sales budget was used for a time before that, but he was unaware of its details. When questioned by the National auditor as to why he had not instituted sales control procedures, the sales manager said he had discussed it with Frank Alderson and they came to the conclusion that the company was moving along very well and there really was no need for tight control. He was, though, on the alert that, should sales results taper off, it might be necessary to have some controls at a future date. The sales manager also pointed out that he was so busy working on a personal basis with the company sales personnel and the sales representatives that he just didn't have the time for budgets, quotas, sales analysis and "things like that."

Was there a need for sales control at Alderson Products, Inc.? Why or why not?

What would have been the components of a good sales control program for Alderson Products? Be specific and give your reasons for each element of sales control.

International Sales Management[1]

24

The expansion of international business has been impressive. Multinational companies—mainly headquartered in the United States, Japan, or Western Europe—have been expanding their foreign production about 10 percent annually, while world exports have been growing more than 7 percent annually. Both the foreign output of multinational corporations (MNCs) and world exports have been expanding faster than gross world product (the total of all nations' GNPs), whose annual growth rate is about 5 percent. Each year more of the world's commerce is international business.

Sales management has increasingly taken on international dimensions. The multinationals and other companies with foreign production and marketing operations look to sales management to implement sales-related marketing policies in each national market. In companies with sophisticated exporting operations, sales management obtains overseas distributors and dealers, maintains relationships with these distributive networks, and monitors continuing changes in marketing conditions and needs in national markets. However, in this chapter, the focus is on those MNCs who maintain subsidiaries and company-owned selling operations in overseas markets.

INTERNATIONAL SALES MANAGEMENT AND CULTURE

International sales management feels the direct impact of many aspects of culture. Culture is defined as the way of life of a people and the whole complex of their learned behavior patterns, attitudes, and material things. Among the as-

[1]We gratefully acknowledge the contributions made to this chapter by Dr. John S. Hill of the University of Alabama, Tuscaloosa.

pects of culture of relevance to sales management are language, religion, values, law, education, social organization, and politics.

Some sales executives assume, almost instinctively, that what has worked in the home market will work elsewhere around the globe. This orientation is called ethnocentrism. Home-country bias and neglect of cross-cultural considerations lead to ineffective sales management both at home and abroad and consequent disappointing sales and profit performances.

Other sales executives, bending over backward to avoid ethnocentric bias, adopt a polycentric orientation—a total "host-country" orientation in each country. Extreme polycentric orientation causes a company to miss opportunities for capitalizing on economies of scale and those that come from some degree of worldwide standardization of policies, practices, and procedures. Tailoring sales management to fit all unique conditions in each market, in other words, leads to high costs and disappointing profit performances. A 100 percent polycentric approach to sales management is not likely to produce optimum sales or profit performances.

To visualize the complications that arise, consider the experiences of one large U.S.-based manufacturer of household appliances. Traditionally, this company had sold its products internationally direct to the household consumer through a sales force recruited for each country. Its system was one in which sales personnel were recruited from direct contacts of management and sales personnel. Sales compensation was entirely in the form of commissions, and sales personnel paid their own expenses. Almost all sales were made on installment plans.

When it entered the Taiwan market, the company, acting ethnocentrically, applied its sales force management system rigidly. Almost at once, difficulties appeared. Local sales personnel turned out to be of very low quality. In Taiwanese culture, type of work and nature of income are the major factors in determining social position. Sales personnel, as in many other societies, rank low in the hierarchy of occupational prestige. Of more importance, the average Taiwanese perceives fixed salary incomes as more desirable and prestigious than commissions, which Taiwanese regard as the "lowest" form of income. Even though a salesperson working for commissions might earn twice the income of an average factory worker, most Taiwanese prefer the factory job at a fixed wage.

Furthermore, Taiwanese sales personnel try to keep their personal friends and family as private sources of introductions to potential customers. So in attempting to recruit sales personnel, management got little help from the existing sales staff. It had to settle for down-and-outers who had nothing to lose from taking low-status jobs. The majority of those recruited turned out to be ex-felons and others who could not hold down regular jobs. These people had little left in the way of the Confucian ethics of honesty and loyalty that permeate most of Taiwanese society.

Those recruited soon found ways to trick the company into paying commissions on "false" sales. One gimmick was to sell an appliance on credit to a "strawman" who would make one or two payments and then disappear along with the appliance. Beset with these and similar difficulties, the company ultimately withdrew from the Taiwanese market.

This nightmare contrasted sharply with the company's experience in Thailand. Thai culture is dominated by Buddhist values, and religion is the historic wellspring from which flow the country's art and literature, its ethics and sense of morality, and many of its customs and folkways. Thai Buddhism proclaims the virtue of gentleness and suppression of desire, not requiring social interactions beyond tolerance and compassion for one's fellow creatures. Suffering is "inevitable" and traces to one's lack of *karma*—the power generated by one's actions to perpetuate transmigration and to determine one's destiny in one's next existence. If one is blessed with high position and comfort, it has been made possible by the merit accumulated in a previous incarnation.

On the company's entering the Thailand market, the country manager was given complete authority to adjust to local conditions, that is, to pursue a totally polycentric approach, Nevertheless, the country manager decided that the company's products should be sold direct to the consumer and that sales personnel should receive straight commissions (i.e., the company's traditional sales system). But sales work in Thailand, as in Taiwan, is regarded as low in prestige. Sales workers, however, are frequently recruited from farm families, which are considered as having low status. For the person with a farm background, then, taking a sales position is a move up the social ladder. Buddhism allows one to move up or down the scale of occupational prestige.

But Thai society is extremely status conscious, and egalitarianism is virtually incomprehensible. Every social relationship is viewed in terms of superior and inferior, and even the syntax of the language requires recognition of this fact. While the company at first had some difficulty in recruiting sales personnel, it did recruit a sizable number.

Early on, however, the country manager was forced to deal with the corruption and theft that was characteristic of much of Thai society. Of particular concern was the fact that there were numerous pawnshops throughout the entire country—over one hundred in Bangkok alone—and the law protected pawnshop owners from liability for items pawned with values of under $500. Management discovered that some departed sales personnel had made fake sales to themselves, paid the first few installments, then pawned the goods and left the company, Furthermore, some customers had obtained the company's products under false pretenses—some had borrowed the use of a friend's house and car to convince the company's salesperson of their creditworthiness. Once granted credit, the customer disappeared and the product showed up in a pawnshop.

The Thailand manager took two actions to correct this situation. He made participation in the company savings plan a condition of continued employment, and he announced that henceforth sales personnel were to be held responsible for "bad accounts." Sales personnel continuing with the company built up their savings accounts, and deductions were made to cover accounts going bad. With the tighter control, the company's Thailand operation became profitable.

HEAD OFFICE INFLUENCE ON OVERSEAS SELLING ACTIVITIES

Head offices of multinational corporations (MNCs) influence decisions made by their overseas subsidiaries. Typically, the head office focuses more upon international sales planning and sales training than upon country-level sales planning, administration, and control. There are several reasons for this emphasis: decisions at the international strategic planning level impact directly upon the entire MNC. Decisions on the type of sales organization (company sales force, distributors, or both) are taken on first market entry, reflecting head office perceptions of the resources necessary to exploit the sales potential in the country. Markets with large sales potentials warrant a multinational sales force. Smaller markets, or countries with political or environmental uncertainties (such as Iran or Libya), receive smaller commitments, usually in the form of distributor or dealer networks. In some case, MNCs create marketing channels totally new to the market as happened, for instance, when IBM entered Japan to sell its Personal Computers.

Many MNC subsidiaries, particularly in the automobile, computer, and electronics industries, are units of integrated worldwide production systems, with operations in each country making components for shipment and assembly elsewhere. Therefore, sales targets, being crucial elements in global plans integrating group manufacturing capabilities and markets, are under strong head office influence.

Other MNCs, especially those in consumer-goods industries, have subsidiaries operating as "free-standing" manufacturing and marketing units. This autonomy, common in such companies as Unilever and Chesebrough-Ponds, has subsidiaries determining their own sales targets and passing them on to the head office for approval.

FORMULATING SALES STRATEGIES AT THE NATIONAL LEVEL

Most MNCs allow local sales managements considerable input into "national-level" decisions on planning, training, administration, and control. This reflects beliefs that success requires localized selling operations, but, of course, head offices still "influence" these decisions. For example, when the product mix of an overseas subsidiary is similar to that of the U.S. parent company, it is likely that U.S. ideas and decisions will be transplanted to the overseas market.

Product mixes are most similar when the company first enters an overseas market. This is because companies enter overseas markets with products already established in the home market; later they diversify as they gain experience in the home market, and still later they diversify as they gain experience in the new markets. Amway, for example, entered Japan with a year-long test market of a few home care and detergent products; as Amway developed Asian markets, exporting from the United States gave way to subcontracting production in Japan (to meet cosmetics testing standards) and in New Zealand (to comply with that country's investment regulations).

The form in which sales management policy is stated influences the likelihood of transfer. When policies are in writing, translations help to moves sales ideas from market to market and give local managers the option of using them. Other documents often transferred internationally include compensation packages, training manuals (which affect training content and method), and administrative reports.

Many MNCs discourage the use of American methods abroad, but in some countries they work well. Both Amway and Electrolux, for instance, take their recognition-oriented "hooplah" management style overseas. Both recognize, however, that hooplah does not go over big with European and Japanese distributors, but they find it is compatible with Hong Kong and Malaysian life-styles and motivation profiles.

SALES ORGANIZATIONAL STRUCTURES

Not often does an MNC use its U.S. sales organization structure as a pattern for overseas use. U.S. sales organizational structures reflect the fact that the United States is an affluent competitive mass market—the fourth largest country in the world, most of its states are reasonably populated and the climate is temperate (made so by air conditioning and central heating). An outstanding infrastructure and superb communications have made the population increasingly culturally homogeneous. These conditions are not duplicated in overseas markets. Smaller national markets, lower stages of economic development, linguistic and cultural diversity, all make U.S. sales force structures unsuitable for overseas markets.

Sales force structures in overseas markets vary with the degree of market development. Electrolux, for example, makes nearly all its sales of vacuums through retail stores in the mature markets of Europe. In its newer markets in Southeast Asia, however, its traditional direct-selling approach is more effective; in India, Indonesia, Thailand, Singapore, and Malaysia (among other markets), Electrolux reps generate demand through in-home demonstrations.

SALES JOB DESCRIPTIONS

Many sales managers and others who construct sales job descriptions for international use write them ethnocentrically in terms of job inputs—"here is what a member of the mainstream culture should do to perform this job." What should be stressed are the job outputs—the purposes of the job (i.e., the job objectives) and the nature of "satisfactory" job performance.

Inadequate sales job descriptions—those that have been put together for little more than window dressing to fool wage and salary administrators—should not be transferred to another culture. Accurate sales job descriptions are transferrable but in terms of desired job outputs only. The inputs—what it takes to do the sales job satisfactorily—are the job components that change from one culture to another. As management in a host country becomes acculturated, then, and only then, should details on "how to do this job" be filled in.

This is almost equivalent to saying that "management by objectives" is culturally transferrable. In fact, MBO is one of the few Western management concepts that is not culture-bound. There are problems in making MBO work as its advocates say it should, but these problems crop up in any culture. Beyond this, in most company environments, the many dimensions that comprise satisfactory sales job performance closely resemble each other from one culture to the next.

Job descriptions developed for U.S. sales forces generally need altering for use in overseas markets. The giant size of the U.S. permits U.S. salespersons to specialize according to selling style; for example, missionary salespersons in the grocery and drug industries make it possible for trade salespersons to concentrate on order-taking and new-business salespersons to concentrate on getting new accounts and new business. The small size of many overseas markets dictates that salespersons call on broad spectrums of customers and prospects, while in other instances, it forces them to perform a wide range of job duties. Throughout Scandinavia, for example, Electrolux salespersons service refrigeration units as well as sell them.

Duties and responsibilities making up the sales job vary with the market, not so much in mainstream activities (such as in obtaining new accounts or handling customer requests) as in peripheral activities. In advanced markets, as in North America, Western Europe, and Japan, middleman efficiency and expertise is recognized and well established, and salespersons perform such peripheral activities as reporting on competitor actions and pricing, arranging and coordinating special promotions within channels, and negotiating special discounts. In the LDCs and other less sophisticated environments, the salesperson's peripheral activities include upgrading middlemen's managerial skills, training dealer sales help, ensuring proper stock rotation, and collecting accounts receivable.

In many overseas markets, job descriptions do not exist. In Japan, "learning by doing" is the normal way new people are trained, generally under tutelage of older, experienced personnel. Oriental management philosophies reflect strong beliefs that job behavior should not be circumscribed by written rules but by the salesperson's dedication to act in the employer's best interest.

RECRUITMENT AND SELECTION

Recruitment and selection of sales forces is the responsibility of local county management. Personal and cultural elements inherent in the selling activity make local orientation a must, particularly since translating U.S. recruitment and selection criteria into local standards is difficult if not wholly impossible.

Levels of educational attainment are difficult to equate cross-culturally. Interviewer impressions, previous experience, and personal appearance mean little unless assessed locally relative to distinctive job requirements and customer characteristics. Psychological tests of personality and sales aptitude, developed mainly to fit American contexts, are dubious measures in overseas markets. The cultural context of selling demands locally oriented recruitment and selection criteria. Variable ethnic, religious, and social conditions dictate local recruiting to minimize potential salesperson-customer differences.

Language and dialect fluency is a prerequisite in selecting salespersons in linguistically heterogeneous markets—a description that fits over 80 percent of all LDCs. In India, Swedish Match recruits from local regions both for language reasons and to take advantage of "local connections." U.S. MNCs in Indonesia hire salespersons to cover as many of the 250 dialects as possible but must still leave much coverage to local culturally oriented sales organizations.

Attracting applicants for sales jobs with advanced educational qualifications is difficult in many markets because of the lack of prestige the local cultures attach to selling. NCR, for example, has worked the Japanese market for over seventy years but has succeeded in recruiting university graduates only in the last twenty. Educated people abroad, especially those resident in developing countries, have many career options, including high-prestige jobs in government, education, and the professions. Consequently, a growing number of multinationals recruit foreign nationals attending U.S. business schools.

Sales Training

Sales training methods should be congruent with each particular culture's view of education. The mainstream U.S. culture sees education as an opportunity. Other cultures view education variously as constituting a privilege, a device for conferring status, or as simply an end in itself (education for education's sake).

Because training and education are viewed differently in different cultures, one must move with extreme caution in transferring sales training methods. The basic purpose of all sales training is to modify the perceptions, attitudes, and behavior of the trainees in ways that are beneficial to the company. But should we utilize any method that involves substituting the ethnocentric values of the trainers for the deeply held culturally rooted values of the trainees?

Sales training methods, like sales job descriptions, all too often are input rather than output oriented. In some cultures, transferring sales training requires major adjustments in training philosophy. The Western approach to problem solving, for example, is extremely difficult to transfer to Oriental cultures. In fact, real doubt exists as to whether we should want to transfer the Western approach. In Japan, for instance, more emphasis is put upon fact finding, listening, and defining the problem than upon developing alternative solutions or reaching compromises. The Japanese do not come to a point of view until everyone who might have something to say agrees on the basic facts of the situation and understands the attitudes of everyone else concerned. Then, and only then, does a *single* course of action emerge from the group—and it is not one individual's idea but the consensus of the group.

Preparation of training materials and programs for use in a different culture presents substantial difficulties. Simply taking English language materials and translating them into Spanish for use in Venezuela and Colombia, for example, is hardly ever the thing to do. Translating from one language to another is a tricky business, as it is next to impossible to avoid "losing something in the translation." Putting complete trust in a translator is not advisable, for even highly competent translators occasionally misinterpret intended meanings of technical terms and concepts.

Lexically and grammatically, there are substantial problems in converting material from one language to another. Lexically, most words have no completely perfect translation equivalent from one language to another—different languages differ even in the number and types of cuts they make on the color continuum—English uses six terms (purple, blue, green, yellow, orange, and red) to describe the same spectrum of color that Bassa (a Liberian language) uses two terms for (hui and ziza). Such grammatical processes as the significance of word order (e.g., The man kicked the horse versus The horse kicked the man) and the grammatical functions performed by parts of words (e.g., straight versus straighter versus straighten versus straightness versus straightener) differ greatly from one language to another. Languages vary so much both in the categories they express, and the particular linguistic means used for representing given categories that communications across cultural lines are inherently difficult and sometimes impossible.

The technical complexity of products is the main influence on sales training methods and content, but market conditions create complications. Literacy levels are a factor in some LDCs, where high illiteracy rates make it difficult to recruit literate salespeople. In the Far East and Southeast Asia, local educated elites look with disdain upon selling jobs and favor more prestigious jobs such as those in government, education, and the professions. Sales training content, particularly product knowledge, and company procedures are readily transferred to overseas markets in written documents, but care is required to assure that they are suitably translated, edited, and adapted to local cultural and environmental conditions.

Sales trainers with cross-cultural responsibilities should be aware of the Whorfian hypothesis, which asserts that certain aspects of language can predispose people to think or act in one way or another. While no one is entirely a prisoner of his or her language, there is no denying the powerful tendency for one's language to guide thought and other behavioral patterns.

SALES COMPENSATION

Sales compensation packages, including salaries, commissions, and benefits, are difficult to standardize in multinational settings. Unlike in the United States, the socialistically oriented governments of Europe legislate benefits: fringe benefits amount to 25 to 40 percent of wages in the United States, rise to 45 percent in West Germany, 55 percent in Belgium, 70 percent in France, and 92 percent in Italy. MNCs, therefore, supplement benefits in Europe with profit sharing, year-end bonuses, most medical and dental expenses, high severance pay, and increased maternity leave. Many of these programs are government mandated and financed through steeply progressive income taxes. This, in turn, affects compensation packages through dulling the positive effects of the commission element on sales performance.

Compensation packages are influenced strongly by culture. For instance, in Southeast Asia, straight salaries are considered more respectable and desirable than larger incomes involving substantial but variable commissions. In Japan, compensation level is more influenced by seniority than by performance, and when commissions are paid they are based on the entire sales force's performance rather than on individual performances, reflecting the strong group orientation of Eastern management philosophies. In Japan, too, the prevalent paternalistic attitude is reflected in certain additional benefits such as reimbursement of commuting expenses and company-provided vacation resort facilities.

Compensation patterns reflect national motivation patterns. Some Indian subsidiaries pay straight salaries plus bonuses based on sales volume generated by the entire sales force. Bonuses, along with contests and special recognition awards are used to boost sales force morale in highly traditional nations such as Burma, Sri Lanka, Pakistan, and Thailand. In these markets, clothing allowances also are common, managers contending that this fosters corporate pride.

SALES PRESENTATIONS

In culturally diverse markets, salespersons tailor their presentations to customers' needs. For instance, in the markets of Southeast Asia, Electrolux salespersons capitalize upon Moslem and Indian pride in owning fine carpets to promote the cleaning efficiency of Electrolux vacuums. To cater to the Chinese preference for polished floors in stores, Electrolux emphasizes its floor polishers in selling to Chinese market segments throughout East Asia.

Especially in Latin American and European markets, salesperson credibility and affability are as important as the presentation itself. Customer entertainment and social skills are often the distinguishing feature between salespersons and companies selling similar lines; this places substantial burdens on off-hours salespersons' activities. International sales managers say that big-ticket salespersons in North European countries including West Germany maintain peak performances for just twelve years before experiencing social burnout.

In door-to-door and party plan selling, cultural values exert strong influences on sales presentations. In Denmark, door-to-door selling is viewed as predatory high-pressure selling and is legally banned. In Southeast Asia, Avon representatives do not go door-to-door but sell mainly according to extended family kinship patterns. In Thailand, Malaysia, and the Philippines, cold calls on strangers are frowned upon and are made only through go-betweens such as business associates or mutual friends. In Nigeria, Tupperware altered its party approach and appointed market "mammies" to sponsor open-air sales events.

SALESPERSON EVALUATION AND CONTROL

Evaluation and control systems and procedures for the most part are local rather than home office oriented, largely because of differences in market conditions, job components, and salespersons' duties and responsibilities. However, it is common for overseas subsidiaries to use such report forms as daily call reports, new business activity reports, and expense reports, but these are designed and adapted to fit local conditions rather than being transplants from the United States. It is also common for salespersons in the subsidiaries to have their performances evaluated in terms of profits on sales, average size of sale, and calls per day or week, and subsidiary management commonly appraises salespersons according to qualitative standards for appearance, personality, attitude, and motivation. In some markets, as in India and Malaysia, salespersons submit call schedules a week in advance, and supervisors rotate surprise visits on field sales personnel on a random basis.

CONCLUSION

International sales management is not simply domestic sales management transplanted overseas. Long-standing cultural forces dictate that the management of overseas sales operations be locally directed in large part. Ethnocentric orientations give way to polycentric considerations, but the optimum represents a fine balance between ethnocentric matters (which promise financial benefits from standardizing policies, practices, and procedures) and polycentric forces (which demand adjustments appropriate to local cultures).

Index

D

E

F

G

H

I

J

Q